HISTORY

OF THE

WAR IN THE PENINSULA

AND IN THE

SOUTH OF FRANCE

FROM THE YEAR 1807 TO THE YEAR 1814

VOLUME I

HISTORY

OF THE

WAR IN THE PENINSULA

AND IN THE

SOUTH OF FRANCE,

FROM THE YEAR 1807 TO THE YEAR 1814.

BY

W. F. P. NAPIER, C.B.

COLONEL H. P. FORTY-THIRD REGIMENT,
MEMBER OF THE ROYAL SWEDISH ACADEMY OF MILITARY SCIENCES.

VOL. I.

THE THIRD EDITION;

CONSTABLE · LONDON

This edition first published in Great Britain 1992
by Constable and Company Limited
3 The Lanchesters, 162 Fulham Palace Road
London W6 9ER

Originally published in London in 1835
by Thomas and William Boone

ISBN 0 09 471680 3

Printed in Great Britain by
St Edmundsbury Press Ltd
Bury St Edmunds, Suffolk

TABLE OF CONTENTS.

BOOK I.

CHAPTER I.

CHAPTER II.

CHAPTER III.

CHAPTER IV.

CHAPTER V.

BOOK II.

CHAPTER I.

BOOK III.

CHAPTER I.

CHAPTER II.

CHAPTER III.

APPENDIX.

LIST OF PLATES.

NOTICE.

Of the manuscript authorities consulted for this history, those marked with the letter S. the author owes to the kindness of marshal Soult.

For the notes dictated by Napoleon, and the plans of campaign sketched out by king Joseph, he is indebted to his grace the duke of Wellington.

The returns of the French army were extracted from the original half-monthly statements presented by marshal Berthier to the emperor Napoleon.

Of the other authorities it is unnecessary to say more, than that the author had access to the original papers, with the exception of Dupont's Memoir, of which a copy only was obtained.

HISTORY

OF THE

PENINSULAR WAR.

BOOK I.

CHAPTER I.

THE hostility of the European aristocracy caused the enthusiasm of republican France to take a military direction, and forced that powerful nation into a course of policy which, however outrageous it might appear, was in reality one of necessity. Up to the treaty of Tilsit, the wars of France were essentially defensive,—for the bloody contest that wasted the continent so many years, was not a struggle for pre-eminence between ambitious powers, not a dispute for some accession of territory, nor for the political ascendency of one or other nation, but a deadly conflict, to determine whether aristocracy or democracy should predominate, whether equality or privilege should henceforth be the principle of European governments.

The French Revolution was pushed into existence before the hour of its natural birth. The power of the aristocratic principle was too vigorous and too much identified with that of the monarchical principle, to be successfully resisted by a virtuous demo-

cratic effort, much less could it be overthrown by a
democracy rioting in innocent blood, and menacing
destruction to political and religious establishments,
the growth of centuries, somewhat decayed indeed,
yet scarcely showing their grey hairs. The first military events of the Revolution, the disaffection of
Toulon and Lyons, the civil war of La Vendée, the
feeble, although successful resistance made to the
duke of Brunswick's invasion, and the frequent and
violent change of rulers whose fall none regretted,
were all proofs that the French revolution, intrinsically too feeble to sustain the physical and moral
force pressing it down, was fast sinking, when the
wonderful genius of Napoleon, baffling all reasonable calculation, raised and fixed it on the basis of
victory, the only one capable of supporting the crude
production.

Nevertheless that great man knew the cause he
upheld was not sufficiently in unison with the feelings
of the age, and his first care was to disarm, or neu-
tralize, monarchical and sacerdotal enmity, by restoring a church establishment, and by becoming a
monarch himself. Once a sovereign, his vigorous
character, his pursuits, his talents, and the critical
nature of the times, inevitably rendered him a
despotic one; yet while he sacrificed political
liberty, which to the great bulk of mankind has
never been more than a pleasing sound, he cherished with the utmost care equality, a sensible
good that produces increasing satisfaction as it descends in the scale of society. But this, the real
principle of his government and secret of his popu-
larity, made him the people's monarch, not the
sovereign of the aristocracy, and hence, Mr. Pitt
called him ' the child and the champion of demo-

cracy,' a truth as evident as that Mr. Pitt and his successors were the children and the champions of aristocracy: hence also the privileged classes of Europe consistently transferred their natural and implacable hatred of the French revolution to his person; for they saw, that in him innovation had found a protector, that he alone having given pre-eminence to a system so hateful to them, was really what he called himself, ' the State.'

The treaty of Tilsit, therefore, although it placed Napoleon in a commanding situation with regard to the potentates of Europe, unmasked the real nature of the war, and brought him and England, the respective champions of equality and privilege, into more direct contact; peace could not be between them while both were strong, and all that the French emperor had hitherto gained, only enabled him to choose his future field of battle.

When the catastrophe of Trafalgar forbade him to think of invading England, his fertile genius had conceived the plan of sapping her naval and commercial strength by depriving her of the markets for her manufactured goods, that is, he prohibited the reception of English wares in any part of the continent, and exacted from allies and dependants the most rigid compliance with his orders; but this ' continental system,' as it was called, became inoperative when French troops were not present to enforce his commands; it was thus in Portugal, where British influence was really paramount, although the terror inspired by the French arms seemed at times to render it doubtful. Fear is however momentary, while self-interest is lasting, and Portugal was but an unguarded province of England; from thence, and from Gibraltar, English goods freely

BOOK
I.

1807.
Monsieur
de Cham-
pagny's
Report,
21st Oct.
1807.
passed into Spain. To check this traffic by force
was not easy, and otherwise impossible.

Spain stood nearly in the same position with regard to France that Portugal did to England; a
warm feeling of friendship for the enemy of Great
Britain, was the natural consequence of the unjust
seizure of the Spanish frigates in a time of peace;
but although this rendered the French cause popular in Spain, and the court of Madrid was from
weakness subservient to the French Emperor, nothing could induce the people to refrain from a
profitable contraband trade; they would not pay that
respect to the wishes of a foreign power, which they
refused to the regulations of their own government.
Neither was the aristocratical enmity to Napoleon
asleep in Spain. A proclamation issued by the
Prince of Peace previous to the battle of Jena,
although hastily recalled when the result of that
conflict was known, sufficiently indicated the tenure
upon which the friendship of the Spanish court was
held.

Napoleon
in Las
Casas, vol.
ii.4th part.
This state of affairs drew the French Emperor's
attention towards the Peninsula, and a chain of remarkable circumstances, which fixed it there, induced him to remove the reigning family, and place
his brother Joseph on the throne of Spain. He
thought that the people of that country, sick of an
effete government, would be quiescent under such a
change; and although it should prove otherwise, the
confidence he reposed in his own fortune, unrivalled
talents, and vast power, made him disregard the
consequences, while the cravings of his military
and political system, the danger to be apprehended
from the vicinity of a Bourbon dynasty, and above
all the temptations offered by a miraculous folly

which outrun even his desires, urged him to a deed, that well accepted by the people of the Peninsula, would have proved beneficial, but being enforced contrary to their wishes, was unhallowed either by justice or benevolence.

In an evil hour, for his own greatness and the happiness of others, he commenced this fatal project. Founded in violence, and executed with fraud, it spread desolation through the fairest portions of the Peninsula, was calamitous to France, destructive to himself; and the conflict between his hardy veterans and the vindictive race he insulted, assumed a character of unmitigated ferocity disgraceful to human nature,—for the Spaniards did not fail to defend their just cause with hereditary cruelty, while the French army struck a terrible balance of barbarous actions. Napoleon observed with surprise the unexpected energy of the people, and therefore bent his whole force to the attainment of his object, while England coming to the assistance of the Peninsula, employed all her resources to frustrate his efforts. Thus the two leading nations of the world were brought into contact at a moment when both were disturbed by angry passions, eager for great events, and possessed of surprising power.

The extent and population of the French empire, including the kingdom of Italy, the confederation of the Rhine, the Swiss Cantons, the Duchy of Warsaw, and the dependant states of Holland and Naples, enabled Buonaparte, through the medium of the conscription, to array an army, in number nearly equal to the great host that followed the Persian of old against Greece; like that multitude also, his troops were gathered from many nations, but they were trained in a Roman discipline, and ruled by a Car-

thaginian genius. Count Mathieu Dumas, in a work
that, with unrivalled simplicity and elegance, tells the
military story of the world for ten years, has shown,
how vigorous and well-contrived was the organization of Napoleon's army ; the French officers, accustomed to victory, were as bold and enterprising, as
the troops they led were hardy and resolute, and
to this power at land, the Emperor joined a formidable marine. The ships of France were, indeed,
chained in her harbours, but her naval strength was
only rebuked, not destroyed. Inexhaustible resources
for building, vast establishments, a coast line of many
thousand miles, and, above all, the creative genius of
Napoleon, were fast nursing up a navy, the efficiency
of which, the war then impending between Great
Britain and the United States promised to aid. Maritime commerce was certainly fainting in France, but
her internal and continental traffic was robust, her
manufactures were rapidly improving, her debt small,
her financial operations conducted on a prudent plan
and with exact economy, the supplies were all raised
within the year without any great pressure from taxation, and from a sound metallic currency. Thus there
seemed no reason to think that Napoleon could fail
of bringing any war to a favourable termination. By
a happy combination of vigour and flattery, of order,
discipline, and moral excitement, admirably adapted
to the genius of his people, he had created a power
which appeared resistless ; and in truth would have
been so if applied to only one great object at a time,
but this the ambition of the man, or rather the force
of circumstances, did not permit.

On the other hand, England, omnipotent at sea,
was little regarded as a military power. Her enormous debt was yearly increasing in an accelerated

Exposé de
l'Empire,
1807-8-9-
13.

Napole-
on's Me-
moirs, Las
Casas, 7th
part.
Lord Col-
lingwood's
letters,
vide Ap-
pendix.

Exposé
1808-9.
Napoleon,
in Las
Casas, vol.
ii. 4th part.

Ibid. 6th
part.

ratio, and this necessary consequence of anticipating

the resources of the country and dealing in a facti-
tious currency, was fast eating into the vital strength
of the state : for although the merchants and great
manufacturers were thriving from the accidental circumstances of the times, the labourers were suffering
and degenerating in character; pauperism, and its
sure attendant crime, were spreading over the land,
and the population was fast splitting into distinct
classes,—the one rich and arbitrary, the other poor
and discontented, the former composed of those who
profited, the latter of those who suffered by the war.
Of Ireland it is unnecessary to speak ; her wrongs
and her misery, peculiar and unparalleled, are too
well known, and too little regarded, to call for
remark.

This general comparative statement, so favourable
to France, would, however, be a false criterion of the
relative strength of the belligerents, with regard to
the approaching struggle in the Peninsula. A cause
manifestly unjust is a heavy weight upon the operations of a general ; it reconciles men to desertion—
it sanctifies want of zeal and is a pretext for cowardice;
it renders hardships more irksome, dangers more obnoxious, and glory less satisfactory to the mind of
the soldier. Now the invasion of the Peninsula,
whatever might have been its real origin, was an
act of violence on the part of Napoleon repugnant to
the feelings of mankind; the French armies were
burthened with a sense of its iniquity, the British
troops exhilarated by a contrary sentiment. All the
continental nations had smarted under the sword of
Napoleon, but, with the exception of Prussia, none
were crushed ; a common feeling of humiliation, the
hope of revenge, and the ready subsidies of Eng-

land, were bonds of union among their governments
stronger than the most solemn treatises. France
could only calculate on their fears, England was
secure in their self-love.

The hatred to what were called French principles
was at this period in full activity. The privileged
classes of every country hated Napoleon, because his
genius had given stability to the institutions that
grew out of the revolution, because his victories had
baffled their calculations, and shaken their hold of
power. As the chief of revolutionary France, he
was constrained to continue his career until the final
accomplishment of her destiny,—and this necessity,
overlooked by the great bulk of mankind, afforded
plausible ground for imputing insatiable ambition to
the French government and to the French nation, of
which ample use was made. Rapacity, insolence,
injustice, cruelty, even cowardice, were said to be
inseparable from the character of a Frenchman, and,
as if such vices were nowhere else to be found, it was
more than insinuated that all the enemies of France
were inherently virtuous and disinterested. Unhap-
pily, history is but a record of crimes, and it is not
wonderful that the arrogance of men, buoyed up by
a spring-tide of military glory, should, as well among
allies, as among vanquished enemies, have produced
sufficient disgust, to insure a ready belief of any accusation however false and absurd.

Napoleon was the contriver and the sole support
of a political system that required time and victory
to consolidate ; he was the connecting link, between
the new interests of mankind and what of the old
were left in a state of vigour, he held them together
strongly, but he was no favourite with either, and
consequently in danger from both ; his power, un-

sanctified by time, depended not less upon delicate
management than upon vigorous exercise; he had to fix the foundations of, as well as to defend, an empire, and he may be said to have been rather peremptory than despotic; there were points of administration with which he durst not meddle even wisely, much less arbitrarily. Customs, prejudices, and the dregs of the revolutionary license, interfered to render his policy complicated and difficult, but it was not so with his inveterate adversaries. The delusion of parliamentary representation enabled the English government safely to exercise an unlimited power over the persons and the property of the nation, and, through the influence of an active and corrupt press it exercised nearly the same power over the public mind. The commerce of England, penetrating, as it were, into every house on the face of the globe, supplied a thousand sources of intelligence,—the spirit of traffic, which seldom acknowledges the ties of country, was universally on the side of Great Britain, and those twin-curses, paper-money and public credit, so truly described as ' strength in the beginning, but weakness in the end,' were recklessly used by statesmen, whose policy regarded not the interests of posterity. Such were the adventitious causes of England's power, and her natural, legitimate resources, were many and great. If any credit is to be given to the census, the increasing population of the United Kingdom amounted at this period to nearly twenty millions, and France reckoned but twenty-seven millions when Frederick the Great declared that, if he were her king, ' not a gun should be fired in Europe without his leave.'

The French army was undoubtedly very formidable

from numbers, discipline, skill, and bravery; but, contrary to the general opinion, the British army was inferior to it in none of these points save the first, and in discipline it was superior, because a national army will always bear a sterner code than a mixed force will suffer. Amongst the latter, military crimes may be punished, but moral crimes can hardly be repressed ; men will submit to death for a breach of great regulations which they know by experience to be useful, but the constant restraint of petty, though wholesome rules, they will escape from by desertion, or resist by mutiny, when the ties of custom and country are removed; for the disgrace of bad conduct attaches not to them, but to the nation under whose colours they serve. Great indeed is that genius that can keep men of different nations firm to their colours, and preserve a rigid discipline at the same time. Napoleon's military system was, from this cause, inferior to the British, which, if it be purely administered, combines the solidity of the Germans with the rapidity of the French, excluding the mechanical dulness of the one, and the dangerous vivacity of the other ; yet, before the campaign in the Peninsula had proved its excellence in every branch of war, the English army was absurdly under-rated in foreign countries, and absolutely despised in its own. It was reasonable to suppose that it did not possess that facility of moving in large bodies which long practice had given to the French, but the individual soldier was most falsely stigmatized as deficient in intelligence and activity, the officers ridiculed, and the idea that a British could cope with a French army, even for a single campaign considered chimerical.

The English are a people very subject to receive,

and to cherish false impressions; proud of their
credulity as if it were a virtue, the majority will
adopt any fallacy, and cling to it with a tenacity
proportioned to its grossness. Thus an ignorant
contempt for the British soldiery had been long
entertained, before the ill-success of the expeditions
in 1794 and 1799 appeared to justify the general
prejudice. The true cause of those failures was
not traced, and the excellent discipline afterwards
introduced and perfected by the duke of York was
despised. England, both at home and abroad, was,
in 1808, scorned as a military power, when she
possessed, without a frontier to swallow up large
armies in expensive fortresses, at least two hundred Appendix, No.XVIII.
thousand of the best equipped and best disciplined
soldiers in the universe, together with an immense
recruiting establishment; and through the medium
of the militia, the power of drawing upon the population without limit. It is true that of this number many were necessarily employed in the defence
of the colonies, but enough remained to compose a
disposable force greater than that with which Napoleon won the battle of Austerlitz, and double that
with which he conquered Italy. In all the materials of war, the superior ingenuity and skill of the
English mechanics were visible, and that intellectual power which distinguishes Great Britain amongst
the nations, in science, arts, and literature, was not
wanting to her generals in the hour of danger.

CHAPTER II.

BOOK
I.
———
1807.
FOR many years antecedent to the French invasion,
the royal family of Spain were distracted with domestic quarrels ; the son's hand was against his
mother, the father's against his son, and the court
was a scene of continual broils, under cover of
which artful men, as is usual in such cases, pushed
their own interest forward, while they seemed to
act only for the sake of the party whose cause they
espoused.   Charles IV. attributed this unhappy
state of his house to the intrigues of his sister-in-
law, the queen of the Two Sicilies ; he himself, a
weak and inefficient old man, was governed by his
wife, and she again by don Manuel Godoy, of
whose person it is said she was enamoured even to
folly.   From the rank of a simple gentleman of the
royal guards, this person had been raised to the
highest dignities, and the title of Prince of the
Peace was conferred upon him whose name must be
for ever connected with one of the bloodiest wars
that fill the page of history.

Nellerto.

The ana-
gram of
Llorente.

Vide
Doblado's
Letters.

Ferdinand, prince of the Asturias, hated this
favourite, and the miserable death of his young
wife, his own youth, and apparently forlorn condition, created such an interest in his favour, that the
people partook of his feelings ; thus the disunion of
the royal family extending its effects beyond the
precincts of the court, involved the nation in ruin.
Those who know how Spaniards hate will compre-

hend why Godoy, who, though sensual, was a CHAP. II.
mild, good-natured man, has been so overloaded
with imprecations, as if he, and he alone, had 1807.
been the cause of the disasters in Spain. It was not
so. The canon, Escoiquiz, a subtile politician, who Napoleon in Las Casas.
appears to have been the chief of Ferdinand's party,
finding the influence of the Prince of the Peace too
strong, looked for support in a powerful quarter,
and under his tuition, Ferdinand wrote upon the
11th of October, 1807, to the emperor Napoleon. Nellerto.
In this letter he complained of the influence which
bad men had obtained over his father, prayed for
the interference of the ' hero destined by Providence,' so run the text, ' to save Europe and to
support thrones;' asked an alliance by marriage
with the Buonaparte family, and finally desired
that his communication might be kept secret from
his father, lest it should be taken as a proof of
disrespect. He received no answer, and fresh matter of quarrel being found by his enemies at home,
he was placed in arrest, and upon the 29th of
October, Charles denounced him to the emperor as
guilty of treason, and of having projected the assassination of his own mother. Napoleon caught
eagerly at this pretext for interfering in the domestic
policy of Spain,—and thus the honour and independence of a great people were placed in jeopardy,
by the squabbles of two of the most worthless persons.

Some short time before this, Godoy; either instigated by an ambition to found a dynasty, or fearing
that the death of the king would expose him to the
vengeance of Ferdinand, had made proposals to the
French court to concert a plan for the conquest and
division of Portugal, promising the assistance of

Spain, on condition that a principality for himself should be set apart from the spoil. Such is the turn given by Napoleon to this affair. But the article which provided an indemnification for the king of Etruria, a minor, who had just been obliged to surrender his Italian dominions to France, renders it doubtful if the first offer came from Godoy, and Napoleon eagerly adopted the project if he did not propose it. The advantages were all on his side. Under the pretext of supporting his army in Portugal, he might fill Spain with his troops; the dispute between the father and the son, now referred to his arbitration, placed the golden apples within his reach, and he resolved to gather the fruit if he had not planted the tree.

A secret treaty was immediately concluded at Fontainebleau, between marshal Duroc on the part of France, and Eugenio Izquerdo on the part of Spain. This treaty, together with a convention dependant on it, was signed the 27th, and ratified by Napoleon on the 29th of October, the contracting parties agreeing on the following conditions.

The house of Braganza to be driven forth of Portugal, and that kingdom divided into three portions. The province of Entre Minho e Duero, including the town of Oporto, to be called the kingdom of North Lusitania, and given as an indemnification to the dispossessed sovereign of Etruria.

The Alemtejo and the Algarves to be erected into a principality for Godoy, who, taking the title of prince of the Algarves, was still to be in some respects dependant upon the Spanish crown.

The central provinces of Estremadura, Beira, and the Tras os Montes, together with the town of

Lisbon, to be held in deposit until a general peace, and then to be exchanged under certain conditions for English conquests.

The ultramarine dominions of the exiled family to be equally divided between the contracting parties, and in three years at the longest, the king of Spain to be gratified with the title of Emperor of the two Americas. Thus much for the treaty. The terms of the convention were :

France to employ 25,000 infantry and 3,000 cavalry. Spain 24,000 infantry, 30 guns, and 3,000 cavalry.

The French contingent to be joined at Alcantara by the Spanish cavalry, artillery, and one-third of the infantry, and from thence to march to Lisbon. Of the remaining Spanish infantry, 10,000 were to take possession of the Entre Minho e Duero and Oporto, and 6,000 were to invade Estremadura and the Algarves. In the mean time a reserve of 40,000 men was to be assembled at Bayonne, ready to take the field by the 20th of November, if England should interfere, or the Portuguese people resist.

If the king of Spain or any of his family joined the troops, the chief command to be vested in the person so joining, but, with that exception, the French general to be obeyed whenever the armies of the two nations came into contact, and during the march through Spain, the French soldiers were to be fed by that country, and paid by their own government.

The revenues of the conquered provinces to be administered by the general actually in possession, and for the benefit of the nation in whose name the province was held.

Although it is evident, that this treaty and con-

vention favoured Napoleon's ulterior operations in
Spain, by enabling him to mask his views, and
introduce large bodies of men into that country
without creating much suspicion, it does not follow,
as some authors have asserted, that they were contrived by the emperor for the sole purpose of rendering the Spanish royal family odious to the world,
and by this far-fetched expedient, to prevent other
nations from taking an interest in their fate, when
he should find it convenient to apply the same
measure of injustice to his associate, that they had
accorded to the family of Braganza. To say nothing of the weakness of such a policy, founded,
as it must be, on the error, that governments acknowledge the dictates of justice at the expense of
their supposed interests, it must be observed that
Portugal was intrinsically a great object. History
does not speak of the time when the inhabitants of
that country were deficient in spirit, the natural
obstacles to an invasion had more than once frustrated the efforts of large armies, and the long line
of communication between Bayonne and the Portuguese frontier, could only be supported by Spanish
co-operation. Add to this, the facility with which
England could, and the probability that she would,
succour her ancient ally, and the reasonable conclusion is, that Napoleon's first intentions were in
accordance with the literal meaning of the treaty
Voice from
St.Helena,
vol. ii. of Fontainebleau, his subsequent proceedings being
the result of new projects, conceived, as the won-
drous imbecility of the Spanish Bourbons became
manifest. Again, the convention provided for the
organization of a large Spanish force, to be stationed in the north and south of Portugal, that is,
in precisely the two places from whence they could

most readily march to the assistance of their country, if it was invaded. In fact the division of the marquis of Solano in the south, and that of general Taranco in the north of Portugal, did, when the Spanish insurrection broke out, form the strength of the Andalusian and Gallician armies, the former of which gained the victory at Baylen, while the latter contended for it, although ineffectually, at Rio Seco.

The French force, destined to invade Portugal, was already assembled at Bayonne, under the title of the " First army of the Garonne," and actually entered Spain before the treaty was signed. It was commanded by general Junot, a young man of a bold, ambitious disposition, but of greater reputation for military talent than he was able to support ; and his soldiers, principally conscripts, were ill fitted to endure the hardships which awaited them. At first by easy marches, and in small divisions, he led his troops through Spain, but the inhabitants, either from a latent fear of what was to follow, or from a dislike of foreigners common to all secluded people, were not friendly. When the head of the columns reached Salamanca, the general halted, intending to complete the organization of his troops in that rich country, and there to await the most favourable moment for penetrating the sterile frontier which guarded his destined prey; but political events marched faster than his calculations, and fresh instructions from the emperor prescribed an immediate advance upon Lisbon ; Junot obeyed, and the family of Braganza, at his approach, fled to the Brazils. The series of interesting transactions which attended this invasion will be treated of hereafter, at present, I must return to Spain,

now bending to the first gusts of that hurricane,
which soon swept over her with destructive violence.

The accusation of treason and intended parricide,
preferred by Charles IV. against his son Ferdinand,
gave rise to some judicial proceedings, which ended
in the submission of the prince, who being absolved
of the imputed crime, wrote a letter to his father
and mother, acknowledging his own fault, but ac-
cusing the persons in his confidence, of being the
instigators of deeds which he himself abhorred.
The intrigues of his advisers, however, continued,
and the plans of Napoleon advanced as a necessary
consequence of the divisions in the Spanish court.

By the terms of the convention of Fontainebleau,
forty thousand men were to be held in reserve at
Bayonne ; but a greater number were assembled on
different points of the frontier, and in the course of
December, two corps had entered the Spanish territory, and were quartered in Vittoria, Miranda,
Briviesca, and the neighbourhood. The one, commanded by general Dupont, was called the second
army of observation of the ' Gironde.' The other,
commanded by marshal Moncey, took the title of
Return of
the French
army. Ap-
pendix.
Journal of
Dupont's
Operations
MSS. the army of observation of the ' Côte d'Océan.' In
the gross, they amounted to fifty-three thousand
men, of which above forty thousand were fit for
duty ; and in the course of the month of December,
Dupont advanced to Valladolid, while a reinforcement for Junot, four thousand seven hundred in
number, took up their quarters at Salamanca. It
thus appeared as if the French troops were quietly
following the natural line of communication between
France and Portugal ; but, in reality, Dupont and
Moncey's positions cut off the capital from all inter-

course with the northern provinces, and secured the
direct road from Bayonne to Madrid. Small divisions under different pretexts continually reinforced
these two bodies, and through the Eastern Pyrenees
twelve thousand men, commanded by general Duhesme, penetrated into Catalonia, and established
themselves in Barcelona.

1808.
March.
Notes of
Napoleon.
Appendix,
No. II.

In the mean time the dispute between the king
and his son, or rather between the Prince of the
Peace and the advisers of Ferdinand, was brought
to a crisis by insurrections at Aranjuez and Madrid,
which took place upon the 17th, 18th, and 19th of
March, 1808. ' The old king, deceived by intrigues,
or frightened at the difficulties which surrounded
him, had determined, as it is supposed by some, to
quit Spain, and take refuge in his American dominions, and preparations were made for a flight to
Seville, when the prince's grooms commenced a
tumult, in which the populace of Aranjuez soon
joined, and were only pacified by the assurance
that no journey was in contemplation.

Upon the 18th, the people of Madrid, following
the example of Aranjuez, sacked the house of the
obnoxious Manuel Godoy, and upon the 19th the
riots having recommenced at Aranjuez, that minister
secreted himself, but his retreat being discovered,
he was maltreated, and on the point of being killed,
when the soldiers of the royal guard rescued him.
Charles IV., terrified by the violent proceedings of
his subjects, had abdicated the day before, and this
event being proclaimed at Madrid on the 20th, Ferdinand was declared king, to the great joy of the
nation at large: little did the people know what
they rejoiced at, and time has since taught them

that the fable of the frogs demanding a monarch had its meaning.

During these transactions, Murat, grand duke of Berg, who had taken the command of all the French troops in Spain, quitted his quarters at Aranda de Duero, passed the Somosierra, and entered Madrid the 23d, with Moncey's corps and a fine body of cavalry; Dupont at the same time, deviating from the road to Portugal, crossed the Duero, and occupied Segovia, the Escurial, and Aranjuez. Ferdinand who arrived at Madrid on the 24th, was not recognised by Murat as king; nevertheless, at the demand of his powerful guest, he delivered to him the sword of Francis I. with much ceremony. Meanwhile Charles protested to Murat that his abdication had been forced, and also wrote to Napoleon in the same strain. This state of affairs being unexpected by the emperor, he sent general Savary to conduct his plans, which appear to have been considerably deranged by the vehemence of the people, and the precipitation with which Murat had seized the capital. But previous to Savary's arrival, Don Carlos, the brother of Ferdinand, departed from Madrid, hoping to meet the emperor Napoleon, whose presence in that city was confidently expected; and upon the 10th of April, Ferdinand, having first appointed a supreme junta, of which his uncle, Don Antonio, was named president and Murat a member, commenced his own remarkable journey to Bayonne. The true causes of this measure have not yet been developed; perhaps, when they shall be known, some petty personal intrigue, may be found to have had a greater influence than the grand machinations attributed to

Napoleon,
in Las
Casas.

Napoleon, who could not have anticipated, much
less have calculated, a great political scheme upon
such a surprising example of weakness.

The people everywhere manifested their anger at
this journey; in Vittoria they cut the traces of Ferdinand's carriage, and at different times several gallant men offered, at the risk of their lives, to carry
him off by sea, in defiance of the French troops
quartered along the road. Unmoved by their entreaties and zeal, and regardless of the warning contained in a letter that he received at this period from
Napoleon, (who, withholding the title of majesty,
sharply reproved him for his past conduct, and
scarcely expressed a wish to meet him,) Ferdinand
continued his progress, and, on the 20th of April,
1808, found himself a prisoner in Bayonne. In the
meantime, Charles, under the protection of Murat,
resumed his authority, obtained the liberty of Godoy,
and quitting Spain, also threw himself his cause
and kingdom, into the emperor's hands.

These events were in themselves quite enough to
urge a more cautious people than the Spaniards into
action; but other measures had been pursued, which
proved, beyond the possibility of doubt, that the
country was destined to be the spoil of the French.
The troops of that nation had been admitted, without reserve or precaution, into the different fortresses
upon the Spanish frontier, and, taking advantage of
this hospitality to forward the views of their chief,
they got possession, by various artifices, of the cita-
dels of St. Sebastian in Guipuscoa, of Pampeluna
in Navarre, and of the forts of Figueras and Mon-
juik, and the citadel of Barcelona in Catalonia.
Thus, under the pretence of mediating between the
father and the son, in a time of profound peace, a

foreign force was suddenly established in the capital, on the communications, and in the principal
frontier fortresses ; its chief was admitted to a share
of the government, and a fiery, proud, and jealous
nation was laid prostrate at the feet of a stranger,
without a blow being struck, without one warning
voice being raised, without a suspicion being excited, in sufficient time, to guard against those acts
upon which all were gazing with stupid amaze-
ment.

It is idle to attribute this surprising event to the
subtlety of Napoleon's policy, to the depth of his
deceit, or to the treachery of Godoy ; such a fatal
calamity could only be the result of bad government,
and the consequent degradation of public feeling. It
matters but little to those who wish to derive a
lesson from experience, whether it be a Godoy or a
Savary that strikes the last bargain of corruption,
the silly father or the rebellious son, that signs the
final act of degradation and infamy. Fortunately,
it is easier to oppress the people of all countries,
than to destroy their generous feelings; when all
patriotism is lost among the upper classes, it may
still be found among the lower ; in the Peninsula it
was not found, but started into life with a fervor and
energy that ennobled even the wild and savage form
in which it appeared ; nor was it the less admirable
that it burst forth attended by many evils ; the good
feeling displayed was the people's own, their cruelty,
folly, and perverseness, were the effects of a long
course of misgovernment.

There are many reasons why Napoleon should
have meddled with the interior affairs of Spain, there
seems to be no good one for his manner of doing it.
The Spanish Bourbons could never have been sincere

friends to France while Buonaparte held the sceptre, and the moment that the fear of his power ceased to operate, it was quite certain that their apparent friendship would change to active hostility; the proclamation issued by the Spanish cabinet just before the battle of Jena was evidence of this fact. But if the Bourbons were Napoleon's enemies, it did not follow that the people sympathized with their rulers; his great error was that he looked only to the court, and treated the nation with contempt. Had he, before he openly meddled in their affairs, brought the people into hostile contact with their government,—and how many points would not such a government have offered!—instead of appearing as the treacherous arbitrator in a domestic quarrel, he would have been hailed as the deliverer of a great people.

The journey of Ferdinand, the liberation of Godoy, the flight of Charles, the appointing Murat to be a member of the governing junta, and the movements of the French troops, who were advancing from all parts towards Madrid, aroused the indignation of the nation, and tumults and assassinations had taken place in various parts; at Toledo a serious riot occurred on the 23d of April, the peasants joined the inhabitants of the town, and it was only by the advance of a division of infantry and some cavalry of Dupont's corps, then quartered at Aranjuez, that order was restored. The agitation of the public mind, however, increased, the French troops were all young men, or rather boys, taken from the last conscription, and disciplined after they had entered Spain; their youth and apparent feebleness excited the contempt of the Spaniards, who pride themselves

Journal of
Dupont's
Operations
MSS.

much upon individual prowess, and the swelling indignation at last broke out.

Upon the 2d of May, a carriage being prepared,
as the people supposed, to convey Don Antonio, the
uncle of Ferdinand, to France, a crowd collected
about it, their language indicated a determination
not to permit the last of the royal family to be
spirited away, the traces of the carriage were cut,
and loud imprecations against the French burst forth
on every side; at that moment colonel La-Grange,
aide-de-camp to Murat, appeared, he was assailed
and maltreated, and in an instant the whole city was
in commotion. The French soldiers, expecting no
violence, were killed in every street, about four
hundred fell, and the hospital was attacked, but the
attendants and sick men defended themselves; and
meanwhile the alarm having spread to the camp
outside the city, the French cavalry galloped in to
the assistance of their countrymen by the gate of
Alcala, while general Lanfranc, with three thousand
infantry, descending from the heights on the north-
west quarter, entered the Calle Ancha de Bernardo.
As he crossed the end of the street Maravelles, Daois
and Velarde, two Spanish officers who were in a state
of great excitement, discharged a cannon at the
passing troops, and were immediately attacked and
killed by some voltigeurs; the column, however,
continued its march, releasing, as it advanced,
several superior officers, who were in a manner besieged by the populace. The cavalry at the other
end of the town, treating the affair as a tumult, and
not as an action, made some hundred prisoners, and
some men were killed or maimed by the horses, but
marshal Moncey, general Harispe, and Gonzalvo

O'Farril, restored order.   Nevertheless, after night-
fall, the peasantry of the neighbourhood, who were
armed and in considerable numbers, beset the city
gates, and the French guards firing upon them,
killed twenty or thirty, and wounded more.

In the first moment of irritation, Murat ordered
all the prisoners to be tried by a military commission, which condemned them to death ; but the municipality interfering, represented to that prince the
extreme cruelty of visiting this angry ebullition of
an injured and insulted people with such severity,
whereupon admitting the weight of their arguments,
he forbade any executions on the sentence.   Yet it is
said that general Grouchy, in whose immediate power
the prisoners remained, after exclaiming that his
own life had been attempted, that the blood of the
French soldiers was not to be spilt with impunity,
and that the prisoners having been condemned by
a council of war, ought and should be executed,
proceeded to shoot them in the Prado.   Forty were
thus slain before Murat could cause his orders
to be effectually obeyed.   The next day some
of the Spanish authorities having discovered that
a colonel, commanding the imperial guards, still
retained a number of prisoners in the barracks,
applied to have them also released.   Murat consented, but it is said by some, although denied
by others of greater authority, that the colonel getting intelligence of what was passing, and being
enraged at the loss of so many choice soldiers, put
forty-five of his captives to death before the order
arrived to stay his bloody proceedings.

See gen.
Harispe's
observa-
tions at the
end of this
volume.

Such were nearly the circumstances that attended
this celebrated tumult, in which the wild cry of
Spanish warfare was first heard, and as many authors,

adopting without hesitation all the reports of the
day, have represented it, sometimes as a wanton and
extensive massacre on the part of the French,
sometimes as a barbarous political stroke to impress
a dread of their power, I think it necessary to
remark—First, that it was commenced by the
Spaniards; their fiery tempers, the irritation produced by passing events, and the habits of violence which they had acquired in their late
successful insurrection against Godoy, rendered
an explosion inevitable. Second, that if the
French had secretly stimulated this disposition,
and had resolved in cold blood to make a
terrible example, they would have prepared
some check on the Spanish soldiers of the garrison; they would not have left their own hospital
unguarded, still less have arranged the plan so, that
their loss should far exceed that of the Spaniards;
and surely nothing would have induced them to
relinquish the profit of such policy after having
suffered all the injury! Yet marshal Moncey, and
general Harispe were actively engaged in restoring
order; and it is certain that, including the peasants
shot outside the gates, and the executions afterwards,
the whole number of Spaniards slain did not amount
to one hundred and twenty persons, while several
hundred French fell. Of the imperial guards
seventy men were wounded, and this fact alone
would suffice to prove that there was no premedita-
tion on the part of Murat; for if he was base enough
to sacrifice his own men with such unconcern, he
would not have exposed the select soldiers of the
French empire in preference to the conscripts who
abounded in his army.

The affair itself was certainly accidental, and not

Manifesto
of the coun-
cil of Cas-
tile.
Page 28.

Surgical
Campaigns
of Baron
Larrey.

very bloody for the patriots, but policy induced both
sides to attribute secret motives, and to exaggerate
the slaughter. The Spaniards in the provinces,
impressed with an opinion of French atrocity, were
thereby excited to insurrection on the one hand;
and, on the other, the French, well aware that such
an impression could not be effaced by an accurate
relation of what did happen, seized the occasion to
convey a terrible idea of their own power and severity. It is the part of history to reduce such amplifications. But it is impossible to remain unmoved in
recording the gallantry and devotion of a populace
that could thus dare to assail the force commanded
by Murat, rather than abandon one of their princes;
such, however, was the character of the Spaniards
throughout this war, they were prone to sudden and
rash actions, and though weak in military execution,
fierce and confident individually, and they had always
an intuitive perception of what was great and
noble.

The commotion of the 2d of May was the fore-
runner of insurrections in every part of 'Spain, few
of which were so honourable to the actors as that of
Madrid. Unprincipled villains hailed the opportunity of directing the passions of the multitude,
and under the mask of patriotism, turned the un-
thinking fury of the people against whomever it
pleased them to rob or to destroy. Pillage, massacres, assassinations, cruelties of the most revolting
kind, were everywhere perpetrated, and the intrinsic
goodness of the cause was disfigured by the enor-
mities committed at Cadiz, Seville, Badajos, and
other places, but chiefly at Valencia, pre-eminent
in barbarity at a moment when all were barbarous!
The first burst of popular feeling being thus mis-

directed, and the energy of the people wasted in assassinations, lassitude and fear succeeded to the insolence of tumult at the approach of real danger ; for it is one thing to shine in the work of butchery, and another to establish that discipline which can alone sustain the courage of the multitude in the hour of trial.

To cover the suspicious measure of introducing more troops than the terms of the convention warranted, a variety of reports relative to the ultimate intentions of the French emperor had been propagated ; at one time Gibraltar was to be besieged, and officers were dispatched to examine the Mediterranean coasts of Spain and Barbary ; at another, Portugal was to become the theatre of great events ; and a mysterious importance was attached to all the movements of the French armies, with a view to deceive a court that fear and sloth disposed to the belief of anything but the truth, and to impose upon a people whose unsuspicious ignorance was at first mistaken for tameness.

In the mean time, active agents were employed to form a French party at the capital ; and, as the insurrections of Aranjuez and Madrid discovered the fierceness of the Spanish character, Napoleon enjoined more caution and prudence upon his lieutenant than the latter was disposed to practise. In fact, Murat's precipitation was the cause of hastening the discovery of his master's real views before they were ripe for execution. For Dupont's first division and cavalry had crossed the Duero as early as the 14th of March, and upon the 10th of April had occupied Aranjuez, while his second and third divisions took post at the Escurial and at Segovia, thus encircling the capital, which was soon occupied by Moncey's corps. It was then evident that Murat designed to control the provisional government left by Ferdinand ; and the riot at Toledo, although promptly quelled by the interference of the French troops, indicated the state of the public mind, before the explosion at Madrid had placed the parties in a state of direct hostility. Murat seems to have been intrusted with only a half confidence, and as his natural impetuosity urged him to play a rash rather than a timid part, he appeared with the air of a conqueror before a ground of quarrel was laid. His policy was too coarse and open for such difficult affairs, yet he was not entirely without grounds for his proceeding ; a letter addressed to him about this time by Napoleon contained these expressions : ' *The duke of Infantado has a party in Madrid ; it will attack you ; dissipate it, and seize the government.*'

At Bayonne the political events kept pace with those of Madrid. Charles IV. having reclaimed his rights in presence of Napoleon, commanded the infant, Don Antonio, to relinquish the presidency of the governing junta to Murat, who, at the same time, received the title of lieutenant-general of the kingdom. This appointment, and the restoration of Charles to the regal dignity, were proclaimed in Madrid, with the acquiescence of the Council of Castile, on the 10th of May ; but five days previous to that period, the old monarch had again ceded his authority to Napoleon, and Ferdinand and himself were consigned, with large pensions, to the tranquillity of private life.

The throne of Spain being now vacant, the right to fill it, was assumed by the French emperor in virtue of the cession made by Charles IV., and he desired that a king might be chosen from his own family. After some hesitation, the council of Castile, in concert with the municipality of Madrid and the governing junta, declared that their choice had fallen upon Joseph Buonaparte, who was then king of Naples. Cardinal Bourbon, primate of Spain, first cousin of Charles IV., and archbishop of Toledo, not only acceded to this arrangement, but actually wrote to Napoleon a letter testifying his adhesion to the new order of things.

As it was easy to foretel the result of the election, the king of Naples was already journeying towards Bayonne; he arrived there on the 7th of June, and the principal men of Spain were invited to meet in that town upon the 15th, with a view to obtain their assent to a constitution prepared by Napoleon. At this meeting, called ' the Assembly of Notables,' ninety-one Spaniards of eminence appeared; they accepted Joseph as their king, proceeded to discuss the constitution in detail, and after several sittings adopted it, and swore to maintain its provisions. Thus finished the first part of this eventful drama.

The new constitution was calculated to draw forth all the resources of Spain: compared to the old system it was a blessing, and it would have been received as such under different circumstances, but now arms were to decide its fate, for in every province the cry of war had been raised. In Catalonia, in Valencia, in Andalusia, Estremadura, Gallicia, and the Asturias, the people were gathering, and fiercely declaring their determination to resist French intrusion. Nevertheless Joseph, apparently contented with the acquiescence of the ninety-one notables, and trusting to the powerful support of his brother, crossed the frontier on the 9th of July; and on the 12th arrived at Vittoria. The inhabitants still remembering the journey to Bayonne, seemed disposed to hinder his entrance; but their opposition did not break out into actual violence, and the next morning he continued his progress by Miranda del Ebro, Breviesca, Burgos, and Buitrago. The 20th of July he entered Madrid, and upon the 24th he was proclaimed king of Spain and the Indies, with all the solemnities usual upon such occasions; thus making himself the enemy of eleven millions of people, the object of a nation's hatred! With a strange accent, from the midst of foreign bands, he called upon a fierce and haughty race to accept of a constitution which they did not understand, and which few of them had ever heard of; his only hope of success resting on the strength of his brother's arms, his claims upon the consent of an imbecile monarch, and the weakness of a few pusillanimous nobles, in contempt of the rights of millions now arming to oppose him. This was the unhallowed part of the enterprise; this it was that rendered his offered constitution odious, covered it with a leprous skin, and drove the noble-minded far from the pollution of its touch!

CHAPTER III.

BOOK
I.
————
1808.
July. JOSEPH being proclaimed king, required the council
of Castile to take the oath of allegiance prescribed
by the constitution; but, with unexpected boldness,
that body, hitherto obsequious, met his orders with
a remonstrance, for war, virtually declared on the 2d
of May, was at this time raging in all parts of the
Memoir of
O'Farril,
and
Azanza. peninsula, and the council was secretly apprized that
a great misfortune had befallen the French arms.
It was no longer a question between Joseph and some
reluctant public bodies; it was an awful struggle
between great nations; and how the spirit of insurrection, breaking forth simultaneously in every province, was nourished in each, until it acquired the
consistence of regular warfare, I will now relate.

Just before the tumult of Aranjuez, the marquis
of Solano y Socoro, commanding the Spanish auxiliary force in the Alentejo, had received an order
from Godoy to withdraw his division, and post
it on the frontier of Andalusia, to cover the
projected journey of Charles IV. Napoleon was
aware of this order, but would not interrupt its
execution, wherefore Solano quitted Portugal without difficulty, and in the latter end of May,
observing the general agitation, repaired to his government of Cadiz, in the harbour of which place
five French sail of the line and a frigate, under
admiral Rossily, had just before taken refuge from
the English fleet. Seville was in a great ferment,
and Solano, in passing through, was required to put
himself at the head of an insurrection in favour of

Ferdinand VII., he refused, and passed on to his own government; but there also the people were ripe for a declaration against the French. A local government was established at Seville, which assuming the title of ' Supreme Junta of Spain and the Indies,' declared war in form against the intrusive monarch, commanded all men between the ages of sixteen and forty-five to take arms, called upon the troops of the camp of San Roque to acknowledge their authority, and ordered Solano to attack the French squadron. That unfortunate man would not acknowledge the authority of this self-constituted government, and as he hesitated to commit his country in war against a power whose strength he knew better than he did the temper of his own countrymen, he was murdered. His ability, his courage, his amiable and unblemished character, have never been denied, and yet there is too much reason to believe that the junta of Seville sent an agent to Cadiz for the express purpose of procuring his assassination. This foul stain upon the cause was enlarged by the perpetration of similar, or worse deeds, in every part of the kingdom. At Seville the conde d'Aguilar was dragged from his carriage, and without even the imputation of guilt, inhumanly butchered; and here again it is said that the mob were instigated by a leading member of the junta, count Gusman de Tilly, a man described as ' capable of dishonouring a whole nation by his crimes,' while his victim was universally admitted to be virtuous and accomplished.

As early as April, general Castaños, then commanding the camp of San Roque, had entered into communication with sir Hew Dalrymple, the governor of Gibraltar. He was resolved to seize any

opportunity that offered to resist the French, and
he appears to have been the first Spaniard, who
united patriotism with prudent calculation; readily
acknowledging the authority of the junta of Seville,
and stifling the workings of self-interest, with a
virtue by no means common to his countrymen at
that period.   When the insurrection first broke out,
admiral Purvis commanded the British squadron off
Cadiz, and in concert with general Spencer, who
happened to be in that part of the world with five
thousand men, offered to co-operate with Solano,
in an attack upon the French ships of war in
the harbour.   Upon the death of that unfortunate
man, this offer was renewed and pressed upon don
Thomas Morla, his successor ; but he, for reasons
hereafter to be mentioned, refused all assistance,
Sir Hew Dalrymple's correspondence. and reduced the hostile ships himself.   Castaños,
however, united himself closely with the British
commanders, and obtained from them supplies of
arms, ammunition, and money; and at the instance
of sir Hew Dalrymple, the merchants of Gibraltar
advanced a loan of forty-two thousand dollars for
the service of the Spanish patriots.

Moniteur. Azanza and O'Far-ril: Nel-lerto. Meanwhile the assassinations at Cadiz and Seville
were imitated in every part of Spain ; hardly can a
town be named in which some innocent and worthy
persons were not slain.   Grenada had its murders ;
Carthagena rivalled Cadiz in ruthless cruelty, and
Valencia reeked with blood.   Don Miguel de
Saavedra, the governor of that city, was killed, not
in the first fury of commotion, which he escaped,
but, having returned, was deliberately sacrificed.
Balthazar Calvo, a canon of the church of San
Isidro, at Madrid, came down to Valencia, and
having collected a band of fanatics, commenced

a massacre of the French residents; and this ruth-less villain continued his slaughters unchecked, until French victims failing, his raging thirst for murder urged him to menace the junta, who with the ex-ception of the English consul Mr. Tupper, had given way to his previous violence, but now readily found the means to crush his power. The canon, while in the act of braving their authority, was seized by stratagem, and soon afterwards stran-gled, together with two hundred of his band. The conde de Serbelloni, captain-general of the province, then proceeded to organize an army, the old count Florida Blanca placed himself at the head of the Murcian insurrection, and his force acted in unison with that of Valencia.

In Catalonia the occupation of Barcelona re-pressed the popular effervescence, but the feeling was the same, and an insurrection, breaking out at the town of Manresa, soon spread to all the un-fettered parts of the province.

In Aragon the arrival of don Joseph Palafox kindled the fire of patriotism. He had escaped from Bayonne, and his family were greatly esteemed in a country where it was of the noblest among a people absurdly vain of their ancient descent. The captain-general, fearful of a tumult, ordered Palafox to quit the province, but this circumstance, joined to some appearance of mystery in his escape from Bayonne, encreased the passions of the multitude; a crowd surrounded his abode, and forced him to assume the command, the captain-general was confined, some persons were murdered, and a junta was formed. Palafox was considered by his companions as a man of slender capacity and great vanity, and there is nothing in his exploits to create a doubt of the justness of this opinion; it was not Palafox that upheld the glory of Aragon, it was the spirit of the people, which he had not excited, and could so little direct, that for a long time after the commencement of the first siege, he was kept a sort of prisoner in Zaragoza, his courage and fidelity being distrusted by the population which he is supposed to have ruled.

The example of Aragon aroused the Navarrese, and Logroño became the focus of an insurrection which extended along most of the valleys of that kingdom. In the northern and western provinces, the spirit of independence was equally fierce and as decidedly pronounced, accompanied also by the same excesses. In Badajos the conde de la Torre del Frenio was butchered by the populace, and his mangled carcass dragged through the streets in triumph. At Talavera de la Reyna, the corregidor with difficulty escaped a similar fate by a hasty flight; Leon presented a wide, unbroken scene of anarchy, and, generally speaking, in all the great towns violent hands were laid upon those who opposed the people's wishes.

Gallicia seemed to hold back for a moment, but the example of Leon, and the arrival of an agent from the Asturias, where the insurrection was in full force, produced a general movement. A junta was formed, and Filanghieri, the governor of Coruña, an Italian, was called upon to exercise the functions of royalty by declaring war in form against France. Like every man of sense in Spain he was unwilling to commence a revolution upon such uncertain grounds, and the impatient populace sought his death; he was saved at the moment by the courage of an officer of his staff, yet his horrible fate was

only deferred.   Being a man of talent and sincerely
attached to Spain, he exerted himself to organize
the military resources of the province, and no suspicion attached to his conduct ; but such was the
inherent ferocity of the people and of the time,
that the soldiers of the regiment of Navarre seized
him at Villa Franca del Bierzo, and, as some say,
stuck him full of bayonets, while others assert that
they planted their weapons in the ground, and then
tossing him on to their points, left him there to
struggle, and disbanded themselves.

The Asturians were the first who proclaimed their
indefeasible right of choosing a new government
when the old one ceased to afford them protection.
They established a local junta, declared war against
the French, and despatched deputies to England to
solicit assistance.   Meanwhile, although the great
towns in Biscay and the Castilés, were overawed by
fifty thousand bayonets, the peasantry commenced a
war, in their own manner, against the stragglers and
the sick, and thus a hostile chain surrounding the
French army was completed in every link.

This universal, and nearly simultaneous effort of
the Spanish people was beheld by the rest of Europe
with astonishment and admiration; astonishment at
the energy thus suddenly put forth by a nation
hitherto deemed unnerved and debased ; admiration
at the devoted courage of an act, which, seen at a
distance and its odious parts unknown, appeared
with all the ideal beauty of Numantian patriotism.
In England the enthusiasm was unbounded ; dazzled
at first with the splendour of such an agreeable,
unlooked-for spectacle, men of all classes gave way
to the impulse of a generous sympathy, and forgot,
or felt disinclined to analyse, the real causes of this

apparently magnanimous exertion. It may, however, be fairly doubted if the disinterested vigour of
the Spanish character was the true source of the
resistance; it was, in fact, produced by several co-
operating causes, many of which were anything but
commendable. Constituted as modern states are,
with little in their systems of government or educa-
tion adapted to nourish intense feelings of patriotism,
it would be miraculous indeed if such a result was
obtained from the pure virtue of a nation, which for
two centuries had groaned under the pressure of
civil and religious despotism.

The Spanish character, with relation to public
affairs, is distinguished by inordinate pride and
arrogance. Dilatory and improvident, the individual
as well as the mass, all possess an absurd confidence
that every thing is practicable which their heated
imaginations suggest, once excited, they can see no
difficulty in the execution of a project, and the
obstacles they encounter are attributed to treachery;
hence the sudden murder of so many virtuous men
at the commencement of this commotion. Kind
and warm in his attachments, but bitter in his anger,
the Spaniard is patient under privations, firm in
bodily suffering, prone to sudden passion, vindictive,
bloody, remembering insult longer than injury, and
cruel in his revenge. With a strong natural perception of what is noble, his promise is lofty, but
as he invariably permits his passions to get the
mastery of his reason, his performance is mean.
In the progress of this war, the tenacity of vengeance peculiar to the nation supplied the want of
cool, persevering intrepidity; but it was a poor sub-
stitute for that essential quality, and led rather to
deeds of craft and cruelty than to daring acts of

patriotism. Now the abstraction of the royal family, and the unexpected pretension to the crown, so in- sultingly put forth by Napoleon, had aroused all the Spanish pride, and the tumults of Madrid and Aranjuez prepared the public mind for a violent movement; the protection afforded by the French to the obnoxious Godoy increased the ferment of popular feeling, because a dearly cherished vengeance was thus frustrated at the moment of its expected accomplishment, and the disappointment excited all that fierceness of anger which with Spaniards is, for the moment, uncontrollable; and then came the tumult of Madrid, which, swollen and distorted, was cast like Cæsar's body before the people to urge them to phrenzy; they arose, not to meet a danger the extent of which they had calculated, and were prepared for the sake of independence to confront, but to gratify the fury of their hearts, and to slake their thirst of blood.

During Godoy's administration the property of the church had been trenched upon, and it was evident, from the example of France and Italy, that, under the new system, the operation would be repeated; this was a matter that involved the interests, and, of course, stimulated the activity of a multitude of monks and priests, who found no difficulty in persuading an ignorant and bigoted people, that the aggressive stranger was also the enemy of religion and accursed of God. With processions, miracles, prophecies, distribution of reliques, and the appointment of saints to the command of the armies, they fanaticised the mass of the patriots, and in every part of the peninsula the clergy were distinguished for their active zeal; monks and friars were invariably, either leaders in the tumults, or at the side of

BOOK
I.

1808.

Napoleon's
Mémoires,
Campagne
d'Italie,
Venise.

Appendix,
No. 9.

those who were, instigating them to barbarous actions. Buonaparte found the same cause produce
similar effects during his early campaigns in Italy;
and if the shape of that country had been as favourable for protracted resistance, and a like support had
been furnished by Great Britain, the patriots of Spain
would have been rivalled by modern Romans.

The continental system of mercantile exclusion
was another spring of this complicated machinery.
It threatened to lessen the already decayed commerce of the maritime towns, and the contraband
trade, which has always been carried on in Spain to
an incredible extent, was certain of destruction; with
that trade the fate of one hundred thousand excise
and custom-house officers was involved. It required
but a small share of penetration to perceive, that a
system of armed revenue officers, organized after
the French manner, and stimulated by a vigorous
administration, would quickly put an end to the
smuggling, which was, in truth, only a consequence
of monopolies and internal restrictions upon the
trade of one province with another—vexations abolished by the constitution of Bayonne: hence all
the activity and intelligence of the merchants engaged in foreign trade, and all the numbers and
lawless violence of the smugglers, were enlisted in
the cause of the country, swelling the ranks of the
insurgent patriots; and hence also, the readiness of
the Gibraltar merchants to advance the loan before
spoken of.

The state of civilization in Spain was likewise
exactly suited to an insurrection, for if the people
had been a little more enlightened, they would have
joined the French, if very enlightened, the invasion
could not have happened at all.   But in a country

where the comforts of civilized society are less needed, and therefore less attended to than in any other
part of Europe; where the warmth and dryness of
the climate render it no sort of privation, or even inconvenience, to sleep for the greatest part of the
year in the open air; and where the universal custom
is to go armed, it was not difficult for any energetic
man to assemble and keep together large masses of
the credulous peasantry. No story could be too
gross for their belief, if it agreed with their wishes.
' Es verdad, los dicen,' ' It is true, they say it,' is
the invariable answer of a Spaniard if a doubt is
expressed of the truth of an absurd report. Tem-
perate, possessing little furniture, and generally
hoarding all the gold he can get, he is less concerned
for the loss of his house than the inhabitant of another country would be, and the effort that he makes
in relinquishing his abode, must not be measured by
the scale of an Englishman's exertion in a like case;
once engaged in an adventure, the lightness of his
spirits and the brilliancy of his sky, make it a matter
of indifference to the angry peasant whither he
wanders.

The evils which had afflicted the country previous
to the period of the French interference also tended
to prepare the Spaniards for violence, and aided in
turning that violence against the intruders. Famine,
oppression, poverty, and disease, the loss of commerce, and unequal taxation, had pressed sorely upon
them. For such a system the people could not be
enthusiastic, but they were taught to believe, that
Godoy was the sole author of the misery they suffered, that Ferdinand would redress their grievances; and as the French were the protectors of the
former, and the oppressors of the latter, it was easy

Historia de
la Guerra
contra Na-
poleon.

to add this bitterness to their natural hatred of the
domination of a stranger, and it was so done.

Such were the principal causes which combined to
produce this surprising revolution, from which so
many great events flowed, without one man of eminent talent being cast up, to control or direct the
spirit thus accidentally excited. Nothing more
directly shows the heterogeneous nature of the feelings and interests, which were brought together, than
this last fact, which cannot be attributed to a deficiency of natural talent, for the genius of the Spanish
people is notoriously ardent, subtle, and vigorous ;
but there was no common bond of feeling, save that
of individual hatred to the French, which a great
man could lay hold of to influence large masses.
Persons of sagacity perceived, very early, that the
Spanish revolution, like a leafy shrub in a violent
gale of wind, greatly agitated, but disclosing only
slight unconnected stems, afforded no sure hold for
the ambition of a master-spirit, if such there were.
It was clear that the cause would fail, unless supported by England, and then England would direct
all, and not suffer her resources to be wielded for
the glory of an individual, whose views and policy
might afterwards thwart her own ; nor was it difficult
to perceive that the downfall of Napoleon, not the
regeneration of Spain, was the object of her cabinet.

The explosion of public feeling was fierce in its
expression, because political passions will always be
vehement at the first moment of their appearance
among a people new to civil commotion, and unused
to permit their heat to evaporate in public discussions. The result was certainly a wonderful change
in the affairs of Europe, it seems yet undecided
whether that change has been for the better or for

the worse; and in the progress of their struggle, the Spaniards certainly developed more cruelty than courage, more violence than intrepidity, more personal hatred of the French than enthusiasm for their own cause. They opened, indeed, a wide field for the exertions of others, they presented a fulcrum upon which a lever was rested that moved the civilized world, but assuredly the presiding genius, the impelling power, came from another quarter; useful accessories they were, but as principals they displayed neither wisdom, spirit, nor skill sufficient to resist the prodigious force by which they were assailed. If they appeared at first heedless of danger, it was not because they were prepared to perish rather than submit, but that they were reckless of provoking a power whose terrors they could not estimate, and in their ignorance despised.

It is, however, not surprising that great expectations were at first formed of the heroism of the Spaniards, and those expectations were greatly augmented by their agreeable qualities. There is not upon the face of the earth a people so attractive in the friendly intercourse of society. Their majestic language, fine persons, and becoming dress, their lively imaginations, the inexpressible beauty of their women, and the air of romance which they throw over every action, and infuse into every feeling, all combine to delude the senses and to impose upon the judgment. As companions, they are incomparably the most agreeable of mankind, but danger and disappointment attend the man who, confiding in their promises and energy, ventures upon a difficult enterprise. ' Never do to-day what you can put off until to-morrow,' is the favourite proverb in Spain, and rigidly followed.

CHAPTER IV.

THE commotion of Aranjuez undeceived the French emperor, he perceived that he was engaged in a delicate enterprise, and that the people he had to deal with were anything but tame and quiescent under insult. Determined, however, to persevere, he pursued his political intrigues, and without relinquishing the hope of a successful termination to the affair by such means, he arranged a profound plan of military operations, and so distributed his forces, that at the moment when Spain was pouring forth her swarthy bands, the masses of the French army were concentrated upon the most important points, and combined in such a manner, that, from their central position, they had the power of overwhelming each separate province, no three of which could act in concert without first beating a French corps. And if any of the Spanish armies succeeded in routing a French force, the remaining corps could unite without difficulty, and retreat without danger. It was the skill of this disposition which enabled seventy thousand men, covering a great extent of country, to brave the simultaneous fury of a whole nation; an army less ably distributed would have been trampled under foot, and lost, amidst the tumultuous uproar of eleven millions of people.

In a political point of view the inconvenience which would have arisen from suffering a regular army to take the field, was evident. To have been able to characterise the opposition of the Spanish people, as a partial insurrection of peasants, instigated by some evil-disposed persons to act against the wishes of

the respectable part of the nation, would have given
some colour to the absorbing darkness of the invasion.
And to have permitted that which was at first an insurrection of peasants, to take the form and consistence of regular armies and methodical warfare, would
have been a military error, dangerous in the extreme. Napoleon, who well knew that scientific war is
only a wise application of force, laughed at the delusion of those who regarded the want of a regular
army as a favourable circumstance, and who hailed
the undisciplined peasant as the more certain de-
fender of the country. He knew that a general insurrection can never last long, that it is a military
anarchy, and incapable of real strength; he knew
that it was the disciplined battalions of Valley Forge,
not the volunteers of Lexington, that established
American independence; that it was the veterans of
Arcole and Marengo, not the republicans of Valmy,
that fixed the fate of the French revolution. Hence
his efforts were directed to hinder the Spaniards from
drawing together any great body of regular soldiers,
an event that might easily happen, for the gross
amount of the organized Spanish force was, in the
month of May, about one hundred and twenty-seven
thousand men of all arms. Fifteen thousand of these
were in Holstein, under the marquis of Romana, but
twenty thousand were already partially concentrated
in Portugal, and the remainder, in which were comprised eleven thousand Swiss and thirty thousand
militia, were dispersed in various parts of the kingdom, principally in Andalusia. Besides this force, Historia de
there was a sort of local reserve called the urban la Guerra
contra
militia, much neglected indeed, and more a name Napoleon
than a reality, yet the advantage of such an institu- Buonaparte.

tion was considerable; men were to be had in abundance, and as the greatest difficulty in a sudden
crisis is to prepare the framework of order, it was
no small resource to find a plan of service ready, the
principle of which was understood by the people.

The French army in the Peninsula about the same
period, although amounting to eighty thousand men,
exclusive of those under Junot in Portugal, had not
more than seventy thousand capable of active operations, the remainder were sick or in depôts.   The
possession of the fortresses, the central position, and
the combination of this comparatively small army,
gave it great strength, but it had also many points
of weakness; it was made up of the conscripts of
different nations, French, Swiss, Italians, Poles, and
even Portuguese whom Junot had expatriated; and
it is a curious fact, that some of the latter remained
in Spain until the end of the war.   A few of the
imperial guards were also employed, and here and
there an old regiment of the line was mixed with
the young troops to give them consistence, yet with
these exceptions the French army must be considered
as a raw levy, fresh from the plough and unacquainted with discipline: so late even as the month
of August, many of the battalions had not completed
the first elements of their drill, and if they had not
been formed upon good skeletons, the difference between them and the insurgent peasantry would have
been very trifling.   This fact explains, in some measure, the otherwise incomprehensible checks and
defeats, which the French sustained at the commencement of the contest, and it likewise proves
how little of vigour there was in Spanish resistance
at the moment of the greatest enthusiasm.

In the distribution of these troops Napoleon at-

Napole-
on's notes.
Appendix,
No. 3.

Thiebault.

Dupont's
Journal,
MSS.

tended principally to the security of Madrid. As the
capital, and the centre of all interests, its importance was manifest, and the great line of communication between it and Bayonne was early and constantly covered with troops. But the imprudence
with which the grand duke of Berg brought up the
corps of Moncey and Dupont to the capital, together
with his own haughty, impolitic demeanour, drew
on the crisis of affairs before the time was ripe, obliged the French monarch to hasten the advance of
other troops, and to make a greater display of his
force than was consistent with his policy. For
Murat's movement, while it threatened the Spaniards
and provoked their hostility, isolated the French
army, by stripping the line of communication, and
the arrival of fresh battalions to remedy this error
generated additional anger and suspicion at a very
critical period.

It was, however, absolutely necessary to fill the
void left by Moncey's advance, and a fresh corps
sent into Navarre, being, by successive reinforcements, increased to twenty-three thousand men, Napoleon's
received in June the name of the ' army of the Appendix,
Western Pyrenees.' Marshal Bessières assumed No. 2.
the command, and, on the first appearance of
commotion, fixed his head quarters at Burgos,
occupied Vittoria, Miranda de Ebro, and other
towns, and pushed advanced posts into Leon. This
position, while it protected the line from Bayonne
to the capital, enabled him to awe the Asturias and
Biscay, and also by giving him the command of the
valley of the Duero to keep the kingdom of Leon
and the province of Segovia in check. The town
and castle of Burgos, put into a state of defence,
contained his depôts, and became the centre and

BOOK
I.

1808.

pivot of his operations, while intermediate posts, and the fortresses, connected him with Bayonne, where a reserve of twenty thousand men was formed under general Drouet, then commanding the eleventh military division of France.

By the convention of Fontainebleau, the emperor was entitled to send forty thousand men into the northern parts of Spain, and though the right thus acquired was grossly abused, the exercise of it, being expected, created at first but little alarm; it was however different on the eastern frontier. Napoleon had never intimated a wish to pass forces by Catalonia, neither the treaty nor the convention authorized such a measure, nor could the pretence of support-ing Junot in Portugal be advanced as a mask;

St. Cyr.
Napoleon's
notes.
Appendix,
No. 2.

nevertheless, so early as the 9th of February, eleven thousand infantry, sixteen hundred cavalry, and eighteen pieces of artillery, under the command of general Duhesme, had crossed the frontier at La Jonquera, and marched upon Barcelona, leaving a detachment at the town of Figueras, the strong citadel of which commands the principal pass of the mountains. Arrived at Barcelona, Duhesme pro-longed his residence there, under the pretext of

Duhesme's
Instruc-
tions,
Jan. 28th.
Vide St.
Cyr.

waiting for instructions from Madrid relative to a pretended march upon Cadiz; but his secret orders were to obtain exact information concerning the Catalonian fortresses, depôts, and magazines,—to ascertain the state of public feeling,—to preserve a rigid discipline,—scrupulously to avoid giving any offence to the Spaniards, and to enter into close communication with marshal Moncey, at that time commanding the whole of the French army in the north of Spain.

The political affairs were then beginning to indicate serious results, and as soon as the troops in the north were in a condition to execute their orders, Duhesme, whose report had been received, was directed to seize upon the citadel of Barcelona, and the fort of Monjuick. The citadel was obtained by stratagem ; the fort, one of the strongest in the world, was surrendered by the governor Alvarez, because that brave and worthy man knew, that from a base court he should receive no support. It is said that, stung by the disgrace of his situation, he was at one time ready to spring a mine beneath the French detachments, yet his mind, betraying his spirit, sunk under the weight of unexpected events. What a picture of human weakness do these affairs present!—the boldest shrinking from the discharge of their trust like the meanest cowards, the wisest following the march of events, confounded, and without a rule of action ! If such a firm man, as Alvarez afterwards proved himself to be, could think the disgrace of surrendering his charge at the demand of an insolent and perfidious guest, a smaller misfortune than the anger of a miserable court, what must the state of public feeling have been, and how can those who, like O'Farril and Azanza, served the intruder, be with justice blamed, if, amidst the general stagnation, they could not perceive the elements of a salutary tempest. At the view of such scenes Napoleon might well enlarge his ambitious designs, his fault was not in the projection, but in the rough execution of his plan ; another combination would have ensured success, and the resistance he encountered only shows, that nations, like individuals, are but the creatures of circumstances, at one moment weak, trembling, and submissive, at another proud,

haughty, and daring; every novel combination of
events has an effect upon public sentiment distinct
from, and often at variance with what is called
national character.

The treacherous game played at Barcelona was
renewed at Figueras, with equal success, the
citadel of that place fell into the hands of the
detachment left there; a free entrance, and a secure
base of operations, was thus established in Catalonia; and when the magazines of Barcelona were
filled, Duhesme, whose corps took the name of the
'army of the Eastern Pyrenees,' concluded that his
task was well accomplished. The affair was indeed
a momentous one, and Napoleon earnestly looked
for its termination, before the transactions at Madrid
could give an unfavourable impression of his ulterior intentions, for he saw the importance which,
under certain circumstances, a war would confer
upon Barcelona, which with its immense population, great riches, good harbour, and strong forts,
might be called the key of the south of France
or Spain, just as it happened to be in the possession
of the one or the other nation. The proximity of
Sicily, where a large British force was kept in a
state of constant preparation, made it more than
probable that an English army would be quickly
carried to Barcelona, and a formidable systematic
war be established upon the threshold of France, and
hence Napoleon, seeing the extent of the danger,
obviated it, at the risk of rendering abortive the
attempt to create a French party in Madrid. The
greater evil of finding an English army at Barcelona
left no room for hesitation; thirty or forty thousand
British troops occupying an intrenched camp in
front of that town, supported by a powerful fleet,

and having reserve depôts in Sicily and the Spanish islands, might have been so wielded as to give ample occupation to a hundred and fifty thousand enemies. Under the protection of such an army, the Spanish levies might have been organized and instructed; and as the actual numbers assembled could have been easily masked, increased, or diminished, and the fleet always ready to co-operate, the south of France, whence the provisions of the enemy must have been drawn, would have been exposed to descents, and all the inconvenience of actual hostilities. The Spanish provinces of Valencia, Murcia, and even Andalusia, being thus covered, the war would have been drawn to a head, and concentrated about Catalonia, the most warlike, rugged, sterile portion of Spain. Duhesme's success put an end to this danger, and the affairs of Barcelona sunk into comparative insignificance; nevertheless, that place was carefully watched, the troops were increased to twenty-two thousand men, their general corresponded directly with Napoleon, and Barcelona became the centre of a system distinct from that, which held the other corps rolling round Madrid as their point of attraction.

The capital of Spain is situated in a sort of basin, formed by a semicircular range of mountains, which, under the different denominations of the Sierra de Guadarama, the Carpentanos, and the Sierra de Guadalaxara, sweep in one unbroken chain from east to west, touching the Tagus at either end of an arch, of which that river is the chord. All direct communications between Madrid and France, or between the former and the northern provinces of Spain, must therefore necessarily pass

over one or other of these Sierras, which are separated from the great range of the Pyrenees by the
valley of the Ebro, and from the Biscayan and Asturian mountains by the valley of the Duero.

Now the principal roads which lead from France
directly upon Madrid are four.

The first a royal causeway, which passing the
frontier at Irun runs under St. Sebastian, and
through a wild and mountainous country, full of
dangerous defiles, to the Ebro; it crosses that river
by a stone bridge at Miranda, goes to Burgos, and
then turning short to the left, is carried over the
Duero at Aranda. Afterwards encountering the
Carpentanos and the Sierra de Guadalaxara, it penetrates them by the strong pass of the Somosierra,
and descends upon the capital.

The second, which is an inferior road, commences
at St. Jean Pied de Port, unites with the first at
Pampelona, runs through Taffalla, crosses the Ebro
at Tudela, and enters the basin of Madrid by the
eastern range of the Sierra de Guadalaxara, where
the declination of the mountains presents a less
rugged barrier than the snowy summits of the
northern and western part of the chain.

The third threads the Pyrenees by the way of
Jaca, passes the Ebro at Zarogoza, and uniting with
the second, likewise crosses the Guadalaxara ridge.

The fourth is the great route from Perpignan by
Figueras, Gerona, Barcelona, Cervera, Lerida, and
Zaragoza, to Madrid.

Thus Zaragoza, which contained fifty thousand
inhabitants and was one of the great Spanish magazines for arms, furnished a point of union for two
great roads and was consequently of strategic importance; an army in position there could operate

on either bank of the Ebro, intercept the communication between the Eastern and Western Pyrenees,
and block three out of the four great routes to
Madrid. If the French had occupied it in force,
their army in the capital would have been free and
unconstrained in its operations, and might have
acted with more security against Valencia; and the
danger from the united forces of Gallicia and Leon
would also have been diminished, when the road of
Burgos ceased to be the only line of retreat from
the capital. Nevertheless, Napoleon neglected
Zaragoza at first, because, having no citadel, a
small body of troops could not control the inhabitants, and a large force, by creating suspicion too
soon, would have prevented the success of the
attempts against Pampelona and Barcelona, objects
of still greater importance; neither was the heroic
defence afterwards made within a reasonable calculation.

The grand duke of Berg and the duke of Rovigo
remained at Madrid, and from that central point
appeared to direct the execution of the French emperor's projects; but he distrusted their judgment,
and exacted the most detailed information of every
movement and transaction. In the course of June,
Murat, who was suffering from illness, quitted
Spain, leaving behind him a troubled people, and a
name for cruelty which was foreign to his character.
Savary remained the sole representative of the new
monarch, and his situation was delicate. He was in
the midst of a great commotion, and as upon every
side he beheld the violence of insurrection, and the
fury of an insulted nation, it behoved him to calculate
with coolness and to execute with vigour. Each
Spanish province had its own junta of government,

and they were alike enraged, yet not alike dangerous in their anger. The attention of the Cata-
lonians was completely absorbed by Duhesme's
operations, but the soldiers which had composed
the Spanish garrisons of Barcelona, Monjuick, and
Figueras, quitted their ranks after the seizure of
those places, and joined the patriotic standards in
Murcia and Valencia ; the greatest part belonged
to the Spanish and Walloon guards, and they
formed a good basis for an army which the riches
of the two provinces and the arsenal of Carthagena
afforded ample military resources to equip. The
French had, however, nothing to fear from any
direct movement of this army against Madrid, as
such an operation could only bring on a battle; but
if, by a march towards Zaragoza, the Valencians
had united with the Aragonese, and then operated
against the line of communication with France, the
insurrection of Catalonia would have been supported, and a point of union for three great provinces fixed. In the power of executing this project
lay the sting of the Valencian insurrection, and to
besiege Zarogoza and prevent such a junction was
the remedy.

The importance of Andalusia was greater. The
regular troops which, under the command of the
unhappy Solano, had been withdrawn from Portugal, were tolerably disciplined; a large veteran force
was assembled at the camp of San Roque under
general Castaños, and the garrisons of Ceuta, Alge-
ziras, Cadiz, Granada, and other places being
united, the whole formed a considerable army, while
a superb cannon foundry at Seville, and the arsenal
of Cadiz, furnished the means of equipping a train
of artillery. An active intercourse was maintained

between the patriots and the English, and the juntas CHAP.
IV.
of Granada, Jaen, and Cordova and the army of 1808.
Estremadura, admitted the supremacy of the junta
of Seville. Thus Andalusia, rich, distant from the MrStuart's
Letters ;
vide Par-
liamentary
capital, and well fenced by the Sierra Morena,
afforded the means to establish a systematic war, Papers,
1810.
by drawing together all the scattered elements of
resistance in the southern and western provinces of
Spain and Portugal. This danger, pregnant with
future consequences, was, however, not immediate; there was no line of offensive moment,
against the flank or rear of the French army, open
to the Andalusian patriots; and as a march to
the front, against Madrid, would have been tedious
and dangerous, the true policy of the Andalusians
was palpably defensive.

In Estremadura neither the activity nor means of
the junta were at first sufficient to excite much attention; but in Leon, Old Castile, and Gallicia, a cloud
was gathering that threatened a perilous storm. Don
Gregoria Cuesta was captain-general of the two
former kingdoms. Inimical to popular movements,
and of a haughty, resolute disposition, he at first
checked the insurrection with a rough hand, and thus
laid the foundation for quarrels and intrigues, which
afterwards impeded the military operations, and split
the northern provinces into factions; yet finally, he
joined the side of the patriots. Behind him the
kingdom of Gallicia, under the direction of Filanghieri, had prepared a large and efficient force,
chiefly composed of the strong and disciplined body
of troops which, under the command of Tarranco,
had taken possession of Oporto, and after that general's death had returned with Belesta to Gallicia;
the garrisons of Ferrol and Coruña, and a number

of soldiers flying from the countries occupied by the French, swelled this army, the agents of Great Britain were active to blow the flame of insurrection, and money, arms, and clothing were poured into the province through their hands, because Coruña afforded an easy and direct intercourse with England. A strict connexion was also maintained between the Gallician and Portuguese patriots, and the facility of establishing the base of a regular systematic war in Gallicia was, therefore, as great as in Andalusia; the resources were perhaps, greater, on account of the proximity of Great Britain, and the advantage of position at this time was essentially in favour of Gallicia, because, while the sources of her strength were as well covered from the direct line of the French operations, the slightest offensive movement upon her part, by threatening the communications of the French army in Madrid, endangered the safety of any corps marching from the capital against the southern provinces. To be prepared against the Gallician forces was, therefore, a matter of pressing importance, a defeat from that quarter would have been felt in all parts of the army; and no considerable, or sustained operation, could be undertaken against the other insurgent forces until the strength of Gallicia had been first broken.

Biscay and the Asturias wanted regular troops and fortified towns, and the contracted shape of those provinces placed them completely within the power of the French, who had nothing to fear as long as they could maintain possession of the sea-ports.

From this sketch it results that Savary, in classing the dangers of his situation, should have rated Gallicia and Leon in the first, Zaragoza in the second, Andalusia in the third, and Valencia in the fourth rank, and by that scale he should have regulated his operations. It was thus Napoleon looked at the affair, but the duke of Rovigo, wavering in his opinions, neglected or misunderstood the spirit of his instructions, lost the control of the operations, and sunk amidst the confusion which he had himself created.

Nearly fifty thousand French and eighty guns were disposable for offensive operations in the beginning of June; collected into one mass, such an army was more than sufficient to crush any or all of the insurgent armies combined, but it was necessary to divide it, and to assail several points at the same time. In doing this, the safety of each minor body depended upon the stability of the central point from whence it emanated, and again the security of that centre depended upon the strength of its communications with France; in other words, Bayonne was the base of operations against Madrid, and Madrid in turn became the base of operations against Valencia, Murcia, and Andalusia. To combine all the movements of a vast plan, which would embrace the operations against Catalonia, Aragon, Biscay, the Asturias, Gallicia, Leon, Castille, Andalusia, Murcia, and Valencia, in such a simple manner, as that the corps of the army working upon one principle might mutually support and strengthen each other, and at the same time preserve their communication with France, was the great problem to be solved. Napoleon felt that it required a master mind, and from Bayonne he put all the different armed masses in motion himself, and with the greatest caution; for it is a mistaken notion, although one very generally entertained, that he plunged headlong into the contest, without foresight, as having to do with adversaries he despised.

In his instructions to the duke of Rovigo he says, ' *In a war of this sort it is necessary to act with patience, coolness, and upon calculation.*' ' *In civil wars it is the important points only which should be guarded—we must not go to all places;*' and he inculcates the doctrine, that to spread the troops over the country without the power of uniting upon emergency, would be a dangerous display of activity. The principle upon which he proceeded may be illustrated by the comparison of a closed hand thrust forward and the fingers afterwards extended : as long as the solid part of the member was securely fixed and guarded, the return of the smaller portions of it and their flexible movement was feasible and without great peril ; whereas a wound given to the hand or arm, not only endangered that part, but paralyzed the action of the whole limb. Hence all the care and attention with which his troops were arranged along the road to Burgos ; hence all the measures of precaution already described, such as the seizure of the fortresses and the formation of the reserves at Bayonne.

The insurrection having commenced, Bessières was ordered to put Burgos into a state of defence, —to detach a division of four or five thousand men, under general Lefebre Desnouettes, against Zaragoza,—to keep down the insurgents of Biscay, Asturias, and Old Castille,—and to observe the army assembling in Gallicia ; he was likewise enjoined to occupy and watch with jealous care the port of St. Ander and the coast towns. A reinforcement of nine thousand men was also prepared for Duhesme, which, it was supposed, would enable him to tranquillize Catalonia, and co-operate with a division marching from Madrid against Valencia.

The reserve under general Drouet was nourished by
drafts from the interior: it supplied Bessières with
reinforcements, and afforded a detachment of four
thousand men to watch the openings of the valleys
of the Pyrenees, especially towards the castle of
Jaca, then in possession of the Spanish insurgents.
A smaller reserve was established at Perpignan,
another body watched the openings of the eastern
frontier; and all the generals commanding corps, or
even detachments, were directed to correspond daily
with general Drouet.

CHAP.
IV.

1808.

Napole-
on's notes,
Appendix,
No. 2.

The security of the rear being thus provided for,
the main body at Madrid commenced offensive operations. Marshal Moncey was directed, with part
of his corps upon Cuenca, to intercept the march of
the Valencian army upon Zaragoza; general Dupont,
with ten thousand men, marched towards Cadiz, and
the remainder of his and Moncey's troops being kept
in reserve, were distributed in various parts of La
Mancha and the neighbourhood of Madrid. Napoleon likewise directed, that Segovia should be occupied and put in a state of defence; that Gobert's
division of Moncey's corps should co-operate with
Bessières on the side of Valladolid, and that moveable columns should scour the country in rear of the
acting bodies, uniting again at stated times, upon
points of secondary interest. Thus linking his operations together, Napoleon hoped, by grasping as it
were the ganglia of the insurrection, to paralyze its
force, and reduce it to a few convulsive motions,
which would soon subside; the execution of his
plan failed in the feeble hands of his lieutenants,
but it was well conceived, embraced every probable
immediate chance of war, and even provided for the
uncertain contingency of an English army landing,

S.
Journal of
Moncey's
Operations
MSS.

Napole-
on's notes,
Appendix,
No. 1.

upon the flanks or rear of his corps, at either extremity of the Pyrenean frontier.

Military men would do well to reflect upon the
prudence which the French emperor displayed upon
this occasion. Not all his experience, his power,
his fortune, nor the contempt which he felt for the
prowess of his adversaries, could induce him to relax
in his precautions; every chance was considered,
and every measure calculated with as much care
and circumspection as if the most redoubtable enemy
was opposed to him. The conqueror of Europe
was as fearful of making false movements before an
army of peasants, as if Frederick the Great had
been in his front, and yet he failed! Such is the
uncertainty of war!

CHAPTER V.

As all the insurrections of the Spanish provinces took place nearly at the same period, the operations of the French divisions were nearly simultaneous; I shall, therefore, narrate their proceedings separately, classing them by the effect each produced upon the stability of the intrusive government of Madrid.

CHAP.
V.

1808.
June.

OPERATIONS OF MARSHAL BESSIERES.

This officer had scarcely fixed his quarters at Burgos when a general movement of revolt took place. On his right, the bishop of St. Ander excited the inhabitants of the diocese to take arms. In his rear, a mechanic assembled some thousand armed peasants at the town of Logroño. In front, five thousand men took possession of the Spanish artillery dépôt at Segovia, and an equal number assembling at Palencia, advanced to the town of Torquemada, while general Cuesta, with some regular troops and a body of organized peasantry, took post on the Pisuerga at Cabeçon.

Moniteur.
Victoires et
Conquêtes
des Français.

Bessières immediately divided his disposable force, which was not more than twelve thousand men, into several columns, and traversing the country in all directions, disarmed the towns and interrupted the combinations of the insurgents, while a division of Dupont's corps, under general Frere, marched from the side of Madrid to aid his efforts. General

Verdier attacked Logroño on the 6th of June, dispersed the peasantry, and put the leaders to death after the action. General Lasalle, departing from Burgos with a brigade of light cavalry, passed the Pisuerga, fell upon the Spaniards at Torquemada on the 7th, broke them, and pursuing with a merciless sword, burnt that town, and entered Palencia on the 8th. Meanwhile Frere defeated the Spanish force at Segovia, taking thirty pieces of artillery; and general Merle marching through the country lying between the Pisuerga and the Duero with a division of infantry, joined Lasalle at Dueñas on the 12th; from thence they proceeded to Cabeçon, where Cuesta accepting battle, was overthrown, with much slaughter, the loss of his artillery, and several thousand musquets.

The flat country being thus subdued, Lasalle's cavalry remained to keep it under, while Merle, marching northward, commenced operations, in concert with general Ducos, against the province of St. Ander. On the 20th, the latter general drove the Spaniards from the pass of Soncillo; the 21st, he forced the pass of Venta de Escudo, and descending the valley of the river Pas, approached St. Ander; on the 22d, Merle, after some resistance, penetrating by Lantueño, followed the course of the Besaya to Torre La Vega, then turning to his right, entered St. Ander on the 23d; Ducos arrived at the same time, the town submitted, and the bishop fled with the greatest part of the clergy. The authorities of Segovia, Valladolid, Palencia, and St. Ander were then compelled to send deputies to take the oath of allegiance to Joseph. By these operations, the above-named provinces were completely disarmed, and so awed by the activity of Bessières that no

further insurrections took place, his cavalry raised
contributions and collected provisions without the
least difficulty ; Frere's division then returned to
Toledo, and from thence marched to San Clemente,
on the borders of Murcia.

While Bessières thus broke the northern insurrections, the march of general Lefebre Desnouettes
against the province of Aragon brought on the first
siege of Zaragoza. To that place had flocked Cavallero.
from the most distant parts, soldiers, flying from
Madrid and Pampelona, the engineers of the school
of Alcala, and all the retired officers in Aragon.
With their assistance Palafox's forces were rapidly
organized, and numerous battalions were posted on
the roads leading to Navarre. The baron de Versage, an officer of the Walloon guards, occupied
Calatayud with a regiment composed of students,
and made a levy there to protect the powder-mills
of Villa Felice, and to keep a communication with
Soria and Siguenza. The arsenal of Zaragoza supplied the patriots with arms ; the people of Tudela
broke their bridge on the Ebro, and Palafox reinforced them with five hundred fuzileers.

It was in this situation of affairs Lefebre commen- S.
ced his march from Pampelona the 7th of June, at Journal of Lefebre's
the head of three or four thousand infantry, some Opera-tions. MS.
field batteries, and a regiment of Polish cavalry. On Moniteur. Victoire et
the 9th he forced the passage of the Ebro, put the Conquêtes des Fran-
leaders of the insurrection to death, after the action, çais. Cavallero.
and then continued his movement by the right bank
to Mallen. On the Huecha, Palafox with ten thousand infantry, two hundred dragoons, and eight
pieces of artillery, disputed the passage, but on
the 13th, he was overthrown. The 14th, the French
reached the Xalon, where another combat and

another victory carried Lefebre across that river. The 15th he was on the Huerba, in front of the heroic city.

FIRST SIEGE OF ZARAGOZA.

Zaragoza contained fifty thousand inhabitants. Situated on the right bank of the Ebro, it was connected with a suburb, on the opposite side, by a handsome stone bridge ; its immediate vicinity was flat, and on the side of the suburb low and marshy. The small river Huerba, running through a deep cleft, cut the plain on the right bank, and taking its course close to the walls, fell into the Ebro nearly opposite to the mouth of the Gallego, which, descending from the mountains on the opposite side, also cut the plain on the left bank. The convent of St. Joseph, built on the right of the Huerba, covered a bridge over that torrent, and, at the distance of cannon-shot, a step of land commenced, which, gradually rising, terminated at eighteen hundred yards from the convent, in a hill called the

Monte Torrero. On this hill, which commanded all the plain and overlooked the town, several storehouses, built for the use of the canal, were entrenched, and occupied by twelve hundred men, and the canal itself, a noble work, furnished water carriage without a single lock from Tudela to Zaragoza.

The city, surrounded by a low brick wall, presented no regular defences, and possessed very few guns in a serviceable state; but the houses were strongly constructed, and for the most part of two stories, each story vaulted, so as to be nearly fireproof. Every house had its garrison, and the

massive convents, rising like castles, around the
circuit and inside the place, were crowded with
armed men. Such was Zaragoza when Lefebre Desnouettes appeared before it, his previous movements
having cut the direct communication with Calatayud,
and obliged the baron Versage to retire to Belchite
with his volunteers and fresh levies.

Palafox had occupied the olive groves and houses
on the step of land between the convent of St. Joseph
and Monte Torrero, but his men, cowed by their
previous defeats, were easily driven from thence on
the 16th. The town was then closely invested on
the right bank of the Ebro, and so great was the
terror of the Spaniards, that some of the French,
penetrating without difficulty into the street of St.
Engracia, were like to have taken the city. Palafox,
accompanied by his brother Francisco, an aide-de-
camp, and one hundred dragoons, endeavoured, under
pretence of seeking succour, to go forth on the side
of the suburb at the moment when the French were
entering on the side of Engracia, but the plebeian
leaders, suspicious of his intentions, would not
suffer him to depart without a guard of infantry,
commanded by *Tio*, or goodman Jorge. It was
this person and *Tio* Marin, who by their energy
contributed most to the defence of the city in the
first siege ; but for them Palafox who has gathered
the honours, would have fled at one gate, while the
enemy was pressing in at another, and Zaragoza
was then on the verge of destruction, for the streets
were filled with clamour, the troops making little
resistance, and all things in confusion. But the
French, either fearful of an ambuscade or ignorant
of their advantages suddenly retired, and then the
people as if inspired, changed from the extreme of

s.
Journal of
Lefebre's
Operations
MSS.

Cavallero.

terror to that of courage, suddenly fell to casting up defences, piercing loop-holes in the walls of the houses, and constructing ramparts with sand-bags, working with such vigour, that under the direction of their engineers, in twenty-four hours they put the place in a condition to withstand an assault. Whereupon Lefebre, confining his operations to the right bank of the Ebro, established posts close to the gates, and waited for reinforcements.

Meanwhile Palafox, crossing the Ebro at Pina, joined Versage at Belchite, and having collected seven or eight thousand men and four pieces of artillery, gained the Xalon in rear of the French. From thence he proposed to advance through Epila and relieve Zaragoza by a battle, but his officers, Cavallero. amazed at this project, resisted his authority, and would have retired upon Valencia. Nevertheless, ignorant of war, and probably awed by Tio Jorge, he expressed his determination to fight, saying, with an imposing air, ' that those who feared might retire.' Touched with shame, all agreed to follow him to Epila, but two French regiments, detached by Lefebre, met him on the march, and the Spaniards, unable to form any order of battle, were, notwithstanding their superior numbers, defeated with the loss of three thousand men. Palafox, who did not display that firmness in danger which his speech promised, must have fled early, for he reached Calatayud in the night, although many of his troops arrived there unbroken the next morning. After this disaster, leaving Versage at Calatayud, to make fresh levies, the Spanish chief repaired, with all the beaten troops that he could collect, to Belchite, and from thence regained Zaragoza on the 2nd of July.

Meanwhile Lefebre had taken the Monte Torrero by assault, and on the 29th of June, was joined by general Verdier with a division of infantry and a large battering train; and being then twelve thousand strong, attacked the convents of St. Joseph and the Capuchins, the very day that Palafox returned. A first assault on St. Joseph's failed, but the second succeeded, and the Capuchins, after some fighting, was set fire to by the Spaniards and abandoned. All this time the suburb was left open and free for the besieged; and Napoleon, who blamed this mode of attack, sent orders to throw a bridge across the Ebro,—to press the siege on the left bank,—and to profit of the previous success, by raising a breaching battery in the convent of St. Joseph. A bridge was accordingly constructed at St. Lambert, two hundred yards above the town, and two attacks were carried on at the same time. A change also took place in the command, for hitherto the French troops employed in the siege formed a part of marshal Bessieres' corps, but the emperor now directed Lefebre to rejoin that marshal with a brigade, and then constituting the ten thousand men who remained with Verdier a separate corps, gave him the command.

S.
Journal of
Lefebre's
Operations
MSS.

Verdier continued to press the siege as closely as his numbers would permit, but around him, the insurgents were rapidly organising small armies, and threatened to enclose him in his camp, wherefore he sent detachments against them; and it is singular that, with so few men, while daily fighting with the besieged, he should have been able to scour the country, and put down the insurrection, as far as Lerida, Barbastro, Tudela, Jacca, and Calatayud, without any assistance save what

Napoleon's notes,
Appendix,
No. 2.

68

HISTORY OF THE

BOOK
I.

1808.
July.

Cavallero.

the garrison of Pampelona could give him from the side of Navarre. In one of these expeditions the powder-mills of Villa Felice, thirty miles distant, were destroyed, and the baron Versage was defeated, and forced to retire with his division towards Valencia.

During the course of July, Verdier made several assaults on the gate of El Carmen, and the Portillo, but he was repulsed in all, and the besieged having been reinforced by the regiment of Estremadura, composed of eight hundred old soldiers, made a sally with two thousand men to retake the Monte Torrero; they were, however, beaten, with the loss of their commander, and regular approaches were then commenced by the French against the quarter of St. Engracia and the castle of Aljaferia. The 2nd of August, the besieged were again reinforced by two hundred men of the Spanish guards and volunteers of Aragon, who brought some artillery with them, but the French also, were strengthened by two old regiments of the line, which increased their numbers to fifteen thousand men;

August. and on the 3rd, the breaching batteries opened against St. Engracia and Aljaferia; the mortars threw shells at the same time, and a Spanish magazine of powder blowing up in the Cosso a public walk formed on the line of the ancient Moorish ramparts, destroyed several houses, and killed many of the defenders. The place was then summoned, but as Palafox rejected all offers, a breach in the convent of St. Engracia was stormed on the

Cavallero. 4th. The French penetrated to the Cosso, and a confused and terrible scene ensued, for while some Spaniards defended the houses and some drew up in the streets, others fled by the suburb to the country, where the cavalry fell upon them. Cries of treason, the sure signals for assassinations, were everywhere heard, and all seemed lost, when a column of the assailants, seeking a way to the bridge over the Ebro, got entangled in the Arco de Cineja, a long crooked street, and being attacked in that situation, were driven back to the Cosso; others began to plunder, and the Zaragozans recovering courage, fought with desperation, and finally set fire to the convent of Francisco : at the close of day the French were in possession of one side of the Cosso, and the Spaniards of the other. A hideous and revolting spectacle was exhibited during this action, for the public hospital being set on fire, the madmen confined there, issued forth among the combatants, muttering, shouting, singing, and moping, each according to the character of his disorder, while drivelling idiots mixed their unmeaning cries with the shouts of contending soldiers.

CHAP.
V.

1808.
August.

Cavallero.

The Spaniards now perceived that, with courage, the town might still be defended, and from that day the fighting was murderous and constant ; one party endeavouring to take, the other to defend the houses. In this warfare, where skill was nearly useless, Verdier's force was too weak to make a rapid progress, and events disastrous to the French arms taking place in other parts of Spain, he received, about the 10th, orders from the king to raise the siege, and retire to Logroña. Of this operation I shall speak in due time.

s.
Journal of
Lefebre's
Operations
MSS.

OBSERVATIONS.

1°. Mere professional skill and enterprise do not constitute a great general. Lefebre Desnouettes, by

his activity and boldness, with a tithe of their numbers, defeated the insurgents of Aragon in several
actions, and scoured the open country ; but the same
Lefebre, wanting the higher qualities of a general,
failed miserably where that intuitive sagacity which
reads passing events aright, was required.   There
were thousands in the French army who could have
done as well as he, probably not three who could
have reduced Zaragoza ; and yet it is manifest that
Zaragoza owed her safety to accident, and that the
desperate resistance of the inhabitants was more the
result of chance than of any peculiar virtue.

2°. The feeble defence made at Mallen, at the
Xalon, at the Monte Torrero, at Epila ; the terror
of the besieged on the 16th, when the French penetrated into the town ; the flight of Palafox under the
pretence of seeking succour; nay, the very assault
which in such a wonderful manner called forth the
energy of the Zaragozans, and failed only because
the French troops plundered, and, by missing the
road to the bridge, missed that to victory, proves,
that the fate of the city was determined by accident,
in more than one of those nice conjunctures, which
men of genius know how to seize, but others leave
to the decision of fortune.   However, it must be
acknowledged that Lefebre and Verdier, especially
the latter, displayed both vigour and talent ; for it
was no mean exploit to quell the insurrections to a
distance of fifty miles on every side, at the same
time investing double their own numbers, and
pushing the attack with such ardour as to reduce
to extremity a city so defended.

3°. The current romantic tales, of women rallying
the troops and leading them forward at the most
dangerous periods of this siege, I have not touched

upon, and may perhaps be allowed to doubt; yet
it is not unlikely, that when suddenly environed
with horrors, the delicate sensitiveness of women,
driving them to a kind of phrenzy, might produce
actions above the heroism of men, and in patient
suffering their superior fortitude is acknowledged by
all nations : wherefore I neither wholly believe, nor
will deny, their exploits at Zaragoza, merely remark-
ing, that for a long time afterwards, Spain swarmed
with heroines from that city, clothed in half uni-
forms, and loaded with weapons.

4°. The two circumstances that principally contributed to the success of the defence were, the bad
discipline of the French soldiers, and the system of
terror which was established by the Spanish leaders,
whoever those leaders were. Few soldiers can be
restrained from plunder when a town is taken by
assault, yet there is no period when the chances of
war are so sudden and so decisive, none where the
moral responsibility of a general is so great. Will
military regulations alone secure the necessary discipline at such a moment ? The French army are
not deficient in a stern code, and the English army,
taken altogether, is probably the best regulated of
modern times ; but here it is seen that Lefebre
failed to take Zaragoza in default of discipline ; and
in the course of this work it will appear, that no
wild horde of Tartars ever fell with more licence
upon their rich effeminate neighbours, than did the
English troops upon the Spanish towns taken by
storm. The inference to be drawn is, that national
institutions only will produce that moral discipline
necessary to make a soldier capable of fulfilling his
whole duty ; yet the late Lord Melville was not
ashamed to declare in parliament that the worst

BOOK I.
1808.
Cavallero.

men make the best soldiers; and this odious, narrow-minded, unworthy maxim, had its admirers. That a system of terror was at Zaragoza successfully employed to protract the defence is undoubted. The commandant of Monte Torrero, ostensibly for suffering himself to be defeated, but according to some for the gratification of private malice, was tried and put to death; a general of artillery was in a more summary manner killed without any trial, and the chief engineer, a man of skill and undaunted courage, was arbitrarily imprisoned. The slightest word, or even gesture, of discontent, was punished with instant death. A stern band of priests, and plebeian-leaders, in whose hands Palafox was a tool, ruled with such furious energy, that resistance to the enemy was less dangerous than disobedience to their orders: suspicion was the warrant of death, and this system once begun, ceased not until the town was taken in the second siege.

CHAPTER VI.

OPERATIONS IN CATALONIA.

WHEN Barcelona fell into the power of the French, the Spanish garrison amounted to nearly four thousand men, wherefore, Duhesme, daily fearing a riot in the city, connived at their escape in parties, and even sent the regiment of Estremadura entire to Lerida; but, strange to relate, the gates were shut against it! and thus discarded by both parties, it made its way into Zaragoza during the siege of that place. Many thousand citizens also fled from Barcelona, and joined the patriotic standards in the neighbouring provinces.

After the first ebullition at Manresa, the insurrection of Catalonia lingered awhile, yet the junta of Gerona continued to excite the people to take arms, and it was manifest that a general commotion approached. This was a serious affair, for there were in the beginning of June, including those who came out of Barcelona, five thousand veteran troops in the province, and in the Balearic islands above ten thousand; Sicily contained an English army, and English fleets covered the Mediterranean. Moreover, by the constitution of Catalonia, the whole of the male population fit for war are obliged to assemble, at certain points of each district, with arms and provisions, whenever the alarum bell, called the *somaten*, is heard to ring, hence the name of *somatenes;* and these warlike peasants, either from tradition or experience, are

CHAP.
VI.
———
1808.

Cabanes,
1st Part.

Napoleon's notes.
Appendix,
No. 2.

Cabanes,
1st Part.

BOOK
I.
1808.
June.
well acquainted with the military value of their mountain holds.

Hostilities soon commenced. Duhesme, following his instructions, detached general Chabran, with five thousand two hundred men, to secure Tarragona and Tortosa, to incorporate the Swiss regiment of Wimpfen with his own troops, and to aid marshal Moncey in an attack on Valencia. At the same

St. Cyr.
Victoire et
Conquê-
tes des
Francois.
Foy.
Cabanes.
time general Swartz having more than three thousand Swiss, Germans, and Italians, under his command, was detached by the way of Martorel and Montserrat to Manresa. His orders were to raise contributions to put down the insurrection, to destroy the powder-mills at the last town, to get possession of Lerida, to incorporate all the Swiss troops found there in his own brigade, to place five hundred men in the citadel, and finally to penetrate into Aragon, and co-operate with Lefebre against Zaragoza.

These two columns quitted Barcelona the 3d and the 4th of June, but a heavy rain induced Swartz to halt the 5th at Martorel; the 6th he resumed his march without any military precautions, although the object of his expedition was known, and, the somaten ringing out among the hills, the
Ibid.
peasants of eight districts were assembled in arms. These men having taken a resolution to defend the pass of Bruch, the most active of the Manresa and Igualada districts, assisted by a few old soldiers, immediately repaired there, and when Swartz came on in a careless manner, opened a heavy but distant fire from the rocks. Some confusion arose, but the Catalans were soon beaten from their fastness, and pursued for four or five miles along the main road, to Casa Mansana, where a cross road leads to

Manresa, here one part broke away, while the others continued their flight to Igualada.

Swartz, a man evidently destitute of talent, halted at the very moment when his success was complete, and the Catalans, seeing his hesitation, first rallied in the rear of Casa Mansana, then returned to the attack, and finally drove the advanced guard back upon the main body. The French general now became alarmed, formed a square, and retired hastily towards Esparraguéra, followed and flanked by clouds of somatenes, whose courage and numbers increased every moment. At Esparraguéra, which was a long single street, the inhabitants had prepared an ambush, but Swartz, who arrived at twilight, getting intelligence of their design, passed to the right and left of the houses, and continuing his flight, reached Martorel the 7th. He lost a gun and many men by this inglorious expedition, from which he returned in such disorder, and with his soldiers so discouraged, that Duhesme thought it necessary to recal Chabran from Tarragona. That general, although the country westward of the Llobregat is rugged and difficult for an army, had reached Tarragona on the 8th without encountering an enemy; but when he attempted to return, the line of his march was intercepted by the insurgents, who took post at Vendrill, Arbos, and Villa Franca, and spread themselves along the banks of the Llobregat. As he approached Vendrill the somatenes fell back to Arbos, and were defeated there, whereupon the French set fire to the town, and proceeded to Villa Franca. Here the excesses so common at this time among the Spaniards were not spared; the governor, an old man, and several of his friends, had been murdered, and the

perpetrators of these crimes, as might be expected,
made little or no defence against the enemy. Meanwhile general Lechi moved out of Barcelona, and
acting in concert with Swartz's brigade, which had
reached Martorel, cleared the banks of the Llobregat
and formed a junction at San Felice with Chabran
on the 11th. The latter, after a day's rest, then
marched with his own and Swartz brigade on Manresa to repair the former disgrace, and he arrived at
Bruch the 14th; but the somatenes assisted by some
regular troops with artillery, were again there, and
Chabran, more timid even than Swartz, finding that
in a partial skirmish he made no impression, took
the extraordinary resolution of retreating, or rather
flying from those gallant peasants, who pursued him
with scoffs and a galling fire back to the very walls
of Barcelona.

These successes spurred on the insurrection.
Gerona, Rosas, Hostalrich, and Tarragona prepared
for defence. The somatenes of the Ampurdan,
obliged the French commandant to quit the town
of Figueras, and shut himself up with three hundred men in the citadel, while others, gathering
between the Ter and the Besos, intercepted all
communication between France and Barcelona.
In this predicament, Duhesme resolved to make
a sudden attempt on Gerona, with six thousand
of his best troops, and eight pieces of artillery ;
but as the fortress of Hostalrich stood in the direct
road, he followed the coast line, and employed a
French privateer, then in the harbour, to attend
his march. The somatenes soon got intelligence
of his designs ; one multitude took possession of
the heights of Moncada, which are six miles from

Barcelona, and overhang the road to Hostalrich ; another multitude was posted on the ridge of Mongat, which, at the same distance from Barcelona abuts on the sea, and these last were protected on the left by an intrenched castle with a battery of fifteen guns, and on the right were slightly connected with the people at Moncada. The 17th, Duhesme, after some false movements, defeated them, and a detachment from Barcelona dispersed those at Moncada the same day ; the 18th, the town of Mattaro was taken and plundered, the somatenes were again defeated at the pass of St. Pol, and at nine o'clock in the morning of the 20th, the French appeared before Gerona.

This town, built on the right bank of the Ter, is cut in two by the Oña. To the eastward it is confined by strong rocky hills, whose points filling the space between the Oña and the Ter, overlook the town at different distances. Fort Mont Jóuy, a regular fortification, crowned the nearest hill or table land, at five hundred yards' distance ; three other forts, namely that of the Constable, that of queen Ann, and that of Capuchins, all connected by a ditch and rampart, formed one irregular outwork, a thousand yards in length, and commanding all the ridge to the south-east. The summit of this ridge is five, eight, and twelve hundred yards from Gerona, and sixteen hundred from Fort Mont Jouy, and is separated from the latter by the narrow valley and stream of the Gallegan.

South-west, between the left of the Oña and the Ter, the country is comparatively flat, but full of hollows and clefts close to the town, and the body of the place, on that side, was defended by a ditch and five regular bastions connected by a wall with towers.

To the west the city was covered by the Ter, and on the east fortified by a long wall with towers having an irregular bastion at each extremity, and some small detached works placed at the opening of the valley of Gallegan. Three hundred of the regiment of Ultonia and some artillery-men composed the garrison of Gerona ; they were assisted by volunteers and by the citizens, and the somatenes also assembled on the left of the Ter to defend the passage of that river.

Duhesme, after provoking some cannon-shot from the forts, occupied the village of St. Eugenia in the plain, and making a feint as if to pass the Ter by the bridge of Salt, engaged the somatenes in a useless skirmish. Great part of the day was spent by him in preparing ladders for the attack ; at five o'clock in the evening the French artillery opened from the heights of Palau, and then a column crossing St. Cyr. the Oña passed between the outworks and the town, threw out a detachment to keep the garrison of the former in check, and assaulted the gate of El Carmen. This attempt failed completely, and with great loss to the assailants. Two hours after, another column advancing by the left of the Oña, assaulted the bastion of Santa Clara, but with so little ar- Lafaille. rangement or discipline, that the storming party had only three or four ladders ; and although by favour of the hollows they reached the walls unperceived, and the Neapolitan colonel Ambrosio and the engineer Lafaille actually gained the top of the ramparts, the confusion amongst the assailants was such, that no success was obtained. Duhesme tried negociation on the following day, yet dread- ing a longer absence from Barcelona, broke up on the 22d, and returned by forced marches, leaving Chabran with some troops in Mattaro as he passed. During his absence the victorious somatenes of Bruch had descended the Llobregat, rallied those of the lower country, and getting artillery from Taragona and other fortresses, planted batteries at the different passages of the river, and entrenched a line from San Boy to Martorel. Regular officers now took the command of the peasants. Colonel Milans assembled a body at Granollers ; don Juan Clàros put himself at the head of the peasants of the Ampurdan ; colonel Baget took the command of those at Bruch.

Chabran, after a few days' rest at Mattaro, made a foraging excursion through the district of El Valles, but Milans, who held the valley of the Congosta, encountered him near Granollers, and both sides claimed the victory ; Chabran, however, retired to Barcelona, and Milans remained on the banks of the Besos. The 30th, Duhesme caused the somatenes on the Llobregat to be attacked, sent Lechi to menace those at the bridge of Molinos del Rey, and the brigades of Bessieres and Goullus, to cross at San Boy; the latter having surprised a battery at that point turned the whole line, and Lechi then crossing the river by the bridge of Molinos, ascended the left bank, took all the artillery, burnt several villages, and put the insurgents to flight. They however rallied again, at Bruch and Igualada, and returning the 6th of July, infested the immediate vicinity of Barcelona, taking possession of all the hills between San Boy and Moncada, and connecting their operations with colonel Milans. Other parties collected between the Besos and the Ter, and the line of insurrection was extended to the Ampurdan ; Juan Clàros occupied the flat country about Rosas, and the French garrison of Figueras having burnt the town, were blocked up in the fort of San Fernando by two thousand somatenes of the Pyrenees; a nest of Spanish privateers was formed in Palamos Bay, and two English frigates, the Imperieuse and the Cambrian, watched the coast from Rosas to Barcelona. A supreme junta was now established at Lerida, and opened an intercourse with Aragon, Valencia, Seville, Gibraltar, and the Balearic islands; it also decreed, that forty tercios, or regiments of one thousand men, to be selected from the somatenes, should be paid and organized as regular troops, and that forty others should be kept in reserve, but without pay.

This state of affairs being made known to Napoleon through the medium of the moveable columns watching the valleys of the eastern Pyrenees, he ordered general Reille, then commanding the reserve at Perpignan, to take the first soldiers at hand and march to the relief of Figueras; after which, his force being increased by drafts from the interior of France to nine thousand, he was to assault Rosas and besiege Gerona; and the emperor imagined, that the fall of the latter place would induce the surrender of Lerida, and would so tranquillize Catalonia, that five thousand men might again be detached towards Valencia. On receiving this order, Reille, with two battalions of Tuscan recruits, conducted a convoy safely to Figueras and raised the blockade, but not without difficulty, for his troops were greatly terrified and could scarcely be kept to their colours. He however relieved the place the 10th of July, and the same day, Duhesme, who had been preparing for a second attack on Ge-

Foy's
History.

rona, quitted Barcelona with six thousand infantry, some cavalry, a battering train of twenty-two pieces, and a great number of country carriages to transport his ammunition and stores, leaving Lechi in the city with five thousand men. Meanwhile Reille, having victualled Figueras and received a part of his reinforcements, proceeded to invest Rosas; but he had scarcely appeared before it, when Juan Clàros raised the country in his rear, and captain Otway, of the Montague, landing with some marines, joined the migueletes, whereupon the French retired with a loss of two hundred men.

Lord Collingwood's despatch, Aug. 27. Foy's History.

Duhesme pursued his march by the coast, but the somatenes broke up the road in his front, Milans hung on his left, and lord Cochrane, with the Imperieuse frigate and some Spanish vessels, cannonaded his right. Thus incommoded, he halted five days in front of Arenas de Mar, and then dividing his force, sent one part across the mountains by Villagorguin, and another by San Isicle. The first column made an attempt on Hostalrich, and failed; the second, beating Milans, dispersed the somatenes of the Tordera, and finally, Duhesme united his forces before Gerona, but he lost many carriages on his march. The 23d he passed the Ter, and dispersed the migueletes that guarded the left bank. The 24th general Reille, coming from Figueras with six thousand men, took post at Puente Mayor, and the town was invested, from that point, by the heights of San Miguel to the Monte Livio; from Monte Livio by the plain to the bridge of Salt; and from thence along the left bank of the Ter to Sarria. The garrison, consisting of five hundred migueletes and four hundred of the regiment of Ultonia, was reinforced on the 25th by thirteen hundred of the

regiment of Barcelona, who entered the town with
two guns; the defences were in bad repair, but
the people were resolute.

In the night of the 27th, a French column passed
the valley of the Galligan, gained the table land of
Mont Jouy, and of three towers, which the Spaniards abandoned in a panic. This advantage so
elated Duhesme, that he resolved, without con-
sulting his engineer, to break ground on that side;
but at this period a great change in the affairs
of Catalonia had taken place. The insurrection
hitherto confined to the exertions of the unorga-
nised somatenes, was now consolidated by a treaty
between lord Collingwood, who commanded the
British navy in the Mediterranean, and the marquis of Palacios, who was captain-general of the
Balearic isles; thus the Spanish fleet and the troops
in Minorca, Majorca, and Ivica, became disposable
for the service of the patriots. Palacios immediately sent thirteen hundred men to the port of
San Felice di Quixols to reinforce the garrison of
Gerona, and these men entered that city, as we
have seen, on the 25th, while Palacios himself
disembarked four thousand others, together with
thirty seven pieces of artillery, at Tarragona, an
event which excited universal joy, and produced
a surprising eagerness to fight the French. The
supreme junta immediately repaired to that town,
declared Palacios their president, and created him
commander-in-chief, subject, however, to their tutelar
saint, Narcissus, who was appointed generalissimo
of the forces by sea and land, the ensigns of authority being, with due solemnity, placed on his coffin.

The first object with Palacios was to re-establish
the line of the Llobregat. To effect this, the count

St. Cyr
Campaign
in Catalo-
nia.
Cabanes'
History.

of Caldagues, with eighteen hundred men and four CHAP. VI. guns, marched from Tarragona in two columns, the —— one moving by the coast way to San Boy, and the 1808. July. other by the royal road, through Villafranca and Ordal. Caldagues, in passing by the bridge of Molino del Rey, established a post there, and then ascending the left bank, fixed his quarters at Martorel, where colonel Baget joined him with three thousand migueletes of the new levy. Now the Llobregat runs within a few miles of Barcelona, but as the right bank is much the steepest, the lateral communications easier, and as the heights command a distinct view of everything passing on the opposite side, the line taken by Caldagues was strong, for the country in his rear was rough with defiles, and very fitting for a retreat after the loss of a battle.

General Lechi, thus hemmed in on the west, was also hampered on the north, because the mountains filling the space between the Llobregat and the Besos, approach in tongues as near as two and three miles from Barcelona, and the somatenes of the Manresa and Valls districts occupying them, skirmished daily with the French outposts. And beyond the Besos, which bounds Barcelona on the eastward, a lofty continuous ridge, extending to Hostalrich, runs parallel to and at the distance of two or three miles from the sea coast, separating the main from the marine roads, and sending its shoots down to the water's edge; this ridge also swarmed with somatenes, who cut off all communication with Duhesme, and lay in leaguer round the castle of Mongat, in which were eighty or ninety French. The Cambrian and the Imperieuse frigates blockaded the harbour of Barcelona itself; and, on the 31st,

BOOK
I.

1808.
August.
Lord Col-
lingwood's
des-
patches.

St. Cyr.

lord Cochrane having brought his vessel alongside of Mongat, landed his marines, and, in concert with the somatenes, took it, blew up the works, and rolled the rocks and ruins down in such a manner as to destroy the road. Thus, at the very moment that Duhesme commenced the siege of Gerona, he was cut off from his own base of operations, and the communication between Figueras and general Reille's division was equally insecure; for the latter's convoys were attacked the 28th of July and the 3d of August; and so fiercely on the 6th, that a Neapolitan battalion was surrounded, and lost one hundred and fifty men.

Palacios, whose forces increased daily, now wished to make an effort in favour of Gerona, and with this view sent the count of Caldagues, at the head of three or four thousand men part migueletes, part regulars, to interrupt the progress of the siege, intending to follow himself with greater forces. Caldagues marched by Tarrasa, Sabadell, Granollers, and San Celoni, and reached Hostalrich the morning of the 10th, where his force was increased to five thousand men and four guns. The 13th, he entered Llagostera, and the 14th Castellar, a small place situated behind the ridges that overlook Gerona and only five miles from the French camps. Here Juan Clàros with two thousand five hundred migueletes, mixed with some Walloon and Spanish Guards from Rosas, met him, as did also Milans with eight hundred somatenes. A communication with the junta of Gerona was then opened, Fort Mont Jouy was upon the point of surrendering, but the French, who were ignorant of Caldagues' approach, had, contrary to good discipline, heaped their forces in the plain between the left of the

Oña and the Ter, but only kept a slender guard on the hills, while a single battalion protected the batteries raised against Mont Jouy. Being an enterprising, man the Spanish general resolved to make an immediate effort for the relief of the place, and, after a careful observation, sent, on the 16th, several columns against the weak part of the besiegers' line, the garrison sallied forth at the same time from Mont Jouy, and the French guards being taken between two fires, were quickly overpowered, and driven first to the Puente Mayor and finally over the Ter. The Catalans re-formed on the hills, expecting to be attacked; but Duhesme and Reille remained quiet until dark, and then breaking up the siege, fled, the one to Figueras, the other to Barcelona, leaving both artillery and stores behind.

Duhesme at first wished to retreat by the coast, but at Callella he learned that the road was cut, that an English frigate was ready to rake his columns, and that the somatenes were on all the heights, wherefore, destroying his ammunition, he threw his artillery over the rocks, and, taking to the mountains, forced a passage through the somatenes to Mongat, where Lechi met him and covered the retreat to Barcelona.

OBSERVATION 1st.—Three great communications pierce the Pyrenean frontier of Catalonia, leading directly upon Barcelona.

The first, or Puycerda road penetrates between the sources of the Segre and the Ter.

The second, or Campredon road, between the sources of the Ter and the Fluvia.

The third, or Figueras road, between the sources of the Muga and the sea-coast.

The first and second unite at Vicque; the second
and third are connected by a transverse road running from Olot, by Castle Follit, to Gerona; the
third also dividing near the latter town, leads with
one branch through Hostalrich, and with the other
follows the line of the coast.   After the union of the
first and second at Vicque, a single route pursues
the stream of the Besos to Barcelona, thus turning
the Muga, the Fluvia, the Ter, the Tordera, Besos,
and an infinity of minor streams, which in their
rapid course to the Mediterranean, furrow all the
country between the eastern Pyrenees and Barcelona.   The third, which is the direct and best communication between Perpignan and the capital of
Catalonia, crosses all the above-named rivers, and
their deep channels and sudden floods offer serious
obstacles to the march of an army.

All these roads, with the exception of that from
Olot to Gerona, are separated by craggy mountain
ridges scarcely to be passed by troops; and the two
first leading through wild and savage districts, are
incommoded by defiles, and protected by a number
of old castles and walled places, more or less capable of resistance.   The third, passing through many
rich and flourishing places, is however completely
blocked, to an invader, by the strong fortresses of
Figueras and Rosas on the Muga, of Gerona on the
Ter, and Hostalrich on the Tordera.   Palamos and
other castles likewise impede the coast road, which
is moreover skirted by rocky mountains, and exposed
for many leagues to the fire of a fleet.   Such is
Catalonia, eastward and northward of Barcelona.

On the west, at five or six miles distance, the
Llobregat cuts it off from a rough and lofty tract,
through which the Cardena, the Noga, the Foix,

Gaya, Anguera, and Francoli rivers, breaking down
deep channels, descend, in nearly parallel lines, to
the coast, and the spaces between are gorged with
mountains, and studded with fortified places which
command all the main roads.

So few and contracted are the plains and fertile
valleys, that Catalonia may, with the exception of
the rich parts about Lerida and the Urgel, be
described as a huge mass of rocks and torrents,
incapable of supplying subsistence even for the
inhabitants, whose prosperity depends entirely upon
manufactures and commerce. Barcelona, the richest
and most populous city in Spain, is the heart of the
province, and who masters it, if he can hold it, may
suck the strength of Catalonia away. But a French
army, without a commanding fleet to assist, can
scarcely take or keep Barcelona; the troops must
be supplied by regular convoys from France, the
fortresses on the line of communication must be
taken and provisioned, and the active intelligent
population of the country must be beaten from the
rivers, pursued into their fortresses, and warred
down by exertions which none but the best troops
are capable of: for the Catalans are robust, numerous, and brave enough after their own manner.

OBSERVATION 2d.—It follows from this exposition, that Duhesme evinced a surprising want of forethought and military sagacity, in neglecting to secure
Gerona, Hostalrich, and Tarragona, with garrisons,
when his troops were received into those places. It
was this negligence that rendered the timid operations of Swartz and Chabran capital errors; it was
this that enabled some poor, injured, indignant peasants to kindle a mighty war, and in a very few

BOOK I. weeks obliged Napoleon to send thirty thousand
men to the relief of Barcelona.

1808.

OBSERVATION 3d.—Duhesme was experienced in
battles, and his energy and resources of mind have
Napoleon. been praised by a great authority ; but undoubtedly
an absence of prudent calculation and arrangement,
a total neglect of military discipline, marked all his
operations in Catalonia, witness his mode of attack
St. Cyr. on Gerona, the deficiency of ladders, and the confusion of the assaults ; witness also his raising of the
second siege, and absolute flight from Caldagues,
whose rash enterprise, although crowned with success, should have caused his own destruction.   In
those affairs it is certain Duhesme displayed neither
Napole- talent nor vigour ; but in the severities he exercised
on's notes,
Appendix, at the sacking of Mattaro, in the burning of villages,
No. 2.
which he executed to the extreme verge of, if not
St. Cyr. beyond what the harshest laws of war will justify, an
Cabanes. odious energy was apparent ; and as the ardour of
the somatenes was rather increased than repressed
by these rigorous proceedings, his conduct may be
deemed as impolitic as it was barbarous.   It is however to be remembered that Duhesme has not wanted
defenders, who, asserting that he was humane and
Lafaille. just, accuse Lechi, his equal in rank, of being the
author of the severities exercised at Barcelona.

OBSERVATION 4th.—In Catalonia all the inherent
cruelty of the Spaniards was as grossly displayed as
in any other province of Spain ; the Catalans were
likewise vain and superstitious.   But their courage
was higher, their patriotism purer, and their efforts
more sustained, the somatenes were bold and active
in battle, the population of the towns firm, and some
of the juntas apparently disinterested ; the praise

merited, and bestowed, upon the people of Zaragoza is great, yet Gerona more justly claims the admiration of mankind. For the Aragonese troops were by Lefebre driven from the open country in crowds to their capital, and little was wanted to induce them to surrender at once; it was not until the last hour that, gathering courage from despair, the people of Zaragoza put forth all their energy, whereas those of Gerona, although attacked by a greater force, and possessing fewer means of defence, without any internal system of terror to counterbalance their fear of the enemy, manfully and successfully resisted from the first. The people of Zaragoza rallied at their hearthstone, those of Gerona stood firm at the porch. But quitting these matters, I must now, following the order I have marked out, proceed to relate the occurrences in Valencia.

OPERATIONS OF MARSHAL MONCEY.

The execution of Calvo and his followers changed the horrid aspect of the Valencian insurrection; the spirit of murder was checked, and the patriotic energy assumed a nobler appearance. Murcia and Valencia were united as one province, and towards the end of June, nearly thirty thousand men, armed and provided with artillery, attested the resources of these rich provinces, and the activity of their chiefs. The Valencians then conceived the plan of marching to the assistance of the Aragonese; but Napoleon had already prescribed the measures which were to render such a movement abortive.

An order, dated the 30th of May, had directed Moncey to move, with a column of ten thousand men, upon Cuenca; from that point he was to watch

BOOK
I.
───────
1808.
June.
8.
Journal of
Moncey's
Operations
MSS.
the country comprised between the lower Ebro and
Carthagena, and he was empowered to act against
the city of Valencia if he judged it fitting to do so.
The position of Cuenca was advantageous; a short
movement from thence to the left would place Moncey's troops upon the direct line between Valencia
and Zaragoza, and enable him to intercept all communication between those towns; and a few marches
to the right would place him upon the junction of
the roads leading from Carthagena and Valencia
to Madrid. If he thought it essential to attack
Valencia, the division of general Chabran was to co-
operate from the side of Catalonia, by which combination the operations of Lefebre Desnouettes at
Zaragoza, and those of Duhesme in Catalonia, were
covered from the Valencians; and at the same time
the flank of the French army at Madrid was protected on the side of Murcia.

The 6th of June Moncey marched from Aranjuez
by Santa Cruz, Tarancon, Carascoso, and Villa del
Osma, and reached Cuenca the 11th. Here receiving information of the rapid progress of the insurrec-
Ibid.
tion, of the state of the Valencian army, and of the
projected movement to relieve Zaragoza, he resolved
to make an attempt against the city of Valencia.
In this view, supposing general Chabran to be at
Tortosa, he ordered him to march upon Castellon de
la Plana, a town situated at some distance eastward
of the river Guadalaviar, proposing himself to clear
the country westward of that river, and he fixed the
25th of June as the latest period at which the two
columns were to communicate in the immediate
vicinity of Valencia.

Halting from the 11th to the 16th at Cuenca, he
marched the 17th to Tortola, the 18th to Buenaches,

the 19th to Matilla, the 20th to Minglanilla, and the 21st to Pesquiera; but from Buenaches to Pesquiera no inhabitants were to be seen, the villages were deserted, and either from fear or hatred, every living person fled before his footsteps. At length, a Swiss regiment, some of the Spanish guards, and a body of armed peasantry, made a stand at the bridge of Pajaso, upon the river Cabriel, and the manner in which the country had been forsaken, the gloomy and desolate marches, and this sudden appearance of an armed force ready to dispute this important pass, prognosticated a desperate conflict; yet the event belied the omens, scarcely any resistance was made.

Moncey, having informed general Chabran of this success, appointed the 27th and 28th for a junction under the walls of Valencia. The next day he Ibid. took a position at Otiel; but hearing that the defeated patriots had rallied and, reinforced, to the number of ten or twelve thousand, were intrenching themselves upon his left, he quitted the direct line of march to attack them in their post of Cabrillas, which was somewhat in advance of the Siete Aguas. The Spanish position was of extraordinary strength, the flanks rested upon steep rocky mountains, and the only approach to the front was through a long narrow defile, formed by high scarped rocks, whose tops, inaccessible from the French side, were covered with the armed peasantry of the neighbourhood. As a direct assault upon such a position could not succeed, and general Harispe was directed to turn it by the right, while the cavalry and artillery occupied the attention of the Spaniards in front; that general soon overcame the obstacles of ground, reached the Spanish troops, and defeated them, with the loss of all their cannon, ammunition, and baggage, and also of the Swiss regiment which came over to the victors. This action happened on the 24th, it freed Moncey's left flank, and he resumed his march by the direct road to Valencia, where he arrived the twenty-seventh. The ancient walls remained, all the approaches were commanded by works hastily repaired or newly raised, the citadel was in a state of defence, and the population were willing to fight.

A city, containing eighty thousand people actuated by violent passions, cannot be easily overcome; and Valencia, built upon low ground, and encircled with numerous canals and cuts, made for the purposes of irrigation, had its deep ditches filled with water, so that no approach could be made except against the gates. An assault seemed hopeless, but it is said that the marshal had corrupted a smuggler, who promised to betray the city during the heat of the assault, and it is probable that some secret understanding of that kind induced him to make an attempt which would otherwise have been rash and unmilitary.

Don Joseph Caro, a brother of the marquis of Romana, was with four thousand men entrenched behind the canal of the Guadalaviar, five miles in advance of the city gates; and as the village of Quarte, and some thickly planted mulberry trees, helped to render this post very strong, Moncey, who attacked it upon the 27th, met with a vigorous resistance. Caro was, however, beaten, and chased into the city, with the loss of some cannon, and on the 28th the French drove in the outposts, and occupied all the principal avenues of the town. Enthusiastic as the Valencians were while the enemy was at a distance, Moncey's appearance filled them with terror, and it is possible that a vigorous assault might have succeeded at the first moment of consternation; yet the favourable opportunity, if it really existed, quickly passed away. Padre Rico, a friar distinguished by his resolution, traversed the streets, with a cross in one hand and a sword in the other, arousing the sinking spirit and exciting the fanaticism of the multitude; the fear of retaliation for the massacre of the French residents, and the certainty that Moncey's troops were few, powerfully seconded his efforts, and as it is usual for undisciplined masses of people to pass suddenly from one extreme to another, fear was soon succeeded by enthusiasm.

After disposing his field-pieces at the most favourable points, Moncey, while the impression of Caro's defeat was fresh, summoned the governor. The latter answered, ' That he would defend the city,' and the French fire then opened; but the heavy guns of the Spaniards soon overpowered it. A warm skirmish about the houses of the suburbs and at the gates ensued, and the Valencians fought so well, that when the night fell, no impression had been made on the defences; the assailants were repulsed with loss at every point, and the situation of the French marshal became delicate. The persons sent to seek Chabran could gain no intelligence of that general's movements; the secret connexions in the town, if any there were, had failed; the ammunition was nearly expended, and the army was encumbered with seven or eight hundred wounded men, and among them the general of engineers. Moncey, swayed by these circumstances, relinquished his attack, and the 29th fell back to Quarte.

When it is considered that in a great city only a

small number of persons can estimate justly the immense advantages of their situation and the comparative weakness of the enemy, it must be confessed
that the spirit displayed by the Valencians upon
this occasion was very great; unfortunately it ended
here, nothing worthy of such an energetic commencement was afterwards performed, although
very considerable armies were either raised or maintained in the province.

Journal of
Moncey.
At Quarte, the French ascertained that the captain-general, Serbelloni, was marching upon Almanza to intercept the communication with Chieva
and Buñol, whereupon Moncey resolved to relinquish the line of Cuenca, and attack him before
he could quit the kingdom of Murcia. This vigorous resolution he executed with great celerity; for,
directing the head of his column towards Torrente,
he continued his march until night, halting a short
distance from that town, and by a forced march
the next day reached Alcira, only one league from
the river Xucar. From his bivouac at that place he
dispatched advice to general Chabran of this change
of affairs, and meanwhile Serbelloni, surprised in
the midst of his movement, and disconcerted
in his calculations by the decision and rapidity
of Moncey, took up a position to defend the passage of the Xucar. The line of that river is strong,
and offers many advantageous points of resistance,
but the Spaniards imprudently occupied both banks,
and in this exposed situation they were attacked
on the morning of the 1st of July. The division on
the French side of the river was overthrown, the
passage forced without loss of time, and Serbelloni
retired to the heights of San Felice, which covered

the main road leading from Alcira to Almanza, hoping to secure the defiles in front of the latter town before the enemy could arrive there. But Moncey was again too quick for him; leaving San Felice to his left, he continued his march on another route, and by a strenuous exertion seized the gorge of the defiles near Almanza late in the night of the 2d, and when the Spanish troops approached his position, he dispersed them at day-break on the 3d, and captured some of their guns. The road being now open, Moncey entered Almanza, and then marched by Bonete, and Chinchilla to Albacete, where he got intelligence that Frere's division, which he expected to find at San Clemente, was gone to Requeña.

To understand this movement of Frere, it must be known, that, when Dupont and Moncey marched against Andalusia and Valencia, two divisions were retained by Savary to scour the country near Madrid, and to connect the operations of the main bodies; but they were ill-managed. General Gobert, who, following Napoleon's orders, should have been at Valladolid, reinforced Dupont; and general Frere was sent to Requeña to reinforce Moncey, when he should have been at San Clemente, a central point, from whence he could have gained the road of Seville, that of Valencia and Cuenca, or that of Carthagena. Meanwhile the people of the Cuenca district having suddenly overpowered a detachment left there by Moncey, Savary ordered Frere to move from San Clemente to Requeña, and sent Caulaincourt from Taracon to quell the insurgents, which was effected with great slaughter on the 3d of July; and the town of Cuenca was pillaged. Hence when

Frere, who quitted San Clemente the 26th, reached
Requeña, he found the country quiet, heard of
Caulaincourt's success, and discovered that Moncey,
having crossed the Xucar, was on the road to San
Clemente. Then retracing his steps, he returned
to the latter place with troops, sickly, wearied, and
exhausted by these long useless marches in the heat
of summer.

Moncey now re-organized his forces, and was
preparing artillery and other means for a second
attempt against Valencia, when he was interrupted
by Savary, who, alarmed at the advance of Cuesta
and Blake, recalled Frere towards Madrid. The
marshal, extremely offended that the duke of Ro-
Foy's
History.
vigo, inflated with momentary power, should treat
him with so little ceremony, then abandoned San
Clemente, and returned by the way of Ocaña to
the capital.

OBSERVATIONS.

1°. The result of marshal Moncey's campaign was
published by the Spaniards, as a great and decisive
failure, and produced extravagant hopes of final
success ; a happy illusion, if the chiefs had not par-
taken of it, and pursued their wild course of mutual
flattery and exaggeration, without reflecting that in
truth there was nothing very satisfactory in the
prospect of affairs. Moncey's operation was in the
nature of a moveable column, the object of which
was to prevent the junction of the Valencian army
with the Aragonese ; the attempt upon the town
of Valencia was, therefore, a simple experiment,
which, successful, would have produced great effects, failing, was of trifling consequence in a
military point of view. Valencia was not the es-

sential object of the expedition, and the fate of the
general campaign depended upon the armies in Old
Castile.

2°. It was consoling that a rich, and flourishing
town, had not fallen into the power of the enemy;
but, at the same time, a want of real nerve in the
Spanish insurrection was visible. The kingdoms of
Murcia and Valencia acted in concert, and contained
two of the richest sea-port towns in the Peninsula;
their united force amounted to thirty thousand organized troops, exclusive of the armed peasants in
various districts, and the populace of Valencia were
deeply committed by the massacre of the French
residents. Here then, if in any place, a strenuous
resistance was to be expected; nevertheless, marshal
Moncey, whose whole force was, at first, only eight
thousand French, and never exceeded ten thousand
men, continued marching and fighting without cessation for a month, forced two of the strongest
mountain passes in the world, crossed several large
and difficult rivers, and carried the war into the
streets of Valencia. Disappointed of assistance
from Catalonia, he yet extricated himself from a
difficult situation, defeated his opponents in five
actions, killed and wounded a number of them,
equal in amount to the whole of his own force, and
made a circuit of above three hundred miles through
a hostile and populous country, without having
sustained any serious loss, without any desertion
from the Spanish battalions incorporated with his
own, and what was of more importance, having
those battalions much increased by desertions from
the enemy. In short, the great object of the expedition had been attained, the plan of relieving

Zaragoza was entirely frustrated, and the organization of an efficient Spanish force retarded. But
Moncey could hardly have expected to succeed
against the town of Valencia; for to use Napoleon's
words, ' *a city, with eighty thousand inhabitants,
barricadoed streets, and artillery placed at the gates,
cannot be* TAKEN BY THE COLLAR.'

3°. General Frere's useless march to Requeña
was very hurtful to the French, and the duke of
Rovigo was rated by the emperor for his want of
judgment upon the occasion : ' It was a folly,' the
latter writes, ' to dream of reinforcing Moncey, because, if that marshal failed in taking the city by
a sudden assault, it became an affair of artillery,
and twenty thousand men, more or less, would not
enable him to succeed.'—' Frere could do nothing
at Valencia, but he could do a great deal at San
Clemente ; because from that post he could support
either Madrid or general Dupont.'

4°. Moncey was slightly blamed by the emperor
for not halting within a day's march of Valencia, in
order to break the spirit of the people, and make
them feel the weight of the war ; but this opinion
was probably formed upon an imperfect knowledge
of the local details. The marshal's line of operations from Cuenca was infested by insurgent bands,
his ammunition was nearly exhausted, he could
hear nothing of Chabran's division, the whole
force of Murcia was collecting upon his flank and
rear, the country behind him was favourable for
his adversaries, and his army was encumbered by a
number of wounded men ; it was surely prudent,
under such circumstances, to open his communication again with Madrid as quickly as possible.

By some authors, the repulse at Valencia has been classed with the inglorious defeat of Dupont at Baylen, but there was a wide difference between the events, the generals, and the results. Moncey, although an old man, was vigorous, active, and decided, and the check he received produced little effect. Dupont was irresolute, slow, and incapable, if not worse, as I shall hereafter show; but before describing his campaign, I must narrate the operations of the Gallician army.

CHAPTER VII.

OPERATIONS OF BESSIERES AGAINST BLAKE AND CUESTA.

WHILE Bessieres' moveable columns, ranging over the Asturian and Biscayan mountains, dispersed the insurgent patriots of those provinces, Cuesta, undismayed by his defeat at Cabezon, collected another army at Benevente, and prepared to advance again towards Burgos; and he was supported by the Gallician army, which Filanghieri had organized without difficulty, because the abundant supplies poured in from England were beginning to be felt, and patriotism is never more efficacious than when supported by large sums of money. Taranco's soldiers joined to the garrisons of Ferrol and Coruña had been reinforced, with new levies, to twenty-five thousand men, and being well equipped, and provided with a considerable train of artillery, were assembled at Manzanal, a strong post in the mountains, twelve miles behind Astorga.

The situation of that city offered great advantages to the Spaniards, for the old Moorish walls which surrounded it were complete, and susceptible of being strengthened, so as to require a regular siege; but a siege could not be undertaken by a small force, while the army of Gallicia was entrenched at Manzanal, and while Cuesta remained at Benevente; neither could Bessieres, with any prudence, attack the Gallicians at Manzanal while Cuesta was at Benevente, and while Astorga contained a strong garrison. Filanghieri, who appears to have had some notion of its value, had commenced forming an entrenched camp in the mountains; but being slain by his soldiers, Joachim Blake succeeded to the command, and probably fearing a similar fate, if the army remained stationary, left one division at Manzanal, and with the remainder marched towards Benevente to unite with Cuesta.

Bessieres immediately collected his scattered columns at Palencia, and his plan, founded upon instructions from Bayonne, was to make a rapid movement against Cuesta, in the hope of beating him, while Blake was still behind Leon; then wheeling to the right, to drive the Gallicians back to the mountains, to overrun the flat country with his numerous cavalry, to open a communication with Portugal, and after receiving certain reinforcements, preparing for him, to subdue Gallicia, or assist Junot, as might seem most fitting at the time.

S.
Journal of
Bessieres'
Operations
MSS.

Napoleon's
notes.
Appendix,
No. 2.

At this period the king was on his journey to Madrid, and the military system of Napoleon was brought to its first great crisis; for unless Bessieres was successful, there could be no sure footing for the French in the capital; and as Madrid was the base of Moncey's and Dupont's operations, the farther prosecution of their plans depended upon the result of the approaching struggle in the plains of Leon. Napoleon, foreseeing this crisis, had directed Savary to occupy Segovia, to send general Gobert's division to Valladolid, and to hold Vedel's and Frere's, the one in La Mancha, a few marches from the capital, and the other at San Clemente, a central

point connecting Moncey, Dupont, and Madrid.
But Savary, unable to estimate justly the relative
importance of the different operations, sent Vedel
and Gobert into Andalusia, to reinforce Dupont,
when he should rather have recalled the latter to
the northern side of the Sierra Morena; he caused
Frere, as we have seen, to quit San Clemente, and
march by Requeña against Valencia, at the moment
when Moncey was retiring from that city through
Murcia to San Clemente; thus he dispersed and
harassed his reserves by long marches to the south
without any definite object, when the essential
interests were at stake in the north. Now, struck
with fear at the approach of Cuesta and Blake,
whose armies he had hitherto disregarded, he pre-
cipitately recalled Frere, Vedel, Gobert, and even
Dupont, to Madrid; too late to take part with
Bessieres in the coming battle, but exactly timed
to frustrate Moncey's projects, and, as we shall
hereafter find, to ensure the ruin of Dupont. In
this manner, steering his vessel against every wind
that blew, he could not fail of storms.

Greatly was Napoleon discontented with these
errors; he relied, and with reason, on the ability of
Bessieres for a remedy, but to Savary he sent the
following instructions, dated the 13th of July:

‘ The French affairs in Spain would be in an excellent state if Gobert's division had marched upon Valladolid, and Frere's had occupied San Clemente, with
a moveable column, three or four marches upon the
route of general Dupont. Gobert having been directed
upon Dupont, Frere being with Moncey, harassed
and enfeebled by marches and countermarches, the
position of the French army is become less advantageous.

' *Marshal Bessieres is this day at Medina del Rio
Seco with fifteen thousand men, infantry, cavalry,
and artillery; the 15th or 16th he will attack Benevente, open a communication with Portugal, drive the
rebels into Gallicia, and seize upon Leon. If his
operations succeed thus, and in a brilliant manner,
the position of the French army will again be as good
as it was.*

' *If general Cuesta retires from Benevente without
fighting, he will move by Zamora and Salamanca to
gain Avila and Segovia, certain that then Bessieres
cannot pursue him, as, in that case, he would be menaced by the army of Gallicia, whose advanced guard
is at Leon. The general who commands at Madrid
must then be able to assemble six or seven thousand
men and march upon Cuesta; the citadel of Segovia
must be occupied by three or four hundred convalescents, with some guns and six weeks' biscuit. It was
a great fault not to have occupied this citadel when
the major-general ordered it; of all the possible positions, Segovia is the most dangerous for the army;
the capital of a province, and situated between two
routes, it deprives the army of all its communications,
and the enemy once posted in the citadel, the French
army cannot dislodge him. Three or four hundred
convalescents, a good commandant, and a squad of
artillery, will render the castle of Segovia impregnable
for some time, and will insure to the army the important position of Segovia.*

' *If general Cuesta throws himself into Gallicia
without fighting or suffering a defeat, the position of
the army will become better; of course it will be still
better if he does so, after having suffered a defeat.*

' *If marshal Bessieres faces Cuesta at Benevente
without attacking him, or if he is repulsed by him,*

*his object will always be to cover Burgos, and to hold
the enemy in check as long as possible; he could, perhaps, be reinforced with the three thousand troops of
the line which accompany the king, but then there
would be no room for hesitation. If Bessieres retires
without a battle, he must be reinforced instantly with
six thousand men. If he retreats after a battle
wherein he has suffered great loss, it will be necessary
to make great dispositions; to recal Frere, Gobert,
Caulaincourt, and Vedel by forced marches to Madrid;
to withdraw Dupont into the Sierra Morena, or even
bring him nearer to Madrid (keeping him always,
however, seven or eight marches off), then to crush
Cuesta and all the Gallician army, while Dupont will
serve as an advanced guard to hold the army of
Andalusia in check.'*

However, before Bessieres could collect his troops,
Blake effected a junction with Cuesta, at Benevente,
and three plans were open to those generals.

1°. To remove into the mountains, and take a
position covering Gallicia.

2°. To maintain the head of the Gallician army in
advance of Astorga, while Cuesta, with his Casti-
lians, pushing by forced marches through Salamanca
and Avila, reached Segovia.

3°. To advance farther into the plains, and try the
fate of a battle.

This last was rash, seeing that Bessieres was well
provided with horsemen, and that the Spaniards had
scarcely any; but Cuesta, assuming the chief command, adopted it. He left a division at Benevente to
protect his stores, and advanced, much against Blake's
wishes, with twenty-five thousand regular infantry,
a few hundred cavalry, and from twenty to thirty
pieces of artillery, in the direction of Palencia. His

march, as we have seen, dismayed Savary. To use Napoleon's expressions, he who had been ' *hitherto acting as if the army of Gallicia was not in existence,*' now acted ' *as if Bessieres was already beaten;*' but that marshal, firm and experienced, rather than risk an action of such importance with insufficient means, withdrew even the garrison from the important post of St. Ander, and having quickly collected fifteen thousand men and thirty pieces of artillery at Palencia, moved forward on the 12th of July to the encounter.

His line of battle consisted of two divisions of infantry, one of light cavalry, and twenty-four guns, his reserve was formed of four battalions and some horse grenadiers of the imperial guards, with six pieces of artillery. On the 13th he halted at Ampudia and Torre de Mormojon, but advancing on the 14th in two columns, he drove in an advanced guard of one hundred and fifty Spanish cavalry, and arrived about nine o'clock in front of Rio Seco, where Cuesta's army was drawn up like some heavy, domestic animal, awaiting the spring of an active wild beast.

S.
Journal of
Bessieres'
Operations

BATTLE OF RIO SECO.

The first line of the Spaniards with all the heavy guns were posted along the edge of a step of land which had an abrupt fall towards the French. The second line, composed of the best troops, augmented but not strengthened by some eighteen thousand armed peasants, was displayed at a great distance behind the first, and the town of Rio Seco was in rear of the centre. Bessieres was at first startled at their numbers, and doubted if he should attack; but soon perceiving the vice of Cuesta's disposition, he

BOOK I.

1808. July.

ordered general Lasalle to make a feint, against the front, with the light cavalry, while he himself, marching obliquely to the right, outstretched the left of the Spaniards, and suddenly thrust Merle's and Mouton's divisions and the imperial guards, horse and foot, between the lines, and threw the first into confusion; at that moment Lasalle charged furiously, the Spanish front went down at once, and fifteen hundred dead bodies strewed the field.

S. Journal of Bessieres' Operations

The victor's ranks were disordered, and Cuesta made a gallant effort to retrieve the day, for, supported by the fire of all his remaining artillery, he advanced with his second line upon the French, and his right wing falling on boldly, took six guns; but his left hung back, and the flank of the right was thus exposed. Bessieres, with great readiness, immediately charged on this naked flank with Merle's division and the horse grenadiers, while the fourteenth provisionary regiment made head against the front; a fierce short struggle ensued, and the Spaniards were overborne, were broken and dispersed: meanwhile the first line rallied in the town of Rio Seco, but being a second time defeated by Mouton's division, fled over the plains, pursued by the light cavalry and suffering severely in their flight.

Ibid.

Five or six thousand Spaniards were killed and wounded on the field, twelve hundred prisoners, eighteen guns, and a great store of ammunition, remained in the hands of the French, and the vanquished sought safety in all directions, chiefly on the side of Benevente. Blake and Cuesta separated in wrath with each other, the former made for the mountains of Gallicia, and the latter towards Leon, while the division left at

MrStuart's Papers.

Benevente dispersed. The French, who had lost fifty killed and three hundred wounded, remained at Rio Seco all the 15th, and the 16th advanced to Benevente, where they found many thousand English muskets and vast quantities of ammunition, clothing, and provisions. The communication with Portugal was now open, and Bessieres at first resolved to give his hand to Junot, but hearing that the fugitives were likely to rally on the side of Leon, he pursued them by the road of Villa-fere. On his march, learning that Cuesta was gone to Mayorga, he turned aside to that place, and on the 22d captured there another great collection of stores; for the Spanish general, with the usual improvidence of his nation, had established all his magazines in the open towns of the flat country.

After this Bessieres entered the city of Leon and remained there until the 29th, during which time he received the submission of the municipality, and prepared to carry the war into Gallicia. Meanwhile the junta of Castile and Leon, whose power had hitherto been restrained by Cuesta, retired to Puente-Ferrada, assumed supreme authority, and the quarrel between the generals having become rancorous, they sided with Blake. This appeared to Bessieres a favourable occasion to tamper with the fidelity of the chiefs. He therefore sent his prisoners back, argued the hopeless state of the insurrection, offered the vice-royalty of Mexico to Cuesta, and promised military ranks and honours to Blake. But as neither would listen to him, he had reached Puente Orbigo the 31st, intending to break into Gallicia, when he was suddenly recalled to protect the king; for Dupont had surrendered with a whole army in

Andalusia. The victory of Rio Seco was rendered useless, the court was in consternation, and Bessieres immediately returned to Mayorga, where he took a defensive position.

OBSERVATIONS.

1°. As Blake was overruled by Cuesta, he is not responsible for the errors of this short campaign; but the faults were gross on both sides, and it seems difficult to decide whether Savary or Cuesta made the greatest number. If Savary had sent Gobert's division to Valladolid, Bessieres would have had twenty-two thousand men and forty pieces of artillery in the field; a force not at all too great, when it is considered that the fate of three French armies depended upon a battle, to which the Spaniards might have brought at least double the number On the other hand, Cuesta having determined upon an offensive movement, disregarded the powerful cavalry of his enemy, and chose a field of battle precisely in the country where that arm would have the greatest advantage; when he should have brought every man to bear upon the quarter which he did attack, he displayed his ignorance of the art of war, by fighting the battle of Rio Seco with twenty-five thousand men only, leaving ten thousand disciplined troops in the rear, to guard positions which could not be approached until he himself was first beaten. Neither was the time well chosen for his advance. Had he waited a few days, the port of St. Ander would have been attacked by eight English frigates, and a detachment of Spanish troops under the command of general da Ponte; an enterprise that would have distracted and weakened Bessieres, but which was relinquished in consequence of the battle of Rio Seco.

2°. Once united to Blake, Cuesta's real base of operations was Gallicia, and he should have kept all his stores within the mountains, and not have heaped them up in the open towns of the flat country, exposed to the marauding parties of the enemy; or covered, as at Benevente, by strong detachments which weakened his troops in the field and confined him to a particular line of operations in the plain.

3°. The activity and good sense of marshal Bessieres overbalanced the errors of Savary, and the victory of Rio Seco was of infinite importance, because, as we have seen, a defeat in that quarter would have shaken the French military system to its centre; it would also have obliged the king, then on his journey to Madrid, to halt at Vittoria, until the distant divisions of the army were recalled to the capital, and a powerful effort made to crush the victorious enemy. Napoleon's observations are full of strong expressions of discontent at the imprudence of his lieutenant.—' *A check given to Dupont,*' he says, ' *would have a slight effect, but a wound received by Bessieres would give a locked jaw to the whole army. Not an inhabitant of Madrid, not a peasant of the valleys that does not feel that the affairs of Spain are involved in the affairs of Bessieres; how unfortunate, then, that in such a great event you have wilfully given the enemy twenty chances against yourself.*' When he heard of the victory, he exclaimed, that it was the battle of Almanza, and that Bessieres had saved Spain. The prospect was indeed very promising; the king had arrived in Madrid, bringing with him

BOOK
I.

1808.

Napoleon's
notes,
Appendix,
No. 3.
the veteran brigade of general Rey and some French guards, and all fears upon the side of Leon being allayed, the affairs of Andalusia alone remained of doubtful issue; for Zaragoza, hard pushed by Verdier, was upon the point of destruction, in despite of the noble courage of the besieged. Nor did the subjugation of Andalusia appear in reason a hard task, seeing that Moncey was then at San Clemente, and from that point threatened Valencia, without losing the power of succouring Dupont, while Frere's and Caulaincourt's troops were disposable for any operation. In fine the French army possessed the centre, the Spaniards were dispersed upon a variety of points on the circumference without any connexion with each other, they were in force only upon the side of Andalusia, and the great combinations of the French emperor were upon the point of being crowned with success, when a sudden catastrophe overturned his able calculations and raised the sinking hopes of Spain.

It was the campaign in Andalusia which produced such important effects, and it offers one of the most interesting and curious examples, recorded by history, of the vicissitudes of war; disorder, unaccompanied by superior valour, triumphed over discipline; inexperienced officers were successful against practised generals, and a fortuitous combination of circumstances enabled the Spaniards, without any skill, to defeat in one day an immense plan, wisely arranged, embracing a variety of interests, and until that moment happily conducted in all its parts. This blow, which felled Joseph from his throne, marked the French army with a dishonourable scar, the more conspicuous, because it was the only one of its numerous wounds that misbecame it.

CHAPTER VIII.

OPERATIONS IN ANDALUSIA.

DUPONT was ordered to march against Cadiz with CHAP. VIII.
a force composed of the Spanish-Swiss regiments 1808.
of Preux and Reding—Barbou's division of French Journal of Dupont's
infantry; Fresia's division of cavalry—a marine bat- Operations MS.
talion of the imperial guards, and eighteen pieces
of artillery. Three thousand infantry, five hundred
cavalry, and ten guns, were to join him at Seville,
from the army of Portugal; three other Swiss regiments were in Andalusia, and it was expected that
both they, and the troops at San Roque, would join
the French army.

In the latter end of May he traversed La Mancha,
entered the Sierra Morena by the pass of Despenas
Perros, and proceeded by Carolina and Baylen to
Andujar, where he arrived the 2d of June. There
he was informed that a supreme junta of government was established at Seville, that minor juntas
ruled in Granada, Jaen, and Cordoba; that war
was formally declared against the French, that the
whole of Andalusia was in arms and the Swiss regiments ranged under the Spanish banners: lastly,
that general Avril, commanding the detachment
expected from Portugal, had halted in Tavora, and
was preparing to return to Lisbon.

Alarmed by this intelligence, Dupont wrote to
Murat and Savary to demand reinforcements, and
in the mean time closed up the rear of his columns,
and established an hospital in Andujar. The 6th he

crossed the Guadalquivir, and continued his march towards Cordoba, following the left bank of the river. But two leagues from that ancient city the road recrossed the Guadalquivir by a long stone bridge, at the farthest end of which stood the village of Alcolea; and when the French general arrived there at daybreak on the 7th, his progress was opposed by the Spanish general Echevaria, who had fortified the head of the bridge, placed twelve guns in battery on the right bank, and was prepared to dispute the passage, with a force, composed of three thousand regulars, supported by ten thousand new levies and smugglers. Besides these troops, a small reserve was left in a camp close to Cordoba, and a cloud of armed peasants, from the side of Jaen, hovered on the hills behind the French, ready to fall on the rear when they should attack the bridge.

Dupont having observed this disposition, placed the cavalry, the Swiss regiments, and the marine battalion in reserve, facing to the hills, and with the division of Barbou stormed the head of the bridge. The Spaniards there, making a feeble resistance, were driven across the river, and their whole line immediately fled to the camp at Cordoba. The multitude on the hills descended during the battle, but were beaten back by the cavalry with loss, and the French general, then leaving the marine battalion at Alcolea, to secure the bridge, marched with the rest of his forces to complete the victory. At his approach the Spaniards took refuge in the town, and opened a fire of musketry from the walls; whereupon the French, bursting the gates with their field-pieces, broke in, and after a short and confused fight Echevaria's men fled along the Seville road, pursued by the cavalry. As the inhabitants took no part in the contest, and received the French without any signs of aversion, the first disorders attendant on the action were soon suppressed, the town was protected from pillage, and Dupont, fixing his quarters there, sent patroles as far as Ecija without finding an enemy.

In Seville the news of this disaster, and the arrival of the fugitives, struck such a terror, that the junta were only prevented from retiring to Cadiz by their dread of the populace, they even entertained thoughts of abandoning Spain altogether, and flying to South America. Castaños, who a few days before had been declared captain-general of the armies, and was at this time in march with seven thousand troops of the line from San Roque, repaired to Seville the 9th, and after a short conference with the junta, proceeded to take the command of Echevaria's forces; the greater part of these were re-assembled at Carmona, but in such confusion, and so moody, that Castaños returned immediately. Having persuaded the president Saavedra to accompany him, he fixed his head-quarters at Utrera, where he gathered two or three thousand regulars from the nearest garrisons, directed all the new levies to repair to him, and hastened the march of his own men from San Roque. He also pressed general Spencer to disembark, and take up a position with the British forces at Xeres; but that officer, for reasons hereafter to be mentioned, sailed to Ayamonte,—a circumstance which augmented the general distrust of the English, prevailing at the time, and secretly fomented by Morla, and by several members of the junta.

Andalusia was lost, if Dupont had advanced. His inactivity saved it. Instead of pushing his

victory, he wrote to Savary for reinforcements, and
to general Avril, desiring that he would, without
delay, come to his assistance, remaining himself
meanwhile in Cordoba, overwhelmed with imagi-
nary dangers and difficulties. For although Castaños had in a few days collected at Carmona and
Utrera, seven or eight thousand regulars, and above
fifty thousand new levies ; and although Dupont's
desponding letters were intercepted and brought to
him, such was the condition of affairs that, resigning all thoughts of making a stand, he had, under
the pretence of completing the defences of Cadiz,
Appendix, embarked the heavy artillery and stores at Seville,
No. 13.
resolving, if Dupont should advance, to burn the
timbers and harness of his field artillery, and retreat to Cadiz.   Nevertheless he continued the organization of his forces, filled up the old regiments
with new levies, and formed fresh battalions, in which
he was assisted by two foreigners; the marquis de
Coupigny, a crafty French emigrant, of some experience in war, and Reding, a Swiss, a bold, enterprising, honest man, but without judgment, and of
very moderate talents as an officer.

Castaños wished to adopt a defensive plan, to make
Cadiz his place of arms, and to form an entrenched
camp, where he hoped to be joined by ten or twelve
thousand British troops, and, in security, to organize
and discipline a large army ; but, in reality, he had
merely the name and the troubles of a commander-in-
chief, without the power.   Morla was his enemy, and
Sir H. Dal- the junta, containing men determined to use their
rymple's
Papers.   authority for their own emolument and the gratification of private enmity, were jealous lest Castaños
should control their proceedings ; they thwarted him,
humoured the caprice and insolence of the populace,

and meddled with affairs foreign to the matter in hand. But as the numbers at Utrera increased, the general confidence augmented, and a retreat was no longer contemplated; plans were laid to surround Dupont in Cordoba, and one detachment of peasants, commanded by regular officers, was sent to occupy the passes of the Sierra Morena, leading into Estremadura; another detachment marched from Grenada, accompanied by a regiment of the line, to seize Carolina, and cut off the communication with La Mancha; a third, under colonel Valderaños, proposed to attack the French in Cordoba without any assistance; and this eagerness for action was increased by a knowledge of the situation of affairs in Portugal, and by rumours exaggerating the strength of Filanghieri and Cuesta. It was believed that the latter had advanced to Valladolid, and had offered Murat the option of abiding an attack, or retiring immediately to France by stated marches, and that, alarmed at Cuesta's power, the grand duke was fortifying the Retiro. These reports, so congenial to the wishes and vanity of the Andalusians, caused the defensive plan proposed by Castaños to be rejected; and when Dupont's despatches, magnifying his own danger, and pressing in the most urgent manner for reinforcements, were again intercepted and brought to head-quarters, it was resolved to attack Cordoba immediately.

Dupont's fears outstripped the Spaniard's impatience. After ten days of inactivity, by which he lost the immediate fruit of his victory at Alcolea,—the lead in an offensive campaign, and all the imposing moral force of the French reputation in arms, he resolved to fall back to Andujar, because Savary would not promise any succour save what Moncey, after

Journal of Dupont's Operations

subduing Valencia, could give by the circuitous route of Murcia. This retreat was commenced the 17th of June, and the French were followed as far as Carpio by the advanced guard of the Andalusians, under general Coupigny.

Along the line of march, and in the town of Andujar, where he arrived the evening of the 18th, Dupont found terrible proofs of Spanish ferocity; his stragglers had been assassinated, and his hospital taken; the sick, the medical attendants, the couriers, the staff officers, in fine, all who had the misfortune to be weaker than the insurgents, were butchered, with circumstances of extraordinary barbarity, and upwards of four hundred men had perished in this miserable manner since the fight of Alcolea. The fate of colonel Renè was horrible. He had been sent on a mission to Portugal, previous to the breaking out of hostilities, and was on his return, travelling in the ordinary mode, without arms, attached to no army, engaged in no operations of war, but being recognised as a Frenchman, he was seized, mutilated, and then being placed, living, between two planks was sawed in two.

At Andujar the French general collected provisions, and prepared to maintain himself until he should be reinforced; yet wishing to punish the city of Jaen, from whence the bands had come to murder his sick, he sent captain Baste, a naval officer, with a battalion of infantry and some cavalry, to accomplish that object. The soldiers, inflamed by the barbarity of their enemies, inflicted a severe measure of retaliation, because it is the nature of cruelty to reproduce itself in war; and for this reason, although the virtue of clemency is to all persons becoming, it

BOOK I.

1808.

Napoleon's notes. Appendix, No. 1.

Whittingham.

Journal of Dupont.

Foy's History.

Victoires et Conquêtes.

is peculiarly so to an officer, the want of it leading to so many and such great evils. Meanwhile the Andalusian army remained quiet, and Dupont, who knew that general Vedel, with a division of infantry, and escorting a large convoy for the army, was marching through La Mancha, sent captain Baste with a second detachment to clear the pass of Despeñas Perros, which was now occupied by insurgents and smugglers from Grenada to the number of three thousand. This pass was of incredible strength, and the Spaniards had artillery, and were partially entrenched; however their commander, a colonel of the line, deserted to the enemy, and before Baste could arrive, Vedel had forced his way to Carolina, where he left a detachment, and then descended to Baylen, a small town sixteen miles from Andujar. But other July. insurgents came from Grenada to Jaen, and would have moved on Despeñas Perros and Carolina, by the Linhares road; wherefore Vedel sent general Cassagne against them, Jaen was again taken, and the Grenadans were driven back with slaughter; but the French who lost two hundred men, returned on the 5th to Baylen without the provisions, to obtain which had been one object of the expedition.

Notwithstanding these successes, and that Vedel, besides his own division, brought reinforcements for Barbou's division and the cavalry, Dupont's fears increased. His position at Andujar covered the main road from Seville to Carolina; but eight miles lower down the river, it could be turned by the bridge of Marmolexo; sixteen miles higher up by the roads leading from Jaen to the ferry of Mengibar and Baylen; and beyond that line by roads from Jaen and Grenada to Uzeda, Linhares, and the passes of El Rey and Despeñas Perros. The dryness of

the season had rendered the Guadalquivir fordable
in many places; the regular force under Castaños
was daily increasing in strength; the population
around was actively hostile, and the young French
soldiers were drooping under privations and the heat

of the climate: six hundred were in hospital, and
the whole were discouraged. It is in such situations

that the worth of a veteran is found; in battle the
ardour of youth often appears to shame the cool indifference of the old soldier, but when the strife is
between the malice of fortune and fortitude, between
human endurance and accumulating hardships, the
veteran becomes truly formidable, when the young
soldier resigns himself to despair.

After the actions at Jaen, Vedel posted general
Ligier Bellair's brigade at the ferry of Mengibar,
with a post beyond the river, but on the 13th this
post was driven across the Guadalquivir, and on
the 15th, Gobert, who should have been at Rio
Seco with Bessieres, arrived at Baylen with a divi-

sion of infantry and some cuirassiers. Vedel then
advanced to Mengibar, and it was full time, seeing
that the whole Spanish army was on the opposite
bank of the river. For when Dupont's retreat from

Cordoba had frustrated the plan of the Spaniards
to surround him, Castaños would have returned to
his old project of a rigorous defensive system, but
the junta, although at first they acquiesced, were
unsettled in their policy, and getting intelligence of
of Vedel's march, had ordered Castaños to attack
Dupont at Andujar before the reinforcements could
arrive.

The Spanish general had twenty-five thousand
regular infantry, two thousand cavalry, and a very
heavy train of artillery. Large bodies of armed

peasantry, commanded by officers of the line, attended this army, and the numbers varied from day to day, but the whole multitude that advanced towards the Guadalquivir could not have been less than fifty thousand men ; hence the intelligence that Vedel had actually arrived did not much allay the general fierceness. Castaños, however, was less sanguine than the rest, and learning that Spencer had again returned to Cadiz with his division, he once more requested him to land and advance to Xeres, to afford a point of retreat in the event of a disaster, and the English general consented to disembark, but refused to advance farther than Port St. Mary.

Whitting-ham's
Correspon-dence.

From the 1st of July the Spanish army occupied a position extending from Carpio to Porcuñas, and the 11th, a council of war being held, it was resolved that Reding's division should cross the Guadalquivir at the ferry of Mengibar, and gain Baylen ; that Coupigny should cross at Villa Nueva, and support Reding ; and that Castaños, with the other two divisions, advancing to the heights of Argonilla, should attack Andujar in front, while Reding and Coupigny should descend from Baylen and attack it in the rear : some detachments of light troops under colonel Cruz were also ordered to pass the Guadalquivir by Marmolexo, and to seize the passes leading through the Morena to Estremadura. The 13th, Reding, with the first division, and three or four thousand peasantry, marched towards Mengibar, and, as I have said, drove the French post over the Guadalquivir, while Coupigny, with the second division, took the road of Villa Nueva. The 15th, Castaños crowned the heights of Argonilla, in front of Andujar, with two divisions of

Ibid.

Ibid.

BOOK
I.

1808.
July.

Dupont's
Journal.

Foy.

Vedel's
Precis.

infantry, and a multitude of irregular troops; Coupigny skirmished with the French picquets at Villa
Nueva, and Reding attacked Ligier Bellair, but
when Vedel came up retired. When Dupont saw
the heights of Argonilla covered with enemies
he sent to Vedel for succour, broke the bridge
of Marmolexo, occupied an old tower on the
bridge of Andujar, and detached cavalry parties to
watch the fords above and below the town. The
15th Castaños cannonaded the bridge of Andujar,
while colonel Cruz, with four thousand men, crossed
the river near Marmolexo. The 16th he attacked,
and Cruz fell upon the French rear, but was chased
into the hills by a single battalion, and about two
o'clock Vedel, who had marched all night, arrived,
which put an end to the action.

During these events, Reding passed the Guadalquivir at Mengibar, and drove Ligier Bellair before
him, Gobert arrived, and renewed the action, but
fell mortally wounded, and general Dufour succeeded him. The French then returned to Baylen,
Reding to Mengibar, and Dufour, finding the
Spaniards did not push their success, rashly credited
a rumour that they were in march by Linhares, and
therefore retreated to Carolina. Meanwhile Dupont,
hearing, on the evening of the 16th, that Mengibar
had been forced, sent Vedel again to Baylen, but
with instructions so vague, that he was induced to
follow Dufour on the 17th, whereupon Reding,
who, strange to say, had remained tranquil at
Mengibar, being now reinforced by Coupigny,
seized Baylen in the night, and throwing out a
detachment on the side of Carolina, took a position
facing Andujar, with about twenty thousand men,
including a multitude of peasants.

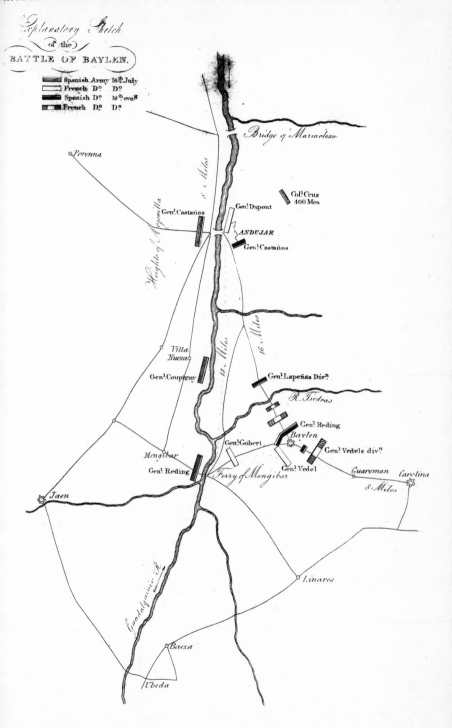

Explanatory Sketch
of the
BATTLE OF BAYLEN.

▬	Spanish Army 16ᵗʰ July
▭	French Dᵒ Dᵒ
▬	Spanish Dᵒ 19ᵗʰ eveᵍ
▨	French Dᵒ Dᵒ

Bridge of Marmolexo

Porcuna

Genˡ Castanos

Genˡ Dupont

Colˡ Cruz
400 Men

ANDUJAR

Genˡ Castaños

Heights of Arquillo

Villa
Nueva

Genˡ Coupigny

Genˡ Lapeña Divⁿ

R. Tiedras

Genˡ Reding

Baylen

Genˡ Gobert

Genˡ Vedels divⁿ

Mengibar

Genˡ Vedel

Genˡ Reding

Guaroman

Carolina

Ferry of Mengibar

8. Miles

Jaen

Guadalquivir R.

Linares

Baexa

Ubeda

The armies were thus interlaced in a singular manner, Dupont between Reding and Castaños, Reding between Dupont and Vedel, and the affair became one of time, yet Castaños remained tranquil in his camp, and Dupont, although he knew on the 17th of Vedel's march to Carolina, did not quit Andujar until the night of the 18th. His movement was unobserved by Castaños, and at day-break he reached the Tiedras, a torrent with rugged banks, only two miles from Reding's position which was strong, well shaded with olive-trees, and intersected by deep ravines. Dupont, hoping that Vedel would return, immediately passed the Tiedras, and leaving Barbou with a few battalions on that stream, to check Castaños if he should arrive during the action, fell on, yet feebly, and with few troops ; for his march had been unmilitary, and his best soldiers were employed guarding the baggage, which was enormous, and mixed with the columns. For some time the French appeared to gain ground, but fatigued by their night's work, and unable to force the principal points, they became discouraged ; the Swiss then went over to the Spaniards, and about twelve o'clock, after losing two thousand men, killed and wounded, Dupont proposed an armistice with a view to a convention, which Reding, hard pressed, willingly granted.

Vedel had quitted Carolina at five in the morning of the 19th. The sound of battle became distinct as he advanced, yet he halted at Guaroman, two leagues from Baylen, and remained there until three o'clock, to refresh his men, and to ascertain if any enemy was at Linhares ; when the firing had entirely ceased, he resumed his march, and coming upon the rear of Reding, attacked, and

Foy.

Journal of
Dupont's
Operations
MSS.

BOOK
I.

1808.
July.
after some fighting, captured two guns and made fifteen hundred prisoners; an aide-du-camp of Dupont's then brought him an order to cease the attack, whereupon he awaited the result of this singular crisis.

Whitting-
ham's
Correspon-
dence.
MSS.
Castaños, who did not discover Dupont's march until eight hours after the latter's departure from Andujar, had sent La Pena's division in pursuit, but remained himself in that town.   La Peña reached the Tiedras about five o'clock, and soon after, one Villoutreys passed his posts, going to ask Castaños' consent to the terms accepted by Reding, and Ibid. on the 20th generals Marescot and Chabert likewise passed to Andujar, being empowered by Dupont to conclude a convention.   They demanded permission for the French army to retire peaceably upon Madrid, and Castaños was ready to grant this, but Savary's letter, written just before the battle of Rio Seco, to recal Dupont, was intercepted, and brought at this moment to the Spanish head-quarters.   The aspect of affairs immediately changed, and a convention was no longer in question.   Dupont's troops were required to lay down their arms, and become prisoners of war, on condition of being sent by sea to France, and Vedel's division was to surrender, and be sent to France likewise, but not as prisoners of war: without hesitation these terms were accepted.

Vedel's
Precis of
Operations
Meanwhile Vedel had proposed to Dupont to make a joint attack upon Reding, and general Privé gave a like counsel, but the French general refused, and sent Vedel orders to give up his prisoners, and retreat to Carolina.   Castaños menaced Dupont with death if Vedel did not return, and the latter, on receiving his commander's orders to

that effect, did come back to Baylen the 22d, and surrendered. Thus above eighteen thousand French soldiers laid down their arms, before a raw army incapable of resisting half that number led by an able man. Nor did this end the disgraceful transaction, for Villoutreys, as if to show how far fear and folly combined, will carry men, passed the Morena with a Spanish escort, and gathering up the detachments left by Dupont in La Mancha, even to within a short distance of Toledo, sent them to Andujar as prisoners under the convention. Nay, he even informed Castaños how to capture two French battalions that had been left to guard the passes into La Mancha; and these unheard-of proceedings were quietly submitted to by men belonging to that army which for fifteen years had been the terror of Europe; a proof how much the character of soldiers depends upon their immediate chief.

This capitulation, shameful in itself, was shamefully broken. The French troops, instead of being sent to France, were maltreated, and numbers of them murdered in cold blood, especially at Lebrixa, where above eighty officers were massacred in the most cowardly manner. Armed only with their swords, they kept the assassins for some time at bay, and gathering in a company, upon an open space in the town, endeavoured to save their lives, but a fire from the neighbouring houses was kept up until the last of those unfortunate gentlemen fell. No distinction was made between Dupont's and Vedel's troops, and all who survived the march to Cadiz, after being exposed to every species of indignity, were cast into the hulks at Cadiz, whence a few hundreds escaped, two years afterwards, by

cutting the cables of their prison-ship, and drifting
in a storm upon a lee shore : the remainder, transported to the desert island of Cabrera, perished by
lingering torments in such numbers, that few remained alive at the termination of the war. Dupont
himself was permitted to return to France, and to
take with him all the generals ; and it is curious
that general Privé, who had remonstrated strongly
against the capitulation, and had pressed Dupont, on
the field, to force a passage through Reding's army,
was the only one left behind.

Victoires et
Conquêtes.

Don Thomas Morla, after a vain attempt to involve lord Collingword and sir Hew Dalrymple in
the transaction, formally defended the conduct of
the junta in breaking the capitulation ; and soon
afterwards betrayed his own country with the readiness that might be expected from his shameless
conduct on this occasion.

OBSERVATIONS.

Return of
the French
army.
Appendix.

1°. The gross amount of Dupont's corps when it
first entered Spain was about twenty-four thousand
men, with three thousand five hundred horses ; of
these twenty-one thousand were fit for duty. It
was afterwards strengthened by a provisionary regiment of cuirassiers, a marine battalion of the guard,
and the two Swiss regiments of Preux and Reding.
It could not therefore have been less than twenty-
four thousand fighting men when Dupont arrived
in Andalusia ; and as the whole of Vedel's, and the
greatest part of Gobert's division, had joined before
the capitulation, and as eighteen thousand men
laid down their arms at Baylen, Dupont must have
lost by wounds, desertion, and deaths in hospital
or the field, above five thousand men.

2°. The order which directed his corps upon Cadiz
was despatched from Bayonne before the Spanish
insurrection broke out ; it was therefore strange that
Dupont should have persevered in his march, when
he found affairs in such a different state, from that
contemplated by Napoleon at the time the instructions for this expedition were framed. If the emperor considered it necessary to reinforce the division, which marched under Dupont's own command,
with a detachment from the army in Portugal,
before the insurrection broke out, it was evident
that he never could have intended, that that general
should blindly follow the letter of his orders, when
a great and unexpected resistance was opposed to
him, and that the detachment from Portugal was
unable to effect a junction. The march to Cordoba
was therefore an error, and it was a great error,
because Dupont confesses in his memoir, he advanced under the conviction that his force was
too weak to obtain success, and, consequently,
having no object, his operations could only lead to
a waste of lives.

3°. At Cordoba, Dupont remained in a state of
torpor for ten days. This was the second error of a
series which led to his ruin ; he should either have
followed up his victory and attacked Seville in the
first moment of consternation, or he should have retired to Andujar while he might do so without the appearance of being compelled to it. If he had followed the first plan, the city would inevitably have fallen
before him, and thus time would have been gained
for the arrival of the second and third division of his
corps. It may be objected, that ten thousand men
dared not penetrate so far into a hostile country ;

but at Alcolea, Dupont boasts of having defeated
forty thousand men without any loss to himself :
from such armies, then, he had nothing to fear, and
the very fact of his having pushed his small force
between the multitudes that he defeated upon the
7th, proves that he despised them. ' He retired
from Cordoba,' he says in his memoir, ' because to
fight a battle when victory can be of no use, is
against all discretion ;' but to make no use of a victory when it is gained, comes to the same thing,
and he should never have moved from Andujar,
unless with the determination of taking Seville.
These errors were, however, redeemable; the position behind the Guadalquivir, the checks given
to the patriots at Jean after the arrival of Vedel
at Carolina upon the 27th, above all, the opportune junction of Gobert at the moment when Castaños and Reding appeared in front of the French
line, proved, that it was not fortune, but common
sense, that deserted Dupont. The Spanish forces
divided, and extended from Argonilla to Mengibar,
were exposed to be beaten in detail; but as their
adversary was indulgent to them, their false movements were successful, and, amidst the mass of greater
errors on both sides, appeared like acts of wisdom.

4°. At Mengibar a variety of roads branch off,
leading to Jaen, to Linhares, to Baylen, and other
places.   From Andujar, a road nearly parallel to the
Guadalquivir runs to the ferry of Mengibar, and forms
the base of a triangle, of which Baylen may be taken
as the apex.   The distance of this latter town from
the ferry is about six miles, from the ferry to Andujar
is about eighteen, and from the latter to Baylen the
distance may be sixteen miles.   Fifteen miles above

Baylen, the town of Carolina, situated in the gorge of the Sierra Morena, was the point of communication with La Mancha, and the line of retreat for the French in the event of a defeat; hence Baylen, not Andujar, was the pivot of operations. The French force was inferior in number to that under Castaños, yet Dupont spread his divisions upon several points, and the natural results followed. The Spaniards, although the most unwieldy body, took the lead and became the assailants; the French divisions were worn out by useless marches; the orders of their chief were mistaken or disobeyed; one position being forced, another was of necessity abandoned, confusion ensued; and finally Dupont says he surrendered with *eighteen thousand* men, because his fighting force was reduced to *two thousand:* such an avowal saves the honour of his soldiers, but destroys his own reputation as a general. The first question to ask is, what became of the remainder? Why had he so few when ten thousand of his army never fired a shot? It must be confessed that Dupont, unless a worse explanation can be given of his conduct, was incapable to the last degree. But this worse explanation has been given. His own officers, as well as the Spaniards, assert that his baggage was filled with plunder, and that he surrendered to save it!

Dupont's Journal, MSS.

5º. There were two plans, either of which promised a reasonable chance of success, under the circumstances in which the French army was placed on the 14th. 1st. To abandon Andujar, send all the incumbrances into La Mancha, secure the passes, unite the fighting men at Carolina, and fall in one mass upon the first corps of Spaniards that advanced: the result of such an attack could hardly

have been doubtful, but if, contrary to all probability, the Spaniards had been successful, the
retreat of the French was open and safe. 2dly. To
secure Carolina by a detachment, and placing small
bodies in observation at Andujar and the ferry of
Mengibar, to unite the army on the 15th at Baylen,
and in that central position await the enemy. If the
two corps of the Spanish army had presented themselves simultaneously upon both roads, the position
was strong for battle, and the retreat open; if one
approached before the other, each might have been
encountered and crushed separately. Dupont had a
force more than sufficient for this object, and fortune
was not against him.

6°. On the Spanish side the direction in which
Reding marched was good, but it should have been
followed by the whole army. The heights of Argonilla would have screened the march of Castaños, and
a few troops with some heavy guns, left in front of the
bridge of Andujar, would have sufficed to occupy Dupont's attention. If the latter general had attacked
Castaños upon the morning of the 16th, when Vedel's
division arrived from Baylen, the twelve thousand
men thus united by accident, would easily have
overthrown the two Spanish divisions in front of
Andujar; and Reding, if he had lost an hour in retreating to Jaen, might have been taken in flank by
the victorious troops, and in front by Gobert, and so
destroyed. Instead of availing himself of this opening, the French general sent Vedel back to Baylen,
followed himself two days after, and being encountered by Reding, vainly hoped that the divisions,
which with so much pains he had dispersed, would
reunite to relieve him from his desperate situation.

7°. In the action, Dupont clung tenaciously to

the miserable system of dividing his troops, when his only chance of safety was to force Reding before Castaños could arrive upon the Tiedras; it was a wretched misapplication of rules, to have a reserve watching that torrent, and to fight a formal battle with a first and second line, and half a dozen puny columns of attack. An energetic officer would have formed his troops in a dense mass, and broken at once through the opposing force upon the weakest point; there are few armies so good, that such an assault would not open a passage through them; seven thousand infantry with cavalry and artillery is a powerful column of attack, and the Spanish line could not have withstood it for a moment. The battle should have been one of half an hour; Dupont, by his ridiculous evolutions, made it one of ten hours, and yet so badly did the patriots fight, that in all that time not a single prisoner or gun fell into their hands, and the fact of Reding's entering at all into a convention, proves his fears for the final result. It is truly astonishing that Dupont, who, from his rank, must have been well acquainted with Napoleon's Italian campaigns, should have caught so little of the spirit of his master. And then the capitulation of Vedel after his retreat was actually effected! Vedel, who might have given battle and disputed the victory by himself without any great imprudence! Joseph called Dupont's capitulation, a '*defection*.' Appendix, No. 6.

8ª. Castaños, although active in preparation, discovered but little talent in the field; his movements were slow, uncertain, and generally false. The attempt to turn the French position at Andujar by detaching four thousand men across the river, was ill conceived and badly supported; it was of that

class of combinations to which the separate march
of Reding's corps belonged.   To the latter general
the chief honour of the victory is due; yet, if Vedel
had returned from Carolina upon the 19th, with the
rapidity which the occasion required, Reding would
have repented taking post at Baylen; it was undoubtedly a daring step; but instead of remaining
at that place, he should have descended instantly
upon the rear of Dupont, leaving a corps of observation to delay the march of Vedel.   Time not being
taken into his calculation, Reding acted like a bold,
but rash and unskilful officer.   Fortune, however,
favoured his temerity, and with her assistance war
is but child's play.

Intelligence of the capitulation of Baylen was
secretly spread among the Spaniards in Madrid as
early as the 23d or 24th of July; but the French,
although alarmed by rumours of some great disaster,
were unable to acquire any distinct information,
until the king sent two divisions into La Mancha
to open the communication;   these troops having

Foy's
History.
reached Madrilejos, one hundred and twenty miles
from Baylen, met Villoutreys with his Spanish escort
collecting prisoners, and apparently intending to proceed in his disgraceful task to the very gates of
Madrid;   the extent of the disaster thus became
known, and the divisions retraced their steps.
Joseph then called a council of war, and it was
proposed to unite all the French forces, place a
small garrison in the Retiro, and fall upon the
Spanish armies in succession as they advanced towards the capital.   But a dislike to the war was
prevalent amongst the higher ranks of the French
army, the injustice of it was too glaring; hence
the reasons for a retreat, which might perchance

induce Napoleon to desist, being listened to with more complacency than this proposal, it was resolved to abandon Madrid and retire behind the Ebro. The operation commenced on the 1st of August. The king marched by the Somosierra, and Bessieres, posted at Mayorga, covered the movement until the court reached Burgos, and then fell back himself; in a short time the French were all behind the Ebro, the siege of Zaragoza was raised, and the triumphant cry of the Spaniards was heard throughout Europe.

This retreat was undoubtedly hasty and ill considered; whether as a military or political measure it was unwise. Bessieres, with seventeen thousand victorious troops, and forty pieces of artillery, paralysed the northern provinces; the Spanish army of Andalusia was too distant from that of Valencia to concert a combined movement, and if they had formed a junction, their united force could not have exceeded forty thousand fighting men, ill provided, and commanded by jealous independent chiefs. Now the king, without weakening Bessieres' corps too much, could have collected twenty thousand infantry, five thousand cavalry, and eighty pieces of artillery; the battle of Rio Seco shows what such an army could have effected, and every motive of prudence and of honour called for some daring action to wipe off the ignominy of Baylen.

Let it be conceded that Joseph could not have maintained himself in Madrid; the line of the Duero was then the true position for the French army. Taking Aranda as a centre, and occupying the Somosierra, Segovia, Valladolid, Palencia, Burgos, and Soria on the circumference, two ordinary marches would have carried the king to the succour of any

part of his position, and the northern provinces would
thus have been separated from the southern. Then
Blake dared not have made a flank march to the
Guadarama, Castaños dared not have remained in the
basin of Madrid, and the siege of Zaragoza might
have been continued ; because from Aranda to Zaragoza the distance is not greater than from Valencia, or
from Madrid, and from Soria it is only three marches;
wherefore the king could have succoured Verdier if the
Valencians attacked him, and it was impossible for
Castaños to have arrived at Zaragoza under a month.
Now by taking up the line of the Ebro, Napoleon's
plan of separating the provinces, and confining each
to its own exertions, was frustrated, and Joseph
virtually resigned the throne; for however doubtful
the prudence of opposing the French might have
been considered before the retreat, it became imperative upon all Spaniards, to aid the energy of the
multitude when that energy was proved to be
efficient.

In this manner Napoleon's first effort against
Spain was frustrated. Yet he had miscalculated
neither the difficulties, nor the means to overcome them; for although Bessieres was the only
general who perfectly succeeded in his operations,
the plan of the emperor was so well combined, that
it required the destruction of a whole army to shake
it at all. Even when the king, by committing the
great fault of abandoning Madrid and raising the
siege of Zaragoza, had given the utmost force to
Dupont's catastrophe, it was only the political position of the French which was shaken ; their military
hold of the country was scarcely loosened, and the
Spaniards were unable to follow up their victory.
But there was another operation, too great indeed

for Joseph, yet such a one as in Napoleon's hands would have fixed the fate of the Peninsula. The king might have directed the troops before Zaragoza, and the detachments upon the communication with France, to have assembled round Pampeluna, while he, uniting with Bessieres, made, not a retreat, but a march with forty thousand men into Portugal. He would have arrived about the period of the battle of Vimiero, and the English would have been overwhelmed; a demonstration against Seville or Cadiz would then have sufficed to keep the Spanish armies from gathering on the Ebro, and three months later, Napoleon was on that river with two hundred thousand men!

The moral effect of the battle of Baylen was surprising; it was one of those minor events which, insignificant in themselves, are the cause of great changes in the affairs of nations. The defeat of Rio Seco, the preparations of Moncey for a second attack on Valencia, the miserable plight of Zaragoza, the desponding view taken of affairs by the ablest men of Spain, and, above all, the disgust and terror excited among the patriots by the excesses of the populace, weighed heavy on the Spanish cause. One victory more, and probably the moral as well as the physical force of Spain would have been crushed; but the battle of Baylen, opening as it were a new crater for the Spanish fire, all their pride, and vanity, and arrogance burst forth, the glory of past ages seemed to be renewed, every man conceived himself a second Cid, and perceived in the surrender of Dupont, not the deliverance of Spain, but the immediate conquest of France. 'We are much obliged to our good friends the English,' was a common phrase among them when conversing with the officers

of Sir John Moore's army ; ' we thank them for their
good-will, and we shall escort them through France
to Calais; the journey will be pleasanter than a
long voyage, we shall not give them the trouble of
fighting the French, but will be pleased at having
them spectators of our victories.'   This absurd confidence might have led to great things if it had been
supported by wisdom, activity, or valour; but it
was ' a voice, and nothing more.'

BOOK II.

CHAPTER I.

THE uninterrupted success that, for so many years, attended the arms of Napoleon, gave him a moral influence doubling his actual force. Exciting at once terror, admiration, and hatred, he absorbed the whole attention of an astonished world, and, openly or secretly, all men acknowledged the power of his genius ; the continent bowed before him, and in England an increasing number of absurd and virulent libels on his person and character, indicated the growth of secret fear. Hence, his proceedings against the Peninsula were viewed, at first, with anxiety rather than with the hope of arresting their progress ; yet when the full extent of the injustice became manifest, the public mind was vehemently excited; a sentiment of some extraordinary change being about to take place in the affairs of the world, prevailed among all classes of society ; and when the Spanish people rose against the man that all feared, the admiration which energy and courage exact, even from the base and timid, became enthusiastic in a nation conscious of the same virtues.

No factious feelings interfered to check this enthusiasm. The party in power, anxious to pursue a warlike system, necessary to their own political existence, saw with joy that the stamp of justice and high feeling would, for the first time, be affixed to their policy. The party out of power having always

CHAP.
I.
——
1808.

derided the impotence of the ancient dynasties, and asserted that regular armies alone were insufficient means of defence, could not consistently refuse their approbation to a struggle originating with, and carried on entirely by the Spanish multitude. The people at large exulted that the superiority of plebeian virtue and patriotism was acknowledged.

The arrival of the Asturian deputies was, therefore, universally hailed as an auspicious event; their wishes were forestalled, their suggestions were attended to with eagerness, their demands were readily complied with; nay, the riches of England were so profusely tendered to them by the ministers, that it can scarcely be doubted, the after arrogance and extravagance of the Spaniards, arose from the manner in which their first applications were met. There is a way of conferring a favour that appears like accepting one, and this secret being discovered by the English cabinet, the Spaniards soon demanded as a right what they had at first solicited as a boon. In politics it is a grievous fault to be too generous; gratitude, in state affairs, is unknown, and as the appearance of disinterested kindness never deceives, it should never be assumed.

The capture of the Spanish frigates had placed Great Britain and Spain in a state of hostility without a declaration of war; the invasion of Napoleon produced a friendly alliance between those countries without a declaration of peace; for the cessation of hostilities was not proclaimed until long after succours had been sent to the juntas. The ministers seemed, by their precipitate measures, to be more afraid of losing the assistance of the Spaniards, than prepared to take the lead in a contest which could only be supported by the power and riches of Great

Britain. Instead of adopting a simple and decisive policy towards Spain; instead of sending a states-man of high rank and acknowledged capacity to sustain the insurrection, and to establish the influ-ence of England by a judicious application of money and other supplies; the ministers employed a num-ber of obscure men in various parts of the Penin-sula, who, without any experience of public affairs, were empowered to distribute succours of all kinds at their own discretion. Instead of sifting carefully the information obtained from such agents, and con-sulting distinguished military and naval officers in the arrangement of some comprehensive plan of ope-rations, which, being well understood by those who were to execute it, might be supported vigorously, the ministers formed crude projects, parcelled out their forces in small expeditions without any definite object, altered their plans with every idle report, and changed their commanders as lightly as their plans.

Entering into formal relations with every knot of Spanish politicians that assumed the title of a su-preme junta, the government dealt, with unsparing hands, enormous supplies at the demand of those self-elected authorities; they made no conditions, took no assurance that the succours should be justly applied; and with affected earnestness disclaimed all intention of interfering with the internal arrange-ments of the Spaniards, when the ablest men in Spain expected and wished for such an interference to repress the folly and violence of their countrymen; and when England was entitled, both in policy and justice, not only to interfere, but to direct the coun-cils of the insurgents. The latter had solicited and obtained her assistance, the cause was become com-

BOOK
II.

1808.
mon to both nations; and for the welfare of both, a
prudent, just, and vigorous interference on the part
of the most powerful and enlightened, was necessary
to prevent that cause from being ruined by a few
ignorant, and conceited men, accidentally invested
with authority.

The numbers and injudicious choice of military
Vide In-
structions
for sir Tho.
Dyer, &c.
Parlia-
mentary
Papers,
1809.
agents were also the source of infinite mischief;
selected, as it would appear, principally because of
their acquaintance with the Spanish language, few
of those agents had any knowledge of war beyond
the ordinary duties of a regiment, and there was no
concert among them, for there was no controlling
power vested in any; each did that which seemed
good to him. Readily affecting to consult men whose
inexperience rendered them amenable, and whose
friendship could supply the means of advancing their
own interest in a disorganized state of society, the
Spanish generals received the agents with a flatter-
ing and confidential politeness, that diverted the
attention of the latter from the true objects of their
mission. Instead of ascertaining the real numbers
and efficiency of the armies, they adopted the inflated language and extravagant opinions of the
chiefs, with whom they lived; and their reports gave
birth to most erroneous notions of the relative
strength and situation of the contending forces in
the Peninsula. Some exceptions there were, but
the ministers seemed to be better pleased with the
sanguine than with the cautious, and made their own
wishes the measure of their judgments. Accordingly, enthusiasm, numbers, courage, and talent,
were gratuitously found for every occasion, but
money, arms, and clothing, were demanded incessantly, and supplied with profusion; the arms were,

however, generally left in their cases to rot, or to fall
into the hands of the enemy ; the clothing seldom
reached the soldier's back ; and the money, in all instances misapplied, was in some embezzled by the
authorities, into whose hands it fell, in others employed to create disunion, and to forward the private
views of the juntas, at the expense of the public
welfare : it is a curious fact, that from the beginning
to the end of the war, an English musket was rarely
to be seen in the hands of a Spanish soldier.   But
it is time to quit this subject, and to trace the progress of Junot's invasion of Portugal, by which the
whole circle of operations in the Peninsula will
be completed, and the reader can then take a general view of the situation of all parties, at the
moment when sir Arthur Wellesley, disembarking
at the Mondego, commenced those campaigns which
furnished the subject of this history.

1807.
November.
Appendix,
No. 13,
5th Sec-
tion.

INVASION OF PORTUGAL BY JUNOT.

Peremptory orders had obliged Junot to commence
operations at an unfavourable time of year, before
his preparations were completed, when the roads
were nearly impracticable, and while some of his
troops were still in the rear of Salamanca.   Hence, Thiebault.
his march from that town to Alcantara, where he
effected his junction in the latter end of November,
1807, with the part of the Spanish force that was to
act under his immediate orders, was very disastrous,
and nearly disorganized his inexperienced army.
The succours he expected to receive at Alcantara
were not furnished, and the repugnance of the Spanish authorities to aid him, was the cause of so much
embarrassment, that his chief officers doubted the

propriety of continuing operations under the accumulating difficulties of his situation; but Junot's
firmness was unabated. He knew that no English
force had landed at Lisbon; and as the cowardice of
the Portuguese court was notorious, he without hesitation undertook one of those hardy enterprises
which astound the mind by their success, and leave
the historian in doubt if he should praise the happy
daring, or stigmatise the rashness of the deed.

Without money, without transport, without ammunition sufficient for a general action, and with an
auxiliary force of Spaniards by no means well disposed to aid him, Junot, at the head of a raw army,
penetrated the mountains of Portugal on the most
dangerous and difficult line by which that country
can be invaded. He was ignorant of what was
passing in the interior, he knew not if he was to be
opposed, nor what means were prepared to resist
him, but trusting to the inertness of the Portuguese
government, to the rapidity of his own movements,
and to the renown of the French arms, he made his
way through Lower Beira, and suddenly appeared
in the town of Abrantes, a fearful and unexpected
guest. There he obtained the first information of
the true state of affairs. Lisbon was tranquil, and
the Portuguese fleet was ready to sail, but the court
still remained on shore. On hearing this, Junot,
animated by the prospect of seizing the prince
regent, pressed forward, and reached Lisbon in time
to see the fleet, having the royal family on board,
clearing the mouth of the Tagus. One vessel dragged
astern within reach of a battery, the French general
himself fired a gun at her, and, on his return to
Lisbon, meeting some Portuguese troops, he reso-
lutely commanded them to form an escort for his

person, and thus attended, passed through the
streets of the capital. Nature alone had opposed
the progress of the invaders, yet such were the
hardships endured, that of a column which
numbered twenty-five thousand at Alcantara, two
thousand tired grenadiers only entered Lisbon
with their general; fatigue, and want, and tem-
pests, had scattered the remainder along two
hundred miles of rugged mountains, inhabited
by a warlike and ferocious peasantry, well acquainted with the strength of their fastnesses,
and proud of the many successful defences made
by their forefathers against former enemies. Lisbon itself contained three hundred thousand inhabitants, and fourteen thousand regular troops
were collected there; a powerful British fleet
was at the mouth of the harbour, and the commander, sir Sidney Smith, had urged the court to
resist, offering to land his seamen and marines to aid
in the defence of the town, but his offers were declined; and the people, disgusted with the pusillanimous conduct of their rulers, and confounded by the
strangeness of the scene, evinced no desire to impede
the march of events. Thus three weak battalions
sufficed to impose a foreign yoke upon this great
capital, and illustrated the truth of Napoleon's
maxim :—*that in war the moral is to the physical
force as three parts to one.*

The prince regent, after having, at the desire of
the French government, expelled the British factory, sent the British minister plenipotentiary away
from his court, sequestered British property, and
shut the ports of Portugal against British merchants; after having degraded himself and his
nation by performing every submissive act which

France could devise to insult his weakness, was still reluctant to forego the base tenure by which he hoped to hold his crown. Alternately swayed by fear and indolence, a miserable example of helpless folly, he lingered until the reception of a Moniteur which, dated the 13th of November, announced, in startling terms, that the ' *house of Braganza had ceased to reign.*' Lord Strangford, the British pleni-potentiary, whose efforts to make the royal family emigrate, had entirely failed, was then on board the squadron, with the intention of returning to England ; but sir Sydney Smith, seizing the favour-able moment, threatened to bombard Lisbon, if the prince regent hesitated any longer, and thus urged on both sides, the latter embarked with his whole court, and sailed for the Brazils on the 29th of November, a few hours before Junot arrived.

Lord Strangford's despatch, relating this event, although dated the 29th of November, on board the Hibernia, was written the 19th December, in London, and was so worded, as to create a notion that his exertions during the 27th and 28th had caused the emigration, a notion quite contrary to the fact. For the prince regent of Portugal, yield-ing to the united pressure of the admiral's menaces, and the annunciation in the Moniteur, had em-barked on the 27th, before lord Strangford reached Lisbon ; and actually sailed on the 29th, without having had an interview with that nobleman, who consequently had no opportunity to advance or re-tard the event in question. Nevertheless, lord Strangford received the red riband, and sir Sydney Smith was neglected.

This celebrated emigration was beneficial to the Brazils in the highest degree, and of vast importance,

to England in two ways, for it ensured great
commercial advantages, and it threw Portugal completely into her power in the approaching conflict;
but it was disgraceful to the prince, insulting to the
brave people he abandoned, and impolitic, inasmuch as it obliged men to inquire how far subjects
were bound to a monarch who deserted them in
their need? how far the nation could belong to a
man who did not belong to the nation? It has been
observed by political economists, that where a gold
and paper currency circulate together, if the paper
be depreciated it will drag down the gold with it,
and deteriorate the whole mass; but after a time,
the metal revolts from this unnatural state, and
asserts its own intrinsic superiority: so a privileged
class, corrupted by power and luxury, drags down
the national character. Yet there is a point when
the people, like the gold, no longer suffering such a
degradation, will separate themselves with violence
from the vices of their effeminate rulers, and until
that time arrives, a nation may appear to be sunk in
hopeless lethargy, when it is really capable of great
and noble exertions; and thus it was with the Portuguese, who were at this time unjustly despised by
enemies, and mistrusted by friends.

The invading army, in pursuance of the con- Thiebault.
vention of Fontainebleau, was divided into three Foy.
corps. The central one, composed of the French
troops, and a Spanish division under general Caraffa,
had penetrated by the two roads, which from Alcantara lead, the one by Pedragoa, the other by
Sobreira Formosa; but at Abrantes, Caraffa's division had separated from the French, and took possession of Thomar, and meantime the right, under
general Taranco, marching from Gallicia, had es-

tablished itself at Oporto, while the marquis of Solano, with the left, entered the Alemtejo, and fixed his quarters at Setuval. The Spanish troops did not suffer on their route; but such had been the distress of the French army, that three weeks afterwards, it could only muster ten thousand men under arms, and the privations encountered on this march led to excesses, which first produced that rancorous spirit of mutual hatred, so remarkable between the French and Portuguese. Young soldiers always attribute their sufferings to the ill-will of the inhabitants, it is difficult to make them understand that a poor peasantry have nothing to spare; old soldiers, on the contrary, blame nobody, but know how to extract subsistence, and in most cases without exciting enmity.

Junot passed the month of December in collecting his army, securing the great military points about Lisbon, and in preparations to supplant the power of a council of regency, to whom the prince at his departure had delegated the sovereign authority. As long as the French troops were scattered on the line of march and the fortresses held by Portuguese garrisons, it would have been dangerous to provoke the enmity, or to excite the activity of this council, hence the members were treated with studious respect; yet they were of the same leaven as the court they emanated from, and the quick resolute proceedings of Junot soon deprived them of any importance conferred by the critical situation of affairs during the first three weeks.

The Spanish auxiliary forces were well received in the north and in the Alemtejo, and as general Taranco died soon after his arrival at Oporto, the French general Quesnel was sent to command that

province. Junot had meanwhile taken possession
of Elvas, and detached general Maurin to the Algarves, with sixteen hundred men; and, when Solano was ordered by his court to withdraw from
Portugal, nine French battalions and the cavalry,
under the command of Kellerman, took possession
of the Alemtejo also, and occupied the fortress of
Setuval. At the same time Caraffa's division, being
replaced at Thomar, by a French force, was distributed in small bodies, at a considerable distance
from each other, on both sides of the Tagus, immediately round Lisbon. As the provisions of the
treaty of Fontainbleau were unknown to the Portuguese, the Spanish troops met with a better reception than the French, and the treaty itself was disregarded by Junot, whose conduct plainly discovered
that he considered Portugal to be a possession entirely belonging to France. For when all the stragglers were come up, and the army recovered from
its fatigues, and when a reinforcement of five thousand men had reached Salamanca, on its march to
Lisbon, the French general assumed the chief authority. Commencing by a forced loan of two hundred thousand pounds, he interfered with the different departments of state, and put Frenchmen into
all the lucrative offices, while his promises, and
protestations of amity, became loud and frequent in
proportion to his encroachments.

At last, being by Napoleon created duke of Abrantes, he threw off all disguise, suppressed the council
of regency, seized the reins of government, and while
he established many useful regulations, made the
nation sensibly alive to the fact that he was a despotic
conqueror. The flag and the arms of Portugal were

replaced by those of France; eight thousand men were selected and sent from the kingdom under the command of the marquis d'Alorna and Gomez Frere, two noblemen of the greatest reputation for military talent among the native officers ; five thousand more were attached to the French army, and the rest were disbanded.   An extraordinary contribution of four millions sterling, decreed by Napoleon, was then demanded under the curious title of a ransom for the state, but this sum was exorbitant, and Junot prevailed on the emperor to reduce it

Foy.

one half.   He likewise, on his own authority, accepted the forced loan, the confiscated English merchandise, the church plate, and the royal property, in part payment ; yet the people were still unable to raise the whole amount, for the court had before taken the greatest part of the church plate and bullion of the kingdom, and had also drawn large sums of money from the people, under the pretext of defending the country; and with this treasure they departed, leaving the public functionaries, the army, private creditors, and even domestic servants, unpaid.

But, although great discontent and misery prevailed, the tranquillity of Lisbon, during the first month after the arrival of the French was remarkable ; no disturbance took place, and the populace were completely controlled by the activity of a police, first established under the prince regent's government by the count de Novion, a French emigrant, and continued by Junot on an extended scale.   No capital city in Europe suffers so much as Lisbon from the want of good police regulations, and the French general conferred an unmixed

benefit on the inhabitants by giving more effect to
Novion's plans ; yet, so deeply rooted is the prejudice in favour of ancient customs, that no act gave
the Portuguese more offence, than the having the
streets cleansed, and the wild dogs, who infested
them by thousands, killed.   A French serjeant, distinguished by his zeal in destroying those disgusting
and dangerous animals, was in revenge assassinated.

In the course of March and April, Junot's military system was completed.   The arsenal of
Lisbon, one of the finest establishments in Europe, contained all kinds of naval and military
stores in abundance, and ten thousand workmen
excellent in every branch of business appertaining
to war ; hence the artillery, the carriages, the ammunition, with all the minor equipments of the
army, were soon renewed and put in the best possible condition, and the hulks of two line-of-battle
ships, three frigates, and seven lighter vessels of
war, were refitted, armed, and moored across the
river to defend the entrance, and to awe the town.
The army itself, perfectly recovered from its fatigues, reinforced, and better disciplined, was
grown confident in its chief from the success of the
invasion, and being well fed and clothed, was become a fine body of robust men, capable of any
exertion.   It was re-organized in three divisions
of infantry and one of cavalry.   General La Borde
commanded the first, general Loison the second,
general Travot the third, general Margaron the
fourth, and general Taviel directed the artillery.
General Kellerman commanded in the Alemtejo,
general Quesnel in Oporto, general Maurin in the
Algarves, and Junot himself in Lisbon.

The fortresses of Faro in Algarve, of Almeida,

BOOK
II.
—————
1807-8.
March. of Elvas, La-Lippe, St. Lucie, Setuval, Palmela, and those between Lisbon and the mouth of the Tagus, of Ericia and Peniche, were furnished with French garrisons; Estremos, Aldea-Gallegos, Santarem, and Abrantes were occupied, and put in such a state of defence as their decayed ramparts would permit.

Return of
the French
army.
Appendix,
No. 28. The whole army, including the French workmen and marines attached to it, amounted to above fifty thousand men, of which above forty-four thousand were fit for duty; that is to say, fifteen thousand five hundred Spaniards, five thousand Portuguese, and twenty-four thousand four hundred French.

Of the latter 1000 were in Elvas and La Lippe,
1000 in Almeida,
1000 in Peniche,
1600 in the Algarves,
2892 in Setuval,
750 in Abrantes,
450 cavalry were kept in Valencia d'Alcantara, in Spanish Estremadura,

and 350 distributed in the proportion of fifteen men to a post, guarded the lines of communication which were established from Lisbon to Elvas, and from Almeida to Coimbra. Above fifteen thousand men remained disposable.

Lisbon, containing all the civil, military, naval, and greatest part of the commercial establishments; the only fine harbour, two-eighths of the population, and two-thirds of the riches of the whole kingdom, formed a centre, which was secured by the main body of the French, while on the circumference a number of strong posts gave support to the operations of their moveable columns. The garrison in

Peniche secured the only harbour between the Tagus
and the Mondego, in which a large disembarkation
of English troops could take place; the little port
of Figueras, held by a small garrison, blocked the
mouth of the latter river; the division at Thomar
secured all the great lines of communication to the
north-east, and in conjunction with the garrison of
Abrantes, commanded both sides of the Zezere.
From Abrantes to Estremos and Elvas, and to
Setuval, the lines of communication were short, and
through an open country suitable for the operations
of the cavalry, which was all quartered on the south
bank of the Tagus.   Thus, without breaking up the
mass of the army, the harbours were sealed against
the English; a great and rich tract was enclosed by
posts, and rendered so pervious to the troops, that
any insurrection could be reached by a few marches,
and immediately crushed; the connexion between
the right and left banks of the Tagus at Lisbon was
secured, and the entrance to the port defended by
the vessels of war which had been refitted and
armed.   A light squadron was also prepared to communicate with South America, and nine Russian line-
of-battle ships and a frigate, under the command of
admiral Siniavin, which had taken refuge some time
before from the English fleet, were of necessity engaged in the defence of the harbour, forming an
unwilling, but not an unimportant auxiliary force.

These military arrangements were Junot's own,
and suitable enough if his army had been unconnected with any other; but they clashed with the
general views of Napoleon, who regarded the force
in Portugal, only as a division of troops to be rendered subservient to the general scheme of subject-
ing the Peninsula; wherefore, in the month of May,

he ordered, that general Avril, with three thousand infantry, five hundred cavalry, and ten guns, should co-operate with Dupont in Andalusia; and that general Loison, with four thousand infantry, should proceed to Almeida, and from thence co-operate with Bessieres in the event of an insurrection taking place in Spain. General Thiebault complains of this order as injurious to Junot, ill combined, and the result of a foolish vanity, that prompted the emperor to direct all the armies himself; yet it would be difficult to show that the arrangement was faulty. Avril's division, if he had not halted at Tavora, for which there was no reason, would have ensured the capture of Seville; and if Dupont's defeat had not rendered the victory of Rio Seco useless, Loison's division would have been eminently useful in controlling the country behind Bessieres, in case the latter invaded Gallicia; moreover it was well placed to intercept the communication between the Castilian and the Estremaduran armies. The emperor's combinations, if they had been fully executed, would have brought seventy thousand men to bear on the defence of Portugal.

Such was the military attitude of the French in May, but their political situation was far from being so favourable. Junot's natural capacity, though considerable, was neither enlarged by study nor strengthened by mental discipline. Of intemperate habits, indolent in business, prompt and brave in action, quick to give offence yet ready to forget an injury, he was, at one moment a great man, the next below mediocrity, and at all times unsuited to the task of conciliating and governing a people like the Portuguese, who, with passions as sudden and vehement as his own, retain a sense of injury or

insult with incredible tenacity. He had many difficulties to encounter, and his duty towards France
was in some instances incompatible with good policy
towards Portugal, yet he was not without resources
for establishing a strong French interest, if he had
possessed the ability and disposition to soothe a
nation that, without having suffered a defeat, was
suddenly bowed to a foreign yoke.

But the pride and the poverty of the Portuguese,
and the influence of ancient usages, interfered with
Junot's policy. The monks, and most of the nobility, were inimical to it, and all the activity of the
expelled British factory, and the secret warfare of
spies and writers in the pay of England, were directed to undermine his plans, and to render him and
his nation odious. On the other hand, he was in
possession of the government and of the capital, he
had a fine army, he could offer novelty, so dear to
the multitude, and he had the name and the fame
of Napoleon to assist him. The promises of power
are always believed by the many, and there were
abundance of grievances to remedy, and wrongs to
redress, in Portugal. Among the best educated
men, especially at the universities, there existed a
strong feeling against the Braganza family, and such
an earnest desire for reformed institutions, that steps
were actually taken to have prince Eugene declared Foy.
king of Portugal : nor was this spirit extinguished
at a much later date.

With these materials and the military vanity of
the Portuguese to work upon, Junot might have established a powerful French interest ; under an active
government, the people would not long have regretted the loss of an independence that had no wholesome breathing amidst the corrupt stagnation of the

old system.   But the arrogance of a conqueror, and
the necessities of an army, which was to be subsisted
and paid by an impoverished people, soon gave rise
to all kinds of oppression ; private abuses followed
close upon the heels of public rapacity, and insolence left its sting to rankle in the wounds of the
injured.   The malignant humours broke out in quarrels and assassinations, and the severe punishments
that ensued, many of them unjust and barbarous in
the highest degree, created rage, not terror, for the
nation had not tried its strength in battle, and would
not believe that it was weak.   Meanwhile the ports
being rigorously blockaded by the English fleet, and
Thiebault. the troubles in Spain having interrupted the commerce in grain, by which Portugal had been usually
supplied from that country, the unhappy people
suffered under the triple pressure of famine, war-
contributions, and a foreign yoke.   With all external
aliment thus cut off, and a hungry army gnawing at
its vitals, the nation could not remain tranquil ; yet
the first five months of Junot's government was, with
the exception of a slight tumult at Lisbon, when the
arms of Portugal were taken down, undisturbed by
commotion.   Nevertheless the whole country was
ripe for a general insurrection.

The harvest proved abundant, and Junot hailed the
prospect of returning plenty as a relief from his principal difficulty ; but as one danger disappeared, another presented itself.   The Spanish insurrection
excited the hopes of the Portuguese, and agents from
the neighbouring juntas communicated secretly with
the Spanish generals in Portugal ; the capture of the
French fleet in Cadiz became known, assassinations
multiplied, the pope's nuncio fled on board the English fleet, and all things tended to an explosion.   The

English agents were, of course, actively engaged in promoting this spirit, and the appearance of two English fleets at different points of the coast, having troops on board, produced great alarm among the French, and augmented the impatient fierceness of the Portuguese.

Among the various ways in which the people discovered their hatred of the invaders, one was very characteristic ; an egg being, by a chemical process, marked with certain letters, was exhibited in a church, and the letters were interpreted to indicate the speedy coming of don Sebastian, king of Portugal, who, like Arthur of Romantic memory, is supposed to be hidden in a secret island, waiting for the destined period to re-appear and restore his country to her ancient glory. The trick was turned against the contrivers ; other eggs prophesied in the most unpatriotic manner, yet the belief of the Sebastianists lost nothing of its zeal ; many people, and those not of the most uneducated classes, were often observed upon the highest points of the hills, casting earnest looks towards the ocean, in the hopes of descrying the island in which their long-lost hero is detained.

CHAPTER II.

BOOK
II.

1808.
June.
THE first serious blow was struck at Oporto.   The
news of what had taken place all over Spain was
known there in June, and general Bellesta, the chief
Spanish officer, immediately took an honourable and
resolute part.   He made the French general Quesnel,
with his staff, prisoners; after which, calling together the Portuguese authorities, he declared that
they were free to act as they judged most fitting for
their own interests, and then marched to Gallicia
with his army and captives.   The opinions of the
leading men at Oporto were divided upon the great
question of resistance, but, after some vicissitudes,
the boldest side was successful; the insurrection,
although at one moment quelled by the French
party, was finally established in Oporto, and soon
extended along the banks of the Douro and the
Minho, and to those parts of Beira which lie between the Mondego and the sea-coast.

Junot being informed of this event, perceived that
no time was to be lost in disarming the Spanish regiments quartered in the neighbourhood of Lisbon,
which was not an easy operation.   Carraffa's division was above six thousand men, and without employing the garrisons of the citadel and forts of Lisbon, it was difficult to collect an equal force of
French; the suspicions of the Spanish regiments
had been already excited, they were reluctant to
Thiebault. obey the French generals, and one, quartered at
Alcacer do Sal, had actually resisted the orders of

the general-in-chief himself. To avoid a tumult was also a great object, because in Lisbon fifteen thousand Gallicians were ordinarily engaged as porters and water-carriers, and if a popular movement had been excited, these men would naturally have assisted their countrymen. Notwithstanding these difficulties, Junot, in the night of that day, upon which he received the information of Bellesta's defection, arranged all his measures, and the next day, the Spanish troops being under various pretexts assembled in such numbers and in such places, that resistance was useless, were disarmed, and placed on board the hulks in the Tagus, with exception of eight hundred of the regiment of Murcia and three hundred of that of Valencia, who escaped. Thus, in the course of twenty-four hours, and with very little bloodshed, Junot, by his promptness and dexterity, averted a very serious danger.

Although this stroke produced considerable effect, it did not prevent the insurrection from becoming general; all couriers and officers carrying orders, or commanding small posts of communications, were suddenly cut off; Junot, reduced by a single blow from fifty to twenty-eight thousand men, found himself isolated, and dependent upon his individual resources, and the courage of his soldiers, for the maintenance of his conquest, and even for the preservation of his army. The Russian squadron, indeed, contained six thousand seamen and marines, but while they consumed a great quantity of provisions, it was evident, from certain symptoms, that they could not be depended upon as useful allies, except in the case of an English fleet attempting to force the entrance of the river. In this situation the duke of Abrantes would have seized Badajos, but

was deterred by the assembling of an Estremaduran
army, then under the command of general Galuzzo.
However, Avril's column, having failed to join Dupont, returned to Estremos, and it is probable that
Junot never intended that it should do otherwise.

Meanwhile Loison, then in Upper Beira, was ordered to march upon Oporto. He had reached Almeida
on the 5th of June, one day previous to Bellesta's
defection, and on the 12th, when he read the order,
partly by menace, partly by persuasion, got possession of Fort Conception, a strong, but ill-placed
Spanish work on that frontier. He first attempted to
penetrate the Entre-Minho e Douro by Amarante,
but as his division was weak, and that it was possible Bellesta might return and fall upon his flank,
he advanced timidly. At Mezam Frias he was opposed, and his baggage was at the same time menaced by other insurgents, whereupon he fell back
to Villa Real, and after a trifling skirmish at that
place, crossed the Douro at Lamego, and marched
to Castro d'Airo, where he turned and defeated the
armed peasants of the mountains, who had particularly harassed his flanks. From Castro d'Airo he
moved upon Coimbra, whence he dislodged a body
of insurgents, and was about to scour the country,
when he received one of twenty-five despatches, the
rest had been intercepted, sent by Junot to recall
him to Lisbon. He immediately united his columns,
placed his sick and weakly men in Almeida, raised
the garrison up to twelve hundred and fifty men,
and then having ruined the defences of Fort Conception, commenced his march to Lisbon by the way
of Guarda.

But while these events were passing in the Beira
an insurrection also broke out in the Algarves

onfused

CHAP.
II.

1808.
July.

where general Maurin commanded. It begun near Faro, and Maurin himself, lying sick in that town, was made prisoner. Some Portuguese troops attached to the French force then joined the insurgents; the Spaniards from Andalusia prepared to cross the Guadiana, and general Spencer appeared off Ayamonte with five thousand British troops. The French colonel Maransin, who had succeeded Maurin, immediately retired to Mertola, leaving his baggage, military chest, and above a hundred prisoners, besides killed and wounded, in the hands of the patriots, who, finding that Spencer would not land, did not pursue beyond the Algarve mountains.

The circle of insurrection was now fast closing round Junot. Emissaries from Oporto excited the people to rise as far as Coimbra, where a French post was overpowered, and a junta was formed whose efforts spread the flame to Condeixa, Pombal, and Leira. A student named Zagalo, mixing boldness with address, obliged a Portuguese officer and a hundred men to surrender the fort of Figueras at the mouth of the Mondego; Abrantes was threatened by the insurgents of the valley of the Zezere, and the Spaniards, under Galuzzo, crossing the Guadiana, at Juramenha, occupied that place and Campo Mayor; thus a great, although confused body of men menaced Kellerman at Elvas, yet, supported by the strength of the town and fort La-Lippe, he easily maintained himself. Avril remained unmolested at Estremos, and Evora, held by a small garrison, was tranquil; but the neighbourhood of Setuval was in commotion, the populace of Lisbon was unquiet, and, at this critical moment, general Spencer, who had quitted Ayamonte and whose force report magnified to ten thousand men, appeared at the mouth of the Tagus.

Junot held a council of war, and after hearing the opinions of the principal general officers decided on the following plan: 1°. To collect the sick in such hospitals as could be protected by the ships of war. 2°. To secure the Spanish prisoners by mooring the hulks in which they were confined as far as possible from the city. 3°. To arm and provision the forts of Lisbon, and remove the powder from the magazines to the ships. 4°. To abandon all other fortresses in Portugal, with exception of Setuval, Almeida, Elvas, and Peniche, and to concentrate the army in Lisbon. In the event of bad fortune, the duke of Abrantes determined to defend the capital as long as he was able, and then crossing the Tagus, move upon Elvas, and from thence retreat to Madrid, Valladolid, or Segovia, as he might find it expedient. This well-conceived plan was not executed, the first alarm soon died away, Spencer returned to Cadiz, and when the insurrection was grappled with, it proved to be more noisy than dangerous.

Kellerman having recalled Maransin from Mertola, was preparing to march on Lisbon, when the inhabitants of the town of Villa Viciosa rose on a company of French troops, and drove them into an old castle; yet when Avril came from Estremos to their succour, the Portuguese fled, and a very few were killed in the pursuit. The town of Beja followed the example of Villa Viciosa, but colonel Maransin, who was ready to retire from Mertola, marched in that direction with such rapidity, that he passed over forty miles in eighteen hours, and falling suddenly upon the patriots,

defeated them with considerable slaughter, and
pillaged the place. He had eighty men killed or
wounded, and general Thiebault writes, that an
obstinate combat took place in the streets. But
the Portuguese never made head for a moment
against a strong body during the whole course of
the insurrection ; how, indeed, was it possible for
a collection of miserable peasants, armed with
scythes, pitchforks, a few old fowling-pieces, and
a little bad powder, under the command of some
ignorant countryman, or fanatic friar, to maintain
a battle against an efficient and active corps of
French soldiers ? For there is this essential difference to be observed in judging between the Spanish
and Portuguese insurrections ; the Spaniards had
many great and strong towns free from the presence
of the French, and large provinces in which to
collect and train forces at a distance from the
invaders ; while in Portugal, the naked peasants
were forced to go to battle the instant even of
assembling. The loss which Maransin sustained
must have arisen from the stragglers, who in a
consecutive march of forty miles would have been
numerous, having been cut off and killed by the
peasantry.

This blow quieted the Alemtejo for the moment,
and Kellerman having cleared the neighbourhood
of Elvas of all Spanish parties, placed a commandant
in La-Lippe, concentrated the detachments under
Maransin and Avril, and proceeded himself towards
Lisbon, where the duke of Abrantes was in great
perplexity. The intercepting of his couriers and
isolated officers being followed by the detection of
all his spies, had exposed him, without remedy, to
every report which the fears of his army, or the

ingenuity of the people, could give birth to; and
there are few nations that can pretend to vie with
the Portuguese and Spaniards in the fabrication of
plausible reports. Among those current, the captivity of Loison was one; but as nothing was
certainly known, except that the insurgents from the
valley of the Mondego were marching towards
Lisbon, general Margaron was ordered to disperse
them, and, if possible, to open a communication
with general Loison. He advanced, with three
thousand men and six pieces of artillery, to Leiria,
whither the patriots had retired, in disorder, when
they heard of his approach; the greater part dispersed at once, but those who remained were
attacked on the 5th of July, and a scene similar to
that of Beja ensued; the French boasted of victory,
the insurgents called it massacre and pillage. In a
combat with armed peasantry, it is difficult to know
where the fighting ceases and the massacre begins;
men dressed in peasant's clothes are observed firing
and moving about without order from place to
place,—when do they cease to be enemies? They
are more dangerous when single than together;
they can hide their muskets in an instant and appear
peaceable; the soldier passes, and is immediately
shot from behind.

Thiebault.
Accursio
de Neves.

The example at Leiria did not however deter the
people of Thomar from declaring against the French,
and the neighbourhood of Alcobaça rose at the same
time. Margaron was thus placed between two new
insurrections at the moment he had quelled one;
English fleets, with troops on board, were said to
be hovering off the coast, and as the most alarming
reports relative to Loison were corroborated, his
safety was despaired of, when, suddenly, authentic

intelligence of his arrival at Abrantes revived the
spirits of the general-in-chief and the army.

After arranging all things necessary for the security of Almeida, he had quitted that town the 2d
of July, at the head of three thousand four hundred
and fifty men, and arrived at Abrantes upon the
8th; having in seven days passed through Guarda,
Attalaya, Sarsedas, Corteja, and Sardoval. During
this rapid march he dispersed several bodies of
insurgents that were assembled on the line of his
route, especially at Guarda and Attalaya, and it
has been said that twelve hundred bodies were
stretched upon the field of battle near the first
town; but twelve hundred slain would give
five thousand wounded, that is to say, six thousand two hundred killed and wounded by a corps
of three thousand four hundred and fifty men
in half an hour! and this without cavalry or artillery, and among fastnesses that vie in ruggedness
with any in the world! The truth is, that the
peasants, terrified by the reports that Loison himself
spread to favour his march, fled on all sides, and
if two hundred and fifty Portuguese were killed and
wounded during the whole passage, it was the
utmost. The distance from Almeida to Abrantes is
more than a hundred and eighty miles, the greatest
part is a mountain pathway rather than a road, and
the French were obliged to gather their provisions
from the country as they passed; to forage, to fight
several actions, to pursue active peasants well acquainted with the country so closely as to destroy
them by thousands, and to march a hundred and
eighty miles over bad roads, and all in seven days,
is impossible.

The whole French army was now concentrated.

BOOK
II.

1808.
July.

Thiebault.

Parlia-
mentary
Papers,
1809.

But though Kellerman had quelled the insurrection
at Alcobaça, and that of Thomar was quieted, the
insurgents from Oporto were gathering strength
at Coimbra, and the last of the native soldiers deserted the French colours; the Spanish troops at
Badajos, strengthened by a body of Portuguese
fugitives, and commanded by one Moretti, were also
preparing to enter the Alemtejo, and that province
was again in commotion; for the English admiral
had opened a communication with the insurgents
on the side of Setuval, and the patriots were assembled in considerable numbers at Alcacer do Sal.

In this dilemma Junot resolved to leave the
northern people quiet for a while, and attack the
Alemtejo, because that was his line of retreat upon
Spain, from thence only he could provision the
capital, and there also his cavalry could act with
the most effect. Accordingly, Loison, with seven
thousand infantry, twelve hundred cavalry, and
eight pieces of artillery, crossed the Tagus the
25th of July, and marched by Os Pegoens, Ven-
danovas, and Montemor. At the latter place he
defeated an advanced guard, which fled to Evora,
where the Portuguese general Leite had assembled
the mass of the insurgents, and assisted by three or
four thousand Spanish troops under Moretti, had taken
a position to cover the town. When Loison discovered them, he directed Margeron and Solignac to turn
their flanks, and fell upon their centre himself; the
battle was short, for the Spanish auxiliaries performed
no service, and the Portuguese soon took to flight, but
there was a great and confused concourse, a strong
cavalry was let loose upon the fugitives, and many
being cut off from the main body, were driven into
the town, which had been deserted by the principal

CHAP.
II.

1808.
July.

inhabitants; there, urged by despair, they endeavoured to defend the walls and the streets for a few
moments, but were soon overpowered, the greater
part slain, and the houses pillaged. The French
lost two or three hundred men, and the number of
the Portuguese and Spaniards that fell was very Thiebault.
considerable; disputes also arose between them,
and the latter ravaged the country in their retreat Appendix,
with more violence than the French.   No. 12.

Loison, after resting two days at Evora, proceeded
to Elvas, and drove away the numerous Spanish
parties which had again infested the neighbourhood
of that fortress, and were become obnoxious alike
to Portuguese and French. He then scoured the
country round, and was accumulating provisions
to form magazines at Elvas, when he was suddenly
interrupted by a despatch from the duke of Abrantes,
recalling him to the right bank of the Tagus, for the
British army, so long expected, had, at last, descended upon the coast, and manly warfare reared
its honest front amidst the desolating scenes of insurrection.

OBSERVATIONS.

1°. Loison's expedition to the Alemtejo was an
operation of military police, rather than a campaign. Junot wished to repress the spirit of insurrection by sudden and severe examples, and hence
the actions of his lieutenant were of necessity
harsh; but they have been represented as a series
of massacres and cruelties of the most revolting
nature, and Loison disseminated such stories to
increase the terror which it was the object of his
expedition to create. The credulity of the nation
that produced the Sebastianists was not easily

shocked, the Portuguese eagerly listened to tales
so derogatory to their enemies, and so congenial to
their own revengeful dispositions; but the anecdotes
of French barbarity current for two years after the
convention of Cintra were notoriously false, and
the same stories being related by persons remote
from each other is no argument of their truth.
The report that Loison was captured, on his march
from Almeida, reached Junot through fifty different
Thiebault. channels; there were men to declare that they had
beheld him bound with cords; others to tell how
he had been entrapped; some named the places he
had been carried through in triumph, and his habitual and characteristic expressions were quoted;
the story was complete, and the parts were consistent, yet the whole was not only false, but the
rumour had not even the slightest foundation of truth.

2°. The Portuguese accounts of the events of
this period are angry amplifications of every real
or pretended act of French barbarity and injustice; the crimes of individuals are made matter of
accusation against the whole army. The French
accounts are more plausible, yet scarcely more safe
as authorities, seeing that they are written by men
who, being for the most part actors in the scenes
they describe, are naturally concerned to defend
their own characters; their military vanity also has
had its share in disguising the simple facts of the
insurrection; for willing to enhance the merit of
the troops, they have exaggerated the number of
the insurgents, the obstinacy of the combats, and
the loss of the patriots. English party writers,
greedily fixing upon such relations, have changed
the name of battle into massacre; and thus prejudice, conceit, and clamour, have combined to

violate the decorum of history, and to perpetuate
error.

3°. It would, however, be an egregious mistake
to suppose, that because the French were not mon-
sters, there existed no cause for the acrimony with
which their conduct has been assailed.   The duke
of Abrantes, although not cruel, nor personally
obnoxious to the Portuguese, was a sensual and
violent person, and his habits were expensive ; such
a man is always rapacious, and as the character of
the chief influences the manners of those under his
command, it may be safely assumed that his vices
were aped by many of his followers.   Now the virtuous general Travot was esteemed, and his person
respected, even in the midst of tumult, by the
Portuguese, while Loison was scarcely safe from
their vengeance when surrounded by his troops;
the execrations poured fourth at the mere mention
of ' the bloody Maneta,' as, from the loss of his
hand, he was called, proves that he must have
committed many heinous acts ; and Kellerman appears to have been as justly stigmatised for rapacity,
as Loison was for violence.

4°. It has been made a charge against the French
generals, that they repressed the hostility of the
Portuguese and Spanish peasants by military executions ; but in doiug so, they only followed the
custom of war, and they are not justly liable to
reproof, save where they may have carried their
punishments to excess, and displayed a wanton
spirit of cruelty.   All armies have an undoubted
right to protect themselves when engaged in hostilities.   An insurrection of armed peasants is a
military anarchy, and men in such circumstances
cannot be restrained within the bounds of civilised

warfare. They will murder stragglers, torture
prisoners, destroy hospitals, poison wells, and break
down all the usages that soften the enmities of modern nations ; they wear no badge of an enemy,
and their devices cannot, therefore, be guarded
against in the ordinary mode ; their war is one of
extermination, and it must be repressed by terrible
examples, or the civilised customs of modern warfare must be discarded, and the devastating system
of the ancients revived. The usage of refusing
quarter to an armed peasantry, and burning their
villages, however unjust and barbarous it may appear at first view, is founded upon a principle of
necessity, and is in reality a vigorous infliction of
a partial evil, to prevent universal calamity: but
however justifiable it may be in theory, no wise
man will hastily resort to it, and no good man will
carry it to any extent.

CHAPTER III.

THE subjugation of Portugal was neither a recent CHAP. III.
nor a secret project of Napoleon's. In 1806, Mr.
Fox, penetrating this design, had sent lord Rosslyn, 1808.
lord St. Vincent, and general Simcoe, on a politico- Parliamentary
Papers,
1809.
military mission to Lisbon, instructing them, to
warn the court that a French army destined to invade Portugal was assembling at Bayonne, and to
offer the assistance of a British force to meet the
attack. The cabinet of Lisbon affected to disbelieve the information, Mr. Fox died during the
negotiation, and as the war with Prussia diverted
Napoleon's attention to more important objects, he
withdrew his troops from Bayonne. The Tory
administration, which soon after overturned the
Grenville party, thought no further of this affair,
or at least did not evince as much foresight and ready
zeal as its predecessors. They, indeed, sent sir
Sydney Smith with a squadron to Lisbon, but their
views seem to have been confined to the emigration
of the royal family, and they intrusted the conduct
of the negotiation to lord Strangford, a young man
of no solid influence or experience.

But, the Russian squadron, under admiral Siniavin, suddenly entered the Tagus, and this unexpected event produced, in the British cabinet, an
activity which the danger of Portugal had not been
able to excite. It was supposed, that as Russia
and England were in a state of hostility, the presence of the Russian ships would intimidate the
prince regent, and prevent him from passing to the

BOOK
II.

1808.

Parlia-
mentary
Papers,
1809.

Sir John
Moore's
Journal,
MS.

Ibid.

Brazils, wherefore sir Charles Cotton, an admiral
of higher rank than sir Sydney Smith, was sent out
with instructions to force the entrance of the Tagus,
and attack Siniavin.   General Spencer, then upon
the point of sailing with five thousand men upon a
secret expedition, was ordered to touch at Lisbon,
and ten thousand men, under sir John Moore, were
withdrawn from Sicily to aid this enterprise ; but
before the instructions for the commanders were
even written, the prince regent was on his voyage
to the Brazils, and Junot ruled in Lisbon.   When
sir John Moore arrived at Gibraltar, he could
hear nothing of sir Sydney Smith, nor of general Spencer, and proceeded to England, which
he reached the 31st of December, 1807.   From
thence, after a detention of four months on ship-
board, he was despatched upon that well-known and
eminently-foolish expedition to Sweden, which ended
in such an extraordinary manner ; and which seems
from the first to have had no other object, than the
factious one of keeping an excellent general and a
superb division of troops at a distance from the only
country where their services were really required.

Meanwhile, general Spencer's armament, long
baffled by contrary winds, and once forced back to
port, was finally dispersed in a storm, and a part
arrived at Gibraltar, by single ships, the latter end
of January, 1808. Sir Hew Dalrymple, the governor
of that fortress, hearing, on the 5th of February, that
a French fleet had just passed the Strait, and run
up the Mediterranean, became alarmed for Sicily,
and caused the first comers to proceed to that island
on the 11th; but Spencer himself, whose instructions
included an attack on Ceuta, did not arrive at Gibraltar until the 10th of March, when the deficiency in

his armament was supplied by a draft from the garrison, and a council was held to arrange the plan of attack on Ceuta; the operation was however finally judged impracticable.

The objects of Spencer's expedition were manifold. He was to co-operate with Moore against the Russian fleet in the Tagus; he was to take the French fleet at Cadiz; he was to assault Ceuta; and he was to make an attempt on the Spanish fleet at Port Mahon! But the wind which brought Moore to Lisbon blowed Spencer from that port, and a consultation with admiral Purvis convinced him that the French fleet in Cadiz was invulnerable to his force; Ceuta was too strong; and it only remained to sail to Port Mahon, when the Spanish insurrection breaking out, drew him back to Cadiz with altered views. In the relation of Dupont's campaign, I have already touched upon Spencer's proceedings at Cadiz; but in this place it is necessary to give a more detailed sketch of those occurrences, which fortunately brought him to the coast of Portugal, at the moment when sir Arthur Wellesley was commencing the campaign of Vimiero.

When the French first entered Spain, general Castaños commanded the Spanish troops at San Roque. In that situation he was an object of interest to Napoleon, who sent two French officers privately to sound his disposition; Castaños, who had secretly resolved to oppose the designs of the emperor, thought those officers were coming to arrest him, and at first determined to kill them, and fly to Gibraltar, but on discovering his mistake, treated them civilly, and prosecuted his original plans. Through the medium of one Viali, a merchant of Gibraltar, he opened a communication with sir Hew

Sir Hew
Dalrymple'sCorrespondence,
MS.

Dalrymple, and the latter, who had been closely
watching the progress of events, encouraged him in
his views, and not only promised assistance, but recommended several important measures, such as the
immediate seizure of the French squadron in Cadiz,
the security of the Spanish fleet at Minorca, and a
speedy communication with South America: however, before Castaños could mature his plans, the
insurrection took place at Seville, and he acknowledged the authority of the junta.

Meanwhile Solano arrived at Cadiz, and general
Spencer, in conjunction with admiral Purvis, pressed
him to attack the French squadron, offering to assist
if he would admit the English troops into the town.
Solano, whose mind was not made up to resist the
invaders, expressed great displeasure at this proposal to occupy Cadiz, and refused to treat at all with
the British, an event not unexpected by sir Hew,
for he knew that most of the Spaniards were mis-
trustful of the object of Spencer's expedition, and
the offer was made without his concurrence.   Thus
a double intercourse was carried on between the
British and Spanish authorities, the one friendly and
confidential between sir Hew and Castaños, the other
of a character proper to increase the suspicions of
the Spaniards.   And when it is considered that
Spain and England were nominally at war; that the
English commanders were acting without the authority of their government; that the troops, which it
was proposed to introduce into Cadiz, were in that
part of the world for the express purpose of attacking Ceuta, and had already taken the island of
Perexil close to that fortress, little surprise can be
excited by Solano's conduct.   When he was killed,
and Morla had succeeded to the command, Spencer

and Purvis renewed their offers; but Morla also declined their assistance, and having himself forced
the French squadron to surrender, by a succession
of such ill-directed attacks, that some doubt was
entertained of his wish to succeed, he commenced a
series of low intrigues calculated to secure his own
personal safety, while he held himself ready to betray his country if the French should prove the
strongest.

After the reduction of the enemy's ships, the people were inclined to admit the English troops, but
the local junta, swayed by Morla's representations,
were averse to it; and he, while confirming this disposition, secretly urged Spencer to persevere in his
offer, saying that he looked entirely to the British
force for the future defence of Cadiz: thus dealing, he passed with the people for an active patriot,
yet made no preparations for resistance, and by his
double falsehoods preserved a fair appearance both
with the junta and the English general. With these
affairs sir Hew Dalrymple did not meddle, he early
discovered that Morla was an enemy of Castaños,
and having more confidence in the latter, carried on
the intercourse at first established between them,
without reference to the transactions at Cadiz. He
also supplied the Spanish general with arms and
two thousand barrels of powder, and placing one
English officer near him as a military correspondent,
sent another in the capacity of a political agent to
the supreme junta at Seville.

When Castaños was appointed commander-in-
chief of the Andalusian army, and had rallied Echevaria's troops, he asked for the co-operation of the
British force, and offered no objection to their entering Cadiz, but he preferred having them landed at

Almeria to march to Xeres. General Spencer confined his offers to the occupation of Cadiz, and when
Morla pretended, that to fit out the Spanish fleet
was an object of immediate importance, colonel sir
George Smith, an officer employed by general
Spencer to conduct the negotiations, promised, on
his own authority, money to pay the Spanish
seamen, who were then in a state of mutiny. However lord Collingwood and sir Hew Dalrymple refused to fulfil this promise, and the approach of
Dupont causing Morla to wish Spencer's troops
away, he persuaded that general to sail to Ayamonte,
under the pretence of preventing Avril's division
from crossing the Guadiana, although he knew
well that the latter had no intention of doing so.
The effect produced upon colonel Maransin by
the appearance of the British force off Ayamonte
has been already noticed. General Thiebault says
that Spencer might have struck an important blow
at that period against the French; but the British
troops were unprovided with any equipment for a
campaign, and to have thrown five thousand infantry, without cavalry and without a single place
of arms, into the midst of an enemy who occupied
all the fortresses, and who could bring twenty
thousand men into the field, would have been imprudent to the greatest degree. General Spencer,
who had by this time been rejoined by his detachment from Sicily, only made a demonstration of
landing, and having thus materially aided the insurrection, returned to Cadiz, from whence he was
almost immediately summoned to Lisbon, to execute
a new project, which proved to be both ill-considered
and fruitless.

Sir Charles Cotton, being unable to force the entrance of the Tagus without troops, had blockaded that post with the utmost rigour, expecting to force the Russian squadron to capitulate for want of provisions. This scheme, which originated with lord Strangford, never had the least chance of success, and only augmented the privations and misery of the wretched inhabitants ; Junot, therefore, had recourse to various expedients to abate the rigour of the blockade with regard to them, and among others, employed a Portuguese, named Sataro, to make proposals to the English admiral. This man, who at first pretended that he came without the privity of the French, led sir Charles to believe that only four thousand French troops remained in Lisbon, and under that erroneous impression, the latter desired general Spencer might join him, for the purpose of attacking the enemy while they were so weak. Spencer, by the advice of sir Hew Dalrymple and lord Collingwood, obeyed the summons, but on his arrival was led to doubt the correctness of the admiral's information ; instead of four thousand, it appeared that there could not be less than fifteen thousand French in or near Lisbon, and the attack was of course relinquished. Spencer returned to Cadiz, Castaños again pressed him to co-operate with the Spanish forces, and he so far consented, as to disembark them at the port of St. Mary, and even agreed to send a detachment to Xeres ; yet deceived by Morla, who still gave him hopes of finally occupying Cadiz, he resolved to keep the greater part close to that city.

At this period the insurrection of Andalusia, attracted all the intriguing adventurers in the Mediterranean towards Gibraltar and Seville, and the confusion of Agramant's camp would have been

CHAP. III.

1808. June.

Mr. Canning to lord Castlereagh, 28th Dec. 1807.

Sir Hew Dalrymple's Correspondence.

Parliamentary Papers, 1809.

Sir Hew Dalrymple's Correspondence.

rivalled, if the prudent firmness of sir Hew Dalrymple had not checked the first efforts of those
political pests. Among the perplexing follies of
the moment, one deserves particular notice, on
account of some curious circumstances that attended
it, the full explanation of which I must, however,
leave to other historians, who may perhaps find in
that and the like affairs, a key to that absurd
policy, which in Sicily so long sacrificed the welfare of two nations to the whims and follies of a
profligate court. The introduction of the salique
law had long been a favourite object with the Bourbons of Spain; but it had never been promulgated
with the formalities necessary to give it validity, and
the nation was averse to change the ancient rule
of succession; this law was, however, now secretly
revived by some of the junta of Seville who wished
to offer the regency to the prince of Sicily, because,
Ferdinand and his brother dying without sons, the
regent would then succeed to the prejudice of the
princess Carlotta of Portugal. With this object in view,
the chevalier Robertoni, a Sicilian agent, appeared
early at Gibraltar, and from thence, as if under the
auspices of England, attempted to forward the views
of his court, until sir Hugh Dalrymple, being
accidentally informed that the British cabinet disapproved of the object of his mission, sent him away.

Meanwhile Castaños, deceived by some person
engaged in the intrigue, was inclined to support the
pretensions of the Sicilian prince to the regency,
and proposed to make use of sir Hew Dalrymple's
name to give weight to his opinions, a circumstance
which would have created great jealousy in Spain,
if sir Hew had not promptly refused his sanction.

The affair then seemed to droop for a moment, but

in the middle of July an English man of war suddenly appeared at Gibraltar, having on board prince
Leopold of Sicily, a complete court establishment
of chamberlains with their keys, and ushers with
their white wands; and the duke of Orleans, who
attended his brother-in-law the prince, making no
secret of his intention to negotiate for the regency
of Spain, openly demanded that he should be
received into Gibraltar. Sir Hew, foreseeing all
the mischief of this proceeding, promptly refused to
permit the prince or any of his attendants to land,
and the captain of the ship, whose orders were
merely to carry him to Gibraltar, refused to take
him back to Sicily. Finally, to relieve his royal
highness from this awkward situation, sir Hew
consented to receive him as a guest, provided that
he divested himself of his public character, and
that the duke of Orleans departed instantly from
the fortress.

Sir William Drummond, British envoy at Palermo, Mr. Viali, and the duke of Orleans, were
the ostensible contrivers of this notable scheme, by
which, if it had succeeded, a small party in a local
junta, would have appointed a regency for Spain,
paved the way for altering the laws of succession in
that country, established their own sway over the
other juntas, and created interminable jealousy between England, Portugal, and Spain. With whom
the plan originated does not very clearly appear.
Sir William Drummond's representations induced Appendix,
No. 8.
sir Alexander Ball to provide the ship of war, nominally for the conveyance of the duke of Orleans,
in reality for prince Leopold, with whose intended
voyage sir Alexander does not appear to have been
made acquainted. That the prince should have

desired to be regent of Spain was natural, but that
he should have been conveyed to Gibraltar in a
British ship of the line, when the English government disapproved of his pretensions, was really curious. Sir William Drummond could scarcely have
proceeded such lengths in an affair of so great consequence, without secret instructions from some
member of his own government, yet lord Castlereagh expressed unqualified approbation of sir Hew's
decisive conduct upon the occasion! Did the ministers act at this period without any confidential communication with each other? or was lord Castlereagh's policy secretly and designedly thwarted by
one of his colleagues? But it is time to quit this
digression and turn to

THE PROCEEDINGS IN PORTUGAL.

The bishop of Oporto being placed at the head
of the insurrectional junta of that town, claimed the
assistance of England. ' We hope,' said he, ' for an
aid of three hundred thousand cruzado novas; of
arms and accoutrements complete, and of cloth for
forty thousand infantry and for eight thousand cavalry; three thousand barrels of cannon powder,
some cargoes of salt fish, and other provisions, and
an auxiliary body of six thousand men at least, including some cavalry.' This extravagant demand
would lead to the supposition that an immense force
had been assembled by the prelate, yet he could
never at any time have put five thousand organized
men in motion against the French, and had probably not even thought of any feasible or rational mode
of employing the succours he demanded; the times
were however favourable for extravagant demands,
and his were not rejected by the English ministers.

who sent agents to Oporto and other parts, with
power to grant supplies. The improvident system
adopted for Spain, being thus extended to Portugal,
produced precisely the same effects, that is, cavils,
intrigues, waste, insubordination, inordinate vanity,
and ambition, among the ignorant upstart men of the
day.

More than half a year had now elapsed since
Napoleon first poured his forces into the Peninsula,
every moment of that time was marked by some extraordinary event, and one month had passed since a
general and terrible explosion, shaking the unsteady
structure of diplomacy to pieces, had left a clear
space for the shock of arms; yet the British cabinet
was still unacquainted with the real state of public
feeling in the Peninsula, and with the Spanish cha-
racter; and although possessing a disposable army, Parl. Pap.
lord Cas-
of at least eighty thousand excellent troops, was tlereagh to
sir A. Wel-
totally unsettled in its plans, and unprepared for any lesley,
21st June.
vigorous effort. Agents were indeed despatched to
every accessible province, the public treasure was
scattered with heedless profusion, and the din of
preparation was heard in every department; but the
bustle of confusion is easily mistaken for the activity
of business, and time removing the veil of official
mystery covering those transactions, has exposed all
their dull and meagre features: it is now clear, that
the treasure was squandered without judgment, and
the troops dispersed without meaning. Ten thousand exiled to Sweden proved the truth of Oxen-
stiern's address to his son; as many more idly kept
in Sicily were degraded into the guards of a vicious
court; Gibraltar was unnecessarily filled with fighting men, and general Spencer, with five thousand
excellent soldiers, was doomed to wander between

Ceuta, Lisbon, and Cadiz, seeking, like the knight of La Mancha, for a foe to combat.

A considerable force remained in England, but it was not ready for service, when the minister resolved to send an expedition to the Peninsula, and nine thousand men collected at Cork, formed the only disposable army for immediate operations. The Grey and Grenville administration, so remarkable for unfortunate military enterprises, had assembled this handful of men with a view to permanent conquests in South America! upon what principle of policy it is not necessary to inquire, but such undoubtedly was the intention of that administration, perhaps in imitation of the Roman senate, who sent troops to Spain when Hannibal was at the gates of the city. The Tory administration relinquishing this scheme of conquest, directed sir Arthur Wellesley to inform general Miranda, the military adventurer of the day, not only that he must cease to expect assistance, but that all attempts to separate the colonies of Spain from the parent state would be discouraged by the English government; thus the troops assembled at Cork became available, and sir Arthur Wellesley being appointed to command them, sailed on the 12th of July, to commence that long and bloody contest in the Peninsula which he was destined to terminate in such a glorious manner.

Two small divisions were soon after ordered to assemble for embarkation at Ramsgate and Harwich, under the command of generals Anstruther and Acland, yet a considerable time elapsed before they were ready to sail, and a singular uncertainty in the views of the ministers at this period subjected all the military operations to perpetual and mischievous changes. General Spencer, supposed to be at Gib-

Parliamentary Papers, 1808.

raltar, was directed to repair to Cadiz, and there CHAP. III.
await sir Arthur's orders, and the latter was permitted to sail under the impression that Spencer was 1808. July.
actually subject to his command; other instructions Parliamentary
empowered Spencer, at his own discretion, to com- Papers, 1808.
mence operations in the south, without reference to Ld Castlereagh to
sir Arthur Wellesley's proceedings; admiral Purvis, sir A. Wellesley,
who, after lord Collingwood's arrival, had no sepa- 30th June.
rate command, was also authorised to undertake any Ibid.
Ld Castle-
enterprise in that quarter, and even to control the reagh to
gen. Spen-
operations of sir Arthur Wellesley by calling for the cer, 28th & 30th June.
aid of his troops, that general being enjoined to ' pay Do.to adm.
Purvis,
all due obedience to any such requisition!' Yet sir 28th June.
Arthur himself was informed, that ' the accounts
from Cadiz were bad;' that ' no disposition to move
either there or in the neighbourhood of Gibraltar
was visible,' and that ' the cabinet were unwilling
he should go far to the southward, whilst the spirit
of exertion appeared to reside more to the northward.' Again, the admiral, sir Charles Cotton, was
informed that sir Arthur Wellesley was to co-operate with him in a descent at the mouth of the Tagus,
but sir Arthur himself had no definite object given
for his own operations, although his instructions
pointed to Portugal. Thus in fact no one officer,
naval or military, knew exactly what his powers
were, with the exception of admiral Purvis, who,
being only second in command for his own service,
was really authorised to control all the operations of
the land forces, provided he directed them to that
quarter which had been declared unfavourable for
any operations at all! These inconsistent orders were
calculated to create confusion and prevent all vigour
of action, but more egregious conduct followed.

In recommending Portugal as the fittest field of

BOOK
II.
————
1808.
July.

Parl. Pap.
Ld Castle-
reagh to
sir A. Wel-
lesley,
30th June.

action, the ministers were chiefly guided by the advice of the Asturian deputies. Yet, having received
sir Hew Dalrymple's despatches to a late date, their
own information must have been more recent and
more extensive than any that they could obtain from
those deputies, who had left Spain at the commencement of the insurrection, who were ill informed of
what was passing in their own province, utterly
ignorant of the state of any other part of the Peninsula, and under any circumstances incapable of
judging rightly in such momentous affairs. But
though sir Arthur Wellesley's instructions were
vague and confined with respect to military operations, he was expressly told that the intention of the
government, was to enable Portugal and Spain to
throw off the French yoke, and ample directions
were given to him as to his future political conduct
in the Peninsula. He was informed how to demean
himself in any disputes that might arise between
the two insurgent nations, how to act with relation
to the settlement of the supreme authority during
the interregnum. He was directed to facilitate communications between the colonies and the mother
country, and to offer his good offices to arrange any
differences between them. The terms upon which
Great Britain would acquiesce in any negotiation
between Spain and France were imparted to him,
and finally he was empowered to recommend the
establishment of a paper system in the Peninsula, as
a good mode of raising money, and attaching the
holders of it to the national cause: the Spaniards
were not, however, sufficiently civilised to adopt
this recommendation, and barbarously preferred gold
to credit, at a time when no man's life, or faith, or
wealth, or power, was worth a week's purchase.

CHAP.
III.

1808.
July.

Parl. Pap.
Ld. Castle-
reagh to
sir H. Dal-
rymple,
28th June.

Sir Hew Dalrymple was also commanded to furnish sir Arthur with every information that might
be of use in the operations, and when the tenor of
these instructions, and the great Indian reputation
enjoyed by sir Arthur Wellesley are considered, it
is not possible to doubt that he was first chosen as
the fittest man to conduct the armies of England at
this important conjuncture. Yet scarcely had he
sailed when he was superseded, not for a man whose
fame and experience might have justified such a
change, but by an extraordinary arrangement, which
can hardly be attributed to mere vacillation of purpose, he was reduced to the fourth rank in that
army, for the future governance of which, he had
fifteen days before received the most extended instructions. Sir Hew Dalrymple was now appointed to
the chief command, and sir John Moore, who had
suddenly and unexpectedly returned from the
Baltic, having by his firmness and address saved
himself and his troops from the madness of the
Swedish monarch, was, with marked disrespect, directed to place himself under the orders of sir Harry
Burrard, and proceed to Portugal. Thus two men,
comparatively unknown and unused to the command
of armies, superseded the only generals in the
British service whose talents and experience were
indisputable. The secret springs of this proceeding
are not so deep as to baffle investigation ; but that
task scarcely belongs to the general historian, who
does enough when he exposes the effects of envy,
treachery, and base cunning, without tracing those
vices home to their possessors.

Notwithstanding these changes in the command,
the uncertainty of the minister's plans continued.

BOOK
II.
———
1808.
July.

Parl. Pap.
Ld. Castle-
reagh to
sir A. Wel-
lesley,
15th July.

The same day that sir Hew Dalrymple was appointed to be commander-in-chief, a despatch, containing the following project of campaign, was sent
to sir Arthur Wellesley : ' The motives which have
induced the sending so large a force to that quarter
(the coast of Portugal), are, 1st, to provide effectually for an attack upon the Tagus ; and, 2dly, to
have such an additional force disposable beyond
what may be indispensably requisite for that operation, as may admit of a detachment being made to
the southward, either with a view to secure Cadiz,
if it should be threatened by the French force under
general Dupont, or to co-operate with the Spanish
troops in reducing that corps, if circumstances
should favour such an operation, or any other that
may be concerted. His Majesty is pleased to direct
that the *attack upon the Tagus should be considered
as the first object to be attended to ;* and as the whole
force, of which a statement is enclosed, when assembled, will amount to not less than thirty thousand, *it is considered that both services may be
provided for amply.* The precise distribution, as
between Portugal and Andalusia, both as to time
and proportion of force, must depend upon circumstances, to be judged of on the spot ; and should it
be deemed advisable to fulfil the assurance which
lieutenant-general sir Hew Dalrymple appears to
have given to the supreme junta of Seville, under
the authority of my despatch of (no date), that it
was the intention of his Majesty to employ a corps
of ten thousand men to co-operate with the
Spaniards in that quarter ; a corps of this mag-
nitude may, I should hope, be detached without
prejudice to the main operation against the Tagus,

and may be reinforced, according to circumstances, after the Tagus has been secured. But if, previous to the arrival of the force under orders from England, Cadiz should be seriously threatened, it must rest with the senior officer of the Tagus, at his discretion to detach, upon receiving a requisition to that effect, such an amount of force as may place that important place out of the reach of immediate danger, *even though it should for the time suspend operations against the Tagus.*'

The inconsistent folly of this despatch is apparent, but the occupation of Cadiz was a favourite project with the Cabinet, which was not discouraged by Spencer's unsuccessful effort to gain admittance, nor by the representations of sir Hew Dalrymple, who had grounds to believe that the attempt would bring down the army under Castaños to oppose it by force. Neither did the minister consider that, in a political view, such a measure, pressed as a preliminary, would give a handle for misrepresentation, and that, in a military view, the burden of Cadiz would clog operations in Portugal. Adopting all projects, and weighing none, they displayed the most incredible confusion of ideas; for the plan of sending ten thousand men to Seville, was said to be in pursuance of a promise made by sir Hew Dalrymple to the junta, whereas the despatch of that general, quoted as authority for this promise of help, contained nothing of the kind, and was even written *before any junta existed!*

In England, at this period, personal enmity to Napoleon, and violent party prejudices, had so disturbed the judgments of men relative to that monarch, that any information speaking of strength or success for him, was regarded with suspicion even by the ministers, who, as commonly happens in such cases, becoming the dupes of their own practices, listened with complacency to all those tales of mutiny among his troops, disaffection of his generals, and insurrections in France, which the cunning or folly of their agents transmitted to them. Hence sprung such projects as the one above, the false calculations of which may be exposed by a short comparative statement.   The whole English force was not much above thirty thousand men, distributed off Cadiz, off the coast of Portugal, on the eastern parts of England, and in the Channel.   The French in Spain and Portugal were about a hundred and twenty thousand men, and they possessed all the Portuguese, and most of the Spanish fortresses. The English army had no reserve, no fixed plan, and it was to be divided, and to act upon a double line of operations.   The French had a strong reserve at Bayonne, and the grand French army of four hundred thousand veterans was untouched, and ready to succour the troops in the Peninsula if they required it.

Happily, this visionary plan was in no particular followed by the generals entrusted with the conduct of it.   A variety of causes combined to prevent the execution.   The catastrophe of Baylen marred the great combinations of the French emperor, fortune drew the scattered divisions of the English army together, and the decisive vigour of sir Arthur Wellesley sweeping away these cobweb projects, obtained all the success that the bad arrangements of the ministers would permit.   In the next chapter, resuming the thread of the history, I shall relate the proceedings of the first British campaign in the Peninsula.   But I judged it necessary to

make an exposition of the previous preparations
and plans of the cabinet, lest the reader's attention
not being fully awakened to the difficulties cast in
the way of the English generals by the incapacity
of the government, should, with hasty censure, or
niggard praise, do the former injustice; for, as a
noble forest hides many noisome swamps and
evil things, so the duke of Wellington's actions
have covered the innumerable errors of the
ministers.

CHAPTER IV.

BOOK
II.
1808.
July.

Sir A.Wel-
lesley's
Narrative.
Court of
Inquiry.
A FEW days after sailing from Cork, sir Arthur
Wellesley, quitting the fleet, repaired in a frigate
to Coruña, where he arrived the 20th of July, and
immediately held a conference with the Gallician
junta, by whom he was informed of the battle of
Rio Seco. The account was glossed over in the
Spanish manner, and the issue of that contest had
caused no change of policy, if policy that may be
called, which was but a desire to obtain money and
to avoid personal inconvenience. The aid of troops
was rejected, but arms and gold were demanded,
and while the conference went on, the last was
supplied, for an English frigate entered the harbour
with two hundred thousand pounds. The junta
recommended that the British should be employed
in the north of Portugal, promised to aid them by
sending a Spanish division to Oporto, and supported
their recommendation with an incorrect statement
of the number of men, Spanish and Portuguese,
who, they asserted, were in arms near that city.
They gave also a still more inaccurate estimate of
the forces under Junot, and in this manner persuaded sir Arthur not to land in their province :
yet, at the moment they were rejecting the assistance of the British troops, the whole kingdom of
Gallicia was lying at the mercy of marshal Bessieres, and there were neither men nor means to
impede the progress of his victorious army.

Mr. Charles Stuart, appointed envoy to the Gallician junta, had arrived with sir Arthur Wellesley

at Coruña, and quickly penetrated the flimsy veil
of Spanish enthusiasm, informed his government of
the true state of affairs ; but his despatches were
unheeded, while the inflated reports of the subordinate civil and military agents were blazoned forth,
and taken as sure guides.   Meanwhile sir Arthur
proceeded to Oporto, where he found colonel
Browne, an active, intelligent officer, employed to
distribute succours.   From his reports it appears
that no Spanish troops were in the north of Portugal, and that all the Portuguese force was upon
the Mondego, to the south of which river the insurrection had already spread.   A French division
of eight thousand men was supposed to be in their
front, and some great disaster was to be expected,
for, to use colonel Browne's words, ' with every
good will in the people, their exertions were so
short-lived, and with so little combination, that
there was no hope of their being able to resist the Parliamentary
advances of the enemy;' in fact, only five thousand Papers,
1809.
regulars and militia, half armed, and associated
with ten or twelve thousand peasants without any
arms, were in the field at all.   A large army was,
however, made out upon paper by the bishop of
Oporto, who, having assembled his civil and military coadjutors in council, proposed various plans Sir A. Wellesley's
of operation for the allied forces, none of which sir Narrative.
Court of
Arthur was inclined to adopt; but after some dis- Inquiry.
cussion it was finally arranged that the prelate and
the paper army should look to the defence of the
Tras os Montes against Bessieres, and that the five
thousand soldiers on the Mondego should co-operate
with the British forces.

   This being settled, sir Arthur Wellesley hastened
to consult with sir Charles Cotton relative to the

descent at the mouth of the Tagus, which had so
long haunted the imaginations of the ministers. The
strength of the French, the bar of the river, the
disposition of the forts, and the difficulty of landing
in the immediate neighbourhood, occasioned by the
heavy surf playing upon all the undefended creeks
and bays, convinced him that such an enterprise
was unadvisable, if not impracticable. There remained a choice of landing to the north of Lisbon
at such a distance as to avoid the danger of a disputed disembarkation; or of proceeding to the
southward to join general Spencer, and commence
operations in that quarter against Dupont. Sir
Arthur Wellesley decided against the latter, which
promised no good result while Junot held Portugal
and Bessieres hung on the northern frontier; for he
foresaw that the jealousy of the Spaniards, evinced
by their frequent refusal to admit English troops
into Cadiz, would assuredly bring on a tedious
negotiation, and waste the season of action before
the army could obtain a place of arms; or that the
campaign must be commenced without any secure
base of operations. Nothing was then known of
the Spanish troops, except that they were inexperienced, and without good aid from them, it
would have been idle with fourteen thousand men
to take the field against twenty thousand, strongly
posted in the Sierra Morena, and communicating
freely with the main body of the French army.
A momentary advance was useless! and if the campaign was protracted, the line of operations running
nearly parallel to the frontier of Portugal, would
have required a covering army on the Guadiana to
watch the movements of Junot.

The double line of operations, proposed by lord

Sir A. Wel-
lesley's
Narrative.
Court of
Inquiry.

Sir H Dal-
rymple's
and lord
Colling-
wood's
Correspon-
dence.

Castlereagh, was contrary to all military principle, and as Spencer's despatches announced that his division was at St. Mary's, near Cadiz, and disengaged from any connexion with the Spaniards— a fortunate circumstance, scarcely to have been expected,—sir Arthur sent him orders to sail to the mouth of the Mondego, whither he himself also repaired, to join the fleet having his own army on board.

Off the Mondego he received the despatches announcing sir Hew Dalrymple's appointment and the sailing of sir John Moore's troops, but this mortifying intelligence did not relax his activity; he directed fast-sailing vessels to look out for Anstruther's armament, and conduct it to the Mondego, and having heard of Dupont's capitulation, resolved, without waiting for general Spencer's arrival, to disembark his own troops and commence the campaign—a determination that marked the cool decisive vigour of his character. He was, indeed, sure that, in consequence of Dupont's defeat, Bessieres would not enter Portugal; yet his information led him to estimate Junot's own force at sixteen to eighteen thousand men, a number, indeed, below the truth, yet sufficient to make the hardiest general pause before he disembarked with only nine thousand men, and without any certainty that his fleet could remain even for a day in that dangerous offing: another man, also, was coming to profit from any success that might be obtained, and a failure would have ruined his own reputation in the estimation of the English public, always ready to deride the skill of an Indian general.

Sir A.Wellesley's Narrative. Court of Inquiry.

It was difficult to find a good point of disembarkation. The coast of Portugal, from the Minho to

the Tagus, presents, with few exceptions, a rugged
and dangerous shore; all the harbours formed by
the rivers have bars, that render most of them difficult of access even for boats; with the slightest
breeze from the seaboard, a terrible surf breaks along
the whole line of coast, forbidding all approach;
and when the south wind, which commonly prevails
from August to the winter months, blows, a more
dangerous shore is not to be found in any part of
the world.

The small peninsula of Peniché, about seventy
miles northward of the Lisbon Rock, alone offered a
safe and accessible bay, perfectly adapted for a disembarkation; but the anchorage was completely
within range of the fort, which contained a hundred
guns and a garrison of a thousand men. The next
best place was the Mondego river, and as the little
fort of Figueras, taken, as I have before related,
by the student Zagalo, and now occupied by English
marines, secured a free entrance, sir Arthur commenced landing his troops there on the 1st of August. The weather was calm, yet the operation
was so difficult, that it was not completed before
the 5th, and at that moment, by singular good fortune, general Spencer arrived; he had not received
sir Arthur's orders, but with great promptitude had
sailed for the Tagus the moment Dupont surrendered, and by sir Charles Cotton had been directed
to Mondego. The united forces, however, only
amounted to twelve thousand three hundred men,
because a veteran battalion, being destined for
Gibraltar, was left on board the ships.

When the army was on shore, the British general
repaired to Montemor Velho, to confer with don
Bernardim Freire de Andrada, the Portuguese com-

Sir A. Wel-
lesley's
Narrative.
Court of
Inquiry.

mander-in-chief, who proposed that the troops of
the two nations should relinquish all communication
with the coast, and throwing themselves into the
heart of Beira, commence an offensive campaign.
He promised ample stores of provisions, but sir
Arthur having already discovered the weakness of
the insurrection, placed no reliance on those promises;
wherefore furnishing Freire with five thousand stand
of arms and ammunition, he refused to separate
from his ships, and seeing clearly that the insurgents were unable to give any real assistance, resolved to act with reference to the probability of
their deserting him in danger. The Portuguese
general, disappointed at this refusal, reluctantly
consented to join the British army, yet pressed sir
Arthur to hasten to Leiria, lest a large magazine
filled, as he affirmed, with provisions for the use
of the British army, should fall into the enemy's
hands. After this the two generals separated, and
the necessary preparations being completed, the
advanced guard of the English army quitted the
banks of the Mondego on the 9th, taking the road
to Leiria, and the 10th, sir Arthur Wellesley followed with the main body.

His plan embraced three principal objects:

1°. To hold on by the sea-coast, as well for the
sake of his supplies, as to avoid the drain upon his
army, which the protection of magazines on shore
would occasion, and also to cover the disembarkation
of the reinforcements expected from England.

2°. To keep his troops in a mass, that he might
strike an important blow.

3°. To strike that blow as near Lisbon as possible,
that the affairs of Portugal might be quickly brought
to a crisis.

BOOK
II.
―――
1808.
August.
Sir A. Wel-
lesley's
Narrative.
Court of
Inquiry.
He possessed very good military surveys of the ground in the immediate neighbourhood of Lisbon, and he was anxious to carry on his operations in a part of the country where he could avail himself of this resource; but the utter inexperience of his commissariat staff, and the want of cavalry, rendered his movements slow, and obliged him to be extremely circumspect; especially as the insurrection, although a generous, was a feeble effort, and its prolongation rather the result of terror than of hope; the blow had been hastily struck in the moment of suffering, and the patriots, conscious of weakness, trembled when they reflected on their own temerity.

Bernardim Freire had received arms and equipments complete for five thousand soldiers, yet his army at Leiria did not exceed six thousand men of all arms fit for action, and besides this force, there were in all the provinces north of the Tagus only three thousand infantry, under the command of the marquis of Valladeres, half of whom were Spaniards : hence it appears, that nothing could be more insignificant than the insurrection, nothing more absurd than the lofty style adopted by the junta of Oporto in their communications with the British ministers.

Upon the other side, Junot, who had received information of the English descent, in the Mondego, as early as the 2d, was extremely embarrassed by the distance of his principal force, and the hostile disposition of the inhabitants of Lisbon. He also was acquainted with the disaster of Dupont, and exaggerated notions of the essential strength of the Portuguese insurgents were generated in his own mind, and in the minds of his principal officers. The patriots of the Alemtejo and Algarves, assisted by some Spaniards, and animated by manifestos and promises assiduously promulgated from the English fleet, had once more assembled at Alcacer do Sal, from whence they threatened the garrisons of St. Ubes, and the French posts on the south bank of the Tagus, immediately opposite to Lisbon. That capital was very unquiet. The anticipation of coming freedom was apparent in the wrathful looks and stubborn manners of the populace, and superstition was at work to increase the hatred and the hopes of the multitude, it was at this time the prophetic eggs, denouncing death to the French, and deliverance to the Portuguese, appeared. But less equivocal indications of approaching danger were to be drawn from the hesitations of Junot, who, wavering between his fear of an insurrection in Lisbon, and his desire to check the immediate progress of the British army, gave certain proof of an intellect yielding to the pressure of events.

Loison, having seven or eight thousand men, was now in the neighbourhood of Estremos; two thousand five hundred men were in the fortresses of Elvas and Almeida, a few hundred were at Abrantes, a thousand in Santarem, and the same number in Peniché; general Thomieres, with one brigade, was in the vicinity of Alcobaça, and the rest of the army was quartered at Lisbon and on a circuit round, including both sides of the river. The Tagus itself was guarded on the north bank by the forts of Cascaes, St. Antonio, St. Julian's, Belem, and the citadel, between which smaller works kept up a continued line of offence against ships entering by the northern passage of the harbour. On the southern bank, fort Bugio, built upon a low sandy point, crossed its fire with St. Julian's in the defence of the entrance. Upon the

heights of Almada or Palmela, stood the fort of
Palmela, and St. Ubes and Traffaria completed the
posts occupied by the French on that side. The communication between the north and south banks was
kept up by the refitted Portuguese ships of war, by
the Russian squadron, and by the innumerable
boats, most of them very fine and large, with which
the Tagus is covered.

Such was the situation of the army on the 3d,
when Junot ordered Loison to march by Portalegre
and Abrantes, and from thence effect a junction with
general Laborde, who, with three thousand infantry,
five or six hundred cavalry, and five pieces of artillery, quitted Lisbon upon the 6th, and proceeded
by Villa Franca, Rio Mayor, and Candeiros; being
charged to observe the movements of the British,
and to cover the march of Loison, with whom he
expected to form a junction at Leiria.   Junot
himself remained in Lisbon thinking to control
Thiebault. the inhabitants by his presence.   He embarked
all the powder from the magazines, took additional precautions to guard his Spanish prisoners,
and put the citadel and forts into a state of siege;
but disquieted by the patriots, assembled at Alcacer
do Sal, he sent general Kellerman with a moveable
column to disperse them, directing him to scour the
country between that place and Setuval, to withdraw the garrison from the latter, to abandon all the
French posts on the south of the Tagus except Palmela, and to collect the whole force in one mass on
the heights of Almada, where an entrenched camp
had been already commenced.   But Kellerman had
scarcely departed, when two English regiments, the
one from Madeira, the other from Gibraltar, arriving
off the bar of Lisbon, distracted anew the attention

of the French, and increased the turbulence of the
populace; and in this state of perplexity the duke
of Abrantes lingered until the 15th, when the progress of sir Arthur Wellesley forced him to assume
the command of the army in the field.

Loison entered Abrantes the 9th, and the same
day Laborde arrived at Candeiros, from which point
he could, with facility, either move upon Alcobaça
and Leiria, or form a junction with Loison upon the
side of Santarem. The 10th, Loison halted at
Abrantes, and Laborde moved to Alcobaça, where
he was joined by Thomieres and the garrison of
Peniché. Hence the armies on both sides were
now in a state of attraction towards each other,
indicated an approaching shock, and while the news
of Bessieres' victory at Rio Seco produced a short-
lived exultation in the French camp, intelligence of
Joseph's flight from Madrid reached the British
army, and increased its confidence of victory.

Sir Arthur's advanced guard entered Leiria, and Proceed-
was there joined by Bernardim Freire and the Portu- ings of the
Court of
guese army, which immediately seized the magazine Inquiry.
without making any distribution to the British
troops, the main body of which only arrived the
11th, but the whole marched in advance upon the
12th. Laborde had employed the 11th and 12th
seeking for a position in the vicinity of Batalha, and
finding the ground too extensive for his force, fell
back in the night of the 12th to Obidos, a town with
a Moorish castle built on a gentle eminence, in the
middle of a valley. Occupying this place with his Thiebault.
piquets, he placed a small detachment at the windmill of Brilos, three miles in front, and retired the
14th to Roriça, a village six miles to the southward,
situated at the intersection of the roads leading to

Torres Vedras, Montechique, and Alcoentre, and overlooking the whole valley of Obidos. This position enabled him to preserve his communication with Loison open, but as it uncovered Peniché, the fourth Swiss regiment, with the exception of the flank companies, was sent to re-garrison that important point, and at the same time three hundred men were detached to the right by Bombarral, Cadaval, and Segura, to obtain intelligence of Loison.

That general, by a demonstration on the side of Thomar the 11th, had ascertained that Leiria was in the hands of the British, and fell back the same day upon Torres Novas, then following the course of the Tagus he arrived at Santarem upon the 13th, but in such an exhausted state, that he was unable to renew his march until the 15th. Sir Arthur Wellesley's first movement had thus cut the line of communication between Loison and Laborde, caused a loss of several forced marches to the former, and obliged the latter to risk an action with more than twice his own numbers. But as the hostile troops approached each other, the Portuguese chiefs became alarmed; for, notwithstanding the confident language of their public manifestos and the bombastic style of their conversation, an internal conviction that a French army was invincible pervaded all ranks of the patriots. The leaders, aware of their own deficiency, and incredulous of the courage of the English soldiers, dreaded the being committed in a decisive contest; because a defeat would deprive them of all hope to make terms with the victors, whereas by keeping five or six thousand men together, they could at any time secure themselves by a capitulation. The junta of Oporto also, who were already aiming at supreme authority, foresaw that, in the event of a successful battle, it would be more advantageous for their particular views to be provided with an army untouched and entirely disconnected with a foreign general; and Freire being well instructed in the secret designs of this party, resolved not to advance a step beyond Leiria. However to cover his real motives, he required the British commander to supply him with provisions, choosing to forget the magazine which he had just appropriated to himself, and as readily forgetting the formal promises of the bishop of Oporto, who had undertaken to feed the English army.

This extraordinary demand, that an auxiliary army, just disembarked, should nourish the native soldiers, instead of being itself fed by the people, was met by sir Arthur Wellesley with a strong remonstrance. He easily penetrated the secret motive which caused it, yet feeling that it was important to have a respectable Portuguese force acting in conjunction with his own, he first appealed to the honour and patriotism of Freire, warmly admonishing him, that he was going to forfeit all pretension to either, by permitting the British army to fight without his assistance. This argument had no effect upon don Bernardim, and he parried the imputations, against his spirit and zeal, by pretending that his intention was to operate independently on the line of the Tagus; hence after some further discussion, sir Arthur, changing his tone of rebuke to one of conciliation, recommended to him not to risk his troops by an isolated march, but to keep in the rear of the British and wait for the result of the first battle. This advice was agreeable to Freire, and at the solicitation of colonel Trant, a military agent, he consented to leave fourteen hundred infantry, and

two hundred and fifty cavalry, under the immediate command of the English general. But the
defection of the native force was a serious evil,
it shed an injurious moral influence, and deprived
sir Arthur of the aid of troops whose means of
gaining intelligence, and whose local knowledge,
might have compensated for his want of cavalry.
Nevertheless, continuing his own march, his advanced guard entered Caldas the 15th, on which day
also Junot reluctantly quitted Lisbon, with a reserve
composed of two thousand infantry, six hundred
cavalry, and ten pieces of artillery, carrying with
him his grand parc of ammunition, and a military
chest, containing forty thousand pounds.

General Travot was left at Lisbon, with above
seven thousand men, of which number two battalions
were formed of stragglers and convalescents. He
held both sides of the Tagus, and Palmela, the Bugio
fort, and the heights of Almada, were occupied by
two thousand men, to protect the shipping from the
insurgents of the Alemtejo, who, under the orders
of the Monteiro Mor, were again gathering at Setuval; a thousand were on board the vessels of war to
guard the Spanish prisoners, and the spare powder;
two thousand four hundred were in the citadel and
supporting the police; a thousand were distributed
in the forts of Belem, St. Julian's, Cascaes, and
Ericeia, which last is situated to the northward of
the Rock of Lisbon, and commands a small harbour
a few miles west of Mafra; finally, a thousand were
at Santarem, protecting a large depôt of stores.
Thus, if the garrisons of Elvas, Peniché, and Almeida
be included, nearly one-half of the French army was,
by Junot's combinations, rendered inactive, and
those in the field were divided into three parts,

without any certain point of junction in advance, yet each too weak singly to sustain an action. The duke of Abrantes seems to have reigned long enough in Portugal, to forget that he was merely the chief of an advanced corps, whose safety depended upon activity and concentration.

The French reserve was transported to Villa Franca by water, from whence it was to march to Otta, but the rope ferry-boat of Saccavem being removed by the natives, it cost twenty-four hours to throw a bridge across the creek at that place; and on the 17th when the troops were on their march, Junot hastily recalled them to Villa Franca, because of a report that the English had landed near the capital. This rumour, proving false, the reserve resumed the road to Otta, under the command of general Thiebault, and Junot himself pushed forward to Alcoentre, where he found Loison, and assumed the personal direction of that general's division. Meanwhile sir Arthur Wellesley was pressing Laborde. The 15th he had caused the post at Brilos to be attacked, and the piquets to be driven out of Obidos, but two companies of the 95th, and two of the 5th battalion, 60th, after gaining the windmill without loss, pursued the retiring enemy with such inconsiderate eagerness, that at the distance of three miles from their support, they were out-flanked by two superior bodies of French, and were only saved by the opportune advance of general Spencer. Two officers and twenty-seven men were killed and wounded in this slight affair, which gave a salutary check to the rashness, without lowering the confidence of the troops, and on the 16th, Laborde's position was examined.

The main road from Obidos passed through a

Sir A. Welles-ley's De-spatch.

valley, which was closed to the southward by some
high table land, on which stood the village of
Roriça, and the French being posted on a small plain
immediately in front of that place, overlooked all
the country as far as Obidos.   All the favourable
points of defence in front, and on the nearest hills at
each side, were occupied by small detachments, and
one mile in the rear, a steep ridge, extending about
three quarters of a mile east and west, and consequently parallel to the French position, offered a
second line of great strength.   The main road led
by a steep defile over this ridge, which was called
the height of Zambugeira or Columbeira.   Beyond
it, very lofty mountains stretching from the sea-
coast to the Tagus like a wall, filled all the space
between that river and the ocean, down to the Rock
of Lisbon ; and the valley leading from Obidos
to Roriça was bounded on the left by a succession
of ridges rising like steps, until they were lost in the
great mass of the Sierra de Baragueda, itself a shoot
from the Monte Junto.

Laborde's situation was truly embarrassing.   Loison was still at Alcoentre, and the reserve at Villa
Franca, that is, one and two marches distant from
Roriça ; hence if he retired upon Torres Vedras, his
communication with Loison would be lost, and to
fall back on Montechique was to expose the line of
Torres Vedras and Mafra ; to march upon Alcoentre,
and unite with Loison, was to leave open the shortest
road to Lisbon, and to remain at Roriça was to
fight three times his own force.   Nevertheless, encouraged by the local advantages of his position,
and justly confident in his own talents, Laborde resolved to abide his enemy's assault, in the feeble
hope that Loison might arrive during the action.

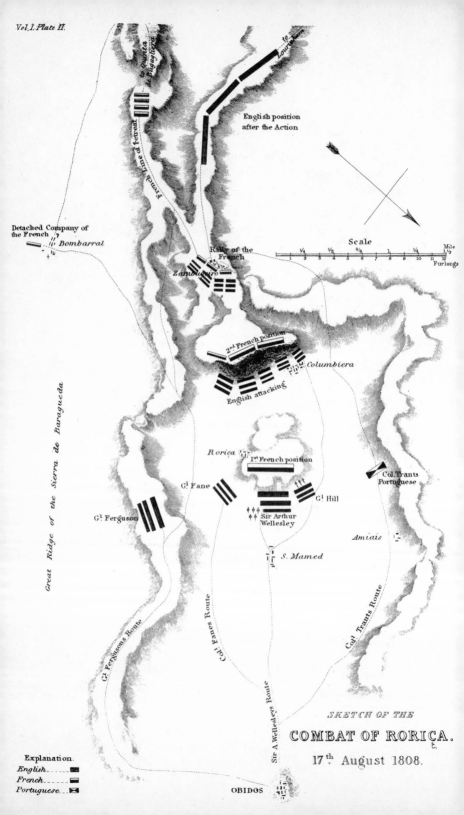

to Quinta
de Bugagliera

to Louriva

English position
after the Action

French Line of retreat

Detached Company of
the French
Bombarral

Scale

Mile
1.1/2

1/4   1/2   3/4   1

Furlongs

Rally of the
French

Zambugeira

2nd French position

Columbiera

English attacking

Rorica

Col. Trants
Portuguese

Rorica

1st French position

Gl. Fane

Gl. Hill

Sir Arthur
Wellesley

Gl. Ferguson

Amiais

S. Mamed

Col. Trants Route

Col. Fanes Route

Gl. Fergusons Route

Great Ridge of the Sierra de Baragueda

Sir A Wellesleys Route

SKETCH OF THE

COMBAT OF RORIÇA.

17th August 1808.

Explanation.
English
French
Portuguese

OBIDOS

COMBAT OF RORIÇA.

Early in the morning of the 17th, thirteen thousand four hundred and eighty infantry, four hundred
and seventy cavalry, and eighteen guns, issued from
Obidos, and soon afterwards broke into three distinct
columns of battle.

The left, commanded by general Ferguson, was
composed of his own and Bowes' brigade of infantry,
reinforced by two hundred and fifty riflemen, forty
cavalry, and six guns, forming a total of four thousand nine hundred combatants.   He marched by the
crests of the hills adjoining the Sierra de Baragueda,
being destined to turn the right flank of Laborde's
position, and to oppose the efforts of Loison, if that
general, who was supposed to be at Rio Mayor,
should appear during the action.

The right, under colonel Trant, composed of a
thousand Portuguese infantry, and fifty horse of the
same nation, moved by the village of St. Amias, with
the intention of turning the left flank of the French.

The centre, nine thousand in number, with twelve
guns, was commanded by sir Arthur in person, and
marched straight against the enemy by the village
of Mahmed.   It was composed of generals Hill's,
Nightingale's, Catlin Crawfurd's, and Fane's brigades of British infantry, four hundred cavalry, two
hundred and fifty of which were Portuguese, and
there were four hundred light troops of the same
nation.

As this column advanced, Fane's brigade, extending to its left, drove back the French skirmishers,
and connected the march of Ferguson's division with
the centre.   When the latter approached the eleva-

ted plain upon which Laborde was posted, general
Hill, who moved upon the right of the main road,
being supported by the cavalry, and covered by the
fire of his light troops, pushed forward rapidly to
the attack; on his left, general Nightingale displayed a line of infantry, preceded by the fire of
nine guns, and Crawfurd's brigade, with the remaining pieces of artillery, formed a reserve. At this
moment, Fane's riflemen crowned the nearest hills
on the right flank of the French, the Portuguese
troops showed the head of a column beyond St.
Amias, upon the enemy's left, and general Ferguson
was seen descending from the higher grounds in the
rear of Fane. Laborde's position appeared desperate, yet with the coolness and dexterity of a practised warrior, he evaded the danger, and, covered
by his excellent cavalry, fell back rapidly to the
heights of Zambugeira, and a fresh disposition of
the English became indispensable to dislodge him
from that formidable post.

Colonel Trant now continued his march to turn the
left of the new field of battle; Ferguson and Fane
were united, and directed through the mountains,
to outflank the French right; Hill and Nightingale advanced against the front, which was of singular strength, and only to be approached by narrow paths winding through deep ravines. A swarm
of skirmishers, starting forward, soon plunged into
the passes, and spreading to the right and left,
won their way among the rocks and tangled ever-
greens that overspread the steep ascent; with still
greater difficulty the supporting columns followed,
their formation being disordered in the confined and
rugged passes, and while the hollows echoed with
a continued roll of musketry, the shouts of the ad-

vancing troops were loudly answered by the enemy,
while the curling smoke, breaking out from the side
of the mountain, marked the progress of the assailants, and showed how stoutly the defence was maintained.

Laborde, watching anxiously for the arrival of
Loison, gradually slackened his hold on the left, but
clung tenaciously to the right, in the hope of yet
effecting a junction with that general, and the ardour
of the 9th and 29th regiments, who led the attack,
favoured this skilful conduct.   It was intended that
those battalions should take the right-hand path of
two leading up the same hollow, and thus have come
in upon Laborde's flank in conjunction with Trant's
column; but as the left path led more directly to
the enemy, the 29th followed it the 9th being close
behind, and both regiments advanced so vigorously,
as to reach the plain above, long before the flank
movements of Trant and Ferguson could shake the
credit of the position.   The right of the 29th arrived
first at the top, under a heavy fire, and ere it could
form, colonel Lake was killed, and some French
companies coming in on the flank, gallantly broke
through, carrying with them a major and fifty or
sixty other prisoners.   The head of the regiment
thus pressed, fell back and rallied on the left wing,
below the brow of the hill, and being there joined
by the 9th, whose colonel, Stewart, also fell in this
bitter fight, the whole pushed forward, and regained
the dangerous footing above.   Laborde, who brought
every arm into action at the proper time and place,
endeavoured to destroy these regiments before they
could be succoured, and, failing in that, he yet
gained time to rally his left wing upon his centre
and right; but the 5th regiment, following the

right-hand path, soon arrived, the English gathered
thickly on the heights, and Ferguson, who had at
first taken an erroneous direction towards the centre,
recovered the true line, and was rapidly passing the
right flank of the position. The French general
commenced a retreat by alternate masses, protecting his movements by vigorous charges of
cavalry, and at the village of Zambugeira he attempted another stand ; but the English bore on
him too heavily, and thus disputing the ground,
he fell back to the Quinta de Bugagliera, where
he halted until his detachments on the side of
Segura rejoined him. After this taking to the
narrow pass of Runa, he marched all night to gain
the position of Montechique, leaving three guns on
the field of battle, and the road to Torres Vedras
open for the victors. The loss of the French was
six hundred killed and wounded, among the latter
Laborde himself; and the British also suffered considerably, for two lieutenant-colonels and nearly
five hundred men were killed, taken, or wounded,
and as not more than four thousand men were actually engaged, this hard-fought action was very
honourable to both sides.

Thiebault.

Appendix,
No. 19.

The firing ceased a little after four o'clock, when
sir Arthur, getting intelligence that Loison's division
was at Bombaral only five miles distant, took up a
position for the night in an oblique line to that
which he had just forced, his left resting upon a
height near the field of battle, and his right covering the road to Lourinham. Believing that Loison
and Laborde had effected their junction at the Quinta
de Bugagliera, and that both were retiring to Montechique, the English general resolved to march the
next morning to Torres Vedras, by which he would

have secured an entrance into the mountains. But
before night-fall he was informed that general
Anstruther's and general Acland's divisions, accompanied by a large fleet of store ships, were off the
coast, the dangerous nature of which rendered it necessary to provide for their safety by a quick disembarkation; he therefore changed his plans, and
resolved to seek for some convenient post, that,
being in advance of his present position, would
likewise enable him to cover the landing of these
reinforcements; the vigour of Laborde's defence had
also an influence upon this occasion, for before an
enemy so bold and skilful, no precaution could be
neglected with impunity.

CHAPTER V.

WHILE the combat of Roriça was fighting, some
Portuguese insurgents attacked Abrantes, and the
garrison, being ill commanded, gave way and was
destroyed ; thus nothing remained for Junot but a
battle, and as sir Arthur marched to Lourinham on
the 18th, the French general quitted Cercal with
Loison's division, and keeping the east side of the
Baragueda ridge, crossed the line of Laborde's
retreat, and pushed for Torres Vedras, which he
reached in the evening of the same day. The 19th
he was joined by Laborde, and the 20th by his
reserve, when he re-organized his army, and prepared for a decisive action. Meanwhile Wellesley
took a position at Vimiero, a village near the
sea-coast, and from thence sent a detachment to
cover the march of general Anstruther's brigade,
which had, with great difficulty and some loss,
been landed on the morning of the 18th on an
open sandy beach called the bay of Maceira. The
20th the French cavalry scouring the neighbouring
country, carried off some of the women from the
rear of the English camp, and hemmed the army
round so closely, that no information of Junot's position could be obtained ; but in the night general
Acland's brigade was disembarked, by which the
army was increased to sixteen thousand fighting
men, with eighteen pieces of artillery, exclusive of
Trant's Portuguese, and of two British regiments,
under general Beresford, which were with the fleet
at the mouth of the Tagus. Thus the principal
mass of the English army was irrevocably engaged

in the operations against Junot, while the ministers
were still so intent upon Cadiz, that they had sent
Anstruther out with an appointment as governor of
that city!

Estimating the whole French army at eighteen
thousand men, sir Arthur Wellesley judged, that
after providing for the security of Lisbon, Junot Appendix,
No. 9,
could not bring more than fourteen thousand into
the field; he designed, therefore, not only to strike
the first blow, but to follow it up so as to prevent
the enemy from rallying and renewing the campaign
upon the frontier. In this view he had, before
quitting the Mondego, written to sir Harry Burrard an exact statement of his own proceedings
and intentions, and recommended that sir John
Moore, with his division, should disembark at the
Mondego, and march without delay to Santarem,
by which he would protect the left of the army,
block the line of the Tagus, and at the same time
threaten the French communication between Lisbon
and Elvas. And without danger, because Junot
would be forced to defend Lisbon against the
coast army; or if, relinquishing the capital, he
endeavoured to make way to Almeida by Santarem,
the ground there was so strong that sir John Moore
might easily maintain it against him. Moreover,
the marquis of Valladeras commanded three thousand men at Guarda, and general Freire, with five
thousand men, was at Leiria, and might be persuaded to support the British at Santarem.

From Vimiero to Torres Vedras was about nine
miles, and although the number and activity of
the French cavalry, completely shrouded Junot's
position, it was known to be strong, and very
difficult of approach, by reason of a long defile

BOOK
II.
———
1808.
August.

Sir A. Wel-
lesley's
evidence.
Court of
Inquiry.
through which the army must penetrate in order to reach the crest of the mountain; there was, however, a road leading between the sea-coast and Torres Vedras, which, turning the latter, opened a way to Mafra. Sir Arthur possessed very exact military surveys of the country through which that road led, and he projected, by a forced march on the 21st, to turn the position of Torres Vedras, and to gain Mafra with a strong advanced guard, while the main body, seizing some advantageous heights, a few miles short of that town, would be in a position to intercept the French line of march to Montechique. The army was therefore reorganized during the 20th in eight brigades of infantry and four weak squadrons of cavalry, and every preparation was made for the next day's enterprise, but at that critical period of the campaign the ministerial arrangements, which provided three commanders-in-chief, begun to work. Sir Harry Burrard arrived in a frigate off the bay of Maceira, and sir Arthur, thus checked in the midst of his operations on the eve of a decisive battle, repaired on board the frigate, to make a report of the situation of affairs, and to renew his former recommendation relative to the disposal of sir John Moore's troops. Burrard, who had previously resolved to bring the latter down to Maceira, condemned this project, and forbade any offensive movement until the whole army should be concentrated, whereupon sir Arthur returned to his camp.

The ground occupied by the army, although very extensive, and not very clearly defined as a position, was by no means weak. The village of Vimiero, situated in a valley, through which the little river of Maceira flows, contained the parc and commissariat stores. The cavalry and the Portuguese were on a small plain close behind the village, and immediately in its front a rugged isolated height, with a flat top, commanded all the ground to the southward and eastward for a considerable distance. Upon this height Fane's and Anstruther's brigades of infantry, with six guns, were posted ; the left of Anstruther's occupied a churchyard which blocked a road leading over the extremity of the height of the village ; the right of Fane's rested on the edge of the other extremity of the hill, the base of which was washed by the Maceira.

A mountain, that commenced at the coast, swept in a half circle close behind the right of the hill upon which these brigades were posted, and commanded, at rather long artillery range, all its upper surface. Eight guns, and the first, second, third, fourth, and eighth brigades of infantry, occupied this mountain, which was terminated on the left by a deep ravine that divided it from another strong and narrow range of heights over which the road from Vimiero to Lourinham passed ; the right of these last heights also overtopped the hill in front of the village, but the left, bending suddenly backward, after the form of a crook, returned to the coast, and ended in a lofty cliff. There was no water upon this last named ridge, wherefore, only the 40th regiment and some piquets were placed there. The troops being thus posted, on the night of the 20th, about twelve o'clock, sir Arthur was aroused by a German officer of dragoons, who galloped into the camp, and with some consternation reported, that Junot, at the head of twenty thousand men, was coming on to the attack, and distant but one hour's march. Undisturbed by this

inflated report, he merely sent out patroles, warned
the piquets to be on the alert, and before day-break
had his troops, following the British custom, under
arms; but the sun rose, and no enemy appeared.
However, at seven o'clock a cloud of dust was
observed beyond the nearest hills, and at eight
o'clock an advanced guard of horse was seen to
crown the heights to the southward, sending forward scouts on every side. Scarcely had this body
been discovered, when a force of infantry, preceded
by other cavalry, was descried moving along the road
from Torres Vedras to Lourinham, and threatening
the left of the British position; column after column
followed in order of battle, and it soon became evident that the French were coming to fight, but that
the right wing of the English was not their object.

The second, third, fourth, and eighth brigades
were immediately directed to cross the valley behind the village, and to take post on the heights
before mentioned as being occupied by the piquets
only; as they reached the ground, the second
and third were disposed in two lines facing to
the left, and consequently forming a right angle
with the prolongation of Fane and Anstruther's
front. The fourth and eighth brigades were to
have furnished a third line, but before the latter
could reach the summit the battle commenced.
From the flank of all these troops, a line of skirmishers was thrown out upon the face of the descent towards the enemy, the cavalry was drawn up
in the plain a little to the right of the village of
Vimiero, and the fifth brigade and the Portuguese
were detached to the returning part of the crook to
cover the extreme left, and to protect the rear of
the army. The first brigade, under general Hill,

remained on the mountain which the others had just quitted, and formed a support for the centre and a reserve for the whole. The ground between the two armies was so wooded and broken, that after the French had passed the ridge where they had been first descried, no correct view of their movements could be obtained, and the British, being weak in cavalry, were forced to wait patiently until the columns of attack were close upon them.

Junot had quitted Torres Vedras the evening of the 20th, intending to fall on the English army at day-break, but the difficulty of the defile in his front retarded his march for many hours, and fatigued his troops. When he first came in sight of the position of Vimiero, the British order of battle appeared to him as being on two sides of an irregular triangle, the apex of which, formed by the hill in front of the village, was well-furnished with men, while the left face appeared naked, for he could only see the piquets on that side, and the passage of the four brigades across the valley was hidden from him. Concluding, then, that the principal force was in the centre, he resolved to form two connected attacks, the one against the apex, the other against the left face ; he thought that the left of the position was an accessible ridge, whereas a deep ravine, trenched as it were along the base, rendered it utterly impervious to an attack, except at the extremity, over which the road from Torres Vedras to Lourinham passed. Junot had nearly fourteen thousand fighting men, organised in four divisions, of which three were of infantry and one of cavalry, with twenty-three pieces of very small

BOOK
II.
———
1808.
August. artillery ; each division was composed of two
brigades, and at ten o'clock, all being prepared, he
commenced the

BATTLE OF VIMIERO.

Thiebault.
Foy. Laborde marched with one brigade against the
centre, general Brennier led another against the
left, and Loison's brigades followed in the same
order at a short distance. Kellerman, with a reserve composed of grenadiers, moved in one body
behind Loison, and the cavalry under Margaron,
about thirteen hundred in number, was divided,
part being on the right of Brennier, part in the rear
of the reserve. The artillery, distributed among the
columns, opened its fire wherever the ground was
favourable. It was designed that Laborde's and
Brennier's attacks should be simultaneous, but
the latter, coming unexpectedly upon the ravine
before mentioned as protecting the English left,
got entangled among the rocks and water-courses,
and thus Laborde alone engaged Fane and Anstruther under a heavy and destructive fire of artillery, which played on his front and flank ; for the
eighth brigade being then in the act of mounting
Sir A. Wel-
lesley's
despatch. the heights where the left was posted, observing the advance of the French columns against the
centre, halted, and opened a battery against their
right.

Junot, perceiving this failure in his combinations,
ordered Loison to support Laborde's attack with
one brigade of his division, and directed general
Solignac, with the other, to turn the ravine in
which Brennier was entangled, and to fall upon the

From Lourinham

Village of Perenza

Line of retreat from right attack

Position of the French when Sir A. Wellesly proposed to follow up the Victory.

G.ˡ Solignac's situation when the order from Sir H. Burrard stopt G.ˡ Ferguson

Fergusons position when his progress was arrested

Breniers attack

5.ᵗʰ Brigade Portuguese

Solignac's attack

Line of retreat from the left attack

Road to Torres Vedras

2 Reg.ᵗˢ that arrived from Lisbon at the close of the attack

G.ˡ Ferguson

G.ˡ Breniers

Kellerman

Cavalry

G.ˡ Nightingale

Kellerman

G.ˡ Bowes

Laborde

G.ˡ Ackland

Cranstruther

Loison

VIMIERO

G.ˡ Fane

Cavalry

to Torres Vedras

G.ˡ Hill

R. Maceira

Original position of the English right

Porto Novo

THE SEA

SKETCH OF THE
BATTLE OF VIMIERO.
21.ˢᵗ August 1808.

Scale

0	¼	½	¾	1	¼	½	¾	2	Miles.
	2	4	6	8	10	12	14	16	Furlongs.

extremity of the English line; general Fane seeing
Loison's advance, and having a discretionary power
to use the reserve artillery, immediately directed colonel Robe to bring it into action, and thus formed
with the divisional guns a most powerful battery in
opposition. Meanwhile, Loison and Laborde formed
a principal and two secondary columns of attack, one
of which advanced against Fane's brigade, while
the other endeavoured to penetrate by a road which
passed between the ravine and the church on the
extreme left of Anstruther; but the main column,
headed by Laborde in person, and preceded by a
multitude of light troops, mounted the face of the
hill with great fury and loud cries. The English
skirmishers were forced in upon the lines in a moment, and the French masses arrived at the summit;
yet shattered by the terrible fire of Robe's artillery,
and breathless from their exertions, and in this
state, first receiving a discharge of musketry from
the fiftieth regiment at the distance of half-pistol
shot, they were vigorously charged in front and
flank, and overthrown. At the same time the remainder of Fane's brigade repulsed the minor
attack, and colonel Taylor, with the very few
horsemen he commanded, passing out by the right,
rode fiercely among the confused and retreating
troops, and scattered them with great execution;
but then Margaron's cavalry came suddenly down
upon Taylor, who was there slain, and the half of
his feeble squadron cut to pieces.

Kellerman took advantage of this check to throw
one half of his reserve into a pine wood flanking the
line of retreat, and the other half he had before sent to
reinforce the attack on the church. The forty-third
regiment were engaged in a hot skirmish amongst

some vineyards, when these French grenadiers arrived, at a brisk pace, and beat back the advanced
companies, but to avoid the artillery which ran-
sacked their left, they dipped a little into the ravine,
and were taken on the other flank by the guns of
the eighth and fourth brigades. Then, when the nar-
rowness of the way and the sweep of the round shot
was disordering the French ranks, the forty-third
rallying in one mass, came furiously down upon the
head of the column, and, after a short, desperate
fight, drove it back in confusion, but the regiment
suffered very severely.

The French were now discomfited in the centre, the
woods and hollows were filled with their wounded
and straggling men, and seven guns were lost. They
retired up the edge of the ravine in a direction almost
parallel to the British line, leaving the road from
Vimiero to Torres Vedras open to their opponents;
sir Arthur Wellesley, however, strictly forbade any
pursuit at that moment, partly because the grenadiers
in the pine wood flanked the line of the French retreat, and partly because Margaron's horsemen, riding
stiffly between the two armies were not to be lightly
meddled with. Meanwhile, Brennier being still hampered in the ravine, general Solignac passed along
the crest of the ridge above, and came upon general
Ferguson's brigade, which was posted at the left of
the English position; but where the French expected to find a weak flank, they encountered a
front of battle, on a depth of three lines, protected
by steep declivities on either side, a powerful artillery swept away their foremost ranks, and on
their right the fifth brigade and the Portuguese
were seen marching by a distant ridge towards the
Lourinham road, threatening the rear.

Ferguson, instantly taking the lead, bore down upon the enemy, the ridge widened as the English advanced, the regiments of the second line running up in succession, increased the front, and constantly filled the ground, and the French, falling fast under the fire, drew back fighting, until they reached the declivity of the ridge; their cavalry made several efforts to check the advancing troops, but the latter were too compact to be disturbed by these attempts. Solignac himself was carried from the field severely wounded, and his retiring column, continually out-flanked on the left, was cut off from the line of retreat, and thrown into the low ground about the village of Perenza, where six guns were captured. General Ferguson leaving the eighty-second and seventy-first regiments to guard those pieces, was continuing to press the disordered columns, when Brennier having at last cleared the ravine, came suddenly in upon those two battalions, and retook the artillery; but his success was only momentary, the surprised troops rallied upon the higher ground, poured in a heavy fire of musquetry, and with a shout returning to the charge, overthrew him and recovered the guns. Brennier himself was wounded and made prisoner, and Ferguson having thus completely separated the French brigades from each other, would have forced the greatest part of Solignac's to surrender, if an unexpected order had not obliged him to halt: the discomfited troops then re-formed under the protection of their cavalry with admirable quickness, and making an orderly retreat, were soon united to the broken brigades which were falling back from the attack on the centre.

Brennier, who, the moment he was taken, was brought to sir Arthur Wellesley, eagerly demanded if the reserve under Kellerman had yet charged? sir Arthur, ascertaining from other prisoners that it had, was then satisfied that all the enemy's attacks were exhausted, that no considerable body of fresh troops could be hidden among the woods and hollows in his front, and that the battle was won. It was only twelve o'clock, thirteen guns had been taken; the fourth and eighth brigades had suffered very little; the Portuguese, the fifth and the first brigades had not fired a shot, and the latter was two miles nearer to Torres Vedras than any part of the French army, which was moreover in great confusion. The relative numbers before the action were considerably in favour of the English, the result of the action had increased that disparity; a portion of the army had defeated the enemy when entire, a portion then could effectually follow up the victory; sir Arthur therefore resolved with the five brigades on the left to press Junot closely, hoping to drive him over the Sierra da Baragueda, and force him upon the Tagus, while Hill, Anstruther, and Fane, seizing the defile of Torres Vedras, should push on to Montechique and cut him off from Lisbon.

If this able and decisive operation had been executed, Junot would probably have lost all his artillery and several thousand stragglers, and then, buffeted and turned at every point, would have been glad to seek safety under the guns of Almeida or Elvas; and even that, he could only have accomplished, because sir John Moore's troops were not landed in the Mondego. But sir Harry Burrard, who was present during the action, although partly from delicacy, and partly from approving of sir Arthur's arrangements, he had not hitherto interfered, now assumed the chief command; from him

the order which arrested Ferguson in his victorious
career had emanated, and by him further offensive
operations were forbidden, for he resolved to wait in
the position of Vimiero until the arrival of sir John
Moore. The adjutant-general Clinton, and colonel
Murray the quarter-master-general, supported sir
Harry's views, and sir Arthur's earnest representations could not alter their determination.

Burrard's decision was certainly erroneous, yet
error is common in an art which at best is but a
choice of difficulties; the circumstances of the moment were imposing enough to sway most generals.
The French had failed in the attacks, yet they ral- Proceedings of the
lied with surprising quickness under the protection Court of
Inquiry.
of a strong and gallant cavalry; sir Harry knew
that his own artillery carriages were so shaken as to
be scarcely fit for service; the draft horses were few
and bad, and the commissariat parc on the plain was
in the greatest confusion, for the hired Portuguese
carmen were making off with their carriages in all
directions; the English cavalry was totally destroyed, and finally, general Spencer had discovered a
line of fresh troops on the ridge behind that occupied by the French army. Weighing all these
things in his mind, with the caution natural to age,
Burrard was reluctant to hazard the fortune of the
day upon what he deemed a perilous throw. Thus
the duke of Abrantes, who had displayed all that
reckless courage to which he originally owed his ele-
vation, was enabled, by this unexpected cessation
of the battle, to re-form his broken infantry; twelve
hundred fresh men joined him at the close of the
contest, and then covered by his cavalry, he retreated
with order and celerity until he regained the command of the pass of Torres Vedras, so that when the

day closed, the relative position of the two armies
was the same as on the evening before.

One general, thirteen guns, and several hundred
prisoners, fell into the hands of the victors, and the
total loss of the French was estimated at three thousand men, an exaggeration, no doubt, but it was certainly above two thousand, for their closed columns
had been exposed for more than half an hour to
sweeping discharges of grape and musquetry, and
the dead lay thickly together. General Thiebault,
indeed, reduces the number to eighteen hundred,
and asserts that the whole amount of the French
army did not much exceed twelve thousand men,
from which number he deducts nearly three thousand
for the sick, the stragglers, and all those other petty
drains which form the torment of a general-in-chief.
But when it is considered that this army was composed of men selected and organized in provisionary
battalions, expressly for the occasion; that one-half
had only been in the field for a fortnight, and that
the whole had enjoyed two days' rest at Torres
Vedras, it is evident that the number of absentees
bears too great a proportion to the combatants. A
French order of battle found upon the field gave a
total of fourteen thousand men, present under arms,
of which thirteen hundred were cavalry; and this
amount agrees too closely with other estimates, and
with the observations made at the time, to leave any
reasonable doubt of its authenticity or correctness.

The arrangements made by sir Harry Burrard did
not remain in force a long time. Early on the morning of the 22d, sir Hew Dalrymple disembarked and
assumed the chief command; thus, in the short
space of twenty-four hours, during which a battle
was fought, the army fell successively into the hands

of three men, who, coming from the ocean, with different views, habits, and information, had not any previous opportunity of communing even by letter, so as to arrange a common plan of operations : and they were now brought together at a critical moment, when it was more than probable they must all disagree, and that the public service must suffer from that want of vigour which is inherent to divided councils.   For when sir Hew Dalrymple was appointed to the command, sir Arthur Wellesley was privately recommended to him, by the minister, as a person who should be employed with more than usual confidence ; and this unequivocal hint was backed up with too much force by the previous reputation and recent exploits of the latter, not to produce some want of cordiality.   Sir Arthur could not do otherwise than take the lead in discussing affairs of which he had more than laid the foundation, and sir Hew would have forfeited all claims to independence in his command, if he had not exercised the right of judging for himself between the conflicting opinions of his predecessors.

After receiving information upon the most important points, and taking a hasty view of the situation of the army,—although the wounded were still upon the ground, and the wains of the commissariat were employed in removing them,—sir Hew decided to advance upon the 23d, and gave orders to that effect. Nevertheless, he entirely agreed in opinion with sir Harry Burrard, that the operation was a perilous one, which it required the concentration of all his troops, and the application of all his means, to bring to a good conclusion ; and for this reason he did not rescind the order directing sir John Moore to fall down to Maceira.   This last measure was dis-

Proceedings of the Court of Inquiry.

Sir H. Dalrymple's Narrative. Court of Inquiry.

approved of by sir Arthur, who observed that the
provisions on shore would not supply more than
eight or nine days' consumption for the troops already at Vimiero ; that the country would be unable
to furnish any assistance, and that the fleet could
not be calculated upon as a resource, because the
first of the gales common at that season of the year
would certainly send it away from the coast, if it
did not destroy a great portion of it. Sir Hew
thought the evil of having the army separated,
would be greater than the chance of distress from
such events. His position was certainly difficult.
The bishop of Oporto had failed in his promise of
Proceed-
ings of the
Court of
Inquiry.
assisting the troops with draft cattle,—as, indeed,
he did in all his promises ; the artillery and commissariat were badly supplied with mules and horses ;
the cavalry was a nullity, and the enemy was, with
the exception of his immediate loss in killed and
wounded, suffering nothing from his defeat, which,
we have seen, did not deprive him of a single position necessary to his defence. While weighing
this state of affairs, he was informed that general
Kellerman, escorted by a strong body of cavalry,
was at the outposts, and demanded an interview.
Thiebault. For Junot, after regaining Torres Vedras, had occupied Mafra, and was preparing to fight again,
when he received intelligence that Lisbon was on
the point of insurrection ; wherefore, sending
forward a false account of the action, he followed
it up with a reinforcement for the garrison, and
called a council of war to advise measures with
respect to the English. It is an old and sound
remark that ' a council of war never fights,' and
Kellerman's mission was the result of the above
consultation.

That general being conducted to the quarters of
the commander-in-chief, demanded a cessation of
arms, and proposed the ground-work of a convention
under which Junot offered to evacuate Portugal
without further resistance. Nothing could be more
opportune than this proposition, and sir Hew
Dalrymple readily accepted of it, as an advantage,
which would accrue, without any drawback to the
general cause of the Peninsula. He knew, from a
plan of operations, sketched by the chief of the
French engineers, colonel Vincent, and taken by
the Portuguese, that Junot possessed several strong
positions in front of Lisbon; and that a retreat
either upon Almeida, or across the river upon
Elvas, was not only within the contemplation of
that general, but considered in this report as a
matter of course, and perfectly easy of execution.
Hence the proposed convention was an unexpected
advantage offered in a moment of difficulty, and
the only subject of consideration was the nature of
the articles proposed by Kellerman as a basis for
the treaty. Sir Hew being necessarily ignorant of
many details, had recourse to sir A. Wellesley for
information, and the latter, taking an enlarged view
of the question in all its bearings, coincided as to
the sound policy of agreeing to a convention, by
which a strong French army would be quietly got
out of a country that it had complete military possession of; and by which, not only a great moral
effect in favour of the general cause would be
produced, but an actual gain made, both of men
and time, for the further prosecution of the war in
Spain. By the convention, he observed,

1°. That a kingdom would be liberated, with all

its fortresses, arsenals, &c., and that the excited
population of the Peninsula might then be pushed
forward in the career of opposition to France, under
the most favourable circumstances.

2°. That the Spanish army of Estremadura, which
contained the most efficient body of cavalry in the
Peninsula, could be reinforced with the four or five
thousand Spanish soldiers who were prisoners on
board the vessels in the Tagus; and would be enabled to unite with the other patriot armies at a
critical period, when every addition of force must
tend to increase the confidence and forward the
impulse, which the victory of Baylen and the flight
of Joseph had given to the Spaniards. Finally,
that the sacrifice of lives to be expected in carrying
the French positions in Portugal, all the difficulties
of reducing the fortresses, and the danger of losing
a communication with the fleet, would be avoided
by this measure, the result of which would be as
complete, as the most sanguine could expect, from
the long course of uncertain and unhealthy operations which must follow a rejection of the proposal.
But, while admitting the utility of the measure
itself, he differed with the commander-in-chief as
to the mode of proceeding, and a long discussion,
in which Sir H. Burrard took a part, followed the
opening of Kellerman's mission. Sir Arthur's first
objection was, that, in point of form, Kellerman
was merely entitled to negotiate a cessation of
hostilities; sir Hew Dalrymple judged that, as
the good policy and the utility of the convention
were recognized, it would be unwise to drive the
French to the wall on a point of ceremony, and
therefore accepted the proposition. The basis of a

definitive treaty was then arranged, subject to the
final approbation of sir Charles Cotton, without
whose concurrence it was not to be binding.

Articles 1st and 2d declared the fact of the armistice, and provided for the mode of future proceedings.

Article 3d indicated the river Sisandre as the line of demarcation betwen the two armies. The position of Torres Vedras to be occupied by neither.

Article 4th. Sir Hew Dalrymple engaged to have the Portuguese included in the armistice, and their boundary line was to extend from Leiria to Thomar.

Article 5th declared, that the French were not to be considered as prisoners of war, and that themselves and their property, public and private, were, without any detainer, to be transported to France. To this article sir Arthur objected, as affording a cover for the abstraction of Portuguese property, whereupon Kellerman said, that it was to be taken in its fair sense of property justly obtained, and upon this assurance it was admitted.

Article 6th provided for the protection of individuals. It guaranteed from political persecution all French residents, all subjects of powers in alliance with France, and all Portuguese who had served the invaders, or become obnoxious for their attachment to them.

Article 7th stipulated for the neutrality of the port of Lisbon as far as the Russian fleet was concerned. At first Kellerman proposed to have the Russian fleet guaranteed from capture, with leave to return to the Baltic, but this was peremptorily refused ; indeed, the whole proceeding was designed to entangle the Russians in the French negociation, that, in case the armistice should be broken, the former might be forced into a co-operation with the latter.

Sir Arthur strenuously opposed this article : he argued, 1°. That the interests of the two nations were not blended, and that they stood in different relations towards the British army. 2°. That it was an important object to keep them separate, and that the French general, if pressed, would leave the Russians to their fate. 3°. That as the British operations had not been so rapid and decisive as to enable them to capture the fleet before the question of neutrality could be agitated, the right of the Russians to such protection was undoubted; and in the present circumstances it was desirable to grant it, because, independent of the chances of their final capture, they would be prevented from returning to the Baltic, which in fact constituted their only point of interest when disengaged from the French ; but, that, viewed as allies of the latter, they became of great weight.   Lastly, that it was an affair which concerned the Portuguese, Russians, and British, but with which the French could have no right to interfere.   Sir Hew finding that the discussion of this question became lengthened, and considering that sir Charles Cotton alone could finally decide, admitted the article merely as a form, without acquiescing in the propriety of it.

Article 8th provided, that all guns of French calibre, and the horses of the cavalry, were to be transported to France.

Article 9th stipulated, that forty-eight hours' notice should be given of the rupture of the armistice.

To this article also sir Arthur objected ; he considered it unnecessary for the interests of the British

army, and favourable to the French; because, if
hostilities recommenced, the latter would have forty-
eight hours to make arrangements for their defence,
for the passage of the Tagus, and for the co-operation of the Russian fleet. Upon the other hand, sir
Hew thought it was an absolute advantage to gain
time for the preparations of the British army, and
for the arrival of sir John Moore's reinforcements.

By an additional article it was provided, that all
the fortresses held by the French, which had not
capitulated before the 25th of August, should be
given up to the British ; and the basis of a convention being thus arranged, general Kellerman returned to his chief, and colonel George Murray was
ordered to carry the proposed articles to the English
admiral.

Previous to his landing, sir Hew had received
none of the letters addressed to him by sir Arthur
Wellesley, he had met with no person during his
voyage from whom he could obtain authentic information of the state of affairs, and his time being
at first occupied by the negotiations with Kellerman,
he was uninformed of many details of importance.
Now, the day after Kellerman's departure, don
Bernardim Freire Andrada, the Portuguese commander-in-chief, came to remonstrate against the
armistice just concluded ; but, from the circumstances before-mentioned, it so happened that sir
Hew was utterly ignorant of the existence of don
Bernardim and his army, at the time the armistice
was discussed, and it was therefore difficult for him
to manage this interview with propriety, because
Andrada had some plausible, although no real,
ground of complaint. His remonstrances were,

however, merely intended for the commencement of an intrigue, to which I shall hereafter revert.

Colonel Murray soon reached the fleet, and presented the articles of convention to sir Charles Cotton, but the latter refused to concur therein, declaring that he would himself conduct a separate treaty for the Russian ships. With this answer colonel Murray returned on the 24th, having first, in reply to a question put by the French officer who accompanied him on board the Hibernia, declared, that nothing had passed between him and sir Charles Cotton which ought to preclude further negotiation.

Sir Hew Dalrymple was now urged by sir Arthur Wellesley to give notice, without further explanation, that hostilities would recommence, leaving it to Junot to renew propositions, if he chose to do so, separately from the Russians. Sir Hew, however, felt himself, in honour, bound by colonel Murray's observation to the French officer, and would not take advantage of the occasion; he likewise felt disinclined to relinquish a negotiation which, from certain circumstances, he deemed upon the point of being crowned with success. He therefore despatched colonel Murray to Lisbon, with directions to inform Junot of the admiral's objection, and to give notice of the consequent rupture of the armistice, Murray himself being provided, however, with full powers to enter into and conclude a definitive treaty upon a fresh basis. The army was, at the same time, pushed forward to Ramalhal, and sir J. Moore's

troops were landed at Maceira Bay, but the order to repair to that place did not reach them until several regiments had been disembarked in the Mondego; the re-shipping of these, together with contrary

winds, had caused a delay of four days, and at
Maceira great difficulty and some loss was sustained
in getting on shore, an operation only effected by five
days of incessant exertion on the part of the navy;
the boats were constantly swamped by the surf, and
such was its fury that not more than thirty remained
fit for service at the conclusion.

On the 27th, information was received, from
colonel Murray, that a fresh treaty was in agitation
upon an admissible basis; and the next day the
army took a new position, a part occupying Torres
Vedras, and the remainder being placed in the rear
of that town.   Meanwhile, in Lisbon, the agitation
of the public mind was excessively great; hope and
fear were magnified by the obscurity of affairs, and
the contradictory news which was spread by the
French, and by those who held communication with
the country, had increased the anxious feeling of
joy or grief almost to phrensy.   Junot made every
effort to engage admiral Siniavin in the negotiation,
and the necessity by which the latter was forced to
put his ships in a hostile and guarded attitude,
contributed powerfully to control the populace, and
give strength to an opinion industriously spread,
that he would make common cause with the
French.   Nevertheless Siniavin had no intention
of this kind, and very early gave notice that he
would treat separately; wherefore the French
being thus left to themselves, had no· resource
but their own dexterity, and brought all the ordinary machinery of diplomatic subtlety into play.
Among other schemes, Junot opened a separate
communication with sir Hew Dalrymple at the
moment when colonel Murray, invested with full
powers, was engaged in daily conferences with

Kellerman; and the difficulty of coming to a conclusion, was much increased by the natural sources
of suspicion and jealousy incident to such a singular transaction, where two foreign nations were
seen bargaining, and one of them honestly bargaining, for the goods and interests of a third,
yet scarcely hinting even at the existence of the
latter. The French being the weakest, were most
subtle, and to protect the vital questions advanced
extravagant claims; on the other hand, the Portuguese leaders, no longer fearing a defeat, protested against the convention, passed the line of
demarcation, attacked the French patroles, and
menaced an attack from the side of Santarem. This
movement, and the breach of faith in attacking the
patroles, were promptly and distinctly disavowed
by sir Hew; yet they kept suspicion awake, and
the mutual misunderstandings arose at last to such
a height, that Junot, seeming for a moment to recover all his natural energy, threatened to burn the
public establishments, and make his retreat good
at the expense of the city; a menace which nothing could have prevented him from executing.
Finally, however, a definitive treaty was concluded
at Lisbon on the 30th, and soon afterwards ratified
in form.

This celebrated convention, improperly called ' of
Cintra,' consisted of twenty-two original, and three
supplementary articles, upon the expediency of
many of which, sir Arthur Wellesley and the commander-in-chief disagreed, but as their disagreement
had reference to the details and not to the general
principle, the historical importance is not sufficient
to call for remark. An informality on the part of
Junot, caused some delay in the ratification of the

Appendix,
No. 13.

instrument; the British army marched notwithstanding to take up the position near Lisbon, assigned to it by the 11th article of the treaty, and
on the march, sir Hew Dalrymple met two Russian
officers, who were charged to open a separate negotiation for the Russian squadron; he, however, refused
to receive their credentials, and referred them to sir
Charles Cotton. Thus baffled in an attempt to carry
on a double treaty, for a naval one was already
commenced, Siniavin, whose conduct appears to
have been weak, was forced to come to a conclusion
with the English admiral. At first he claimed the
protection of a neutral port, but as singly he possessed none of that weight which circumstances
had given him before the convention with Junot,
his claim was answered by an intimation, that a
British flag was flying on the forts at the mouth of
the Tagus; and this was true, for the third and
forty-second regiments, under the command of
major-general Beresford, having landed and taken
possession of them, in virtue of the convention, the
British colours were improperly hoisted instead of
the Portuguese. Foiled again by this proceeding,
the justice of which is somewhat doubtful, Siniavin finally agreed to surrender upon the following
terms :

1°. The Russian ships, with their sails, stores,
&c. were to be held by England, as a deposit,
until six months after the conclusion of a peace
between the two governments of the contracting
parties.

2°. The admiral, officers, and seamen, without any
restriction as to their future services, were to be
transported to Russia, at the expense of the British
government.

BOOK
II.

1808.
August.

Parl. Pap.
1809.

Parl. Pap.
1809.
Admiralty
Instruc-
tions to sir
C. Cotton,
16th April,
1808.
Ibid.
Mr. Wel-
lesley Pole
to sir C.
Cotton,
17th Sept.
1808.

But two additional articles were, subsequently to the ratification of the original treaty, proposed by the Russians, and assented to by the English admiral. The first stipulated that the imperial flag should be displayed, even in the British harbours, as long as the Russian admiral remained on board. The second provided that the ships themselves and their stores should be delivered again at the appointed time, in the same state as when surrendered. The rights of the Portuguese were not referred to, but sir Charles Cotton was justified by his instructions, which authorised him to make prize of the Russian fleet. Siniavin thus suffered all the inconvenience of hostilities, and the shame of striking his colours without having violated in any manner the relations of amity in which his nation stood with regard to Portugal. On the other hand, for the sake of a few old and decaying ships, the British government made an injudicious display of contempt for the independence of their ally, because, with singular inconsistency, they permitted the officers and crews, the real strength of the squadron, to return to the Baltic, although scarcely a year had elapsed, since the national character was defiled in that quarter, to suppress a navy inimical to Great Britain. This inconsistency belonged wholly to the ministers; for the two original articles of the treaty only were confirmed by them, and they were copied from the Admiralty instructions delivered to sir Charles Cotton four months previous to the transaction. Yet that officer, by the very men who had framed those instructions, was, with matchless effontery, rebuked for having adopted a new principle of maritime surrrender !

On the 2d of September head-quarters were established at Oyeras ; the right of the army occupied
the forts at the mouth of the river, the left rested
upon the heights of Bellas. The French army
concentrated in Lisbon, posted their piquets and
guards as if in front of an enemy, and at night the
sentries fired upon whoever approached their posts,
the police disbanded of their own accord, and the
city became a scene of turbulence, anarchy, and
crime. Notwithstanding the presence of their enemies, the inhabitants of the capital testified their
joy, and evinced their vengeful feelings in a remarkable manner; they refused to sell any provisions,
or to deal in any manner with the French ; they
sung songs of triumph in their hearing, and in their
sight fabricated thousands of small lamps for the
avowed purpose of illuminating the streets at their
departure ; the doors of many of the houses occupied by the troops were marked in one night ; men
were observed bearing in their hats lists of Portuguese or Frenchmen designed for slaughter, and the
quarters of Loison were threatened with a serious
attack. Yet amidst all this disorder and violence,
general Travot, and some others of the French
army, fearlessly and safely traversed the streets,
unguarded save by the reputation of their just
and liberal conduct when in power, a fact extremely honourable to the Portuguese, and conclusive of the misconduct of Loison. Junot himself was menaced by an assassin, but he treated
the affair with magnanimity, and in general he
was respected, although in a far less degree than
Travot.

The dread of an explosion, which would have
compromised at once the safety of his army and of

the city, induced the French general to hasten the period when an English division was to occupy the citadel and take charge of the public tranquillity. Meanwhile emissaries from the junta of Oporto fomented the disposition of the populace to commit themselves by an attack upon the French, the convention was reprobated, and endeavours were fruitlessly made to turn the tide of indignation even against the English, as abettors of the invaders. The judge of the people, an energetic, but turbulent fellow, issued an inflammatory address, in which, calling for a suspension of the treaty, he designated the French as robbers and insulters of religion ; the Monteiro Mor, who commanded a rabble of peasantry, which he dignified with the title of an army, took possession of the south bank of the Tagus, and from his quarters issued a protest against the convention, the execution of which he had the audacity to call upon sir Charles Cotton to interrupt ; the latter sent his communications to sir Hew Dalrymple, who treated them with the contemptuous indignation they merited.

Sir John Hope being appointed English commandant of Lisbon, took possession of the castle of Belem on the 10th, and of the citadel the 12th, and, by his firm and vigorous conduct, reduced the effervescence of the public mind, and repressed the disorders which had arisen to a height that gave opportunity for the commission of any villany. The duke of Abrantes, with his staff, embarked the 13th. The first division of his army sailed the 15th ; it was followed by the second and third divisions ; and on the 30th, all the French, except the garrisons of Elvas and Almeida, were out of Portugal.

But the execution of the convention had not been
carried on thus far without much trouble and con-
testation.   Lord Proby, the English commissioner
appointed to carry the articles of the treaty into
effect, was joined by major-general Beresford on the
5th, and their united labours were scarcely sufficient to meet the exigences of a task, in the prosecution of which disputes hourly arose.   Anger,
the cupidity of individuals, and opportunity, combined to push the French beyond the bounds of
honour and decency, and several gross attempts
were made to appropriate property which no inter-
pretation of the stipulations should give a colour
to; amongst the most odious were the abstraction
of manuscripts, and rare specimens of natural history, from the national museum ; and the invasion
of the deposito publico, or funds of money awaiting
legal decision for their final appropriation.   Those
dishonest attempts were met and checked with a
strong hand, and at last a committee, consisting of
an individual of each of the three nations, was appointed by the commissioners on both sides.   Their
office was to receive reclamations, to investigate
them, and to do justice by seizing upon all contraband baggage embarked by the French; a measure
attended with excellent effect.   It must, however,
be observed, that the loud complaints and violence
of the Portuguese, and the machinations of the
bishop of Oporto, seem to have excited the suspicions of the British and influenced their acts,
more than the real facts warranted ; for the national character of the Portuguese was not then
understood, nor the extent to which they supplied
the place of true reports by the fabrication of false
ones, generally known.

Party writers have not been wanting since to exaggerate the grounds of complaint. The English have imputed fraud and evasions of the most dishonourable kind to the French, and the latter have retorted by accusations of gratuitous insult, and breach of faith, inasmuch as their soldiers, when on board the British ships, were treated with cruelty in order to induce them to desert. It would be too much to affirm that all the error was on one side, but it does appear reasonable and consonant to justice to decide, that as the French were originally aggressors and acting for their own interest, and that the British were interfering for the protection of the Portuguese, an indecorous zeal on the part of the latter, if not commendable, was certainly more excusable than in their opponents. Upon the ground of its being impossible for Junot to know what was doing in his name, the British commissioners acquitted him of any personal impropriety of conduct, and his public orders, which denounced severe punish-

ments for such malpractices corroborated this testimony; yet Kellerman, in his communications with sir Hew Dalrymple, did not scruple to insinuate matters to the duke's disadvantage. But, amidst all these conflicting accusations, the British commander's personal good faith and scrupulous adherence to justice has never been called in question.

To define the exact extent to which each party should have pushed their claims is not an easy task, yet an impartial investigator would begin by carefully separating the original rights of the French, from those rights which they acquired by the convention; and much of the subsequent clamour

in England against the authors of that treaty sprung
from the error of confounding these essentially distinct grounds of argument.   Conquest being the
sole foundation of the first, defeat, if complete, extinguished them; if incomplete, nullified a part
only.   Now the issue of the appeal to arms not
having been answerable to the justice of the cause,
an agreement ensued, by which a part was sacrificed for the sake of the remainder, and upon the
terms of that agreement the whole question of
right hinges.   If the French were not prisoners of
war, it follows that they had not forfeited their
claims, founded on the right of conquest, but they
were willing to exchange an insecure tenure of the
whole, for a secure tenure of a part.   The difficulty
consisted in defining exactly what was conceded,
and what should be recovered from them.   With respect to the latter, the restitution of plunder acquired
anterior to the convention was clearly out of the
question; if officially obtained, it was part of the
rights bargained for, if individually, to what tribunal could the innumerable claims which would
follow such an article be referred?   Abstract notions of right in such matters are misplaced.   If an
army surrenders at discretion, the victors may say
with Brennus, ' Woe to the vanquished ;' but a
convention implies some weakness, and must be
weighed in the scales of prudence, not in those of
justice.

CHAPTER VI.

THE interview that took place at Vimiero, between
don Bernardin Freire d'Andrada and sir Hew Dalrymple, has been already noticed as the commence-
men of an intrigue of some consequence. The
Portuguese chief objected at the time to the
armistice concluded with Kellerman, ostensibly
upon general grounds, but really, as it appeared to
sir Hew, because the bishop and junta of Oporto
were not named in the instrument. At the desire
of Freire, one Ayres Pinto de Souza was received at
the English head-quarters as the protector of Portuguese interests during the subsequent negotiation, and he was soon apprised that a treaty for
a definitive convention was on foot, himself and his
general being invited to state their views and
wishes before any further steps were taken.
Neither of them took any notice of this invitation,
but when the treaty was concluded clamoured
loudly against it. The British army was, they
said, an auxiliary force, and should only act
as such; nevertheless, it had assumed the right
of treating with the French for Portuguese interests, and a convention had been concluded
which protected the enemy from the punishment
due to his rapine and cruelty; it was more favourable than the strength of the relative parties
warranted, and no notice had been taken of the
Portuguese government, or of the native army in
the Alemtejo; men who were obnoxious to their

countrymen, for having aided the invaders, were
protected from a just vengeance ; finally the fortresses were bargained for, as acquisitions appertaining to the British army : a circumstance which
must inevitably excite great jealousy both in Portugal and Spain, and injure the general cause, by
affording an opportunity for the French emissaries
to create disunion among the allied nations.   They
dwelt also upon the importance of the native forces,
the strength of the insurrection, and insinuated that
separate operations were likely to be carried on notwithstanding the treaty.

Noble words often cover pitiful deeds; this
remonstrance, apparently springing from the feelings of a patriot whose heart was ulcerated by
the wrongs his country had sustained, was but a
cloak for a miserable interested intrigue.   The
bishop of Oporto, a meddling ambitious priest, had
early conceived the project of placing himself at the
head of the insurrectional authorities, and transfer-
ring the seat of government from Lisbon to
Oporto.   He was aware that he should encounter
great opposition, and he hoped that by inveigling
the English general to countenance these pretensions, he might, with the aid of Freire's force, and
his own influence, succeed in the object of his
wishes.   With this view he wrote a letter to sir
Charles Cotton, dated the 4th of August, in which
was enclosed, as the letter describes it, " The form
of government with which they, the junta of
Oporto, meant to govern Portugal when the city of
Lisbon should be free from the French ; and this
letter, together with its enclosure, being transmitted
to sir Arthur Wellesley, he placed them among
other public documents in the hands of sir Hew

Dalrymple when the latter first landed at Maceira.
In the document itself it was declared that " The
body of government had taken the glorious resolution of restoring the Portuguese monarchy in all
its extent, and of recovering the crown of Portugal
for its lawful sovereign, don Juan VI., their prince."
But this " glorious resolution" was burthened with
many forms and restrictions; and although the junta
professed the intention of re-establishing a regency,
they declared, " that if this new regency should be
interrupted by a new invasion of the French, or by
any other thing, the junta would immediately take
the government on itself, and exercise the authority
and jurisdiction which it had done ever since its
institution."

Thus prepared for some cabal, sir Hew Dalrymple was at no loss for an answer to Freire's remonstrance. He observed, that if the government of
Portugal had not been mentioned in the treaty,
neither had that of England, nor that of France.
The convention was purely military, and for the
present concerned only the commanders in the field.
With regard to the occupation of the fortresses, and
the fact of the British army being an auxiliary
force, the first was merely a measure of military
precaution absolutely necessary, and the latter was
in no way rendered doubtful by any act which had
been committed; he sir Hew was instructed by his
government to assist in restoring the prince regent
of Portugal to his lawful rights, without any secret
or interested motives; finally, the Portuguese general had been invited to assist in the negotiations,
and if he had not done so, the blame rested with
himself. To this sir Hew might have justly added,
that the conduct of Freire in withdrawing his troops

at the most critical moment of the campaign, by no
means entitled him to assume a high tone towards
those whom he had so disgracefully deserted in the
hour of danger.

The Portuguese general was silenced by this
plain and decided answer; yet the English general
was quickly convinced that the bishop and his coadjutors, however incapable of conducting great
affairs, were experienced plotters. In his first interview with Andrada, sir Hew Dalrymple had
taken occasion to observe, that " no government
lawfully representing the prince regent actually
existed in Portugal:" in fact, a junta, calling itself independent, was likewise established in
Algarvé, and the members of the regency legally
invested by the prince with supreme authority were
dispersed, and part of them in the power of the
French. This observation, so adverse to the prelate's views, was transmitted to him by Freire, together with a copy of the armistice; and he was
well aware that a definite convention, differing materially from the armistice, was upon the point of
being concluded, the refusal of sir Charles Cotton
to concur in the latter, having rendered it null and
void. Nevertheless, preserving silence on that point,
the bishop forwarded the copy of the armistice to
the chevalier Da Souza, Portuguese minister in
London, accompanied by a letter filled with invectives and misrepresentations of its provisions; the
chevalier placed this letter with its inclosures, in
the hands of Mr. Canning, the English secretary of
state for foreign affairs, and at the same time delivering to him an official note, in which, adopting the
style of the prelate and junta, he spoke of them as

the representatives of his sovereign, and the possessors of the supreme power in Portugal.

Nor were the efforts of the party confined to
formal communications with the ministers, the
daily press teemed with invectives against the
English general's conduct ; ex-parte statements,
founded on the provisions of an armistice that was
never concluded, being thus palmed upon a public,
always hasty in judging of such matters, a prejudice against the convention was raised before either
the terms of, or the events which led to it, were
known. For sir Hew, forgetting the ordinary
forms of official intercourse, had neglected to transmit information to his government until fifteen days
after the commencement of the treaty, and the
ministers, unable to contradict or explain any of
Souza's assertions, were thus placed in a mortifying
situation, by which their minds were irritated and
disposed to take a prejudiced view of the real
treaty. Meanwhile the bishop pretended to know
nothing of the convention, hence the silence of
Freire during the negotiation; but that once concluded, a clamour was, by the party, raised in
Portugal, similar to what had already been excited in England : thus both nations appeared to
be equally indignant at the conduct of the general,
when, in fact, his proceedings were unknown to
either.

It would appear that the bishop had other than
Portuguese coadjutors. The baron Von Decken, a
Hanoverian officer, was appointed one of the mili-
tary agents at Oporto ; he was subject to sir Hew
Dalrymple's orders, but as his mission was of a de-
tached nature, he was also to communicate directly

with the secretary of state in England. Von
Decken arrived at Oporto upon the 17th August,
and the same evening, in concert with the bishop,
concocted a project admirably adapted to forward
the views of the latter; they agreed that the prelate
was the fittest person to be at the head of the
government, and that as he could not, or pretended
he could not, quit Oporto, the seat of government
ought to be transferred to that city.

Two obstacles to this arrangement were foreseen;
first, the prince regent at his departure had nomi-
nated a regency, and left full instructions for the
filling up of vacancies arising from death or other
causes; secondly, the people of Lisbon and of the
southern provinces would certainly resist any plan
for changing the seat of government; hence to obviate these difficulties, Von Decken wrote largely in
commendation of the proposed arrangement, villifying
the conduct of the regency, and urging sir Hew not Appendix,
No. 11.
only to give his sanction to the ambitious project,
but to employ the British troops in controlling the
people of Lisbon, should they attempt to frustrate
the bishop's plans. To conciliate the members of
the regency, it was proposed to admit a portion of
them into the new government, and Francisco
Noronha, Francisco da Cunha, the Monteiro Mor,
and the principal Castro, were named as being the
only men who were faithful to their sovereign.
Now the last had accepted the office of minister of
worship under the French, and was consequently
unfaithful; but he was the half-brother of the
bishop, Castro being legitimately born. Under the
pretext of sparing the feelings of the people of
Lisbon, it was further proposed to appoint a Portuguese commandant, subject to the British gover-

nor, yet with a native force under his orders, to conduct all matters of police, and the bishop took the ocasion to recommend a particular general for that office. Finally, civil dissension and all its attendant evils were foretold as the consequences of rejecting this plan.

Sir Hew Dalrymple's answer was peremptory and decisive. He reprimanded general Von Decken, and at once put an end to the bishop's hopes of support from the English army. This second repulse, for sir Hew's answer did not reach Oporto until after Freire's report had arrived there, completed the mortification of the prelate and his junta, and they set no bounds to their violence. Efforts were made to stimulate the popu-lace of Lisbon to attack both French and English, in the hope that the terrible scene which must have ensued, would effectually prevent the re-establish-ment of the old regency, and at the same time render the transfer of the seat of government to Oporto an easy task. Hence the outrageous con-duct of the Monteiro Mor and of the judge of the people, and the former's insolent letter calling upon sir Charles Cotton to interrupt the execution of the convention.

The 3d of September, sir Hew Dalrymple re-ceived instructions, from home, relative to the for-mation of a new regency, which were completely at variance with the plan arranged between the bishop and general Von Decken, yet no difficulty attended the execution; and here, as in the case of prince Leopold, we are arrested by the singularity of the transaction. General Charles Stewart, brother of lord Castlereagh, was the bearer of Von Decken's first letter; he would not knowingly have lent himself to an intrigue, subversive of his brother's views, as explained in the official instructions sent to sir Hew; neither is it likely that Von Decken should plunge into such a delicate and important affair in one hour after his arrival at Oporto, if he had not been secretly authorised by some member of the English cabinet: are we then to seek for a clue to these mysteries, in that shameful Machiavelian policy that soon afterwards forced lord Castlereagh to defend his public measures by a duel?

But the usual fate of plans laid by men more cunning than wise, attended the bishop of Oporto's projects; he was successful for a moment in rendering the convention of Cintra odious to the Portuguese, yet the great mass of the people soon acknowledged with gratitude the services rendered them by the English, rejoicing at the fulfilment of a treaty which freed their country at once from the invaders. And well might they rejoice when they beheld above twenty-five thousand bold and skilful soldiers, reluctantly quitting the strong holds of the kingdom, and to the last maintaining the haughty air of an army unsubdued, and capable, on the slightest provocation, of resorting once more to the decision of battle. The Portuguese people were contented, but the Spanish general Galluzzo appears to have favoured the views of the Oporto faction. Detachments of his troops, and Portuguese refugees principally from the northern provinces and commanded by a Spaniard, were acting in conjunction with the insurgents of the Alemtejo. Many disputes had arisen between the two nations, as I have already related, for the Spaniards treated Portugal as a conquered country, denied the authority of the Portuguese

Appendix, No. 23.

BOOK
II.
——
1808.
September
Appendix,
No. 12.
general Leite, who was not of the bishop's party, and insulted him personally; they even seized his military chest at Campo Mayor, and in all things acted with the utmost violence and rapacity.

Galluzzo himself was required by his own government to join the Spanish armies concentrating on the Ebro; but instead of obeying, he collected his forces near Elvas, and when he heard of the convention concluded at Lisbon, invested Fort Lalippe, and refused to permit the execution of the treaty relative to that impregnable fortress. Colonel Girod de Novillard commanded the French garrison, and profiting from its situation, had compelled the inhabitants of Elvas to shut their gates also against the Spaniards, and to supply the fort daily with provisions. Galluzzo's proceedings were therefore manifestly absurd in a military point of view, for his attacks were confined to a trifling bombardment of Lalippe from an immense distance, and the utmost damage sustained or likely to be sustained by that fortress, was the knocking away the cornices and chimneys of the governor's house, every other part being protected by bomb proofs of the finest masonry.

Through lord Burghersh, who had been appointed to communicate with the Spanish troops in Portugal, Galluzzo was, early in September, officially informed of the articles of the convention, and that the troops of his nation, confined on board the hulks at Lisbon, were by that treaty released, and would be clothed, armed, and sent to Catalonia. Sir Hew Dalrymple also wrote to the Spanish general on the 5th of September to repeat this intelligence and to request that his detachment might be withdrawn from the Alemtejo, where they were living at the expense of the people; Galluzzo, however, took no notice of either communication; pretending that he had opened his fire against Lalippe before the date of the convention, and that no third party had a right to interfere, he declared he would grant no terms to the garrison, nor permit any but Portuguese to enter the fort. Yet at this moment the Spanish armies on the Ebro were languishing for cavalry, which he alone possessed; and his efforts were so despised by Girod, that the latter made no secret of his intention, if the fate of the French army at Lisbon should render such a step advisable, to blow up the works, and march openly through the midst of Galluzzo's troops.

Colonel Ross being finally detached, with the 20th regiment to receive the fort from colonel Girod, and to escort the garrison to Lisbon under the terms of the convention, sent a flag of truce, and major Colborne, who carried it, was also furnished with an autograph letter from Kellerman; he was received with civility, but Girod refused to surrender his post without more complete proof of the authenticity of the treaty, and with the view of acquiring that, he proposed that a French officer should proceed to Lisbon to verify the information. He did not affect to disbelieve Colborne's information, but he would not surrender his charge while the slightest doubt, capable of being removed, was attached to the transaction; and so acting he did well, and like a good soldier. General D'Arcy, who commanded the Spanish investing force, was persuaded to grant a truce for six days, to give time for the journey of the officers appointed to go to Lisbon, but on their return it was not without great difficulty and delay that they were permitted to communicate with colonel Girod ; and no argument could prevail upon the obstinate Galluzzo to relinquish the siege.   After a warm intercourse of letters, sir Hew Dalrymple ordered sir John Hope to advance to Estremos with a considerable body of troops, to give weight to his remonstrances, and, if pushed to extremity, even to force the Spaniard to desist from his unwarrantable pretensions ; for it must be observed, that Galluzzo was not only put- Appendix, No. 12. ting aside the convention by which he profited himself, but violating the independence of the Portuguese, who desired his absence from their territory.   He was likewise setting at nought the authority of his own government; for the army of Estremadura pretended to act under the orders of the junta of Seville, and Laguna, an accredited agent of that junta, was at the moment receiving, from sir Hew Dalrymple, the Spanish prisoners liberated by the effect of the convention, together with money and arms, to prepare them for immediate service in Catalonia, whither they were to be transported in British vessels.   One more effort was, however, made to persuade the intractable Galluzzo to submit to reason, before recourse was had to violent measures, which must have produced infinite evil.   Colonel Graham repaired upon the 25th of September to Badajos, and his arguments backed up by the approach of the powerful division under Hope, were finally successful.

Colonel Girod evacuated the forts, and his garrison proceeded to Lisbon, attended by the 52d regiment as an escort; the rival troops agreed very well together, striving to out-do each other by the vigour and the military order of their marches,

but the Swiss and French soldiers did not accord,
and many of the latter wished to desert. At Lisbon
the whole were immediately embarked, and the
transports being detained for some time in the river,
major de Bosset, an officer of the Chasseurs Britan-
niques, contrived to persuade near a thousand of
the men to desert, who were afterwards received
into the British service. Girod complained of this
as a breach of the convention, and it must be confessed that it was an equivocal act, yet one common
to all armies, and if done simply by persuasion very
excusable.

Almeida surrendered without any delay, and the
garrison being marched to Oporto, were proceeding
to embark, when the populace rose and would have
slain them if great exertions had not been made
by the British officers to prevent such a disgraceful breach of faith. The escort, although weak,
was resolute to sustain the honour of their nation,
and would have fired upon the multitude if the
circumstances had become desperate, yet several
of the French soldiers were assassinated, and, in
spite of every effort, the baggage was landed, and
the whole plundered, the excuse being, that church
plate was to be found amongst it; an accusation
easily made, difficult to be disproved to the satisfaction of a violent mob, and likely enough to be
true.

This tumult gives scope for reflection upon the
facility with which men adapt themselves to circumstances, and regulate their most furious passions, by
the scale of self-interest. In Oporto, the suffering,
in consequence of the invasion, was trifling compared to the misery endured in Lisbon, yet the inhabitants of the former were much more outrageous in

their anger.   In Lisbon, the very persons who had
inflicted the worst evils upon the people were daily
exposed, more or less, to violence, yet suffered none;
while in Oporto, it was with extreme difficulty that
men, until that moment unseen of the multitude,
were rescued from their frantic revenge.   In both
cases fear regulated the degree of hatred shown,
and we may conclude from hence, that national insurrections, however spontaneous and vehement, if
the result of hatred only, will never successfully
resist an organized force, unless the mechanical
courage of discipline be grafted upon the first enthusiasm.

While the vexatious correspondence with Galluzzo
was going on, sir Hew Dalrymple renewed his intercourse with Castaños, and prepared to prosecute
the war in Spain.   The Spanish prisoners, about
four thousand in number, were sent to Catalonia,
and the British army was cantoned principally in
the Alemtejo along the road to Badajos; some officers
were despatched to examine the roads through Beira,
with a view to a movement on that line, and general
Anstruther was directed to repair to the fortress of
Almeida, for the purpose of regulating every thing
which might concern the passage of the army, if it
should be found necessary to enter Spain by that
route.   Lord William Bentinck was also despatched
to Madrid, having instructions to communicate with
the Spanish generals and with the central junta, and
to arrange with them the best line of march, the
mode of providing magazines, and the plan of campaign.   But in the midst of these affairs, and before
the garrison of Elvas arrived at Lisbon, sir Hew
Dalrymple was called home to answer for his conduct relative to the convention; the command then

devolved upon sir Harry Burrard, and he, after holding it a short time, also returned to England, there to abide the fury of the most outrageous and disgraceful public clamour that was ever excited by the falsehoods of venal political writers.

The editors of the daily press, adopting all the misrepresentations of the Portuguese minister, and concluding that the silence of government was the consequence of its dissatisfaction at the convention, broke forth with such a torrent of rabid malevolence, that all feelings of right and justice were overborne, and the voice of truth entirely stifled by their obstreperous cry. Many of the public papers were printed with mourning lines around the text which related to Portuguese affairs, all called for punishment, and some even talked of death to the guilty, before it was possible to know if any crime had been committed; the infamy of the convention was the universal subject of conversation, a general madness seemed to have seized all classes, and, like the Athenians after the sea-fight of Arginusæ, the English people, if their laws would have permitted the exploit, would have condemned their victorious generals to death.

A court was assembled at Chelsea to inquire into the transactions relating to the armistice and the definite convention. Sir Arthur Wellesley, sir Harry Burrard, sir Hew Dalrymple, and the principal generals engaged at Vimiero, were called before it; a minute investigation of all the circumstances took place, and a detailed report was made, at the end of which, it was stated that no further judicial measures seemed to be called for. This was not satisfactory to the government, and the members of the court were required to state, individually, whether they

approved or disapproved of the armistice and convention. It then appeared, that four approved and
three disapproved of the convention, and among the
latter the earl of Moira distinguished himself by a
laboured criticism, which, however, left the pith of
the question entirely untouched. The proceedings
of the board were dispassionate and impartial, but
the report was not luminous; a circumstance to be
regretted, because the rank and reputation of the
members were sufficiently great to secure them from
the revenge of party, and no set of men were ever
more favourably placed for giving a severe and just
rebuke to popular injustice.

Thus ended the last act of the celebrated convention of Cintra, the very name of which will always
be a signal record of the ignorant and ridiculous
vehemence of the public feeling; for the armistice,
the negotiations, the convention itself, and the execution of its provisions, were all commenced, conducted, and concluded, at the distance of thirty
miles from Cintra, with which place they had not
the slightest connexion, political, military, or local.
Yet lord Byron has gravely sung, that the convention was signed in the marquis of Marialva's house
at Cintra, and the author of the ' Diary of an Inva-
lid,' improving upon the poet's discovery, detected
the stains of ink spilt by Junot upon the occasion!

OBSERVATIONS.

1°. General Thiebault says, that the scattered
state of the French army in the beginning of August
rendered its situation desperate, and that the slowness of sir Arthur Wellesley saved it. Others again
have accused the latter of rashness and temerity.
Neither of these censures appear to be well founded.

It is true that Junot's army was disseminated; yet to beat an army in detail, a general must be perfectly acquainted with the country he is to act in, well informed of his adversary's movements, and rapid in his own. Now rapidity in war depends as much upon the experience of the troops as upon the energy of the chief; but the English army was raw, the staff and commissariat mere novices, the artillery scantily and badly horsed, few baggage or draft animals were to be obtained in the country, and there were only a hundred and eighty cavalry mounted. Such impediments are not to be removed in a moment, and therein lies the difference betwixt theory and practice, between criticism and execution.

2°. To disembark the army without waiting for the reinforcements, was a bold yet not a rash measure. Sir Arthur Wellesley knew that the French troops were very much scattered, although he was not aware of the exact situation of each division, and, from the bishop of Oporto's promises, he had reason to expect good assistance from the Portuguese, who would have been discouraged if he had not landed at once. Weighing these circumstances, he was justified in disembarking his troops, and the event proved that he was right; he had full time to prepare his army, his marches were methodical, and he was superior in numbers to his enemy in each battle; his plans were characterized by a due mixture of enterprise and caution, well adapted to his own force, and yet capable of being enlarged without inconvenience when the reinforcement should arrive.

3°. In the action of Roriça there was a great deal to admire, and some grounds for animadversion. The movement against Laborde's first position was well conceived and executed, but the subsequent attack,

against the heights of Zambugeira, was undoubtedly
faulty, as the march of Ferguson's and Trant's divisions would have dislodged Laborde from that strong
ridge without any attack on the front. It is said that
such was sir Arthur's project, and that some mistake
in the orders caused general Ferguson to alter the
direction of his march from the flank to the centre.
This, if true, does not excuse the error, because the
commander-in-chief being present at the attack in
front, might have restrained it until Ferguson had
recovered the right direction; it is more probable
that sir Arthur did not expect any very vigorous
resistance, that wishing to press the French in their
retreat he pushed on the action too fast, and Laborde,
who was unquestionably no ordinary general, made
the most of both time and circumstances.

4°. Towards the close of the day, when the French
had decidedly taken to the mountains, the line of
Loison's march was in the power of the English
general. If he had sent two thousand men in pursuit of Laborde, left one thousand to protect the
field of battle, and with the remaining ten thousand
marched against Loison, whose advanced guard could
not have been far off, it is probable that the latter
would have been surprised and totally defeated; at
all events he could only have saved himself by a
hasty retreat, which would have broken Junot's combinations and scattered his army in all directions.
Sir Arthur Wellesley, however, marched to Lourinham, to cover the immediate landing of his reinforcement and stores, and this was prudent, because
a south-west wind would in one night have sent half
the fleet on shore in a surf unequalled for fury; such
indeed was the difficulty of a disembarkation, that a
detachment from the garrison of Peniché would have

sufficed to frustrate it. The existence of a French reserve, estimated by report at four thousand men, was known, its situation was unknown, and it might have been on the coast line; hence great danger to Anstruther, if he attempted a landing without being covered, greater still if he remained at sea. The reasons then for the march to Lourinham were cogent, and, perhaps, outweighed the advantages of attacking Loison, yet it seems to have been an error not to have occupied Torres Vedras on the 18th; the disembarkation of Anstruther's force would have been equally secured, while the junction of the French army, and the consequent battle of Vimiero would have been prevented.

5°. It is an agreeable task to render a just tribute of applause to the conduct of a gallant although unsuccessful enemy, and there is no danger of incurring the imputation of ostentatious liberality, in asserting, that Laborde's operations were exquisite specimens of the art of war. The free and confident manner in which he felt for his enemy—the occupation of Brilos, Obidos, and Roriça in succession, by which he delayed the final moment of battle, and gained time for Loison—the judgment and nice calculation with which he maintained the position of Roriça—the obstinacy with which he defended the heights of Zambugeira, were all proofs of a consummate knowledge of war, and a facility of command rarely attained.

6°. Sir Arthur Wellesley estimated Laborde's numbers at six thousand men, and his estimation was corroborated by the information gained from a wounded French officer during the action. It is possible that at Alcobaça there might have been so many, but I have thought it safer to rate them at five thousand, for the following reasons :—First, it is

at all times very difficult to judge of an enemy's force
by the eye, and it is nearly impossible to do so cor-
rectly when he is skilfully posted, and as in the present case, desirous of appearing stronger than he
really was; secondly, the six hundred men sent on
the 14th to Peniché, and three companies employed
on the 16th and 17th to keep open the communica-

tion with Loison by Bombaral, Cadaval, and Segura
must be deducted; thirdly, Laborde himself, after the
convention, positively denied that he had so many as
six thousand. General Thiebault indeed says, that
only one thousand nine hundred were present under
arms, but this assertion is certainly inaccurate, and
even injurious to the credit of Laborde, because
it casts ridicule upon his really glorious deed of
arms; it is surprising that a well-informed and
able writer should disfigure an excellent work by
such trifling.

7°. Vimiero was merely a short combat, yet it led
to important results, because Junot was unable to
comprehend the advantages of his situation. Profitable lessons may however be drawn from
every occurrence in war, and Vimiero is not deficient in good subjects for military speculation.
To many officers the position of the British appeared weak from its extent, and dangerous from its
proximity to the sea, into which the army must
have been driven if defeated. The last objection is
well founded, and suggests the reflection that it is
unsafe to neglect the principles of the art even for
a moment. The ground having been occupied
merely as a temporary post, without any view to
fighting a battle, the line of retreat by Lourinham
was for the sake of a trifling convenience left uncovered a few hours. The accidental arrival of sir

Harry Burrard arrested the advanced movement projected by sir Arthur Wellesley for the 21st, and in the mean time Junot took the lead, and had he been successful upon the left, there would have been no retreat for the British army. But the extent of the position at Vimiero, although considerable for a small army, was no cause of weakness, because the line of communication from the right to the left was much shorter and much easier for the British defence than it was for the French attack; and the centre was very strong and perfectly covered the movement of the right wing. Sir Arthur, when he placed the bulk of the combatants in that quarter, did all that was possible to remedy the only real defect in his position, that of having no line of retreat.

8°. The project of seizing Torres Vedras and Mafra, at the close of the battle, was one of those prompt daring conceptions that distinguish great generals, and it is absurd to blame sir Harry Burrard for not adopting it. Men are not gifted alike, and even if the latter had not been confirmed in his view of the matter by the advice of his staff, there was in the actual situation of affairs ample scope for doubt; the facility of executing sir Arthur's plan was not so apparent on the field of battle as it may be in the closet. The French cavalry was numerous, unharmed, and full of spirit; upon the distant heights behind Junot's army, a fresh body of infantry had been discovered by general Spencer, and the nature of the country prevented any accurate judgment of its strength being formed; the gun-carriages of the British army were very much shaken, and they were so badly and so scantily horsed, that doubts were entertained if they could keep up with the infantry in a long march; the commissariat was in great confusion, the natives, as we have seen, were flying with the country transport; the Portuguese troops gave no promise of utility, and the English cavalry was destroyed. To overcome obstacles in the pursuit of a great object is the proof of a lofty genius; but the single fact that a man of sir George Murray's acknowledged abilities was opposed to the attempt, at once exonerates sir Harry Burrard's conduct from censure, and places the vigour of sir Arthur Wellesley's in the strongest light. It was doubtless ill-judged of the former, aware as he was of the ephemeral nature of his command, to interfere at all with the dispositions of a general who was in the full career of victory, and whose superior talents and experience were well known; yet it excites indignation to find a brave and honourable veteran borne to the earth as a criminal, and assailed by the most puerile, shallow writers, merely because his mind was not of the highest class. Sir Arthur Wellesley himself was the first to declare before the court of inquiry that sir Harry Burrard had decided upon fair military reasons.

GENERAL PLAN OF THE CAMPAIGN.

1°. Although double lines of operation are generally disadvantageous and opposed to sound principles, the expediency of landing sir John Moore's troops at the mouth of the Mondego, and pushing them forward to Santarem, was unquestionable; unless the probable consequences of such a movement are taken into consideration, sir Arthur Wellesley's foresight can not be justly appreciated.

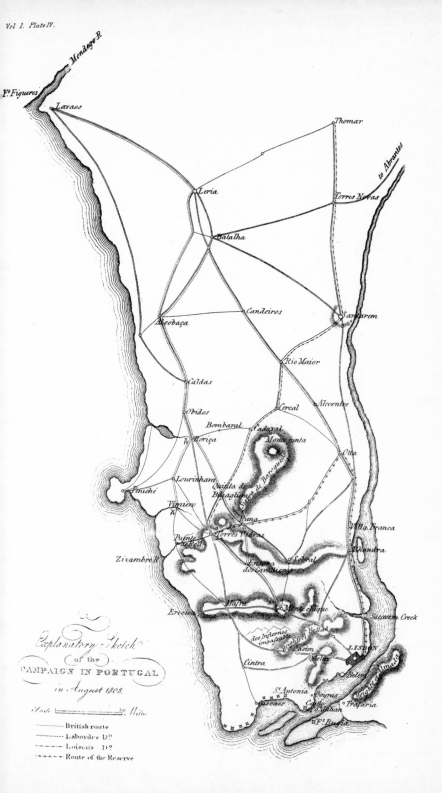

Mondego R.

Ft Figueres

Lavaos

Themar

to Abrantes

Leria

Torres Novas

Batalha

Candeiros

Santarem

Alcobaça

Rio Maior

Caldas

Alcoentre

Obidos

Cercal

Bombaral

Cadaval

Roriça

Monte junta

Otta

Leurinham

Quinta de
Brisagliana

Serra de Baragueda

Peniché

Villa Franca

Vimiero

Ruma

Puente
Rateiro

Torres Vedras

Alhandra

Zizambre R.

Ensara
dos cavalleiros

Sobral

Ereceira

Mafra

Monte chique

Sacavem Creek

dos Infiernos
impassable

Bellas

Casim

LISBON

Cintra

Belen

Belem

St Antonia

Oeyras

Trafaria

Cascaes

Cabeça
Ft Sylchan

Ft Bugi

Explanatory Sketch

of the

CAMPAIGN IN PORTUGAL

in August 1808.

Scale [————] 10 Miles

——— British route
········· Labordes Do
-·-·-·- Loisons Do
+++++ Route of the Reserve

London, Published by T. & W. Boone, New Bond Street.

Lisbon, situated near the end of the tongue of land
lying between the sea-coast and the Tagus, is defended to the northward by vast mountains, that,
rising in successive and nearly parallel ranges, end
abruptly in a line extending from Torres Vedras to
Alhandra on the Tagus ; and as these ridges can
only be passed at certain points by an army, the in-
tersections of the different roads form so many
strong positions. Moreover the great mass of the
Monte Junto which appears to lead perpendicularly
on to the centre of the first ridge, but stops short
at a few miles distance, sends a rugged shoot,
called the Sierra de Barragueda, in a slanting direction towards Torres Vedras, from which it is
only divided by a deep defile.

From this conformation it results, that an army
marching from the Mondego to Lisbon, must
either pass behind the Monte Junto, and follow the
line of the Tagus, or keeping the western side of
that mountain, come upon the position of Torres
Vedras.

If sir Arthur Wellesley had adopted the first line
of operations, his subsistence must have been drawn
by convoys from the Mondego, the enemy's numerous
cavalry would then have cut his communications,
and in that state he would have had to retreat, or to
force the positions of Alhandra, Alverca, and finally
the heights of Bellas, a strong position, the right
flank of which was covered by the creek of Saccavem, and the left flank by the impassable Sierra
dos Infiernos. On the other line, Torres Vedras
was to be carried, and then Mafra or Montechique,
following the direction of Junot's retreat. If Mafra
was forced, and it could not well be turned, a line
of march, by Cassim and Quelus, upon Lisbon,

would have been opened to the victors ; but that
route, besides being longer than the road through
Montechique and Loures, would, while it led the
English army equally away from the fleet, have entangled it among the fortresses of Ereceira, Sant
Antonio, Cascaes, St. Julian's, and Belem. Again,
supposing the position of Montechique to be
stormed, the heights of Bellas offered a third line
of defence ; and lastly, the citadel and forts of
Lisbon itself would have sufficed to cover the passage of the river, and a retreat upon Elvas would
have been secure.

Thus it is certain, that difficulties of the most
serious nature awaited the English army while
acting on a single line of operations, and the double
line proposed by sir Arthur was strictly scientific.
For if sir John Moore, disembarking at the Mondego, had marched first to Santarem and then to
Saccavem, he would have turned the positions
of Torres Vedras and Montechique ; and   sir
Arthur, on the other side, would have turned the
heights of Bellas by the road of Quelus, and
Junot's central situation could not have availed
him, because the distance between the British corps
would be more than a day's march, and their near
approach to Lisbon would have caused an insurrection of the populace. The duke of Abrantes must then
either have abandoned that capital and fallen vigorously upon sir John Moore, with a view to over-
whelm him and gain Almeida or Elvas, or he must
have concentrated his forces, and been prepared to
cross the Tagus if he lost a battle in front of Lisbon.
In the first case, the strength of the country afforded
Moore every facility for a successful resistance, and
sir Arthur's corps would have quickly arrived upon

the rear of the French.   In the second case, Junot
would have had to fight superior numbers, with an
inveterate populace in his rear, and if, fearing the
result of such an encounter, he had crossed the
Tagus, and pushed for Elvas, sir John Moore's
division could likewise have crossed the river,
and harassed the French in their retreat.
The above reasoning being correct, it follows
that to re-embark sir John Moore's army after it
had landed at the Mondego, and to bring it down
to Maceira bay, was an error which, no convention
intervening, might have proved fatal to the success
of the campaign; and this error was rendered more
important by the danger incurred from the passage,
for, as the transports were not sea-worthy, the
greatest part would have perished had a gale of
wind come on from the south-west.

Captain
Pulteney
Malcolm's
evidence.
Court of
Inquiry.

2°. Sir Arthur Wellesley's project of seizing
Mafra by a rapid march on the morning of the
21st, was exceedingly bold ; its successful execution would have obliged Junot to make a hurried
retreat by Enxara dos Cavalleiros to Montechique,
at the risk of being attacked in flank during his
march; if he had moved by the longer route of
Ruña and Sobral, it is scarcely to be doubted that
the British army would have reached Lisbon before him.   But was it possible so to deceive an
enemy, inured to warfare, as to gain ten miles in a
march of sixteen? was it possible to evade the
vigilance of an experienced general, who, being
posted only nine miles off, possessed a formidable
cavalry, the efforts of which could neither be
checked nor interrupted by the small escort of
horse in the British camp? was it, in fine, possible
to avoid a defeat, during a flank march, along a

road, crossed and interrupted by a river, and several deep gullies which formed the beds of mountain torrents? These are questions which naturally occur to every military man. The sticklers for a rigid adherence to system would probably decide in the negative; sir Arthur Wellesley was, however, not only prepared to try at the time, but he afterwards deliberately affirmed that, under certain circumstances of ground, an operation of that kind would succeed. To investigate such questions is the best study for an officer.

A night march is the most obvious mode of effecting such an enterprise, but not always the best in circumstances where expedition is required; great generals have usually preferred the day-time, trusting to their own skill in deceiving the enemy, while their army made a forced march to gain the object in view; thus Turenne, at Landsberg, was successful against the archduke Leopold in broad day-light, and Cæsar in a more remarkable manner overreached Afranius and Petrieus, near Lerida. Nor were the circumstances at Vimiero unfavourable to sir Arthur Wellesley. He might have pushed a select corps of light troops, his cavalry, the marines of the fleet, the Portuguese auxiliaries, and a few field pieces, to the entrance of the defile of Torres Vedras before daybreak, with orders to engage the French outposts briskly, and to make demonstrations as for a general attack. There is no doubt that such a movement, if skilfully conducted, would have completely occupied the enemy's attention, while the main body of the army, marching in great coats, and hiding the glitter of their arms, might have profited from the woods and hollows through which the by-road to Mafra led, and

gained such a start as would have insured the suc- CHAP.
VI.
cess of the enterprise.

1808.

Let us, however, take a view of the other side.
Let us suppose that Junot, instructed by his spies
and patroles, or divining the intention of the British
general, held the masking division in check with a
small force, and carrying the remainder of his army
by the Puente de Roll, or some other cross road,
and there were several, against the flank of the
English, had fallen upon the latter while in march
hemmed in, as they would be, between the sea and
the mountains, and entangled among hollows and
torrents.   What then would have been the result?
History answers, by pointing to Condé and the
battle of Senef.   It must, however, be confessed,
that it could be no ordinary general that conceived
such a project, and notwithstanding the small numbers of the opposing armies, success would have
ranked sir Arthur high among the eminent commanders of the world, if he had never performed
any other exploit.   'The statue of Hercules, cast
by Lysippus, although only a foot high, expressed,'
says Pliny, ' the muscles and bones of the hero
more grandly than the colossal figures of other
artists.'

3°.   So many circumstances combine to sway the
judgment of an officer in the field which do not
afterwards appear of weight, that caution should
always be the motto of those who censure the conduct of an unfortunate commander; nevertheless,
the duke of Abrantes' faults, during this campaign,
were too glaring to be mistaken.   He lingered too
long at Lisbon; he was undecided in his plans; he
divided his army unnecessarily; he discovered no
skill on the field of battle.   When the English

army was landed, affairs were brought to a crisis, and
Junot had only two points to consider. Could the
French forces under his command defend Portugal
without assistance, and if not, how were its operations to be made most available for furthering
Napoleon's general plans against the Peninsula?
The first point could not be ascertained until a
battle with sir Arthur had been tried; the second
evidently required that Junot should keep his army
concentrated, preserve the power of retreating into
Spain, and endeavour to engage the British troops
in the sieges of Elvas and Almeida. If the two
plans had been incompatible, the last was certainly
preferable to the chance of battle in a country universally hostile. But the two plans were not incompatible.

The pivot of Junot's movements was Lisbon; he
had therefore to consider how he might best fall
upon and overthrow the English army, without resigning the capital to the Portuguese insurgents
during the operation. He could not hope to accomplish the first effectually without using the great
mass of his forces, nor to avoid the last except by
skilful management, and the utmost rapidity. Now
the citadel and forts about Lisbon, were sufficiently
strong to enable a small part of the French army
to control the populace, and to resist the insurgents
of the Alemtejo for a few days. The Russian admiral, although not hostile to the Portuguese, or
favourable to the French, was forced, by his fear of
the English, to preserve a guarded attitude, and in
point of fact, did materially contribute to awe the
multitude, who could not but look upon him as an
enemy. The Portuguese ships of war which had
been fitted out by Junot, were floating fortresses

requiring scarcely any garrisons, yet efficient instruments to control the city, without ceasing to
be receptacles for the Spanish prisoners, and safe
depôts for powder and arms, which might otherwise
have fallen into the power of the populace. Wherefore, instead of delaying so long in the capital, instead of troubling himself about the assemblage of
Alcacer do Sal, instead of detaching Laborde with a
weak division to cover the march of Loison, Junot
should have taken the most vigorous resolutions in
respect to Lisbon, the moment he heard of the
English descent. He should have abandoned the
left bank of the Tagus, with the exception of Palmela
and the Bugio, which was necessary to the safety
of his shipping; he should have seized upon the
principal families of the capital, as hostages for
the good behaviour of the rest; he should have
threatened, and been prepared, to bombard the city
if refractory; then, leaving nothing more than the
mere garrisons of the citadel, forts, and ships behind
him, have proceeded, not to Leiria, which was too
near the enemy to be a secure point of junction with
Loison, but to Santarem, where both corps might
have been united without danger and without fatigue.
General Thomieres, in the mean time, putting a
small garrison in Peniché, could have watched the
movement of the British general, and thus from
eighteen to twenty thousand men would have been
assembled at Santarem by the 13th at farthest,
and from thence, one march would have brought
the whole to Batalha, near which place the lot of
battle might have been drawn without trembling.
If it proved unfavourable to the French, the ulterior
object of renewing the campaign on the frontier
was in no manner compromised. The number of

BOOK II.
1808.

large boats that Lisbon can always furnish, would have sufficed to transport the beaten army over the Tagus from Santarem in a few hours, especially if the stores had been embarked before Junot moved towards Batalha; and the French army, once in the Alemtejo, with a good garrison in Abrantes, could not have been followed until the forts at the mouth of the Tagus were reduced, and the fleet sheltered in the river. Thus, long before the British could have appeared in force in the Alemtejo, the fortress of Elvas would have been provisioned from the magazines collected by Loison after the battle of Evora, and the campaign could have been easily prolonged until the great French army, coming from Germany, crushed all opposition.

The above is not a theory broached after the event. That Junot would attempt something of the kind, was the data upon which the English general formed his plans, and the intercepted memoir of colonel Vincent treated such an operation as a matter of course. Junot's threats during the negotiation prove that he was not ignorant of his own resources, but his mind was depressed, and his desponding mood was palpable to those around him; it is a curious fact, that Sattaro, the Portuguese agent, who, for some purpose or other was in the British camp, told sir Arthur Wellesley before the battle of Vimiero, that Junot would willingly evacuate Portugal upon terms.

4°. When the French, being fourteen thousand in number, occupied Torres Vedras, that position was nearly impregnable; but though seventeen thousand British could scarcely have carried it by force, they might have turned it in a single march by the coast road, and Junot neither placed a detachment on that side, nor kept a vigilant watch by his patroles; hence, if sir Arthur Wellesley's intended movement had not been arrested by orders from Burrard, it must have succeeded, because Junot was entangled in the defiles of Torres Vedras from six o'clock in the evening of the 20th, until late in the morning of the 21st. The two armies would thus have changed camps in the space of a few hours, without firing a shot; Junot would have lost Lisbon, and have been placed in the most ridiculous situation.

5°. In the battle, the duke of Abrantes showed great courage, but no talent. His army was inferior in numbers, yet he formed two separate attacks, an evident error, that enabled sir Arthur to beat him in detail without difficulty. He was the less excusable, because the comparatively easy nature of the ground over which the road from Torres Vedras to Lourinham led, and the manner in which the English army was heaped to the right when the position first opened to the view, plainly indicated the true line of attack. Junot should, with all his forces concentrated for one effort, have fallen in upon the left of his opponent's position: if victorious, the sea would have swallowed those who escaped his sword, if repulsed, his retreat was open, and his loss could not have been so great in a well-conducted single effort, as it was in the ill-digested, unconnected attacks that took place.

6°. The rapidity with which the French soldiers rallied, and recovered their order after such a severe check, was admirable, but their habitual method of attacking in column cannot be praised. Against the Austrians, Russians, and Prussians, it may have been successful, but against the British it must always fail; because the English infantry is suffi-

ciently firm, intelligent, and well-disciplined, to
wait calmly in lines for the adverse masses, and sufficiently bold to close upon them with the bayonet. The column is undoubtedly excellent for all
movements short of the actual charge, but as the
Macedonian phalanx was unable to resist the open
formation of the Roman legion, so will the close
column be unequal to sustain the fire and charge of
a good line aided by artillery. The natural repugnance of men to trample on their own dead and
wounded, the cries and groans of the latter, and the
whistling of the cannon-shots as they tear open the
ranks, produce the greatest disorder, especially in
the centre of attacking columns, which blinded by
smoke, unstedfast of footing, and bewildered by
words of command, coming from a multitude of
officers crowded together, can neither see what is
taking place, nor make any effort to advance or
retreat without increasing the confusion : hence no
example of courage can be useful, no moral effect
can be produced by the spirit of individuals, except
upon the head, which is often firm, and even victorious at the moment when the rear is flying in
terror. Nevertheless, well managed columns are
the very soul of military operations, in them is the
victory, and in them also is safety to be found after
a defeat ; the secret consists in knowing when and
where to extend the front.

ARMISTICE.—CONVENTION.

1°. It is surprising, that Junot having regained
Torres Vedras, occupied Mafra, and obtained an
armistice, did not profit by the terms of the latter
to prepare for crossing the Tagus and establishing
the war on the frontiers. Kellerman ascertained

during his negotiation, that sir John Moore was not arrived; it was clear that, until he did arrive, the position of Montechique could neither be attacked nor turned, and there was nothing in the armistice itself, nor the war in which it had been agreed to, which rendered it dishonourable to take such an advantage. The opening thus left for Junot to gain time, was sir Arthur Wellesley's principal objection to the preliminary treaty.

2°. With regard to the convention, although some of its provisions were objectionable in point of form, and others imprudently worded, yet taken as a whole, it was a transaction fraught with prudence and wisdom. Let it be examined upon fair military and political grounds, let it even be supposed for the sake of argument, that sir Arthur, unimpeded by sir Harry Burrard, had pursued his own plan, and that Junot, cut off from Lisbon and the half of his forces, had been driven up the Tagus; he was still master of flying to Almeida or Elvas, the thousand men left in Santarem would have joined him in the Alemtejo, or fallen down to the capital, and what then would have been the advantages that could render the convention undesirable? The British army, exclusive of Moore's division, had neither provisions, nor means of transporting provisions for more than ten days, and the fleet was the only resource when that supply should be exhausted; but a gale from any point between south and north-west, would have driven the ships away or cast them on a lee-shore. It was therefore indispensable first to secure the mouth of the Tagus, for the safety of the fleet; and this could only be done by occupying Cascaes, Bugio, and St. Julian's, the last of which would alone have required

BOOK
II.

1808.

Proceed-
ings of the
Court of
Inquiry.
ten days open trenches, and a battering train, which
must have been dragged by men over the mountains; for the artillery horses were scarcely able
to draw the field guns, and no country animals
were to be found. In the mean time, the French
troops in Lisbon, upon the heights of Almada, and
in the men-of-war, retiring tranquilly through the
Alemtejo, would have united with Junot, or, if he
had fallen back upon Almeida, they could have
retired upon Elvas and La-Lyppe. In this argument the Russians have not been considered, but
whatever his secret wishes might have been, Siniavin
must have surrendered his squadron in a disgraceful
manner, or joined the French with his six thousand
men; and it may here be observed, that even after
the arrival of sir John Moore, only twenty-five
thousand British infantry were fit for duty.

Let it now be supposed that the forts were taken,
the English fleet in the river, the resources of
Lisbon organized, the battering guns and ammunition necessary for the siege of Elvas transported to
Abrantes by water; seventy miles of land remained
to traverse, and then three months of arduous operations in the sickly season, and in the most pestilent
of situations, would have been the certain consequences of any attempt to reduce that fortress.
Did the difficulty end there? No! Almeida remained, and in the then state of the roads of Portugal, and taking into consideration only the certain
and foreseen obstacles, it is not too much to say,
that six months more would have been wasted before
the country would have been entirely freed from
the invaders; but long before that period Napoleon's
eagles would have soared over Lisbon again! The
conclusion is inevitable; the convention was a great

and solid advantage for the allies, a blunder on the part of the French.

With the momentary exception of Junot's threat to burn Lisbon if his terms were not complied with, we look in vain for any traces of that vigour which urged the march from Alcantara; we are astonished to perceive the man, who, in the teeth of an English fleet, in contempt of fourteen thousand Portuguese troops, and regardless of a population of three hundred thousand souls, dared, with a few hundred tired grenadiers, to seize upon Lisbon, so changed in half a year, so sunk in energy, that, with twenty-five thousand good soldiers, he declined a manly effort, and resorted to a convention to save an army which was really in very little danger. But such and so variable is the human mind, a momentary slave of every attraction, yet ultimately true to self-interest. When Junot entered Portugal, power, honours, fame, even a throne was within his view; when he proposed the convention, the gorgeous apparition was gone; toil and danger were at hand, fame flitted at a distance, and he easily persuaded himself that prudence and vigour could not be yoked together. A saying attributed to Napoleon perfectly describes the convention in a few words. " I was going to send Junot before a council of war, when, fortunately, the English tried their generals, and saved me the pain of punishing an old friend !"

BOOK III.

CHAPTER I.

THE convention of Cintra followed by the establishment of a regency at Lisbon, disconcerted the
plans of the bishop and junta of Oporto, and Portugal was restored to a state of comparative tranquillity; for the Portuguese people, being of a
simple character, when they found their country
relieved from the presence of a French army
readily acknowledged the benefit derived from the
convention, and refused to listen to the pernicious
counsels of the factious prelate and his mischievous
coadjutors. Thus terminated what may be called
the convulsive struggle of the Peninsular war. Up
to that period a remarkable similarity of feeling and
mode of acting betrayed the common origin of the
Spanish and Portuguese people; a wild impatience
of foreign aggression, extravagant pride, vain
boasting, and a passionate reckless resentment,
were common to both; but there the likeness
ceased, and the finer marks of national character
which had been impressed upon them by their
different positions in the political world, became
distinctly visible.

Spain, holding, from time immemorial, a high
rank among the great powers, and more often an
oppressor than oppressed, haughtily rejected all
advice. Unconscious of her actual weakness and

ignorance, and remembering only her former dignity, she, ridiculously, assumed an attitude which
would scarcely have suited her in the days of
Charles V. ; whereas Portugal, always fearing the
ambition of a powerful neighbour, and relying for
safety as much upon her alliances as upon her own
intrinsic strength, was from habit inclined to prudent calculation, and readily submitted to the
direction of England. The turbulence of the first
led to defeat and disaster ; the docility and patience of the second were productive of the most
beneficial results.

The difference between these nations was, however, not immediately perceptible, at the period
of the convention the Portuguese were despised,
while a splendid triumph was anticipated for the
Spaniards. It was affirmed and believed, that from
every quarter enthusiastic multitudes of the latter
were pressing forward to complete the destruction
of a baffled and dispirited enemy ; the vigour, the
courage, the unmatched spring of Spanish patriotism, was in every man's mouth, Napoleon's power
and energy seemed weak in opposition. Few persons doubted the truth of such tales, and yet
nothing could be more unsound, more eminently
fallacious, than the generally entertained opinion of
French weakness and of Spanish strength. The
resources of the former were unbounded, almost
untouched ; those of the latter were too slender
even to support the weight of victory ; in Spain the
whole structure of society was shaken to pieces by
the violence of an effort which merely awakened
the slumbering strength of France. Foresight,
promptitude, arrangement, marked the proceedings
of Napoleon, but with the Spaniards the counsels

of prudence were punished as treason, and personal interests, everywhere springing up with incredible force, wrestled against the public good. At a distance the insurrection appeared of towering proportions and mighty strength, when in truth, it was a fantastic object, stained with blood, and tottering from weakness. The helping hand of England alone was stretched forth for its support, all other assistance was denied, for the continental powers, although nourishing secret hopes of profit from the struggle, with calculating policy, turned coldly from the patriots' cause. The English cabinet was, indeed, sanguine, and resolute to act, yet the ministers, while anticipating success in a preposterous manner, displayed little industry, and less judgment, in their preparations for the struggle; nor does it appear that the real freedom of the Peninsula was much considered in their councils. They contemplated this astonishing insurrection as a mere military opening through which Napoleon might be assailed, and they neglected, or rather feared, to look towards the great moral consequences of such a stupendous event,—consequences which were, indeed, above their reach of policy: they were neither able, nor willing, to seize such a singularly propitious occasion for conferring a benefit upon mankind.

It is, however, certain, that this opportunity for restoring the civil strength of a long degraded people, by a direct recurrence to first principles, was such as had seldom been granted to a sinking nation. Enthusiasm was aroused without the withering curse of faction; the multitude were ready to follow whoever chose to lead, the weight of ancient authority was, by a violent external shock, thrown off, the ruling power fell from the hands of the few, and was caught by the many, without the latter having thereby incurred the odium of rebellion, or excited the malice of mortified grandeur. There was nothing to deter the cautious, for there was nothing to pull down ; the foundation of the social structure was already laid bare, and all the materials were at hand for building a noble monument of human genius and virtue, the architect alone was wanting : no anxiety to ameliorate the moral or physical condition of the people in the Peninsula was evinced by the ruling men of England, and if any existed amongst those of Spain, it evaporated in puerile abstract speculations.   Napoleon, indeed, offered the blessing of regeneration in exchange for submission, but in that revolting form, accompanied by the evils of war, it was rejected, and amidst the clamorous pursuit of national independence, the independence of man was trampled under foot. The mass of the Spanish nation, blinded by personal hatred, thought only of revenge ; the leaders, arrogant and incapable, neither sought nor wished for any higher motive of action : without unity of design, devoid of arrangement, their policy was mean and personal, their military efforts were abortive, and a rude, unscientific warfare disclosed at once the barbarous violence of the Spanish character, and the utter decay of Spanish institutions.

After Joseph's retreat from Madrid, the insurrection of Spain may be said to have ceased ; from that period it became a war between France and the Peninsula ; the fate of the latter was entrusted to organized bodies of men, and as the first excitement subsided, and danger seemed to recede, all the meaner passions resumed their empire.   Hence

the transactions of the memorable period which in-
tervened between the battles of Baylen and Coruña
were exceedingly confused, and the history of them
must necessarily partake somewhat of that confusion.   The establishment of a central supreme junta,
the caprices of the Spanish generals, and their interminable disputes; the proceedings of the French
army before the arrival of the emperor; the operations of the grand army after his arrival, and the
campaign of the British auxiliary force; form so
many distinct actions, connected indeed by one great
catastrophe, yet each attended by a number of minor
circumstances of no great historical importance taken
separately, but when combined, showing the extent
and complicated nature of the disease which destroyed the energy of Spain.   For the advantage of
clearness, therefore, it will be necessary to sacrifice
chronological order; and as frequent reference must
be made to the proceedings of a class of men whose
interference had a decided, and in many cases a very
disastrous influence upon the affairs of that period,
I shall first give a brief account of the English
agents, under which denomination both civil and
military men were employed; yet the distinction
was rather nominal than real, as generally speaking,
each person assumed the right of acting in both
capacities.

The envoy, Mr. Charles Stuart, was the chief of
the civil agents; the persons subordinate to him
were, Mr. Hunter, Mr. Duff, and others, consuls
and vice-consuls.

Mr. Stuart sailed with sir A. Wellesley, and was
left at Coruña when that officer touched there, previous to the operations in Portugal.

Mr. Hunter was stationed at Gihon in the Asturias.

Mr. Duff proceeded to Cadiz, and the others in like manner were employed at different ports. They were all empowered to distribute money, arms, succours of clothing and ammunition, and the want of system and forethought in the cabinet was palpable from the injudicious zeal of these inferior agents, each of whom conceived himself competent to direct the whole of the political and military transactions; Mr. Stuart was even put to some trouble in establishing his right to control their proceedings.

The military agents were of two classes; those sent from England by the government, and those employed by the generals abroad.

Sir Thomas Dyer, assisted by major Roche and captain Patrick, proceeded to the Asturias. The last officer remained at Oviedo, near the junta of that province; major Roche went to the head-quarters of Cuesta; sir Thomas Dyer, after collecting some information, returned to England.

Colonel Charles Doyle, having organized the Spanish prisoners at Portsmouth, sailed with them to Coruña. He was accompanied by captain Carrol and captain Kennedy, and during the passage a singular instance of turbulent impatience occurred : the prisoners, who had been released, armed, and clothed by England, and who had been as enthusiastic in their expressions of patriotism as the most sanguine could desire, mutinied, seized the transports, carried them into different ports of the Peninsula, disembarked, and proceeded each to his own home.

Colonel Browne was despatched to Oporto, and major Green to Catalonia.

Those employed by the generals commanding armies were captain Whittingham, who was placed by sir Hew Dalrymple near general Castaños, he accompanied the head-quarters of the Andalusian army until the battle of Tudela put an end to his functions.   Major Cox, appointed also by sir Hew Dalrymple, remained near the junta of Seville, where his talents and prudent conduct were of great service; it would have been fortunate if all the persons employed as agents had acted with as much judgment and discretion.

All the above-named gentlemen were in full activity previous to the commencement of the campaign in Portugal; but when the convention of Cintra opened a way for operations in Spain, sir Hew Dalrymple sent lord William Bentinck to Madrid, that he might arrange a plan of co-operation with the Spanish generals, and transmit exact intelligence of the state of affairs.   Such a mission was become indispensable.   Up to the period of lord William's arrival in Madrid, the military intelligence received was very unsatisfactory.   The letters from the armies contained abundance of common-place expressions relative to the enthusiasm and patriotism visible in Spain; vast plans were said to be under consideration, some in progress of execution, and complete success was confidently predicted ; but by some fatality, every project proved abortive or disastrous, without lowering the confidence of the prognosticators, or checking the mania for grand operations, which seemed to be the disease of the moment.

The English ministers confirmed the appointment of lord William Bentinck, and at the same time re-organized the system of the military agents, by marking out certain districts, and appointing a general officer to superintend each.   Thus, major-general Broderick was sent to Gallicia; major-general Leith, with a large staff, proceeded to the Asturias; major-

general Sontag went to Portugal. At the same
time, sir Robert Wilson, being furnished with
arms, ammunition, and clothing for organizing three
or four thousand men levied by the bishop of Oporto,
took with him a large regimental staff, and a number of Portuguese refugees, and succeeded in forming a partizan corps, afterwards known as the Lusitanian legion. Brigadier-general Decken, also a
German, being first destined for Spain, was coun-
termanded at sea, and directed to Oporto, where
he arrived on the 17th of August, and immediately
commenced that curious intrigue which has been
already mentioned in the campaign of Vimiero. The
scope of general Leith's mission was wide; Biscay,
Castille, Leon, and even Catalonia, were placed
under his superintendence, and he appears to have
had instructions to prepare the way for the disembarkation of an English army on the coast of
Biscay.

When sir John Moore assumed the command of
the army, he sent colonel Graham to reside at the
Spanish head-quarters on the Ebro, and directed
lord William Bentinck to remain at Madrid to forward the arrangements for commencing the campaign. Lord William found in Mr. Stuart an able
coadjutor, and in the letters of these two gentlemen,
and the correspondence of major Coxe, then at
Seville, is to be found the history of the evils which
at this period afflicted unhappy Spain, and ruined
her noble cause. But the power of distributing
supplies, and the independent nature of their ap-
pointments, gave to the military agents immediately
employed by the minister, an extraordinary influence,
which was very injudiciously exercised. They forgot the real objects of their mission, and in many

cases took a leading part in affairs with which it was not politic in them to have meddled at all.

Thus Colonel Doyle having left captain Kennedy at Coruña, and placed captain Carrol at the head-quarters of Blake's army, repaired in person to Madrid, where he was received with marked attention, obtained the rank of a general officer in the Spanish service for himself, that of lieutenant-colonel for captains Carrol and Kennedy, and from his letters it would appear, that he had a large share in conducting many important measures, such as the arrangement of a general plan of operations, and the formation of Sir John Moore's Correspondence, MS. a central and supreme government. He seems to have attached himself principally to the duke of Infantado, a young man of moderate capacity, but with a strong predilection for those petty intrigues which constituted the policy of the Spanish court. Captain Whittingham likewise gained the confidence of Castaños to such a degree, that he was employed by him to inspect the different Spanish corps on the Whittingham's Letters, MS. Ebro early in September, and to report upon their state of efficiency previous to entering upon the execution of the plan laid down for the campaign. But notwithstanding the favourable position in which these officers stood, it does not appear that either of them obtained any clear idea of the relative strength of the contending forces; their opinions, invariably and even extravagantly sanguine, were never borne out by the result.

The Spaniards were not slow to perceive the advantages of encouraging the vanity of inexperienced men who had the control of enormous supplies; and while all outward demonstrations of respect and confidence were by them lavished upon subordinate functionaries, especially upon those who had ac-

cepted of rank in their service, the most strenuous
exertions of lord William Bentinck and Mr. Stuart
were insufficient to procure the adoption of a single
beneficial measure, or even to establish the ordinary
intercourse of official business. The leading Spaniards wished to obtain a medium through which to
create a false impression of the state of affairs, and
thus to secure supplies and succours from England,
without being fettered in the application of them;
the subordinate agents answered this purpose, and,
satisfied with their docility, the generals were far
from encouraging the residence of more than one
British agent at their head-quarters. Captain Birch,
an intelligent engineer officer, writing from Blake's
camp, says, ' General Broderick is expected here;
but I have understood that the appearance of a British general at these head-quarters, to accompany
the army, might give jealousy. General Blake is
not communicative, yet captain Carrol appears to
be on the best footing with him and his officers; and
captain Carrol tells me that he informs him of more
than he does any of his generals.' Soon after this,
general Broderick did arrive, and complained, that
' general Blake's reserve was such that he could
only get answers to the most direct and particular
questions, but by no means candid and explicit
replies to general inquiries '

No object could be more perfectly accomplished;
nothing could be more widely different than Spanish
affairs, judged of by the tenor of the military agents'
reports, and Spanish affairs when brought to the test of
battle; yet the fault did not attach so much to the
agents as to the ministers who selected them. It was
difficult for inexperienced men to avoid the snare.
Living with the chiefs of armies actually in the
field, being in habits of daily intercourse with

CHAP.
I.

1808.
MrStuart's
Letters,
MS.
Lord W.
Bentinck's
Letters,
MS.
Appendix,
No. 13, §6.

Sir John
Moore's
Correspon-
dence, MS.

Letter to
Mr. Stuart,
MS.
Sept. 13.

them, holding rank in the same service, and dependent upon their politeness for every convenience,
the agent was in a manner forced to see as the
general saw, and to report as he wished; a simple
spy would have been far more efficacious!

Sir John Moore, perceiving the evil tendency of
such a system, recalled all those officers who were
under his immediate control, and strongly recommended to ministers that only one channel of communication should exist between the Spanish authorities and the British army.   He was convinced of
the necessity of this measure, by observing, that
each of the military agents considered the events
passing under his own peculiar cognizance as the
only occurrences of importance.   Some of those
officers treated sir Hew Dalrymple and himself, as
persons commanding an auxiliary force which was
to be moved, divided, and applied at the requisition
of every inferior agent, and all the military stores of
the British empire, as placed at their disposal. Mr.
Hunter demanded English cavalry and horse artillery to act with the Spaniards in the Asturian plains,
and infantry to garrison their seaport towns.   Sir
Thomas Dyer was convinced that the horsemen and
guns should have been at Rio Seco, in Leon, and
that, with the aid of two thousand British cavalry
and twenty pieces of artillery, the Spaniards would
in six weeks have all the French troops ' in a state
of siege.'   General Leith says: ' Whatever may be
the plan of operations, and whatever the result, I
beg leave, in the strongest manner, to recommend to
your consideration, the great advantage of ordering
all the disposable force, of horse or car artillery, and
light infantry, mounted on horses or mules of the
country, without a moment's delay to move on
Palencia, where the column or columns will receive

Sir John
Moore's
Papers,
MSS.

such intelligence as may enable them to give the
most effectual co-operation.' Captain Whittingham,
at the same period, after mentioning the wish of
general Castaños that some British cavalry should
join him, writes, ' I cannot quit this subject without
once more repeating, that the efforts of the cavalry
will decide the fate of the campaign. Should it be
possible for your excellency to send one thousand or
fifteen hundred horse, the advantages that would
result are incalculable.' And while these pressing
recommendations came the one from Oviedo, the
other from Tudela, colonel Doyle, writing from
Madrid, thus expresses himself: ' Certain it is, that
if your army were here, the French would evacuate
Spain before you got within a week's march of them;
indeed, even the light cavalry and two thousand
light troops sent on cars, to keep up with the cavalry,
to show our friends the nature of outpost duty,
would, I think, decide the question.'—' A respectable corps of British troops, landed in Catalonia,
would so impose, that I have no doubt of the good
effects.' This last proposition relative to Catalonia
was a favourite plan of all the leading men at
Madrid ; so certain were they of success on the
Ebro, that, finding no British force was likely to be
granted, they withdrew eight or nine thousand men
from the army near Tudela, and directed them upon
Lerida.

Thus much I have thought it necessary to relate
about the agents, and now quitting that subject, I
shall narrate

THE OPERATIONS OF THE SPANISH ARMIES IMME-
DIATELY AFTER THE BATTLE OF BAYLEN.

When that victory caused Joseph to abandon
Madrid, the patriotic troops, guided by the caprice

of the generals, moved in a variety of directions, without any fixed object in view, and without the slightest concert; all persons seemed to imagine that the war was at an end, and that rejoicing and triumph alone ought to occupy the minds of good Spaniards.

The Murcian and Valencian army separated. General Llamas, with twelve thousand infantry, and a few cavalry, took the road to Madrid, and arrived there before any of the other generals. St. Marc, a Fleming by birth, with greater propriety, carried the Valencians to the relief of Zaragoza. On the road he joined his forces with those of the baron de Versage, and the united troops, amounting to sixteen thousand, entered Zaragoza on the 15th, one day after Verdier and Lefebre had broken up the siege and retired to Tudela, leaving their heavy guns and many stores behind them; they were pursued by the Valencians and Aragonese, but on the 19th their cavalry turned and defeated the Spanish advanced guard. On the 20th Lefebre abandoned Tudela, and took a position at Milagro. On the 21st, St. Marc and Versage occupied Tudela, and the peasantry of the valleys, encouraged by the approach of a regular army, and by the successful defence of Zaragoza, assembled on the left flank of the French, and threatened their communications. Meanwhile Palafox gave himself up to festivity and rejoicing, and did not begin to repair the defences of Zaragoza until the end of the month; he also Cavallero. assumed supreme authority, and in various ways discovered inordinate and foolish presumption, decreeing, among other acts, that no Aragonese should be liable to the punishment of death for any crime.

The army of Andalusia was the most efficient

body of men in arms throughout Spain, it contained
thirty thousand regular troops, provided with a good
train of artillery and flushed with recent victory;
yet it was constrained to remain idle by the junta
of Seville, who detained it to secure a supremacy
over the other juntas of Andalusia, and even brought
back a part to assist at an ostentatious triumph in
that city. It was not until a full month after the
capitulation of Dupont, that Castaños made his entry
into the capital, at the head of a single division of
seven thousand men ; another of the same force was
left at Toledo, and the rest of his army quartered
at Puerto del Rey, St. Helena, and Carolina, in the
Sierra Morena.

Of the Estremaduran army the infantry was at
first composed only of new levies, but it was afterwards strengthened by some battalion of the Walloon and Royal Guards; and supplied by sir Hew
Dalrymple with every needful equipment. Following the terms of a treaty between the juntas of
Badajoz and Seville, the cavalry, four thousand
strong, was to be given to Castaños, but, Cuesta
excepted, no other general had any horsemen. This
cavalry was useless in Estremadura, yet orders and
entreaties and the interference of sir Hew Dalrymple, alike failed to make Galluzzo send it either to
the capital or to Blake ; nor would he, as we have
seen, desist from his pretended siege of La-Lyppe,
although it delayed the evacuation of Portugal.
Meanwhile the Spanish captives, released by the
convention of Cintra, were clothed, armed, and
sent to Catalonia in British transports, which also
carried ten thousand musquets, with ammunition,
for the Catalans.

It has been before stated, that one thousand five

hundred Spaniards, commanded by the marquis of Valladeras, co-operated with the Portuguese during the campaign of Vimiero; they never penetrated beyond Guarda, and being destitute of money, were reduced to great distress, for they could not subsist where they were, nor yet march away: sir Hew, by a timely advance of ten thousand dollars, relieved them, and Valladeras joined Blake, when, after the defeat of Rio Seco, that general had separated from Cuesta, and sheltered himself from the pursuit of Bessieres in the mountains behind Astorga. Blake's reserve division had not been engaged in that battle, and the resources of the province, aided by the succours from England, were sufficient to place him again at the head of thirty thousand infantry. Hence, when Bessieres retired after the defeat of Baylen, Blake occupied Leon, Astorga, and the pass of Manzanal; and as he dared not enter the plains without cavalry, the junta of Castille and Leon, then at Ponteferrada, ordered Cuesta, who had one thousand dragoons at Arevalo, to transfer them to the Gallician army. Instead of obeying, the arbitrary old man, exasperated by his defeat, and his quarrel with Blake, retired to Salamanca, collected and armed ten thousand peasants, annulled the proceedings of the junta, and menaced the members with punishment for resisting his authority as captain-general. On the other hand, Blake protected them, and while the generals disputed, three thousand French cavalry, descending the Douro, scoured the plains, and raised contributions in face of both their armies.

Sir H. Dalrymple's Papers. MSS.

Doyle's Letters.

Mr Stuart's Correspondence.

Finally, Blake, finding the obstinacy of Cuesta invincible, quitted his cantonments early in September, and

skirting the plains on the north-east, carried his army
by forced marches to the Moñtana St. Ander, a rugged district, dividing Biscay from the Asturias. The
junta of the latter province had received enormous
and very timely succours from England, but made
no exertions answerable to the amount of the assistance granted, or to the strength and importance of
the district ; eighteen thousand men were said to be
in arms, but only ten thousand were promised to
Blake, and but eight thousand joined his army.

CHAP.
I.

1808.
August.

Capt.
Carrol's
Letters.

In Catalonia the war was conducted by both sides
without much connexion, or dependance on the
movements of the main armies, and at this period
it had little influence on the general plan of campaign. Thus it appears, that one month after the
capitulation of Dupont, only nineteen thousand
infantry without cavalry, and those under the command of more than one general, were collected at
Madrid ; that only sixteen thousand men were in
line upon the Ebro, and that the remainder of the
Spanish armies, exclusive of that in Catalonia,
computed at eleven thousand men, were many days'
march from the enemy, and from one another ; that
the chiefs, at discord with their respective juntas,
and at variance among themselves, were inactive,
or, as in the case of Galluzzo, doing mischief.

These feeble and dilatory operations of the armies,
were partly owing to the inaptitude of the generals,
but the principal causes were the unbounded vanity,
arrogance, and selfishness of the local governments,
among whom the juntas of Gallicia and Seville were
remarkable for their ambition. The time which
should have been passed in concerting measures for
pushing the victory of Baylen, was spent by them
in devising schemes to ensure the permanency of

BOOK
III.
—————
1808.
August.
their own power, and the money and resources, both of England and Spain, were applied to further this pernicious object; in every part of the country a spirit of interested violence prevailed, the ardour of patriotism was chilled, and the exertions of sensible men were rendered nugatory, or served as a signal for their own destruction.

The argument to be drawn from this state of affairs is conclusive against the policy of Joseph's retreat. Without drafting a man from the garrisons of Pampeluna and St. Sebastian; without interfer- Appendix, No. 6. ing with the moveable columns employed on the communications of Biscay and Navarre, that monarch drew together about fifty thousand good troops, in twenty days after he had abandoned his capital. At the head of such a force, or even of two-thirds of it, he might have bid defiance to the inactive, half-organized, and scattered Spanish armies, and it was so necessary to have maintained himself in Madrid, that scarcely any disproportion of numbers should have induced him to abandon it without an effort; but the disaster of Dupont had created in Joseph's mind a respect for Spanish prowess, while from his sagacious brother it only drew the following observation: ' *The whole of the* Appendix, No. 4. *Spanish forces are not capable of beating twenty-five thousand French in a reasonable position.*' The error of abandoning the capital would, if the Spaniards had been capable of pursuing any general plan of action, been fatal; but the stone of Cadmus had been cast among them, and the juntas, turning upon one another in hate, forgot the common enemy.

Ferdinand was now again proclaimed king of Spain, and the pomp and rejoicing, attendant on this event, put an end to all business, except that of intrigue. Castaños assumed the title of captain-general of Madrid ; a step which seems to have been taken by him, partly to forward his being appointed generalissimo, and partly with a view to emancipate himself from the injurious control of the Seville junta ; for, although the authority of the captains-general had been superseded in most of the provinces by the juntas, it was not universally the case. He expected, and with reason, to be appointed generalissimo of the Spanish armies, but he was of an indolent disposition, and it was manifest that until a central and supreme government was establsihed, such a salutary measure would not be adopted. In the mean time, the council of Castille, although not generally popular with the people, and hated by the juntas, was accepted as the provisional head of the state in the capital ; yet its authority was merely nominal, and the necessity of showing some front to the enemy seems to have been the only link of connexion between the Spanish armies.

The evil consequences flowing from this want of unity were soon felt.   Scarcely had the French quitted Madrid, when the people of Biscay prepared to rise, and such an event, prudently conducted and well supported, would have been of incalculable advantage, but the nicest arrangement, and the utmost prudence, were necessary to insure success ; for the Biscayans had neither arms nor ammunition, the French were close to them, and the nearest Spanish force was the feeble Asturian levy. A previous junction of Blake's army with the latter was indispensable ; that once effected, and due preparation made, the insurrection of Biscay, protected by forty thousand regular troops, and

supplied from the sea-board with money and stores,
would have forced the French to abandon the Ebro
or to fight a battle, which Blake might have risked,
provided that the Andalusian, Murcian, Valencian,
and Aragonese troops assembling about Tudela,
were prepared to move at the same time against the
left flank of the enemy. In every point of view it
was an event pregnant with important consequences, and the impatience of the Biscayans
should have been restrained rather than encouraged ; yet the duke of Infantado, colonel Doyle,
and others, at Madrid, made strenuous efforts to
hasten the explosion, and the crude manner in
which they conducted this serious affair is exposed
in the following extracts from colonel Doyle's
despatches :—

'I proposed to general Blake that he should
send officers to Biscay to stir up the people there,
and into the Asturias to beg that, of their 15,000
men, 8,000 might be pushed into Biscay to Bilbao,
to assist the people, who were all ready, and only
waited for arms and ammunition, for both of which
I wrote to Mr. Hunter at Gihon, and learned from
him that he had sent a large supply of both, and
some money to Bilbao, where already 14,000 men
had enrolled themselves. The remainder of the
Asturians I begged might instantly occupy the
passes from Castille into the Asturias and Biscay,
that is to say, from Reynosa in the direction of
Bilbao.' Some days after he says, 'My measures
in Biscay and Asturias have perfectly succeeded ;
the reinforcements of arms, ammunition and men
(5,000 stand of arms, and ammunition in proportion), have reached Bilbao in safety, and the Asturians have taken possession of the passes I

pointed out, so that we are all safe in that part of
the world.'

In this fancied state of security affairs remained
until the 16th of August; Blake was still in the
mountains of Gallicia, but the English succours arrived in the port of Bilbao, and the explosion took
place. General Merlin, with three thousand grenadiers, immediately came down on the unfortunate
Biscayans, Bilbao was taken, and to use the gloomy
expression of king Joseph, ' the fire of insurrection
was quenched with the blood of twelve hundred
men.' Fortunately, the stores were not landed, and
the vessels escaped from the river. Thus, at a
blow, one of the principal resources which Blake
had a right to calculate upon in his future operations was destroyed; and although the number
admitted by the Spaniards to have fallen was less
than the above quotation implies, the spirit of
resistance was severely checked, and the evil was
unmixed and deplorable. This unfortunate event,
however, created little or no sensation beyond the
immediate scene of the catastrophe; triumphs and
rejoicings occupied the people of Madrid and
Zaragoza, and it is difficult to say how long the
war would have been neglected, if Palafox had not
been roused by the re-appearance of a French corps,
which retook Tudela, and pushed on to the vicinity
of Zaragoza itself.

This movement took place immediately after the
expedition against Bilbao, it was intended to suppress the insurrection of the valleys, and to clear the
left flank of the French army. Palafox thus roughly
aroused, wrote intemperately to the council of Castille, ordering that all the troops in the capital should
be forwarded to the Ebro, and menacing the members

Appendix,
No. 8.

Whitting-
ham's
Letters.
MSS.

personally for the delay which had already occurred. Being a young man without any weight
of character, and his remonstrances founded only
upon his own danger, and not supported by any
general plan or clear view of affairs, the presumptuous tone of his letters gave general offence: he
chiefly aimed at Castaños, who was not under his
command, and moreover, the junta of Seville refused to pay, or to subsist the Andalusian army, if
it moved beyond the capital before a central
government should be established. But the same
junta resorted to every kind of intrigue, to retard, if
not entirely to prevent the execution of the latter measure. It was, however, necessary to do something,
and a council of all the generals commanding armies
was held at Madrid on the 5th of September.
Castaños, Llamas, Cuesta, the duke of Infantado,
and some others assembled; Blake gave his proxy
to the duke, Palafox was represented by a colonel
of his own staff. Cuesta proposed that a commander-in-chief should be appointed, the others
were too jealous to adopt this proposal, yet
they agreed to pursue the following plan of
operations :—

Llamas, with the Murcians, to occupy Taranzona,
Agreda, and Borja. La-Peña, with the two divisions
of Andalusia already in the capital, to march by
Soria, and take possession of Logroña and Najera.
The other divisions of that army to follow in due
time, and when La-Peña should be established in
Logroña, Llamas was to advance to Cascante, Co-
rella, and Calahorra.

This united force was to be called the army of
the centre, and once securely fixed in its positions,
Palafox, under whose command St. Marc's division

acted, was to push forward to Sanguessa by the left bank of the Ebro, and thus turn the enemy on the Aragon river. In the mean time it was hoped that Blake would arrive at Palencia, and form his junction with the Asturians, and Cuesta promised to march upon Burgo del Osma, to fill up the space between Blake and the army of the centre. The head of La-Peña's column was to be at Soria on the 15th of September, and the junta confidently expected that this vicious plan, in which every sound military principle was violated, and the enemy's troops, considered with regard to position, as a fixed immoveable mass, would cause the total destruction of the French army: the only fear entertained was, that a hasty flight into France would save it from Spanish vengeance! And captain Whittingham, echoing the sentiments of the Spanish generals with reference to this plan, writes, ' As far as my poor judgment leads me, I am satisfied that if the French persist in maintaining their present position, we shall, in less than six weeks, have a second edition of the battle of Baylen !'

But to enable La-Peña and Llamas to march, pecuniary aid was requisite, there was a difficulty in raising money at Madrid, and the maritime provinces intercepted all the English supplies. In this dilemma, colonel Doyle drew bills upon the English treasury, and upon the government at Seville, making the latter payable out of two millions of dollars just transmitted to the junta through Mr. Duff. It is probable that such an unprincipled body would have dishonoured the bills, if, just before they were presented, major Cox had not remonstrated strongly upon the destitute condition of the army, and his representations, although at first

Sir Hew Dalrymple's Correspondence. Doyle's Letters. Cox's Do.

haughtily and evasively received, became effectual when the junta discovered that a plot against their lives, supposed to have been concocted at Madrid, was on the eve of execution : in fact, they had become hateful from their domineering insolence and selfishness, and the public feeling was strongly against them. Alarmed for the consequences, they sent off 200,000 dollars to Madrid, and published a manifesto, in which they inserted a letter, purporting to be from themselves to Castaños, dated on the 8th, and giving him full powers to act as he judged fitting for the public good. Their objects were to pacify the people, and to save their own dignity by appearing to have acted voluntarily, but Castaños published the letter in Madrid with its true date of the 11th, and then it became manifest, that to major Cox's remonstrance, and not to any sense of duty, this change of conduct was due.

Doyle's bills having been negotiated, the troops in the capital were put in motion, and 40,000 fresh levies were enrolled, yet the foresight and activity of Napoleon in disarming the country had been so effectual, that only 3,200 firelocks could be procured. A curious expedient then presented itself to the imagination of the duke of Infantado, and other leading persons in Madrid : colonel Doyle, at their desire, wrote to sir Hew Dalrymple, in the name of the supreme council, to request that *the firelocks of Junot's army, and the arms of the Portuguese people*, might be forwarded to the frontier, and from thence carried by post to the capital. And this novel proposition was made at a time when England had already transmitted to Spain 160,000 muskets, a supply considerably exceeding the

whole number of men organized throughout the
country. Fifty thousand of these arms had been sent
to Seville, where the junta shut them up in the arsenals, and left the armies defenceless ; for to neglect
or misuse real resources, and to fasten with avidity
upon the most extravagant projects, is peculiarly
Spanish. No other people could have thought of
asking for a neighbouring nation's arms at such
a conjuncture. No other than Spanish rulers
could have imagined the absurdity of supplying
their levies, momentarily expecting to fight upon
the Ebro, with the arms of a French army still
unconquered in Portugal. But this project was
only one among many proofs afforded at the time,
that Cervantes was as profound an observer as he
was a witty reprover of the extravagance of his
countrymen.

CHAPTER II.

INTERNAL POLITICAL TRANSACTIONS.

BOOK
III.

1808.

WITH the military affairs, thus mismanaged, the civil and political transactions proceeded step by step, and in the same crooked path. Short as the period was between the first breaking forth of the

MrStuart's
Letters.
Parlia-
mentary
Papers.

insurrection, and the arrival of Mr. Stuart at Coruña, it was sufficient to create disunion of the worst kind. The juntas of Leon, of the Asturias, and of Gallicia, were at open discord, and those provinces were again split into parties, hating each other with as much virulence as if they had been of a hundred years' growth. The money and other supplies sent by the English ministers were considered, by the authorities into whose hands they fell, as a peculiar donation to themselves, and appropriated accordingly. The junta of one province would not assist another with arms when there was a surplus, nor permit their troops to march against the enemy beyond the precincts of the particular

Ibid.

province in which they were first organized. The ruling power was in the hands of the provincial nobility and gentry, men of narrow contracted views, unused to business, proud, arrogant—as extreme ignorance suddenly clothed with authority will always be—and generally disposed to employ their newly acquired power in providing for their relations and dependants at the expense of the common cause, which with them was quite subor-

dinate to the local interests of their own particular CHAP. II.
province. A jealousy of their neighbours regulated
the proceedings of all the juntas, and the means
they resorted to for increasing their own, or de-
pressing a rival government's influence, were
equally characterised by absurdity and want of
principle.

The junta of Gallicia did their utmost to isolate
that province, as if with a view to a final separation
from Spain and a connexion with Portugal. They
complained, as of an injury, that the army of Estre- Mr Stuart's
madura had obeyed the orders of the junta of Letters. MS.
Seville, yet they formed an independent alliance
with the junta of Oporto, and sent troops, as we
have seen, under Valladeras, to aid the war in Portugal; but, at the same time, they refused to unite
in any common measure of defence with the provinces of Castille, until a formal treaty of alliance
between them was negotiated, signed, and ratified;
and their selfishness and incapacity created so
much disgust in their own district, that plots
were formed to overthrow their authority. The
bishop of Orense and the archbishop of St. Jago
were their decided enemies. The last-named prelate,
an intriguing man, secretly endeavoured to draw
Blake, with the army, into his views, and even wrote
to him to desire that he would lead the troops against
the government of Coruña; the junta having inter- Ibid.
cepted the letters, arrested the archbishop, yet their
own stability and personal safety were still so insecure, that many persons applied to Mr. Stuart to
aid in changing the form of government by force.
The Asturians were even worse; they refused to
assist Blake when his army was suffering, although
the stores required by him, and supplied by England,

were rotting in the harbours where they were first landed; money also, sent out in the Pluto frigate for the use of Leon, was detained at Gihon, and Leon itself never raised a single soldier for the cause. Thus, only two months after the first burst of the insurrection, corruption, intrigue, and faction, even to the verge of civil war, were raging in the northern parts of Spain.

Like passions being at work in the south, the same consequences followed.   The junta of Seville, still less scrupulous than that of Gallicia, made no secret of their ambitious views. They stifled all local publications, and even suppressed the public address of Florida Blanca, who, as president of the Murcian junta, had recommended the formation of a supreme central government; they wasted their time in vain and frivolous disputes, and, neglecting every concern of real importance, sacrificed the general welfare to views of private advantage and interest. They made promotions in the army without regard to public opinion or merit; they overlaid all real patriotism, and bestowed on their own creatures places of emolument, to the patronage of which they had not a legal right; they even usurped the royal prerogative of appointing canons in the church, and their cupidity equalled their ambition. They intercepted, as I have already related, the pecuniary supplies necessary to enable the army to act, and they complained that La Mancha and Madrid, in whose defence they said ' *their* troops were sacrificing themselves,' did not subsist and supply the force with Castaños.   Under the pretence of forming a nucleus for disciplining thirty thousand levies as a reserve, they retained five battalions at Seville, and, having by this draft weakened the army in the field, they neglected the

Appendix,
No.13, § 5.

Ibid.

Sir H. Dalrymple's Papers.
Coxe's Correspondence.

rest, and never raised a man. The canonries filled up by them had been vacant for several years, and the salaries attached to those offices had been appropriated to the public service; the junta now applied the money to their own and their creatures' emolument, and at one period they appear to have contemplated an open partition of the funds received from England among themselves. Against this flagitious junta also, the public indignation was rife. A plot was formed to assassinate the members; the municipal authorities remonstrated with them, the archbishop of Toledo protested against their conduct, the junta of Grenada refused to acknowledge their supremacy; and yet so great was their arrogance, so unprincipled their ambition, that the decided and resolute opposition of Castaños alone prevented them from commencing a civil war, by marching the victorious army of Baylen against the refractory Grenadans. Such was the real state of Spain, and such the patriotism of the juntas, who were at this time filling Europe with the sound of their own praise.

In the northern parts, Mr. Stuart endeavoured to reduce the chaos of folly and wickedness to some degree of order, and to produce that unity of design and action, without which, it was impossible to resist the mighty adversary that threatened the independence of the Peninsula. He judged that to abate the conflicting passions of the moment, a supreme authority, upon which the influence of Great Britain could be brought to bear with full force, was indispensable; and that to convoke the ancient cortes of the realm was the most certain and natural method of drawing the strength and energy of the nation into one compact mass; but there Napoleon again

CHAP.
II.

1808.
August.

Sir H. Dalrymple's Papers.
Coxe's Correspondence.
Appendix, No. 13, §5.

Ibid.

interfered, for by an able distribution of the French
forces, all direct communication between the northern and southern provinces was intercepted. Bessieres, Dupont, and Moncey at that time occupied
a circle round Madrid, and would have prevented the
local governments of the north from uniting with those
of the southern, if they had been inclined to do so.

A union of deputies from the nearest provinces,
to be called the northern cortes, then suggested itself to Mr. Stuart as a preliminary step, which would
ensure the convocation of a general assembly when
such a measure should become practicable; accordingly he strenuously urged its adoption, but his
efforts, at first, produced no good results. It was in
vain that he represented the danger of remaining in
a state of anarchy, when so many violent passions
were excited, and such an enemy was in the heart
of the country. It was in vain that he pointed out
the difficulties that the want of a supreme authority
fastened on the intercourse with the British cabinet,
which could not enter into separate relations with
every provincial junta. The Spaniards, finding that
the supplies were not withheld, that their reputation
for patriotism was not lowered in England by actions
which little merited praise; finding, in short, that
the English cabinet was weak enough to gorge their
cupidity, flatter their vanity, and respect their folly,
assented to all Mr. Stuart's reasoning, but forwarded
none of his propositions, and continued to nourish
the disorders that were destroying the common
cause.

The jarring interests which agitated the northern
provinces were not even subdued by the near approach of danger; the result of the battle of Rio
Seco rather inflamed than allayed the violence of

Stuart's
Corre-
spondence.
Parlia-
mentary
Papers.

party feeling, and if Bessieres had not been checked by the disaster of Dupont, he would have encountered few obstacles in establishing Joseph's authority in Gallicia and Old Castille. For the enthusiasm of those provinces never rose to a great pitch, and as Bessieres was prepared to use address as well as force, he would have found support amongst the factions, and the reinforcements continually arriving from France would have enabled him to maintain his acquisition. The ability of the emperor's dispositions would then have been apparent; for while Bessieres held Gallicia, and Dupont hung on the southern frontier of Portugal with twenty-five thousand men, Junot could have securely concentrated his army in the neighbourhood of Lisbon, and have rendered an English disembarkation on the coast nearly impracticable.

Napoleon's combinations were overturned by the disgraceful capitulation of Baylen, and when Joseph evacuated Madrid a fresh impulse was given to the spirit of the people; but, unfortunately for Spain, as a wider scope for ambition was obtained, the workings of self-interest increased, fresh parties sprung up, and new follies and greater absurdities stifled the virtue of the country, and produced irremediable confusion, ending in ruin. The fact of Dupont's capitulation was made known to the council of Castille before King Joseph was informed of it, and the council, foreseeing all the consequences of such an event, immediately refused, as I have already related, to promulgate officially his accession to the throne. The king permitted this act of disobedience to pass without much notice, for he was naturally averse to violence, and neither he, nor his brother Napoleon, did at any period of the contest for Spain

Azanza
and
O'Farril,
Mem.

constrain a Spaniard to accept or retain office under
the intrusive government. Joseph went further. Before he abandoned Madrid, he released his ministers
from their voluntary oath of allegiance to himself,
leaving them free to choose their party once more.
Don Pedro Cevallos and the marquis of Pinuelo
seized the occasion to change with, what appeared
to them, changing fortune; the five others remained
steadfast, preferring an ameliorated government,
under a foreign prince, to what they believed to be
a hopeless struggle, but which, if successful, they
knew must end in a degrading native despotism:
perhaps, also, a little swayed by their dislike to
England, and by the impossibility of obtaining that
influence among their countrymen, which, under
other circumstances, their talents and characters
would have ensured.

The boldness of the council of Castille was not
publicly chastised by the intruding monarch, yet
secretly he punished the members by a dexterous
stroke of policy. General Grouchy wrote to Castaños, saying, that as circumstances required the presence of the French troops in another quarter, he
invited the Spanish general to take immediate possession of Madrid, for the preservation of public
tranquillity. This was construed to mean the entire
evacuation of Spain, and a report so congenial to
the vanity and indolence of the Spaniards was greedily received; it contributed to the subsequent
supineness of the nation in preparing for its defence,
and Joseph, by appealing to Castaños, and affecting
to treat the council of Castille as a body who had
lost all influence with the nation, gave a handle to
its enemies, which the latter failed not to lay hold
of. The juntas dreaded that the influence of the

council would destroy their own. That of Gallicia would not even communicate with them,
but affirmed that, individually, the members were
attached to the French, and that, collectively, they
had been the most active instrument of the usurper's
government. The junta of Seville endeavoured not
only to destroy the authority of the existing members, but to annul the body, as an acknowledged
tribunal of the state. This proscribed council, however, was not wanting to itself, the individuals composing it did not hesitate to seize the reins of government the moment the French had departed ; and
the prudence with which they preserved tranquillity
in the capital, preventing all re-action, while it
proves that they were not without merit, forms a
striking contrast to the conduct of the provincial
juntas, under whose savage sway every kind of
excess was committed, and even encouraged.

Aware of the hostility they had to encounter, the
members of the council lost no time in forming a
party to support themselves. Don Arias Mon y
Velarde, dean or president for the time being, wrote
a circular letter to the local juntas, pointing out the
necessity of establishing a central and supreme
power, and proposing that deputies from each province, or nation, as they were sometimes called,
should repair to Madrid, and there concert with the
council the best mode of carrying such a measure
into effect. If this proposal had been adopted, all
power would inevitably have fallen into the hands
of the proposers. Confessedly the first public body
in the state, and well acquainted with the forms of
business, the council must necessarily have had a
preponderating influence in the assembly of dele-
gates ; and it appeared so reasonable that it should

BOOK
III.
────
1808.
August. take the lead, when an efficient authority was required to direct the violence of the people in a useful channel, before the moment of safety was passed,
that all the juntas trembled at the prospect of losing
their misused power. The minor ones submitted, and
agreed to send deputies, the stronger and more
ambitious felt that subtlety would avail more than
open opposition to the project.

The council followed up this blow by the publi-
cation of a manifesto, containing an accurate detail
of the events of the revolution, defending the part
taken by its members, and claiming a renewal of the
confidence formerly reposed in them by the nation.
MrStuart's
Correspon-
dence. This important state paper was so ably written, that
a large party, especially at Valladolid, was immediately formed in favour of its authors, and the junta
of Seville were so sensible of the increasing influence of the council, that they intercepted a copy of
Coxe's
Correspon-
dence.
Appendix,
No. 13, §5. this manifesto, addressed to sir Hew Dalrymple, and
strictly suppressed all writings favourable to the
formation of a supreme central authority, nothing
they dreaded more. But it was no longer possible to
resist the current, which had set strongly in favour
of such a measure ; the juntas, however they might
oppose its progress, could not openly deny the propriety of it, and in every province, individuals of
MrStuart's
Correspon-
dence. talent and consideration called for a change in the
Hydra polity, which oppressed the country, and was
inefficient against the enemy. Every British func-
tionary, civil or military, in communication with the
Spaniards, also urged the necessity of concentrating
the executive power.
Ibid.   All the provincial juntas were become universally odious ; some of the generals alone, who had
suddenly risen to command under their rule, were

favourable to them. Palafox was independent, as
a captain-general, whose power was confirmed by
success; Castaños openly declared that he would
no longer serve under their control; Cuesta was
prepared to put them down by force, and to re-establish the royal audienzas and the authority of the
captains-general according to the old practice. In
this state of affairs, the retreat of Bessieres' army
having freed the communication with the southern
parts, removed all excuse for procrastination, and
the juntas of Gallicia, Castille, Leon, and the Asturias, giving way to the unceasing remonstrances of
Mr. Stuart, at his instance agreed to meet in cortes,
at Lugo; Gallicia, however, first insisted upon a
formal ratification of that treaty with Castille which
has been already mentioned.

When the moment of assembling arrived, the Asturians, without assigning any reason, refused to
fulfil the engagement they had entered into, and
the three remaining juntas held the session without
them. The bishop of Orense, and the junta of
Gallicia, were prepared to assert the supremacy of
that province over the others. But the Baily Valdez
of Castille, an able and disinterested man, being
chosen president of the convocation, proposed, on
the first day of assembly, that deputies should be
appointed to represent the three provinces in a supreme junta, to be assembled in some central place,
for the purpose of convoking the ancient cortes of
the whole kingdom, according to the old forms,
and of settling the administration of the interior,
and the future succession to the throne. This proposition was immediately carried by the superior
number of the Castillians and Leonese, although
the bishop of Orense protested against it, and the

Gallician members strongly opposed an arrangement,
by which their province was placed on the same
footing as others ; a glaring injustice, they urged,
when the numbers of the Gallician army were taken
into consideration, for the local feeling of ambition
was uppermost, and the general cause disregarded.
The other party answered, with great force, that the
Gallician army was paid, armed, and clothed by
England, and fed by Castille and Leon.

Meanwhile the influence of the council of Castille
greatly increased, and the junta of Seville, quickened
by fear, took the lead in directing what they could
not prevent ; the convocation of the cortes they
knew would be fatal to their own existence. Wherefore, in a public letter, addressed to the junta of
Gallicia, dated one day previous to the circular of
don Arias Mon, but evidently written after the
receipt of the latter, they opposed the assembling
of the cortes, on the ground that it was ' the prerogative of the king to convoke that body ; and if
it was called together by any other authority, the
provinces would not obey ;' ' there would be no
unanimity.' The futility of this argument is apparent ; the question was not one of form, but of expediency. If the nation was in favour of such a
step, and after facts proved that the people were
not opposed to it, the same necessity which constituted the right of the junta to declare war against
the French, another prerogative of the monarch,
would have sufficed to legalize the convocation of
the national assembly. But their sole object was
to preserve their own power. They maintained that
the juntas, being chosen by the nation, were the only
legitimate depositaries of authority, that to members
of their own bodies only could any of that autho-

rity be delegated ; then adopting the suggestion contained in the letter of Arias Mon, they proposed that two deputies from each supreme junta should repair, not to Madrid, but to Ciudad Real, or Almagro, and at the moment of meeting be in fact constituted governors-general of the kingdom, and as such obeyed ; nevertheless, the local governments were, with due subordination to the central junta, to retain and exercise in their own provinces all the authority with which they had already invested themselves. Thus they had only to choose subservient deputies, and their power would be more firmly fixed than before; and this arrangement would, doubtless, have been adopted by the junta of Gallicia, had not the rapidity with which Valdez carried his proposition, prevented that cause of discord from being added to the numerous disputes which already distracted the northern provinces.

Mr. Stuart proceeded to Madrid, and, wherever he passed, found the same violence of local party feeling, the same disgust at the conduct of the oligarchical provincial governments. Pride, vanity, corruption, and improvidence, were everywhere obtrusively visible. The dispute between Blake and Cuesta, which was raging at the period of the battle of Rio Seco, a period when division was most hurtful to the military operations, was now allayed between the generals ; yet their political partizans waged war with more bitterness than ever, as if with the intent to do the greatest possible mischief, by continuing the feud among the civil branches of the government, when union was most desirable in that quarter. The seeds of division had taken deep root. On the one side was the Baily Valdez, deputy to the

MrStuart's
Corre-
spondence.

supreme junta, on the other Cuesta; a man not
to be offended with impunity when he had power
to punish, for he was haughty and incredibly obstinate. He had been president of the council of
Castille, and he was captain-general of Castille
and Leon when the insurrection first broke out;
but disliking all revolutionary movements, although
as inimical to a foreign domination as any of his
countrymen, he endeavoured to repress the public
effervescence, and to maintain the tranquillity of the
country at the risk of losing his life as a traitor.

Cuesta was an honest man, insomuch as the Spanish and French interests being put in competition,
he would aid the former, yet, between his country's
cause and his own passions, he was not honest.
He disliked, and with reason, the sway of the local
juntas, and, with consistency of opinion, wished
to preserve the authority of the captains-general
and the royal audienzas, both of which had been
overturned by the establishment of those petty governments. But, sullen and ferocious in his temper,
he supported his opinion with an authority and
severity which had no guide save his own will; and
he was prepared, if an opportunity offered, to exercise military influence over the supreme, as well
as over the subordinate juntas. He had himself
appointed one for Leon and Castille as a sort of
council, subordinate to the authority of the captain-general ; yet, after the battle of Rio Seco, the
members fled to Ponteferrada, assumed the supreme
authority, and, putting themselves under the protection of his enemy Blake, disregarded Cuesta's
orders, and commanded him, their superior, to deliver up his cavalry to the former general. Upon
this he annulled all their proceedings at Pon-

Appendix,
No. 13. §6.

teferrada, and now asserting that the election of Valdez and his colleagues was void, as being contrary to the existing laws, directed new juntas to be assembled in a manner more conformable to existing usages, and a fresh election to be made.

His mandates were disregarded ; Valdez and the other deputies proceeded in defiance of them towards the place appointed for the assembly of the central and supreme government. Cuesta, in return, without hesitation, abandoned the operations of the campaign, which, in the council of war held at Madrid, he had promised to aid, and falling back to Segovia with twelve thousand men, seized the deputies, and shut up Valdez a close prisoner in the tower of that place, declaring his intention to try him by a military tribunal for disobedience. And such was the disorder of the times, that he was not without plausible arguments to justify this act of stubborn violence, for the original election of members to form the junta of Castille and Leon had been anything but legal ; several districts had been omitted altogether in the representation of those kingdoms, many deputies had been chosen by the city of Leon alone, and Valdez was named president, although neither a native nor a proprietor, and for those reasons ineligible to be a deputy at all : the kingdom of Leon also had appointed representatives for those districts in Castille which were under the domination of the French, and when the enemy retired, the Castillians in vain demanded a more equitable arrangement.

However, amidst all this confusion and violence, the plan of uniting to form a central government gained ground all over the kingdom. Seville, Catalonia, Aragon, Murcia, Valencia, and Asturias, appointed their deputies, and although fresh disputes relative to the place of assembly arose, after some time it was agreed to meet at Aranjuez. This royal residence was chosen contrary to the wishes of many, and notably against the opinion of Jovellanos, an eloquent person, and of great reputation for integrity, but of a pertinacious temper, unsuitable to the times : he urged, that the capital was the meetest spot, and he was answered, that the turbulent disposition of the inhabitants of Madrid would impede the formation of a government, and that the same objection would exist against the choice of any other large town. It is extraordinary that such an argument should be held in Spain at a moment when the people were, in all the official and public papers, represented as perfectly enthusiastic and united in one common sacred pursuit, and in the British parliament were denominated the ' universal Spanish nation !'

To seek thus for protection in a corner, instead of manfully and confidently identifying themselves with the people, and courting publicity, augured ill for the intentions of the deputies, nor was the augury belied by the event. The junta of Seville, who had so bitterly reviled the council of Castille,
for having partially submitted to the usurper, had, notwithstanding, chosen for their own deputies, don Vincent Hore, a known creature of the prince of peace, and the count de Tilly Guzman, who was under the stigma of a judicial sentence for robbery. Hore declined the appointment, but Tilly, braving the public disgust, repaired to Aranjuez, and his place as resident with the head-quarters of the Andalusian army was filled up by Miñiano, another member of the junta, who received an enormous

salary for performing the mischievous duties of that office. The instructions given by the different provinces to the deputies were to confine their deliberations and votes to such subjects as they should, from time to time, receive directions from their constituents to treat of, and Seville again took the lead in this fraudulent policy; and when public indignation, and the remonstrances of some right-minded persons, obliged the juntas of that town and of Valencia, to rescind these instructions, both substituted secret orders of the same tenor. In short, the greater part of the deputies were the mere tools of the juntas, agents, watching over the interests of their employers, and, conscious of demerit, anxious to hide themselves from the just indignation of the public until they had consolidated their power; hence the dislike to large towns, and the intrigues for fixing the government at Aranjuez. Count Florida Blanca, a man in the last stage of decrepitude, was chosen first president in rotation for three months, and all idea of forming an independent executive was abandoned; for when Jovellanos proposed to establish a regency selected from their own body, his plan was rejected on the ground that the members were not authorised to delegate their powers even to one another: it was palpable that the juntas had merely appeared to comply with the public wish for a central government, but were determined not to part with one iota of their own real power.

The first act of authority executed by the assembly, was a necessary assertion of its own dignity, which had been violated in the case of Valdez. Cuesta, who was personally unpopular, and feared

Appendix,
No. 13, §6.

by the central, as well as by the provincial juntas,
was summoned to release his captive, and to repair
to Aranjuez, that cognizance might be taken of his
proceedings; he was at the same time denounced by
the juntas of Castille and Leon as a traitor, and exposed to great danger of popular commotion. At
MrStuart's
Corre-
spondence.
Colonel
Graham's
Ditto. first, he haughtily repelled the interference of Castaños and Florida Blanca, yet finally he was forced
to bend, and after a sharp correspondence with Mr.
Stuart, whose influence was usefully employed to
strengthen the central government, he released his
prisoner, and quitting the command of the army,
appeared at Aranjuez. No formal proceedings were
had upon the case, but after much mutual recrimi-
nation, Valdez was admitted to the exercise of his
functions, and the old general was detained at the
seat of government, a kind of state prisoner at large,
until, for the misfortune of his country, he was, by
subsequent events, once more placed at the head of
an army. About this time lord William Bentinck
joined Mr. Stuart at Madrid. Perfectly coinciding
in opinions, they laboured earnestly to give a favourable turn to affairs, by directing the attention of the
central junta to the necessity of military preparations, and active exertion for defence; but the
picture of discord, folly, and improvidence exhibited
in the provinces, was here displayed in more glaring
colours. The lesser tribunals being called upon to
acknowledge the authority of the assembled deputies, readily obeyed, and the council of Castille, reluctant to submit, yet too weak to resist, endeavoured
to make terms, but was forced to an unconditional
submission. A good management of the revenue,
a single chief for the army, and, above all, the total

suppression of the provincial juntas, were the three
next objects of public anxiety. With respect to the
army, no doubt was at first entertained that Castanos would be appointed commander-in-chief, his
services entitled him to the office, and his general
moderation and conciliating manners fitted him for
it at a time when so much jealousy was to be
soothed, and so many interests to be reconciled.
The past expenditure of the money received from
England was also a subject of great importance,
and it was loudly required that an account of its
disbursement should be demanded of the local
juntas, and a surrender of the residue instantly enforced.

These just expectations lasted but a short time.
Scarcely were the deputies assembled, when every
prospect of a vigorous administration was blasted.
Dividing themselves into sections, answering in
number to the departments of state under the old
king, they appointed a secretary not chosen from
their own body, to each, and declared all and every
one of these sections supreme and independent,
having equal authority.

Florida Blanca informed Mr. Stuart and lord
William Bentinck that Castaños would be named
generalissimo, and the two last named were even
directed to confer upon the plan of campaign for the
British troops, then marching from Portugal to the
assistance of the Spaniards. The necessity of having
a single chief at the head of the armies was imperious, and acknowledged by every individual, military or civil, yet such was the force of jealousy, and
so stubborn were the tools of the different juntas,
that in despite of the exertions of Mr. Stuart and
lord William Bentinck, and the influence of the

British cabinet, the generals were all confirmed in
their separate and independent commands. The
old and miserable system of the Dutch deputies
in Marlborough's time, and of the commissaries
of the convention during the French revolution,
was partially revived; and the English government were totally disregarded, at a time when
it had supplied Spain with two hundred thousand
muskets, clothing, ammunition of all kinds, in proportion, and sixteen millions of dollars. Such ample
succours, if rightly managed, ought to have secured unlimited influence; but as the benefits came
through one set of persons, and the demands through
another, the first were taken as of right, the last
unheeded, and thus the resources of Great Britain
were wasted without materially improving the condition of Spain. The armies were destitute, the
central government was without credit, and notwithstanding the ample subsidies, had contracted a
large debt; yet with an insolence of tone appertaining rather to conquerors dictating terms, than
to grateful allies demanding further assistance, they
required from England an instant gift of ten millions of dollars, and stores to an amount that would
have sufficed a well-governed army for many years.

The provincial juntas were still permitted to retain
their power within their own districts, and the
greatest timidity marked all the proceedings of the
central government in relation to those obnoxious
bodies. Attentive, however, to their own interests,
the members of the supreme junta decreed, 1st. that
their persons should be inviolable; 2d. that the president should have the title of highness, with a salary
of 25,000 crowns a-year; 3d. that each of the deputies, taking the title of excellency, should have a

Stuart's
Correspon-
dence.
Lord W.
Bentinck's
Ditto.

yearly salary of 5000 crowns.; lastly, that the col-
lective body should be addressed by the title of
majesty. Thinking that they were then sufficiently
confirmed in power to venture upon a public entry
into Madrid, they made preparations to ensure a
favourable reception from the populace; that is, they
resolved to declare a general amnesty, to lower the
duties on tobacco, and to fling large sums among the
people during the procession; and in the midst of all Lord W.
Bentinck's
this pomp and vanity, the presence of the enemy on Correspondence.
the soil was scarcely remembered, and the details of Appendix,
No. 13, §6.
business were totally neglected. This last was a pro-
minent evil which extended to the lowest branches
of administration; self-interest, indeed, produced
abundance of activity, but every department, almost
every man, seemed struck with torpor when the
public welfare was at stake, and withal, an astonishing presumption was common to the highest and
the lowest.

To supply the place of a generalissimo, a council,
or board of general officers was projected, on whose
reports the junta proposed to regulate the military
operations. Castaños was destined to be president,
but some difficulty arising relative to the appointment
of the other members, the execution of the plan was Lord W.
Bentinck's
deferred, with the characteristic remark, 'that when Correspondence.
the enemy was driven across the frontier, Castaños
would have leisure to take his seat.' The idea of a
defeat, the possibility of failure, never entered their
minds; the government, evincing neither apprehension, nor activity, nor foresight, were contented if
the people believed the daily falsehoods they promulgated relative to the enemy, and the people, equally
presumptuous, were content to be so deceived; in
fine, all the symptoms of a ruined cause were already

visible to discerning eyes. The armies neglected
even to nakedness; the soldier's constancy under
privations cruelly absurd; disunion, cupidity, incapacity, in the higher orders; the patriotic ardour
visibly abating among the lower classes; the rulers
grasping, improvident, boasting; the enemy powerful, the people insubordinate, the fighting men
without arms or bread; as a whole, and in all its
parts, the government unfitted for its task; the system, cumbrous and ostentatious, was, to use the comprehensive words of Mr. Stuart, ' neither calculated
to inspire courage nor to increase enthusiasm.'

The truth of this picture will be recognized by
men who are yet living, and whose exertions were
as incessant as unavailing to remedy those evils at
the time; it will be recognized by the friends of a
great man, who fell a victim to the folly and base
intrigues of the day; it will be recognized by that
general and army, who, winning their own unaided
way through Spain, found that to trust Spaniards
in war was to lean against a broken reed. To others
it may appear exaggerated, for without having seen,
it is difficult to believe the extent of a disorder that
paralyzed the enthusiasm of a whole people.

EXTERNAL POLITICAL RELATIONS OF SPAIN.

At first these were of necessity confined to England, Sicily, and Portugal; the rest of the Old
World was either subject to Buonaparte or directly
under his influence, but in the New World it was
different. The Brazils, after the emigration of the
royal family of Braganza, became important under
every point of view, and relations were established
between the junta and that court, that afterwards,
under the cortez, created considerable interest, and

threatened serious embarrassments to the operations
of the duke of Wellington. The ultra-marine possessions of Spain were also, of course, a matter of great anxiety to both sides, and Napoleon's activity balanced the natural preponderance of the mother-country. The slowness of the local juntas, or rather their want of capacity to conduct such an affair, gave the enemy a great advantage, and it was only owing to the exertions of Mr. Stuart in the MrStuart's Correspondence, MS. Sir Hew Dalrymple north, and of sir Hew Dalrymple and lord Collingwood in the south, that, after the insurrection broke out, vessels were despatched to South America to confirm the colonists in their adherence to Spain, and to arrange the mode of securing the resources of those great possessions for the parent state. The hold which Spain retained over her colonies was, however, very slight; her harsh restrictive system had long before weakened the attachment of the South Americans, and the expedition of Miranda, although unsuccessful, had kindled a fire which could not be extinguished; it was apparent to all able statesmen, that Spain must relinquish her arbitrary mode of governing, or relinquish the colonies altogether; the insurrection at home only rendered this more certain, every argument, every public manifesto put forth in Europe, to animate the Spaniards against foreign aggression, told against them in America: yet for a time the latter transmitted the produce of the mines, and many of the natives served in the Spanish armies.

Napoleon, notwithstanding his activity, and the offers which he made of the viceroyalty of Mexico to Cuesta, Castaños, Blake, and probably to others residing in that country, failed to create a French party of any consequence; for the Americans were unwilling to plunge into civil strife for a less object than their own independence. The arrogance and injustice of Old Spain, however, increased, rather than diminished, under the sway of the insurrectional government; and at last, as it is well known, a general rebellion of the South American states established the independence of the fairest portion of the globe, and proved how little the abstract love of freedom influenced the resistance of the old country to Napoleon.

The Spanish intercourse with the English court, which had been hitherto carried on through the medium of the deputies, who first arrived in London to claim assistance, was now placed upon a regular footing. The deputies themselves, at the desire of Mr. Canning, were recalled, admiral Apodaca was appointed minister plenipotentiary at St. James's, and Mr. John Hookham Frere was accredited, with the same diplomatic rank, near the central junta. Mr. Stuart, whose knowledge of the state of the country, whose acquaintance with the character of the leading persons, and whose able and energetic exertions had so much contributed to the formation of a central government, was superseded by this injudicious appointment; and thus the great political machine, with every wheel in violent action, was, at the most critical moment, left without any controlling power or guiding influence. For Mr. Stuart, who, on his own responsibility, had quitted Coruña, and repaired to Madrid, and had remitted the most exact and important information of what was passing, remained for three months without receiving a single line from Mr. Canning, approving or disapproving of his proceedings, or giving him instructions how to act at this important crisis : a

strange remissness, indicating the bewildered state
of the ministers, who slowly and with difficulty followed, when they should have been prepared to lead.
Their tardy abortive measures demonstrated, how
wide the space between a sophist and a statesman,
and how dangerous to a nation is that public feeling,
which, insatiable of words, disregards the actions of
men, esteeming more the interested eloquence and
wit of an orator like Demades, than the simple integrity, sound judgment, and great exploits, of a
general like Phocion.

Such were the preparations made by Spain, in
September and October, to meet the exigencies of a
period replete with danger and difficulty. It would
be instructive to contrast the exertions of the ' enthusiastic Spaniards' during these three months of
their insurrection, with the efforts of ' discontented
France' in the hundred days of Napoleon's second
reign. The junta were, however, not devoid of
ambition, for before the battle of Baylen, that of
Seville was occupied with a project of annexing
the Algarves to Spain, and the treaty of Fontainebleau was far from being considered as a dead
letter.

CHAPTER III.

BOOK
III.
1808.

Letter to
Murat.
Las Cases. NAPOLEON, surprised and chagrined at the disgrace which, for the first time, his armies had sustained, was yet nothing dismayed by a resistance
which he had early contemplated as not impro-
bable. With a piercing glance he had observed the
efforts of Spain, calculated the power of foreign
influence in keeping alive the spirit of resistance,
and assigning a just value to the succours which
England could afford, foresaw the danger which
might accrue, if he suffered an insurrection of
peasants, which had already dishonoured the glory
of his arms, to attain the consistency of regular
government, to league with powerful nations, and
to become disciplined troops. To defeat the raw
levies which the Spaniards had hitherto opposed to
his soldiers was an easy matter, but it was necessary to crush them to atoms, that a dread of his
invincible power might still pervade the world, and
the secret influence of his genius remain unabated.
The constitution of Bayonne would, he was aware,
weigh heavy in the scale against those chaotic
governments, neither monarchical, nor popular, nor
aristocratic, nor federal, which the Spanish revolution was throwing up; but before the benefit of
that could be felt by the many, before he could
draw any advantages from his moral resources, it
was necessary to develop all his military strength.

The moment was critical and dangerous. He was

surrounded by enemies whose pride he had wounded,
but whose means of offence he had not destroyed; if he bent his forces against the Peninsula, England might again excite the continent to arms, and Russia and Austria, once more banding together, might raise Prussia, and renew the eternal coalitions. The designs of Austria, although covered by the usual artifices of that cunning, rapacious court, were not so hidden but that, earlier or later, a war with her was to be expected as a certain event, and the inhabitants of Prussia, subdued and oppressed, could not be supposed tranquil. The secret societies that, under the name of Tugenbunde, Gymnasiasts, and other denominations, have since been persecuted by those who were then glad to avail themselves of such assistance, were just beginning to disclose their force and plans. A baron de Nostiz, Stein the Prussian councillor of state, generals Sharnhost and Gneizenau, and colonel Schill, appear to have been the principal contrivers and patrons of these societies, so characteristic of Germans, who, regular and plodding even to a proverb in their actions, possess the most extravagant imaginations of any people on the face of the earth. But whatever the ulterior views of these associations may have been, at this period they were universally inimical to the French; their intent was to drive the latter over the Rhine, and they were a source of peril to the emperor, the more to be feared, as the extent of their influence could not be immediately ascertained. Russia, little injured by her losses, was more powerful perhaps from her defeats, because more enlightened as to the cause of them. Napoleon felt that it would tax all his means to repel the hostility of such a great empire, and that, consequently, his Spa-

nish operations must be confined in a manner
unsuitable to the fame of his arms.   With a long-
sighted policy, he had, however, prepared the means
of obviating this danger, by what has been called
the conference at Erfurth, whither he now repaired
to meet the czar, confiding in the resources of his
genius for securing the friendship of that monarch.

At this period, it may be truly said, that Napoleon
supported the weight of the world; every movement
of his produced a political convulsion; yet so sure,
so confident was he, of his intellectual superiority,
that he sought but to gain one step, and doubted
not to overcome all resistance, and preserve his ascendancy; time was to him victory, if he gained the
one, the other followed: hence, sudden and prompt
in execution, he made one of those gigantic efforts
which have stamped this age with the greatness of
antiquity.   His armies were scattered over Europe.
In Italy, in Dalmatia, on the Rhine, the Danube,
the Elbe; in Prussia, Denmark, Poland, his legions
were to be found; over that vast extent, above five
hundred thousand disciplined men maintained the
supremacy of France.   From those bands he drew
the imperial guards, the select soldiers of the warlike nation he governed, the terror of the other
continental troops; these and the veterans of Jena,
of Austerlitz, of Friedland, reduced in number,
but of confirmed hardihood, were marched towards
Spain; a host of cavalry, unequalled for enterprise
and knowledge of war, were also directed against
that devoted land, and a long train of gallant soldiers followed, until two hundred thousand men,
accustomed to battle, had penetrated the gloomy
fastnesses of the western Pyrenees, while forty thousand of inferior reputation, drawn from the interior

of France, from Naples, from Tuscany, and from
Piedmont, assembled on the eastern ridges of those
gigantic hills. The march of this multitude was
incessant, and as the troops passed the capital, Napoleon, neglectful of nothing which could excite
their courage, and swell their military pride, addressed to them one of his nervous orations. In
the tranquillity of peace it may seem inflated, but
on the eve of battle it is thus a general should speak.

‘ Soldiers! after triumphing on the banks of the
Vistula and the Danube, with rapid steps you have
passed through Germany. This day, without a mo-
ment of repose, I command you to traverse France.
Soldiers! I have need of yōu! The hideous presence
of the leopard contaminates the peninsula of Spain
and Portugal. In terror he must fly before you.
Let us bear our triumphal eagles to the pillars of
Hercules; there also we have injuries to avenge!
Soldiers! you have surpassed the renown of modern
armies, but have you yet equalled the glory of those
Romans, who, in one and the same campaign, were
victorious upon the Rhine and the Euphrates, in
Illyria and upon the Tagus? A long peace, a lasting
prosperity, shall be the reward of your labours, but
a real Frenchman could not, ought not, to rest until
the seas are free and open to all. Soldiers! all that
you have done, all that you will do, for the happiness of the French people, and for my glory, shall
be eternal in my heart!’

Thus saying, he sent his army towards the frontiers of Spain, and himself hastened to meet the
emperor Alexander at Erfurth. Their conference,
conducted upon the footing of intimate friendship,
produced a treaty of alliance offensive and defensive,
and the fate of Spain was, by the one, with calm

indifference, abandoned to the injustice of the other;
but the accession of strength with this treaty, and
the manifest personal partiality of Alexander, gave
to the French emperor, inspired him perhaps with
the idea, that the English cabinet would, if a fair
occasion offered, gladly enter into negotiations for a
general peace.

The two emperors wrote a joint letter to the king
of England. ' The circumstances of Europe had,'
they said, ' brought them together; their first
thought was to yield to the wish and the wants of
every people, and to seek, in a speedy pacification,
the most efficacious remedy for the miseries which
oppressed all nations. The long and bloody war
which had torn the continent was at an end, without the possibility of being renewed. If many
changes had taken place in Europe, if many states
had been overthrown, the cause was to be found in
the state of agitation and misery in which the stagnation of maritime commerce had placed the greatest nations; still greater changes might yet take
place, and all of them contrary to the policy of the
English nation. Peace, then, was, at once, the interest of the people of the continent, as it was the
interest of the people of Great Britain. We entreat
your majesty,' they concluded, ' we unite to entreat
your majesty to listen to the voice of humanity, to
silence that of the passions, to seek, with the intention of arriving at that object; to conciliate all
interests, and thus, preserving all powers which
exist, insure the happiness of Europe and of this
generation, at the head of which Providence has
placed us.'

To this joint letter Mr. Canning replied by two
letters addressed to the French and Russian mini-

sters, accompanied by an official note. In that addressed to the Russian, he observed that, ' however
desirous the king might be to reply personally to the
emperor, he was prevented by the unusual mode of
communication adopted, which had deprived it of a
private and personal character. It was impossible to
pay that mark of respect to the emperor, without at
the same time acknowledging titles which he had
never acknowledged. The proposition for peace
would be communicated to Sweden, and to the existing government of Spain. It was necessary that
his majesty should receive an immediate assurance,
that France acknowledged the government of Spain
as a party to the negotiation. That such was the
intention of the emperor could not be doubted, when
the lively interest manifested by his imperial majesty
for the welfare and dignity of the Spanish monarchy
was recollected. No other assurance was wanted,
that the emperor could not have been induced to
sanction by his concurrence or approbation, usur-
pations, the principles of which were not less unjust
than their example was dangerous to all legitimate
sovereigns.'

The letter addressed to Mons. de Champagny,
duke of Cadore, merely demanded that Sweden and
Spain should be admitted as parties to the negotiation. The official note commenced by stating the
king's desire for peace, on terms consistent with his
honour, his fidelity to his engagements, and the permanent repose of Europe. " The miserable condition of the continent, the convulsions it had
experienced, and those with which it was threatened, were not imputable to his majesty. If the
cause of so much misery was to be found in the
stagnation of commercial intercourse, although his

majesty could *not be expected to hear with unqualified regret*, that the system, devised for the destruction of the commerce of his subjects, had recoiled
upon its authors or its instruments; yet, as it was
neither the disposition of his majesty, nor in the
character of the people over whom he reigned, to
rejoice in the privations and unhappiness even of
the nations which were combined against him, he
anxiously desired the termination of the sufferings
of the continent." The note then, after stating that
the progress of the war had imposed new obli-
gations upon Great Britain, claimed for Sicily, for
Portugal, for Sweden, and for Spain, a participation
in the negotiations. "Treaties, it stated, existed
with the three first, which bound them and England in peace and war. With Spain indeed no
formal instrument had yet been executed, but the
ties of honour were, to the king of England, as
strong as the most solemn treaties; wherefore it
was assumed, that the central junta, or government
of Spain, was understood to be a party to any
negotiation in which his majesty was invited to
engage."

The reply of Russia was peremptory. The
claims of the sovereigns, allies of Great Britain, she
would readily admit. But the insurgents of Spain,
Russia would not acknowledge as an independent
power. The Russians, and England it was said
could recollect one particular instance, had always
been true to this principle; moreover, the emperor
had acknowledged Joseph Buonaparte as king of
Spain, and was united to the French emperor for
peace and for war; he was resolved not to separate
his interests from those of Napoleon. After some
further arguments touching the question, the reply

concluded by offering to treat upon the basis of the
' uti possidetis,' and the respective power of the bel-
ligerent parties, or upon *any basis*, for the conclusion
of an honourable, just, and equal peace.

The insulting tone of Mr. Canning's communication produced an insulting reply from Mons. de
Champagny, which also finished by proposing the
' uti possidetis' as a basis for a treaty, and expressing a hope, that without losing sight of the
inevitable results of the force of states, it would be
remembered, that between great powers there could
be no solid peace but that which was equal and
honourable for both parties. Upon the receipt
of these replies, the English minister broke off
the negotiations, and all chance of peace vanished ;
but previous to the conclusion of this remarkable correspondence, Napoleon had returned to
Paris.

What his real views in proposing to treat were, it
is difficult to determine. He could not have expected
that Great Britain would relinquish the cause of
Spain ; he must therefore have been prepared to
make some arrangement upon that head, unless the
whole proceeding was an artifice to sow distrust
among his enemies. The English ministers asserted
that it was so, but what enemies were they among
whom he could create this uneasy feeling ? Sweden,
Sicily, Portugal ! the notion as applied to them was
absurd ; it is more probable that he was sincere.
He said so at St. Helena, and the peculiar circum- O'Meara.
stances of the period at which the conferences of Voice from St.Helena,
Erfurth took place, warrant a belief in that asser- Vol. ii.
tion. The menacing aspect of Austria, the recent
loss of Portugal, the hitherto successful insurrection of Spain, the secret societies of Germany, the

desire of consolidating the Polish dominions, and
placing, while he might, a barrier to the power of
Russia on that side, the breach which the events of
the Peninsula made in his continental system of excluding British goods, and the commercial distresses
of Europe, were cogent reasons for a peace; they
might well cause him to be suspicious of the future,
and render him anxious for an excuse to abandon an
unjust contest, in which he could not fail to suffer
much, and to risk more than he could gain.   In securing the alliance of Russia, he only disentangled
a part of the Gordian knot of politics; to cut the
remainder with his sword was, at this conjuncture,
a task which even he might have been doubtful of.
The fact that his armies were marching upon Spain,
proves nothing to the contrary of this supposition.
Time was to him of the utmost consequence.   His
negotiations proving abortive, it would have been
too late to have reinforced his troops on the Ebro,
and the event evinced the prudence of his measures
in that respect.

The refusal to admit the Spaniards as a party to
the conferences for peace is scarcely more conclusive; to have done that would have been to resign
the weapon in his hands before he entered the lists.
That England could not abandon the Spaniards is
unquestionable, but that was not a necessary consequence of continuing the negotiations.   There was
a bar put to the admission of a Spanish diplomatist,
but no bar was thereby put to the discussion of
Spanish interests; the correspondence of the English
minister would not of necessity have compromised
Spanish independence, it need not have relaxed in
the slightest degree the measures of hostility, nor
retarded the succours preparing for the patriots.

And when we consider the great power of Napo- leon's arms, the subtlety and force of his genius, the good fortune which had hitherto attended his progress in war, the vast additional strength which the alliance of Russia conferred at the moment; and when, to oppose all this, we contrast the scanty means of Spain, and the confusion into which she was plunged, it does appear as if her welfare would have been better consulted by an appeal to negotiation rather than to battle. It is true that Austria was arming, yet Austria had been so often conquered, was so sure to abandon the cause of the patriots, and every other cause when pressed; so certain to sacrifice every consideration of honour or faith to the suggestions of self-interest, that the independence of Spain through the medium of war could only be regarded as the object of uncertain hope; a prize to be gained, if gained at all, by wading through torrents of blood, and sustaining every misery that famine and the fury of devastating armies could inflict. To avoid, if possible, such dreadful evils by negotiating was worth trial, and the force of justice, when urged by the minister of a great nation, would have been difficult to withstand; no power, no ambition, can resist it and be safe.

But such an enlarged mode of proceeding was not in accord with the shifts and subterfuges that characterized the policy of the day, when it was thought wise to degrade the dignity of such a correspondence by a ridiculous denial of Napoleon's titles; and praiseworthy to render a state paper, in which such serious interests were discussed, offensive and mean, by miserable sarcasm, evincing the pride of an author rather than the gravity of a statesman. There is sound ground also for believing that hope, derived from a silly intrigue carried on through the princess of Tour and Taxis, with Talleyrand and some others, who were even then ready to betray Napoleon, was the real cause of the negotiation having been broken off by Mr. Canning. Mr. Whitbread declared in the House of Commons, that he saw no reason for refusing to treat with France at that period, and although public clamour afterwards induced him to explain away this expression, he needed not to be ashamed of it; for if the opinion of Cicero, that an unfair peace is preferable to the justest war, was ever worthy of attention, it was so at this period, when the success of Spain was doubtful, her misery certain, her salvation only to be obtained through the baptism of blood !

Upon the 18th of October Napoleon returned to Paris, secure of the present friendship and alliance of Russia, but uncertain of the moment when the stimulus of English subsidies would quicken the hostility of Austria into life; yet, if his peril was great, his preparations to meet it were likewise enormous. He called out two conscriptions. The first, taken from the classes of 1806, 7, 8, and 9, afforded eighty thousand men arrived at maturity; these were destined to replace the veterans directed against Spain. The second, taken from the class of 1810, also produced eighty thousand, which were disposed of as reserves in the dépôts of France. The French troops left in Germany were then concentrated on the side of Austria; Denmark was evacuated, and one hundred thousand soldiers were withdrawn from the Prussian states. The army of Italy was powerfully reinforced, and placed under the command of prince Eugene, who was assisted by

marshal Massena.   Murat also, who had succeeded
Joseph in the kingdom of Naples, was directed to
assemble a Neapolitan army on the shores of
Calabria, and to threaten Sicily.   In short, no measures that prudence could suggest were neglected
by this wonderful man, to whom, the time required
by Austria for the mere preparation of a campaign
seemed sufficient for the subjection of the whole
Peninsula.

The session of the legislative body was opened
on the 24th of October; the emperor, in his speech
from the throne, after giving a concise sketch of the
political situation of Europe, touched upon Spain.
' In a few days I go,' said he, ' to put myself at
the head of my armies, and, with the aid of God, to
crown the king of Spain in Madrid ! to plant my
eagles on the towers of Lisbon !'   Then departing
from Paris he repaired to Bayonne, but the labours
of his ministers continued ; their speeches and
reports more elaborately explicit than usual, exposed
the vast resources of France, and were well calculated to impress upon the minds of men the danger
of provoking the enmity of such a powerful nation.
From those documents it appeared that the expenses of the year, including the interest of the
national debt, were under thirty millions sterling,
and completely covered by the existing taxes,
drawn from a metallic currency ; that no fresh
burthens would be laid upon the nation ; that
numerous public works were in progress; that internal trade, and the commerce carried on by land
were flourishing, and nearly one million of men
were in arms !

The readiness with which Mr. Canning broke off
the negotiation of Erfurth, and defied this stupen-

dous power, would lead to the supposition that on the side of Spain at least he was prepared to encounter it with some chance of success ; yet no trace of a matured plan is to be found in the instructions to the generals commanding in Portugal previous to the 25th of September, nor was the project then adopted, one which discovered any adequate knowledge of the force of the enemy, or of the state of affairs : indeed the conduct of the cabinet relative to the Peninsula was scarcely superior to that of the central junta itself. Several vague projects, or rather speculations, were communicated to the generals in Portugal, but in none of them was the strength of the enemy alluded to, in none was there a settled plan of operations visible! it was evident that the prodigious activity of the emperor was not taken into consideration, and that a strange delusion relative to his power, or to his intentions, existed among the English ministers.

It was the 6th of October before a despatch, containing the first determinate plan of campaign, arrived at Lisbon. Thirty thousand infantry and five thousand cavalry were to be employed in the north of Spain, of which ten thousand were to be embarked at the English ports, and the remainder to be composed of regiments, drafted from the army then in Portugal ; sir John Moore was appointed to command the whole, and he was authorised, at his own discretion, to effect a junction by a voyage round the coast, or by a march through the interior. He chose the latter, 1°. because a voyage at that season of the year would have been tedious and precarious ; 2°. because the intention of sir Hew Dalrymple had been to enter Spain by Almeida, and

the few arrangements which that general had power
to make were made with a view to such a march;
3°. because he was informed that the province of Gallicia would be scarcely able to equip the force coming from England, under the command of sir David
Baird. But Moore was directed to take the field immediately, to fix upon some place, either in Gallicia
or on the borders of Leon, for concentrating the
whole army, and the specific plan of operations was
to be concerted afterwards with the Spanish generals! This was a light and idle proceeding, promising no good result, for the Ebro was to be the
theatre of war, and the head of the great French host
coming from Germany, was already in the passes of
the Pyrenees; the local difficulties impeding the
English general's progress were also abundant, and
of a nature to render that which was ill begun,
end worse, and that which was well arranged, fail.
To be first in the field is a great and decided
advantage, yet here the plan of operations was not
even arranged, when the enemy's first blows were
descending.

Sir John Moore had much to execute, and with
little help. He was to organize an army of raw
soldiers, and in a poor and unsettled country; just
relieved from the pressure of a harsh and griping
enemy, he was to procure the transport necessary
for his stores, ammunition, and even for the conveyance of the officers' baggage. Assisted by an
experienced staff, such obstacles do not very much
impede a good general, but here, few of the subordinate officers had served a campaign, and every
branch of the administration, civil and military, was
composed of men, zealous and willing indeed, yet
new to a service, where no energy can prevent the

BOOK
III.

1808.
October.
Appendix,
No. 13,
§§ 1 & 3.
effects of inexperience from being severely felt. The roads through Portugal were very bad, and the rainy season, so baleful to an army, was upon the point of setting in; time pressed sorely when it was essential to be quick, and gold, which turneth the wheels of war, was wanting. And this, at all times a great evil, was the more grievously felt at the moment, inasmuch as the Portuguese, accustomed to fraud on the part of their own government, and to forced contributions by the French, could not readily be persuaded that an army of foreigners, paying with promises alone, might be trusted: nor was this natural suspicion allayed by observing that, while the general and his troops were thus kept without money, all the subordinate agents dispersed throughout the country were amply supplied. Sir David Baird, who, with his portion of troops, was to land at Coruña, and to equip in a country already exhausted by Blake's army, was likewise encompassed with difficulties; for from Coruña, to the nearest point, where he could effect a junction with the forces marching from Lisbon, was two hundred miles, and he also was without money.

No general-in-chief was appointed to command the Spanish armies, nor was sir John Moore referred, by the English ministers, to any person with whom he could communicate at all, much less concert a plan of operations for the allied forces. He was unacquainted with the views of the Spanish government; and he was alike uninformed of the numbers, composition, and situation of the armies with whom he was to act, and those with whom he was to contend. Twenty-five thousand pounds in his military chest, and his own genius, constituted his resources for a campaign, which was to lead

him far from the coast, and all its means of supply.
He was first to unite the scattered portions of his
forces by a winter march of three hundred miles;
another three hundred were to be passed before he
reached the Ebro; there he was to concert a plan of
operations with generals acting each independent of
the other, their corps reaching from the northern sea-
coast to Zaragoza, themselves jealous and quarrel-
some, their men insubordinate, differing in customs,
discipline, language, and religion from the English,
and despising all foreigners; and all this was to be
accomplished in time to defeat an enemy who was
already in the field, accustomed to great movements,
and conducted by the most rapid and decided of men.
It must be acknowledged that the ministers' views
were equally vast and inconsiderate, and their mis-
calculations are the more remarkable, as there was
not wanting a man, in the highest military situation,
to condemn their plan at the time, and to propose a
better.

The duke of York, in a formal minute, drawn
up for the information of the government, observed,
that the Spanish armies being unconnected, and occupying a great extent of ground, were weak; that
the French being concentrated, and certain of reinforcement, were strong; that there could be no
question of the relative value of Spanish and French
soldiers, and that, consequently, the allies might be
beaten before the British could arrive at the scene
of action; the latter would then unaided have to
meet the French army, and it was essential to provide a sufficient number of troops to meet such an
emergency. That number he judged should not be
less than sixty thousand men, and by a detailed
statement, he proved that such a number could Appendix, No. 24.

have been furnished without detriment to any other service, but his advice was unheeded.

At this period, also, the effects of that incredible folly and weakness, which marked all the proceedings of the central junta, were felt throughout Spain. In any other country, the conduct of the government would have been attributed to insanity. So apathetic with respect to the enemy as to be contemptible, so active in pursuit of self-interest as to become hateful; continually devising how to render itself at once despotic and popular, how to excite enthusiasm and check freedom of expression; how to enjoy the luxury of power without its labour, how to acquire great reputation without trouble, how to be indolent and victorious at the same moment. Fear prevented the members from removing to Madrid after every preparation had been made for a public entrance into that capital. They passed decrees, repressing the liberty of the press on the ground of the deceptions practised upon the public, yet themselves never hesitated to deceive the British agents, the generals, the government, and their own countrymen, by the most flagitious falsehoods upon every subject, whether of greater or less importance. They hedged their own dignity round with ridiculous and misplaced forms, opposed to the vital principle of an insurrectional government, devoted their attention to abstract speculations, recalled the exiled Jesuits, and inundated the country with long and laboured state papers, while the pressing business of the moment was left uncared for. Every application on the part of lord William Bentinck and Mr. Stuart, even for an order to expedite a common courier, was met by difficulties and delays, and it was necessary to have recourse to the most painful

MrStuart's
Letters,
MS.

Appendix,
No.13, §6.

solicitations to obtain the slightest attention; nor
did that mode always succeed.

Sir John Moore strenuously grappled with the difficulties besetting him, and well knowing the value of time in military transactions, urged forward the preparations with all possible activity. He was very desirous that troops who had a journey of six hundred miles to make previous to meeting the enemy, should not, at the commencement, be overwhelmed by the torrents of rain, which, in Portugal, descend at this period with such violence as to destroy the shoes, ammunition, and accoutrements of a soldier, and render him almost unfit for service. The Spanish generals recommended that the line of march should be conducted by Almeida, Ciudad Rodrigo, Salamanca, Vallodolid, and Burgos; and that the magazines for the campaign should be formed at one of the latter towns. This coincided with the previous preparations, and the army was therefore organized in three columns, two of which were directed upon Almeida, by the routes of Coimbra and Guarda, while the third, comprising the artillery, the cavalry, and the regiments quartered in the Alemtejo, was destined to move by Alcantara, upon Ciudad Rodrigo. Almeida itself was chosen for a place of arms, and all the reserve-stores, and provisions, were forwarded there, as time and circumstances would permit; but the want of money, the unsettled state of the country, and the inexperience of the commissariat, rendered it difficult to procure the means of transport even for the light baggage of the regiments, although the quantity of the latter was reduced so much as to create discontent. One Sataro, the same person who has been already mentioned as an agent of Junot's in the negotiation with sir Charles Cotton, engaged to Appendix, No.13, § 3.

supply the army, but dishonestly failing in his con-
tract, so embarrassed the operations, that the general resigned all hope of being able to move with
more than the light baggage, the ammunition necessary for immediate use, and a scanty supply of medicines; the formation of the magazines at Almeida
was also retarded, and the future subsistence of the
troops was thus thrown upon a raw commissariat,
unprovided with money. The general, however,
relying upon its increasing experience, and upon the
activity of lord William Bentinck and Mr. Stuart,
did not delay his march, and he sent agents to
Madrid and other places to make contracts, and to
raise money; for such was the policy of the ministers, that they supplied the Spaniards with gold,
and left the English army to get it back in loans.

Many of the regiments were actually in movement when an unexpected difficulty forced the commander-in-chief to make a fresh disposition of the
troops. The state of the Portuguese roads north of
the Tagus was unknown, but the native officers and
the people had alike declared that they were impracticable for artillery; the opinion of colonel
Lopez, a military commissary sent, by the Spanish
government, to facilitate the march of the British,
coincided with this information; and the report of
captain Delancey, one of the most intelligent and
enterprising of those officers of the quarter-master-
general's department, who were employed to examine
the lines of route, corroborated the general opinion.
Junot had indeed, with infinite pains, carried his
guns along these roads, but his carriages had been
broken, and the batteries rendered unserviceable by
the operation; wherefore Moore reluctantly determined to send his artillery and cavalry by the south

bank of the Tagus, to Talavera de la Reyna, from whence they might gain Naval Carneiro, the Escurial, the pass of the Guadarama mountains, Espinar, Arevalo, and Salamanca. He would have marched the whole army by the same route, if this disagreeable intelligence respecting the northern roads had been obtained earlier; but when the arrangements were all made for the supplies to go to Almeida, and when most of the regiments were actually in movement towards that town, it was too late to alter their destination.

This separation of the artillery, although it violated a great military principle, which prescribes that the point of concentration for an army should be beyond the reach of the enemy, was here a matter of apparent necessity; and no danger was apprehended from the offensive operations of an adversary, represented to be incapable of maintaining his own line of defence. Valladolid and Burgos were considered by the Spaniards as safe places for the English magazines; Moore shared so much of the universal confidence in the Spanish enthusiasm and courage, as to suppose, that Salamanca would not be an insecure point of concentration for his columns, while covered by such numerous patriotic armies as were said to be on the Ebro. One brigade of six-pounders he retained with the head-quarters, but the remainder of his artillery, consisting of twenty-four pieces, the cavalry, amounting to a thousand troopers, the great parc of the army, containing many hundred carriages and escorted by three thousand infantry, he sent by the road of Talavera, under the command of sir John Hope, an officer qualified by his talents, firmness, and zeal, to conduct the most important enterprises.

The rest of the army marched in three columns.
The first by Alcantara and Coria, the second by
Abrantes, the third by Coimbra, all having Ciudad
Rodrigo as the point of direction; and with such
energy did the general overcome all obstacles, that
the whole of the troops were in movement, and
head-quarters quitted Lisbon the 26th of October, just twenty days after the receipt of the despatch which appointed him to the chief command;
a surprising diligence, but rendered necessary by
the pressure of circumstances.   ' The army,' to use
his own words, ' run the risk of finding itself in
front of the enemy with no more ammunition than
the men carried in their pouches:' ' but had I waited,'
he adds, ' until every thing was forwarded, the troops
would not have been in Spain until the spring, and
I trust that the enemy will not find out our wants
as soon as they will feel the effects of what we have.'

The Spaniards, however, who expected ' every
body to fly, except themselves,' thought him slow,
and were impatient, and from every quarter indeed
letters arrived, pressing him to advance.   Lord William Bentinck and Mr. Stuart, witnesses of the slug-
gish incapacity of the Spanish government, judged
that such a support was absolutely necessary to
sustain the reeling strength of Spain.   The central
junta was awakened for a moment.   Hitherto, as
a mask for its ignorance, it had treated the French
power with contempt, and the Spanish generals and
the people echoed the sentiments of the government;
but now, a letter addressed by the governor of
Bayonne to general Jourdan, stating that sixty thousand infantry, and seven thousand cavalry, would
reinforce the French armies between the 16th of
October and the 16th of November, was intercepted,

and made the junta feel that a crisis for which it CHAP.
III.
was unprepared was approaching: then with the folly 1808.
usually attendant on improvidence, these men, who November
had been so slow themselves, required that others
should be supernaturally quick as danger pressed.

In the mean time sir David Baird's forces arrived
at Coruña. Lord William Bentinck had given intimation of their approach, and the central junta
had repeatedly assured him, that every necessary
order was given, and that every facility would be
afforded, for their disembarkation and supply. This
was untrue; no measures of any kind had been
taken, no instructions issued, no preparations made;
the junta of Coruña disliked the personal trouble of Capt.
a disembarkation in that port, and in the hope that Kennedy's
Baird would be driven to another, refused him per- Letter.
mission to land, until a communication was had Parl. Pap.
with Aranjuez; yet fifteen days elapsed, before an
answer could be obtained from a government, who
were daily pestering sir John Moore with complaints
of the tardiness of his march.

Sir David Baird came without money; sir John Appendix,
could only give him £8000, a sum which might No.13, § 1.
have been mistaken for a private loan, if the fact of Sir John
its being public property were not expressly men- Moore to
tioned; yet at this time Mr. Frere, the plenipoten- lord Cas-
tiary, arrived at Coruña, with two millions of dollars, 27th Oct.
intended for the use of the Spaniards; and while
such large sums, contrary to the earnest recommendations of Mr. Stuart and major Cox, were lavished Appendix,
in that quarter, the penury of the English general No. 13,
obliged him to borrow from the funds in Mr. Frere's §§ 5 & 6.
hands. Thus assisted, the troops were put in motion, but wanting all the equipments essential to an
army, they were forced to march by half battalions,

conveying their scanty stores on country cars, hired
from day to day; nor was that meagre assistance
obtained but at great expense, and by compliance
with a vulgar mercenary spirit predominant among
the authorities of Gallicia. The junta frequently
promised to procure the carriages, but did not; the
commissaries, pushed to the wall by the delay,
offered an exorbitant remuneration; the cars were
then forthcoming, and the procrastination of the
government proved to be a concerted plan to defraud
the military chest. In fine, the local rulers were
unfriendly, crafty, fraudulent, the peasantry suspicious, fearful, rude, disinclined toward strangers,
and indifferent to public affairs; a few shots only
were required to render theirs a hostile instead of a
friendly greeting.

With Mr. Frere came a fleet, conveying a Spanish
force, under the marquis of Romana. When the
insurrection first broke forth, that nobleman commanded fourteen or fifteen thousand troops, who
were serving with the French armies, and how to

recover this disciplined body of men from the enemy
was a subject of early anxiety with the junta of
Seville. Castaños, in his first intercourse with sir
Hew Dalrymple, signified his wish that the British
government should adopt some mode of apprising
Romana, that Spain was in arms, and should endeavour to extricate him and his army from the toils of
the enemy, and finally a gentleman named M'Kenzie
was employed by the English ministers to conduct
the enterprise. The Spanish troops were quartered
in Holstein, Sleswig, Jutland, and the islands of
Funen, Zealand, and Langeland; Mr. M'Kenzie,
through the medium of one Robertson, a catholic
priest, opened a communication with Romana, and

as neither the general, nor the soldiers he commanded, hesitated, a judicious plan was concerted. Sir
Richard Keats, with a squadron detached from the
Baltic fleet, suddenly appeared off Nyborg, in the
island of Funen, and a majority of the Spanish regiments quartered in Sleswig immediately seized all
the craft in the different harbours of that coast,
and pushed across the channel to Funen; Romana,
with the assistance of Keats, had already seized the
port and castle of Nyborg without opposition, save
from a small Danish ship of war that was moored
across the mouth of the harbour, and from thence the
Spaniards passed to Langeland, where they embarked
above nine thousand strong, on board the English
fleet, commanded by sir James Saumarez. The rest
of the troops either remained in Sleswig or were
disarmed by the Danish force in Zealand. This
enterprise was conducted with prudent activity, and
the unhesitating patriotism of the Spanish soldiers
was very honourable, but the danger was slight to
all but Mr. Robertson. Romana, after touching at
England, repaired to Coruña; his troops did not,
however, land at that port, but at St. Andero, where
they were equipped from the English stores, and
proceeded by divisions to join Blake's army in
Biscay.

Among the various subjects calling for sir John
Moore's attention, there was none of greater interest
than the appointment of a generalissimo to the
Spanish armies. Impressed with the imminent danger of procrastination or uncertainty in such a matter, he desired lord William Bentinck and Mr. Stuart
to urge the central government with all their force
upon that head; to lord Castlereagh he represented
the injury that must accrue to the cause, if the mea-

sure was delayed; and he proposed to go himself
to Madrid, with a view of adding weight to these
representations.   Subsequent events frustrated this
intention, and there seems no reason to imagine,
that his personal remonstrances would have influenced a government, described by Mr. Stuart, after
a thorough experience of its qualities, as ' never
having made a single exertion for the public good,
neither rewarding merit nor punishing guilt,' and
being for all useful purposes ' absolutely null.' The
junta's dislike to a single military chief was not an
error of the head, and reason is of little avail against
the suggestions of self-interest.

The march of the British troops was as rapid as
the previous preparations had been; but general
Anstruther had, unadvisedly, halted the leading column in Almeida, and when Moore reached that
town on the 8th of November, he found the whole
of the infantry assembled there, instead of being on
the road to Salamanca.   The condition of the men
was, however, superb, and their discipline exem-
plary; on that side all was well, yet from the obstacles encountered by sir David Baird, and the change
of direction in the artillery, it was evident that no
considerable force could be brought into action
before the end of the month.   Meanwhile, the Spaniards were hastening events.   Despatches from
lord William Bentinck announced that the enemy
remained stationary on the Ebro, although reinforced
by ten thousand men; that Castaños was about to
cross that river at Tudela; and that the army of
Aragon was moving by Sor upon Roncevalles, with
a view to gain the rear of the French, while Castaños assailed their left flank. Moore, judging that
such movements would bring on a battle, the success

of which must be very doubtful, became uneasy for his own artillery. His concern was increased by observing, that the guns might have kept with the other columns; ' and if any thing adverse happens, I have not,' he wrote to general Hope, ' necessity to plead ; the road we are now travelling, that by Villa Velha and Guarda, is practicable for artillery ; the brigade under Wilmot has already reached Guarda, and, as far as I have already seen, the road presents few obstacles, and those easily surmounted ; this knowledge was, however, only acquired by our own officers, when the brigade was at Castello Branco, it was not certain if it could proceed.' He now desired Hope no longer to trust any reports, but seek a shorter line, by Placentia, across the mountains to Salamanca.

Up to this period, all reports from the agents, all information from the government at home, all communications public and private, coincided upon one subject. *The Spaniards were an enthusiastic, an heroic people, a nation of unparalleled energy ! their armies were brave, they were numerous, they were confident ! one hundred and eighty thousand men were actually in line of battle, extending from the sea-coast of Biscay to Zaragoza; the French, reduced to a fourth of this number, cooped up in a corner, were shrinking from an encounter ; they were deserted by the emperor, they were trembling, they were spiritless!* Nevertheless, the general was somewhat distrustful; he perceived the elements of disaster in the divided commands, and the lengthened lines of the Spaniards, and early in October he had predicted the mischief that such a system would produce. ' As long as the French remain upon the defensive,' he observed, ' it will not be so much felt, but the mo-

ment an attack is made, some great calamity must
ensue:' however, he was not without faith in the
multitude and energy of the patriots, when he considered the greatness of their cause.

Castaños was at this time pointed out by the central junta as the person with whom to concert a plan
of campaign, and sir John Moore, concluding that
it was a preliminary step towards making that officer
generalissimo, wrote to him in a conciliatory style,
well calculated to ensure a cordial co-operation. It
was an encouraging event, the English general believed it to be the commencement of a better system,
and looked forward with more hope to the opening
of the war, but this favourable state soon changed;
far from being created chief of all, Castaños was
superseded in the command he already held, the
whole folly of the Spanish character broke forth,
and confusion and distress followed. At that moment also clouds arose in a quarter, which had
hitherto been all sunshine; the military agents, as
the crisis approached, lowered their sanguine tone,
and no longer dwelt upon the enthusiasm of the
armies; they admitted, that the confidence of the
troops was sinking, and that even in numbers they
were inferior to the French. In truth, it was full
time to change their note, for the real state of affairs
could no longer be concealed; a great catastrophe
was at hand; but what of wildness in their projects,
or of skill in the enemy's, what of ignorance, vanity,
and presumption in the generals, what of fear
among the soldiers, and what of fortune in the
events, combined to hasten the ruin of the Spaniards,
and how that ruin was effected, I, quitting the English army for a time, will now relate.

Appendix,
No. 13, §7.

CHAPTER IV.

In the preceding chapters I have exposed the weak- ness, the folly, the improvidence of Spain, and shown how the bad passions and sordid views of her leaders were encouraged by the unwise prodigality of England.   I have dissected the full boast and meagre preparations of the governments in both countries, laying bare the bones and sinews of the insurrection, and by comparing their loose and feeble structure, with the strongly knitted frame and large proportions of the enemy, prepared the reader for the inevitable issue of a conflict between such ill-matched champions.   In the present book, I shall recount the sudden and terrible manner in which the Spanish armies were overthrown, during the tempestuous progress of the French emperor.   Yet, previous to relating these disasters, I must revert to the period immediately following the retreat of king Joseph, and trace those early operations of the French and Spanish forces, which, like a jesting prologue to a deep tragedy, unworthily ushered in the great catastrophe.

CAMPAIGN OF THE FRENCH AND SPANISH ARMIES BEFORE THE ARRIVAL OF THE EMPEROR.

After general Cuesta was removed from the command, and the junta of Seville had been forced by major Coxe to disgorge so much of the English subsidy as sufficed for the immediate relief of the troops in Madrid, all the Spanish armies closed upon the Ebro.

General Blake, reinforced by eight thousand Asturians, established his base of operations at Reynosa, opened a communication with the English vessels off the port of St. Andero, and directed his views towards Biscay.

The Castilian army, conducted by general Pignatelli, resumed its march upon Burgo del Osma and Logroña.

The two divisions of the Andalusian troops under Lapeña, and the Murcian division of general Llamas, advanced to Taranzona and Tudela.

Palafox, with the Aragonese and Valencian divisions of St. Marc, operated from the side of Zaragoza.

The conde de Belvidere, a weak youth, not twenty years of age, marched with fifteen thousand Estremadurans upon Logroña, as forming part of Castaños' army, but soon received another destination.

Between all these armies there was neither concert nor connexion, their movements were regulated by some partial view of affairs, or by the silly caprices of the generals, who were ignorant of each other's plans, and little solicitous to combine operations. The weak characters of many of the chiefs, the inexperience of all, and this total want of system, opened a field for intriguing men, and invited unqualified persons to interfere in the direction of affairs ; thus we find colonel Doyle, making a journey to Zaragoza, and priding himself upon having prevailed with Palafox to detach seven thousand men to Sanguessa. Captain Whittingham, without any knowledge of Doyle's interference, earnestly dissuading the Spaniards from such an enterprise.

The first affirming that the movement would ' turn
the enemy's left flank, threaten his rear, and have
the appearance of cutting off his retreat.' The second arguing, that Sanguessa, being seventy miles
from Zaragoza, and only a few leagues from Pampeluna, the detachment would itself be cut off. Doyle
judged that, drawing the French from Caparosa and
Milagro, it would expose those points to Llamas
and La-Peña; that it would force the enemy to recall the reinforcements said to be marching against
Blake, enable that general to form a junction
with the Asturians, and then with the forty thousand men thus collected, possess himself of the
Pyrenees; and if the French army, estimated at
thirty-five thousand men, did not fly, cut it off from
France, or, by moving on Miranda, sweep clear
Biscay and Castille. Palafox, pleased with this plan,
sent Whittingham to inform Llamas and La-Peña,
that O'Neil would, with six thousand men, march
on the 15th of September to Sanguessa. Those ge- Whittingham's
nerals disapproved of the movement as dangerous, Correspondence.
premature, and at variance with the plan arranged
in the council of war held at Madrid, but Palafox,
regardless of their opinion, persisted; O'Neil accordingly occupied Sanguessa, drew the attention of
the enemy, and was immediately driven across the
Alagon river.

In this manner all their projects, characterized by
a profound ignorance of war, were lightly adopted
and as lightly abandoned, or ended in disasters; yet
victory was more confidently anticipated, than if consummate skill had presided over the arrangements;
and this vain-glorious feeling, extending to the military agents, was by them propagated in England,
where the fore-boasting was nearly as loud, and as

BOOK
III.
————
1808.
September
Lord W.
Bentinck's
Corre-
spondence.
MS.
Doyle's
Corre-
spondence.
MS.

absurd, as in the Peninsula.   The delusion was universal ; even lord William Bentinck and Mr. Stuart,
deceived by the curious consistency of the Spanish
falsehoods, doubted if the French army was able to
maintain its position, and believed that the Spaniards
had obtained a moral ascendancy in the field.

Drunk with vanity and folly, and despising the 'remnants' of the French army on the Ebro, which they
estimated at from thirty-five to forty thousand men,
the Spanish government proposed that the British
army should be directed upon Catalonia; and when
they found that this proposal was not acceded to, they
withdrew ten thousand men from the Murcian division, and sent them to the neighbourhood of Lerida.
The innate pride and arrogance of the Spaniards
were also nourished by the timid and false operations
of king Joseph.   Twenty days after the evacuation
of Madrid, that monarch was at the head of above
fifty thousand fighting men, exclusive of eight thousand employed to maintain the communications, and
to furnish the garrisons of Pampeluna, Tolosa, Irun,
St. Sebastian and Bilbao; exclusive also of the
Catalonian army, which was seventeen thousand
strong, and distinct from his command.   A strong
reserve, assembled at Bayonne, under general Drouet,
supplied reinforcements, and was itself supported by
drafts from the interior of France; six thousand
men, forming moveable columns, watched the openings of the Pyrenees, from St. John Pied de Port to
Rousillon, and guarded the frontier against Spanish
incursions; and a second reserve, composed of Nea-
politans, Tuscans, and Piedmontese, was commenced
at Belgarde, with a view of supporting Duhesme in
Catalonia.   How the king quelled the nascent insurrection at Bilbao, and how he dispersed the in-

surgents of the valleys in Aragon, I have already
related; but after those operations, the French
army made no movement. It was re-organized, and
divided into three grand divisions and a reserve.
Bessieres retained the command of the right wing,
Moncey assumed that of the left, and Ney, arriving
from Paris, took charge of the centre; the reserve,
chiefly composed of detachments from the imperial
guard, remained near the person of the king, and
the old republican general, Jourdan, a man whose
day of glory belonged to another æra, re-appeared
upon the military stage, and filled the office of
major-general to the army.

With such a force, and so assisted, there was nothing in Spain, turn which way he would, capable of
opposing king Joseph's march, but the incongruity
of a camp with a court is always productive of indecision and of error; the truncheon does not fit every
hand, and the French army soon felt the inconvenience of having at its head a monarch who was not
a warrior. Joseph remained on the defensive, without understanding the force of the maxim, ' *that
offensive movements are the foundation of a good defence;*' he held Bilbao, and, contrary to the advice Napoleon's notes.
of the generals who conducted the operations on Appendix, Nos. 4 & 5.
his left, abandoned Tudela, to choose for his field
of battle, Milagro, a small town situated near the
confluence of the Arga and Aragon with the Ebro.
While Bessieres held Burgos in force, his cavalry
commanded the valley of the Duero, menaced Palencia and Valladolid, and scouring the plains, kept
Blake and Cuesta in check; instead of reinforcing
a post so advantageous, the king relinquished Burgos
as a point beyond his line of defence, and Bessieres'
troops were posted in successive divisions behind it,

as far as Puente Lara on the Ebro. Ney's force
then lined that river down to Logroño, the reserve
was quartered behind Miranda, and Trevino, a small,
obscure place, was chosen as the point of battle, for
the right and centre.

In this disadvantageous situation the army, with
some trifling changes, remained from the middle of
August until late in September, during which time
the artillery and carriages of transport were repaired,
magazines were collected, the cavalry remounted,
and the preparations made for an active campaign
when the reinforcements should arrive from Germany.
But the line of resistance thus offered to the Spaniards evinced a degree of timidity, which the relative
strength of the armies by no means justified ; the
left of the French evidently leaned towards the great
communication with France, and seemed to refuse
the support of Pampeluna; Tudela was abandoned,
and Burgos resigned to the enterprise of the Spaniards; all this indicated fear, a disposition to retreat if the enemy advanced. The king complained
with what extreme difficulty he obtained intelligence, yet he neglected by forward movements to
feel for his adversaries ; wandering as it were in the
dark, he gave a loose to his imagination, and conju-
ring up a phantom of Spanish strength, which had no
real existence, anxiously waited for the development
of their power, while they were exposing their weakness by a succession of the most egregious blunders.

Joseph's errors did not escape the animadversion of his brother, whose sagacity enabled him,
although at a distance, to detect, through the
glare of the insurrection, all its inefficiency; he
dreaded the moral effect produced by its momentary
success, and was preparing to crush the rising hopes

of his enemies; but, despising the Spaniards as soldiers, Joseph's retreat, and subsequent position, displeased him, and he desired his brother to check the exultation of the patriots, by acting upon a bold and well-considered plan, of which he sent him the outline. His notes, dictated upon the occasion, are replete with genius, and evince his absolute mastery of the art of war. ' It was too late,' he said, ' to discuss the question, whether Madrid should have been retained or abandoned; idle to consider, if a position, covering the siege of Zaragoza, might not have been formed; useless to examine, if the line of the Duero was not better than that of the Ebro for the French army. The line of the Ebro was actually taken, and it must be kept; to advance from that river without a fixed object would create indecision, this would bring the troops back again, and produce an injurious moral effect. But why abandon Tudela, why relinquish Burgos? Those towns were of note, and of reputation, the possession of them gave a moral influence, and moral force constituted two-thirds of the strength of armies. Tudela and Burgos had also a relative importance; the first, possessing a stone bridge, was on the communication of Pampeluna and Madrid, it commanded the canal of Zaragoza, it was the capital of a province. When the army resumed offensive operations, their first enterprise would be the siege of Zaragoza; from that town to Tudela, the land carriage was three days, but the water carriage was only fourteen hours, wherefore to have the besieging artillery and stores at Tudela, was the same as to have them at Zaragoza; if the Spaniards got possession of the former, all Navarre would be in a state of insurrection, and Pampeluna

Appendix,
No. 5.

exposed. Tudela then was of vast importance, but Milagro was of none, it was an obscure place, without a bridge, and commanding no communication; in short, it was without interest, defended nothing! led to nothing! A river,' said this great commander, ' though it should be as large as the Vistula, and as rapid as the Danube at its mouth, is nothing, unless there are good points of passage, and a head quick to take the offensive; the Ebro as a defence was less than nothing, a mere line of demarcation! and Milagro was useless. The enemy might neglect it, be at Estella, and from thence gain Tolosa, before any preparation could be made to receive him; he might come from Soria, from Logroño, or from Zaragoza.

' Again, Burgos was the capital of a province, the centre of many communications, a town of great fame, and of relative value to the French army; to occupy it in force, and offensively, would threaten Palencia, Valladolid, Aranda, and even Madrid. It is necessary,' observed the emperor, ' to have made war a long time to conceive this; it is necessary to have made a number of offensive enterprises, to know how much the smallest event, or even indication, encourages or discourages, and decides the adoption of one enterprise instead of another.' ' In short, if the enemy occupies Burgos, Logroño, and Tudela, the French army will be in a pitiful position. It is not known if he has left Madrid; it is not known what has become of the Gallician army, and there is reason to suspect that it may have been directed upon Portugal; in such a state, to take up, instead of a bold, menacing, and honourable position like Burgos, a confined, shameful one like Trevino, is to say to the enemy, you have nothing to fear, go

elsewhere, we have made our dispositions to go farther; or we have chosen our ground to fight, come
there, without fear of being disturbed. But what
will the French general do if the enemy marches
the next day upon Burgos? Will he let the citadel
of that town be taken by six thousand insurgents?
if the French have left a garrison in the castle, how
can four or five hundred men retire in such a vast plain?
and, from that time, all is gone; if the enemy masters
the citadel, it cannot be retaken. If, on the contrary,
we should guard the citadel, we must give battle to
the enemy, because it cannot hold out more than three
days, and if we are to fight a battle, why should Bessieres abandon the ground where we wish to fight?

These dispositions appear badly considered, and
when the enemy shall march, our troops will
meet with such an insult as will demoralize
them if there are only insurgents or light troops
advancing against them. If fifteen thousand insurgents enter Burgos, retrench themselves in the
town, and occupy the castle, it will be necessary to
calculate a march of several days to enable us to post
ourselves there, and to retake the town, which cannot
be done without some inconvenience; and if, during
this time, the real attack is upon Logroño or Pampeluna, we shall have made countermarches without
use, which will have fatigued the army. If we hold
it with cavalry only, is it not to say we do not intend
stopping, and to invite the enemy to come there?
It is the first time that an army has quitted all
its offensive positions to take up a bad defensive
line, and to affect to choose its field of battle, when
the thousand and one combinations which might take
place, and the distance of the enemy, did not leave a
probability of being able to foresee if the battle would

take place at Tudela, between Tudela and Pampeluna, between Soria and the Ebro, or between Burgos and Miranda.   Then followed an observation which may be studied with advantage by those authors who, unacquainted with the simplest rudiments of military science, censure the conduct of generals, and are pleased, from some obscure nook, to point out their errors to the world ; authors who, profoundly igno- rant of the numbers, situation, and resources of the opposing armies, pretend, nevertheless, to detail with great accuracy the right method of executing the most difficult and delicate operations of war.   As the rebuke of Turenne, who frankly acknowledged to Louvois that he could pass the Rhine at a particular spot, if the latter's finger were a bridge, has been lost upon such men, perhaps the more recent opinion of Napoleon may be disregarded.   ' But it is not per- mitted,' says that consummate general, ' *it is not permitted, at the distance of three hundred leagues, and without even a state of the situation of the army, to direct what should be done !*'

After having thus protected himself from the charge of presumption, the emperor proceeded to re- commend certain dispositions for the defence of the Ebro.   The Spaniards, he said, were not to be feared in the field ; twenty-five thousand French in a good position would suffice to beat all their armies united, and this opinion he deduced from the events of Dupont's campaign, of which he gave a short analysis.   Let Tudela, he said, be retrenched if possible ; at all events it should be occupied in force, and offensively towards Zaragoza.   Let the general commanding there, collect provisions on all sides, secure the boats, with a view to future ope- rations when the reinforcements should arrive, and

maintain his communication with Logroño by the
right bank if he can, but certainly by the left ; let
his corps be considered as one of observation. If a
body of insurgents only approach, he may fight
them, or keep them constantly on the defensive by
his movements against their line or against Zaragoza ; if regular troops attack him, and he is forced
across the Ebro, let him then operate about Pampeluna until the general-in-chief has made his dispositions for the main body : in this manner no
prompt movement upon Estella and Tolosa can take
place, and the corps of observation will have amply
fulfilled its task.

Let marshal Bessieres, with all his corps
united, and reinforced by the light cavalry of
the army, encamp in the wood near Burgos; let
the citadel be well occupied, the hospital, the
dépôts, and all encumbrances sent over the Ebro ;
let him keep in a condition to act, be under arms
every day at three o'clock in the morning, and remain until the return of his patroles : he should
also send parties to a great extent, as far as two
days' march. Let the corps of the centre be placed
at Miranda and Briviesca, and all the encumbrances
be likewise sent across the Ebro behind Vittoria;
this corps should be under arms every morning, and
send patroles by the road of Soria, and wherever
the enemy may be expected : and it must not be
lost sight of, that these two corps, being to be
united, they should be connected as little as possible
with Logroño, and consider the left wing as a corps
detached, having a line of operations upon Pampeluna, and a separate part to act. Tudela is preserved as a post contiguous to the line. Be well
on the defensive, he continues, in short, make war !
that is to say, get information from the alcaldes, the

curates, the posts, the chiefs of convents, and the principal proprietors, you will then be perfectly informed. The patroles should always be directed upon the side of Soria, and of Burgos, upon Palencia, and upon the side of Aranda, they could thus form three posts of interception, and send three reports of men arrested; these men should be treated well, and dismissed after they had given the information desired of them. Let the enemy then come, and we can unite all our forces, hide our marches from him, and fall upon his flank at the moment he is meditating an offensive movement.'

With regard to the minor details, the emperor thus expressed himself: ' Soria is not, I believe, more than two short marches from the actual position of the army, and that town has constantly acted against us; an expedition sent there to disarm it, to take thirty of the principal people as hostages, and to obtain provisions, would have a good effect. It would be useful to occupy St. Ander, it will be of advantage to move by the direct road of Bilbao to St. Ander. It will be necessary

Navarre and Biscay being within the French line of defence, the inhabitants were, according to the civilians, *de facto* French subjects.

to occupy and disarm Biscay and Navarre, and every Spaniard taken in arms there should be shot. The manufactories of arms at Placencia should be watched, to hinder them from working for the rebels. The port of Pancorbo should be armed and fortified with great activity, ovens and magazines of provisions and ammunition should be placed there; situated nearly half way between Madrid and Bayonne, it is an intermediate post for the army, and a point of support for troops operating towards Gallicia. The interest of the enemy,' he resumes, ' is to mask his forces; by hiding the true point of attack, he operates in such a manner, that the blow he means to strike is never indicated

in a positive way, and the opposing general can
only guess it by a well-matured knowledge of his
own position, and of the mode in which he makes
his offensive system act, to protect his defensive
system.

We have no accounts of what the enemy is
about, it is said that no news can be obtained, as
if this case was extraordinary in an army, as if spies
were common; they must do in Spain as they do in
other places. Send parties out. Let them carry
off, sometimes the priest, sometimes the alcalde, the
chief of a convent, the master of the post or his
deputy, and, above all, the letters. Put these persons under arrest until they speak; question them
twice each day, or keep them as hostages; charge
them to send foot messengers, and to get news.
When we know how to take measures of vigour and
force, it is easy to get intelligence. All the posts,
all the letters must be intercepted; the single
motive of procuring intelligence will be sufficient
to authorise a detachment of four or five thousand
men, who will go into a great town, will take the
letters from the post, will seize the richest citizens,
their letters, papers, gazettes, &c. It is beyond
doubt, that even in the French lines, the inhabitants
are all informed of what passes, of course, out of
that line they know more; what, then, should prevent you from seizing the principal men? Let them
be sent back again without being ill treated. It is
a fact, that when we are not in a desert, but in a
peopled country, if the general is not well instructed, it is because he is ignorant of his trade.
The services which the inhabitants render to an
enemy's general are never given from affection,
nor even to get money; the truest method to ob-

tain them is by safeguards and protections to preserve their lives, their goods, their towns, or their
monasteries! '

Joseph, although by no means a dull man,
seems to have had no portion of his brother's
martial genius. The operations recommended by
the latter did not appear to the king to be applicable to the state of affairs; he did not adopt
them, but proposed others, in discussing which, he
thus defended the policy of his retreat from Madrid.
' When the *defection* of twenty-two thousand men
(Dupont's) caused the king to quit the capital, the
disposable troops remaining were divided in three
corps, namely, his own, marshal Bessieres', and
general Verdier's, then besieging Zaragoza; but
these bodies were spread over a hundred leagues of
ground, and with the last the king had little or no
connexion. His first movement was to unite the
two former at Burgos, afterwards to enter into
communication with the third, and then the
line of defence on the Ebro was adopted; an
operation said the king dictated by sound reason
—Because when the events of Andalusia fore-
boded a regular and serious war, prudence did
not permit three corps, the strongest of which was
only eighteen thousand men, to separate to a greater
distance than six days' march, in the midst of
eleven millions of people in a state of hostility. But
fifty thousand French could defend with success a
line of sixty leagues, and could guard the two grand
communications of Burgos and Tudela, against enemies who had not, up to that period, been able to
carry to either point above twenty-five thousand
men.   In this mode fifteen thousand French could
be united upon either of those roads.'

Appendix,
No. 6.

Joseph was dissatisfied with Napoleon's plans, and preferred his own. The disposable troops at his command, exclusive of those in Bilbao, were fifty thousand, which he distributed as follows. The right wing occupied Burgos, Pancorbo, and Puente Lara. The centre was posted between Haro and Logroño. The left extended from Logroño to Tudela, and the latter town was not occupied. He contended, that this arrangement, at once offensive and defensive, might be advantageously continued if the great army, directed upon Spain, arrived in September, since it tended to refit the army already there, and menaced the enemy; but that it could not be prolonged until November, because in three months the Spaniards must make a great progress, and would very soon be in a state to take the offensive, with grand organized corps obedient to a central administration, which would have time to form in Madrid. Everything announced, he said, that the month of October was one of those decisive epochs which gave, to the party who knew how to profit from it, the priority of movements and success, the progress of which it was difficult to calculate.

In this view of affairs, the merits of six projects were discussed by the king.

First project. To remain in the actual position. This was declared to be unsustainable, because the enemy could attack the left with forty thousand, the centre with forty thousand, the right with as many. Tudela and Navarre, as far as Logroño, required twenty-five thousand men to defend them. Burgos could not be defended but by an army in a state to resist the united forces of Blake and Cuesta, which would amount to eighty thousand men; it was doubtful if the twenty thousand bayonets which could be opposed to them, could completely beat them; if they did not, the French would be harassed by the insurgents of the three provinces, Biscay, Navarre, and Guipuscoa, who would interpose between the left wing and France.

Second project. To carry the centre and reserve by Tudela, towards Zaragoza or Albazan. United with the left, they would amount to thirty thousand men, who might seek for, and, doubtless, would defeat the enemy, if he was met with on that side. In the meantime, the right wing, leaving garrisons in the citadel of Burgos and the fort of Pancorbo, could occupy the enemy, and watch any movements in the Montaña St. Ander, or disembarkations that might take place at the ports. But this task was considered difficult, because Pancorbo was not the only defile accessible to artillery; three leagues from thence another road led upon Miranda, and there was a third passage over the point of the chain which stretched between Haro and Miranda.

Third project. To leave the defence of Navarre to the left wing. To carry the centre, the reserve, and the right wing, to Burgos, and to beat the enemy before he could unite; an easy task, as the French would be thirty thousand strong. Meanwhile, Moncey would keep the Spaniards in check on the side of Tudela, or, if unable to do that, he was to march up the Ebro, by Logroño and Briviesca, and join the main body : the communication with France would be thus lost, but the army might maintain itself until the arrival of the emperor. A modification of this project was, that Moncey, retiring to the entrenched camp of Pampeluna, should there await either the arrival of

the emperor, or the result of the operations towards
Burgos.

Fourth project. To pass the Ebro in retreat, and
to endeavour to tempt the enemy to fight in the
plain between that river and Vittoria.

Fifth project. To retire, supporting the left upon
Pampeluna, the right upon Montdragon.

Sixth project. To leave garrisons, with the
means of a six weeks' defence, in Pampeluna, St.
Sebastian, Pancorbo, and Burgos. To unite the rest
of the army, march against the enemy, attack him
wherever he was found, and then wait, either near
Madrid or in that country, into which the pursuit
of the Spaniards, or the facility of living should
draw the army. This plan relinquished the communications with France entirely, but it was said
that the grand army could easily open them
again; the troops, already in Spain, would be sufficiently strong to defy all the efforts of the enemy,
to disconcert all his projects, and to wait in a noble
attitude the general impulse which would be given
by the arrival of the emperor.

Of all these projects, the last was the favourite
with the king, who strongly recommended it, and
asserted, that if it was followed, affairs would be
more prosperous when the emperor arrived than
could be expected from any other plan. Marshal
Ney and general Jourdan approved of it, but it
would appear that Napoleon had other views,
and too little confidence in his brother's military
judgment, to entrust so great a matter to his
guidance.

OBSERVATIONS.

1°. It is undoubted, that there must always be
some sympathy of genius in the man who is to

execute another's conception in military affairs. Without that species of harmony between their minds, the thousand accidental occurrences and minor combinations which must happen contrary to expectation, will inevitably embarrass the executor to such a degree, that he will be unable to see the most obvious advantages; and in striving to unite the plan he has received with his own views, he will adopt neither, but steering an unsteady reeling course between both, will fail of success. The reason of this appears to be, that a strong, and, if the term may be used, inveterate attention must be fixed upon certain great principles of action in war, to enable a general to disregard the minor events and inconveniences which cross his purpose; minor they are to the great object, but in themselves sufficient to break down the firmness and self-possession of any but extraordinary men.

2°. The original memoir from which Joseph's projects have been extracted, is so blotted and interlined, that it would be unfair to consider it as a mature production. The great error which pervades it, is the conjectured data upon which he founds his plans, and the little real information which he appears to have had relative to the Spanish forces, views, or interior policy. His plans were based upon the notion that the central junta would be able and provident, the Spaniards united, the armies strong and well guided, none of which was true. Again, he estimated Cuesta and Blake's armies at eighty thousand, and considered them as one body; but they were never united at all, and if they had, they would scarcely have amounted to sixty thousand. The bold idea of throwing himself into the interior came too late, he should have

thought of that before he quitted Madrid, or at
least before the central government was established
at that capital. His operations might have been successful against the miserable armies opposed to him,
but against good and moveable troops they would
not, as the emperor's admirable notes prove. The
first project, wanting those offensive combinations
discussed by Napoleon, was open to all his objections, as being timid and incomplete. The
second was crude and ill-considered, for, according
to the king's estimate of the Spanish force, thirty
thousand men on each wing might oppose the heads
of his columns, while sixty thousand could still
have been united at Logroño; these might pass the
Ebro, excite an insurrection in Navarre, Guipuscoa,
and Biscay, seize Tolosa and Miranda, and fall
upon the rear of the French army, which, thus cut
in two, and its communications intercepted, would
have been extremely embarrassed. The third was
not better judged. Burgos, as an offensive post,
protecting the line of defence, was very valuable,
and to unite a large force there was so far prudent;
but if the Spaniards retired, and refused battle with
their left, while the centre and right operated by
Logroño and Sanguessa, what would have been the
result? the French right must, without any definite
object, either have continued to advance, or remained stationary without communication, or returned to fight a battle for those very positions
which they had just quitted. The fourth depended
entirely upon accident, and is not worth argument.
The fifth was an undisguised retreat. The sixth
was not applicable to the actual situation of affairs,
the king's force was no longer an independent
body, it was become the advanced guard of the

great army, marching under Napoleon. It was absurd, therefore, to contemplate a decisive movement,
without having first matured a plan suitable to the
whole mass that was to be engaged in the execution : in short, to permit an advanced guard to determine the operations of the main body, was to
reverse the order of military affairs, and to trust to
accident instead of design. It is curious, that while
Joseph was proposing this irruption into Spain, the
Spaniards and the military agents of Great Britain
were trembling lest he should escape their power
by a precipitate flight. *War is not a conjectural
art !*

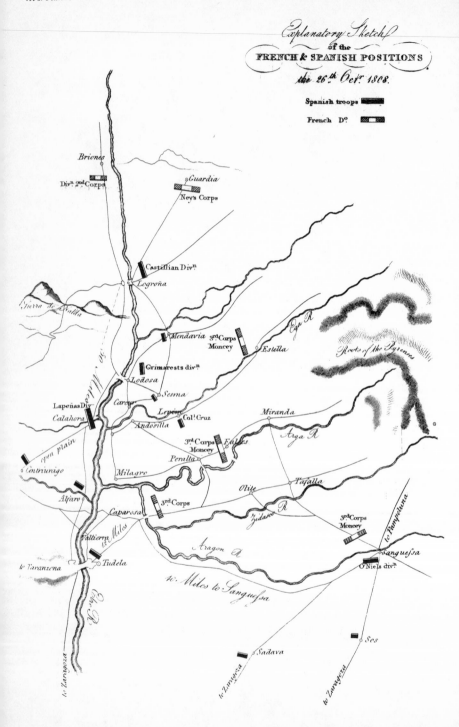

Explanatory Sketch
of the
FRENCH & SPANISH POSITIONS
the 26th Octr. 1808.

Spanish troops
French Do.

Briones

Divn 2nd Corps

Guardia

Ney's Corps

Castilian Divn

Logroño

Sierra de Codila

Mendavia

3rd Corps Moncey

Estella

Ego R.

Roots of the Pyrenees

Grimarests divn

Lodosa

Sesma

Carcas

Lapeñas Div

Calahora

Andorilla

Lerin

Coll Cruz

Miranda

Arga R.

3rd Corps Moncey

Falces

Peralta

open plain

Centriunigo

Milagro

Olite

Tafalla

3rd Corps Moncey

Alfaro

3rd Corps

Idasco R.

to Pampeluna

Caparosa

Aragon R.

Sanguessa

Valtierra 12 Miles

to Tavanzena

Tudela

O'Niels divn

Ebro R.

40. Miles to Sanguessa

to Zaragoza

Sadava

Ses

to Zaragoza

to Zaragoza

London Published by T.&W. Boone, New Bond Street.

CHAPTER V.

THE emperor overruled the offensive projects of the king, and the latter was forced to distribute the centre and right wing in a manner more consonant to the spirit of Napoleon's instructions; but he still neglected to occupy Tudela, and covered his left wing by the Aragon river.

The 18th of September, the French army was posted in the following manner:—

V.

1808.
September

Journal of
the king's
operations,
MS.

	Under Arms.	
Right wing, Marshal Bessieres	15,595	Three divisions of infantry in front of Pancorbo, at Briviesca, Santa Maria, and Cuba; light cavalry behind Burgos.
Centre . Marshal Ney . . .	13,756	Logrono, Nalda, and Najera.
Left wing Marshal Moncey . .	16,636	Milagro, Lodosa, Caparosa, and Alfaro. The garrison of Pampeluna was also under Moncey's command.

Reserve of the king.
General Saligny. . 5,413
Imperial guard.
General Dorsenne . 2,423
Total—— 7,833 } Miranda, Haro, and Puente Lara.

Appendix,
No. 28.

Garrisons	6,004	Pampeluna.
General Monthion.	1,500	Bilbao.
General La Grange	6,979	Composed of small garrisons and moveable columns, guarding the communications of Biscay, Alava, and Guipuscoa.

Grand reserve.
Moveable columns . 1,984
Stationary 20,005
Total, commanded by }
General Drouet . } —— 21,989 } Bayonne, and watching the valleys of the Pyrenees opening into Navarre.

Total 90,289 present under arms, exclusive of the troops in Catalonia; and when the communications were secured, the fortresses garrisoned, and the fort of Pancorbo armed, there remained above fifty thousand sabres and bayonets disposable on a line of battle extending from Bilbao to Alfaro.

To oppose this formidable force the Spanish troops were divided into three principal masses, denominated the armies of the right, centre, and left.

	Infantry.	Cavalry.	Guns.	First Line.	
The first, composed of the divisions of St. Marc and O'Neil, numbered about	17,500	500	24	Men. 75,400	Guns. 86
The second, composed of the divisions of La-Pena, Llamas, and Caro	26,000	1,300	36		
The third, consisting entirely of Gallicians, about	30,000	100	26		
				Second Line.	
In the second line the Castillians were at Segovia	12,000	—	—		
The Estremadurans at Talavera	13,000	—	—	57,000	—
Two Andalusian divisions were in La Mancha	14,000	—	—		
And the Asturians (posted at Llanes) were called	18,000	—	—		

This estimate, founded upon a number of contemporary returns and other documents, proves the monstrous exaggerations put forth at this time to deceive the Spanish people and the English government. The Spaniards pretended that above one hundred and forty thousand men in arms were threatening the French positions on the Ebro, whereas less than seventy-six thousand were in line of battle, and those exceedingly ill-armed and provided. The right, under Palafox, held the country between Zaragoza and Sanguessa, on the Aragon river; the centre, under Castaños, occupied Borja, Taranzona, and Agreda; the left, under Blake, was posted at Reynosa, near the sources of the Ebro. The relative position of the French and Spanish armies was also very disadvantageous to the latter. From the right to the left of their line, that is, from Reynosa to Zaragoza, was twice the distance between Bayonne and Vittoria, and the roads more difficult; the re-

serve under Drouet was consequently in closer military communication with king Joseph's army than
the Spanish wings were with another.

The patriots were acting without concert upon
double external lines of operation, and against an
enemy far superior in quickness, knowledge, and
organization, and even in numbers.

The French were superior in cavalry, and the
base of their operations rested on three great fortresses,—Bayonne, St. Sebastian, and Pampeluna;
they could in three days carry the centre and the
reserve to either flank, and unite thirty thousand
combatants without drawing a man from their garrisons.

The Spaniards held but one fortress, Zaragoza,
and being divided in corps, under different generals
of equal authority, they could execute no combined
movement with rapidity or precision, nor under any
circumstances could they unite more than 40,000
men at a given point.

In this situation of affairs, general Blake, his army
organized in six divisions, each five thousand strong,
broke up from Reynosa on the 17th of September.
One division advanced on the side of Burgos, to
cover the march of the main body, which, threading
the valley of Villarcayo, turned the right of marshal
Bessieres, and reached the Ebro; two divisions occupied Traspaderna and Frias, and established a
post at Oña, on the right bank of that river; a third
division took a position at Medina; a fourth held
the town of Erran and the Sierra of that name; a
fifth halted in the town of Villarcayo, to preserve
the communication with Reynosa; and at the same
time, 8000 Asturians, under general Acevedo, quitted the camp at Llanes, and advanced to St. Ander.

Correspon-
dence of
Captain
Carrol.
Ibid.
General
Broderick.

General Broderick arrived in the Spanish camp,
Blake importuned him for money, and obtained it;
but treated him otherwise with great coldness, and
withheld all information relative to the movements
of the army. English vessels hovering on the coast
were prepared to supply the Biscayans with arms
and ammunition, and Blake thinking himself in a
situation to revive the insurrection in that province,
and to extend it to Guipuscoa, detached his fourth
division, and five guns, under the command of the
marquis of Portazgo, to attack general Monthion at
Bilbao. The king getting knowledge of the march
of this division, ordered a brigade from his right
wing to fall on its flank by the valley of Orduña,
and caused general Merlin to reinforce Monthion by
the valley of Durango, while Bessieres aided these
dispositions with a demonstration on the side of Frias.
The combination was made too late, Portazgo was
already master of Bilbao; Monthion had retired on
the 20th to Durango, and Bessieres fell back with
his corps to Miranda, Haro, and Puente Lara, having
first injured the defences of Burgos.

Corre-
spondence
of general
Leith.

Journal of
the king's
Operations
MS.

The king then took post with the reserve at Vittoria, and Ney immediately abandoning his position
on the Ebro, carried his whole force, by a rapid
march, to Bilbao, where he arrived on the evening of
the 26th; at the same time, general Merle's division
executed a combined movement from Miranda upon
Osma and Barbaceña. Portazgo being thus overmatched, occupied the heights above Bilbao, until
nightfall, and then retreated to Valmaceda, where he
found the third division, for Blake had changed his
position, and now occupied Frias with his right,
Quincoes with his centre, and Valmaceda with his
left; all the Spanish artillery was in the town of

Villarcayo, guarded by a division; and in this situation, holding the passes of the mountains, Blake
awaited the arrival of the Asturians, who were
marching by the valley of Villarcayo. Thus the
second effort to raise Biscay failed of success.

In the mean time, O'Neil, following colonel Doyle's
plan before mentioned, entered Sanguessa, and was
beaten out of it again, with the loss of two guns.
However, the Castillian army approached the Ebro
by the road of Soria ; General La-Peña occupied
Logroño, Nalda, and Najera; Llamas and Caro
occupied Corella, Cascante, and Calahorra, and
O'Neil took post in the mountains, on the left bank
of the Aragon, facing Sanguessa. The peasantry of
the valleys assembled in considerable numbers, the
country between Zaragoza and the Aragon river
appeared to be filled with troops, and Moncey
withdrawing from the Ebro, took a position, with
his left flank at the pass of Sanguessa, his centre at
Falces, and his right at Estella. Ney also, leaving
Merlin with three thousand men at Bilbao, returned
to the Ebro, but finding that Logroño was occupied
in force by the Spaniards, halted at Guardia on the
5th of October, and remained in observation.

On the 4th, the king and Bessieres, at the head
of Mouton's and Merle's divisions, quitted Miranda,
and advanced along the road of Osma, with the intention of feeling for Blake on the side of Frias and
Medina; the Spaniards were then in force at Valmaceda, but Joseph, deceived by false information,
imagined that they were again in march towards
Bilboa, and therefore pushed on to Lodio, with the
intention of attacking Blake during the movement ;
at Lodio he ascertained the truth, and being uneasy
about Moncey, returned the 7th to Murquia, where

BOOK
III.
————
1808.
October.

Journal of
the king's
Operations
MS.
he left Merle to protect the rear of the troops at
Bilbao, and then proceeded to Miranda with the
division of Mouton. On the 12th, Blake, still intent upon the insurrection of Biscay, placed a division at Orduña, and attacked Bilbao with eighteen
thousand men. Merlin retired fighting up the valley
of Durango as far as Zornosa, but being joined there
by general Verdier, with six battalions, turned and
checked the pursuit. At this time, however, the
leading columns of the great French army were
passing the Spanish frontier; Laval's division advanced to Durango; Sebastiani, with six thousand
men, relieved Merle at Murquia, who repaired
to Miranda; Verdier returned to Vittoria, and Lefebre, duke of Dantzic, assumed the command of
the three divisions posted at Durango.

On the Spanish side, the marquis of Romana's
division had disembarked on the 9th at St. Ander,
and the infantry, eight thousand strong, completely
equipped and provided from the English stores, proceeded by slow marches to join Blake. The Asturians
had halted at Villarcayo, but the Estremaduran army,
under the conde de Belvedere, was put in motion, and
the Castillian forces arrived upon the Ebro; the first
and third divisions of the Andalusian army were on
the march from La Mancha, and Castaños, quitting
Madrid, proceeded towards Tudela. All things
announced the approach of a great crisis, yet such
was the apathy of the supreme junta, that the best
friends of Spain hoped for a defeat, as the only
mode of exciting sufficient energy in the government to save the state, and by some it was thought
that even that sharp remedy would be insufficient.

See page
328. A momentary excitement was, however, caused by
the intercepted letter to Jourdan before spoken of;

the troops in the second line were ordered to proceed to the Ebro by forced marches, letters were
written, pressing for the advance of the British army,
and Castaños was enjoined to drive the enemy, without delay, beyond the frontier.   But this sudden
fury of action ended with those orders.   Sir David
Baird's corps was detained in the transports at Coruña, waiting for permission to land ; no assistance
was afforded to sir John Moore; and although the
subsidies, already paid by England, amounted to
ten millions of dollars, and that Madrid was rich,
and willing to contribute to the exigencies of the
moment, the central junta, while complaining of
the want of money, would not be at the trouble of
collecting patriotic gifts, and left the armies ' to all
the horrors of famine, nakedness, and misery.'   The
natural consequence of such folly and wickedness
ensued ; the people ceased to be enthusiastic, and
the soldiers deserted in crowds.

The conduct of the generals was not less extraordinary.   Blake had voluntarily commenced the
campaign without magazines, and without any plan,
except that of raising the provinces of Biscay and
Guipuscoa.   With the usual blind confidence of a
Spaniard, he pressed forward, ignorant of the force
or situation of his adversaries, never dreaming of a
defeat; and so little experienced in the detail of command, that he calculated upon the ordinary quantity
of provisions contained in an English frigate, which
cruised off the coast, as a resource for his army, if
the country should fail to supply him with subsistence; his artillery had only seventy rounds for each
gun, his men were without great-coats, many without
shoes, and the snow was beginning to fall in the
mountains.   That he was able to make any impres-

sion is a proof that king Joseph possessed little
military talent; the French, from the habitude of
war, were indeed able to baffle Blake without difficulty, but the strategic importance of the valley of
Orduña they did not appreciate, or he would have
been destroyed : the lesson given by Napoleon,
when he defeated Wurmser in the valley of the
Brenta, might have been repeated, under more
favourable circumstances, at Orduña and Durango.

But if genius was asleep with the French, it was
dead with the Spaniards. As long as Blake remained
between Frias and Valmaceda, his position was
tolerably secure from an attack, because the Montaña St. Ander is exceedingly rugged, and the line
of retreat by Villarcayo was open ; nevertheless he
was cooped up in a corner, and ill placed for offensive movements, which were the only operations he
thought of. Instead of occupying Burgos, and repairing the citadel, he descended on Bilbao with
the bulk of his army, thereby discovering his total
ignorance of war ; for several great valleys, the
upper parts of which were possessed by the French,
met near that town, and it was untenable, the flank
of his army was always exposed to an attack from
the side of Orduña, and his line of retreat was in
the power of Bessieres. To protect his flank and
rear, Blake detached largely, but that weakened
the main body without obviating the danger ; nor
did he make amends for his bad dispositions by
diligence ; for his movements were slow, his attacks
without vigour, and his whole conduct displayed
temerity without decision, rashness without enterprise.

The armies of the centre and right were not
better conducted. Castaños having quitted Madrid

on the 8th of October, arrived at Tudela on the 17th, and on the 20th held a conference with Palafox at Zaragoza. The aggregate of their forces did not much exceed forty-five thousand men, of which from two to three thousand were cavalry, and sixty pieces of artillery followed the divisions; which were posted in the following manner :—

Appendix,
No. 27.

ARMY OF THE CENTRE,
27,000.

General Pignatelli, with ten thousand Castillian infantry, one thousand five hundred cavalry, and fourteen guns, at Logroño.

General Grimarest, with the second division of Andalusia, five thousand men, at Lodosa.

General La-Peña, with the fourth division, five thousand infantry, at Calahorra.

The parc of artillery, and a division of infantry, four thousand, at Centruenigo.

The remainder at Tudela and the neighbouring villages.

ARMY OF ARRAGON.
18,000.

O'Neil with seven thousand five hundred men, held Sor, Lumbar, and Sanguessa.

Thirty miles in the rear, St. Marc occupied Exca, with five thousand five hundred men.

Palafox, with five thousand men, remained in Zaragoza.

The Ebro rolled between these two corps, but viewed as one army their front lines occupied two sides of an irregular triangle, of which Tudela was

the apex, Sanguessa and Logroño the extremities
of the base.   From the latter points, the rivers
Ebro and Arragon, which meet at Milagro, describe,
in their double course, an arc, the convex of which
was opposed to the Spaniards. The streams of the
Ega, the Arga, and the Zidasco rivers, descending
from the Pyrenees in parallel courses, cut the chord
of this arc at nearly equal distances, and fall, the
two first into the Ebro, the last into the Aragon, and
all the roads leading from Pampeluna to the Ebro
follow the course of those torrents.

Marshal Moncey's right was at Estella on the
Ega, his centre held Falces and Tafalla on the
Arga and the Zidasco, his left was in front of San-
guessa on the Aragon; the bridges of Olite and
Peralta were secured by advanced parties, and
Caparosa, where there was another bridge, was oc-
cupied in force.   In this situation he could operate
freely between the torrents, which intersected his
line, he commanded all the roads leading to the
Ebro, and he could, from Caparosa, at any moment,
issue forth against the centre of the Spanish armies.
Now from Tudela to Sanguessa is fifty miles, from
Tudela to Logroño sixty miles, but from Tudela to
Caparosa is only twelve miles of good road;
wherefore, the extremities of the Spanish line were
above one hundred miles, or six days' march from
each other, while a single day would have sufficed
to unite the French within two hours' march of the
centre.   The weakness of the Spaniards' position
is apparent.

If Palafox, crossing the Aragon at Sanguessa,
advanced towards Pampeluna, Moncey would be
on his left flank and rear; if he turned against
Moncey, the garrison of Pampeluna would fall upon

his right ; if Castaños, to favour the attack of Palafox, crossed the Ebro at Logroño, Ney, being posted
at Guardia, was ready to take him in flank ; if the
two wings endeavoured to unite, their line of march
was liable to be intercepted at Tudela by Moncey, and
the rear of Castaños be attacked by Ney, who could
pass the Ebro at Logroño or Lodosa. If they remained
stationary, they might easily be beaten in detail.

Any other than Spanish generals would have
been filled with apprehension on such an occasion;
but Palafox and Castaños, heedless of their own Sir John Moore's
danger, tranquilly proceeded to arrange a plan Papers. Colonel
of offensive operations singularly absurd. They Graham's Corre-
agreed that the army of the centre, leaving a di- spondence.
vision at Lodosa and another at Calahorra, should
make a flank march to the right, and take a position
along the Aragon, the left to be at Tudela, the right
at Sanguessa ; that is, with less than twenty thousand men to occupy fifty miles of country close to a
powerful and concentrated enemy. In the mean- Ibid. Colonel
time, Palafox, with the Aragonese, crossing the Doyle's Correspon-
river at Sanguessa, was to extend in an oblique line dence.
to Roncesvalles, covering the valleys of Talay,
Escay, and Roncal, with his centre, and reinforcing
his army by the armed inhabitants, who were ready
to flock to his standard. Blake was invited to
co-operate, in combination, by Guipuscoa, so
as to pass in the rear of the whole French army,
unite with Palafox, and thus cut off the enemy's
retreat into France, and intercept his reinforcements at the same time.

Castaños returned to Tudela on the 23d, and
proceeded to Logroño on the 25th, the grand movement being to commence on the 27th. But on the
21st, Grimarest had pushed forward strong detach-

BOOK
III.

1808.
October.
ments across the Ebro to Mendavia, Andosilla,
Sesma, and Carcur, and one over the Ega to
Lerim—the Castillian outposts occupied Viana on
the left bank of the Ebro—the Aragonese divisions
were already closing upon Sanguessa, and a multitude of peasants crowded to the same place in the
hope of obtaining arms and ammunition.   Moncey,
deceived by this concourse of persons, estimated the
force in Sanguessa at twenty thousand, when, in
fact, it was only eight thousand regular troops; and
his report, and the simultaneous movements of the
Spaniards on both extremities, made the king to apprehend a triple attack from Logroño, Lodosa, and
Journal of
the king's
operations.
MS. Sanguessa.   He immediately reinforced Ney with
Merlin's division from Bessieres' corps, and directed
him to clear the left bank of the Ebro, while Bonnet's division, also taken from Bessieres, descended
the right bank from Haro to Briones.   A division of
Moncey's corps, stationed at Estella, received orders
to follow the course of the Ega, and second Ney's
operations; and a part of the garrison of Pampeluna,
posted at Montreal and Salinas, was commanded to
advance upon Nardues, and make a demonstration
against Sanguessa.

   When Castaños arrived at Logroño these operations were in full activity.   Ney had, on the 24th,
driven back the Castillian outposts, crowned the
height opposite that town on the 25th, and was can-
nonading the Spaniards' position.   On the 26th, he
renewed his fire briskly until twelve o'clock, at
Whitting-
ham's
Corre-
spondence.
MS. which time Castaños, after giving Pignatelli strict
orders to defend his post unless he was turned by a
force descending the right bank of the Ebro, proceeded himself to Lodosa and Calahorra.   Meanwhile the French from Estella falling down the

Ega, drove the Spanish parties out of Mendavia,
Andosilla, Carcur, and Sesma; and Grimarest retired from Lodosa to La Torre with such precipitation, that he left colonel Cruz, a valuable officer,
with a light battalion, and some volunteers, at
Lerim, where he was taken after a creditable resistance.

Pignatelli, regardless of Castaños' orders, retired
from Logroño, and abandoned all his guns at the
foot of the Serra de Nalda, only a few miles from
the enemy; then crossing the mountains, he gained
Centruenigo in such disorder, that his men continued to arrive for twenty-four hours consecutively.
On the right, O'Neil skirmished with the garrison
of Pampeluna, and lost six men killed, and eight
wounded, but in the Spanish fashion, announced,
that, after a hard action of many hours, the enemy
was completely overthrown. On the 27th, Merlin's
division rejoined Bessieres at Miranda, and Bonnet,
retiring from Briones, took post in front of Pancorbo. Castaños, incensed at the ill conduct of the
Castillians, dismissed Pignatelli and incorporated
his troops with the Andalusian divisions; fifteen
hundred men of the latter, being sent back to
Nalda under the conde de Cartoajal, recovered the
lost guns, and brought them safe to Centruenigo.

Dissensions followed these reverses. Palafox ar-
rogantly censured Castaños, and a cabal, of which
general Coupigny appears to have been the principal mover, was formed against the latter. The
junta, exasperated that Castaños had not already
driven the enemy beyond the frontier, encouraged
his traducers, and circulated slanderous accusations
themselves, as if his inaction alone had enabled the
French to remain in Spain; they sent Francisco

Palafox, brother of the captain-general, and a member of the supreme junta, to head-quarters, avow-
edly to facilitate, but really to control the military
operations, and he arrived at Alfaro on the 29th, accompanied by Coupigny, and the conde de Montijo,
a turbulent factious man, shallow and vain, but

designing and unprincipled. Castaños waited upon
this representative of the government, and laid
before him the denuded state of the army; the captain-general, Palafox, also came up from Zaragoza,
and a council of war was held at Tudela on the 5th
of November. The rough manner in which the
Spaniards had just been driven from the left bank of
the Ebro, made no impression on the council, which
persisted in the grand project of getting in the rear
of the French, although it was known that sixty
thousand fresh men had joined the latter. Deeming

it, however, fitting that Blake should act the first, it
was resolved to await his time, and, as an intermediate operation, it was agreed that the army of
the centre, leaving six thousand men at Calahorra,
and a garrison at Tudela, should cross the Ebro and

attack Caparosa: French parties had, however,
pushed as far as Valtierra, and in the skirmishes
which ensued, the conduct of the Castillian battalions was discreditable. Joseph Palafox then
returned to Zaragoza, and the deputy separated
himself from Castaños.

The loss sustained by desertion and the previous combats was considerable, but some Murcian
levies, and a part of the first and third Andalusian
divisions joined the army of the centre, which now
mustered twenty-six thousand infantry, and nearly
three thousand cavalry under arms, with fifty or
sixty pieces of artillery. The positions of the army

extended from Calahorra, by Haro, to Tudela.
La-Peña held the first town with five thousand
men; Grimarest and Caro commanded eight
thousand at the second; head-quarters, with thirteen thousand five hundred men, were fixed in the
last; Cartoajal remained with eleven hundred in
the Sierra de Nalda, and eight hundred were
posted at Ansejo. From these points, in pursuance
of the plan arranged, the troops were actually in
movement to cross the Ebro, when despatches from
Blake announced that he had met with some disaster on the 31st, the extent of which he did not
communicate.

This news arrested the attack, and the preposterous transactions that ensued, resembled the
freaks of Caligula rather than the operations of
real war. First, it was arranged that the army
should abandon Tudela, and take a position in
two lines, the extremities of the one to rest on
Calahorra and Amedo, the second to extend from
Alfaro to Fitero, and the deputy ordered O'Neil,
with the army of Aragon, to occupy the latter
of these lines forthwith; O'Neil, however, refused
to stir without instructions from the captain-general. This was on the 9th, on the 10th the plan
was changed. Castaños fixed his head-quarters at
Centruenigo, and the deputy proposed that O'Neil
should descend the right bank of the Aragon river,
and attack Caparosa in the rear; that the troops in
Tudela should attack it in front; and that a division
should make a demonstration of passing the Ebro in
boats, opposite to Milagro, in order to favour this attack. Castaños assented, and on the 12th a division
assembled opposite Milagro, while La-Peña, with two
divisions, marched against Caparosa; suddenly, the

whimsical deputy sent them orders to repair to Lodosa, forty miles higher up the Ebro, to attack the
bridge at that place, while Grimarest, crossing in
the boats at Calahorra, should ascend the left bank
of the Ebro, and take it in rear. La Peña and Vil-

larcayo, confounded by this change, wrote to Castaños for an explanation, and this was the first
intimation that the latter, who was lying sick at
Centruenigo, received of the altered dispositions.
He directed his lieutenants to obey; but being provoked beyond endurance, wrote sharply to the junta,
demanding to know who was to command the army;
and after all this insolence and vapouring no ope-

ration took place: Francisco Palafox declaring, that
his intention was merely to make a demonstration,
ordered the troops to their quarters, and then, without assigning any reason, deprived La-Peña of his
command, and appointed Cartoajal in his place.

It was at this time that sir John Moore's letter arrived, but Castaños, no longer master of his own operations, could ill concert a plan of campaign with
the general of another army; he could not even tell
what troops were to be at his nominal disposal! for
the Estremaduran force, originally destined for his
command, was now directed by the junta upon
Burgos, and the remainder of his first and third
division was detained in Madrid. His enemies, especially Montijo, were active in spreading reports
to his disadvantage, the deserters scattered over the
country declared that all the generals were traitors;

and the people of the towns and villages, deceived
by the central junta, and excited by false rumours,
respected neither justice nor government, and committed the most scandalous excesses. Blake's situation was not more prosperous. The road from

Bayonne to Vittoria was encumbered with the advancing columns of the great French army.

An imperial decree, issued early in September, incorporated the troops already in Spain with the grand army then marching from Germany, and the united forces were to compose eight divisions, called ' Corps d'Armée,' an institution analogous to the Roman legion ; because each ' Corps d'Armée,' although adapted for action as a component part of a large army, was also provided with light cavalry, a parc, and train of artillery, engineers, sappers and miners, and a complete civil administration, to enable it to take the field as an independent force. The imperial guards and the heavy cavalry of the army were, however, not included in this arrangement; the first had a constitution of their own, and at this time all the heavy cavalry, and all the artillery, not attached to the ' Corps d'Armée,' were formed into a large reserve. As the columns arrived in Spain, they were united to the troops already there, and the whole was disposed conformably to the new organization.

Marshal Victor, duke of Belluno, commanded the	First Corps.
Marshal Bessieres, duke of Istria . .	Second Corps.
Marshal Moncey, duke of Cornegliano . .	Third Corps.
Marshal Lefebre, duke of Dantzic . .	Fourth Corps.
Marshal Mortier, duke of Treviso . .	Fifth Corps.
Marshal Ney, duke of Elchingen . .	Sixth Corps.
General St. Cyr . .	Seventh Corps.
General Junot, duke of Abrantes . .	Eighth Corps.

The seventh corps was appropriated to Catalonia, but the remainder were, in the latter end of October, assembled or assembling in Navarre and Biscay. General Merlin, with a division, held Zornosa, and observed Blake, who remained tranquilly at Bilbao. Two divisions of the fourth corps occupied Durango and the neighbouring villages.

BOOK
III.
————
1808.
S.
Journal of
the king's
operations.
MS.
One division and the light cavalry of the first corps
was at Vittoria, a second division of the same corps
guarded the bridge of Murguia on the river Bayas,
and commanded the entrance to the valley of Orduña.   Haro, Puente, Lara, Miranda, and Pancorbo
were maintained by the infantry of the king's body
guard and the second corps ; and the light cavalry
of the latter covered the plains close up to Briviesca.   The reinforcements were daily crowding up to
Vittoria, and the king, restrained by the emperor's
orders to a rigorous system of defence, occupied
himself with the arrangements attendant on such an
immense accumulation of force, and left Blake in
quiet possession of Bilbao.   The latter mistook this
apparent inactivity for timidity ; he was aware that
reinforcements, in number equal to his whole army,
had joined the enemy, yet, with wonderful rashness,
resolved to press forward, and readily agreed to
attempt a junction with Palafox, in the rear of the
French position.

At this time Romana's infantry were approaching
Bilbao, and the Estremadurans were in march for
Burgos ; but the country was nearly exhausted
of provisions, both armies felt the scarcity, desertion prevailed among the Spaniards, and the
Biscayans, twice abandoned, were fearful of a
third insurrection.   Prudence dictated a retreat
towards Burgos, but Blake resolved to advance.
First he posted general Acevedo with the Astu-
Carrol's
Correspon-
dence. rians and the second division at Orduña ; then he
left a battalion at Miravelles, to preserve the communication with Bilbao ; finally he marched himself, on the 24th, at the head of seventeen thousand
fighting men, divided in three columns, to attack
Zornosa.   The right column ascended the valley of

Explanatory Sketch of BLAKE'S POSITION at the Battle of Zornoza

Spanish troops
French Do.

London, Published by T. & W. Boone, New Bond Street.

Durango by Galdacano, the centre by Larabezua, the left by Rigoytia; and general Acevedo penetrated through the mountains of Gorbea by Ozoco and Villaro, with a view to seize Manares and St. Antonia d'Urquitiola. It was intended by this operation to cut the communication between Miranda on the Ebro, and the town of Durango, and thus to inter- cept the retreat of marshal Ney, and oblige him to surrender with sixteen thousand men; for Blake was utterly ignorant of his adversary's position, and imagined that he had only two corps to deal with. He believed that the king, with one, was in his front at Durango and Mont Dragon, and that Ney, with the other, was at Miranda; but, in fact, the latter was at that moment attacking Pignatelli at Logroño.

Brodrick's
Correspon-
dence.

As the Spanish army approached Zornosa, Merlin, abandoning the town, drew up on some heights in the rear. Bad weather, and the want of provisions, checked further operations until the evening of the 25th, when the Spanish division at Rigoytia attempted to turn the right flank of the French; at the same time Blake marched against the centre and left, and Merlin fell back to Durango. The duke of Dantzic, alarmed by these movements, concentrated Sebastiani's and Laval's division, and a Dutch brigade of infantry at Durango; and as his third division, under general Valence, was not come up, the king reinforced him with Villatte's division of the first corps, and ordered Merlin's force, which was composed of detachments, to join their respective regiments.

S.
Journal of
the king's
operations.
MS.

Until the 30th the armies remained quiet, but at day-break on the 31st, the Spaniards were formed in a checquered order of battle across the Durango

BOOK
III.

1808.
October.
S.
Journal of
the king's
operations,
MS.
road, five miles beyond Zornosa, and close to the
enemy's position. The duke of Dantzic, apprised
by the previous movements that he was going to be
attacked, became impatient; the state of the atmos-
phere prevented him from discovering the order of
march, or the real force of the Spaniards, but he
knew that Blake had the power of uniting nearly
fifty thousand men, and concluding that such a
force was in his front, he resolved to anticipate his
adversaries by a sudden and vigorous assault. In
fact, the Spanish generals were so little guided by
the rules of war, that before their incapacity was
understood, their very errors being too gross for
belief, contributed to their safety. Blake had commenced a great offensive movement, intending to
beat the troops in his front, and to cut off and capture Ney's corps of sixteen thousand men. In six
days, although unopposed, he advanced less than
fifteen miles ; and so disposed his forces, that out of
thirty-six thousand men, he had only seventeen
thousand infantry, without artillery, upon the field
Carrol's
Correspon-
dence.
of battle. His adversary, at the head of twenty-
five thousand men, formed in three columns of
attack, then descended from the heights.

COMBAT OF DURANGO.

A thick fog covering the mountain sides, filled all
the valleys, and a few random shots alone indicated
the presence of the hostile armies, when suddenly
Villatte's division appearing close to the Spanish
vanguard, with a brisk onset forced it back upon
the third division ; Sebastiani's and Laval's followed in succession; a fire of artillery, to which
Blake could make no reply, opened along the road,

the day cleared, and the Spanish army, heaped in confused masses, was, notwithstanding the example of personal courage given by Blake, and the natural strength of the country, driven from one position to another. At mid-day it was beyond Zornosa, and at three o'clock in full flight for Bilbao, which place it gained, in a state of great confusion, during the night; but the next day Blake crossed the Salcedon, and took a position at Nava. The duke of Dantzic pursued as far as Gueñes, and then leaving general Villatte, with seven thousand men, to observe the enemy, returned to Bilbao. Twelve vessels, laden with English stores, were in the river, but contrived to escape.

S.
Journal of
operations
MS.
Leith's
Correspon-
dence.
MS.

The king was displeased with the precipitancy of marshal Lefebre, but to aid him ordered the division of the first corps, stationed at Murguia, to descend the valley of Orduña, as far as Amurio ; at the same time, Mouton's division was detached from the second corps towards Barbareña, from whence it was, according to circumstances, either to join the troops in the valley of Orduña, or to watch Medina and Quincoes, and press Blake in his retreat, if he retired by Villarcayo. The French were ignorant of the situation of general Acevedo, but the day of the action at Zornosa, that general was at Villaro, from whence he endeavoured to rejoin Blake, by marching to Valmaceda ; he reached Miravalles, in the valley of Orduña, on the 3d, at the moment when the head of the French troops coming from Murguia appeared in sight, and after a slight skirmish, the latter, thinking they had to deal with the whole of Blake's army, retired to Orduña.

Acevedo immediately pushed for the Salcedon

BOOK
III.
——————
1808.
November
5.
Journal of
operations
MS.
Captain
Carrol.

river, and Villatte who first got notice of his march, dividing his own troops, posted one half at Orantia, on the road leading from Miravelles to Nava, the other on the road to Valmaceda, thus intercepting the Spaniards' line of retreat. Blake, informed of Acevedo's danger, in the night of the 4th, promptly passed the bridge of Nava, meaning to fall suddenly upon the nearest French; but they were aware of his intention, and sending a detachment to occupy Gordujuela, a pass in the mountains, leading to Bilbao, rejoined Villatte on the Valmaceda road. Five Spanish divisions and some of Romaña's troops were now assembled at Orantia, Blake left two in reserve, detached one against Gordujuela, and with the other two drove Villatte across the Salcedon. That general rallied on the left bank and renewed the action, but at this moment Acevedo appeared in sight, and sending two battalions by a circuit to gain the rear of the French, with the remainder joined in the combat. Villatte then retired fighting, and encountering the two battalions in his retreat, broke through them, and reached Guenes, yet with considerable loss of men, and he also left one gun and part of his baggage in the hands of the Spaniards. Thus ended a series of operations and combats, which had lasted for eleven days.

OBSERVATIONS.

1°. The duke of Dantzic's attack at Durango was founded upon false data; it was inconsistent with the general plan of the campaign, hasty, ill-combined, and feebly followed up; and it was an unpardonable fault to leave Villatte without support, close to an army that had met with no signal defeat,

and that was five times his strength. The march of
Victor's division was too easily checked at Miravalles, and for five days, general Acevedo, with at
least eight thousand men, wandered unmolested in
the midst of the French columns, and finally escaped without any extraordinary effort.

2°. General Blake's dispositions, with the exception of his night-march from Nava to Orantia, will,
if studied, afford useful lessons in an inverse sense.
From the 24th of October to the 4th of November,
he omitted no error that the circumstances rendered
it possible to commit; and then, as if ashamed of
the single judicious movement that occurred, he
would not profit by it. When Romana's infantry
had partly arrived, and the remainder were in the
vicinity of Nava, the whole Spanish army was, contrary to all reasonable expectation, concentrated;
above thirty thousand fighting men were united in
one mass, harassed, but not much discouraged, and
the conde de Belvedere, with twelve thousand infantry, twelve hundred cavalry, and thirty pieces of
artillery, was close to Burgos. If Blake had been
at all acquainted with the principles of his art, he
would then have taken advantage of Villatte's retreat,
to march by Espinosa, and Villarcayo, to the upper
Ebro; from thence he could have gained Burgos,
brought up the artillery from Reynosa, and uniting
Belvedere's troops to his own, have opened a communication with the English army. In that position,
with a plentiful country behind him, his retreat
open, and his army provided with cavalry, he might
have commenced a regular system of operations;
but with incredible obstinacy and want of judgment, he now determined to attack Bilbao again,
and to renew the ridiculous attempt to surround the

French army and unite with Palafox at the foot of the Pyrenees.

Such were the commanders, the armies, the rulers, upon whose exertions the British cabinet relied for the security of sir John Moore's troops, during their double march from Lisbon and Coruña! It was in such a state of affairs that the English ministers, anticipating the speedy and complete destruction of the French forces in Spain, were sounding the trumpet for an immediate invasion of France! Of France, defended by a million of veteran soldiers, and governed by the mightiest genius of two thousand years! As if the vast military power of that warlike nation had suddenly become extinct, as if Baylen were a second Zama, and Hannibal flying to Adrumetum instead of passing the Iberus! But Napoleon, with an execution more rapid than other men's thoughts, was already at Vittoria, and his hovering eagles cast a gloomy shadow over Spain.

Lord W.
Bentinck's
Correspon-
dence.
Appendix,
No. 13, §8.

BOOK IV.

CHAPTER I.

AFTER the opening of the legislative sessions, the emperor repaired to Bayonne. He arrived there on the 3d of November. It was his intention that the presumption of the Spanish generals should be encouraged by a strict defensive system until the moment when the blow he was prepared to strike could fall with the greatest effect; hence the precipitate attack at Zornosa displeased him, nor was he satisfied with the subsequent measures of the king, for he thought that Mouton's division would be endangered between the army of Blake and that of the conde de Belvedere. To prevent any accident, he judged it necessary that Bessieres should advance with the whole of the second corps to Burgos; that marshal Victor should march by Amurio to Valmaceda; and that marshal Lefebre should immediately renew his attack on that position from the side of Bilbao. Thus at the very moment when Blake was leading his harassed and starving troops back to Bilbao, two corps, amounting to fifty thousand men, were in full march to meet him, and a third, having already turned his right flank, was on his rear.

The Spanish general advanced from Valmaceda on the 7th, and thinking that only fifteen hundred men were in Gueñes, prepared to surround them. Two divisions, making a circuit to the left, passed

CHAP.
I.

1808.
November

S.
Journal of
the king's
operations.
MS.

Captain
Carrol's
Correspon-
dence.

through Abellana and Sopoerte, with a view to gain
the bridge of Sodupe, in the rear of Gueñes, while
two other divisions attacked that position in front;
the remainder of the army followed at some distance, but the advanced guard of the 4th corps was
in Gueñes, and after an action of two hours, the
Spaniards were thrown into such confusion that
night alone saved them from a total rout. The
same day, one of their flanking divisions was encountered and beaten near Sopoerte, and the retreat
of the other being intercepted on the side of Abellana, it was forced to make for Portagalete on the
sea-coast, and from thence to St. Andero. Blake,
whose eyes were now opening to the peril of his
situation, resolved to retire upon Espinosa de los
Monteros, a mountain position, two marches distant,
where he designed to rest his troops, and draw
supplies from his magazines at Reynosa. Falling
back to Valmaceda in the night, he gained Nava
the next day, and on the 9th was at Espinosa. The
late division of Romana's infantry joined him on the
march, and with exception of the men cut off at
Abellana; the whole army was concentrated on
strong ground commanding the intersection of the
roads from St. Andero, Villarcayo, and Reynosa.

Napoleon, accompanied by the dukes of Dalmatia
and Montebello, quitted Bayonne the morning of the
8th, and reached Vittoria in the evening. He was
met by the civil and military chiefs at the gates of
the town, but refusing to go to the house prepared
for his reception, jumped off his horse, entered the
first small inn that he observed, and calling for his
maps, and a report of the situation of the armies on
both sides, proceeded to arrange the plan of his
campaign.

The first and fourth corps, after uniting at Val-
maceda, had separated again at Nava on the 9th,
Victor was therefore pursuing the track of Blake,
and Lefebre was marching upon Villarcayo by
Medina. The second corps was concentrating at
Briviesca. The third corps occupied Tafalla,
Peraltes, Caparosa, and Estrella. The sixth corps,
the guards, and the reserve, were distributed from
Vittoria to Miranda, and a division, under the command of general La Grange, was at Guardia, connecting the positions of the third and sixth corps.
The fifth corps was still behind the frontier, and the
eighth, composed of the troops removed from Portugal
by the convention of Cintra, was marching from the
French sea-ports, where it had disembarked.

On the Spanish side, the conde de Belvedere
was at Burgos; Castaños and Palafox, unknowing
of their danger, were planning to cut off the French
army, and Blake was flying to Espinosa. The
English army were scattered from Coruña to Talavera de la Reyna. On these facts, and in two
hours the emperor had arranged his plans.

Moncey was directed to leave a division in front of
Pampeluna, in observation of the Spaniards on the
Aragon, to concentrate the remainder of the third
corps at Lodosa, and remain on the defensive until
further orders. La Grange was reinforced by Colbert's brigade of light cavalry from the sixth corps,
and directed upon Logroño. The first and fourth
corps were to press Blake without intermission.
The sixth to march towards Arando de Duero. The
duke of Dalmatia appointed to command the
2d corps, was ordered to fall headlong upon the
conde de Belvedere, and the emperor, with the imperial guards and the reserve, followed the movement
of the second corps.

These instructions being issued, the enormous
mass of the French army was put in motion with
a celerity that marked the vigour of Napoleon's
command. Marshal Soult departed on the instant
for Briviesca, arrived at day-break on the 9th,
received the second corps from Bessieres, and in a
few hours was in full march for the terrace of
Monasterio, which overlooks the plains of Burgos;
head-quarters were established there, during the
night, and Franceschi's light cavalry took the road
of Zaldueño to Arlanzon, with orders to cross the
river of that name, to descend the left bank, cut
the communication with Madrid, and prevent the
Spaniards rallying at the convent of the Chartreuse,
if defeated near Burgos.

At four o'clock on the morning of the 10th,
Soult was again in march from Monasterio, and at
six o'clock general Lassalle's cavalry reached Villa
Fria. The conde de Belvedere, being informed of
their approach, posted the Spanish army at Gamonal, and taking four thousand infantry, eight
guns, and the whole of his cavalry, fell upon
Lassalle. The latter skirmished for a while, and
then, following his orders, retired slowly to Rio
Bena, but at eight o'clock, the French infantry,
which had advanced by two roads, was reunited at
this town, and immediately pushed forward on Villa
Fria, Belvedere was driven back upon Gamonal,
and the Spanish army was discovered in line of
battle. The right was in a wood, leaving a clear
space of some extent unoccupied between it and
the river Arlanzon; the left was posted in the
walled park of Vellimer; thirty pieces of artillery
covered the front, and seven or eight thousand armed
peasants were arrayed on the heights, immediately
behind the regular troops; these latter amounted

to eleven thousand one hundred and fifty infantry,
and eleven hundred and fifty cavalry. This was
the best army at that time in Spain; it was composed of the Walloon and Spanish guards, the regiments of Mayorca, Zafra, and Valencia de Alcantara;
the hussars of Valencia, the royal carbineers, and
some volunteers of good families; it was completely
equipped, and armed principally from the English
stores, yet its resistance was even more feeble than
that made by the half-famished peasants of Blake's
force.

BATTLE OF GAMONAL.

Lassalle, with the light cavalry, leading down
upon the Spanish right, filled the plain between the
river and the wood, and at the same moment the
Spanish artillery opened along the whole of the
line; then the French infantry, formed in columns
of regiments, arrived, and Mouton's division, composed of old soldiers, broke at once into the wood
at a charging pace. General Bonnet followed closely,
but so rapid and effectual was the assault of Mouton's veterans that the Spaniards fled in disorder
before Bonnet's troops could fire a shot; their left
wing, although not attacked, followed the example
of the right, and the whole mass, victors and vanquished, rushed into the town of Burgos with extraordinary violence and uproar. Bessieres, who retained
the command of all the heavy cavalry, passed at full
gallop toward the Madrid road, where it crosses
the Arlanzon, sabring the fugitives, and taking
all the guns which had escaped Mouton, while,
on the other side of the river, Franceschi was
seen cutting in pieces some Catalonian light troops
stationed there, and barring all hopes of flight.

BOOK
IV.

1808.
November Never was a defeat more instantaneous, or more complete. Two thousand five hundred Spaniards were killed; twenty guns, thirty ammunition waggons, six pair of colours, and nine hundred men were taken on the field; four thousand musquets were found unbroken, and the fugitives dispersed far and wide. Belvedere himself escaped to Lerma, where he arrived in the evening of the day on which the battle was fought, and meeting some battalions, principally composed of volunteers, on their march to join his army, retired with them to Aranda de Duero during the night; but first, with true Spanish Appendix, No. 15. exaggeration, wrote a despatch, in which he asserted that the French, repulsed in two desperate attacks, had, after thirteen hours' hard fighting, succeeded in a third.

All the ammunition and stores of the defeated army were captured in Burgos; and the indefatigable Soult, who was still upon the post-horse which he had mounted at Briviesca, who had travelled from Bayonne to Burgos, taken the latter town, and gained a decisive victory all within the space of fifty hours, now detached one column in pursuit on the side of Lerma, another towards Palencia and Valladolid, and marched himself with a third, on Carrol's Correspondence. the very day of the battle, towards Reynosa, where he hoped to intercept Blake's line of retreat to the plains of Leon. This last-mentioned general had reached Espinosa, as we have seen, on the evening of the 9th, with six divisions, including Romana's infantry, who also dragged with them six guns of a small calibre; but the separation of the fourth division at Abellana, the deserters, and the losses sustained in battle, had reduced his army below twenty-five thousand fighting men; and the parc of ammunition

and artillery, guarded by two thousand infantry,
were behind Reynosa, at Aquilar del Campo, on
the road to Leon; yet his position was strong, and
he hoped to remain in it for some days unmolested.
His left wing, composed of the Asturians and the
first division, occupied some heights which covered
the road of St. Andero; the centre, consisting of
the third division and the reserve, formed a line
across the road of Reynosa, which leads through
Espinosa directly to the rear; the second division
was established on a commanding height, a little on
the right hand of the town; Romana's infantry were
posted in a wood, two miles in advance of the right,
and the vanguard, with six guns, formed a reserve
behind the centre of the position.

BATTLE OF ESPINOSA.

On the 10th, the duke of Belluno came up, and
at two o'clock in the afternoon, the head of a French
column driving back Romana's infantry, seized the
wood, but the Spaniards, reinforced by the third
division, renewed the combat; a second column
then opened its fire upon the Spanish centre, thus
weakened by the advance of the third division, and
at the same time some light troops ascending the
heights on the left, menaced that wing of Blake's
army.   Meanwhile the contest on the right was
maintained with vigour, and the Spaniards supported by the fire of the six guns in their centre,
even appeared to be gaining ground, when the
night closed and put an end to the action, leaving
the French in possession of the wood, and of a
ridge of hills, which at the distance of a cannon
shot, run parallel to the centre of the position.

The generals S. Roman and Riquielmé were mortally wounded on the Spanish side, and at daylight the next morning, Victor, who had relieved his left with fresh troops during the night, renewed the attack. General Maison, throwing out a cloud of skirmishers along the front of the Spanish centre and left wing, under cover of their fire, passed rapidly to his own right, and fell upon the Asturians and the first division. Blake, observing this movement, detached a column of grenadiers to reinforce the latter, and advanced in person with three regiments from the centre to take Maison in flank during his march, but it was too late; three Asturian generals fell at the first fire, and the troops of that kingdom fled without waiting for the enemy : they were soon followed by the first division, and Maison continuing his course without a check, intercepted the line of retreat by St. Andero, and also that by the town of Espinosa. In the mean time, the French troops posted on the parallel ridge, before spoken of, attacked the centre, and when the division in the wood also advanced against the right, the whole Spanish army gave way in terrible confusion ; crowding heavily towards the river Trueba which swept with a bound round the rear, the men endeavoured to escape, some by the fords, some by the town, some by the hills on the right ; but the weather was bad, the road steep, the overthrow fatal. Those whom the sword missed, went to their own provinces, carrying dismay into the remotest parts of Gallicia, Leon, Castille, and the Asturias. Blake himself reached Reynosa on the 12th, and then rallied about seven thousand fugitives, without artillery, without arms, without spirit, and without hope.

It has been said that, Spartan-like, Romana's soldiers died to a man in their ranks ; yet in 1812, captain Hill of the royal navy, being at Cronstadt, to receive Spaniards taken by the Russians during Napoleon's retreat, found that the greater portion were men who had escaped with Romana from the Danish Isles in 1808 ; captives at Espinosa, they had served Napoleon for four years, passed the ordeal of the Moscow retreat, and were still above four thousand strong !

A line of retreat by Aguilar del Campo, where his artillery remained, was still open to Blake, who thought to remain at Reynosa, to restore order, and then retire through Leon upon sir David Baird's division, the head of which was now near Astorga. But his total ignorance of the French operations and strength again misled him ; he looked only to the side of Espinosa, and already Soult's cavalry was upon his line of retreat, and the duke of Dantzic was hastening by the valley of Villarcayo towards Reynosa. Upon the 13th, he was attacked by Soult's advanced guard, and being now utterly confounded, he fled with four or five thousand men through the valley of Cabuerniga, and took refuge at Arnedo, in the heart of the Asturian mountains, where the marquis of Romana joined him, and assumed the command of all that remained of this unfortunate army.

S.
Journal of
operations.
MS.

Blake being thus disposed of, marshal Lefebre, after a halt of a few days to refresh his troops, took the road of Carrion and Valladolid, while Soult concentrated the 2d corps at Reynosa, and seized St. Ander where he captured a quantity of English stores. This done, the duke of Dalmatia spread his columns over the whole of the Montaña, pursuing,

BOOK
IV.
────────
1808.
November attacking, and dispersing every body of Spaniards
which yet held together, and filling all places with
alarm.   Everything military belonging to the patriots was thus driven over the snowy barrier of the
Asturian hills, and Soult having left a detachment
at San Vincente de Barqueira, scoured the banks of
S.
Journal of
operations
MS. the Deba, took the town of Potes, and overrun Leon
with his cavalry as far as Sahagun and Saldana.
Meanwhile the duke of Belluno, quitting Espinosa,
joined the emperor, whose head-quarters were fixed
at Burgos, after the defeat of Belvedere.

These battles of Espinosa and Gamonal, and the
subsequent operations of marshal Soult, laid the
north of Spain prostrate, secured the whole coast
from St. Sebastian to the frontier of the Asturias, and by a judicious arrangement of small garrisons, and moveable columns, the provinces of
Guipuscoa, Navarre, Biscay, and the Baston de
Laredo were fettered.   Thus the communication
of the army with France could no longer be
endangered by insurrections in the rear; the wide
and fertile plains of Old Castille and Leon were
thrown open to the French, and forbidden to the
separated divisions of the British army.   These
great advantages, the result of Napoleon's admirable
combinations, the fruits of ten days of active exertion,
obtained so easily, and yet so decisive of the fate of
the campaign, prove the weakness of the system
upon which the Spanish and British governments
were at this time acting; if that can be called a
system where no one general knew what another
had done, was doing, or intended to do.

But Burgos, instead of Vittoria, was now become
the pivot of operations, and the right of the army being
secured, the emperor prepared to change his front,

and bear down against the armies of Castaños and
Palafox, with a similar impetuosity. It was however
first necessary to ascertain the exact situation of the
British force. Napoleon believed that it was concentrated at Valladolid, and he detached three divisions of cavalry and twenty-four pieces of artillery,
by Lerma and Palencia, with orders to cross the
Douero, to turn the flank of the English, threaten
their communications with Portugal, and thus force
them to retire; it was, however, soon discovered
that the heads of their columns had not penetrated
beyond Salamanca and Astorga, and that many days
must elapse before they could be concentrated, and
in a condition to act offensively. Certain of this
fact, the emperor let loose his three divisions of
cavalry, and eight thousand horsemen sweeping over
the plains, vexed all Leon and Castille; the captain general Pignatelli shamefully fled, and the authorities everywhere shrunk from the tempest; the
people displayed no enthusiasm, and discontented by
the rapid movements of the French spread a thousand confused and contradictory reports, while the
incursions of the cavalry extended to the neighbourhood of Astorga, to Benevente, Zamora, Toro, Tor-
desilla, and even to the vicinity of Salamanca. Such
was the fear or the apathy of the inhabitants, that Sir John Moore's Papers.
thirty dragoons were sufficient to raise contributions
at the gates of the largest towns; and after the
overthrow of Espinosa was known, ten troopers
could safely traverse the country in any direction.

The front of the French army being now changed,
the second corps, hitherto the leading column of
attack, became a corps of observation, covering
the right flank, and protecting the important point
of Burgos, where large magazines were establishing,

and upon which the reinforcements continually arriving from France were directed. Of the other corps, the first, the guards, and a part of the reserve were at Burgos; Ney, with the sixth, was at Aranda de Douero; this officer's march from Ebro had been made to intercept the Estremadurans on the side of Madrid, and although their sudden destruction at Gamonal rendered this unnecessary, Ney was equally well placed to cut Castaños off from the capital. Meanwhile as Lagrange had occupied Logroño, and Moncey was with three divisions of infantry and one of cavalry at Lodosa, the Spanish army of the centre was turned, menaced, and excised from Madrid, before Castaños was even aware that the campaign had commenced.

In passing the mountains near Tolosa, Lasnes, duke of Montebello, fell from his horse, and was left at Vittoria, and his hurts were dangerous; a rapid and interesting cure was however effected by wrapping him in the skin of a sheep newly slain, and the emperor then directed him to assume the command of Lagrange's division and Colbert's light cavalry, to unite them with the third corps at Lodosa, and to fall upon Castaños in front. At the same time he ordered Ney to ascend the course of the Douero with the light cavalry and two divisions of the sixth corps, to connect his left with the right of Lasnes, and to gain Agreda by the road of Osma and Soria, from whence he could intercept the retreat of Castaños, and place himself on the rear of the Spanish army. To support this operation, the first corps, and Latour Maubourg's division of heavy cavalry being drawn from the reserve, proceeded by Lerma and Aranda, and from thence slowly followed the direction of Ney's march. The emperor, with the

CHAP.
I.

1808.
November

guards, and the remainder of the reserve, continued at Burgos, where the citadel was repaired and armed, magazines formed, and arrangements made to render it the great depôt of the army; all the reinforcements coming from France were directed upon this town, and proclamations were issued, assuring the country people of protection, if they would be tranquil and remain in their houses.

Ten days had now elapsed since Napoleon, breaking forth from Vittoria, had deluged the country with his troops, and each day was marked by some advantage gained over the Spaniards, but these misfortunes were still unknown at Tudela and disregarded at the capital. The remnants of Belvedere's army had rallied in the pass of the Somosierra, and on the side of the Segovia; the troops belonging to the army of the centre, which had been detained in Madrid, were forwarded to the former place, those left behind from Cuesta's levies were ordered to the latter. General St. Juan, an officer of reputation, took the command at the Somosierra, general Heredia repaired to Segovia, an intermediate camp of detachments was formed at Sepulveda, and the men thus collected were, by the junta, magnified into a great army sufficient to protect Madrid. That the left wing of the French army was still unbroken upon the Ebro, the central junta attributed, not to the enemy's strength, but to the dilatory proceedings of Castaños; wherefore depriving him of the command, they gave it to Romana, precisely at the moment when it was impossible for the latter general to reach the army he was to lead; but the junta wanted a battle, and, uncorrected by Blake's destruction, doubted not of victory.

Mr. Stuart.
Lord W.
Bentinck.
MSS.

Ibid.

Ibid.

BOOK
IV.
―――――
1808.
November The proceedings at Tudela also continued to be
worthy of the time, for the madness of the generals,
and the folly of the deputy had increased rather
than abated. The freaks of Francisco Palafox, and
their ridiculous termination on the 12th of November, I have already related, and a few days sufficed
to give birth to new plans equally absurd, but more
dangerous, as the crisis approached nearer. This
time Castaños took the lead. He knew upon the
10th that the Estremaduran army was at Burgos,
and that the French were marching on that town ;
from that moment, despairing of the junction of the

Castanos'
Vindica-
tion. British army, and likewise of his own first and third
divisions which had been left in Madrid, he sent
orders to Belvedere to unite himself with Blake.
His letters never reached that officer, who was
defeated before they were written, and Castaños,
feeling that he himself was in a dangerous position,
and that some decided measure was required, conceived so extraordinary a plan, that it would be
difficult to credit it upon any authority but his own.

Ibid. He proposed to carry the army of the centre, reduced
in numbers and ill-disciplined as it was, by the
Concha de Haro and Soria, towards Burgos, to fall
upon the emperor's rear-guard, and, as a preliminary
step, he determined to beat the army in his front ;
but Palafox had also a plan for attacking Moncey
on the side of Sanguessa, and the first measure necessary was to combine these double operations. It
was agreed therefore that Caparosa should be garrisoned by four thousand infantry, that the bridge
head at that place should be fortified, and that

Colonel
Graham's
Corre-
spondence.
MSS. O'Neil should be reinforced at Sanguessa by detachments from the centre until his troops amounted to
nineteen thousand infantry and twelve hundred

cavalry; he was then to break down the bridge, place guards at all the passages on the Aragon, come down to Caparosa, cross the river, and threaten Peraltes and Olite on the 17th; but on the 18th, he was to turn suddenly to the left, and get in rear of Lodosa, while La-Peña and Coupigny, marching from Centruenigo, should attack Moncey in front.

This great movement was openly talked of at the head-quarters of the Spanish generals for several days before its execution; and these extraordinary commanders, who were ignorant of Blake's disasters, announced their intention of afterwards marching towards Vittoria to lighten the pressure on that officer if he should be in difficulty; or if, as his dispatches of the 5th had assured them he was successful, to join in a general pursuit. Castaños, however, concealed his real project, which was to move by the Concha de Haro towards Burgos.

It was found impossible to procure a sufficient number of boats to lay a bridge over the Ebro at Alfaro, thus the reinforcements, intended for O'Niel, were forced to make a circuit by Tudela, and lost three or four days; however, on the 14th O'Neil arrived at Caparosa, after breaking the bridge of Sanguessa, and on the 15th the reinforcements joined him. The 17th, the day appointed for the execution of the plan, Castaños received notice of his own dismissal from the command, yet he persevered in his project. La-Peña and Coupigny were put in motion to pass the bridges of Logroño and Lodosa, and the fords between them, but general O'Neil, instead of executing his part, first refused to stir without an order from Joseph Palafox, who was at Zaragoza, and then changing his ground, complained that he was without bread. Castaños besought him

CHAP. I.

1808.
November

Colonel Graham's Correspondence. MSS.

Ibid.

Castanos' Vindication.

to move upon the 18th, urging the necessity of the measure, and the danger of delay; but the deputy, Palafox, who had hitherto approved of the project, suddenly quitted the head-quarters, and went to Caparosa, from whence, in concert with O'Neil, he wrote to demand a further reinforcement from the centre, of six thousand infantry and some more cavalry, without which, they affirmed that it would be dangerous to pass the Aragon river. Castaños preserved his temper, invited the deputy to return to the right bank of the Ebro, and opposed the demand for more troops on the ground of the delay it would cause; but now the captain-general Palafox, agreeing with neither side, proposed a new plan, and it is difficult to say how long these strange disputes would have continued, if an umpire had not interposed, whose award was too strongly enforced to be disregarded.

Castaños was with the divisions of Coupigny and
La-Peña at Calahorra on the 19th, when he received information that a French corps was advancing upon Logroño; it was Lasnes, with Lagrange's and Colbert's troops, yet the Spaniard concluded it to be Ney, for he was ignorant of the changes which had taken place since the 8th of the month. It was likewise reported, that Moncey, whose force he estimated at twelve thousand, when it really was above twenty thousand, had concentrated at Lodosa, and, at the same time, the bishop of Osma announced that twelve thousand men, under Dessolles, were marching from
the side of Aranda de Duero. On the 21st, the intelligence that Dessolles had passed Almazan, and that Moncey was in motion, was confirmed; Castaños then relinquishing his offensive projects, prepared to retire, and it was full time; for marshal

Ney, who left Aranda on the 19th, had passed Almazan on the 20th, dispersed several small bands of
insurgents, and entered Soria on the 21st, so that
when Castaños determined to fall back on the 21st,
his flank was already turned, and his retreat upon
Madrid in the enemy's power.   The Spanish artillery was at Centruenigo, and a large detachment
was with O'Neil at Caparosa; but during the night
of the 21st and 22d Castaños retired to the heights
which extend from Tudela by Cascante, Novellas,
Taranzona, and Monteguda.

On the morning of the 22d Lasnes was seen marching upon Calahorra ; at this moment the only supply
of money which the central junta had transmitted
for his army arrived at Tudela, and, to complete
the picture of distracted councils, O'Neil refused to
fall back upon Caparosa without the order of Palafox.   Fortunately the latter arrived at the moment
in Tudela, and a conference taking place between
him and Castaños the same day, they agreed that
the Aragonese army should cross the Ebro, and
occupy the heights over Tudela, while the rest
of the troops should stretch away in line as far as
Taranzona ; nevertheless, in defiance of all orders,
entreaties, or reasoning, the obstinate O'Neil remained in an olive-wood on the right bank of the
river during the night of the 22d, leaving the key
of the position open to the enemy.

A council of war was held, the discussion was
turbulent, and the opinions discordant; Palafox insisted on the defence of Aragon, as the principal
or rather the only object to be attended to ; and he
wished the whole army to pass to the left bank of the
Ebro, and confine its operations to the protection of

Zaragoza on that side,—a proposal which alone was sufficient to demonstrate his total incapacity for military affairs. Castaños reasoned justly against this absurdity, but the important moments passed in useless disputation, and the generals came to no conclusion. Meanwhile, marshal Lasnes, bringing with him Maurice Mathieu's division of the sixth corps, which had just arrived from France, concentrated above thirty thousand infantry, four or five thousand cavalry, and sixty pieces of artillery, and marching by Alfaro, appeared, at eight o'clock in the morning of the 23d, in front of the Spanish outposts, close to Tudela, just at the moment when the Aragonese were passing the bridge and ascending their position.

BATTLE OF TUDELA.

From forty to fifty guns were distributed along the front of the Spanish army, which, numbering about forty-five thousand fighting men, was extended on a range of easy hills from Tudela to Taranzona, a distance of more than ten miles. Two divisions of the army of the centre connected the Aragonese with the fourth division, which occupied Cascante, three divisions were in Taranzona, and there were no intermediate posts between these scattered bodies. The weakness attendant on such an arrangement being visible to the enemy at the first glance, Lasnes hastened to make his dispositions, and at nine o'clock general Morlot, with one division, attacked the heights above the town. Maurice Mathieu, supported by the cavalry of Lefebre Desnouettes, assailed the centre, and general Lagrange advanced against Cascante. The Aragonese resisted Morlot with vigour, and even pressed him in the

plain at the foot of the hills, but Maurice Mathieu
having gained possession of an olive-wood, and a
small ridge which was connected with the centre of
the Spanish position, after some sharp fighting
pierced the line, and then Lefebre, breaking through
the opening with his cavalry, wheeled up to the
left, and threw the right wing into hopeless confusion. The defeated soldiers fled towards the
bridge of Tudela, pursued by the victorious horsemen. In the meantime La-Peña, descending from
Cascante with the fourth division, drove in Lagrange's advanced guard of cavalry, yet he was soon
encountered at a charging pace by the infantry,
was beaten, and fell back to Taranzona, where three
divisions had remained during the whole of the action, which, strictly speaking, was confined to the
heights above Tudela. Palafox was not in the
battle, and O'Neil, with the right wing and the
centre, fled to Zaragoza with such speed, that some
of the fugitives are said to have arrived there the
same evening.

When La Peña was driven back upon Taranzona,
the left wing had commenced an orderly retreat
towards Borja, when some cavalry, detached by Ney
from the side of Soria, coming in sight, caused great
confusion; a magazine blew up, in the midst of
the disorder cries of treason were heard, the columns
dissolved in a few moments, and the road to Borja
was covered with a disorganized multitude. This
ended the celebrated battle of Tudela, in which
forty thousand men were beaten and dispersed by
an effort that, being in itself neither very vigorous
nor well sustained, was nevertheless sufficient to
demonstrate the incapacity of Spanish generals, and
the want of steadiness in Spanish soldiers.

BOOK
IV.
——
1808.
November

Eleventh
Bulletin.
Victoires
et Con-
quêtes.

Several thousand prisoners, thirty pieces of artillery, and all the ammunition and baggage, fell into
the hands of the French, who rated the killed and
wounded very high.   The total loss may be estimated
at eight or nine thousand men.   Fifteen thousand
escaped to Zaragoza ; a detachment of two thousand,
under the conde de Cartoajal and general Lilli, left
in the mountains of Nalda, were cut off by the result of the action, and two divisions, whose numbers
were increased by fugitives from the others, were
rallied at Calatayud on the 25th, but they were half
starved and mutinous.   At Calatayud, Castaños

Castanos'
Account of
the Battle
of Tudela,
and Vindi-
cation.

received two despatches from the central junta, virtually restoring him to the command, for the first
empowered him to unite the Aragonese army with
his own, and the second desired him to co-operate
with St. Juan in the Somosierra to protect the capital.   The battle of Tudela disposed of the first despatch, the second induced Castaños to march by
Siguenza upon Madrid.

In the meantime, Napoleon, recalling the greatest
part of his cavalry from the open country of Castille,
and having left seven or eight thousand men in
Burgos, had fixed his head-quarters at Aranda de
Duero on the 23d ; but from the difficulty of trans-

S.
Journal of
operations
MS.

mitting despatches through a country in a state of
insurrection, intelligence of the victory at Tudela only
reached him on the 26th, and he was exceedingly dis-

Eleventh
Bulletin.

contented that Castaños should have escaped the
hands of Ney.   That marshal had been instructed to
reach Soria by the 21st, to remain there until Lasnes
should be in front of the Spaniards, and then to
pass by Agreda, and intercept the retreat of the
latter, and on the evening of the 21st, general
Jomini and colonel D'Esmenard, staff-officers of the

sixth corps, arrived with an escort of eighty cavalry at Soria. This town is situated upon a rocky
height, with a suburb below, and the conde de
Cartoajal, who was retiring from the mountains of
Nalda, happening to be in the upper part, the
magistrates endeavoured to entrap the French officers. For this purpose, they were met at dusk by
the municipality, and invited to enter the town with
great appearance of cordiality; but their suspicions
were excited, the plan failed, Cartoajal marched
during the night, and the next day the sixth corps
occupied the place.

General Jomini, whose profound knowledge of
the theory of war enabled him to judge accurately
of the events that were likely to occur, urged Ney
to continue his march upon Calatayud, without any
rest; the marshal, however, either offended with
the heat of Jomini's manner, or from some other
cause, resolved to follow the letter of his instructions, and remained at Soria the 23d and 24th,
merely sending out some light cavalry on the side
of Medina Celi and Agreda. On the 25th he
marched to the latter town, and the 26th crossed
the field of battle, passing through Cascante; the
27th, he arrived with one division, at Mallen, a
town between Tudela and Zaragoza, his advanced
guard being at Arlazon on the Xalon. To the
erroneous direction and dilatory nature of these
movements, Castaños owed the safety of the troops,
which were reassembled at Calatayud.

Ney must have been acquainted with the result of
the battle on the 25th, and it is remarkable that
he should have continued on the road towards
Agreda, when a single march by Medina Celi
would have brought him upon the line of retreat

from Calatayud to Siguenza.   By some writers
these errors have been attributed to Ney's jealousy
of marshal Lasnes; by others it has been asserted
that the plunder of Soria detained him.   The falsehood of the latter charge is, however, evident from
the fact, that with the exception of a requisition
for some shoes and great coats, no contribution was
exacted from Soria, and no pillage took place at
all; and with respect to the former accusation, a
better explanation may be found in the peculiar
disposition of this extraordinary man, who was
notoriously indolent, and unlearned in the abstract
science of war.   It was necessary for him to see, in
order to act, and his character seemed to be asleep
until some imminent danger aroused all the mar-
vellous energy and fortitude with which nature had
endowed him.

The success at Tudela fell short of what Napoleon had a right to expect from his previous dispositions, yet it sufficed to break the Spanish
strength on that side, and to lay open Aragon,
Navarre, and New Castille, as the northern part of
Spain had been before opened by the victory of
Espinosa.   From the frontiers of France to those
of Portugal, from the sea-coast to the Tagus, the
country was now overwhelmed; Madrid, Zaragoza,
and the British army, indeed, lifted their heads a
little way above the rising waters, but the eye
looked in vain for an efficient barrier against the
flood, which still poured on with unabated fury.
And as the divided, weak state of the English troops
led the emperor to conclude that sir John Moore
would instantly retire into Portugal, he ordered
Lasnes to pursue Palafox—to seize the important
position of Monte Torrero—to summon Zaragoza,

and to offer a complete amnesty to all persons in the
town, without reservation, thus bearing testimony
to the gallantry of the first defence.   His own attention was fixed on Madrid.   That capital was the
rallying point of all the broken Spanish, and of all
his own pursuing divisions, and it was the centre of
all interests; a commanding height from whence a
beneficial stream of political benefits might descend
to allay, or a driving storm of war pour down to ex-
tinguish the fire of insurrection.

CHAPTER II.

BOOK
IV.
_____
1808.
November THE French patroles sent towards the Somosierra
ascertained, on the 21st, that above six thousand
men were entrenching themselves in the gorge of the
mountains ; that a small camp at Sepulveda blocked
the roads leading upon Segovia; and that general
Heredia was preparing to secure the passes of the
Guadarama.   Napoleon having, however, resolved
to force the Somosierra, and reach the capital before
Castaños could arrive there, ordered Ney to pursue
the army of the centre without intermission, and
directed the fourth corps to continue its march from
Carrion by Palencia, Valladolid, Olmedo, and Segovia.   The movement of this corps is worthy of the
attention of military men. We shall find it confusing
the spies and country people—overawing the flat
country of Leon and Castille—protecting the right
flank of the army — menacing Gallicia and Salamanca—keeping the heads of Moore's and Baird's
columns from advancing and rendering it dangerous
for them to attempt a junction — threatening the
line of Hope's march from the Tagus to the Guadarama — dispersing Heredia's corps, and finally
turning the pass of Somosierra, without ever ceasing
to belong to the concentric movement of the great
army upon Madrid.

s.
Journal of
operations
MS. But the time lost in transmitting intelligence of
the victory at Tudela was productive of serious consequences.   The officer despatched with these fresh

instructions, found Ney and Moncey (Lasnes was CHAP. sick at Tudela), each advanced two days' march in the wrong direction. The first, as we have seen, was at Mallen, preparing to attack Zaragoza; the second was at Almunio, near Calatayud, pursuing Castaños. They were consequently obliged to countermarch, and during the time thus lost, the people of Zaragoza, recovering from the consternation into which they were at first thrown by the appearance of the flying troops, made arrangements for a vigorous defence. Castaños also escaped to Siguenza, without any further loss than what was inflicted in a slight action at Burvieca, where general Maurice Mathieu's division came up with his rear-guard.

The emperor quitted Aranda on the 28th with the guards, the first corps, and the reserve, and marched towards Somosierra. Head-quarters were at Boucequillas on the 29th, and a detachment being sent to attack the camp at Sepulveda, was beaten, with a loss of fifty or sixty men; yet the Spaniards, struck with a panic after the action, quitted their post, which was very strong, and fled in disorder towards Segovia. The 30th, the French advanced guard reached the foot of the Somosierra, where general St. Juan, whose force now amounted to ten or twelve thousand men, was judiciously posted. Sixteen pieces of artillery, planted in the neck of the pass, swept the road along the whole ascent, which was exceedingly steep and favourable for the defence; the infantry, advantageously placed on the right and left, were in lines, one above another, and some entrenchments, made in the more open parts, strengthened the whole position.

PASSAGE OF THE SOMOSIERRA.

At day-break, three French battalions attacked
St. Juan's right, three more assailed his left, and as
many marched along the causeway in the centre,
supported by six guns. The French wings, spreading over the mountain side, commenced a warm
skirmishing fire, which was as warmly returned,
while the frowning battery at the top of the causeway was held in readiness to crush the central
column, when it should come within range. At
that moment Napoleon rode into the mouth of the
pass, and attentively examined the scene before him ;
the infantry were making no progress, and a thick
fog mixed with smoke hung upon the ascent ; suddenly, as if by inspiration, he ordered the Polish
cavalry of his guard to charge up the causeway, and
seize the Spanish battery. In an instant the foremost ranks of the first squadron were levelled with
the earth by the fire of the great battery, and the
remainder were thrown into confusion, but general
Krazinski as suddenly rallied them, and covered by
the smoke and the morning vapour led them sword
in hand up to the mountain. As these gallant horsemen passed, the Spanish infantry on each side fired
and fled towards the summit of the causeway, and
when the Poles, cutting down the gunners, took the
battery, the whole army was in flight abandoning
arms, ammunition, and baggage.

This surprising exploit, in the glory it conferred
upon one party, and the disgrace it heaped upon
the other, can hardly be paralleled in the annals of
war. It is indeed almost incredible, even to those
who are acquainted with Spanish armies, that a

CHAP.
II.

1808.
November

position, in itself nearly impregnable, and defended by twelve thousand men, should, without any panic, but merely from a deliberate sense of danger, be abandoned, at the wild charge of a few squadrons, which two companies of good infantry would have effectually stopped : yet some of the Spanish regiments so shamefully beaten here, had been victorious at Baylen a few months before, and general St. Juan's dispositions at Somosierra were far better than Reding's at the former battle! The charge itself, viewed as a simple military operation, was extravagantly rash ; but taken as the result of Napoleon's sagacious estimate of the real value of Spanish troops, and his promptitude in seizing the advantage offered by the smoke and fog that clung to the side of the mountain, it was a most felicitous example of intuitive genius. The routed troops were pursued towards Buitrago by the French cavalry. St. Juan himself broke through the French on the side of Sepulveda, and gained the camp of Heredia at Segovia, but the cavalry of the fourth corps approached, and the two generals crossing the Guadarama, united some of the fugitives from Somosierra, on the Madrid side of the mountains, and were about to enter that capital, when the appearance of a French patrole terrified the vile cowards that followed them ; the multitude once more fled to Talavera de la Reyna, and there consummated their intolerable villany by murdering their unfortunate general, and fixing his mangled body to a tree, after which, dispersing, they carried dishonour and fear into their respective provinces.

Colonel Graham's Correspondence.

The Somosierra being forced, the imperial army came down from the mountains—the sixth corps hastened on from the side of Alcala and Guada-

laxara—the central junta fled from Aranjuez, and the
remnant of the forces under Castaños, being intercepted on the side of Madrid, and pressed by Ney
in the rear, turned towards the Tagus. The junta
flying with indecent haste, spread a thousand false
reports, and with more than ordinary pertinacity,
endeavoured to deceive the people and the English
general; a task in which they were strongly aided
by the weak credulity of Mr. Frere, the British
plenipotentiary, who accompanied them in their
flight toward Badajos; Mr. Stuart, however, being
endowed with greater discretion and firmness, remained at Madrid until the enemy had actually
commenced the investment of that town.

Castaños, after the combat of Burvieca, had continued his retreat unmolested by Ney, who never
recovered the time lost by the false movement upon
Mallen; but although the Spaniards escaped the
sword, their numbers daily diminished, their sufferings increased, and their insubordination kept
pace with their privations. At Alcazar del Rey,

Castanos'
Vindica-
tion. Castaños resigned the command to general La-Peña,
and proceeded to Truxillo himself, with an escort of
thirty infantry and fifteen dragoons, a number
scarcely sufficient to protect his life from the ferocity
of the peasants, who were stirred up and prepared,
by the falsehoods of the central junta, and the villany of the deserters, to murder him. Meanwhile
Madrid was in a state of anarchy seldom equalled.
A local and military junta were formed to conduct
the defence, the inhabitants took arms, a multitude
of peasants from the neighbourhood entered the place,
and the regular forces, commanded by the marquis
of Castellar, amounted to six thousand men, with a
train of sixteen guns; the pavement was taken up,

the streets were barricadoed, the houses were
pierced, and the Retiro, a weak irregular work,
which commanded the city, was occupied in strength.
Don Thomas Morla and the prince of Castelfranco
were the chief men in authority ; the people demanded ammunition, and when they received it,
discovered, or said, that it was mixed with sand,
and as some person accused the marquis of Perales,
a respectable old general, of the deed, a mob
rushed to his house, murdered him, and dragged his
body about the streets ; many others of inferior note
also fell victims to this fury, for no man was safe,
none dared assume authority to control, none dared
give honest advice ; the houses were thrown open,
the bells of the convent and churches rung incessantly, and a band of ferocious armed men traversed
the streets in all the madness of popular insurrection. Eight days had now elapsed since the first
preparations for defence were made, and each day
the public effervescence had increased, the dominion
of the mob had become more decisive, their violence more uncontrollable ; the hubbub was extreme, when, on the morning of the 2d of December,
three heavy divisions of French cavalry suddenly
appeared on the high ground to the north-west,
and like a dark cloud overhung the troubled city.

At twelve o'clock the emperor arrived, and the
duke of Istria, by his command,* summoned the
town, but the officer employed was upon the point
of being massacred by the irregulars, when the
Spanish soldiers, ashamed of such conduct, rescued
him. This determination to resist was, however,
notwithstanding the fierceness displayed at the
gates, very unpalatable to many of the house-
holders, numbers of whom escaped from different

quarters; deserters also came over to the French, and Napoleon, while waiting for his infantry, examined all the weak points of the city.

Madrid was for many reasons incapable of defence. There were no bulwarks; the houses, although strong and well built, were not, like many Spanish towns, fire proof; there were no outworks, and the heights on which the French cavalry were posted, the palace, and the Retiro, completely commanded the city; the perfectly open country around would have enabled the French cavalry to discover and cut off all convoys, and no precaution had been taken to provide subsistence for the hundred and fifty thousand people contained within the circuit of the place. The desire of the central junta, that this metropolis should risk the horrors of a storm, was therefore equally silly and barbarous; their own criminal apathy had deprived Madrid of the power of procrastinating its defence until relieved from without, and there was no sort of analogy between the situation of Zaragoza and this capital. Napoleon knew it well; he was not a man to plunge headlong into the streets of a great city, among an armed and excited population; he knew that ad-
Appendix,
No. 3. dress in negotiation, a little patience, and a judicious employment of artillery, would soon reduce the most outrageous to submission, and he had no wish to destroy the capital of his brother's kingdom.

In the evening the infantry and artillery arrived, and were posted at the most favourable points. The night was clear and bright, and in the French camp all was silent and watchful, but a tumultuous noise was heard from every quarter of the
Four-
teenth
Bulletin. city, as if some mighty beast was struggling and howling in the toils. At midnight a second summons was sent through the medium of a prisoner,

and the captain-general Castellar attempted to gain
time by an equivocal reply; but the French light
troops stormed the nearest houses, and one battery
of thirty guns opened against the Retiro, while another threw shells from the opposite quarter, to dis-
tract the attention of the inhabitants. This building,
situated on a rising ground, was connected with
another range of buildings erected on the same side
of the Prado, which is a public walk nearly encircling the town, and into which some of the principal
streets opened, upon the above-mentioned range.
In the morning, a practicable breach was made in
the Retiro wall, and the difference between military
courage and ferocity became apparent; for Villatte's
division breaking in, easily routed the garrison, and,
pursuing its success, seized all the public buildings
connected with it, and then crossing the Prado,
gained the barriers erected at the entrance of the
streets, and took possession of the immense palace
of the duke of Medina Celi, which was in itself the
key to the city on that side.

Such a vigorous commencement created great terror, the town was summoned for the third time, and
in the afternoon, Morla and another officer came
out to demand a suspension of arms, necessary, they
said, to persuade the people to surrender. The emperor addressed Morla in terms of great severity,
reproaching him for his scandalous conduct towards
Dupont's army. ‘Injustice and bad faith,’ he exclaimed, ‘always recoil upon those who are guilty
of either.’ A saying well applied to that Spaniard,
and Napoleon himself confirmed its philosophic truth
in after times. ‘The Spanish ulcer destroyed me!’
was an expression of deep anguish which escaped
from him in his own hour of misfortune.

Morla returned to the town, his story was soon
told : before six o'clock the next morning Madrid
must surrender or perish ! Dissensions arose. The
violent excitement of the populace was considerably
abated, but the armed peasantry from the country,
and the poorest inhabitants, still demanded to be
led against the enemy, and a constant fire was kept
up from the houses in the neighbourhood of the
Prado, by which the French general Maison was
wounded, and general Bruyeres killed. Nevertheless the disposition to fight became each moment
weaker, and finally Morla and Castelfranco prepared a capitulation ; the captain-general Castellar,
however, refused to sign it, and as the town was
only invested on one side, he effected his escape
with the regular troops during the night, carrying
with him sixteen guns. The people then sunk into a
quiescent state, and at eight o'clock in the morning
of the 4th, Madrid surrendered.

That Morla was a traitor there is no doubt, and
his personal cowardice was excessive ; but Castelfranco appears to have been rather weak and ignorant than treacherous, and certainly the surrender of
Madrid was no proof of his guilt ; that event was
inevitable. The boasting uproar of the multitude,
when they are permitted to domineer for a few days,
is not enthusiasm ; the retreat of Castellar with the
troops of the line during the progress of the negotiation was the wisest course to pursue, and proves
that he acquiesced in the propriety of surrendering.
That the people neither could nor would defend the
city is quite evident ; for it is incredible that Morla
and Castelfranco should have been able to carry
through a capitulation in so short a period, if the
generals, the regular troops, the armed peasantry,

and the inhabitants, had been all, or even a part of
them, determined to resist.

Napoleon, cautious of giving offence to a population so lately and so violently excited, carefully
provided against any sudden reaction, and preserved
the strictest discipline; a soldier of the imperial
guard was shot in one of the squares for having
a plundered watch in his possession; the infantry
were placed in barracks and convents, the cavalry
were kept ready to scour the streets on the first
alarm, and the Spaniards were all disarmed. The
emperor then fixed his own quarters at Chamartin,
a country house four miles from Madrid, and in a
few days everything presented the most tranquil
appearance, the shops were opened, the public
amusements recommenced, and the theatres were
frequented. The inhabitants of capital cities are
easily moved, and easily calmed, self-interest and
sensual indulgence unfit them for noble and sustained efforts; they can be violent, ferocious, cruel,
but are seldom constant and firm.

During the operations against Madrid, La-Peña,
after escaping from the sixth corps, arrived at Guadalaxara with about five thousand men; on the 2d,
the dukes of Infantado and Albuquerque leaving the
capital, joined him; and, on the 4th, Venegas came up
with two thousand men. While these generals were
hesitating what course to pursue, Napoleon, apprized
of their vicinity, directed Bessieres with sixteen
squadrons upon Guadalaxara, supporting him by
Ruffin's division of the first corps; at the approach of this cavalry, the main body retired
through the hills by Sanctorcaz towards Aranjuez,
and the artillery crossed the Tagus at Sacedon;
Ruffin's division immediately changed its direction,

BOOK
IV.
————
1808.
December. and cut the Spaniards off from La Mancha by the
line of Ocaña.   Meanwhile a mutiny among the
Spanish troops forced La-Peña to resign, and the
duke of Infantado was chosen in his place.   The
Tagus was then crossed at several points, and after
some slight actions with the advanced cavalry of the
French, this miserable body of men finally saved
themselves at Cuenca, where many deserters and
fugitives, and the brigades of Cartoajal and Lilli,
which had escaped the different French columns,
also arrived, and the duke proceeded to organize
another army.

On the French side, the fourth corps reached
Segovia, passed the Guadarama, dispersed some
armed peasants assembled at the Escurial, and then
marched toward Almaraz, to attack general Galluzzo,
who, having assembled five or six thousand men to
defend the left bank of the Tagus, had, with the
usual skill of a Spanish general, occupied a line of
Sir John
Moore's
Papers. forty miles.   The first French corps entered La
Mancha at the same time, and Toledo immediately
shut its gates ; but, although the junta of that town
publicly proclaimed their resolution to bury themselves under the ruins of the city, at the approach
of a French division, they betrayed a most contemptible cowardice.   Thus, six weeks had sufficed to
dissipate the Spanish armies ; the glittering bubble
was bursted, and a terrible reality remained.   From
St. Sebastian to the Asturias, from the Asturias to
Talavera de la Reyna, from Talavera to the gates of
the noble city of Zaragoza, all was submission, and
beyond that boundary, all was apathy or dread.
Ten thousand French soldiers could safely, as regarded the Spaniards, have marched from one extremity of the Peninsula to the other.

After the fall of Madrid, king Joseph remained at
Burgos, issuing proclamations, and carrying on a
sort of underplot, through the medium of his native
ministers; the views of the latter naturally turned
towards the Spanish interests as distinct from the
French, and a source of infinite mischief to Joseph's
cause was thus opened, for that monarch, anxious to
please and conciliate his subjects, ceased to be a
Frenchman without becoming a Spaniard. At this
time, however, Napoleon assumed and exercised all
the rights of conquest, and it is evident, from the
tenor of his speeches, proclamations, and decrees,
that some ulterior project, in which the king's personal interests were not concerned, was contemplated
by him. It appeared as if he wished the nation, in
imitation of the old king, to offer the crown to himself a second time, that he might obtain a plausible
excuse for adopting a new line of policy by which
to attract the people, or at least to soften their pride,
which was now the main obstacle to his success.

An assemblage of the nobles, the clergy, the cor-
porations, and the tribunals of Madrid, waited upon
him at Chamartin, and presented an address, in
which they expressed their desire to have Joseph
among them again. The emperor's reply was an
exposition of the principles upon which Spain was
to be governed, and offers a fine field for reflection
upon the violence of those passions which induce men
to resist positive good, and eagerly seek for danger,
misery, and death, rather than resign their prejudices.

' I accept,' said he, ' the sentiments of the town
of Madrid. I regret the misfortunes that have befallen it, and I hold it as a particular good fortune
that I am enabled, under the circumstances of the

moment, to spare that city, and to save it from yet greater misfortunes.

' I have hastened to take measures fit to tranquillize all classes of citizens, knowing well that to all people, and to all men, uncertainty is intolerable.

' I have preserved the religious orders, but I have restrained the number of monks ; no sane person can doubt that they are too numerous. Those who are truly called to this vocation by the grace of God will remain in their convents ; those who have lightly or from worldly motives adopted it, will have their existence secured among the secular ecclesiastics, from the surplus of the convents.

' I have provided for the wants of the most interesting and useful of the clergy, the parish priests.

' I have abolished that tribunal against which Europe and the age alike exclaimed.   Priests ought to guide consciences, but they should not exercise any exterior or corporal jurisdiction over men.

' I have taken the satisfaction which was due to myself and to my nation, and the part of vengeance is completed.   Ten of the principal criminals bend their heads before her ; but for all others there is absolute and entire pardon.

' I have suppressed the rights usurped by the nobles during civil wars, when the kings have been too often obliged to abandon their own rights to purchase tranquillity and the repose of their people.

' I have suppressed the feudal rights, and every person can now establish inns, mills, ovens, weirs, and fisheries, and give free play to their industry ; only observing the laws and customs of the place. The self-love, the riches, and the prosperity of a

small number of men, was more hurtful to your agri-
culture than the heats of the dog-days.
' As there is but one God, there should be in one
estate but one justice ; wherefore all the particular
jurisdictions having been usurped, and being contrary to the national rights, I have destroyed them.
I have also made known to all persons that which
each can have to fear, and that which they may
hope for.

' The English armies I will drive from the Peninsula. Zaragoza, Valencia, Seville, shall be reduced
either by persuasion or by the force of arms.

' There is no obstacle capable of retarding for
any length of time the execution of my will. But
that which is above my power, is to constitute the
Spaniards a nation, under the orders of the king, if
they continue to be imbued with the principle of
division, and of hatred towards France, such as the
English partizans and the enemies of the continent
have instilled into them. I cannot establish a nation,
a king, and Spanish independence, if that king is
not sure of the affection and fidelity of his subjects.

' The Bourbons can never again reign in Europe.
The divisions in the royal family were concerted by
the English ; it was not either king Charles or his
favorite, but the duke of Infantado, the instrument
of England, that was upon the point of overturning
the throne. The papers recently found in his
house prove this ; it was the preponderance of
England that they wished to establish in Spain.
Insensate project ! which would have produced a
land war without end, and caused torrents of blood
to be shed.

' No power influenced by England can exist upon
the continent ; if any desire it, their desire is folly,

and sooner or later will ruin them ; I shall be obliged to govern Spain, and it will be easy for me to
do it by establishing a viceroy in each province.
However, I will not refuse to concede my rights of
conquest to the king, and to establish him in
Madrid, when the thirty thousand citizens assemble
in the churches, and on the holy sacrament take an
oath, not with the mouth alone, but with the heart,
and without any jesuitical restriction, " to be true to
the king, to love and to support him." Let the
priests from the pulpit and in the confessional, the
tradesmen in their correspondence and their dis-
courses, inculcate these sentiments in the people ;
then I will relinquish my rights of conquest, then I
will place the king upon the throne, and I will take
a pleasure in showing myself the faithful friend of
the Spaniards.

' The present generation may differ in opinions ;
too many passions have been excited ; but your de-
scendants will bless me as the regenerator of the
nation : they will mark my sojourn among you as
memorable days, and from those days they will
date the prosperity of Spain. These are my sentiments, go consult your fellow citizens, choose
your part, but do it frankly, and exhibit only true
colours.'

The ten criminals were the dukes of Infantado, of
Hijar, Medini Celi, and Ossuna ; marquis Santa
Cruz ; counts Fernan, Miñez, and Altamira ; prince
of Castello Franco, Pedro Cevallos, and the bishop
of St. Ander, were proscribed, body and goods, as
traitors to France and Spain.

Napoleon now made dispositions indicating a vast
plan of operations. It would appear that he intended
to invade Gallicia, Andalusia, and Valencia, by his

lieutenants, and to carry his arms to Lisbon in person. Upon the 20th December the sixth corps, the guards, and the reserve, were assembled under his own immediate control. The first corps was stationed at Toledo, and the light cavalry attached to it scoured the roads leading to Andalusia, up to the foot of the Sierra Morena. The fourth corps was at Talavera, on the march towards the frontier of Portugal. The second corps was on the Carrion river, preparing to advance against Gallicia. The eighth corps was broken up; the divisions composing it were ordered to join the second, and Junot, who commanded it, repaired to the third corps, to supply the place of marshal Moncey, who was called to Madrid for a particular service,—doubtless an expedition against Valencia. The fifth corps, which had arrived at Vittoria, was directed to reinforce the third, then employed against Zaragoza. The seventh was always in Catalonia.

Vast as this plan of campaign appears, it was not beyond the emperor's means; for, without taking into consideration his own genius, activity, and vigour, there were on his muster rolls, above three hundred and thirty thousand men, and above sixty thousand horses; two hundred pieces of field artillery followed the corps to battle, and as many more remained in reserve. Of this monstrous army, two hundred and fifty-five thousand men, and fifty thousand horses, were actually under arms, with their different regiments, while thirty-two thousand were detached or in garrisons, preserving tranquillity in the rear, and guarding the communications of the active force. The remainder were in hospital, and so slight had been the resistance of the Spanish armies, that only nineteen hundred prisoners were

Appendix
No. 28.

to be deducted from this multitude.   Of the whole
host two hundred and thirteen thousand were native
Frenchmen, the residue were Poles, Germans, and
Italians; thirty-five thousand men and five thousand
horses, were available for fresh enterprise, without
taking a single man from the service of the lines of
communication.   What was there to oppose this
fearful array ?   What consistency or vigour in the
councils ?   What numbers ?   What discipline and
spirit in the armies of Spain?   What enthusiasm
among the people?   What was the disposition, the
means, what the activity of the allies of that
country ?   The answers to these questions demonstrate that the fate of the Peninsula hung at this
moment upon a thread, and that the deliverance of
that country was due to other causes than the
courage, the patriotism, or the constancy of the
Spaniards.

　　First, with regard to their armies.   The duke of
Infantado resided with, rather than commanded, a
few thousand wretched fugitives at Cuenca, destitute, mutinous, and cowed in spirit.   At Valencia
there was no army, for that which belonged to the
province was shut up in Zaragoza, and dissentions
had arisen between Palafox and the local junta in
consequence.   In the passes of the Sierra Morena
were five thousand raw levies, hastily made by the
junta of Seville, after the defeat of St. Juan.   Galluzzo, who had undertaken to defend the Tagus,
with six thousand timid and ill-armed soldiers, was
at this time in flight, having been suddenly attacked and defeated at Almarez by a detachment of
the fourth corps.   Romana was near Leon, at the
head of eighteen or twenty thousand runaways, collected by him after the dispersion at Reynosa; but

of this number only five thousand were armed, and
none were subordinate, or capable of being disciplined, for, when checked for misconduct, the
marquis complained that they deserted. In Gallicia
there was no army, and in the Asturias the local
government were so corrupt, so faithless, and so op-
pressive, that the spirit of the people was crushed,
and patriotism reduced to a name.

The members of the central junta had at first
thought of going to Badajos, but, being terrified,
fled to Seville, and their inactivity was more conspicuous in this season of adversity than before,
contrasting strangely with the pompous and inflated
language of their public papers : all their promises
were fallacious, their incapacity glaring, their exertions ridiculous, abortive, and the junta of Seville, still actuated by their own ambitious views,
had now openly reassumed all their former authority. In short, the strength and spirit of Spain was
broken, the enthusiasm was null, except in a few
places, and the emperor was, with respect to the
Spaniards, perfectly master of his operations. He
was in the centre of the country ; he held the
capital the fortresses the command of the great
lines of communication between the provinces ; and
on the wide military horizon, no cloud intercepted
his view, save the heroic city of Zaragoza on the
one side, and a feeble British army on the other.
Sooner or later, he observed, and with truth, that the
former must fall, as it was an affair of artillery calculation. The latter he naturally supposed to be in
full retreat for Portugal ; but as the fourth corps
was nearer to Lisbon than the British general, a
hurried retreat alone could bring the latter in time
to that capital, and consequently no preparations for

defence could be made sufficient to arrest the sixty thousand Frenchmen which the emperor could carry there at the same moment. The subjugation of Spain appeared inevitable, when the genius and vigour of Sir J. Moore frustrated Napoleon's plans at the very moment of execution; the Austrian war breaking out at the instant, drew the master-spirit from the scene of contention, and England then put forth her vast resources, which being fortunately wielded by a general equal to the task of delivering the Peninsula, it was delivered. But through what changes of fortune, by what unexpected helps, by what unlooked-for and extraordinary events, under what difficulties, by whose perseverance, and in despite of whose errors, let posterity judge, for in that judgment only will impartiality and justice be found.

CHAPTER III.

OPERATIONS OF THE BRITISH ARMY.

WHILE at Madrid, Napoleon heard that sir John Moore, having relinquished his communication with Lisbon, was menacing the French line of operations on the side of Burgos; this intelligence obliged him to suspend all his designs against the south of Spain and Portugal, and to fix his whole attention upon that general's movements. The reasons which induced Moore to divide his army, and to send general Hope with one column by the Tagus, while the other marched under his own personal command, by Almeida and Ciudad Rodrigo, have been already related; as likewise the arrangements which brought sir David Baird to Coruña, without having permission to land his troops, and without money to equip them, when they were suffered to disembark.

The 8th of November, sir John Moore was at Almeida, on the frontier of Portugal, his artillery was at Truxillo, in Spanish Estremadura, and sir David Baird's division was at Coruña. General Blake, pursued by fifty thousand enemies, was that day flying from Nava to Espinosa; Castaños and Palafox were quarrelling at Tudela. The conde de Belvedere was at Burgos, with thirteen thousand bad troops, and Napoleon was at Vittoria, with one hundred and seventy thousand good troops.

At this time the letters of lord William Bentinck
and colonel Graham, exposing all the imprudence
of the Spanish generals, were received, and disquieted the English general.   He already foresaw
that his junction with the other divisions of his
army might be impeded by the result of an action,
which the Spaniards appeared to be courting, contrary to all sound policy; but as no misfortune had
yet befallen them, he continued his march, hoping
' that all the bad which might happen, would not
happen.'

The 11th he crossed the frontier of Spain, and
marched to Ciudad Rodrigo; on that day Blake was
completely discomfited at Espinosa, and the Estremaduran army, beaten the day before at Gamonal,
was utterly ruined and dispersed.

The 13th the head of the British columns entered
Salamanca, at the moment when Blake's fugitive
force was finally disorganized at Reynosa, leaving
the first, second, and fourth, French corps, amounting to near seventy thousand men, free to act against
any quarter.

Sir John Moore participated at first in the universal belief, that the nation was enthusiastic, and
fixed in a determination to dispute every step with
the invaders ; and after he had detected the exaggerations of the military agents, and perceived
the want of capacity in the Spanish generals and
rulers, he still trusted that the spirit of the people
Appendix,
No. 14. would compensate for their deficiency of skill. What
then was his surprise to find, that the defeat of the
conde de Belvedere, an event which laid Castille
open to the incursions of the enemy, which uncovered the march of the British, and compromised
their safety, had created no sensation among the

people; that the authorities had spread no alarm,
taken no precautions, delivered out no arms, although many thousands were stored in the principal towns, and neither encouraged the inhabitants
by proclamations, nor enrolled any of them for defence! He himself was not informed of this important occurrence until a week after it happened,
and then only through a single official channel.

Valladolid, where the enemy's cavalry were, was
but three marches from Salamanca, and as not more
than four thousand of Moore's infantry had come
up to the latter town, it was evident that if the
French advanced in force, the British must fall
back towards Ciudad Rodrigo. Nevertheless the
general, assembling the local authorities, explained
the nature of his position, endeavoured to excite
their ardour, and, notwithstanding the apathetic
state of the public mind, resolved not to retire unless forced back by superior numbers; he even hastened the arrival of his rear divisions, but sent
orders to both Hope and Baird to concentrate their
troops and be prepared for a retreat. His exhor-
tations produced no effect upon the junta or the
people; the former were stupified and timid,
the latter, although declaring their hatred of the
invaders, would not stir in defence; the first feeling
of indignation against the French was exhausted,
and there was nothing to supply its place; the
fugitives from the armies passed daily without
shame, and unreproached by their countrymen. In
this state the English general remained until the
18th, his army was closing up, and the French
cavalry withdrew from Valladolid to Palencia, when
the news of Blake's defeat reached Salamanca, not
by rumour, or by any direct communication from

BOOK
IV.

1808.
November
Mr. Frere's
Letter to
the Junta.
the Montaña St. Ander, but through Mr. Stuart, eight days subsequent to the date of the action; the central junta did not even inform the minister plenipotentiary until thirty hours after having received official intelligence of it themselves.

Want of transport and supplies had obliged the British to march in small and successive divisions, it was, therefore, the 23d of November before the centre, consisting of twelve thousand infantry, and a battery of six guns, was concentrated at Salamanca. On that day, Castaños and Palafox being defeated at Tudela, and their armies scattered without a chance of rallying again in the field, the third and sixth French corps became disposable. The emperor also, victorious on both flanks, and with a fresh base of operations fixed at Burgos, was then free to move, with the guards and the reserve, either against Madrid or in the direction of Salamanca; detachments of his army were already in possession of Valladolid, the very town

which, a few days before, the Spanish government had indicated for the base of sir John Moore's operations, and the formation of his magazines. The 26th the head of sir David Baird's column was in Astorga, but the rear extended beyond Lugo, while the head of Hope's division was at the Escurial, and the rear at Talavera. But the second French corps was on the Deba, threatening Leon and the Asturias; the cavalry covered the plains; the fourth corps was descending by Carrion and Valladolid, to seize the pass of the Guadarama; the emperor himself was preparing to force the Somosierra.

From this summary of contemporary events, it is evident, that, notwithstanding sir John Moore had organised, equipped, and supplied his army, and

marched four hundred miles, all in the space of six weeks, he was too late in the field ; the campaign was decided against the Spaniards before the British had, strictly speaking, entered Spain as an army. And it is certain, that if, instead of being at Salamanca, Escurial, and Astorga, on the 23d, the troops had been united at Burgos on the 8th, such was the weakness of the Spanish forces, the strength of the enemy, and such the skill with which Napoleon directed his movements, that a difficult and precarious retreat was the utmost favour that could be expected from Fortune by the English.

Sir John Moore's situation on his arrival at Salamanca, gave rise to serious reflections. He had been sent forward without a plan of operations, or any data upon which to found one ; his instructions merely directed him to open communication with the Spanish authorities, for the purpose of ' framing the plan of campaign'. But general Castaños, with whom he was desired to correspond, was superseded immediately afterwards, and the marquis of Romana, his successor, was engaged in rallying the remains of Blake's force in the Asturias, at a distance of two hundred miles from the only army with which any plan of co-operation could be formed, and of whose proceedings he also Appendix, No.13, § 1 and 4. was ignorant. No channel of intelligence had been pointed out to Moore, and as yet a stranger in the country, and without money, he could not establish any certain one for himself. It was the will of the people of England, and the orders of the government, that he should push forward to the assistance of the Spaniards, and he had done so, without magazines, and without money to form them ;

BOOK
IV.

1808.
November
trusting to the official assurance of the minister, that above a hundred thousand Spanish soldiers covered his march, that the people were enthusiastic and prepared for any exertion to secure their own deliverance, but he found them supine and unprepared ; the French cavalry, in parties as weak as twelve men, traversed the country, and raised contributions, without difficulty or opposition.

Appendix
No. 13, § 5
and 6.
This was the state of Castille, and the letters of Mr. Stuart and lord William Bentinck amply exposed the incapacity, selfishness, and apathy of the supreme government at Aranjuez. The correspondence of colonel Graham painted in the strongest colours the

Ibid.
confusion of affairs on the Ebro, the jealousy, the discord of the generals, the worse than childish folly of the deputy Palafox and his creatures. Sir David Baird's experience proved, that in Gallicia the people were inert as in Castille and Leon, and the authorities more absurd and more interested.

Ibid.
General Hope expressed a like opinion as to the ineptitude of the central junta ; and even the military agents, hitherto so sanguine, had lowered their tone of exultation in a remarkable manner.

Napoleon's enormous force was unknown to sir John Moore, but he knew that it could not be less than eighty thousand fighting men, and that thirty thousand more were momentarily expected, and might have arrived ; he knew that Blake and the conde de Belvedere were totally defeated, and that Castaños must inevitably be so if he hesitated to retreat. The only conclusion to be drawn from these facts was, that the Spaniards were unable, or unwilling, to resist the enemy, and that the British would have to support the contest alone, unless they could form a junction with Castaños, before the latter was entirely discomfited and destroyed; but there was no time for such an operation, and the first object was, to unite the parcelled divisions of the English army.

From Astorga to Salamanca was five marches; from Salamanca to the Escurial was six marches; but it would have required five days to close up the rear upon Salamanca, six days to enable Hope to concentrate at the Escurial, and sixteen to enable Baird to assemble at Astorga. Hence twenty days were required for the English army to unite and act in a body, and to have advanced in their divided state would have been equally contrary to military principle and to common sense. A retreat, although it was prescribed by the rules of scientific war, and in unison with the instructions of the government, which forbad the general to commit his troops in any serious affair before the whole were united, would have been, while the Spanish army of the centre still held the field, ungenerous : the idea was repugnant to the bold and daring spirit of Moore. Rather than resort to such a remedy for the false position his government had placed him in, he contemplated a hardy and dangerous enterprise, such as none but great minds are capable of. He proposed, if he could draw the extended wings of his army together in good time, to abandon all communication with Portugal, and throwing himself into the heart of Spain, to rally Castaños' army, if it yet existed, upon his own, to defend the southern provinces, and trust to the effect which such an appeal to the patriotism and courage of the Spaniards would produce.

Appendix, No. 14.

But Moore also considered, that the question was not purely military; the Spanish cause was not one which could be decided by the marches of a few auxiliary troops; its fate rested on the vigour of the rulers, the concert of the generals, the unity of the exertions, and the fixed resolution of the people to suffer all privations, and die rather than submit; to him it appeared doubtful that such a spirit, or the means of creating it, existed, and more doubtful that there was capacity in the government to excite or to direct it when aroused; no men of talent had yet appeared, and good-will was in itself nothing if improperly treated. Wherefore he turned to the English plenipotentiary, who had just superseded Mr. Stuart near the central junta; for he had been directed by the ministers to communicate with him upon all important points, to receive with deference his opinion and advice, and the present was an occasion to which those instructions were peculiarly applicable.   Mr. Frere had come fresh from the English government, he was acquainted with its views, he was in the most suitable position to ascertain what degree of elasticity the Spanish cause really possessed, and the decision of the question belonged as much to him as to the general, because it involved the whole policy of the English cabinet with respect to Spain; it was likewise the more proper to consult him because, as a simple operation of war, the proposed movement was rash.   All the military and many political reasons called for a retreat upon Portugal, which would take the army back upon its own resources, ensure its concentration, increase its strength, protect British interests, and leave it free either to return to Spain, if a favourable opportunity should occur, or to pass by sea to Andalusia, and commence the campaign in the south.

Such were the reflections that induced sir John Moore to solicit Mr. Frere's opinion upon the general policy of the proposed operation. But in so doing he never had the least intention of consulting him upon the mode of executing the military part, of which he conceived himself to be the best judge, and while awaiting the reply, he directed sir David Baird, if the enemy showed no disposition to molest him, to push the troops on to Salamanca as fast as they should arrive at Astorga. Sir David was proceeding to do so, when Blake advised him that a considerable French force was collecting at Rio Seco and Ampudia, with a view of interrupting the march ; this arrested his movement, he was even preparing to fall back, when he was stopped by Moore, whose information led him to believe that Blake's report was false. Valuable time was thus lost, but it was the march of the fourth corps then traversing the line from Carrion to the Guadarama, that gave rise to this contradictory intelligence, for the many various changes in the French positions, and the continual circulation of their light cavalry through the plains, bewildered the spies and the peasants. The force of the enemy on different points also confused the higher agents, who, believing the greatest amount of the invading army to be from a hundred to a hundred and twenty thousand men, could never reconcile the reports with this standard, and therefore concluded that Napoleon exaggerated his real numbers to create terror.

Moore had written to Mr. Frere on the 27th of November, Baird was to march by Benevente on the 1st, and Hope by Tordesillas ; the troops at Salamanca by Zamora and Toro, and all the arrangements for the execution of the project were completed when, in the night of the 28th, a despatch from Mr. Stuart made known the disaster at Tudela. This again changed the aspect of affairs ; the question proposed to Mr. Frere was no longer doubtful. The projected movement had been founded upon *the chance of rallying the Spanish armies behind the* Appendix, No. 14. *Tagus,* a hazardous and daring experiment when first conceived, but now that Castaños had no longer an army, now that the strength of Spain was utterly broken, to have persisted in it would have been insanity ; the French could be over the Tagus before the British, and there were no Spanish armies to rally. The defeat at Tudela took place the 23d of November ; Baird's brigades could not be united at Astorga before the 4th of December, and to concentrate the whole of the army at Salamanca, required a flank march of several days over an open plain ; an operation not to be thought of, within a few marches of a skilful enemy, who possessed such an overwhelming force of artillery and cavalry.

As long as Castaños and Palafox kept the field, there was reason to believe that the French stationed at Burgos would not make any serious attempt on the side of Astorga, but that check being now removed, an unmilitary flank march would naturally draw their attention, and bring them down upon the parcelled divisions of the English troops. The object of succouring the Spaniards called for great, but not for useless sacrifices. The English general was prepared to confront any danger and to execute any enterprise which held out a chance of utility, but he also remembered that the best blood of England was committed to his charge, that not an English army, but the very heart, the pith of the military power of his country was in his

keeping, it was entrusted to his prudence, and his
patriotism spurned the idea of seeking personal renown by betraying that sacred trust. The political
reasons in favour of marching towards Madrid,
scarcely balanced the military objections before the
battle of Tudela; after that event, the latter acquiring
double force, left no room for hesitation in the mind
of any man capable of reasoning at all, and sir John
Moore resolved to fall back into Portugal.

He ordered sir David Baird to regain Coruña or
Vigo, and to carry his troops by sea to Lisbon ; yet
wishing, if possible, to unite with Hope before the
retrograde movement commenced, he directed Baird
to show a bold front for a few days in order to attract
the enemy's attention. The negligence, the false
intelligence, the frauds, the opposition approaching
to hostility, experienced by sir David Baird during
his march from Coruña, had so reduced that general's hopes, that he prepared for this retreat without
reluctance ; he was in direct communication with
Romana, but the intercourse between them had
rather confirmed than weakened the impression on
Baird's mind, that it was impossible to depend upon
the promises, the information, or the judgment of Appendix, No. 13, § 5.
any Spanish general. In the mean time, Napoleon
forced the Somosierra, and summoned Madrid : the
supreme junta fled towards Badajos ; St. Juan was
murdered at Talavera, the remnant of Castanos's
army was driven towards the Tagus ; the fourth
corps approached Segovia, and sir John Hope's
situation became very critical.

His column, consisting of three thousand in- Sir John Moore's
fantry, nine hundred cavalry, the artillery, and Papers. Hope's
the great parc of ammunition had been obliged, Letters.

from the want of money and supplies, to move in six divisions, each being a day's march behind the other.   At Almaraz, he endeavoured to discover a way across the mountains to Ciudad Rodrigo, and a road did exist, but the peasants and muleteers declared it to be impracticable for carriages, and consequently unfit for the convoy; the truth of their assertions was much doubted, but sir John was daily losing horses from the glanders, and, with a number but just sufficient to drag his guns and convoy along a good road, he feared to explore a difficult passage over the Sierras.

When his leading division had reached Talavera, don Thomas Morla, then secretary at war, anxious to have the troops more minutely divided, proposed that the regiments should march through Madrid in ten divisions on as many successive days, the first to reach the capital on the 22d of November, which would exactly have brought the convoy into the jaws of the French army.   Hope immediately repaired in person to Madrid, held a conference with Morla, and quickly satisfied himself that everything was in confusion, and that the Spanish government had neither arranged a general plan, nor was capable of conducting one.   Convinced of this unfortunate truth, he paid no attention to Morla's proposition, but carried his troops at once by the road of Naval Carnero to the Escurial, where he halted to close up the rear, and to obtain bullocks to assist in dragging the parc over the Guadarama. The 28th, he crossed the mountain, and entered the open flat country; the 28th and 29th the infantry and guns were at Villa Castin and St. Antonia, the parc was at Espinar, and the cavalry

advanced on the road to Arevalo. General Heredia
was then at Segovia, but the duke of Dantzic was
at Valladolid and Placentia, and his patroles were
heard of at Coca, only a few miles from Arevalo, and
in the course of the day a despatch from Mr. Stuart
announced the catastrophe at Tudela, and the dispersion of the camp at Sepulveda; at the same
time the outposts of cavalry in the front reported
that four hundred French horse were at Olmedo,
only twelve miles from Arevalo, and that four thousand others were in the neighbourhood; the scouts
at St. Garcia, on the right, also tracked the French
again at Añaya, near Segovia.

Hope's situation was now truly embarrassing.
If he fell back to the Guadarama, the army at
Salamanca would be without ammunition or artillery. If he advanced, it must be by a flank
movement of three days, with a heavy convoy,
over a flat country, and within a few hours' march
of a very superior cavalry. If he delayed where
he was, even for a few hours, the French on
the side of Segovia might get between him and the
pass of Guadarama, and then, attacked in front,
flank, and rear, he would be reduced to the shameful necessity of abandoning his convoy and guns
to save his men in the mountains of Avila. A
man of less intrepidity and calmness would have
been ruined. Hope, as enterprising as he was prudent, without any hesitation ordered the cavalry to
throw out parties cautiously towards the French,
and maintain a confident front if the latter approached, then moving the infantry and guns from
Villacastin, and the convoy from Espinosa, by cross
roads, to Avila, he continued his march day and
night until they reached Peneranda. Meanwhile the

cavalry to cover this movement closed gradually to
the left, and finally occupied Fontiveros on the 2d of
December.   The infantry and the draught animals
were greatly fatigued ; but the danger was not over ;
the patroles reported that the enemy, to the number of ten thousand infantry, two thousand cavalry,
and forty guns, were still in Olmedo ; this was the
eternal fourth corps, which thus traversing the
country, continually crossed the heads of the English columns, and seemed to multiply the forces
of the French at all points.   Hope immediately
drew his infantry and cavalry up in position, and
obliged the artillery and the convoy to proceed
without rest to Alba de Tormes, where a detachment from Salamanca met them, and covered
their march to that town.   This vigorous and skilful
march was thus concluded, for the division remaining at Peneranda collected its stragglers, and
pushed outposts to Medino del Campo, Madrigal,
and Torecilla, while the fourth corps unwittingly
pursued its march to the Guadarama.

Sir John Moore's resolution to retreat upon Portugal created a great sensation at Madrid and at
Aranjuez.   The junta feared, and with reason, that
such a palpable proof of the state to which their
MrStuart's negligence and incapacity had reduced the country,
Corre-
spondence. would endanger their authority and perhaps their
lives ; and although they were on the point of flying
to Badajos themselves, they were anxious that others
should rush headlong into danger.   Morla, and
those who, like him, were prepared to abandon the
cause of their country, felt mortified at losing an
opportunity of commemorating their defection by
a signal act of perfidy ; and the English plenipotentiary was surprised and indignant that a general of

experience and reputation should think for himself,
and decide upon a military operation without a
reference to his opinion.

Mr. Frere, although a person of some scholastic
attainments, was very ill qualified for the duties of his
situation, which at this moment required temper, sagacity, and judgment.   Greatly overrating his own
talents for public affairs, he had come out to Spain
impressed with false notions of what was passing in
that country, and tenaciously clinging to the pictures
of his imagination, resented the intrusion of reason,
and petulantly spurned at facts.   The defeat of the
conde de Belvedere at Gamonal, a defeat that broke
the centre of the Spanish line uncovered the flank
and rear of Castaños' army opened a way to
Madrid and rendered the concentration of the
British divisions unsafe if not impossible, he
curiously called the 'unlucky affair of the 10th at
Burgos.'   After the battle of Tudela he estimated
the whole French army on the side of Burgos and
Valladolid at eleven thousand men, when they were
above one hundred thousand; and yet, with information so absurdly defective, he was prompt to
interfere with, and eager to control, the military
combinations of the general, which were founded
upon the true and acknowledged principles of the
art of war.

Moore, while anxiously watching the dangerous
progress of sir John Hope, was suddenly assailed by
the representations and remonstrances of all these
offended, mortified, and disappointed persons, and as
the question of retiring was, by the defeat of Tudela,
rendered so purely military, and the necessity of it so
palpable, the general, although anticipating some expressions of discontent from the Spanish government,

was totally unprepared for the torrent of puerile im-
pertinencies with which he was overwhelmed.

Morla, a subtle man, endeavoured first to deceive Mr. Stuart, by treating the defeat of Castaños lightly, and stating officially that he had
saved the greatest part of his army at Siguenza,
and was on the march to join St. Juan at the
Somosierra; to this he added, that there were only
small bodies of French cavalry in the flat country
of Castille and Leon, and no force on that side
capable of preventing the junction of sir John
Moore's army.   This was on the evening of the
30th, but the emperor had forced the pass of the
Somosierra on that morning, and the duke of
Dantzic was at Valladolid.   The same day Mr.
Frere, writing from Aranjuez in answer to the
general's former communication, and before he was
acquainted with his intention to fall back, depre-
cated a retreat upon Portugal, and asserted that the
enthusiasm of the Spaniards was unbounded, except in Castille and Leon, where, he admitted, they
were more passive than they should be.   He even
stated, that twenty thousand men were actually
assembled in the vicinity of the capital, and that
Castaños was falling back upon them; that reinforcements were arriving daily from the southern
provinces, and that the addition of the British army
would form a force greatly superior to any the
French could bring against that quarter, in sufficient time.   It was certain, he said, that the latter
were very weak, and would be afraid to advance,
while the whole country, from the Pyrenees to
the capital, was in arms upon their left flank.
Rumours also were rife that the conscription had
been resisted, and this was the more probable,

because every great effort made by France was accompanied by weakness and internal disturbance, and a pastoral letter of the bishop of Carcassonne seemed to imply that it was so at that time. ' Good policy, therefore, required, that the French should be attacked before their reinforcements joined them, as any success obtained at that moment would render a conscription for a third attempt infinitely difficult, if not impracticable ; but if, on the other hand,' said this inconsiderate person, ' the French are allowed, with their present forces, to retain their present advantages, and to wait the completion of their conscription, they would pour into Spain with a number of troops which would give them immediate possession of the capital and the central provinces.' Two days after the date of this letter, the emperor was actually at the capital; and Mr. Frere, notwithstanding the superior Spanish force which his imagination had conjured up, was, with the junta, flying in all haste from those very central provinces, France remaining, meanwhile, strong, and free from internal dissension.

This rambling epistle was not despatched when the general's intention to fall back upon Portugal was made known to Mr. Frere, but he thought it so admirably calculated to prevent a retreat, that he forwarded it, accompanied by a short explanatory note, which was offensive in style, and indicative of a petulant disposition. At the same time, Augustin Bueno and Ventura Escalente, two generals deputed by the junta to remonstrate against sir John Moore's intended retreat, arrived at head-quarters, and they justified the choice of their employers, being in folly and presumptuous ignorance the very types of the government they represented. Asserting, that

BOOK
III.
———
1808.
December.
St. Juan, with twenty thousand men under his command, had so fortified the pass of the Somosierra,
that it could not be forced by any number of
enemies, and that reinforcements were daily joining
him, they were proceeding to create immense
Spanish armies, when the general stopped their
Moore's
Papers.
garrulity by introducing colonel Graham, who had
been a witness of the dispersion of Castaños's
army, and had just left the unfortunate St. Juan
at Talavera, surrounded by the villanous runagates,
who murdered him the next day. It may be easily
supposed, that such representations, and from such
men, could have no weight with the commander of
an army; in fact, the necessity of retreating was
rendered more imperious by these glaring proofs
that the junta and the English plenipotentiary were
totally ignorant of what was passing around them.

But Napoleon was now in full career; he had
raised a hurricane of war, and, directing its fury as
he pleased, his adversaries were obliged to conform
their movements to his, and as the circumstances
varied from hour to hour, the determination of one
moment was rendered useless in the next. The
appearance of the French cavalry in the plains of
Madrid, had sent the junta and Mr. Frere headlong
towards Badajos, yet the people of Madrid, as we
have seen, shut their gates, and displayed the outward signs of a resolution to imitate Zaragoza; the
neighbouring peasants flocked in to aid the citizens,
and a military junta, composed of the duke of
Infantado, the prince of Castel Franco, the marquis
of Castellar, and don Thomas Morla, was appointed to manage the defence. Morla, being resolved to make a final effort to involve the British
army in the destruction of his own country, easily

persuaded the duke of Infantado to quit Madrid on
a mission to the army of the centre; and thus
the traitor was left sole master of the town, because
the duke and himself only, had any influence with
that armed mob which had murdered the marquis
of Perales, and filled the city with tumult.

When the French emperor summoned the junta
to surrender, Morla, in concert with the prince of
Castel Franco, addressed a paper to sir John Moore,
in which it was stated that ' twenty-five thousand
men under Castaños, and ten thousand from the
Somosierra, were marching in all haste to the capital, where forty thousand others were in arms.
Nevertheless, apprehending an increase of force
on the enemy's side, the junta hoped the English
army would either march to the assistance of
Madrid, or take a direction to fall upon the rear
of the French; and not doubting that the English
general had already formed a junction with Blake's
army,' which they well knew had been dispersed,
' they hoped he would be quick in his operations.'
This paper was sent by a government messenger
to Salamanca, but ere he could reach that place,
Morla, who had commenced negotiations before the
despatch was written, capitulated, and Napoleon
was in Madrid. This communication alone would
not have been sufficient to arrest Moore's retrograde
movement, for he was become too well acquainted
with what facility Spanish armies were created
on paper, to rely on any statement of their numbers; but Mr. Stuart also expressed a belief that
Madrid would make a vigorous resistance, and the
tide of false information having set in with a strong
current, every moment brought fresh assurances
that a great spirit had arisen.

On the day that Morla's communication arrived, there also appeared at head-quarters, one Charmilly, a French adventurer. This man, who has been since denounced in the British parliament as an organizer of assassination in St. Domingo, and a fraudulent bankrupt in London, came as the confidential agent of Mr. Frere. He had been in Madrid during the night of the first, and left it immediately after having held a conference with Morla, the next morning. Taking the road to Talavera, he met with the plenipotentiary, to whom he spoke with such enthusiasm of the spirit and preparations of the inhabitants in the capital, that Mr. Frere, readily confiding in him, and imparting his own views, not only entrusted him, a stranger, with letters to the British general, but charged him with a mission to obstruct the retreat into Portugal. Thus instructed, Charmilly hastened to Salamanca, and presented Mr. Frere's first missive, in which that gentleman, after alluding to former representations, and to the information of which colonel Charmilly was the bearer, viz. the enthusiasm in the capital, made a formal remonstrance, to the effect that propriety and policy demanded an immediate advance of the British to support this generous effort. Charmilly also demanded a personal interview, which was granted, yet Moore, having some suspicion of the man, whom he had seen before, listened to his tale of the enthusiasm and vigorous character displayed at Madrid, with an appearance of coldness that baffled the penetration of the adventurer, who retired under the impression that a retreat was certain.

But for many years so much ridicule had been attached to the name of an English expedition, that weak-headed men claimed a sort of prescriptive right to censure, without regard to subordination, the conduct of their general. It had been so in Egypt, where a cabal was formed to deprive lord Hutchinson of the command, it had been so at Buenos Ayres, at Ferrol, and in Portugal, it was so at this time in sir John Moore's army; and it will be found, in the course of this work, that the superlative talents, vigour, and success of the duke of Wellington, could not even at a late period of the war secure him from such vexatious folly. The three generals who commanded the separate divisions of the army, and who were in consequence acquainted with all the circumstances of the moment, were perfectly agreed as to the propriety of a retreat, but in other quarters indecent murmurs were so prevalent among officers of rank as to call for rebuke; and Charmilly, ignorant of the decided character of the general-in-chief, concluding that this temper was favourable to the object of his mission, presented a second letter, which Mr. Frere had charged him to deliver, should the first fail of effect. The purport of it was to desire, that if sir John Moore still persisted in his intention of retreating, ' *the bearer might be previously examined before a council of war;*' in other words, that Mr. Frere, convinced of sir John Moore's incapacity and want of zeal, was determined to control his proceedings even by force. And this to a British general of long experience and confirmed reputation, and by the hands of a foreign adventurer!!! The indignation of a high spirit at such a foolish, wanton insult, may be easily imagined. He ordered Charmilly to quit the cantonments of the British army instantly.

His anger, however, soon subsided. Quarrels,
among the servants of the public, could only prove
detrimental to his country, and he put his personal
feelings on one side. The information brought by
Charmilly, separated from the indecorum of his
mission, was in itself important; it confirmed the
essential fact, that Madrid was actually resisting,
and that the spirit and energy of the country was
awaking.

Hitherto his own observation had led sir John
Moore to doubt, if the people took sufficient
interest in the cause to make any effectual
effort, all around himself was apathetic and incapable; his correspondents, with the exception
of Mr. Frere, nay, even the intercepted letters of
French officers, had agreed in describing the general feeling of the country as subsiding into indifference, and to use his own words, ' *Spain was
without armies, generals, or a government.*' But
now the fire essential to the salvation of the nation
seemed to be kindling, and Moore feeling conscious of ability to lead a British army, hailed the
appearance of an enthusiasm which promised success to a just cause, and a brilliant career of glory to
himself. That the metropolis should thus abide the
fury of the conqueror was indeed surprising, it was
a great event and full of promise, and the situation
of the army was likewise improved, general Hôpe's
junction was accomplished; and as the attention of
the French was turned towards Madrid, there was
no reason to doubt that Baird's junction could likewise be effected. On the other hand, there was no
certainty that the capital would remain firm when
danger pressed, none that it would be able to resist,
none that the example would spread; yet without

Appendix,
No. 13, §7.

Appendix,
No. 14.

it did so, nothing was gained, because it was only

by an union of heart and hand throughout the whole country, that the great power of the French could be successfully resisted.

In a matter so balanced, Moore, as might be expected from an enterprising general, adopted the boldest and most generous side. He ordered Baird, who, after destroying some stores, had fallen back to Villa Franca, to concentrate his troops at Astorga, and he himself prepared for an advance; but as he remained without any further information of the fate of Madrid, he sent colonel Graham to obtain intelligence of what was passing, and to carry his answer to Morla. This resolution being taken, he wrote to Mr. Frere, calmly explaining the reasons for his past conduct, and those which actuated him in forming a fresh plan of operation. ' I wish anxiously,' said this noble-minded man in conclusion, ' I wish anxiously, as the king's minister, to continue upon the most confidential footing with you, and I hope as we have but one interest, the public welfare, though we occasionally see it in different aspects, that this will not disturb the harmony which should subsist between us. Fully impressed as I am with these sentiments, I shall abstain from any remarks upon the two letters, from you, delivered to me last night and this morning by colonel Charmilly, or on the message which accompanied them. I certainly at first did feel and expressed much indignation at a person like him being made the channel of a communication of that sort from you to me. Those feelings are at an end, and I dare say they never will be created towards you again.'

The plan of operations now occupied his mind.

The Somosierra and the Guadarama were both in possession of the enemy, wherefore no direct movement could be made towards Madrid, and as the rear of Baird's troops was still several marches behind Astorga, a general movement on the side of the capital could not commence before the 12th of the month. Zaragoza, the general knew, was determined to stand a second siege, and he had the guarantee of the first that it would be an obstinate stand; he had received from the junta of Toledo a formal assurance of their resolution to bury themselves under the ruins of the town, sooner than submit; and he was informed from several quarters that the southern provinces were forwarding crowds of fresh levies. Romana at this time also was in correspondence with him, and, with the usual exaggeration of a Spaniard, declared his ability to aid him with an army of twenty thousand men. Upon this data sir John Moore formed a plan, bearing the stamp of genuine talent and enterprise, whether it be examined as a political or a military measure.

He supposed the French emperor to be more anxious to strike a heavy blow against the English, and to shut them out of Spain, than to overrun any particular province, or get possession of any town in the Peninsula. He resolved, therefore, to throw himself upon the communications of the French army, hoping, if fortune was favourable, to inflict a severe loss upon the troops which guarded them before aid could arrive. If Napoleon, suspending his operations against the south, should detach them largely, Madrid would thereby be succoured; if he did not detach largely, the British could hold their ground. Moore knew well that a great com-

mander would in such a case be more likely to unite
his whole army, and fall upon the troops which
thus ventured to place themselves on his line of
operations; but, to relieve the Spaniards at a critical
moment, and to give time for the southern provinces
to organize their defence and recover courage, he
was willing thus to draw the whole of the enemy
upon himself. He felt that, in doing so, he compromised the safety of his own army, that he must
glide along the edge of a precipice, that he must
cross a gulf on a rotten plank; but he also knew
the martial qualities of his soldiers, he had confidence in his own genius, and the occasion being
worthy of a great deed, he dared essay it even
against Napoleon.

Colonel Graham returned on the 9th, bringing
the first intimation of the capitulation of the capital.
He had been able to proceed no farther than Talavera, where he encountered two members of the
supreme junta. By them he was told that the
French, being from twenty to thirty thousand
strong, possessed the Retiro; that the people retained their arms, and that La-Peña, with thirty
thousand men of the army of the centre, was at
Guadalaxara; that fourteen thousand of St. Juan's
and Heredia's forces were assembled at Almaraz;
and that Romana, with whom they anxiously desired the English should unite, had likewise an
army of thirty thousand fighting men: finally, they
assured colonel Graham that the most energetic
measures were in activity wherever the enemy's
presence did not control the patriots.

Mortifying as it was to find that Madrid, after
so much boasting, should have held out but one

day, the event itself did not destroy the ground of Moore's resolution to advance. Undoubtedly it was so much lost; it diminished the hope of arousing the nation, and it increased the danger of the British army, by letting loose a greater number of the enemy's troops; but as a diversion for the south it might still succeed, and as long as there was any hope, the resolution of the English general was fixed, to prove that he would not abandon the cause, even when the Spaniards were abandoning it themselves.

CHAPTER IV.

THE forward movement of the British army commenced on the 11th of December. Moore's first
intention was to march with his own and Hope's
division to Valladolid, with a view to cover the
advance of his stores and to protect the junction of
sir David Baird's troops, the rear of which was still
behind Astorga; nevertheless preparations for a
retreat upon Portugal were continued, and sir David
was ordered to form magazines at Benevente, Astorga, Villa Franca, and Lugo, by which arrangement two lines of operation were secured, and a
greater freedom of action obtained.

The 13th head-quarters were at Alaejos; two
brigades and Lord Paget's cavalry at Toro; general Hope at Torrecilla; general Charles Stewart's
horsemen at Rueda, having the night before surprised there fifty infantry and thirty dragoons,
who declared, that in the French army it was
believed that the English were retreating to
Portugal.

At Alaejos an intercepted despatch of the prince
of Neufchatel was brought to head-quarters, and
the contents were important enough to change the
direction of the march. It was addressed to the
duke of Dalmatia, and described Madrid as perfectly tranquil, the shops open, and the public
amusements going forward as in a time of profound
peace. The fourth corps of the army was said to
be at Talavera, on its way towards Badajos, and

this movement, it was observed, would force the English to retire to Portugal, if, contrary to the emperor's belief, they had not already done so. The fifth corps was on the march to Zaragoza, and the eighth to Burgos. Soult was therefore directed to drive the Spaniards into Gallicia, to occupy Leon, Benevente, and Zamora, and to keep the flat country in subjection, for which purpose his two divisions of infantry, and the cavalry brigades of Franceschi and Debelle, were considered sufficient.

It is remarkable that this the first correct information of the capitulation of Madrid should have been thus acquired from the enemy, ten days after the event had taken place; nor is it less curious, that while Mr. Frere's letters were filled with vivid descriptions of Spanish enthusiasm, Napoleon should have been so convinced of their passiveness, as to send this important despatch by an officer, who rode post, without an escort, and in safety, until his abusive language to the post-master at Valdestillos created a tumult, in which he lost his life. Captain Waters, an English officer sent to obtain intelligence, happening to arrive in that place, heard of the murder, and immediately pur-
Appendix,
No. 13, § 4. chased the despatch for twenty dollars; and the accidental information thus obtained was the more valuable, as neither money nor patriotism had hitherto induced the Spaniards to bring any intelligence of the enemy's situation, and each step the army had made was in the dark. It was now however certain that Burgos was or would be strongly protected, and that Baird's line of march was unsafe if Soult, following these instructions, advanced. On the other hand, as the French appeared to be ignorant of the British movements,

there was some chance of surprising and beating
the second corps before Napoleon could come to
its succour. Hope, therefore, was ordered to pass
the Duero at Tordesillas, and direct his march upon
Villepando; head-quarters were removed to Toro;
and Valderas was given as the point of junction to
Baird's division, the head of which was now at
Benevente.

The 16th Mr. Stuart arrived at Toro, accompanied by don F. X. Caro, a member of the Spanish
government, who brought two letters, the one from
the junta, the other from Mr. Frere. That from
the junta complained, that when Romana proposed
to unite fourteen thousand picked men to the
British army, with a view to make a forward movement, his offer had been disregarded, and a retreat
determined upon, in despite of his earnest remonstrances; this retreat they declared to be uncalled
for, and highly impolitic, ' as the enemy was never
so near his ruin as in that moment ' If the Spanish
and British armies should unite, they said, it would
give ' liberty to the Peninsula,' that ' Romana, with
his fourteen thousand select men,' was still ready to
join sir John Moore, and that ' thirty thousand fresh
levies would, in a month, be added to the ranks of
the allied force.'

This tissue of falsehoods, for Romana had approved of the intention to retreat, and never had
above six thousand men armed, was addressed to
Mr. Frere, and by him transmitted to the general,
together with one from himself, which, in allusion
to the retreat upon Portugal, contained the following extraordinary passages: ' I mean the immense
responsibility with which you charge yourself by
adopting, upon a supposed military necessity, a

measure which must be followed by immediate, if
not final, ruin to our ally, and by indelible disgrace to the country with whose resources you are
entrusted.' ' I am unwilling to enlarge upon a
subject in which my feelings must be stifled, or
expressed at the risk of offence, which, with such
an interest at stake, I should feel unwilling to
excite, but this much I must say, that if the British
army had been sent abroad for the express purpose of doing the utmost possible mischief to the
Spanish cause, with the single exception of not
firing a shot against their troops, they would,
according to the measures now announced as about
to be pursued, have completely fulfilled their purpose.'

These letters were dated at Truxillo ; for the
junta, not thinking themselves safe at Badajos, had
proceeded so far on their way to Seville, and on
that side the French had continued to advance, the
remnants of the Spanish armies to fly, and every
thing bore the most gloomy appearance. Mr. Frere
knew this. In a subsequent letter he acknowledged
that the enthusiasm was extinguished, and a general panic commencing at the moment when he
was penning these offensive passages. He was
utterly ignorant of the numbers, the situation, and
the resources of the enemy, but he formed hypo-
theses, and upon the strength' of them insulted
sir John Moore, and endangered the interests of
his country. In this manner the British general,
while struggling with unavoidable difficulties, had
his mind harassed by a repetition of remonstrances
and representations, in which common sense, truth,
and decency were alike disregarded ; but he did
not fail to shew how little personal feelings weighed

Appendix,
No. 13, §7.

with him in opposition to the public welfare. He
had reason to suppose Mr. Frere had received his
letter relative to Charmilly's mission, yet as it was
not acknowledged, he took advantage of the omis-
sion, and with singular propriety and dignity thus
noticed the plenipotentiary's second insulting communication. ' *With respect to your letter delivered
to me at Toro by Mr. Stuart, I shall not remark
upon it. It is in the style of the two which were
brought to me by colonel Charmilly, and consequently
was answered by my letter of the 6th, of which
I send you a duplicate; that subject is I hope at
rest!*'

At Toro sir John Moore ascertained that Romana,
although aware of the advance of the British, and
engaged to support them, was retiring into Gallicia.
Nominally commander-in-chief of the Spanish armies, he was at the head of a few thousand miserable soldiers, for the Spaniards, with great ingenuity, contrived to have no general when they
had an army, and no army when they had a general. After the dispersion of Blake's people at
Reynosa, Romana rallied about five thousand men
at Renedo, in the valley of Cabernuigo, and endeavoured to make a stand on the borders of the
Asturias, but without any success, for the vile conduct of the Asturian junta, joined to the terror
created by the French victories, had completely
subdued the spirit of the peasantry, and ruined the
resources of that province. Romana complained
that, when checked for misconduct, his soldiers
quitted their standards, indeed, that any should
have been found to join their colours is to be ad-
mired; for, among the sores of Spain, there were
none more cankered, more disgusting, than the

Sir John
Moore's
Papers.
Colonel
Syme's
Correspon-
dence.

General
Leith.

BOOK
IV.
————
1808.
December.
Appendix.
No.13, §5. venality, the injustice, the profligate corruption of the Asturian authorities. Without a blush, they openly divided the English subsidies, and defrauded, not only the soldiers of their pay and equipments, but the miserable peasants of their hire, doubling the wretchedness of poverty, and deriding the misery they occasioned by pompous declarations of their own virtue.

From the Asturias Romana had led the remnants of Blake's force to Leon about the period of Moore's arrival at Salamanca; like others, he had been deceived as to the real state of the country, and at this time repented that he had returned to Spain. He was a person of talent, quickness, and information, but disqualified by nature for military command; a lively principle of error pervaded all his notions of war, and no man ever bore the title of a general who was less capable of directing an army. Neither was he exempt from the prevailing weakness of his countrymen. At this moment, when he had not strength to stand upright, his letters were teeming with gigantic offensive projects; and although he had before approved of the intention to retreat, he was now as ready to urge a forward movement, promising to co-operate with twenty thousand soldiers when he could scarcely muster a third of that number, and those only half armed, and scarcely capable of distinguishing their own standards : and at the very time he made the promise, he was retiring into Gallicia, not meaning to deceive, for he was as ready to advance as to retreat, but this species of boasting is inherent in his nation. It has been asserted that Caro offered the chief command of the Spanish armies to sir John Moore, and that the latter refused it. This

is not true. Caro had no power to do so, and
there were no armies to command; but that gentleman, in his interview, either was, or affected
to be, satisfied of the soundness of the English
general's views, and ashamed of the folly of the
junta.

The 18th, head-quarters were at Castro Nuevo,
from which place Moore wrote to Romana, in-
forming him of his intention to fall upon Soult;
he desired his co-operation, and requested that the
marquis would, according to his own plan given
to the British minister in London, reserve the
Asturias for his own line of communication, and
leave Gallicia to the British. The latter were now
in full march. Baird was at Benevente, Hope at
Villepando, and the cavalry scouring the country
on the side of Valladolid, had several successful
skirmishes and took a number of prisoners; the
French could be no longer ignorant of the movement, and the English general brought forward his
columns rapidly. On the 20th, the whole of the
forces were united, the cavalry at Melgar Abaxo,
the infantry at Mayorga and as much concentrated
as the necessity of obtaining cover in a country
devoid of fuel, and deep with snow, would permit;
the weather was exceedingly severe, and the
marches long, but a more robust set of men never
took the field, their discipline was admirable, and
there were very few stragglers, the experience of
one or two campaigns alone was wanting to make
a perfect army. The number was however small;
nominally it was nearly thirty-five thousand, but
four regiments were still in Portugal, and three
more were left by sir David Baird at Lugo and
Astorga; one thousand six hundred and eighty-

seven men were detached, and four thousand and five were in hospital; hence the actual number present under arms on the 19th of December, was only nineteen thousand and fifty-three infantry, two thousand two hundred and seventy-eight cavalry, and one thousand three hundred and fifty-eight gunners; forming a total of twenty-three thousand five hundred and eighty-three men, with sixty pieces of artillery. They were organized in three divisions, a reserve, two light brigades of infantry, and one division of cavalry; four batteries were attached to the infantry, two to the cavalry, and one was kept in reserve. Meanwhile Romana, who had been able to bring forward very few men, promised to march in two columns by Almanzer and Guarda, and sent some information of the enemy's position. But sir John Moore depended little upon his intelligence, when he found him, even so late as the 19th of December, upon the faith of information from the junta, representing Madrid as still holding out; and, when the advanced posts were already engaged at Sahagun, proposing an interview at Benevente to arrange the plan of operations.

On the French side, Soult was concentrating his force on the Carrion. After his rapid and brilliant success at the opening of the campaign, his corps

was ordered to remain on the defensive, until the movements against Tudela and Madrid were completed, and the despatches directing him to recommence his offensive operations, were, as we have seen, intercepted on the 12th; but on the 16th he became acquainted with the advance of the English army. At that period general Bonnet's division occupied Barquera de San Vincente and

Potes, on the Deba, watching some thousand
Asturians whom Ballasteros had collected near
Llanes; Merle's and Mermet's divisions were
on the Carrion, Franceschi's dragoons at Valladolid, Debelle's at Sahagun. The whole formed
a total of sixteen or seventeen thousand infantry,
and twelve hundred cavalry, present under arms,
of which only eleven thousand infantry and twelve
hundred cavalry could, without uncovering the
important post of St. Andero, be opposed to
the advance of the British. Soult, alarmed at
this disparity of force, required general Mathieu
Dumas, commandant at Burgos, to direct all the
divisions and detachments, passing through that
town, whatever might be their original destination,
upon the Carrion, and this decisive conduct was approved of by the emperor.

On the 21st, Bonnet's division was still on the
Deba, but Mermet's was in the town of Carrion,
Merle's at Saldaña; Franceschi's cavalry had retired
from Valladolid to Riberos de la Cuesca, Debelle's
continued at Sahagun, and thirteen hundred dragoons, under general Lorge, arrived at Palencia from
Burgos. Meantime, the fifteenth and tenth British hussars having quitted Melgar Abaxo during the night,
came close to Sahagun before daylight on the 21st.
The tenth marched straight to the town, while the
fifteenth turned it by the right, and endeavoured to
cut off the enemy; a patrole gave the alarm, and
when four hundred of the fifteenth had reached the
rear of the village, they were opposed by a line of
six hundred French dragoons. The tenth were not
in sight, but lord Paget, after a few movements,
charged with the 15th, broke the enemy's line, and
pursued them for some distance. Some twenty killed,

two lieutenant-colonels, and eleven other officers, with a hundred and fifty-four men prisoners, were the result of this affair, which lasted about twenty minutes. Debelle then retired to Santerbas; the English infantry occupied Sahagun, and head-quarters were established there. During these events Romana remained at Mancilla, and it was evident that no assistance could be expected from him. The truth was, that, ashamed of exposing the weakness and misery of his troops, he kept away, for, after all his promises, he could not produce six thousand fighting men. His letters however, were, as usual, extremely encouraging. *The French force in Spain was exceedingly weak, Palafox had not been defeated at Tudela; Soult, including Bonnet's division, had scarcely nine thousand men of all arms; it was an object to surround and destroy him before he could be succoured;*—and other follies of this nature.

The English troops having now outmarched their supplies, halted the 22d and 23d, and Soult, whose intention was to act on the defensive, hastened the march of the reinforcements from the side of Burgos, yet being fearful for his communication with Placentia, he abandoned Saldaña on the 23d, and concentrated his infantry at Carrion. Debelle's cavalry again advanced to Villatilla and Villacuenda, Franceschi remained at Riberos, the dragoons of general Lorge occupied Paredes, and general Dumas pushed on the divisions of the eighth corps, of which Laborde's was already arrived at Palencia; Loison's and Heudelet's followed at the distance of two days' march, but they were weak. Sir John Moore's plan was to move during the night of the 23d, so as to arrive at Carrion by daylight on the 24th, to force the bridge, and afterwards

ascending the river, to fall upon the main body of
the enemy, which his information led him to believe
was still at Saldaña. This attack was, however, but
a secondary object, his attention was constantly
directed towards Madrid. To beat the troops in his
front would be a victory of little value beyond the
honour, because the third and fourth corps were
so near; the pith of the operation was to tempt
the emperor from Madrid, and his march from that
capital was to be the signal for a retreat, which
sooner or later was inevitable.

To draw Napoleon from the south was Moore's
design, and it behoves the man to be alert who inter-
poses between the lion and his prey. On the 23d,
Romana first gave notice that the French were in motion from the side of Madrid; and in the night of the
23d, when the troops were actually in march towards
Carrion; this intelligence was confirmed by the general's own spies, all their reports agreed that the whole
French army was in movement to crush the English;
the fourth corps had been halted at Talavera, the
fifth at Vittoria, the eighth was closing up to reinforce the second, and the emperor in person was
marching towards the Guadarama. The principal
objects of sir John Moore's advance were thus attained; the siege of Zaragoza was delayed, the
southern provinces were allowed to breathe, and it
only remained for him to prove, by a timely retreat,
that this offensive operation, although hazardous,
was not the result of improvident rashness, nor
weakness of mind, but the hardy enterprise of a
great commander acting under peculiar circumstances. As a military measure, his judgment condemned it; as a political one, he thought it of
doubtful advantage, because Spain was really pas-

sive; but he had desired to give the Spaniards an
opportunity of making one more struggle for independence. That was done. If they could not, or
would not profit of the occasion, if their hearts
were faint or their hands feeble, the shame and the
loss were their own ; the British general had done
enough ; enough for honour, enough for utility,
more than enough for prudence, the madness of the
times required it. His army was already on the
verge of destruction, the enemy's force was hourly
increasing in his front, the first symptoms of a retreat would bring it headlong on, and in the mean
time the emperor threatened the line of communication with Gallicia, and by the rapidity of his
march left no time for consideration.

After the first burst, by which he swept the
northern provinces, and planted his standards on
the banks of the Tagus, that monarch had put all
the resources of his subtle genius into activity,
endeavouring to soften the public mind, and by
engrafting benefits on the terror his victories had
created, to gain over the people ; but, at the same
time, he was gathering in his extended wings, and
preparing for a new flight, which would have carried him over the southern kingdoms of the
Peninsula, and given him the rocks of Lisbon as a
resting-place for his eagles. Madrid was tranquil,
and Toledo, notwithstanding her heroic promises,
had never shut her gates ; one division of the first
corps occupied that town, another was in Ocaña,
and the light cavalry scoured the whole of La
Mancha, even to the borders of Andalusia; the
fourth corps, and Milhaud's and Lasalle's horsemen, were at Talavera, preparing to march to Badajos, and sixty thousand men, with one hundred

and fifty guns and fifteen days' provisions in carts,

were reviewed at the gates of Madrid upon the 19th ; three days afterwards they were in full march to intercept the line of sir John Moore's retreat.

Napoleon was informed of that general's advance on the 21st, and in an instant the Spaniards, their juntas, and their armies, were dismissed from his thoughts ; his corps were arrested in their different movements, ten thousand men were left to control the capital, and on the evening of the 22d, fifty thousand men were at the foot of the Guadarama. A deep snow choked the passes of the Sierra, and, after twelve hours of ineffectual toil, the advanced guards were still on the wrong side ; the general commanding reported that the road was impracticable, but Napoleon, dismounting, placed himself at the head of the column, and, amidst storms of hail and drifting snow, led his soldiers over the mountain. Many men and animals died during the passage, which lasted two days, but the emperor personally urging on the troops with unceasing vehemence, reached Villacastin, fifty miles from Madrid, on the 24th, and the 26th he was at Tordesillas with the guards and the divisions of Lapisse and Dessoles ; the dragoons of La Houssaye entered Valladolid on the same day, and marshal Ney, with the sixth corps, was at Rio Seco.

From Tordesillas Napoleon communicating with Soult, informed him of these movements, concluding his despatch thus : *' Our cavalry scouts* S.
Journal of
operations
MS. *are already at Benevente. If the English pass today in their position, they are lost ; if, on the contrary, they attack you with all their force, retire one*

day's march; the farther they proceed, the better
for us. If they retreat, pursue them closely.' Then,
full of hope, he hastened himself to Valderas, but
had the mortification to learn that, notwithstanding
his rapid march, having scarcely rested night or
day, he was twelve hours too late. The British
were across the Esla! In fact Soult was in full
pursuit when this letter was written, for sir John
Moore, well aware of his own situation, had given
orders to retreat the moment the intelligence of
Napoleon's march from Madrid reached him, and
the heavy baggage was immediately moved to the
rear, while the reserve, the light brigades, and the
cavalry remained at Sahagun, the latter pushing
patroles up to the enemy's lines, and skirmishing
to hide the retrograde march.

The 24th, general Hope, with two divisions, had
gone back by the road of Mayorga, Baird, with
another, by that of Valencia de San Juan, where
there was a ferry-boat to cross the Esla river. The
marquis of Romana undertook to guard the bridge
of Mansilla. The enemy's dragoons, under Lorge,
arrived the same day at Frechilla, and the division of
Laborde entered Paredes. The 25th the general-in-
chief, with the reserve and light brigades, followed
the route of Hope's column to Valderas, and the
26th Baird passed the Esla at Valencia, and took post
on the other side, but with some difficulty, for the
boat was small, the fords deep, and the river rising.
The troops, under the commander-in-chief, approached the bridge of Castro Gonzalo early in the
morning of the 26th, but the stores were a long
time passing, a dense fog intercepted the view, and
so nicely timed was the march, that the scouts of

the imperial horsemen were already infesting the
flank of the column, and even carried off some of
the baggage.

As the left bank of the river commanded the
bridge, general Robert Crawfurd remained with
a brigade of infantry and two guns to protect the
passage, for the cavalry was still in the rear, watching Soult, who, aware of the retreat, was pressing
forward in pursuit. Meanwhile lord Paget, after
passing Mayorga, was intercepted by a strong body
of horse, which belonged to Ney's corps and was
embattled on a swelling ground close to the road.
Though the soil was deep, and soaked with snow
and rain, two squadrons of the tenth, riding stiffly up,
gained the summit, and notwithstanding the enemy's
advantage of numbers and position, killed twenty
men and captured one hundred. This was a bold
and hardy action; but the English cavalry had
been engaged more or less for twelve successive
days, with such fortune and bravery, that above
five hundred prisoners had already fallen into their
hands, and their leaders being excellent, their confidence was unbounded.

From Mayorga lord Paget proceeded to Benevente; but the duke of Dalmatia, with great judgment, now pushed for Astorga by the road of
Mancilla, whereupon Romana, leaving three thousand men and two guns to defend the bridge at the
latter place, fell back to Leon. Thus, by a critical
march, Moore recovered his communications with
Gallicia, and had so far baffled the emperor, but
his position was by no means safe, or even tenable.

The town of Benevente, a rich open place, remarkable for a small, but curious Moorish castle,

S.
Journal of
operations.
MS.

containing a fine collection of ancient armour, is situated in a plain that, extending from the Gallician mountains to the neighbourhood of Burgos, appears to be boundless. The river Esla winded through it, about four miles in front of Benevente, and the bridge of Castro Gonzalo was the key to the town; but the right bank of the Esla was completely commanded from the further side, and there were many fords. Eighteen miles higher up, at Valencia de San Juan, a shorter road from Mayorga to Astorga, crossed the river by the ferry-boat; and at Mancilla, the passage being only defended by Spaniards, was, in a manner, open to Soult, for Romana had not destroyed the arches of the bridge. Beyond Mancilla, under the hills skirting this great plain, stood the town of Leon, which was inclosed with walls and capable of resisting a sudden assault.

Moore aware of his incapacity resolved to remain no longer than was necessary to clear out his magazines at Benevente, and to cover the march of his stores. But the road to Astorga by Leon was much shorter than that through Benevente, and as Romana was inclined to retreat to Gallicia Sir John requested that he would maintain himself at Leon as long as he could, and repeated his desire to have that province left open for the English army. Romana, who assented to both these requests, had a great rabble with him, and as Leon was a walled place, and a number of citizens and volunteers were willing, and even eager to fight, the town might have made resistance. Moore hoped that it would do so, and gave orders to break down the bridge at Castro Gonzalo in his own front, the moment the stragglers and baggage should have passed; but at this time the bad example of murmuring given by men of high rank had descended lower, many regimental officers neglected their duty, and what with the dislike to a retreat, the severity of the weather, and the inexperience of the army, the previous fine discipline of the troops was broken down: such disgraceful excesses had been committed at Valderas, that the general issued severe orders, justly reproaching the soldiers for their evil deeds, and appealing to the honour of the army to amend them.

On the night of the 26th, the light cavalry of the imperial guard, riding close up to the bridge of Castro Gonzalo, captured some women and baggage, and endeavoured to surprise the post, which gave rise to a remarkable display of courage and discipline. John Walton and Richard Jackson, private soldiers of the forty-third, being posted beyond the bridge, were directed, on the approach of an enemy, the one to stand firm, the other to fire and run back to the brow of the hill, to give notice whether there were many or few. Jackson fired, but was overtaken, and received twelve or fourteen sabre cuts in an instant; nevertheless he came staggering on, and gave the signal, while Walton, with equal resolution, stood his ground, and wounded several of the assailants, who then retired, leaving him unhurt, but his cap, knapsack, belts, and musket were cut in above twenty places, his bayonet was bent double, and notched like a saw. The 27th, the cavalry and the stragglers being all over the river, general Crawfurd commenced the destruction of the bridge amidst torrents of rain and snow, and while half the troops worked the other half kept the

CHAP. IV.

1808. December.

enemy at bay from the heights on the left bank, for the cavalry scouts of the imperial guard were spread over the plain.

At ten o'clock at night a large party of French following some waggons, again endeavoured to pass the piquets and gallop down to the bridge; that failing, a few dismounted, and extending to the right and left, commenced a skirmishing fire, while others remained ready to charge, if the position of the troops, which they expected to ascertain by this scheme, should offer an opportunity. The event did not answer their expectations, and this anxiety to interrupt the work induced general Crawfurd to destroy two arches of the bridge, and to blow up the connecting buttress; yet the masonry was so solid and difficult to pierce, that it was not until twelve o'clock in the night of the 28th that all the preparations were completed. The troops then descended the heights on the left bank, and passing with the greatest silence, by single files, over planks laid across the broken arches, gained the other side without loss; an instance of singular good fortune, for the night was dark and tempestuous, the river rising rapidly with a roaring noise, was threatening to burst over the planks, and the enemy was close at hand. To have resisted an attack in such an awkward situation would have been impossible, but happily the retreat of the troops was undiscovered, and the mine was sprung with good effect.

Crawfurd marched to Benevente, where the cavalry and the reserve still remained. Here several thousand infantry slept in the upper part of an immense convent built round a square, and a frightful catastrophe was impending; for the lower galleries were so thickly stowed with the horses of the cavalry, that it was scarcely possible to pass them, there was but one entrance, and two officers of the forty-third, returning from the bridge, on entering the convent, perceived that a large window-shutter was on fire, that in a few moments the straw under the horses would ignite, and six thousand men and animals must inevitably perish in the flames. One of these officers, captain Lloyd, a man of great strength, activity, and of a presence of mind which never failed, made a sign of silence to his companion, and then springing on to the nearest horse, run along the backs of the others, until he reached the blazing shutter, which he tore off its hinges and cast out of the window, and then awakening a few men, cleared the passage without any alarm, which in such a case would have been as destructive as the fire.

Two days' rest had been gained at Benevente, but as very little could be done to remove the stores, the greatest part were destroyed. The army was and had been from the first without sufficient means of transport, the general had no money to procure it, and the ill-will of the Spaniards, and the shuffling conduct of the juntas added infinitely to their difficulties. But time pressed. Hope and Fraser marched by Labaneza, and reached Astorga the 29th, where Baird joined them from Valencia de San Juan; on the same day the reserve and Crawfurd's brigade quitted Benevente. The cavalry remained in the town, having parties to watch the fords of the Esla. In this state of affairs general Lefebre Desnouettes, seeing only a few cavalry posts on the great plain, rather hastily concluded that there was nothing to support them, and crossing the river at daybreak, by a ford a little way above the

bridge, with six hundred horsemen of the imperial guard, advanced into the plain. The piquets
under major Loftus Otway retired fighting, and
being joined by a part of the third German hussars, even charged the leading French squadrons with some effect. General C. Stewart then
took the command, and the ground was obsti-
nately disputed, but the enemy advanced. At
this moment the plain was covered with stragglers, baggage-mules, and followers of the army,
the town was filled with tumult, the distant piquets and videttes were seen galloping in from
the right and left, the French were pressing forward boldly, and every appearance indicated that
the enemy's whole army was coming up and passing
the river.

Lord Paget ordered the tenth hussars to mount
and form under the cover of some houses at
the edge of the town, for he desired to draw the
enemy, whose real situation he had detected at
once, well into the plain before he attacked; in
half an hour, every thing was ready, and he gave the
signal. Then the tenth hussars galloped forward, the
piquets that were already engaged closed together,
and the whole charged. The scene changed instantly; the enemy were seen flying at full speed
towards the river, the British following close at their
heels, until the French squadrons, without breaking
their ranks, plunged into the stream, and gained
the opposite heights, where, like experienced soldiers, they wheeled instantly, and seemed inclined
to come forward a second time, but a battery of
two guns opened upon them, and after a few rounds
they retired. During the pursuit in the plain, an
officer was observed separating himself from the

main body, and making towards another part of the
river, being followed, and refusing to stop, he was
wounded and brought in a prisoner. It was general
Lefebre Desnouettes.

Although the imperial guards were outnumbered
in the end, they were very superior at the commencement of this action, which was stiffly fought
on both sides, for the British lost fifty men, and the
French left fifty-five killed and wounded on the
field, besides the general and other officers ; according to Baron Larrey, seventy of those who recrossed
the river were also wounded, making a total loss of
above two hundred excellent soldiers. Lord Paget
maintained his posts on the Esla, under an occasional cannonade, until the evening, and then withdrew to La Baneza ; and while these things were
passing, Napoleon arrived at Valderas, Ney at Vil-
laton, and Lapisse at Toro. The French troops were
worn down with fatigue, yet the emperor still urged
them on. The duke of Dalmatia, he said, would intercept the English at Astorga, and their labours
would be finally rewarded. Nevertheless, the destruction of the bridge of Castro Gonzalo was so well
accomplished, that twenty-four hours were required
to repair it, the fords were now impassable, and
it was the 30th before Bessieres could cross the
Esla, but on that day he passed through Benevente
with nine thousand cavalry, and bent his course towards La Baneza ; the same day Franceschi carried
the bridge of Mansilla de las Mulas by a single
charge of his light horsemen, and captured the
artillery and one half of the Spanish division left to
protect it. Romana immediately abandoned Leon
and many stores, and the 31st the duke of Dal-

BOOK
IV.
————
1808.
December

S.
Journal of
operations.
MS.

matia entered that town without firing a shot, while
the duke of Istria, with his cavalry, took possession of La Baneza; the advanced posts were then
pushed forward to the Puente d'Orvigo on one side,
and the Puente de Valembre on the other. The
rear of the English army was still in Astorga, the
head-quarters having arrived there only the day
before.

In the preceding month large stores had been
gradually brought up to this town by sir David
Baird, and as there were no means of transport to
remove them, orders were given, after supplying the
immediate wants of the army, to destroy them; but
Romana, who would neither defend Leon nor Mansilla, had, contrary to his promises, pre-occupied
Astorga with his fugitive army, and when the
English divisions marched in, such a tumult and
confusion arose, that no orders could be executed
with regularity, no distribution made, nor the destruction of the stores be effected. The disorder
thus unexpectedly produced was very detrimental
to the discipline of the troops, which the unwearied
efforts of the general had partly restored; the resources which he had depended on for the support
of his soldiers became mischievous, and contributed
to disorganise instead of nourishing them. And he
had the further vexation to hear Romana, the principal cause of this misfortune, proposing, with
troops unable to resist a thousand light infantry, to
recommence offensive operations on a plan, in comparison with which the visions of Don Quixote were
wisdom.

On the 31st, the flank brigades separated from
the army at Bonillas, and bent their course by cross

roads towards Orense and Vigo, being detached to
lessen the pressure on the commissariat, and to cover
the flanks of the army; Fraser's and Hope's divisions entered Villa Franca, and Baird's division was
at Bembibre; the reserve, with the head-quarters,
halted at Cambarros, a village six miles from Astorga, until the cavalry fell back in the night to the
same place, and then the reserve marched to Bembibre. The marquis of Romana, after doing so
much mischief by crossing the line of march, left
his infantry to wander as they pleased, and retired
with his cavalry and some guns to the valley of the
Minho, and the rest of his artillery mixed with the
British army, but most of it was captured before
reaching Lugo.

Upon the 1st of January the emperor took possession of Astorga, where seventy thousand French
infantry, ten thousand cavalry, and two hundred
pieces of artillery, after many days of incessant
marching, were now united. The congregation of
this mighty force, while it evinced the power and
energy of the French monarch, attested also the
genius of the English general, who, with a handful
of men, had found the means to arrest the course of
the conqueror, and to draw him, with the flower of
his army, to this remote and unimportant part of the
Peninsula, at the moment when Portugal, and the
fairest provinces of Spain, were prostrate beneath
the strength of his hand. That Spain, being in her
extremity, sir John Moore succoured her, and in the
hour of weakness intercepted the blow, which was
descending to crush her, no man of candour and
honesty can deny. For what troops, what preparations, what courage, what capacity was there in

the south to have resisted, even for an instant, the progress of a man, who, in ten days, and in the depth of winter, crossing the snowy ridge of the Carpentinos, had traversed two hundred miles of hostile country, and transported fifty thousand men from Madrid to Astorga in a shorter time than a Spanish courier would have taken to travel the same distance?

This stupendous march was rendered fruitless by the quickness of his adversary; but Napoleon, though he had failed to destroy the English army, resolved, nevertheless, to cast it forth of the Peninsula, and being himself recalled to France by tidings that the Austrian storm was ready to burst, had fixed upon the duke of Dalmatia to continue the pursuit. For this purpose three divisions of cavalry, and three of infantry were added to his former command ; but of these last, the two commanded by generals Loison and Heudelet were several marches in the rear, and general Bonnet's remained always in the Montaña de St. Ander. Hence the whole number bearing arms which the duke led immediately to the pursuit, was about twenty-five thousand men, of which four thousand two hundred were cavalry, composing the divisions of Lorges, La Houssaye, and Franceschi. Fifty-four guns were with the columns, Loison's and Heudelet's divisions followed by forced marches, and Soult was supported by Ney with the sixth corps, wanting its third division, but mustering above sixteen thousand men under arms, the flower of the French army, together with thirty-seven pieces of artillery. Thus including Laborde, Heudelet, and Loison's division, nearly sixty thousand men and ninety-one guns

s.
Journal of
operations
MS.

were put on the track of the English army. Meanwhile the emperor returned to Valladolid, where he
received the addresses of the notables and deputies
from Madrid and other great towns, and strove, by
promises and other means, to win the good opinion
of the public. Appointing Joseph to be his lieutenant-general, he allotted separate provinces for
each 'corps d'armée,' and directing the imperial
guard to return to France, after three days delay he
departed himself with scarcely any escort, but with
an astonishing speed that frustrated the designs
which the Spaniards had as some say formed against
his person.

CHAPTER V.

BOOK
IV.

1809.
January.

S.
Journal of
operations
MS.

THE duke of Dalmatia, a general, who, if the emperor be excepted, was no wise inferior to any of
his nation, commenced his pursuit of the English
army with a vigour that marked his eager desire to
finish the campaign in a manner suitable to the
brilliant opening at Gamonal. The main body of
his troops followed the route of Foncevadon and
Ponteferrada; a second column took the road of
Cambarros and Bembibre; Franceschi entered the
valley of the Syl, and moving up that river, turned
the position of Villa Franca del Bierzo.

Thus sir John Moore, after having twice baffled
the emperor's combinations, was still pressed in his
retreat with a fury that seemed to increase every
moment. The separation of his light brigades, a
measure which he reluctantly adopted by the advice
of his quarter-master-general, had weakened the army
by three thousand men, yet he still possessed
nineteen thousand of all arms, good soldiers to
fight, and strong to march, although shaken in discipline by the disorders at Valderas and Astorga;
for the general's exertions to restore order and regularity were by many officers slightly seconded, and
by some with scandalous levity disregarded. There
was no choice but to retreat. The astonishing
rapidity with which the emperor had brought up
his overbearing numbers, and thrust the English

army into Gallicia, had rendered the natural strength of that country unavailing; the resources were few, even for an army in winter quarters, and for a campaign in that season, there were none at all. All the draught cattle that could be procured would scarcely have supplied the means to transport ammunition for two battles, whereas the French, sweeping the rich plains of Castille with their powerful cavalry, might have formed magazines at Astorga and Leon, and from thence have been supplied in abundance, while the English were starving.

Before he advanced from Salamanca, Moore, foreseeing that his movement must sooner or later end in a retreat, had sent officers to examine the roads of Gallicia and the harbours which offered the greatest advantages for embarkation; by the reports of those officers, which arrived from day to day, and by the state of the magazines which he had directed to be formed, his measures were constantly regulated. The magazines of Astorga, Benevente, and Labaneza, were, by untoward circumstances, and the deficiency of transport, rendered, as we have seen, of no avail beyond the momentary supply they afforded, and part of their contents falling into the enemy's hands, gave him some cause of triumph; but those at Villa Franca and Lugo contained about fourteen days' consumption, and there were other small magazines formed on the line of Orense and Vigo.

Appendix,
No. 13.
sections 2
and 8.

Sir John
Moore's
Papers,
MSS.

More than this could not have been accomplished. It was now only the fifteenth day since sir John Moore had left Salamanca, and already the torrent of war, diverted from the south, was foaming among the rocks of Gallicia. Nineteen thousand

BOOK
IV.
————
1809.
January.
Appendix,
No. 28,
section 3.
British troops, posted in strong ground, might have
offered battle to very superior numbers, but where
was the use of merely fighting an enemy who had
three hundred thousand men in Spain? Nothing
could be gained by such a display of courage,
and the English general, by a quick retreat, might
reach his ships unmolested, embark, and carrying his
army from the narrow corner in which it was
cooped to the southern provinces, establish there a
good base of operations, and renew the war under
favourable circumstances. It was by this combination of a fleet and army, that the greatest assistance could be given to Spain, and the strength of
England become most formidable. A few days'
sailing would carry the troops to Cadiz, but six
weeks' constant marching would not bring the
French army from Gallicia to that neighbourhood.
The northern provinces were broken, subdued in
spirit, and possessed few resources; the southern
provinces had scarcely seen an enemy, were rich
and fertile, and there also was the seat of government. Sir John Moore reasoning thus, resolved to
fall down to the coast and embark, with as little
loss or delay as might be; but Vigo, Coruña, and
Ferrol were the principal harbours, and their relative advantages could not be determined except by
the reports of the engineers, none of which, so
rapidly had the crisis of affairs come on, were yet
received; and as those reports could only be obtained from day to day, the line of retreat became
of necessity subject to daily change.

When the duke of Dalmatia took the command of
the pursuing army, Hope's and Fraser's divisions
were, as I have said, at Villa Franca, Baird's at
Bembibre, the reserve and cavalry at Cambarros,

Appendix,
No. 13,
section 2d.
See colonel
Carmi-
chael
Smith's
report.

six miles from Astorga. Behind Cambarros the mountains of Gallicia rose abruptly, but there was no position, because, after the first rise at the village of Rodrigatos, the ground continually descended to Calcabellos, a small town, only four miles from Villa Franca, and the old road of Foncevadon and Ponteferrada, which turned the whole line, was choked with the advancing columns of the enemy. The reserve and the cavalry therefore marched during the night to Bembibre, and on their arrival Baird's division proceeded to Calcabellos; but in the immense wine vaults of Bembibre many hundred of his men remained behind inebriated, the followers of the army crowded the houses, and a number of Romana's disbanded men were mixed with this heterogeneous mass of marauders, drunkards, muleteers, women, and children; the weather was dreadful, and, notwithstanding the utmost exertions of the general-in-chief, when the reserve marched the next morning, the number of those unfortunate wretches was not diminished. Leaving a small guard to protect them, sir John Moore proceeded to Calcabellos, yet scarcely had the reserve marched out of the village, when some French cavalry appeared, and in a moment the road was filled with the miserable stragglers, who came crowding after the troops, some with shrieks of distress and wild gestures, others with brutal exclamations, while many, overcome with fear, threw away their arms, while those who preserved them were too stupidly intoxicated to fire, and kept reeling to and fro, alike insensible to their danger and to their disgrace. The enemy's horsemen perceiving this, bore at a gallop through the disorderly mob, cutting to the right and left as they passed, and riding so close to the columns, that the infantry were forced to halt in order to check their audacity.

At Calcabellos the reserve took up a position, Baird then marched to Herrerias, and the general-in-chief went on to Villa Franca. But in that town great excesses had been committed by the preceding divisions; the magazines were plundered, the bakers driven away from the ovens, the wine stores forced, and the commissaries prevented from making the regular distributions; the doors of the houses were broken, and the scandalous insubordination of the soldiers proved that a discreditable relaxation of discipline on the part of the officers had taken place. Moore arrested this disorder, and caused one man taken in the act of plundering a magazine to be hanged in the market-place; then issuing severe orders to prevent a recurrence of such inexcusable conduct, he returned to Calcabellos, which the enemy were now approaching.

The Guia, a small, but at this season of the year a deep stream, run through that town, and was crossed by a stone bridge. On the Villa Franca side a lofty ridge, rough with vineyards and stone walls, was occupied by two thousand five hundred infantry, with a battery of six guns; four hundred riflemen, and about the same number of cavalry, were posted on a hill two miles beyond the river, to watch the two roads of Bembibre and Fonce-vadon. In this situation, on the 3d of January, a little after noon, the French general Colbert approached with six or eight squadrons, but observing the ground behind Calcabellos so strongly occupied, demanded reinforcements. Soult, believing that the English did not mean to make a stand, replied by ordering Colbert to charge without delay, and

the latter, stung by the message, obeyed with precipitate fury. From one of those errors so frequent
in war, the British cavalry, thinking a greater
force was riding against them, retired at speed to
Calcabellos, and the riflemen, who, following their
orders, had withdrawn when the French first came
in sight, were just passing the bridge, when a
crowd of staff officers, the cavalry, and the enemy,
came in upon them in one mass; in the confusion
thirty or forty men were taken, and Colbert, then
crossing the river, charged on the spur up the road.
The remainder of the riflemen had however thrown
themselves into the vineyards, and when the enemy
approached within a few yards, opened such
a deadly fire, that the greatest number of the
French horsemen were killed on the spot, and
among the rest Colbert himself; his fine martial
figure, his voice, his gestures, and, above all, his
great valour, had excited the admiration of the
British, and a general feeling of sorrow was predominant when the gallant soldier fell. Some French
voltigeurs now crossed the river, and a few of the
52d regiment descended from the upper part of the
ridge to the assistance of the riflemen, when a sharp
skirmish commenced, in which two or three hundred men of both sides were killed or wounded.
Towards evening, Merle's division of infantry appeared on the hills in front of the town, and made
a demonstration of crossing opposite to the left of
the English position, but the battery of the latter
checked this movement, and night coming on the
combat ceased.

As the road from Villa Franca to Lugo led through
a rugged country, the cavalry were now sent on to the
latter town at once, and during the night the French

patroles breaking in upon the rifle piquets, wounded some men, but were beaten back without being able to discover that the English troops had abandoned the position. This however was the case, and the reserve reached Herrerias, a distance of eighteen miles, on the morning of the 4th, Baird's division being then at Nogales, Hope's and Fraser's near Lugo.

At Herrerias, the English general, who constantly directed the movements of the rearguard himself, received the first reports of the engineers relative to the harbours. It appeared that Vigo, besides its greater distance, offered no position to cover the embarkation, but Coruña and Betanzos did. The march to Vigo was of necessity abandoned, the ships were directed round to Coruña, and Moore, who now deeply regretted the separation of his light brigades, sent forward instructions for the leading division to halt at Lugo, where he designed to rally the army, and give battle if the enemy would accept it. These important orders were carried to sir David Baird by one of the aides de camp of the commander-in-chief, but sir David forwarded them by a private dragoon, who got drunk and lost the despatch. This blameable irregularity was ruinous to general Frazer's troops; in lieu of resting two days at Lugo, that general, unwitting of the order, pursued his toilsome journey towards St. Jago de Compostella, and then returning without food or rest, lost more than four hundred stragglers.

On the 5th, the reserve having, by a forced march of thirty-six miles, gained twelve hours' start of the enemy, reached Nogales, at which place they met a large convoy of English clothing, shoes, and ammunition, intended for Romana's army, yet moving towards the enemy,—a circumstance characteristic of the Spanish mode of conducting public affairs. There was a bridge at Nogales which the engineers failed to destroy, but this was a matter of little consequence ; the river was fordable above and below, and the general was unwilling, unless for some palpable advantage, which seldom presented itself, to injure the communications of a country that he was unable to serve: moreover, the bridges were commonly very solidly constructed, and the arches having little span, could be rendered passable again in a shorter time than they could be destroyed. At this period of the retreat also the road was covered with baggage, sick men, women, and plunderers, all of whom would have been thus sacrificed ; for the peasantry, although armed, did not molest the enemy, but fearing both sides alike, carried their effects into the mountains: even there the villanous marauders followed them, and in some cases were by the Spaniards killed,—a just punishment for quitting their colours. Under the most favourable circumstances, the tail of a retreating force exhibits terrible scenes of distress, and on the road near Nogales the followers of the army were dying fast from cold and hunger. The soldiers, barefooted, harassed, and weakened by their excesses at Bembibre and Villa Franca, were dropping to the rear by hundreds, while broken carts, dead animals, and the piteous appearance of women with children, struggling or falling exhausted in the snow, completed a picture of war, which, like Janus, has a double face.

Franceschi, who, after turning Villa Franca, had scoured the valley of the Syl and captured many

Spanish prisoners and baggage, now regained the
line of march at Becerea, and towards evening the
French army, recovering their lost ground, passed
Nogales, galling the rear-guard with a continual
skirmish, and here it was that dollars to the amount
of twenty-five thousand pounds were abandoned.
This small sum was kept near head-quarters to
answer sudden emergencies, and the bullocks that
drew it being tired, the general, who could not save
the money without risking an ill-timed action, had
it rolled down the side of the mountain, whence
part of it was gathered by the enemy, part by the
Gallician peasants. The returns laid before parliament in 1809 made the sum 60,000*l*., and the whole
loss during the campaign nearly 77,000*l*., but it is
easier to make an entry of one sum for a treasury
return, than to state the details accurately; the
money-agents were, like the military-agents, acting
independently, and all losses went down under the
head of abandoned treasure. Officers actually present, agree, that the only treasure *abandoned* by the
army was that at Nogales, and that the sum was
25,000*l*. When it was ordered to be rolled over
the brink of the hill, two guns, and a battalion of
infantry, were engaged with the enemy to protect
it, and some person in whose charge the treasure
was, exclaiming, 'It is *money!*' the general replied,
' so are shot and shells.' Accidents will happen in
wars. An officer of the guards had charge of the
cars that drew this treasure, and in passing a village,
another officer observing that the bullocks were exhausted, took the pains to point out where fresh and
strong animals were to be found, but the escorting officer, either ignorant of, or indifferent
to his duty, took no notice of this recommen-

dation, and continued his march with the exhausted
cattle.

Towards evening the reserve approached Constantino, the French were close upon the rear, and
a hill within pistol-shot of the bridge offered them
such an advantage, that there was little hope to effect
the passage without great loss.   Moore however
posted the riflemen and the artillery on the hill, so
as to mask the hasty passage of the reserve, and
the enemy, ignorant of the vicinity of a river,
were cautious, until they saw the guns go off at
a trot, and the riflemen follow at full speed; then
they pursued briskly, but when they reached the
bridge the British were over, and a good line of
battle was formed on the other side.   A fight commenced, and the assailants were continually reinforced as their columns of march arrived, yet general Paget maintained the post with two regiments
until nightfall, and then retired to Lugo, in front
of which the whole army was now assembled.

A few of the French cavalry showed themselves
on the 6th, but the infantry did not appear, and, the
7th, sir John Moore, in a general order, gave a severe but just rebuke to the officers and soldiers for
their previous want of discipline, at the same time
announcing his intention to offer battle.   It has
been well said, that a British army may be gleaned
in a retreat, but cannot be reaped, whatever may be
their misery, the soldiers will always be found clean
at review, ready at a fight; and scarcely was this
order issued, when the line of battle, so attenuated
before, was filled with vigorous men, full of confidence and valour.   Fifteen hundred had fallen in
action or dropped to the rear, but as three fresh
battalions, left by sir David Baird when he first

advanced from Astorga, had rejoined the army between Villa Franca and Lugo, nineteen thousand
combatants were still under arms.

The right of the English position was in comparatively flat ground, and partially protected by a
bend of the Minho. The centre was amongst vineyards, with low stone walls. The left, which was
somewhat withdrawn, rested on the mountains, being
supported and covered by the cavalry. It was the
intention of the general to engage deeply with his
right and centre, before he closed with his left wing,
in which he had posted the flower of his troops,
thinking thus to bring on a decisive battle, and
trusting to the valour of the men to handle the
enemy in such sort as that he should be glad to let
the army continue its retreat unmolested. Other
hope, to re-embark the troops without loss,
there was none, save by stratagem. Soult, an experienced general, commanding soldiers habituated
to war, might be tempted, but could never be
forced, to engage in a decisive battle among those
rugged mountains, where whole days would pass in
skirmishing, without any progress being made towards crippling an adversary.

It was mid-day before the French marshal arrived
in person at the head of ten or twelve thousand men,
and the remainder of his power followed in some dis-
array, for the marches had not been so easy but that
many even of the oldest soldiers had dropped behind.
As the columns came up, they formed in order of
battle along a strong mountainous ridge fronting the
English, and as the latter were not distinctly seen,
from the inequalities of the ground, Soult doubted
if they were all before him; wherefore taking four
guns, and some squadrons commanded by colonel Lal-

lemande, he advanced towards the centre, and opened
a fire, which was immediately silenced by a reply from
fifteen pieces. The marshal being then satisfied that
something more than a rear-guard was in his front,
retired. About an hour after he made a feint on
the right, and at the same time sent a column of
infantry and five guns against the left. On that
side the three regiments which had lately joined
were drawn up, and the French pushing the outposts hard, were gaining the advantage, when
Moore arrived, rallied the light troops, and with
a vigorous charge breaking the adverse column,
treated it very roughly in the pursuit. The estimated loss of the French was between three and
four hundred men.

As it was now evident that the British meant to
give battle, the duke of Dalmatia hastened the march
of Laborde's division, which was still in the rear,
and requested marshal Ney, who was then at Villa
Franca, to detach a division of the sixth corps by the
Val des Orres to Orense; Ney, however, merely sent
some troops into the valley of the Syl, and pushed his
advanced posts in front as far as Nogales, Poyo, and
Dancos. At daybreak on the 8th the two armies
were still embattled. On the French side, seventeen
thousand infantry, four thousand cavalry, and fifty
pieces of artillery were in line, but Soult deferred the
attack until the 9th. On the English part, sixteen
thousand infantry, eighteen hundred cavalry, and
forty pieces of artillery, impatiently awaited the assault, and blamed their adversary for delaying a
contest which they ardently desired; yet the darkness fell without a shot having been fired, and with
it fell the English general's hope to engage his enemy

on equal terms. What was to be done? assail the
French position? remain another day in expectation
of a battle? or, in secresy, gain a march, and get on
board without being molested, or at least obtain
time to establish the army in a good situation to
cover the embarkation? The first operation was
warranted neither by present nor by future advantages, for how could an inferior army expect to crip-
ple a superior one, posted as the French were, on a
strong mountain, with an overbearing cavalry to
protect their infantry, should the latter be beaten;
and when twenty thousand fresh troops were at the
distance of two short marches in the rear? The
British army was not provided to fight above one
battle; there were no draught cattle, no means of
transporting reserve ammunition, no magazines, no
hospitals, no second line, no provisions, a defeat
would have been ruin, a victory useless. A battle
is always a serious affair, but two battles under such
circumstances, though both should be victories,
would have been destruction. But why fight at all,
after the army had been rallied, and the disasters of
the march from Astorga had been remedied? What,
if beating first Soult and then Ney, the British had
arrived once more above Astorga, with perhaps ten
thousand infantry, and half as many hundred cavalry.
From the mountains of Gallicia their general might
have cast his eyes as far as the Sierra Morena,
without being cheered by the sight of a single
Spanish army, none existed to aid him, none to
whom he might give aid. Even Mr. Frere acknowledged that at this period six thousand ill-armed
men collected at Despeñas Peros, formed the only
barrier between the French and Seville, and sir John

Moore was sent out not to waste English blood in
fruitless battles, but to assist the universal Spanish
nation !

The second proposition was decided by the state of the magazines ; there was not bread for another day's consumption remaining in the stores at Lugo. It was true that the army was in heart for fighting,
but distressed by fatigue and bad weather, and each moment of delay, increased privations that would soon have rendered it inefficient for a campaign in the south, the only point where its services could now be effectual. For two whole days Moore had offered battle, this was sufficient to rally the troops, to restore order, and to preserve the reputation of the army. Lugo was strong ground in itself, but it did not cover Coruña, the road leading from Orense to St. Jago da Compostella turned it, the French ought to have been on that line, and there was no reason to suppose that they were not ; Soult, as we have seen, pressed Ney to follow it. It was then impossible to remain at Lugo, and useless if it had been possible. The general adopted the third plan, and prepared to decamp in the night ; he ordered the fires to be kept bright, and exhorted the troops to make a great exertion, which he trusted would be the last required of them.

The country immediately in the rear of the posi-tion was intersected by stone walls and a number of intricate lanes, precautions were taken to mark the right tracks, by placing bundles of straw at certain distances, and officers were appointed to guide the columns. At ten o'clock the regiments silently quit-ted their ground, and retired in excellent order ; but a moody fortune pursued sir John Moore throughout this campaign, baffling his prudence, and thwarting his views, as if resolved to prove the unyielding firmness of his mind. A terrible storm of wind and rain, mixed with sleet, commenced as the army broke up from the position, the marks were destroyed, and the guides lost the true direction; only one of the divisions gained the main road, the other two were bewildered, and when daylight broke, the rear columns were still near to Lugo. The fatigue, the depression of mind, occasioned by this misfortune, and the want of shoes, broke the order of the march, and the stragglers were becoming numerous, when, unfortunately, Baird, who was with the leading division, thinking to relieve the men during a halt which took place in the night, desired them to take refuge from the weather in some houses a little way off the road. Complete disorganization followed this imprudent act, from that moment it became impossible to make the soldiers keep their ranks, plunder succeeded, the example was infectious, and what with real suffering, and evil propensity encouraged by this error of inexperience, the main body of the army, which had bivouacked for six hours in the rain, arrived at Betanzos on the evening of the 9th, in a state very discreditable to its discipline.

Mr. James Moore's Narrative. The commander-in-chief, with the reserve and the cavalry, as usual, covered the march, and in the course of it he ordered several bridges to be destroyed, but the engineers failed of success in every attempt. Fortunately, the enemy did not come up with the rear before the evening, and then only with their cavalry, otherwise many prisoners must have fallen into their hands; for the number of stragglers uncovered by the passage of the reserve was so numerous, that when pressed, they united, under Sergeant Newman, of the 43d regiment, and repulsed

the French cavalry themselves : a signal proof that
the disorder was occasioned as much by insubordination in the regiments as by the fatigue of the
march. The reserve commanded by general Edward
Paget, an officer distinguished during the retreat by
his firmness, ability, and ardent zeal, remained in
position, during the night, a few miles from Betanzos ; the rest of the army was quartered in that
town, and as the enemy could not gather in strength
on the 10th, the commander-in-chief halted that day,
and the cavalry passed from the rear-guard to the
head of the column. The 11th, the French interrupted those employed to destroy the bridge of
Betanzos, but from some mismanagement, although
the twenty-eighth regiment repulsed the first skirmishers, the bridge, constructed of wood, was only
partially destroyed. In the meantime sir John Moore
assembled the army in one solid mass. The loss of
men in the march from Lugo to Betanzos had been Appendix,
greater than that in all the former part of the retreat, No. 27.
added to all the waste of the movement in advance and
the loss sustained in the different actions : nevertheless, fourteen or fifteen thousand infantry were still
in column, and by an orderly march to Coruña under
the personal direction of the commander-in-chief,
demonstrated, that inattention and the want of experience in the officers, was the true cause of those
disorders, which had afflicted the army far more
than the sword of the enemy or the rigour of the
elements.

As the troops approached Coruña, the general's
looks were directed towards the harbour, but an open
expanse of water painfully convinced him, that to
Fortune at least he was no way beholden; con-

trary winds still detained the fleet at Vigo, and the last consuming exertion made by the army was rendered fruitless! The men were put into quarters, and their leader awaited the progress of events.

The bridge of El Burgo was destroyed, and also that of Cambria, situated a few miles up the Mero river, but the engineer employed at the latter, mortified at the former failures, was so anxious to perform his duty in an effectual manner, that he remained too near the mine, and was killed by the explosion. Meanwhile three divisions occupied the town and suburbs of Coruña, and the reserve was posted between the village of El Burgo, and the road of St. Jago de Compostella. For twelve days these hardy soldiers had covered the retreat, during which time they had traversed eighty miles of road in two marches, passed several nights under arms in the snow of the mountains, were seven times engaged with the enemy, and now assembled at the outposts, having fewer men missing from the ranks, including those who had fallen in battle, than any other division in the army: an admirable instance of the value of good discipline, and a manifest proof of the malignant injustice with which sir John Moore has been accused of precipitating his retreat beyond the measure of human strength.

The town of Coruña, although sufficiently strong to oblige an enemy to break ground before it, was weakly fortified, and to the southward commanded by some heights close to the walls. Sir John Moore therefore caused the land front to be strengthened, and occupied the citadel, but disarmed the sea face of the works, and the inhabitants cheerfully and honourably joined in the labour, although they were fully aware that the English intended to embark, and that they would incur the enemy's anger by taking a part in the military operations. Such flashes of light from the dark cloud which at this moment covered Spain may startle the reader, and make him doubt if the Spaniards could have been so insufficient to their own defence as they have been represented in the course of this history. I answer, that the facts were as I have told them, and that it was such paradoxical indications of character that deceived the world at the time, and induced men to believe that that reckless, daring defiance of the power of France so loudly proclaimed by the patriots would be strenuously supported. Of proverbially vivid imagination and quick resentments, the Spaniards feel and act individually rather than nationally, and during this war, that which appeared constancy of purpose, was but a repetition of momentary fury; a succession of electric sparks generated by a constant collision with the French army, and daily becoming fainter as custom reconciled them to those injuries and insults which are commonly the attendants of war.

Procrastination and improvidence are the besetting sins of the nation. At this moment large magazines of arms and ammunition, which had been sent in the early part of the preceding year from from England, were still in Coruña unappropriated and unregarded by a nation infested with three hundred thousand enemies, and having a hundred thousand soldiers unclothed and without weapons. Three miles from the town they had piled four thousand barrels of powder in a magazine built upon a hill, and a smaller quantity, collected in another storehouse, was at some distance from the first. To prevent them falling a prey to the enemy,

Moore caused both to be exploded on the 13th, and
the inferior one blew up with a terrible noise, which
shook the houses in the town; but when the train
reached the great store, there ensued a crash like
the bursting forth of a volcano; the earth trembled
for miles, the rocks were torn from their bases, and
the agitated waters rolled the vessels as in a storm;
a vast column of smoke and dust, shooting out fiery
sparks from its sides, arose perpendicularly and
slowly to a great height, and then a shower of
stones, and fragments of all kinds, bursting out of
it with a roaring sound, killed many persons who
remained too near the spot. Stillness, slightly interrupted by the lashing of the waves on the shore,
succeeded, and the business of the war went on.
The next measure was a painful one; for the ground
in front of Coruña is impracticable for cavalry,
and as the horses were generally foundered, and
it was impossible to embark them all in the face
of an enemy, a great number were reluctantly
ordered to be shot; these poor animals, already
worn down and feet broken, would otherwise have
been distributed among the French cavalry, or used
as draft cattle, until death relieved them from pro-
crastinated sufferings.

But the French were now collecting in force on
the Mero, and it became necessary to choose a
position of battle. A chain of rocky elevations,
commencing on the sea-coast north-west of the
place, and ending on the Mero just behind the
village of El Burgo, offered an advantageous line
of defence, covered by a branch of the Mero, which
washing a part of the base, would have obliged
the enemy to advance by the road of Compostella.
This ridge was however too extensive for the English

army, and if not wholly occupied, the French might have turned it by the right, and moved along a succession of eminences to the very gates of Coruña. There was no alternative, but to take possession of an inferior range, enclosed as it were within the other, and completely commanded by it within cannon-shot ; here therefore the army was posted. Meanwhile the French army had been so exhausted with continual toil, that it was not completely assembled on the Mero before the 12th. On that day the infantry took post opposite El Burgo, the cavalry of La Houssaye lined the river as far as the ocean, and Franceschi, crossing at the bridge of Celas, seven miles higher up the river, intercepted some stores arriving from St. Jago, and made a few prisoners. The 14th, the bridges at El Burgo being rendered practicable for artillery, two divisions of infantry, and one of cavalry, passed the river, and to cover this march some guns opened on the English posts but were soon silenced by a superior fire. In the evening, the transports from Vigo hove in sight, and soon after entered the harbour of Coruña, and the dismounted cavalry, the sick, all the best horses, and fifty-two pieces of artillery, were embarked during the night, eight British and four Spanish guns only being retained on shore ready for action.

On the 15th, Laborde's division arrived. The French then occupied the great ridge enclosing the British position, placed their right on the intersection of the roads leading from St. Jago and Betanzos, and their left upon a rocky eminence which overlooked both lines ; after this they extended their cavalry, supported by some troops on their own left, and a slight skirmish took place in the valley below. The English piquets opposite the right of the French also

got engaged, and were so galled by the fire of two
guns, that colonel M'Kenzie, of the fifth regiment,
pushed out with some companies to seize the battery; a line of infantry, hitherto concealed by
some stone walls, immediately arose, and poured in
such a fire of musquetry, that the colonel was killed,
and his men forced back with loss.

In the course of the night, Soult with great difficulty established a battery of eleven heavy guns on
the rocks which closed the left of his line of battle,
and then formed his order of battle. Laborde's division was posted on the right, having one half
on the high ground, and the other half on the
descent towards the river. Merle's division was
in the centre. Mermet's division formed the left.
The position was covered in front of the right by the
villages of Palavia Abaxo and Portosa, and in front
of the centre by a wood. The left was secured by
the rugged heights where the great battery was established, which was about twelve hundred yards from
the right of the British line, and midway the little
village of Elvina was held by the piquets of the fiftieth British regiment. The late arrival of the transports, the increasing force of the enemy, and the
disadvantageous nature of the ground had greatly
augmented the difficulty and danger of the embarkation, and several general officers now proposed to
the commander-in-chief, that he should negotiate
for leave to retire to his ships upon terms. There
was little chance of such a proposal being agreed to
by the enemy, and there was no reason to try. The
army had suffered, but not from defeat, its situation
was dangerous, but far from desperate; wherefore
the general would not consent to remove the stamp
of energy and prudence, which marked his retreat,
by a negotiation that would have given an appear-

ance of timidity and indecision to his previous operations, as opposite to their real character as light is
to darkness ; his high spirit and clear judgment re-
volted at the idea, and he rejected the degrading
advice without hesitation.

All the encumbrances of the army were shipped
in the night of the 15th and morning of the 16th,
and everything was prepared to withdraw the fighting men as soon as the darkness would permit
them to move without being perceived ; and the
precautions taken would, without doubt, have insured the success of this difficult operation, but a
more glorious event was destined to give a melan-
choly but graceful termination to the campaign.
About two o'clock in the afternoon a general
movement along the French line gave notice of an
approaching battle, and the British infantry, fourteen thousand five hundred strong immediately
occupied the inferior range of hills already spoken
of. The right was formed by Baird's division, and,
from the oblique direction of the ridge, approached
the enemy, while the centre and left were of neces-
sity withheld in such a manner that the French bat- ^{Vide Plan of the}
tery on the rocks raked the whole of the line. ^{Battle.}
General Hope's division, crossing the main road,
prolonged Baird's line to the left, and occupied
strong ground abutting on the muddy bank of the
Mero. A brigade of Baird's division remained in
column behind the right wing, and in like manner a
brigade of Hope's division was behind the left wing,
while Paget's reserve, posted at Airis, a small village in rear of the centre, looked down the valley
which separated Baird's right from the hills occupied by Franceschi's cavalry ; a battalion detached
from the reserve kept these horsemen in check, and

was itself connected with the main body by a chain
of skirmishers extended across the valley.   Fraser's
division held the heights immediately before the
gates of Coruña, watching the coast road, but it was
also ready to succour any point.

These dispositions were dictated by the nature of
the ground, which was very favourable to the enemy;
for Franceschi's cavalry reached nearly to the village
of San Cristoval, a mile beyond Baird's right, and
hence sir John Moore was forced to weaken his
front and keep Frazer's division in reserve until
Soult's attack should be completely unfolded.   There
was, however, one advantage on the British side;
many thousand new English musquets, found in the
Spanish stores, were given to the troops in lieu of
their rusty, battered arms, and as their ammunition
was also fresh, their fire was far better sustained
than that of the enemy.

BATTLE OF CORUNA.

When Laborde's division arrived, the French
force was not less than twenty thousand men, and
the duke of Dalmatia made no idle evolutions of display, for distributing his lighter guns along the front
of his position, he opened a fire from the heavy battery on his left, and instantly descended the mountain with three columns, covered by clouds of
skirmishers.   The British piquets were driven back
in disorder, and the village of Elvina was carried by
the first French column, which then dividing, attempted to turn Baird's right by the valley, and to
break his front at the same time.   The second column
made against the English centre, and the third attacked Hope's left at the village of Palavia Abaxo.
The weight of Soult's guns overmatched the English

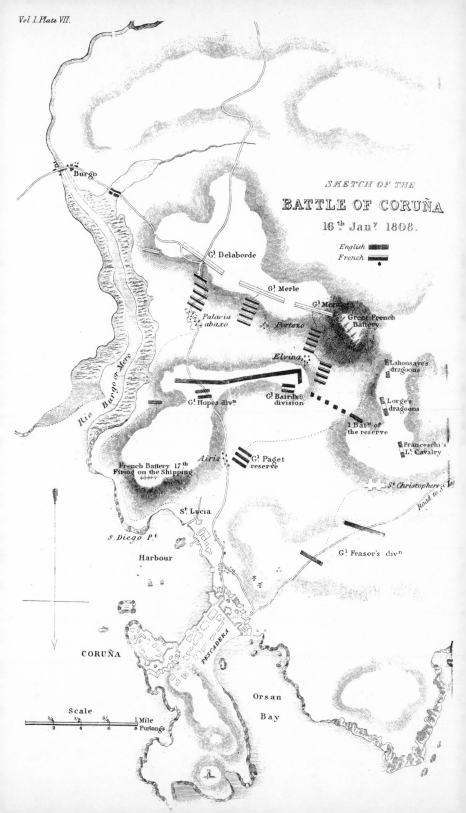

SKETCH OF THE

BATTLE OF CORUÑA

16ᵗʰ Janʸ 1808.

English
French

Burgo

Gˡ Delaborde

Gˡ Merle

Gˡ Mermet

Great French Battery

Palavia abaxo

Puttozo

Elvina

Lahousaye's dragoons

Gˡ Hopes divⁿ

Gˡ Bairds division

Lorge's dragoons

1.Battⁿ of the reserve

Franceschi's Lᵗ Cavalry

Airis

Gˡ Paget reserve

French Battery 17ᵗʰ Firing on the Shipping

Stᵗ Christophers

Road to S.

Stᵗ Lucia

S. Diego Pᵗ

Harbour

Gˡ Fraser's divⁿ

CORUÑA

PESCADERA

Orsan Bay

Rio Burgo or Mero

Scale
¼   ½   ¾   1 Mile
2   4   6   8 Furlongs

six-pounders, and the shot swept the position to the centre; but sir John Moore observing that, according to his expectations, the enemy did not show any body of infantry beyond that which moving up the valley outflanked Baird's right, ordered general Paget to carry the whole of the reserve to where the detached regiment was posted, and, as he had before arranged with him, to turn the left of the French attack and menace the great battery. Meanwhile, he directed Fraser to support Paget, and then throwing back the fourth regiment, which formed the right of Baird's division, he opened a heavy fire upon the flank of the troops penetrating up the valley, while the fiftieth and forty-second regiments met those breaking through Elvina. The ground about that village being intersected by stone walls and hollow roads, a severe scrambling fight ensued, the French were forced back with great loss, and the fiftieth regiment entering the village with them, after a second struggle drove them beyond it. Seeing this, the general ordered up a battalion of the guards to fill the void in the line made by the advance of those regiments, whereupon the forty-second, with the exception of its grenadiers, mistaking his intention, retired, and at that moment the enemy, being reinforced, renewed the fight beyond the village; the officer commanding the fiftieth * was wounded

---

* The author's eldest brother; he was said to be slain. When the French renewed the attack on Elvina, he was somewhat in advance of that village, and alone, for the troops were scattered by the nature of the ground. Being hurt in the leg, he endeavoured to retire, but was overtaken, and thrown to the ground with five wounds; a French drummer rescued him, and when a soldier with whom he had been struggling made a second attempt to kill him, the drummer once more interfered. The morning after the battle marshal Soult sent his own surgeon to major Napier, and, with a kindness and consideration very uncommon, wrote to Napoleon, desiring that his prisoner might not be sent to France, which, from the system of refusing exchanges, would have ruined his professional prospects; the drummer also received the cross of the legion of honour. When the second corps quitted Coruna, marshal Soult recommended his prisoner to the attention of marshal Ney, and the latter treated him rather with the kindness of a friend than the civility of an enemy; he lodged him with the French consul,

and taken prisoner, and Elvina then became the scene of a second struggle, which being observed by the commander-in-chief, he addressed a few animating words to the forty-second, and caused it to return to the attack.   During this time Paget, with the reserve, had descended into the valley, and the line of the skirmishers being thus supported, vigourously checked the advance of the enemy's troops in that quarter, while the fourth regiment galled their flank ; at the same time the centre and left of the army also became engaged, sir David Baird was severely wounded, and a furious action ensued along the line, in the valley, and on the hills.

Sir John Moore, while earnestly watching the result of the fight about the village of Elvina, was struck on the left breast by a cannon shot; the shock threw him from his horse with violence, but he rose again in a sitting posture, his countenance unchanged, and his stedfast eye still fixed upon the regiments engaged in his front, no sigh betraying a sensation of pain.   In a few moments, when he was satisfied that the troops were gaining ground, his countenance brightened, and he suffered himself to be taken to the rear.   Then was seen the dreadful nature of his hurt.   The shoulder was shattered to pieces, the arm was hanging by a piece of skin, the ribs over the heart were broken, and bared of flesh, and the muscles of the breast torn into long strips,

supplied him with money, gave him a general invitat on to his house, and not only refrained from sending him to France, but when by a flag of truce he knew that major Napier's mother was mourning for him as dead, he permitted him, and with him the few soldiers taken in the action, to go at once to England, merely exacting a promise that none should serve until exchanged.   I would not have touched at all upon these private adventures, were it not that gratitude demands a public acknowledgment of such generosity, and that demand is rendered more imperative by the after misfortunes of marshal Ney.   That brave and noble-minded man's fate is but too well known !   He who had fought five hundred battles for France, not one against her, was shot as a traitor !   Could the bitterest enemy of the Bourbons have more strongly marked the difference between their interests and those of the nation ?

which were interlaced by their recoil from the dragging of the shot. As the soldiers placed him in a
blanket his sword got entangled, and the hilt entered the wound; captain Hardinge, a staff officer,
who was near, attempted to take it off, but the
dying man stopped him, saying, ' *It is as well as it*
is. I had rather it should go out of the field with
me;' and in that manner, so becoming to a soldier,
Moore was borne from the fight.

Meanwhile the army was rapidly gaining ground.
The reserve, overthrowing everything in the valley,
obliged La Houssaye's dragoons, who had dismounted, to retire, turned the enemy on that side, and
even approached the eminence upon which the great
battery was posted; on the left, colonel Nicholls,
at the head of some companies of the fourteenth,
carried Palavia Abaxo, which general Foy defended
but feebly; in the centre, the obstinate dispute for
Elvina had terminated in favour of the British, and
when the night set in, their line was considerably
advanced beyond the original position of the morning, while the French were falling back in confusion.
If at this time general Fraser's division had been
brought into action along with the reserve, the enemy
could hardly have escaped a signal overthrow; for
the little ammunition Soult had been able to bring
up was nearly exhausted, the river Mero, with a full
tide, was behind him, and the difficult communication by the bridge of El Burgo was alone open for a
retreat. On the other hand, to continue the action
in the dark was to tempt fortune; the French were
still the most numerous, and their ground was
strong, moreover the disorder they were in, offered
such a favourable opportunity to get on board the
ships, that sir John Hope, upon whom the command

of the army had devolved, satisfied with having repulsed the attack, judged it more prudent to pursue
the original plan of embarking during the night.
This operation was effected without delay, the arrangements being so complete that neither confusion
nor difficulty occurred. The piquets, kindling a
number of fires, covered the retreat of the columns,
and being themselves withdrawn at daybreak, were
embarked, under the protection of general Hill's
brigade, which was posted near the ramparts of the
town.

When the morning dawned, the French, observing
that the British had abandoned their position, pushed
forward some battalions to the heights of St. Lucie,
and about midday succeeded in establishing a battery, which playing upon the shipping in the harbour
caused a great deal of disorder among the transports; several masters cut their cables, and four vessels went ashore, but the troops being immediately
removed by the men of war's boats, the stranded
vessels were burnt, and the whole fleet at last got
out of harbour. General Hill's brigade then embarked from the citadel, while general Beresford, with
a rear guard, kept possession of that work until the
18th, when the wounded being all put on board, his
troops likewise embarked ; the inhabitants faithfully
maintained the town against the French, and the fleet
sailed for England. The loss of the British was never
officially published, but was estimated at eight hundred, and that of the French at three thousand. The
latter is undoubtedly an exaggeration, yet it must have
been very great, for the arms of the English were all
new, the ammunition fresh, and whether from the
peculiar construction of our musquets, the physical
strength and coolness of the men, or from all com-

bined, it is certain that the fire of an English line
is the most destructive known. The nature of the
ground also prevented any movement of artillery on
either side, and the French columns in their attack
were exposed to grape, which they could not return
because of the distance of their batteries.

Thus ended the retreat to Coruña; a transaction
which, up to this day, has called forth as much of
falsehood and malignity as servile and interested
writers could offer to the unprincipled leaders of a
base faction, but which posterity will regard as a
genuine example of ability and patriotism. From
the spot where he fell, the general, who had conducted it, was carried to the town by a party of
soldiers, his blood flowed fast, and the torture of his
wound was great, yet such was the unshaken firmness of his mind, that those about him, judging
from the resolution of his countenance that his hurt
was not mortal, expressed a hope of his recovery;
hearing this, he looked stedfastly at the injury for
a moment, and then said, ' *No, I feel that to be im-*
possible.' Several times he caused his attendants to
stop and turn him round, that he might behold the
field of battle, and when the firing indicated the
advance of the British, he discovered his satisfaction, and permitted the bearers to proceed. Being
brought to his lodgings, the surgeons examined his
wound, but there was no hope, the pain increased,
and he spoke with great difficulty. At intervals he
asked if the French were beaten, and addressing his
old friend, colonel Anderson, he said, ' *You know*
that I always wished to die this way.' Again he
asked if the enemy were defeated, and being told
they were, observed, ' *It is a great satisfaction to*
me to know we have beaten the French.' His coun-

Captain
Hardinge's
Letter.

Mr. James
Moore's
Narrative.

tenance continued firm and his thoughts clear, once only, when he spoke of his mother, he became agitated; but he often inquired after the safety of his friends, and the officers of his staff, and he did not even in this moment forget to recommend those whose merit had given them claims to promotion. His strength failed fast, and life was just extinct, when, with an unsubdued spirit, as if anticipating the baseness of his posthumous calumniators, he exclaimed, ' *I hope the people of England will be satisfied! I hope my country will do me justice!*' In a few minutes afterwards he died, and his corpse, wrapped in a military cloak, was interred by the officers of his staff in the citadel of Coruña; the guns of the enemy paid his funeral honours, and Soult, with a noble feeling of respect for his valour, raised a monument to his memory.

Thus ended the career of sir John Moore, a man whose uncommon capacity was sustained by the purest virtue, and governed by a disinterested patriotism more in keeping with the primitive than the luxurious age of a great nation. His tall graceful person, his dark searching eyes, strongly defined forehead, and singularly expressive mouth, indicated a noble disposition and a refined understanding, while the lofty sentiments of honour habitual to his mind, being adorned by a subtle playful wit, gave him, in conversation, an ascendency that he always preserved by the decisive vigour of his actions. He maintained the right with a vehemence bordering upon fierceness, and every important transaction in which he was engaged increased his reputation for talent, and confirmed his character as a stern enemy to vice, a steadfast friend to merit, a just and faithful servant of his country. The honest loved him, the dishonest feared him; for while he lived he did not shun, but scorned and spurned the base, and, with characteristic propriety, they spurned at him when he was dead.

A soldier from his earliest youth, Moore thirsted for the honours of his profession, and feeling that he was worthy to lead a British army, hailed the fortune that placed him at the head of the troops destined for Spain. As the stream of time passed, the inspiring hopes of triumph disappearèd, but the austerer glory of suffering remained, and with a firm heart he accepted that gift of a severe fate. Confiding in the strength of his genius, he disregarded the clamours of presumptuous ignorance, and opposing sound military views to the foolish projects so insolently thrust upon him by the ambassador, he conducted his long and arduous retreat with sagacity, intelligence, and fortitude; no insult disturbed, no falsehood deceived him, no remonstrance shook his determination; fortune frowned without subduing his constancy; death struck, but the spirit of the man remained unbroken when his shattered body scarcely afforded it a habitation. Having done all that was just towards others, he remembered what was due to himself; neither the shock of the mortal blow, nor the lingering hours of acute pain which preceded his dissolution, could quell the pride of his gallant heart, or lower the dignified feeling with which, conscious of merit, he at the last moment asserted his right to the gratitude of the country he had served so truly.

If glory be a distinction, for such a man death is not a leveller [1]

CHAPTER VI.

OBSERVATIONS.

GENERAL VIEW OF THE CAMPAIGN.

BOOK
IV. MR. CANNING, in an official communication to the Spanish deputies in London, observed, that 'the conduct of the campaign in Portugal was unsatisfactory, and inadequate to the brilliant successes with which it opened.' In the relation of that campaign, it has been shown how little the activity and foresight of the cabinet contributed to those successes, and the following short analysis will prove that, with respect to the campaign in Spain also, the proceedings of the ministers were marked alike by tardiness and incapacity.

Joseph abandoned Madrid the 3d of August, and on the 11th of the same month the French troops from the most distant parts of Europe were in motion to remedy the disasters in the Peninsula.

The 1st of September a double conscription, furnishing one hundred and sixty thousand men, was called out to replace the troops withdrawn from Poland and Germany.

The 4th of September the emperor announced to the senate, that 'he was resolved to push the affairs of the Peninsula with the greatest activity, and to destroy the armies which the English had disembarked in that country.'

The 11th, the advanced guard of the army coming from Germany reached Paris, and was there publicly harangued by the emperor.

The 8th of November that monarch broke into Spain at the head of three hundred thousand men, and the 5th of December, not a vestige of the Spanish armies remaining, he took possession of Madrid.

Now the Asturian deputies arrived in London the 6th of June, and yet on the 20th of August—the battle of Vimiero being then unfought, and, consequently, the fate of the campaign in Portugal uncertain,—the English minister invited sir Hew Dalrymple to discuss three plans of operations in Spain, each founded upon data utterly false, and all objectional in detail. He also desired that sir Arthur Wellesley should go to the Asturias to ascertain what facilities that country offered for the disembarkation of an English army ; and the whole number of troops disposable for the campaign, exclusive of those already in Portugal, he stated to be twenty thousand, of which one half was in England and the other in Sicily. He acknowledged that no information yet received had enabled the cabinet to decide as to the application of the forces at home, or the ulterior use to be made of those in Portugal, yet, with singular rashness, the whole of the southern provinces, containing the richest cities, finest harbours, and most numerous armies, were discarded from consideration; and sir Hew Dalrymple, who was well acquainted with that part of Spain, and in close and friendly correspondence with the chiefs, was directed to confine his attention to the northern provinces, of which he knew nothing.

The reduction of Junot's army in Portugal, and
the discomfiture of Joseph on the Ebro, were regarded as certain events, and the observations of
the minister were principally directed, not to the
best mode of attack, but to the choice of a line of
march that would ensure the utter destruction or
captivity of the whole French army; nay, elated
with extravagant hopes, and strangely despising
Napoleon's power, he instructed lord William Bentinck to urge the central junta to an invasion of
France, as soon as the army on the Ebro should be
annihilated.   Thus it appears that the English
ministers were either profoundly ignorant of the
real state of affairs, or that, with a force scattered
in England, Portugal, and Sicily, and not exceeding forty-five thousand men, they expected in one
campaign, first to subdue twenty-six thousand
French under Junot, then to destroy eighty thousand under Joseph, and turning the tide of war, to
invade France.

The battle of Vimiero took place, and sir Arthur
Wellesley naturally declined a mission more suitable
to a staff captain than a victorious commander; but
before sir Hew's answer, exposing the false calculations of the minister's plans, could be received in
England, a despatch, dated the 2d of September, announced the resolution of the government to employ
an army in the northern provinces of Spain, and
directed twenty thousand men to be held in readiness to unite with other forces to be sent from
England.   Nevertheless, this project also was so
immature, that no intimation was given how the
junction was to be effected, whether by sea or land;
nor had the minister even ascertained that the
Spaniards would permit English troops to enter

Spain at all. Three weeks later, lord William
Bentinck, writing from Madrid, says, 'I had an
interview with Florida Blanca, he expressed his
surprise that there should be a doubt of the
Spaniards wishing for the assistance of the English
army.' Such also was the confusion at home, that
lord Castlereagh repeatedly expressed his fears lest
the embarkation of Junot's troops should have absorbed all the means of transport in the Tagus,
when a simple reference to the transport office in
London would have satisfied him, that although
the English army should also be embarked, there
would still remain a surplus of twelve thousand
tons.

When the popular cry rose against the convention of Cintra, the generals-in-chief were recalled in
succession, as rapidly as they had been appointed,
the despatches addressed to one generally fell into
the hands of his successor; but the plans of the
ministers becoming at last mature, on the 6th of
October sir John Moore was finally appointed to
lead the forces into Spain. At this period the head
of the grand French army was already in the passes
of the Pyrenees, the hostile troops on the Ebro
coming to blows, the Spaniards weak and divided,
and the English forty marches from the scene of
action : yet, said the minister to sir John Moore,
'there will be full time to concert your plan of
operations with the Spanish generals before the
equipment of your army can be completed.' Was
this the way to oppose Napoleon? Could such
proceedings lead to aught but disaster? It has
been said that sir Hew Dalrymple's negligence
was the cause of this delay, that he should have
had the troops in readiness. But that general

could not prudently incur the expense of equipping, for a march, an army that was likely to be embarked; he could not, in short, divine the plans of the ministers before they were formed, and it is evident that the error attaches entirely to the government.

The incapacity of the Spanish generals has been already sufficiently exposed by occasional observations in the narrative, their faults, glaring and fatal, call for no further remark; but the exact combinations, the energy and rapidity of the French emperor, merit the most careful examination. His operations were not, as they have been generally considered, a pompous display of power, to create an appearance of conquest that was unreal; not a mere violent irruption with a multitude of men, but a series of skilful and scientific movements, worthy of so great a general and politician. It is true that his force was immense, and that the Spaniards were but contemptible soldiers, yet he never neglected the lessons of experience, nor deviated from the strictest rules of art. With astonishing activity, and when we consider the state of his political relations on the continent, we may add, with astonishing boldness, he first collected ample means to attain his object; then deceiving his enemies with regard to his numbers, position, and intentions, and choosing his time with admirable judgment, he broke through the weak part of their line, and seized Burgos, a central point, which enabled him to envelope and destroy the left wing of the Spaniards, before their right could hear of his attack, the latter being itself turned by the same movement, and exposed to a like fate. This position also enabled him to menace the capital, to keep the English army in check, and to cover the formation of those magazines and stores which were necessary to render Burgos the base and pivot of further operations.

Napoleon's forces were numerous enough to have attacked Castaños and Palafox, while Blake was being pursued by the first and fourth corps; but trusting nothing to chance, he waited for twelve days, until the position of the English army was ascertained, the strength of the northern provinces quite broken, and a secure place of arms established. Then leaving the second corps to cover his communication, and sending the fourth corps into the flat country, to coast, as it were, the heads of the English columns, and to turn the passes of the Carpentino mountains, he caused the Spanish right wing to be destroyed, and himself approached the capital, at a moment when not a vestige of a national army was left; when he had good reason to think that the English were in full retreat; when the whole of his own corps were close at hand, and consequently when the greatest moral effect could be produced, and the greatest physical power concentrated at the same time to take advantage of it. Napoleon's dispositions were indeed surprisingly skilful; for, although marshal Lefebre's precipitation at Zornoza, by prolonging Blake's agony, lost six days of promise, it is certain, that even reverses in battle could neither have checked the emperor, nor helped the Spaniards.

If Soult had been beaten at Gamonal, Napoleon was close at hand to support the second corps, and the sixth corps would have fallen upon the flank and rear of the Spaniards.

If the first corps had been defeated at Espinosa, the second and fourth corps, and the emperor's

troops, would have taken Blake in flank and
rear.

If Lasnes had been defeated at Tudela, he could
have fallen back on Pampeluna, the fifth and eighth
corps were marching to support him, and the sixth
corps would have taken the Spaniards in flank.

If the emperor had been repulsed at the Somosierra, the sixth corps would have turned that
position by Guadalaxara, and the fourth corps by
Guadarama.

If sir John Moore had retreated on Portugal, the
fourth corps was nearer to Lisbon than he was ; and
if he had overthrown Soult, the fifth and eighth
corps were ready to sustain that marshal, while Napoleon, with fifty thousand men, as we have seen,
was prepared to cut the British line of retreat into
Gallicia. In short, no possible event could have
divided the emperor's forces, and he constantly preserved a central position which enabled him to unite
his masses in sufficient time to repair any momentary disaster. By a judicious mixture of force and
policy also, he obliged Madrid to surrender in two
days, and thus prevented the enthusiasm which
would doubtless have arisen if that capital had
been defended for any time, and the heart burnings
if it had been stormed. The second sweep that he
was preparing to make when sir John Moore's
march called off his attention from the south would
undoubtedly have put him in possession of the remaining great cities of the Peninsula. Then the
civil benefits promised in his decrees and speeches
would have produced their full effect, and the
result may be judged of by the fact, that in 1811
and 12, Aragon, Valencia, and Andalusia were,
under the able administration of marshals Soult

and Suchet, as submissive as any department of
France. Both generals raised Spanish battalions,
and employed them not only to preserve the public
peace, but to chase and put down the guerillas of
the neighbouring provinces.

Sir John Moore's talents saved the Peninsula at
this crisis; and here only a military error of
Napoleon's may be detected. Forgetting his own
maxim that war is not a conjectural art, he took for
granted that the English army was falling back to
Portugal, and without ascertaining that it was so,
acted upon the supposition. This apparent negligence, so unlike his usual circumspection, leads to
the notion, that through Morla he might have become acquainted with the peculiar opinions and
rash temper of Mr. Frere, and trusted that the
treacherous arts of the Spaniard, in conjunction
with the presumptuous disposition of the plenipotentiary, would so mislead the English general, as to
induce him to carry his army to Madrid, and thus
deliver it up entire and bound. It was an error;
but Napoleon could be deceived or negligent only
for a moment. With what vigour he recovered
himself, and hastened to remedy his error! How in-
stantaneously he relinquished his intentions against
the south, turned his face away from the glittering
prize, and bent his whole force against the only
man among his adversaries that had discovered
talent and decision! Let those who have seen the
preparations necessary to enable a small army to
act, even on a pre-conceived plan, say what uncontrollable energy that man possessed, who, suddenly interrupted in such great designs, could, in
the course of a few hours, put fifty thousand men
in movement on a totally new line of operations,

and in the midst of winter execute a march of two
hundred miles, with a rapidity hardly to be equalled
under the most favourable circumstances.

The indefatigable activity of the duke of Dalmatia
greatly contributed to the success of the whole
campaign; and it is a remarkable circumstance,
that Soult and Napoleon, advancing from different
bases, should have so combined their movements,
that, after marching, the one above a hundred, and
the other above two hundred miles, through a
hostile country, they effected their junction at a
given point, and at a given hour, without failure:
nor is it less remarkable, that such a decided and
well-conducted operation should have been baffled
by a general at the head of an inexperienced
army.

When Sylla, after all his victories, styled himself
a happy, rather than a great general, he discovered
his profound knowledge of the military art. Experience had taught him that the speed of one
legion, the inactivity of another, the obstinacy, the
ignorance, or the treachery of a subordinate officer,
was sufficient to mar the best concerted plan—nay,
that the intervention of a shower of rain, an unexpected ditch, or any apparently trivial accident,
might determine the fate of a whole army. It
taught him that the vicissitudes of war are so many,
that disappointment will attend the wisest combinations; that a ruinous defeat, the work of chance,
often closes the career of the boldest and most
sagacious of generals, and that to judge of a commander's conduct by the event alone, is equally
unjust and unphilosophical, a refuge for vanity and
ignorance.

These reflections seem to be peculiarly applicable

to sir John Moore's campaign, which has by sundry
writers been so unfairly discussed. Many of the
subsequent disasters of the French can now be distinctly traced to the operations of the British army.
It can be demonstrated that the reputation of that
excellent man was basely sacrificed at the period of
his death, and that the virulent censures passed
upon his conduct have been as inconsiderate as
they were unmerited and cruel. The nature of the
commands held by sir John Moore in the years
1807-8-9 forced him into a series of embarrassments, from which few men could have extricated
themselves. After refusing the charge of the absurd expedition to Egypt in 1806, which ended, as
he judged it must do, unfavourably, he succeeded
to the command of the troops in Sicily, a situation
which immediately involved him in unpleasant discussions with the queen of Naples and the British
envoy; discussions to which the subsequent well-
known enmity of the cabinet of that day may be
traced. By his frank conduct, clear judgment, and
firm spirit, he soon obtained an influence over the
wretched court of Palermo that promised the hap-
piest results; the queen's repugnance to a reform
was overcome, the ministers were awed, and the
miserable intrigues of the day abated, the Sicilian
army was reorganized, and a good military system
was commenced under the advice of the British
general.

This promising state of affairs lasted but a short
time; the Russian fleet put into the Tagus, the
French threatened Portugal, and Sicily was no
longer considered! Sir John Moore was ordered
to quit that island, and to assemble a large
force at Gibraltar for a special service; but

BOOK.
IV.
the troops to be gathered were dispersed in the
Mediterranean from Egypt to the straits, and their
junction could not be effected at all, unless the
English ambassador at Constantinople should succeed in bringing a negotiation, then pending be-
Sir John
Moore's
Journal.
MS.
tween the Turks and Russians, to a happy issue.
Now this special service in question had two objects, 1°. to aid sir Sydney Smith in carrying off the
the royal family of Portugal to the Brazils; 2°.
to take possession of Madeira; yet neither were
made known to the general before his arrival at
Gibraltar, which was not until after Junot had
taken possession of Lisbon.   Sir John Moore then,
following his instructions, proceeded home, and
thus our interests in Sicily were again abandoned
to the vices and intrigues of the court of Palermo.
On the passage he crossed general Spencer going
with a force against Ceuta, and soon after he had
reached England, he was despatched to Sweden,
without any specific object, and with such vague
instructions, that an immediate collision with the
unfortunate Gustavus was the consequence.

Having with much dexterity and judgment withdrawn himself and his army from the capricious violence of that monarch, sir John was superseded and
sent to Portugal, with the third rank in an army which
at that time no man had such good claims to command
as himself; the mode of doing this was also offensive, and it was evident that the ministers desired
to drive him into private life.   Their efforts were,
however, powerless against his pure and elevated
patriotism.   In a personal conference with lord
Castlereagh, he expressed his indignation at the
insults offered to him, and then repaired to his
station at Portsmouth, where an official letter fol-

lowed him, the purport being that his remonstrance being disrespectful, it would be referred to the king for reprehension, and that measures would be taken to remove him from what appeared to be a disagreeable situation: in other words, that his resignation was demanded. Without a moment's hesitation, he replied to this menace, in a letter which breathed the very spirit of manly dignity and patriotism. 'I am,' he wrote, 'this moment honoured with your lordship's letter (by messenger) of yesterday's date. As I have already had the honour to express my sentiments to your lordship fully at my last interview, it is, I think, unnecessary to trouble you with a repetition of them now. I am about to proceed on the service on which I have been ordered, and it shall be my endeavour to acquit myself with the same zeal by which I have ever been actuated when employed in the service of my country. The communication which it has been thought proper to make to his majesty cannot fail to give me pleasure; I have the most perfect reliance on his majesty's justice, and shall never feel greater security than when my conduct, my character, and my honour are under his majesty's protection.' He heard no more on that subject.

The good fortune of England was never more conspicuous than at this period, when her armies and fleets were thus bandied about, and a blind chance governed the councils at home. For first a force collected from all parts of the Mediterranean was transported to the Baltic at a time when an expedition composed of troops, which had but a short time before come back from the Baltic, were sailing from England to the Mediterranean. An army intended to conquer South America was happily as-

sembled in Ireland at the moment when an unexpected event called for their services in Portugal.
A division destined to attack the Spaniards at
Ceuta, arrived at Gibraltar, at the instant when the
insurrection of Andalusia fortunately prevented them
from making an attempt that would have materially
aided Napoleon's schemes against the Peninsula.
Again, three days after sir John Moore had withdrawn his army from Sweden, orders arrived to
employ it in carrying off the Spanish troops under
Romana,—an operation for which it was not required, and which would have retarded, if not
entirely frustrated, the campaign in Portugal; but
the ministers were resolved at any cost to prevent
Moore from commanding the army destined for
Portugal.   Nor was it the least part of England's
fortune that in such long-continued voyages in bad
seasons, no disaster befel the huge fleets thus
employed in bearing her strength from one extremity of Europe to the other.

After the convention of Cintra, Moore was again
placed at the head of an army, an appointment
unexpected by him, for the frank and bold manner
in which he expressed himself to the ministers left
him little to hope; but the personal goodwill of the
king, and his own towering reputation, crushed all
opposition.   Thus, in a few months after he had
quitted Sweden, Moore, with an army not exceeding
twenty-four thousand men, was in the heart of Spain,
opposed to Napoleon, who having passed the Pyrenees at the head of three hundred and thirty thousand
men, could readily bring two hundred thousand to
bear on the British; a vast disproportion of numbers,
and a sufficient answer to all the idle censures passed
upon the retreat to Coruña.

The most plausible grounds of accusation against
sir John Moore's conduct rest on three alleged
errors:—

1st. That he divided his forces;

2dly. That he advanced against Soult;

3dly. That he made a precipitate and unnecessary
retreat.

When a general, aware of the strength of his adversary, and of the resources to be placed at his own
disposal, arranges a plan of campaign, he may be
strictly judged by the rules of art; but if, as in the
case of sir John Moore, he is suddenly appointed to
conduct important operations without a plan being
arranged, or the means given to arrange one, then
it is evident that his capacity or incapacity must be
judged of by the energy he displays, the comprehensive view he takes of affairs, and the rapidity with
which he accommodates his measures to events, that
the original vice of his appointment will not permit
him to control. Sir Walter Scott, in his Life of Napoleon, with that intrepidity of error which marks the
work, has asserted, ' That Moore sent ten thousand
men, under sir D. Baird, by sea, to Coruña.' That
' the general science of war, upon the most extended
scale, seems to have been so little understood or practised by the English generals at this time, that instead of the country being carefully reconnoitred by
officers of skill, the march of the army was arranged
by such hasty and inaccurate information as could
be collected from the peasants;' and that ' by these
reports sir John Moore was induced to divide his
army.'

The second of these assertions is devoid of reason,
and both are contrary to fact. Sir David Baird

was never at Lisbon, but was sent with his troops, by the ministers, direct from England to Coruña. The ' general science of war upon the most extended scale,' is an inflated and unmeaning expression, the most contracted operation requires that good information should be obtained; and as to the fact, sir John Moore employed his own staff officers
to examine the roads, sought information equally from noble and peasant, and, like all great commanders, regulated his proceedings by the general result of his inquiries.

The first dividing of the army was, therefore, the act of the ministers, who sent Baird to Coruña; the after separation of the artillery was sir John Moore's, the reasons for which have been already stated; but it is worth while to examine what the effect of that measure was, and what it might have been. And here it may be observed, that, although a brigade of light six-pounders did accompany the troops to Almeida, the road, in a military sense, was *not practicable*, for the guns were in some places let down the rocks by ropes, and in others carried over the difficult places; a practicable affair with one brigade, but how could the great train of guns and ammunition-waggons that accompanied sir John Hope, have passed such places, without a loss of time that would have proved more injurious to the operations than the separation of the artillery? The advance of the army was guided by three contingent cases, any one of which arising would have immediately influenced the operations; 1°. Blake on the left, or Castaños and Palafox upon the right, might have beaten the French, and advanced to the Pyrenees. 2°. They might have maintained their position on the Ebro. 3°. The arrival of reinforcements from France might have forced the Spaniards to fall back upon the upper Duero, on one side, and to the mountains of Guadalaxara on the other. In the first case, there was no risk of marching by divisions towards Burgos, which was the point of concentration given by the British and Spanish ministers. In the second case, the army could safely unite at Valladolid. In the third case, if the division of sir David Baird had reached Toro early in November and this it was reasonable to expect, because that general arrived at Coruña the 13th of October, the retrograde movement of the Spanish armies would probably have drawn the English to the Guadarama, as a safe and central point between the retiring Spanish wings.

Now the artillery marching from the Alemtejo by the roads of Talavera and Naval Carnero, to Burgos, would pass over one hundred and two Spanish leagues; to Aranda de Duero, eighty-nine leagues; to Valladolid, ninety-two leagues; while the columns that marched by Almeida and Salamanca would pass over one hundred and sixteen leagues to Burgos, and ninety-eight to Valladolid. Wherefore, supposing the Spaniards successful, or even holding their own, the separation of the artillery was an advantage, and if the Spaniards were driven back, their natural line of retreat would have brought them towards Madrid, Blake by Aranda to the Somosierra, and Castaños and Palafox by Siguenza and Tarancon, to cover the capital, and to maintain an interior communication between the Somosierra and the Henares river. The British artillery would then have halted at Espinar, after a march of only eighty leagues, and Baird and Moore's corps uniting at Salamanca early in November, might, by a flank march to Arevalo, have insured the concentration of the whole army.

Thus, in the three anticipated cases, the separation of the artillery was prudent, and promised to be advantageous. There was, indeed, a fourth case, that which really happened. All the Spanish armies were dispersed in an instant! utterly effaced! But sir John Moore could not have divined such a catastrophe, while his ears were ringing with the universal clamour about the numbers and enthusiasm of the patriots, and if he had foreseen even a part of such disasters, he would never have advanced from Portugal. With the plans of the Spanish government he was unacquainted, but he was officially informed that above one hundred and forty thousand Spanish soldiers were between him and a feeble, dispirited enemy; and as the intercepted letter from the governor of Bayonne stated, that the reinforcements would only arrive between the 18th of October and the 18th of November, it was reasonable to suppose the French would not commence offensive operations before the latter period, and that ample time would be afforded to concentrate the English troops under the protection of the Spanish armies.

If sir John Moore could have suspected the delusion under which the British government acted; if he could have divined the incredible folly of the central junta and the Spanish generals, or the inaccuracy of the military agents; if he could have supposed that the Spanish armies were weak in numbers, weaker in spirit, and destitute of food and clothing, or that, while the Spanish authorities were pressing him to advance, they would wantonly detain sir David Baird's troops seventeen days on board the transports; if he could

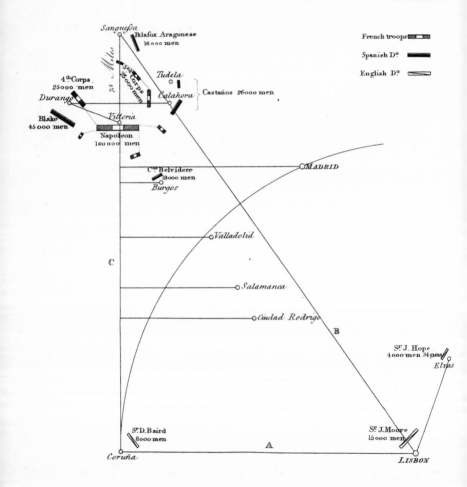

London. Published by T. & W. Boone. New Bond Street.

have imagined all this, undoubtedly his arrangements ought and would have been different, his
army would have been kept together, and the road
to Salamanca through Coria, however difficult,
would have been preferred to a divided march.

Now the dangerous and absurd position of the
Spanish armies, and the remote situation of the
British troops in October, may be explained by the
annexed diagram. Lisbon being taken as a centre,
and the distance A between Lisbon and Coruña,
being the radius, let a circle passing through
Madrid be described, and let the tangential line c
be drawn perpendicular to the radius A, meeting
the secant B at Sanguessa. Then it will be seen
that as the extreme right of the Spaniards
was posted at Sanguessa, and Castaños at Calahorra, while Blake was near Durango, and the main
body of the French was at Vittoria, the latter not
only divided the Spaniards, but was actually twenty-
five miles nearer to Burgos and Valladolid (the
points of concentration for Moore's and Baird's
corps,) than either Castaños or Blake; and seventy-
five miles nearer than Palafox. On the 10th, the
emperor struck the first blow, by beating Belvedere
and seizing Burgos; but sir David Baird did not
quit Coruña until the 12th, and did not bring
up the whole of his troops to Astorga before the
4th of December; hence it is clear, that whatever
road the artillery had taken, the British army
could not have averted the ruin of the Spaniards.

Let us suppose the troops assembled at Salamanca on the 13th of November. They must have
advanced either to Valladolid or to Madrid. If to
Valladolid, the emperor was at Burgos with the
imperial guards, ten or twelve thousand cavalry

and a hundred pieces of artillery; the first corps
was within a day's march, the second and fourth
corps within three marches, and the sixth corps
within two marches.   Above a hundred thousand
French soldiers could, therefore, have been concentrated in three days, and it is to be observed that sir
John Moore never had twenty-five thousand in the
field.   It is said, he might have gone to Madrid; in
that case the separation of the artillery would have
been a decided advantage, and the separation of
Baird's corps, which was not the general's arrangement, the error.   The army could not have marched
from Salamanca to Madrid in less than seven days,
and hence before the 21st of November, twenty-
four thousand British soldiers could not have been
collected in the capital; but the fourth French
corps, which reached Segovia the 1st of December,
would meanwhile have cut off the communication
with Portugal, and the emperor with forty thousand
men was at Aranda de Duero.   Castaños, who had
been defeated on the 23d of November, was indeed with the remnant of an army at Guadalaxara
about the 1st of December, but the sixth corps was
close in pursuit.

Moore must then have done one of three
things.   Advanced to the succour of Castaños,
joined St. Juan at the Somosierra, or retreated
across the Tagus.   In the first case, the emperor would have forced the Somosierra, and
uniting with the fourth corps, have placed sixty
thousand men upon the English rear; in the second
case, the sixth and fourth corps, turning both
flanks, would have effected a junction behind the
Somosierra, and cut them off from Madrid, while
Napoleon, with forty thousand men, assailed them

in front. To retreat over the Tagus was to adopt
the southern provinces for a new base of operations,
and might have been useful if the Spaniards would
have rallied round him with enthusiasm and courage ; but would they have done so when the emperor was advancing with his enormous force ?
After-experience proves that they would not. The
duke of Dalmatia, in 1810, with an army very
inferior to that under Napoleon, reached the gates
of Cadiz without a serious blow being struck to
oppose him, and at this time the people of the
south were reckless of the opportunity procured for
them by sir John Moore's march on Sahagun.

It has, however, been said, that twenty-four thousand British troops acting vigorously, could have
checked the emperor, and raised the courage of the
Spaniards. To such an observation I will oppose a
fact. In 1815, Napoleon crossed the Sambre with
one hundred and fifteen thousand men, and the
two hundred and ten thousand regular troops in his
front, among which were more than thirty thousand
English, could with difficulty stop his progress after
four days' fighting, in three of which he was successful. If sir John Moore, at a subsequent period,
was willing to risk the danger of a movement on the
capital, it was because he was misinformed of the
French strength, and the Spaniards were represented to be numerous and confident ; he was also
unacquainted with the defeat at Tudela. His object was, by assisting Castaños, to arouse the spirit
of the patriots, and nothing more strongly evinces
his hardihood and prompt judgment ; for, in his
letter to Mr. Frere, he distinctly stated the danger
to be incurred, and carefully separating the military

from the political reasons, only proposed to venture
the army, if the envoy was satisfied that the Spanish
government and people would answer to such an
appeal, and that the British cabinet would be willing
to incur the risk for such an object. If he did not
follow up his own proposal, it was because he had
discovered that the army of Castaños was, not simply
defeated, but destroyed ; because the Somosierra
had been forced by a charge of cavalry ; and because the passes of the Guadarama, on his line of
march to Madrid, were seized by the enemy before
his own army could be concentrated.

Why then did he not retreat into Portugal?   Because Napoleon, having directed his forces against
the capital, the British army was enabled to concentrate ; because Madrid had shut her gates ; because
Mr. Frere and the Spanish authorities endeavoured
to deceive him by false information ; because the
solemn declaration of the junta of Todelo, that they
would bury themselves under the ruins of that
town rather than surrender, joined to the fact that
Zaragoza was fighting heroically, seemed to guarantee the constancy and vigour of that patriotic
spirit which was apparently once more excited ;
because the question was again become political,
and it was necessary to satisfy the English people,
that nothing was left undone to aid a cause which
they had so much at heart ; because the peculiar position of the French army at the moment,
afforded the means of creating a powerful diversion
in favour of the southern provinces. These are the
unanswerable reasons for the advance towards Sahagun. In the details of execution, that movement
may be liable to some trifling objections ; perhaps
it would have been better to have carried the army

on the 21st at once to Carrion and neglected
Sahagun and Saldanha; but in its strategic and
political character, it was well conceived and well
timed, hardy and successful.

The irritating interference that sir John Moore
was called upon to repel, and the treachery and the
folly, equal in its effects to treachery, that he was
obliged to guard against have been sufficiently
dwelt upon already; yet before discussing the retreat from Astorga, it may be of some military
interest to show that the line of Portugal, although
the natural one for the British army to retire upon,
was not at this period necessarily either safe or
useful, and that greater evils than those incurred by
a retreat through Gallicia would probably have
attended a retrograde march upon Lisbon.

The rugged frontier of Portugal lying between
the Duero and the Tagus, is vulnerable in many
points to an invading army of superior force. It
may be penetrated between the Duero and Pinhel,
and between Pinhel and Guarda, by roads leading
into the valleys of the Zezere and the Mondego.
Between the Sierra de Estrella and the Sierra de
Gata, by the road from Alfayates to Sabugal and
Penamacor, or that by Guarda and Coria. Again,
it may be pierced between the Sierra de Gata and
the Tagus by Idanha Velha, Castello Branco, and
Sobreira Formosa; and from the Tagus to the
Guadiana, a distance of about twenty leagues,
the Alentejo presents an open country without
any strong fortress, save La-Lippe, which may be
disregarded and passed without danger. Now
sir John Moore commenced his forward movement
from Salamanca on the 12th of December, and
at that period the fourth corps, being at Tala-

vera de la Reyna, was much nearer to Lisbon than the British army was, and the emperor was preparing to march on that capital with the sixth corps, the guards, and the reserve. He could, as the Duke of Berwick did, penetrate by both sides of the Tagus; and what was to prevent him from reaching Lisbon before the British force, if the latter had retreated from Salamanca? he marched on a shorter line and a better road, and he could supply his troops by requisitions, a system that, however fatal it may be in the end, is always advantageous at first; but Moore must, from a scanty military chest, have purchased his supplies from a suspicious peasantry, rendered more distrustful by the retreat.

It is true that in Lisbon, sir John Craddock commanded six thousand infantry and two hundred and fifty-eight cavalry; but the Portuguese provisional government, who had only organized a few ill-composed battalions, were so inactive, that it was not until the 11th of December that a proclamation, calling on the people to arm, was issued. In the arsenal there were scarcely musquets and equipments for eight thousand men, and the new levies were only required to assemble when the country should be actually invaded. Sir Robert Wilson, having with great activity organized about two thousand of the Lusitanian legion, had marched in the middle of December from Oporto, and this was all that could be opposed to an army more numerous, more favourably situated for invasion, and incomparably better commanded than that with which Massena invaded the country in 1810. Thus it may be affirmed, that if a retreat upon Lisbon was advisable before Napoleon took Madrid, it was not a safe operation after that event, and it is clear that sir John Moore neither lightly nor injudiciously adopted the line of Gallicia.

The arguments of those who deny the necessity of falling back, even behind the Esla, are scarcely worth notice, a simple reference to the numbers under the emperor, and the direction of his march, is sufficient to expose their futility; but the necessity of the continued and, as it has been unjustly called, the precipitate retreat to Coruña, may not be quite so obvious. The advance to Sahagun was intended to create a diversion, and give the Spaniards an opportunity of making head in the south, it succeeded in drawing away the enemy, yet the Spaniards did not make any head, the central junta displayed no energy or wisdom; a few slight demonstrations by the marquis of Palacios, on the side of the Sierra Morena, and by the duke of Infantado on the side of Cuenca, scarcely disturbed the first corps which remained in La Mancha; ten thousand men were sufficient to maintain Madrid in perfect tranquillity, and a part of the fourth corps even marched from Talavera by Placentia on Salamanca. By the letters of Mr. Stuart, and the reports of his own spies, the English general was informed of all these disheartening circumstances, yet the intelligence arrived slowly and at intervals, and he, hoping that the Spaniards would finally make an effort, announced his intention to hold the Gallicias; Mr. Stuart's correspondence at last deprived him of that hope, and the presence of the emperor, the great amount of his force, and the vehemence with which he pressed forward, confirmed the unhappy truth that nothing could be expected from the south.

Sir John Moore could not with twenty-three thousand men maintain himself against the whole French army, and until he reached Astorga his flanks were always exposed; from thence he retreated in comparative security, but the natural strength of the country between that town and Coruña misled persons of shallow judgment, who have since inconsiderately advanced many vague accusations, such as that passes where a hundred men could stop an army were lightly abandoned; that the retreat was a flight, and the general's judgment clouded by the danger of his situation. There might be some foundation for such observations if military commanders were like prize-fighters, bound to strike always at the front, but as long as armies are dependent for their subsistence and ammunition upon lines of communication, the safety of their flanks and rear must be considered as of consequence. Moore was perfectly aware that he could fight any number of men in some of the mountainous positions on the road to Coruña; yet unless he could make a permanent defence, such battles would have been worse than useless, and a permanent defence was impossible, inasmuch as there were none but temporary magazines nearer than Coruña, and there were neither carriages of transport, nor money to procure them; moreover a severe winter had just set in, the people were disinclined to aid the troops, and as the province was poor, few resources could be drawn from the vicinity. Neither was there a single position that could be maintained for more than a few days against a superior force.

That of Rodrigatos could be turned by the old road leading to Villa Franca, Villa Franca itself by the valley of the Syl, and from thence the whole line to

Coruña might be turned by the road of Orense, which also led directly to Vigo; and until he reached Nogales, Moore's intention was to retire to Vigo. The French could have marched through the richest part of Gallicia to St. Jago and Coruña on the left, or from the Asturias, by the way of Mondonedo, on the right; and if it be asked, why they did not do so? the answer is prompt, the emperor having quitted the army, the jealousies and misunderstandings usual between generals of equal rank impeded the operations. A coolness subsisted between marshal Ney and the duke of Dalmatia, and without entering into the grounds of their difference, it is plain that, in a military point of view, the judgment of the latter was the soundest. The former committed a great error by remaining at Villa Franca instead of pushing his corps, or a part of it as recommended by Soult, along the valley of Orense to St. Jago de Compostella, the British army would have been lost if the sixth corps had reached Coruña before it; and what would have been the chances in the battle if three additional French divisions had been engaged? Granting, therefore, that the troops could have been nourished during the winter, Villa Franca, Nogales, Constantino and Lugo, were not permanently defensible by an army whose base of operations was at Coruña. Hence it was that sir John Moore resolved to regain his ships with the view to renew the war in the south, and Hannibal himself could have done no more.

Nor was the mode of executing the retreat at all unbecoming the character of an able officer. Lord Bacon observes, that ' honourable retreats are no ways inferior to brave charges, as having less of fortune, more of discipline, and as much of valour.'

That is an honourable retreat in which the retiring
general loses no trophies in fight, sustains every
charge without being broken, and finally, after a
severe action, re-embarks his army in the face of a
superior enemy, without being seriously molested.
It would be honourable to effect this before a foe
only formidable from numbers, but it is infinitely
more creditable, when the commander, while struggling with bad weather and worse fortune, has to
oppose veterans with inexperienced troops, and to
contend against an antagonist of eminent ability,
who scarcely suffers a single advantage to escape
him during this long and vigorous pursuit.   All
this sir John Moore did, and finished his work by
a death as firm and glorious as any that antiquity
can boast of.

Put to lord Bacon's test, in what shall the retreat to Coruña be found deficient? something in
discipline perhaps, but that fault does not attach
to the general.   Those commanders who have been
celebrated for making fine retreats were in most
instances well acquainted with their armies; and
Hannibal, speaking of the elder Scipio, derided
him, although a brave and skilful man, for that,
being unknown to his own soldiers, he should pre-
sume to oppose himself to a general who could
call to each man under his command by name;
thus inculcating, that unless troops be trained in
the peculiar method of a commander, the latter can
scarcely achieve any thing great.   Now Moore had
a young army suddenly placed under his guidance,
and it was scarcely united, when the superior
numbers of the enemy forced it to a retrograde
movement under very harassing circumstances; he
had not time, therefore, to establish a system of

discipline, and it is in the leading events, not the
minor details, that the just criterion of his merits is
to be sought for.

Was the retreat uncalled for? Was it unnecessarily precipitate? Was any opportunity of crippling
the enemy lost? Was any weakness to be discovered
in the personal character of the general? These are
the questions that sensible men will ask. The first
has been already examined, the second is a matter
of simple calculation. The rear guard quitted Astorga on the 1st of January, on the 3d it repulsed
the enemy in a sharp skirmish at Calcabelos, the
6th it rejoined the main body at Lugo, having three
times checked the pursuers during the march; it was
unbroken, had lost no gun, suffered no misfortune.
The whole army offered battle at Lugo for two successive days, it was not accepted, and the retreat
recommencing, the troops reached Betanzos on the
morning of the 10th, and Coruña on the 11th; thus
in eleven days, three of which were days of rest, a
small army passed over a hundred and fifty miles of
good road. Now Napoleon, with fifty thousand men,
left Madrid on the 22d of December, and the 28th
he was at Villapando, having performed a march, on
bad roads, of a hundred and sixty-four miles in
seven days. The retreat to Coruña was consequently not precipitate, unless it can be shown, that
it was unnecessary to retreat at all beyond Villa
Franca; neither can it be asserted, that any opportunity of crippling the enemy was lost. To fight a
battle was the game of the French marshal, and if
any censure will apply to his able campaign, it is
that he delayed to attack at Lugo; victorious or
beaten, it would have increased the embarrassments
of his adversary, who must have continued his

retreat encumbered with the wounded, or the latter
must have been abandoned without succour in the
midst of winter.

At Coruña the absence of the fleet necessarily
brought on a battle. That it was honourable to
the British troops is clear from the fact that they
embarked without loss after the action. That it
was absolutely necessary to embark notwithstanding the success, is a certain proof how little advantage could have been derived from any battle
fought farther inland; and sir John Moore's prudence in declining an action the moment he had
rallied his army at Lugo, and restored that discipline which the previous movements had shaken.
But, notwithstanding the clamour with which this
campaign has been assailed, as if no army had ever
yet suffered such misfortunes, it is certain that the
nominal loss was small, the real loss smaller, and
that it sinks into nothing when compared with the
advantages gained. An army which, after marching
in advance or retreat above five hundred miles before an enemy of immensely superior force, has only
lost, including those killed in battle, four thousand
men, or a sixth part of its numbers, cannot be said
to have suffered severely, nor would the loss have
been so great but for the intervention of the accidental occurrences mentioned in the narrative.
Night marches are seldom happy, that from Lugo
to Betanzos cost the army in stragglers more than
double the number of men lost in all the preceding
operations; nevertheless, the reserve in that, as in
all the other movements, suffered little, and it is a
fact, that the light brigades detached by the Vigo
road, which were not pursued, made no forced
marches, slept under cover, and were well supplied;

Appendix,
No. 26.

Ibid.

left, in proportion to their strength, as many men behind as any other part of the army; thus proof upon proof accumulates that inexperience was the primary and principal cause of the disorders which attended the retreat. Those disorders were sufficiently great, but many circumstances contributed to produce an appearance of suffering and disorganization which was not real.

Sir John Moore's intention was to have proceeded to Vigo, in order to restore order before he sailed for England, instead of which the fleet steered home directly from Coruña, and a terrible storm scattered it; many ships were wrecked, and the remainder, driving up the Channel, were glad to put into any port. The soldiers, thus thrown on shore, were spread from the Land's End to Dover. Their haggard appearance, ragged clothing, and dirty accoutrements, things common enough in war, struck a people only used to the daintiness of parade with surprise; the usual exaggerations of men just escaped from perils and distresses were increased by the uncertainty in which all were as to the fate of their comrades; a deadly fever, the result of anxiety, and of the sudden change from fatigue to the confinement of a ship, filled the hospitals at every port with officers and soldiers, and thus the miserable state of sir John Moore's army became the topic of every letter, and the theme for every country newspaper along the coast. The nation, at that time unused to great operations, forgot that war is not a harmless game, and judging of the loss positively, instead of comparatively, was thus disposed to believe the calumnies of interested men, who were eager to cast a shade over one of the brightest characters that ever adorned the country.

Those calumnies triumphed for a moment, but
Moore's last appeal to his country for justice will
be successful; posterity, revering and cherishing
his name, will visit such of his odious calumniators
as are not too contemptible to be remembered with
a just and severe retribution, for thus it is that
time freshens the beauty of virtue and withers the
efforts of baseness. And if authority be sought
for in a case where reason speaks so plainly, future
historians will not fail to remark, that the man
whose talents exacted the praises of Soult, of Wellington, and of Napoleon, could be no ordinary
soldier.

"Sir John Moore," says the first, "took every
advantage that the country afforded to oppose an
Appendix, active and vigorous resistance, and he finished
No. 14.   by dying in a combat that must do credit to his
memory."

Vivian's   Napoleon more than once affirmed, that if he
Conversa-
tions at   committed a few trifling errors, they were to be
Elba.
Voice from attributed to his peculiar situation, for that his
St.Helena. talents and firmness alone had saved the English
army from destruction.

"In sir John Moore's campaign," said the duke
of Wellington, "I can see but one error; when he
advanced to Sahagun he should have considered it
as a movement of retreat, and sent officers to the
rear to mark and prepare the halting-places for
every brigade. But this opinion I have formed after
long experience of war, and especially of the pecu-
liarities of a Spanish war, which must have been
seen to be understood; finally, it is an opinion
formed after the event."

OBSERVATIONS ON SOME PASSAGES IN CHAPTERS II. & VI.

WITH respect to the tumult of the 2nd of May, 1808, I drew my information from officers, some French, some Italian, who were present. On the veracity of my informants I had the firmest reliance, their accounts agreed well, and the principal facts were confirmed by the result of my personal enquiries at Madrid in the year 1812. But since the first edition of this work the following notes from general Harispe have been sent to me, and I insert them in justice to the colonel of the Imperial Guard. At the same time, I have to remark that, in respect to the latter my statement was made upon the authority of an officer of Murat's staff.

Bayonne, May 22, 1831.

Au Colonel (Anglais) George Napier.

' Monsieur,—J'ai lu avec un véritable intérêt les passages de l'ouvrage de monsieur votre frère, que vous m'aviez prié d'examiner. Je vous remercie de cette communication. J'ai porté en marge les rectifications nécessaires pour rétablir la vérité.——Recevez, monsieur, &c. &c.

' Le Lieut. Général, Comte HARISPE.'

Marginal Notes by General Harispe.

Chap II., page 24. Aucun des quartiers de troupes Françaises à Madrid ne fut attaqué, mais 350 à 400 hommes environ, qui se trouvaient isolés ou occupés à des distributions de pain, furent assassinés.

Page 25. Le colonel de la Garde Impériale ne fit mettre à mort personne.

Chap. VI., page 90. Le battailon Suisse ne fût pas pris au pont de Pajaso, mais bien le lendemain de l'attaque de los Cabrillos.

Page 92. L'attaque de la ville (Valencia) se termina à la nuit, sans que les Espagnols eussent fait aucune sortie.

APPENDIX.

[The following five Notes, dictated by the emperor Napoleon, and signed by general Bertrand, were found in king Joseph's portfolio, at the battle of Vittoria.]

No. I.

OBSERVATIONS ADDRESSÉES AU GÉNÉRAL SAVARY SUR LES AFFAIRES D'ESPAGNE.

Le 13 *Julliet,* 1808.

1ere *Observation.*—Les affaires des Français en Espagne seroient dans une excellente position si la division Gobert avait marché sur Valladolid, et si la division Frère eut occupé San Clemente, ayant une colonne mobile à trois ou quatre journées sur la route général Dupont.

Le g^{al} Gobert ayant été dirigé sur le général Dupont, le g^{al} Frère étant avec le maréchal Moncey, harassé et affaibli par des marches et des contremarches, la position de l'armée Française est devenue moins belle.

2e *Observation.*—Le maréchal Bessières est aujourd'hui à Medina del Rio Secco avec 15 mille hommes, infanterie, cavalerie, artillerie. Le 15 ou le 16, il attaquera Bénavente, se mettra en communication avec le Portugal, jettera les rebelles et Galice, et s'emparera de Léon. Si toutes les opérations réussissent ainsi, et d'une manière brillant, la position de l'armée Française redeviendra ce qu'elle était.

Si le général Cuesta se retire de Bénavente sans combattre, il se retirait sur Zamora, Salamanque, pour venir gagner Avila et

Segovia, certain qu'alors le maréchal Bessières ne pourrait point le poursuivre, puisque, dans cette supposition, il serait menacé par l'armée de Galice, dont l'avant garde est réunie à Léon.

Alors il faut que le général qui commande à Madrid puisse promptement réunir 6 à 7000 hommes pour marcher sur le général Cuesta.   Il faut que la citadelle de Ségovie soit occupée par quelques pièces de canon, trois à 400 convalescens, avec six semaines de biscuit.

C'est une grande faute de n'avoir pas occupé cette citadelle, quand le major-général l'a mandé.   De toutes les positions possibles, Ségovie est la plus dangéreuse pour l'armée : capitale d'une province, assise entre les deux routes, elle ôterait à l'armée toutes ses communications, et l'ennemi une fois posté dans cette citadelle, l'armée Française ne pourrait plus l'en déloger.   Trois ou 400 convalescens et un bon chef de bataillon, une escouade d'artillerie, rendront le château de Ségovie imprégnable pendant bien de tems, et assureront à l'armée l'importante position de Ségovie.

Si le général Cuesta se jette en Galice, sans combattre, sans éprouver de défaite, la position de l'armée devient toujours meilleure ; à plus forte raison, s'il est jetté en Galice après avoir éprouvé une forte défaite.

3e *Observation.*—Si le maréchal Bessières, arrivé devant Bénavente, reste en présence sans attaquer le g^{al} Cuesta, ou s'il est repoussé, son but sera toujours de couvrir Burgos, en tenant le plus possible l'ennemi en échec ; il peut être renforcé de 3000 hommes de troupes de ligne, qui accompagnent le roi, mais alors il n'y a point à hésiter.   Si le maréchal Bessières a fait une marche rétrograde sans bataille, il faut sur le champ lui envoyer 6000 hommes de renforts.   S'il a fait son mouvement après une bataille, où il ait éprouvé de grandes pertes, il faudra faire de grandes dispositions: rappeller à marche forcée sur Madrid le g^{al} Frère, le g^{al} Caulaincourt, le g^{al} Gobert, le g^{al} Vedel, et laisser le g^{al} Dupont sur les montagnes de la Sierra Morena, ou le rapprocher même de Madrid, en le tenant toujours, cependant, à sept ou huit marches, afin de pouvoir écraser le g^{al} Cuesta et toute l'armée de Galice, pendant que le g^{al} Dupont servira d'avant-garde pour tenir l'armée d'Andalousie en échec.

4e *Observation.*—Si le général Dupont éprouvait un échec, cela serait de peu de conséquence.   Il n'aurait d'autre résultat que de lui faire repasser les montagnes ; mais le coup qui serait porté au maréchal Bessières serait un coup porté au cœur de l'armée, qui donnerait le *tetanos,* et qui se ferait sentir à toutes les points extrêmes de l'armée. Voila pourquoi il est très malheureux que toutes les dispositions ordonnées n'aient pas été suivis   L'armée du maréchal Bessières devrait se trouver avoir au moins huite mille hommes de plus, afin qu'il n'y eut aucune espèce de chance contre l'armée du marechal Bessières.

La vraie manière de renforcer le général Dupont, ce n'est pas de lui envoyer des troupes, mais c'est d'envoyer des troupes au maréchal Bessières.   Le général Dupont et le général Vedel sont suffisans pour se maintenir dans les positions qu'ils ont retranchés ; et si le maréchal Bessières avait été renforce, et l'armée de Galice écrasée, le général Dupont immédiatement après se trouverait dans le meilleure position, non seulemont par des forces qu'on pourrait alors lui envoyer, mais encore par la situation morale des affaires.   Il n'y a pas un habitant de Madrid, pas un paysan des vallées qui ne sente que toutes les affaires d'Espagne aujourd'hui sont dans l'affaire du maréchal Bessières.   Combien n'est-il pas malheureux que dans cette grande affaire on se soit donné volontairement 20 chances contre soi.

5e Observation.—L'affaire de Valence n'a jamais été d'aucun considération.   Le maréchal Moncey seul était suffisant.   C'était une folie que de songer à le secourir.   Si le m^al Moncey ne pouvait pas prendre Valence, 20 mille hommes de plus ne le lui auraient pas fait prendre, parcequ'alors c'était un affaire d'artillerie, et non une affaire d'hommes : car on ne prend pas d'un corp de collier une ville de 80 ou 100 mille âmes, qui a barricadé ses rues, mis de l'artillerie à toutes les portes et dans toutes les maisons.   Or, dans cette hypothèse, le m^al Moncey était suffisant pour former une colonne mobile, faire face à l'armée de Valence, et faire sentir dans toute leur force les horreurs de la guerre.

Le g^al Frère ne pouvait donc rien pour faire prendre Valence, et le g^al Frère pouvait beaucoup posté à San Clemente, soit qu'il dût revenir à Madrid, soit qu'il dût prendre une position intermédiaire pour secourir le g^al Dupont.

C'était une autre erreau que de songer à faire aller le m^al Moncey à Valence pour ensuite le faire marcher en Murcie et sur Grenade. C'était vouloir fondre ce corps d'armée en détail et sans fruit. Comme le dit fort bien le général Dupont, il valait mieux lui envoyer directement un régiment que de lui envoyer trois dans cette direction là.

Dans les guerres civiles ce sont les points importans qu'il faut garder : il ne faut pas aller partout.   Si cependant on a dirigé le m^al Moncey sur Valence, c'était à une époque où la situation des affaires n'était pas la même ; c'était lorsque l'armée de Valence pouvait envoyer en Catalogne ou à Saragosse comme elle en menaçait.

6e *Observation.*—Le but de tous les efforts de l'armée doit être de conserver Madrid. C'est là qu'est tout. Madrid ne peut être menacé que par l'armée de Galice. Elle peut l'être aussi par l'armée de l'Andalousie, mais d'une manière beaucoup moins dangereux, parcequ'elle est simple et directe, et que par toutes les marches que fait le g^{al} Dupont sur ses derrières, il se renforce. Les généraux Dupont et Vedel étaient suffisans, ayant plus de 20,000 hommes : le m^{al} Bessières ne l'est pas proportionnellement, vû que sa position est plus dangereuse. Un échec que recevrait le g^{al} Dupont serait peu de chose ; un échec que recevrait le m^{al} Bessières serait plus considérable et se ferait sentir à l'extremité de la ligne.

Resumé.—Faire reposer et rapprocher de Madrid le g^{al} Frère, le g^{al} Caulaincourt le g^{al} Gobert, afin qu'ils puissant arriver à Madrid avant le g^{al} Cuesta, si celui-ci battait le m^{al} Bessières. Immédiatement après l'événement qui aura lieu le 15 ou le 16, prendre un part selon les événemens qui auront eu lieu, et dans le but d'écraser l'armée ennemie en Galice.

Si le maréchal Bessières a eu grand succès, sans éprouver de grandes pertes, tout sera bien dans la direction actuelle. S'il a un succès aprés avoir éprouvé beaucoup de pertes, il faut se mettre en mesure de la renforcer. S'il se tient en observation sans attaquer, il faut le renforcer. S'il a été défait et bien battu, il faut se concentrer et rassambler toutes ses troupes dans le cercle de sept ou huit journées de Madrid, et étudier les dispositions dans les différentes directions pour savoir où placer les avant-gardes, afin de profiter de l'avantage qu'on a d'être au milieu, pour écraser successivement avec toutes ses forces les divers corps de l'ennemi. Si on n'ordonne pas sur le champ au g^{al} Dupont de repasser les montagnes, ci est qu'on espère que malgré la faute faite, le m^{al} Bessières a la confiance (qu'on partage) qu'a la rigueur il est suffisant pour écraser l'ennemi. Le m^{al} Bessières a eu le bon esprit de tellement réunir toutes ses forces, qu'il n'a pas même laissé un seul homme à St. Ander. Quelqu'avantage qu'il y eut à laisser là un millier d'hommes, il a senti qu'un millier d'hommes pouvait décider sa victoire.

Quant à la division du g^{al} Verdier devant Saragosse, elle a rempli aux trois quarts son but. Elle a désorganisé tous les Arragoniens, a porté le découragement parmi eux, les a reduits à défendre les

maisons de leur capitale, a soumis tous les environs, a bloqué la
ville, et réuni tous les moyens pour s'en emparer sans que cela
devienne trop couteux.

Voilà l'esprit de la guerre d'Espagne.

—————

[Dictated by the emperor Napoleon.]

No. II.

NOTE POUR LE ROI D'ESPAGNE.

Bayonne, Juillet, 1808.

L'armée d'Espagne a son quartier-général à Madrid ; voici sa
composition actuelle :

1°. *Corps des Pyrénées Occidentales.*

Le maréchal Bessières commande le corps des Pyrénées Occidentales, qui est fort de 23 mille hommes, infanterie, cavalerie,
artillerie, occupe la place de St. Sébastien, les troys Biscayes, les
montagnes de St. Ander, la place de Burgos, et est chargée de
combattre l'armée ennemie des Asturies et de Galice.

Toutes les troupes sont en mouvement pour composer l'armée
de la manière suivante.

Division du g^{al} Mouton			
Division du g^{al} Mouton	1ere *brigade* le g^{al} Reynaud.	le 4 reg^t d'infanterie légère 15e d'infanterie de ligne 1er bat^{on} de Paris en marche	5100 h^{es}
	total 3000 hom. présens sous les armes, et 6 pièces de canon, ci 3000 h^{es} (*Cette brigade marche sur Bénévent.*) 2e *brigade,* { 2e reg^t d'infanterie légère le g^{al} Rey. { 12e idem total 2100 hommes et 6 pièces de canon, ci . . . 2100 (*Cette brigade est à Burgos avec le roi, et doit joindre sa division.*)		

A reporter   5100 h^{es}

De l'autre part . . 5100 h^{es}

Division du g^{al} Merle.	Brigade d'Armagnac . .	1800	
	Brigade Gaulois . . .	1800	8400 h^{es}
	Brigade Sabathier . .	2800	
	Brigade Ducos . . .	2000	

Total . 8400 h^{es}

et 16 pièces de canon.

Garde. { Infanterie . . . . . 1900 h^{es}
{ et 6 pièces de canon.

(Toutes ces troupes marchent sur Bénévent.)

Cavalerie.	10e de chasseurs . .	450	
	22e id.	450	
	Garde	300	
	(Ces troupes marchent sur Bénévent.)		
	Escadrons de dragons .	200	1950 h^{es}
	(Ces escadrons sont en marche et ont dépassé la frontière.)		
	26e de chasseurs . .	450	
	(Arrivant à Bayonne sous peu de jours.)		
	Total de la cavalrie .	1950 h^{es}	

Les forces actives du maréchal Bessières sont donc de 17,000 h^{es}. Il n'en a guères que 15,000 pour l'affaire de Bénévent.

S'il obtenait à Bénévent et à Léon un grand succès contre l'armée de Galice, peut-être serait-il convenable pour profiter de la victoire et de la terreur des premiers momens de se jetter dans la Galice. Toutefois, il devrait d'abord prendre position à Léon, en s'emparant de la plaine, jettant l'ennemi dans les montagnes, et intesceptant au moins à Astorga la communication de la grande route.

Garnison de Burgos.—Il y a dans le château de Burgos une garnison *de dépôt.** . . . 600 h^{es}

A reporter . 17,950 h^{es}

* Note.—These two words are added in Napoleon's own hand-writing.

De l'autre part . . 17,950 h^{es}

Colonne du général Bonnet.—Il y a encore à
Burgos le g^{al} de division Bonnet, faisant partie
du corps du m^{al} Bessières : ce g^{al} va avoir
sous ses ordres une colonne mobile de 1200
hommes, pour maintenir la tranquillité dans
la ville et ses environs. Cette colonne est
composée comme il suit :

4e bataillon du 118e, formant . 450 h^{es}

(Actuellement existant à Burgos.)

3e bataillon du dépôt g^{al} actuellement
à Vittoria . . . . 450 15,00 h^{es}

2 comp^{ies} du 4e d'infanterie légère,
formant un petit bataillon . . 400

(En marche, ayant passé la fron-
tière.)

_____
1300 h^{es}

Escadron de dragons (en marche) . 200

2 pièces de canon en marche . . . .
_____
1500 h^{es}

Colonne d'Aranda.—Cette colonne, formée du 1er
bataillon de marche, fort de 1000 h^{es} et de 4
pièces de canon, peut se réunir au besoin avec la
colonne du g^{al} Bonnet : elles doivent assurer la
communication jusqu'aux montagnes en avant
d'Aranda, ci . . . . 1000 h^{es}

Colonne de Vittoria. — Le général de brigade
Monthion, et le colonel Barerre, occupent Vittoria avec une colonne composée comme il suit :

2 compagnies du 15e de ligne, formant un petit
bataillon de . . . . 300 h^{es}

Le 2e bat^{on} du 12e d'infanterie légère 600

Le 2e bat^{on} du 2e id. . . . 600
_____
(Ce qui fait en infanterie) . . 1500 h^{es}

1 escadron de dragons (en marche) . 200

2 pièces de canon.
_____
(Tous ces corps sont en marche) . 1700 ci 1700
_____
A reporter . 22,150 h^{es}

De l'autre part   .   .   22,150 h^{es}

Garnison de St. Sébastien.—Le général Thouvenot commande à St. Sébastien avec mille
hommes de garnison, ci   1000

Récapitulation.—Le corps du m^{al} Bessières est
de   23,150
Et 36 pièces de canon.

Les détachemens et troisièmes bataillons des corps qui sont
aux divisions actives du m^{al} Bessières pourront sous 15 jours le
rejoindre, vû qu'ils seront remplacés à Vittoria et à Burgos par
d'autres corps.

2° *Arragon.*

Jusqu'à cette heure les troupes qui sont en Arragon faisaient
partie du corps des Pyrénées Occidentales. Mais le corps des
Pyrénées Occidentales se portant sur la Galice, il devient indispensable d'en faire une division à part.

Aujourd'hui, ce commandement comprend Pampelune, la Navarre, et les troupes qui forment le siège de Saragosse, sous les
ordres du général Verdier.

Ces troupes sont divisées en quatre brigades, et sont composées
ainsi qu'il suit :

3 régimens d'infaterie de ligne de la Vistule, ayant
sous les armes   .   .   .   .   .   3600 h^{es}
Les 4e, 6e et 7e bataillons de march   .   .   1500
Le 3e bataillon du 14e provisoire   .   .   1300
Le 1er regiment supplémentaire   .   .   900
Les 47e, 15e et 70e   1600
Un bataillon des gardes nationales d'élite   .   600

Total   .   .   9500 h^{es}

La cavalerie consiste dans un régiment de
lanciers Polonais   .   .   .   700 }
Plus un escadron de marche   .   .   400 }   1100

A Pampelune le g^{al} Dagout commande. Indépendamment d'un dépôt de 800 hommes, formant   (ci 800
la garnison de la citadelle ; il a une colonne
mobile composée du 1er bataillon de marche du
Portugal, du troisième bataillon du 118e, fort de
650 hommes, et d'un escadron de dragons, ce qui
forme un total de 1400 hommes disponibles pour
se porter sur tous les points de la Navarre, et sur

A reporter   .   11,400 h^{es}

De l'autre part . 11,400 h^{es}

les communication de Saragosse, pour y mettre

l'odre : ci . . . 1400

Artillerie 200

Il y a donc en cernement en Arragon et en
Navarre . . . 13,000 h^{es}

Aussitôt que Saragosse sera pris, et que le corps de l'Arragon sera constitué, il sera nécessaire de faire entrer au corps du mar_l Bessières le bataillon du 47e, celui du 15e, et les trois bataillons du 14e provisoire ; ce qui augmentera le m^{al} Bessiéres de deux mille hommes, afin de tenir les corps réunis. Il est possible qu'on fasse partir de Bayonne les 19,300 hommes de bonnes troupes de ligne, pour se diriger sur Saragosse et enlever la prise de cette place, si toutefois elle n'est pas encore prise.

Si Saragosse était pris, le corps du m^{al} Bessières pourrait être renforcé de ces trois mille hommes d'élite et de 2000 hommes du corps de Saragosse, ce qui lui ferait un corps nombreux pour la campagne de Galice.

Indépendamment de Saragosse, les rebelles occupent la ville de Jaca et plusieurs ponts dans les vallées. A tous les débouchés des vallées en France il y a un général de brigade avec une colonne mobile. On attendra la prise de Saragosse pour entrer dans ces vallées et y marcher dans les deux sens. Un général l'esprit des vallées est bon ; mais des troupes de contrebandiers que les chefs des rebelles ont enregimentés les vexent.

3°. *Catalogne.*

Le général Duhesme occupe Barcelone, qui est une place qui a deux très belles forteresses, qui la dominent. C'est la plus grande ville de la monarchie.

Le général Duhesme a deux divisions, la division Chabran et la division Lechi, formant 11,000 h^{es} d'infanterie, 1600 h^{es} de cavalerie et 18 pièces de canon.

Le général Duhesme a eu plusieurs événemens ; il a brûlé un grand nombre de villages, et maintenu en respect le pays à 15 lieues à la ronde.

La ville de Géronne, n'ayant pas été occupée, les insurgés de la Catalogne ont établis là leur Junte, d'où ils donnent le mouvement au reste de la province. 2000 insurgés assiégeaient le fort de Figuéras. On y avait heureusement laissé 300 Français : ils

ont été o obligés de tirer beaucoup de coups de canon et de brûler
le village

Le g^al de division Reille, avec deux bataillons Toscans, a marché
sur Figuéras, l'a débloqué, le 6 du mois, et y a fait entrer une
grande quantité de vivres, dont on manquait. Le 10, il réunissait
sa division, qui arrivait de divers points de la France; il avait
déjà 6000 hommes, et il doit avoir aujourd'hui 9000 h^es; il doit
s'assurer de Roses et marcher sur Géronne, établir ses communications avec le général Duhesme et ensemble pacifier la
Catalogne.

Les forces réunies des généraux Duhesme et
   Reille s'élèvent donc à 22,000 h^es
Ainsi le corps des Pyrénées Occidentales est

fort de .	.	.	. 23,000
Celui d'Arragon, de	.	.	. 13,000
Celui de Catalogne, de	.	.	. 22,000

Total . 68,000 h^es.

Nous venons de faire connaître la situation de l'armée dans les
provinces de la Biscaye, de St. Ander, de la Castille, de la Navarre,
de l'Arragon, et de la Catalogne; c'est à dire, sur toute la frontière
de France.

Vaici actuellement la situation dans les autres points:

Les deux corps qui se sont rendus à Madrid sous les ordres du
général Dupont et du m^al Moncey portaient, et portent encore;
le premier, le nom de corps d'observation de la Gironde commandé
par le g^al Dupont; le second, le nom de corps d'observation des
Côtes de l'Océan, commandé par le m^al Moncey.

Le corps d'observation de la Gironde est composé de trois
divisions: deux sont en Andalousie avec le général Dupont; la
3eme, celle du général Frère, doit être à present, à San Clemente.

Le corps d'observation des Côtes de l'Océan est composé également de trois divisions. La première est avec le maréchal Moncey, sous Valence: les deux autres sont à Madrid, et disséminés
en différentes colonnes, pour maintenir la communication avec le
général Dupont. Les états de situation vous feront connaître la
force de ces divisions: mais on peut en général les considérer les
unes dans les autres comme fortes de 6000 hommes présens sous
les armes.

Il y a *à Madrid* deux bataillons de la garde, formant 1000 hommes, et à-peu-près 900 hommes de cavalerie de la garde.

Ainsi il y a *à Madrid*, et du côte *de Valence* et *de l'Andalousie*, la valeur de 40,000 hommes d'infanterie, huit mille hommes de cavalerie et 80 pièces de canon attelées.

Le général Junot a en Portugal trois divisions, formant présens sous les armes, compris son artillerie, sa cavalerie, 23 mille hommes.[*]

Telle est la situation de l'armée en Espagne et en Portugal.

1ere *Observation.*—Les événemens qui se passent aujoud'hui et demain amélioreront beaucoup la situation de toutes les affaires, en jettant dans la Galice le général Cuesta, en lui ôtant ses communications avec l'Estramadure, Madrid et l'Andalousie, en assurant notre communication avec le Portugal, et en assurant la soumission des provinces de Salamanque, Zamora, Toro, &^{a}.

La manière dont ces événemens auront lieu décideront à entrer sur le champ en Galice, à soumettre les Asturies, ou à différer encore quelques jours.

2e *Observation.*—La Navarre et la Biscaye se sont maintenues tranquilles.

En Arragon le plat pays a été soumis, les rebelles ont été battus plusieurs fois ; avec deux seuls bataillons, 8 à 10 mille insurgés ont été détruits ou dispersés ; le découragement est a dernier point parmi eux. Ils se sont défendus dans leurs maisons à Saragosse ; on les a bombardé ; on leur a fait beaucoup de mal ; on achève aujourd'hui de bloquer la ville en jettant un pont sur l'Ebre. Une fois cette ville soumise, il n'y a pas de doute que tout l'Arragon ne devienne tranquille. Une partie des troupes sera cependant nécessaire pour maintenir la province ; une petite partie pourra aider à la soumission de la Catalogne. La partie qui est nécessaire pour le bien du service du maréchal Bessières ira le rejoindre. Ainsi cet événement équivaudra à un secours considérable.

3eme *Observation.*—La première opération du général Reille a débloqué Figuéras : il soumet à présent tous les environs. Il ne tardera pas sans doute à s'emparer de Géronne et à établir sa communication par terre avec le général Duhesme. La reduction de Géronne éntamera probablement celle de Lerida ; on pourra avoir alors une colonne de dex trois, ou mille hommes, qu'on dirigera par Tortose sur Valence.

---

[*] *Note by the author.* This calculation was made under the supposition that general Avril had joined Dupont.

4ᵉᵐᵉ *Observation.*—On n'a point de nouvelles de l'expédition de Valence, et le maréchal Moncey a huit mille hommes. Avec ces forces il n'a rien à craindre. Il peut ne pas prendre la ville, qui est très grande, si les paysans s'y sont renfermés et ne craignent point de la ruiner : mas le mᵃˡ Moncey se maintiendra dans le plat pays, occupera les révoltés, qu'il empêchera de se porter ailleurs, et fera porter au pays tout le poids de la guerre.

5ᵉ *Observation.* — On compte que le général Dupont a aujourd'hui près de 20,000 hommes. Si les opérations du maréchal Bessières reussissent bien, il n'y aurapas d'inconvénient à appuyer encore le général Dupont et à lui permettre de reprendre l'offensive. Ainsi les deux points importans, et où on fera une véritable guerre réglée, sont la Galice et l'Andalousie, parceque les troupes du camp de St. Roche, de Cadiz, des Algarves, sont près de 25 mille hommes, qu'elles ont pris parti pour la sédition de Seville en Andalousie, et que tout ce qui était à Porto a pris parti pour les rebelles de Galice.

Le point le plus important de tous est celui du mᵃˡ Bessières, comme on l'a déjà vu dans la note qu'on a envoyé. On doit tout faire pour que ce corps n'éprouve aucun mouvement rétrograde, aucun échec ; celui du général Dupont vient après.

Les affaires de Saragosse sont au 3ᵉ ordre ; celles de Valence ne sont qu'au 4ᵐᵉ.

Violà la véritable situation des affaires militaires du royaume.

Il parait convenable de former dans l'Arragon une division de 10 à 12 mille hommes que pourra commander le gᵃˡ Verdier. Il devra correspondre directement avec l'état major du roi, avec le mᵃˡ Bessières (pour s'éntendre), avec le gᵃˡ Duhesme pur se concerter, et avec le général de la 11ᵉ division militaire, qui se tiendra à Bayonne, afin de connaître toujours la situation de cette frontière. Son commandement doit embrasser la Navarre et tout l'Arragon.

Alors l'armée sera composée du corps des Pyrénées Occidentales, de la division de l'Arragon (il est inutile d'en faire un corps), du corps de la Catalogne composé de trois divisions, y compris celle du général Reille, et des six division que forment les corps d'observation de la Gironde et des Côtes de l'Océan.

Cela fera à-peu-près 12 divisions réunies, et en outre un certain nombre de petites colonnes mobiles et de garnisons.

[Dictated by the emperor Napoleon.]

N°. III.

NOTE SUR LA POSITION ACTUELLE DE L'ARMÉE EN
ESPAGNE.

Bayonne, ce 21 *Juillet*, 1808.

1ere *Observation.*—La bataille de Medina del Rio Seco a mis
les affaires de l'armée dans la meilleure situation. Le maréchal
Bessières ne donne plus aucune inquiétude, et toutes les sollici-
tudes doivent se tourner du côté du général Dupont.

2de *Observation.*—Dans la position actuelle des affaires, l'armée
Française occupe le centre ; l'ennemi, un grand nombre de points
de la circonférence.

3me *Observation.*—Dans une guerre de cette nature, il faut du
sang froid, de la patience, et du calcul ; et il ne faut pas épuiser
les troupes en fausses marches et contremarches ; il ne faut pas
croire, quand on a fait une fausse marche de trois à quatre jours,
qu'on l'aie réparé par une contremarche : c'est ordinairement deux
fautes au lieu d'une.

4me *Observation.*—Toutes les opérations de l'armée ont réussies
jusqu'à cette heure, autant qu'elles devaient réussir. Le général
Dupont s'est maintenu au-delà des montagnes, et dans le bassin
de l'Andalousie ; trois fois il a défait les insurgés. Le maréchal
Moncey a défait les insurgés à Valence ; il n'a pas pu prendre la
ville, ce qui est une chose qui n'est pas extraordinaire. Peut-être
eût-on pu désirer qu'il eût pu se camper à une journée de la ville,
comme a fait le général Dupont ; mais, enfin, qu'il soit à une
journée ou à cinq, comme à Saint Clement, la différence n'est pas
très grande. En Arragon, on a battu sur tous les points, et dans
toutes les circonstances, l'ennemi, et porté le découragement partout.
Saragosse n'a pas été pris ; il est aujourd'hui cerné ; et une ville de
40 à 50 mille âmes, défendue par un mouvement populaire, ne se
prend qu'avec du tems et de la patience. Les histoires des guerres
sont pleines des catastrophes des plus considérables pour avoir
brusqué et s'être enfourré dans les rues étroites des villes. L'exemple de Buenos Ayres, et des 12 milles Anglais d'élite qui y ont
péri, en est une preuve.

5me *Observation.*—Ainsi la position de l'armée est bonne, le ma-

réchal Moncey étant à Saint Clément, ou environ, et les généraux
Gobert et Vedel réunis au général Dupont en Andalousie ; ce
serait une faute, à moins d'incidens et d'un emploi immédiat à
donner à ces troupes dans un autre point, que de concentrer toutes
les troupes trop près de Madrid. L'incertitude des événemens
du maréchal Bessières, et les 25 chances qu'il avoit contre lui
sur cent, pouvaient déterminer à faire arrêter la marche de toutes
les troupes qui s'éloignaient de la capitale, afin que les colonnes
pussent être rapellés à Madrid si le maréchal Bessières était battu,
et pussent arriver dans cette ville avant l'ennemi ; mais ce serait
une faute si on eût fait rétrograder ces colonnes, et si on eût agi
comme si le maréchal Bessières avait été battu, lorsque quelques
jours avant on agissait comme si l'armée de Galice n'existait pas.
500 chevaux et 1800 hommes d'infanterie dirigés sur Valladolid
étaient tous ce qu'il fallait. Si cette colonne était partie trois jours
plutôt, elle y serait arrivé le 15. Le maréchal Bessières a été
vainqueur, et avait pour être vainqueur 75 chances contre 25 ;
mais la fatigue qu'on a donné à l'armée, et les mouvemens rétro-
grades qu'on a ordonné inutilement, puisque même le maréchal
Bessières battu, on avait 8 à 10 jours pour réunir l'armée, ont
fait un mal moral et physique. Il faut espérer que la nouvelle de
la victoire arrivée à tems aura mis l'état major à même d'arrêter
tout mouvement sur Madrid, et que chaque colonne se trouvera
plus près du point où elle doit se trouver.

6me *Observation.*—Dans la situation actuelle des affaires, le plus
important de tous est le général Dupont. On doit lui envoyer le
reste de la division Gobert, et employer d'autres troupes pour maintenir la communication ; il faut tenir la tête de la division du
maréchal Moncey sur Saint Clement, et menacer toujours la province de Valence. Si le maréchal Bessières a battu sans effort et
avec peu de perte, l'armée de Galice, et a eu moins de huit milles
hommes engagés, il n'y a pas de doute qu'avec 20 milles le général
Dupont ne culbute tout ce qu'il a devant lui.

7me *Observation.*—La brigade du général Rey rend à l'armée plus
qu'elle n'a perdu par le dètachement qui a été fait sur Valladolid.
Toutes les probabilités humaines sont que le maréshal Bessières
n'a plus besoin d'aucun renfort, du moins pour être maître de toute
la Castille et du royaume de Léon. Ce n'est que lorsqu'on aura
reçu la nouvelle de ce qu'il aura fait à Bénévent et à Léon qu'on
pourra décider s'il doit attaquer la Galice.

8me *Observation.*—Le général Verdier, en Arragon, a cerné
Saragosse : le 14eme et le 44eme de ligne partent demain pour s'y
rendre. Les partis Français vont jusqu'à moitié chemin de Lerida,

de Barbastro, et de Jaca.   Dans dix jours toute l'artillerie sera
arrivée.   Cette belle et bonne brigade de troupes de ligne porte à
près de quinze mille hommes l'armée du général Verdier.   Il est
probable que Saragosse tombera bientôt, et que les deux tiers de
ces 15 milles hommes deviendront disponibles.

9eme *Observation.*—Ainsi le corps du maréchal Bessières a pris
l'offensive, il est depuis sa victoire renforcé de la brigade Lefebre
et de la brigade Gaulois ; il est donc dans le cas de conserver
l'offensive.   Le corps du général Verdier en Arragon a battu partout les insurgés, a cerné la ville avec des forces beaucoup moindres ;
il vient d'être considérablement renforcé ; ainsi il peut donner une
nouvelle activité aux opérations du siège, et conserver son activité
offensive sur les deux rives de l'Ebre.   Le corps de Catalogne a
joliment agi, ayant pour point d'appui Barcelonne, la jonction sera
faite aujourd'hui ou demain devant Géronne, avec le génl Reille.

10eme *Observation.*—Voilà pour les trois corps d'armée situés
du côte de la France.   La communication de Madrid avec la France
est importante sous tous les points de vue.   Il faut donc que les
colonne qui viennent d'être organisées à Burgos et à Vittoria et
qui seront journellement renforcées et augmentées, soient laissées
dans ces stations.

Ci joint la note de la formation de ces colonnes.   Elles sont
presque toutes composées de 3eme bataillons et de conscrits, mais
avec de bons cadres ; 15 à 20 jours de stations à Burgos et à
Vittoria les mettront à-peu-près à l'école de bataillon.   Ce serait
une très grande faute que de rapeller trop tôt ces troupes pour
en renforcer les cadres principaux ; il faut attendre jusqu'à ce
qu'on ait pu les remplacer à Vittoria et à Burgos par de nouvelles
troupes.

11eme *Observation.*—Il n'y a donc rien à craindre du côté du
maréchal Bessiéres, ni dans le nord de la Castille, ni dans le
royame de Léon.

Il n'y a rien à craindre en Arragon ; Saragosse tombera un jour
plus tôt ou un jour plus tard.

Il n'y a rien à craindre en Catalogne.

Il n'y a rien à craindre pour les communications de Burgos à
Bayonne, moyennant les deux colonnes organisées dans ces deux
villes, et qui seront renforcées.   S'il y avait des événemens en
Biscaye, la force qui se réunit à Bayonne, formant une réserve,
seroit suffisante pour mettre tout en ordre.

S'il arrive à Burgos quelque événement trop considérable pour
que la colonne mobile qui est à Burgos puisse y mettre ordre, le

maréchal Bessières ne sera pas assez loin pour ne pouvoir faire un détachement.

Le général Monthion a la surveillance de toutes les Biscayes. Le général Bonnet à Burgos est chargé de maintenir la communication de Vittoria avec le maréchal Bessières et avec Madrid. Il est nécessaire que ces deux généraux correspondent tous les jours entr'eux et avec le général Drouet, qui est laissé en réserve à Bayonne, de même que le gén[l] Verdier de Saragosse et le gén[l] Dagoult de Pampelune doivent correspondre tous les jours avec le général Drouet à Bayonne, et avec Madrid, par le canal de Bayonne et de Vittoria : jusqu'à ce que les communications directes soient rétablies, un courier partant de Madrid peut se rendre par Vittoria, Tolosa, Pampelune, devant Saragosse. Le seul point important donc aujourd'hui est le général Dupont. Si l'ennemi parvenait jamais à s'emparer des défilés de la Sierra Morena, il serait difficile de l'en chasser; il faut donc renforcer le gén[l] Dupont, de manière qu'il ait 25 mille hommes, compris ce qu'il faudra pour garder les passages des montagnes et une partie du chemin de La Manche. Il pourra disposer les troupes de manière que le jour où il voudra attaquer, la brigade de deux à trois mille hommes, destinée à garder les montagnes, arrive au camp du gén[l] Dupont à marches forcées, et soit successivement remplacée par les colonnes qui seraient en arrière, de sorte que le gén[l] Dupont ait pour le jour de la bataille plus de 23 mille hommes à mettre en ligne.

Une fois qu'ou aura bien battu l'ennemi, une partie des troupes se dissipera, et selon que la victoire sera plus ou moins decidée, on pourra faire continuer le mouvement à d'autres troupes sur le général Dupont.

12[e ne] *Observation.*—Saragosse pris, on aura des troupes disponibles, soit pour renforcer l'armée de Catalogne, soit pour marcher sur Valenne de concert avec le maréchal Moncey, soit pour renforcer le maréchal Bessières et marcher en Galice, si après la victoire qu'il a déjà remporté, et celle qu'il remportera à Léon, il ne croit pas assez fort pour s'y porter d'abord.

13eme *Observation.*—Il serait important de choisir deux points intermédiaires entre Andujar et Madrid, pour pouvoir y laisser garnison permanente, un commandant, un dépôt de cartouches, munitions, canons, magasins de biscuit, des fours, du farine, et un hôpital, de sorte que 3 à 400 hommes défendent le magasin et l'hôpital contre tout une insurrection. Il est difficile de croire qu'il n'y ait point quelque château ou donjon, pouvant être retranché promptement et propre à cela. C'est par ce seul moyen qu'on peut raccourcir la ligne d'opération, et être sûr d'avoir toutes les trois ou quatre grandes marches, une manutention et un point de repos.

14eme *Observation.*—En résumé, le partage de l'armée paraît devoir être celui-ci :

Corps de Catalogne, tel qu'il existe à-peu-près .	20,000 h^{es}
Corps d'Arragon, tel qu'il existe à-peu-près, 15 mille hommes, jusqu'à ce que Saragosse soit prit	15,000

Corps du maréchal Bessières, ce qu'il a

à-peu-près . . .	17,000	
Colonne de Burgos . .	2,000	
Colonne de Vittoria . .	2,000	
Garnison de St. Sébastien . .	1,500	
Corps d'Aranda . . .	1,000	

Total du corps du mar^l Bessiéres . 24,000 h^{es}

Après le prise de Saragosse, lorsque les affaires de Catalogne seront un peu appaisées, on pourra, selon les circonstances, ou renforcer le maréchal Bessières, ou renforcer le général Dupont, ou entrependre l'opération de Valence.

Aujourd'hui, le seul point qui menace, où il faut promptement avoir un succès, c'est du côté du général Dupont, avec 25 mille hommes, infanterie, cavalerie, et artillerie comprise : il a beaucoup plus qu'il ne faut pour avoir de grands résultats ; à la rigueur, avec 21 mille hommes présens sur le champ de bataille, il peut hardiment prendre l'offensive, il ne sera pas battu, et il aura pour lui plus de 80 chances.

[Dictated by Napoleon.]

No. IV.

NOTE SUR LES AFFAIRES D'ESPAGNE.

St. Cloud, ce 30 Août, 1808.

1ere *Observation.*—Dans la position de l'armée d'Espagne on a à craindre d'être attaqué sur la droite par l'armée de Galice, sur le centre par l'armée venant de Madrid, sur la gauche par l'armée venant de Saragosse et Valence. Ce serait une grande faute que de laisser l'armée de Saragosse et de Valence prendre position à Tudela.

Tudela doit être occupée, parceque c'est une position honorable, et Milagro une position obscure.

Tudela est sur les communications de Pampelune, a un beau
pont en pierre, et est l'aboutissant d'un canal sur Saragosse.
C'est une position offensive sur Saragosse telle que l'ennemi ne
peut pas la négliger; cette position seule couvre la Navarre.   En
gardant Tudela, on garde une grande quantité de bateaux, qui
nous seront bientôt nécessaires pour le siège de Saragosse.

Si l'ennemi était maître de Tudela, toute la Navarre s'insurgerait, l'ennemie pourrait arriver à Estella, en négligeant la position de Milagro et en coupant la communication avec Pampelune.

D'Estella il serait sur Tolosa; il y serait sans donner le tems
de faire les dispositions convenables; il n'est pas à craindre, au
contraire, que l'ennemi fasse aucune opération sur Pampelune;
tant que nous aurons Tudela, il serait lui-même coupé sur Saragosse.

Le général qui commande à Tudela peut couvrir les hauteurs
de redoutes; si c'est une armée d'insurgés, s'en approcher et la
battre, la tenir constamment sur la défensive par les reconnois-
sances et ses mouvemens sur Saragosse.

Et si, au lieu de cela, une partie de l'armée de ligne Espagnole
marchait sur Tudela, le général Français repassera l'Ebre, s'il y
est forcé, disputera le terrein sur Pampelune, et donnera le tems
au général en chef de l'armée Française de prendre ses mesures.
Ce corps d'observation remplira alors son but, et aucune opération
prompte sur Tolosa ni Estella n'est à craindre.

Au lieu qu'en occupant la position de Milagro, l'ennemi sera
à Estella, le même jour qu'on l'apprendra au quartier-général.
Si on occupe Tudela, il faut s'y aider de redoutes, et s'y établir,
n'y conserver aucune espèce d'embarras, et les tenir tous dans
Pampelune. Si l'ennemi l'occupe, il faut l'en chasser, et s'y
établir; car dans l'ordre défensif, ce serait une grande faute, qui
entraînerait de fâcheuses conséquences.

2e *Observation.*—La position de Burgos était également importante à tenir, comme ville de haute réputation, comme centre de
communication et de rapports.

De là des partis non seulement de cavalerie, mais encore de
deux ou de trois mille hommes d'infanterie, et même quatre ou
cinq mille hommes en échelons, peuvent poster les premières
patrouilles d'housards dans toutes les directions jusqu'à deux
marches, et parfaitement informés de tout ce qui se fait, en
instruire le quartier-général, de manière que si l'ennemi se pré-
sente en force sur Burgos, les différentes divisions puissent à temps
s'y porter pour le soutenir et livrer la bataille, ou si cela n'est pas

jugé convenable, éclairer les mouvemens de l'ennemi, lui laisser
croire qu'on veut se porter sur Burgos, et pouvoir ensuite faire sa
retraite pour se porter ailleurs.

Un corps de 12 à 15 mille hommes ne prend-il pas 20 positions
dans la journée au seul commandement d'un adjudant major? et
nos troupes seraient-elles devenues des levées en masse, qu'il
faudroit placer 15 jours d'avance dans les positions où on voudroit
qu'elles se battent?

Si cela eût été jugé ainsi, le corps du maréchal Bessières eût
pris la position de Miranda ou de Briviesca; mais lorsque l'ennemi
est encore à Madrid, lorsqu'on ignore où est l'armée de Galice, et
qu'on a le soupçon que les rebelles pourront employer une partie
de leurs efforts contre le Portugal, prendre, au lieu d'une position
menaçante, offensive, honorable, comme Burgos, une position
honteuse, borgne comme Trevino, c'est dire à l'ennemi, " Vous
n'avez rein à craindre; portez vouz ailleurs; nous avons fait nos
dispositions pour aller plus loin, ou bien nous avons choisi un
champ de bataille pour nous battre; venez ici, vous ne craignez
pas d'être inquiétés." Mais que fera le général Français, si l'on
marche demain sur Burgos? laissera-t-il prendre par 6,000 insurgés
la citadelle de cette ville, ou si les Français ont laissés garnison
dans le château (car on ignore la position et la situation de l'armée),
comment une garnison de 4, 6, ou 800 hommes se retira-t-elle
dans une si vaste plaine? Et dès lors c'est comme s'il n'y avoit
rien: l'ennemi maître de cette citadelle, on ne la reprendra plus.

Si, au contraire, on veut garder la citadelle, on veut donc
livrer bataille à l'ennemi; car cette citadelle ne peut pas tenir plus
de trois jours; et si on veut livrer bataille à l'ennemi, pourquoi le
ma¹ Bessières abandonne-t-il le terrein où on veut livrer bataille?

Ces dispositions paraissent mal raisonnées, et quand l'ennemi
marchera on fera essuyer à l'armée un affront qui démoralisera
les troupes, n'y eût-il que des corps légers ou des insurgés qui
marchassent.

En résumé, la position de Burgos devait être gardée; tous les
jours à trois heures du matin on devait être sous les armes, et à
une heure du matin il devait partir des reconnaissances dans toutes
les directions. On devait ainsi recueillir des nouvelles à huit ou
dix lieues à la ronde, pour qu'on pût prendre ensuite le parti que
les circonstances indiqueraient.

C'est la première fois qu'il arrive à une armée de quitter toutes
les positions offensives, pour se mettre dans de mauvaises positions
défensives, d'avoir l'air de choisir des champs de bataille, lorsque

l'éloignement de l'ennemi, les mille et une combinaisons différentes qui peuvent avoir lieu, ne laissent point la probabilité de prévoir si la bataille aura lieu à Tudela, entre Tudela et Pampelune, entre Soria et l'Ebre, ou entre Burgos et Miranda.

La position de Burgos, tenue en force et d'une manière offensive, menace Palencia, Valladolid, Aranda, Madrid même. Il faut avoir longtems fait la guerre pour la concevoir; il faut avoir entrepris un grand nombre d'opérations offensives pour savoir comme le moindre événement ou indice encourage ou décourage, décide une opération ou une autre.

En deux mots, si 15 mille insurgés entrent dans Burgos, se retranchent dans la ville, et occupent le château, il faut calculer une marche de plusieurs jours pour pouvoir s'y poster et reprendre la ville; ce qui ne sera pas sans quelque inconvénient; si pendant ce tems-là la véritable attaque est sur Logrono ou Pampelune, on aura fait des contremarches inutiles, qui auront fatigué l'armée; et enfin, si l'ennemi occupe Logrono, Tudela, et Burgos, l'armée Française serait dans une triste et mauvaise position.

Quand on tient à Burgos de la cavalerie sans infanterie, n'est-ce pas dire à l'ennemi qu'on ne veut pas y tenir; n'est-ce pas l'engager à y venir? Burgos a une grande influence dans le monde par son nom, dans la Castille parceque c'en est la capitale, dans les opérations parcequ'elle donne une communication directe avec St. Ander. Il n'est pas permis à 300 lieues, et n'ayant pas même un état de situation de l'armée, de prescrire ce qu'on doit faire; mais on doit dire que si aucune force majeure ne l'empêche, il faut occuper Burgos et Tudela.

Le corps détaché de Tudela a son mouvement assuré sur Pampelune, a le rôle de garder la Navarre, a ses ennemis à tenir en échec, Saragosse et tous les insurgés. Il était plus que suffisant pour surveiller Tudela, l'Ebre, et Pampelune, pour dissiper les rassemblemens s'il n'y avait que des insurgés, contenir l'ennemi, donner des renseignemens, et retarder la marche sur Pampelune. Si, au lieu des insurgés, c'est l'armée ennemie qui marche de ce côté, il suffit encore pour donner le tems à l'armée de Burgos, à celle de Miranda, de marcher réunie avec 36 mille hommes, soit pour prendre l'offensive, soit pour prendre en flanc l'ennemi qui marche sur Pampelune, soit pour se replier et rentrer dans la Navarre, si toute l'armée ennemie avait pris cette direction.

Si ces observations paraissent bonnes et qu'on les adopte, que l'ennemi n'ait encore montré aucun plan, il faut que le général qui commande le corps de Saragosse fasse construire quelques redoutes autour de Tudela, pour favoriser ses champs de bataille, réunisse des vivres de tous les côtés, et soit là dans une position offensive sur Saragosse en maintenant sa communication avec Logroño par sa droite, mais au moins par la rive gauche de l'Ebre. Il faut que le maréchal Bessières, avec tout son corps, renforcé de la cavalerie légère, soit campé dans le bois près Burgos, la citadelle bien occupée; que tous les hôpitaux, les dépôts, les embarras soient au delà de l'Ebre; qu'il soit là en position de manœuvrer, tous les jours, à trois heures du matin, sous les armes, jusqu'au retour de toutes les reconnaissances, et éclairant le pays dans la plus grande étendue; que le corps du ma^l Moncey soit à Miranda et à Briviesca, tous ses embarras et hôpitaux derrière Vittoria, toujours en bataille avant le jour, et envoyant des reconnaissances sur Soria et les autres directions de l'ennemi.

Il ne faut pas perdre de vue que les corps des maréchaux Bessières et Moncey devant être réunis, il faut se lier le moins possible avec Logroño, et cependant considérer le corps du général Lefebre comme un corps détaché, qui a une ligne d'opération particulière sur Pampelune et un rôle séparé; vouloir conserver Tudela comme une partie contigue de la ligne, c'est se disséminer beaucoup. Enfin, faire la guerre, c'est à dire, avoir des nouvelles par les curés, les alcades, les chefs de couvent, les principaux propriétaires, les postes: on sera alors parfaitement informé.

Les reconnaissances qui tous les jours se dirigeront du côté de Soria, de Burgos, sur Palencia, et du côté d'Aranda, peuvent former tous les jours trois postes d'interception, trois rapports d'hommes arrêtés, qu'on traitera bien, et qu'on relachera quand ils auront donné les renseignemens qu'on désire. On verra alors venir l'ennemi, on pourra réunir toutes ses forces, lui dérober des marches, et tomber sur ses flancs au moment où il méditera un projet offensif.

3me *Observation.*—L'armée Espagnole d'Andalousie était peu nombreuse. Toutes les Gazettes Anglaises, et les rapports de l'officier Anglais qui était au camp, nous le prouvent. L'inconcevable ineptie du général Dupont, sa profonde ignorance des calculs d'un général en chef, son tâtonnement, l'ont perdu: 18 mille hommes ont posé les armes, six mille seulement se sont battus, et encore ces 6000 hommes que le gen^l Dupont a fait battre à la point du jour, après les avoir fait marcher toute la nuit, étaient un contre trois. Malgré tout cela, l'ennemi s'est si mal battu, qu'il n'a pas fait un prisonnier, pris une pièce de canon, gagné un pouce de terrain, et l'armée de Dupont est restée intacte dans sa position: ce qui sans doute a été un malheur; car il eût mieux

valu que cette division eût été mise en déroute, éparpillée, et
détruite, puisque les divisions Vedel et Dufour, au lieu de se
rendre par la capitulation, auraient fait leur retraite.   Comment
ces deux divisions ont-elles été comprises dans la capitulation ?
c'est par la lacheté insultante et l'imbécillité des hommes qui
ont négocié, et qui porteront sur l'échaffaud la peine de ce grand
crime national.

Ce que l'on vient de dire prouve que les Espagnols ne sont pas à
craindre ; toutes les forces Espagnoles ne sont pas capables de
culbuter 25 mille Français, dans une position raisonnable.

Depuis le 12 jusqu'au 19, le général Dupont n'a fait que des
bétises, et malgré tout cela, s'il n'avait pas fait la faute de se
séparer de Vedel, et qu'il eût marché avec lui, les Espagnols
aurarient été battus et culbutès.   A la guerre les hommes ne sont
rien, c'est un homme qui est tout.   Jusqu'à cette heure nous
n'avons trouvé ces exemples que dans l'histoire de nos ennemis :
aujourd'hui, il est fâcheux que nous puissions les trouver dans la
nôtre.

Une rivière, fût-elle aussi large que la Vistule, aussi rapide que
le Danube à son embouchure, n'est rien si on n'a des débouchés
sur l'autre rive, et une tête prompte à reprendre l'offensive.   Quand
à l'Ebre, c'est moins que rien ; on ne la regarde que comme une
trace.

Dans toutes ces observations, on a parlé dans la position où se
trouvait l'armée du 20 au 26, lorsqu'elle n'avait nulle part nouvelle
de l'ennemi.

Si on continue à ne prendre aucune mesure pour avoir des nouvelles, on n'apprendra que l'armée de ligne Espagnole est arrivée
sur Tudela et Pampelune, qu'elle est sur les communications, sur
Tolosa, que lorsqu'elle y sera déjà rendue.   On a fait connaître
dans la note précédente comment on faisait à la guerre pour avoir
des nouvelles.   Si la position de Tudela est occupée par l'ennemi,
on ne voit pas que l'Ebre soit tenable.   Comment a-t-on évacué
Tudela, lorsqu'on avait mandé dans des notes précédentes qu'il
fallait garder ce point, et que l'opinion même des généraux qui
venaient de Saragosse était d'occuper cette importante position ?

[Dictated by Napoleon.]

No. V.

NOTE SUR LES AFFAIRES D'ESPAGNE.

St. Cloud, Août, 1808.

1ere *Observation.*—Tudela est importante sous plusieurs points de vue: il a un pont sur l'Ebre, et protège parfaitement la Navarre : c'est le point d'intersection du canal qui va à Saragosse.

Les convois d'artillerie et de vivres mettent pour se rendre de Pampelune à Tudela trois jours, de Tudela à Saragosse trois jours. Mais en se servant du canal, on va de Tudela à Saragosse en 14 heures. Lorsque donc les vivres, les hôpitaux, sont à Tudela, c'est comme s'ils étaient à Saragosse.

La première opération que doit faire l'armée lorsqu'elle reprendra son système d'offensif, et qu'elle sera forte de tous ses moyens, ce doit être d'invester et de prendre Saragosse ; et si cette ville résiste comme elle l'a fait la première fois, en donner un exemple qui retentisse dans toute l'Espagne.

Une vingtaine de pièces de 12 de campagne, une vingtaine d'obusiers de six pièces de campagne, une douzaine de mortiers, et une douzaine de pièces de 16 et de 24, parfaitement approvisionée, seront nécessaires, ainsi que des mineurs pour remplir ce but.

Il n'est aucun de ces bouches de feu qui doive consommer son approvisionnement de campagne.

Un approvisionnement extraordinaire de 80 mille coups de canon, bombes ou obus, parait nécessaire pour prendre cette ville.

Il faudrait donc, pour ne pas retarder la marche de la grande armée, 15 jours avant qu'elle ne puisse arriver, commencer le transport de Pampelune à Tudela, et que dans les 48 heures après l'investissement de Saragosse, l'artillerie y arrivât sur des bâteaux, de manière que quatre jours après on pût commencer trois attaques à la fois, et avoir cette ville en peu de jours, ce qui serait une partie des succès, en y employant 25 à 30 mille hommes, ou plus s'il était nécessaire.

On suppose que, si l'ennemi a pris position entre Madrid et Burgos, il aura été battu.

Il faut donc occuper Tudela. Ce point est tellement important qu'il serait à désirer qu'on pût employer un mois à le fortifier et à s'y retrancher, de manière qu'un millier d'hommes avec 8 à 10 pièces de canon s'y trouvassent en sureté et à l'abri de toutes les insurrections possibles. Il ne faut pas surtout souffrir que les révoltés s'y retranchassent ; ce serait deux sièges au lieu d'une ; et il serait impossible de prendre Saragosse avant d'avoir Tudela, à cause du canal.

On trouvera ci-joint des observations du colonel Lacoste sur Tudela ; puisque les localités empêchent de penser à le fortifier, il eût été utile de l'occuper au lieu de Milagro, qui n'aboutit à rien.

2de. Soria n'est je crois qu'à deux petites marches des positions actuelles de l'armée. Cette ville s'est constamment mal comportée. Une expédition qui se porterait sur Soria, la désarmerait, en prendrait une trentaine d'hommes des plus considérables, qu'on enverrait en France pour ôtages, et qui enfin lui ferait fournir des vivres pour l'armée, serait d'un bon effet.

3me. Une troisième opération qui serait utile serait l'occupation de St. Ander. Il serait bien avantageux qu'elle pût se faire par la route directe de Bilbao à St. Ander.

4me. Il faut s'occuper de désarmer la Biscaye et la Navarre ; c'est un point important ; tout Espagnol pris les armes à la main doit être fusillé.

Il faut veiller sur la fabrique d'armes de Placencia, ne point laisser travailler les ouvriers pour les rebelles.

Le fort de Pancorvo doit être armé et fortifié avec la plus grande activité. Il doit y avoir dans ce fort des fours, des magasins de bouches et de guerre. Situé presqu'à mi-chemin de Bayonne à Madrid, c'est une poste intermédiaire pour l'armée, et un point d'appui pour les opérations de la Galicie.

Il y a dans l'armée plus de généraux qu'il n'en faut ; deux seraient nécessaires au corps qui était sous Saragosse. Les généraux de division La Grange, Belliard, et Grandjean sont sans emploi, et tous trois bons généraux.

Il faut renvoyer, le plus promptement possible, le régiment et le général Portugais pour joindre leurs corps à Grenobles, où il doit se former.

5me. On ne discutera pas ici si la ligne de l'Ebre est bonne, si elle a la configuration requise pour être défendue avec avantage.

On discutera encore moins si on eût pu ne pas évacuer Madrid, conserver la ligne du Duero, ou prendre une position qui eût couvert le siège de Saragosse et eût permis d'attendre que cette ville fût prise ; toutes ces questions sont oiseuses.

Nous nous contenterons de dire, puisqu'on a pris la ligne de l'Ebre, que les troupes s'y desout et s'y reposent, qu'elle a au moins l'avantage que le pays est plus sain, étant plus élevé, et qu'on peut y attendre que les chaleurs soient passées.

Il faut surtout ne point quitter cette ligne sans avoir un projet déterminé, qui ne laisse aucune incertitude dans les opérations à suivre. Ce serait un grand malheur de quitter cette ligne pour être ensuite obligé de la reprendre.

A la guerre les trois quarts sont des affaires morales ; la balance des forces réelles n'est que pour un autre quart.

6me. En gardant la ligne de l'Ebre il faut que le général ait bien prévu tout ce que l'ennemi peut faire dans tous les hypothèses.

L'ennemi peut se présenter devant Burgos, partir de Soria, et marcher sur Logroño, ou, en partant de Saragosse, se porter sur

Estella, et menacer ainsi Tolosa. Il faut, dans tous ces hypothèses, qu'il n'y ait point un long tems perdu en délibérations, qu'on puisse se ployer de sa droite à sa gauche, et de sa gauche à sa droite, sans faire aucun sacrifice : car dans les manœuvres combinées, les tâtonnemens, l'irrésolution qui naissent des nouvelles contradictoires qui se succèdent rapidement, conduisent à des malheurs.

Cette diversion de Saragosse sur Tolosa est une des raisons qui a longtems fait penser que la position de Tudela devait être gardée, soit sur la rive droite, soit avec la faculté de repasser sur la rive gauche. Elle est offensive sur Sarragosse, elle previent à tems de tous les mouvemens qui pourraient se faire de ce côté.

7me. Une observation qu'il n'est pas hors de propos de faire ici c'est, que l'ennemi, qui a intérêt de masquer ses forces, en cachant le véritable point de son attaque, opère de manière que le coup qu'il veut porter n'est jamais indiqué d'une manière positive, et le général ne peut deviner que par la connaissance bien approfondie de sa position, et la manière dont il fait entrer son système offensif, pour protéger et garantir son système défensif.

8me. On n'a point de renseignemens sur ce que fait l'ennemi. On dit toujours qu'on ne peut pas avoir des nouvelles, comme si cette position était, extraordinaire dans une armée, comme si on trouvait ordinairement des espions. Il faut en Espagne, comme partout ailleurs, envoyer des parties qui enlèvent tantôt le curé ou l'alcalde, tantôt un chef de couvent ou le maître de poste, et surtout toutes les lettres ; quelquefois le maître de la poste, aux douanes, ou celui qui en fait les fonctions ; on les met aux arrêts jusqu'à ce qu'ils parlent, en les faisant interroger deux fois par jour ; on les garde en ôtage, et on les charge d'envoyer des piétons, et de donner des nouvelles.

Quand on saura prendre des mesures de force et de vigueur, on aura des nouvelles ; il faut intercepter toutes les postes, toutes les lettres.

Le seul motif d'avoir des nouvelles peut déterminer à faire un gros détachement de quatre à cinq milles hommes, qui se portent dans une grande ville, prennent les lettres à la poste, se saissisent des citoyens les plus aisés de leurs lettres, papiers, gazettes, etc.

Il est hors de doute que même dans la ligne des Français les habitans sont tous informés de ce qui se passe : à plus forte raison hors de la ligne. Qui empêche donc, qu'on prenne les hommes marquans, et qu'on les renvoye ensuite sans les maltraiter ?

Il est donc de fait, lorsqu'on n'est point dans un désert, et qu'on est dans un pays peuplé, que si le général n'est pas instruit, c'est qu'il n'a pas su prendre les mesures convenables pour l'être.

Les services que les habitans rendent à un général ennemi, ils ne le font jamais par affection, ni même pour avoir de l'argent; les plus réels qu'on obtient c'est pour avoir de sauve-gardes, et de protections; c'est pour conserver ses biens, ses jours, sa ville, son monastère.

[The original of the following memoir is a rough draft, written by king Joseph. It has many erasures and interlineations, and was evidently composed to excuse his retreat from Madrid. The number of the French troops was undoubtedly greater than is here set down, unless the infantry alone be meant.]

No. VI.

Lorsqu'on a quitté Madrid à la nouvelle de *la défection* d'un corps de vingt-deux mille hommes, il y avoit dans Madrid dix-sept mille hommes, au corps du maréchal Bessières quinze mille cinq cent, au corps de Saragosse onze mille sept cent: l'armée se composait donc de quarante-cinq mille hommes; mais ces trois corps étaient distans entre eux de près de cent lieues.   La première idée fut de réunir le corps de Madrid à celui de Léon, à Burgos, et par suite d'entrer en communication avec celui de Saragosse, avec lequel l'état major de Madrid n'avait jamais eu aucune relation directe, et dont il ignorait absolument la situation et la composition.

Vingt jours après sa sortie de Madrid le roi s'est trouvé à la tête d'une armée de cinquante mille hommes.   Le feu de la sédition n'a pas pu se communiquer sur les points parcourus par les trois corps d'armée alors réunis; les communications avec la France ont été gardées; l'insurrection de Bilbao a été éteinte dans le sang de 1200 insurgés.   Peu de jours après, 20,000 d'entre eux réunis à 60 lieues delà, à Tudela, à l'autre extremité de la ligne, ont été dispersés et poursuivis rigoureusement.   Les provinces de la Biscaye, de Burgos, et le royaume de Navarre ont été contenus. Une organisation intérieure a préparé les moyens de nourrir l'armée, d'approvisionner les places de Pampelune, St. Sébastien, les forts de Pancorvo et de Burgos, en rendant le moins insupportable possible à ces provinces cette charge évidemment disproportionnée à leurs moyens.

Le matériel de l'artillerie a été réparé et mis en état d'agir, l'armée réorganisée, les hommes et les chevaux sont aujourd'hui en bon état.

C'est ainsi que s'est passé le mois d'Août et partie de Septembre.   Les renforts arrivés de France ont à peine indemnisé l'armée des pertes qu'elle a éprouvées par les maladies et le siège de Saragosse.

Voici sa force, et son organisation actuelle :

Le corps de droite, commandé par m^r le mar^{al} Bessières, est forte de 18,000 hommes.

Celui de gauche, commandé par m^r le mar^{al} Moncey, est de 18,000 hommes.

Celui du centre, aux ordres de m^r le mar^{al} Ney, est de onze mille hommes.

La réserve du roi est de quatre mille hommes.[*]

Le corps de droite occupe le pays depuis Burgos jusqu'à Pancorvo, et Ponte de Lara.

Le corps de gauche depuis Tudela jusqu'à Logroño.

Le corps du centre depuis Logroño jusqu'à Haro.

La réserve Miranda.

La nouvelle position prise par l'armée depuis que les événemens de l'Andalousie avaient fait présager une guerre réelle en Espagne, était évidemment commandée par les simples notions de la saine raison, qui ne pouvait permettre sa séparation á plus de dix jours de marche, de trois corps d'armée, dont le plus fort n'arrivait pas à 18,000 hommes, au milieu d'une nation de onze millions d'habitans, qui se déclarait ennemi, et se mettait universellement en état de guerre.

Cinquante mille Français ont pu se tenir avec succès sur une ligne de plus de 60 lieues, gardant les deux grandes communications de Burgos et de Tudela contre des ennemis qui n'ont pu jusqu'ici porter sur l'un ou l'autre de ces points plus de 25,000 hommes ; puisque 15,000 Français pouvaient être réunis sur l'une ou l'autre de ces deux communications principales en 24 heures.

Si les corps d'armée dirigés sur l'Espagne devaient arriver dans le mois de Septembre, ce système défensif et offensif à la fois se continuerait avec avantage, puisqu'il tend à refaire l'armée, à attendre celle qui doit arriver, et continue à menacer l'ennemi ; mais il ne saurait se prolonger jusqu'au mois de Novembre. L'ennemi n'a pu rester trois mois sans faire de grands progrès ; bientôt il sera en état de prendre l'offensif avec de grands corps organisés, obéissans à une administration centrale, qui aura eu le tems de se former à Madrid. Tout nous annonce que le mois d'Octobre est une de ces époques décisives qui donne à celui qui

---

[*] On ne comprend pas dans ces calculs les garnisons de Pampelune, St. Sébastien, Vittoria, Tolosa, Bilbao, &c. : il n'est pas question non plus de l'armée de Catalogne.

sait s'en emparer la priorité des mouvemens et des succès dont la
progression est inealculable.

Quel est le parti à prendre dans la position où se trouve l'armée,
et avec l'assurance qu'elle a ? de voir entrer en Espagne dans le
mois de Novembre deux cent mille Français.

Six manières de voir se présentent à l'esprit.

1ere. D'essayer de rester encore dans l'état où l'on est.

Ce systême est évidemment insoutenable.   De Tudela à Burgos
et à Bilbao il y a plus de 60 lieues.   L'ennemi pourra attaquer la
gauche de cette ligne avec quarante mille hommes, la droite avec
quarante mille hommes, le centre avec des forces égales.   Tudela
et la Navarre jusqu'à Logroño demandent 25,000 hommes pour
être défendues.   Burgos ne peut être défendue que par une armée
en état de résister aux forces réunis de MM. Blake, Cuesta,
qui peuvent presenter 80,000 hommes.   Il est douteux que les
20,000 bayonettes qu'il serait possible de leur présenter puissent les
battre complètement.   Si le succès est douteux, ces 20,000 hommes
seront harcelés par les insurgés, qui pourront alors soulever les trois
provinces, les séparer totalement d'avec le corps de gauche et de la
France.

2de. Porter le corps du centre et la réserve par Tudela au devant
de l'ennemi sur la route de Saragosse, ou sur celle d'Albazan ; on
réunirait ainsi 30,000 hommes, on chercherait l'ennemi, et nul
doute on le battrait si on le rencontrait de ce côté.

Le maréchal Bessières serait chargé d'observer la grande communication de Burgos à Miranda, laisserait garnison dans le château
de Burgos, dans le fort de Pancorvo, occuperait l'ennemi, surveil-
lerait les mouvemens des montagnes de Reynosa, les débarquemens
possibles de Santander.   Sa tâche serait difficile si l'on considère
que le défilé de Pancorvo n'est pas le seul accessible à l'artillerie,
qu'à trois lieues de là on arrive sur Miranda par une route praticable
à l'artillerie, que quelques lieues plus loin l'Ebre offre un troisième
passage sur le point de la chaine qu'il traverse entre Haro et
Miranda.

3eme. Laisser le maréchal Moncey à la défense de la Navarre, et
se porter avec le corps du centre et la réserve sur Burgos.   Réuni
au maréchal Bessières on pourroit chercher l'ennemi, et attaquer
avec avantage, on marcherait à lui avec trente mille hommes, et on
n'attendrait pas qu'il fût réuni avec toutes ses forces. Il serait peut-
être possible de donner pour instruction au maréchal Moncey, dans
le cas où il serait débordé sur sa gauche, et qu'il ne verrait pas
probabilité de battre l'ennemi, de faire un mouvement par sa droite,
et se porter par Logroño sur Briviesca, où il se réunirait au reste de

l'armée. Dans ce cas, la Navarre s'insurgerait, les communications avec la France seraient coupées, mais l'armée réunie dans la plaine serait assez forte pour attendre les corps qui arrivent de France, et qui seront asses forts pour pénétrer partout. Il serait aussi possible que, dans tous les cas, le maréchal Moncey se maintienne dans le camp retranché de Pampelune; manœuvrant autour de cette place, il y attendrait le résultat des opérations des deux corps d'armée qui auraient été au devant de l'ennemi dans la plaine de Burgos, et l'arrivée des corps de la grand armée.

4eme. Passer l'Ebre, et chercher à amener l'ennemi à une bataille dans la plaine qui est entre Vittoria et l'Ebre.

5eme. Se retirer, appuyant sa gauche sur Pampelune, et sa droite sur les montagnes de Mondragone.

6eme. Laisser une garnison en état de se défendre pendant six semaines à Pampelune, St. Sébastien, Pancorvo, et Burgos, réunir le reste de l'armée, marcher à la rencontre de l'ennemi sur l'une ou l'autre des grandes communications, le battre partout où on le trouverait, attendre, ou près de Madrid, ou dans le pays où les mouvemens de l'ennemi et la possibilité de vivre aurait porté l'armée, les troupes de France; on abandonnerait ses derrières, ses communications; mais la grande armée serait assez forte pour en ouvir pour elle-même. Et quant à l'armée qui est en Espagne, réunie ainsi elle serait en état de braver tous les efforts, de déconcerter tous les projets de l'ennemi, et d'attendre dans une noble attitude le mouvement général qui sera imprimé par votre majesté lors de l'arrivée de toutes les troupes dans ce pays.

De tous les projets le dernier parait préférable; il est plus noble et aussi sûr que le 5eme.

Ces deux projets sont seuls absolument offensifs ou absolument défensifs. On peut les regarder, l'un et l'autre, comme propres à assurer la conservation de armée jusqu'à l'arrivée des renforts. Le dernier a sur l'autre l'avantage d'arrêter le progrès de l'ordre nouveau qui s'établit en Espagne; il est plus digne des troupes Françaises, et du frère de votre majesté. Il est aussi sûr que celui de la sévère et honteuse défensive proposée par l'article cinq. Je l'ai communiqué au maral Jourdan et au maral Ney, qui l'un et l'autre sont de cet avis. Je ne doute point que les autres maréchaux ne partagent leur opinion.

Au premier Octobre je puis avoir la réponse de V. M., et même avant, puisque je lui ai manifesté cette opinion par ma lettre du 14 Septembre.

Si V. M. approuve ce plan, il sera possible qu'elle n'ait pas de

mes nouvelles jusqu'à l'arrivée des troupes ; mais je suis convaincu
qu'elle trouvera les affaires dans une bien meilleure situation qu'en
suivant aucun des autres cinq projets.

Miranda, le 16 *Sept.* 1808.

No. VII.

S.

EXTRAITS DES LETTRES DU MAJOR GENERAL AU GENERAL SAVARY, A MADRID.

Bayonne, 12 *Juillet,* 1808.

Section 1.—J'ai rendu compte à l'empereur, général, de votre
lettre du 8. S. M. trouve que vous êtes dégarni, de trop de
monde à Madrid, que vous avez fait marcher trop de troupes au secours du g^{al} Dupont, qu'on ne doit pas agir offensivement jusqu'à
ce que les affaires de la Galice soient éclairées.   De tous les points
de l'armée, général, le plus important est la Galice, parceque c'est
la seule province qui ait réellement conclu un traité avec l'Angleterre.   La division de ligne des troupes Espagnoles qui était à
Oporto s'est joint à celle qui était en Galice, et enfin par la position
de cette province extrêmement près de l'Angleterre.   Indépendamment de ces considérations, la position la rend encore plus intéres-
sante ; car les communications de l'armée se trouveraient com-
promises si le maréchal Bessières n'avait pas un entier succès, et il
faudrait bien alors reployer toutes vos troupes, et marcher isolément
au secours du maréchal Bessières.   Encore une fois, général, vous
vous êtes trop dégarni de Madrid, et si un bon régiment de cuirassiers, quelques pièces d'artillerie et 1000 à 1200 hommes d'infanterie
avaient pu arriver à l'appui du maréchal Bessières, le 14, cela lui
aurait été d'un éminent secours.   *Q'importe que Valence soit
soumis? Q'import que Saragosse soit soumis ?*   Mais, général,
le moindre succès de l'ennemi du côté de la Galice aurait des incon-
véniens immenses.   Instruit comme vous l'étiez des forces du
général Cuesta, de la désertion de troupes d'Oporto, &ª . . . .
S. M. trouve que pour bien manœuvrer il aurait fallu vous arranger
de manière à avoir du 12 au 15 8000 hommes pour renforcer le
maréchal Bessières.   Une fois nos derrièrs débarassés, et cette
armée de Galice détruite, tout le reste tombe et se soumet de soi-
même, &c. &c.

S.

EXTRAIT DE LA LETTRE, &c.

Bayonne, 13 *Juillet*, 1808.

Section 2.—Nous recevons vos lettres de 9 et du 10, général.
L'empereur me charge de vous faire connaître que si le général
Gobert était à Valladolid, le général Frère à San Clemente, ayant
une colonne dans la Manche ; si 300 à 400 convalescens, un bon
commandant, 4 pièces de canon, une escouade d'artillerie, et vingt
mille rations de biscuit étaient dans le château de Ségovie, la
position de l'armée serait superbe et à l'abri de toute sollicitude.
La conduite du général Frère ne paraît pas claire. Les nouvelles
qu'il a eues du maréchal Moncey paraissent apocryphes. Il est
possible que ses 8000 hommes et son artillerie n'aient pas été
suffisans pour enlever la ville de Valence. Cela étant, le maréchal
Moncey ne l'enleverait pas d'avantage avec 20,000 hommes, parcequ'alors c'est une affaire de canons et de mortiers, &ᵃ. &ᵃ. ····
Valence est comme la Catalogne et l'Arragon ; ces trois points
sont secondaires. Les deux vrais points importans sont le général
Dupont et particulièrement le maréchal Bessières, parceque le
premier a devant lui le corps du camp de St. Roch et le corps de
Cadiz, et le maréchal Bessières parcequ'il a devant lui les troupes
de la Galice et celles qui étaient à Oporto. Le général Dupont a
près de 20,000 hommes ; il ne peut pas avoir contre lui un pareil
nombre de troupes ; il a déjà obtenu des succès tres marquans, et
au pis aller il ne peut être contraint qu'à repasser les montagnes,
ce qui n'est qu'un événement de guerre. Le maréchal Bessières
est beaucoup moins fort que le général Dupont, et les troupes Espagnoles d'Oporto et de la Galice sont plus nombreuses que celles
de l'Andalousie, et les troupes de la Galice n'ont pas encore été enta-
mées. Enfin le moindre insuccès du maréchal Bessières intercepte
toutes les communications de l'armée et compromettrait même sa
sureté. Le général Dupont se bat pour Andujar, et le maréchal
Bessières se bat pour les communications de l'armée et pour les
opérations les plus importantes aux affaires d'Espagne, &c. &c.

S.

EXTRAIT DE LA LETTRE, &c. &c.

Bayonne, 18 *Juillet*, 1808, *à dix heures du soir.*
Section 3.—Je reçois, général, vos lettres du 14. L'aide-de-
camp du maréchal Moncey a donné à sa majesté tous les détails sur

ce qui s'est passé.   La conduite du maréchal a été belle.   Il a bien battu les rebelles en campagne.   Il est tout simple qu'il n'ait pu entrer à Valence ; c'était une affaire de mortiers et de pièces de siège.   Sa position à San Clemente est bonne, de là il est à même de remarcher sur Valence.   Du reste, général, *l'affaire de Valence est une affaire du second ordre, même celle de Saragosse*, qui cependant est plus importante.   L'affaire du maréchal Bessières était d'un intérêt majeur pour les affaires d'Espagne, et la prémière après cette affaire c'est celle du général Dupont, et c'est le moment de laisser le général Gobert suivre la route.   Le maréchal Moncey se repose ; le général Reille marche sur Gironne : ainsi trois colonnes pourront marcher ensemble sur Valence ; le corps du général Reille, celui de Saragosse, et celui du maréchal Moncey, ce qui formera les 20,000 hommes que ce maréchal croit nécessaires.   Mais l'empereur, général, trouve que vous avez tort de dire qu'il n'y a rien été fait depuis six semaines. On a battu les rassemblemens de la Galice, de St. Ander ceux d'Arragon et de Catalogne, qui dans leur aveuglement croyaient qu'ils n'avaient qu'à marcher pour détruire les Français : le maréchal Moncey, les généraux Duhesme, Dupont, Verdier, ont fait de bonne besogne, et tous les hommes sensés en Espagne ont changé dans le fonds de leur opinion, et voient avec la plus grande peine l'insurrection.   Au reste, général, les affaires d'Espagne sont dans la situation la plus prospère depuis la bataille de Medina del Rio Seco, &c. &c.   Le 14e et le 44e arrivent demain ; après demain ils partent pour le camp de Saragosse ; *non pas que ses troupes puissent avancer la reddition, qui est une affaire de canon*, mais elles serviraient contre les insurgés de Valence, s'ils voulaient renforcer ceux de Saragosse.   Enfin, si le général Gobert et les détachemens qui sont à moitié chemin pour rejoindre le général Dupont font juger à ce général qu'il a des forces suffisantes pour battre le général Castaños, il faut qu'elles continuent leur direction, et qu'il attaque l'ennemi, s'il croit devoir le faire, &a. &a.

(Cette lettre a été écrite le jour de la bataille de Baylen.)

EXTRAIT DE LA LETTRE, &c.

Bourdeaux, 3 *Août*, 1808.

Section 4.—Les événemens du général Dupont sont une chose sans exemple, et la rédaction de sa capitulation est de niveau avec la conduite tenue jusqu'à cette catastrophe.   L'empereur pense qu'on n'a pas tenu compte du vague de la rédaction de l'acte, en permet-

tant que les corps en échellons sur la communication entre vous et
le général Dupont aient marché pour se rendre aux Anglais : car
on ne doit pas présumer qu'ils aient la loyauté de laisser passer les
troupes qui s'embarquent. Comme vous ne parlez pas de cela, on
pense que vous avez retiré ces échellons sur Madrid. Aprés avoir
lu attentivement la relation du général Dupont, on voit qu'il n'a
capitulé que le lendemain de la bataille, et que les corps des généraux Vedel et Dufour, qui se trouvent compris pour quelque chose
dans la capitulation (on ne sait pourquoi), ne se sont pas battus.
Par la relation même du général Dupont, tout laisse penser que
l'armée du général Castaños n'était pas à beaucoup près aussi forte
qu'on le dit, et qu'il avait réuni à Baylen tout ce qu'il avait de
forces. S. M. ne lui calcule pas plus de 25,000 hommes de
troupes de ligne et plus de 15,000 paysans. Par la lettre du
général Belliard *il paraît que l'ordre est donné de lever le siège
de Saragosse,* ce qui serait prématuré ; car vous comprendrez qu'il
n'est pas possible qu'on ne laisse un corps d'armée, qui couvre
Pampelune, et contienne la Navarre, sans quoi l'ennemi peut
cerner Pampelune, insurger la Navarre, et alors la communication
de France par Tolosa serait coupée, et l'ennemi sur les derrières
de l'armée. Supposant l'ennemi réuni à Pampelune, la ville
bloquée, il peut se trouver en cinq à six marches sur les derrières
de Burgos. L'armée qui assiège Saragosse est donc à peu près
nécessaire pour contenir la Navarre, les insurgés de l'Arragon et
de Valence, et pour empêcher de percer sur notre flanc gauche ;
car si, comme le dit le général Belliard, le général Verdier se
porte avec ses troupes à Logroño, en jetant 2000 hommes dans
Pampelune, la communication de Bayonne, qu'eut sur le champ
interceptée le général Verdier, serait mieux à Tudela qu'à Logroño.
Si le général Castaños s'avance, et que vous puissiez lui livrer la
bataille, on ne peut en prévoir que les plus heureux résultats : mais
de la manière dont il a marché vis-à-vis du général Dupont, tout
donne à croire qu'il mettra la plus grande circonspection dans ses
mouvemens. Si par le canal des parlementaires l'on peut établir
une suspension d'armes sans que le roi y soit pour rien en appa-
rence cette espèce d'armistice pourrait se rompre en se prévenant
de part et d'autre huit jours d'avance, donnant aux Français la ligne
du Duero passant par Almazan pour joindre l'Ebre. Cette suspension d'armes, que les insurgés pourraient regarder comme
avantageuse, afin de s'organiser à Madrid, ne nous serait pas dé-
favorable, parcequ'on verrait pendant ce temps l'organisation que
prendraient les parties insurgés de l'Espagne, et ce que veut la
nation, &c. &c.

LE MAJOR GÉNÉRAL AU ROI D'ESPAGNE.

Nntes, 11 *Août,* 1808.

Section 5.—Sire, le général Savary ni vos ministres Azanza et Urquijo ne sont arrivés : il paraît qu'il y a des rassemblemens à Bilbao d'après les nouvelles que nous recevons. S. M. pense qu'il est important d'y faire marcher le plutôt possible une colonne pour y rétablir l'ordre. *V. M. sait que la moitié de Saragosse était en notre pouvoir, et que sous peu on espérait avoir le reste de la ville. Lorsque le général Belliard a donné l'ordre de lever le siège, il eût été à désirer que cet ordre fût conditionnel, comme cela paraissait être l'intention de V. M., ainsi qu'on le voit dans sa correspondance ; c'est à dire, que le siège ne fût levé que dans le cas où l'on n'aurait pas cru être maître de la ville avant cinq ou six jours.* Cela aurait présenté des circonstances meilleures ; car si le général Verdier évacue en entier la Navarre et l'Arragon, il est à craindre que le Navarre ne s'insurge, et Pampelune ne tarderait pas à être cernée. J'ai mandé à V. M. que déja des corps entiers de la grande armée sont en mouvement pour sa rendre en poste en Espagne. Les dispositons les plus vigoureuses sont prises de tous côtés, et *dans six semaines ou deux mois l'Espagne sera soumise.* L'empereur, qui continue à jouir d'une bonne santé, quoiqu'il soit très occupé, part dans une heur pour continuer sa route sur Angers, Tours, et Paris. V. M. doit être persuadée que toutes nos pensées sont sur elle et sur l'arméee qu'elle commande.

No. VIII.

LETTER FROM MR. DRUMMOND TO SIR ALEXANDER BALL.

Palermo, July 4th, 1808.

MY DEAR SIR,

His highness the duke of Orleans has applied to me to write to you on a subject about which he appears to be extremely interested. I take it for granted that you are acquainted with all the events which have lately happened in Spain. The duke thinks that the appearance of a member of the house of Bourbon in that country might be acceptable to the Spaniards, and of great service to the common cause. In this I perfectly concur with his highness, and if you be of the same opinion you will probably have no objection to send a ship here to carry his highness to Gibraltar. He himself is exceedingly sanguine. We have letters from London down to the 5th of June. Portugal has followed the example of Spain, and Lisbon is probably now in other hands. An invitation has been sent to sir Charles Cotton.

(Signed) WILLIAM DRUMMOND.

P.S. Weigh well what is said here, written at the side of the person.

MR DRUMMOND TO SIR HEW DALRYMPLE.

Palermo, July 24th, 1808.

DEAR SIR,

This letter will be delivered to you by his royal highness prince Leopold, second son of the king of the Two Sicilies. This prince goes immediately to Gibraltar to communicate immediately with the loyal Spaniards, and to notify to them that his father will accept the regency, if they desire it, until his nephew Ferdinand the Seventh be delivered from captivity. Don Leopold and his cousin the duke of Orleans will offer themselves as soldiers to the Spaniards, and will accept such situations as may be given to them suitable to their illustrious rank. If their visit should not be acceptable to the Spaniards, don Leopold will return to Sicily, and his serene highness the duke of Orleans will proceed to England. Being of opinion that the appearance of an infant of Spain may be of the greatest utility at the present crisis, and in all events can hardly be productive of harm, I have urged his Sicilian majesty to determine upon this measure, which I conceive to be required at his hands, in consequence of the manifesto of Palafox, which you have probably seen. At the distance of 1000 miles, however, we cannot be supposed to be accurately informed here of many circumstances with which you probably may be intimately acquainted; prince Leopold therefore will be directed to consult with you, and to follow your advice, which I have no doubt you will readily and cheerfully give him. I take the liberty at the same time of recommending him to your care and protection.

(Signed) WM. DRUMMOND.

EXTRACT OF A LETTER FROM SIR HEW DALRYMPLE TO LORD CASTLEREAGH.

Gibraltar, August 10th, 1808.

MY LORD,

Last night the Thunderer arrived here, having on board the duke of Orleans, the second prince of the Two Sicilies, and a considerable number of noblemen and others, the suite of the latter. As the ship

came to anchor at a late hour, I had not the honour of seeing the
duke of Orleans until near ten at night, when he came accompanied
by captain Talbot.   The duke first put into my hands a letter from
Mr. Drummond, as captain Talbot did a despatch from sir Alexander
Ball, copies of which I have the honour to enclose.   As the latter
seemed bulky, I did not immediately open it, and therefore did not
immediately remark that sir Alexander Ball *did not seem aware* that
the prince of the Two Sicilies was comming down, much less that he
meditated establishing his residence at Gibraltar for the avowed purpose of negociating for the regency of Spain.   Of this object the
duke of Orleans made no mystery, and proceeded to arrange the time
and manner of the prince's reception in the morning, and the
accommodation that should be prepared for him, suited to his rank,
and capable of containing his attendants.   I took early occasion
first to remark the ill effect this measure might produce in Spain at
the moment when the establishment of a central government had
become obviously necessary, and would naturally lead to much
intrigue and disunion, until the sentiments of the people and the
armies (which would naturally assemble for the purpose of expelling
the enemy from their territory) should be pronounced.   .   .   .

EXTRACT OF A LETTER FROM LORD CASTLEREAGH TO SIR HEW DALRYMPLE.

Downing Street, Nov. 4th, 1808.

' I have great pleasure, however, in assuring you that the measures pursued by you on that delicate and important subject' (the
unexpected arrival of prince Leopold and the duke of Orleans at
Gibraltar) ' received his majesty's entire appprobation.'   .   .   .

(Signed)   CASTLEREAGH.

No. IX.

SIR ARTHUR WELLESLEY TO SIR HARRY BURRARD.

Head-quarters, at Lavos, August 8th, 1808.

SIR,

Having received instructions from the secretary of state that you
were likely to arrive on the coast of Portugal with a corps of 10,000
men, lately employed in the north of Europe under the orders of
sir John Moore, I now submit to you such information as I have

received regarding the general state of the war in Portugal and Spain, and the plan of operations which I am about to carry into execution.

The enemy's force at present in Portugal consists, as far as I am able to form an opinion, of from 16,000 to 18,000 men, of which number there are about 500 in the fort of Almeida, about the same number in Elvas, about 6 or 800 in Peniché, and 16 or 1800 in the province of Alemtejo, at Setuval, &c.; and the remainder are disposable for the defence of Lisbon, and are in the forts of St. Julian and Cascaes, in the batteries along the coast as far as the Rock of Lisbon, and the old citadel of Lisbon, to which the enemy have lately added some works.

Of the force disposable for the defence of Lisbon, the enemy have lately detached a corps of about 2000, under general Thomieres, principally I believe to watch my movements, which corps is now at Alcobaça; and another corps of 4000 men, under general Loison, was sent across the Tagus into Alemtejo on the 26th of last month, the object of which detachment was to disperse the Portuguese insurgents in that quarter, to force the Spanish corps, consisting of about 2000 men, which had advanced into Portugal as far as Evora from Estremadura, to retire, and then to be enabled to add to the force destined for the defence of Lisbon the corps of French troops which had been stationed at Setuval and in the province of Alemtejo; at all events Loison's corps will return to Lisbon, and the French corps disposable for the defence of that place will probably be about 14,000 men, of which at least 3000 must be left in the garrisons and forts on the coast and in the river.

The French army under Dupont, in Andalusia, surrendered on the 20th of last month to the Spanish army under Castaños; so that there are now no French troops in the south of Spain. The Spanish army of Gallicia and Castille, to the northward, received a check at Rio Seco, in the province of Valladolid, on the 14th of July, from a French corps supposed to be under the command of general Bessieres, which had advanced from Burgos.

The Spanish troops retired on the 15th to Benevente, and I understand there has since been an affair between the advanced posts in that neighbourhood, but I am not certain of it; nor am I acquainted with the position of the Spanish army, or of that of the French, since the 14th July. When you will have been a short time in this country, and will have observed the degree to which the deficiency of real information is supplied by the circulation of unfounded reports, you will not be surprised at my want of accurate knowledge on these subjects.

It is, however, certain that nothing of importance has occurred in that quarter since the 14th of July ; and from this circumstance I conclude that the corps called Bessieres' attacked the Spanish army at Rio Seco solely with a view to cover the march of King Joseph Buonaparte to Madrid, where he arrived on the 21st July. Besides their defeat at Andalusia, the enemy, as you may probably have heard, have been beat off in an attack upon Zaragoza, in Aragon, in another upon the city of Valencia; (in both of which it is said that they have lost many men;) and it is reported that, in Catalonia, two of their detachments have been cut off, and that they have lost the fort of Figueras in the Pyrenees, and that Barcelona is blockaded. Of these last-mentioned actions and operations I have seen no official accounts, but the report of them is generally circulated and believed ; and at all events, whether these reports are founded or otherwise, it is obvious that the insurrection against the French is general throughout Spain ; that large parties of Spaniards are in arms ; amongst others, in particular, an army of 20,000 men, including 4000 cavalry, at Almaraz on the Tagus, in Estremadura, and that the French cannot carry on their operations by means of small corps, I should imagine, from their inactivity, and from the misfortunes they have suffered, that they have not the means of collecting a force sufficiently large to oppose the progress of the insurrection and the efforts of the insurgents, and to afford supplies to their different detached corps, or that they find that they cannot carry on their operations with armies so numerous as they must find it necessary to employ without magazines.

In respect to Portugal, the whole kingdom, with the exception of the neighbourhood of Lisbon, is in a state of insurrection against the French; their means of resistance are, however, less powerful than those of the Spaniards, their troops have been completely dispersed, their officers had gone off to the Brazils, and their arsenals pillaged, or in the power of the enemy, and their revolt under the circumstances in which it had taken place is still more extraordinary than that of the Spanish nation.

The Portuguese may have in the northern part of the kingdom about 10,000 men in arms, of which number 5000 are to march with me towards Lisbon. The remainder with a Spanish detachment of about 1500 men which came from Gallicia, are employed in a distant blockade of Almeida, and in the protection of Oporto, which is now the seat of government.

The insurrection is general throughout Alemtejo and Algarve to the southward, and Entre Minho e Duero and Tras os Montes and

Beira to the northward ; but for want of arms the people can do nothing against the enemy.

Having consulted sir C. Cotton, it appeared to him and to me that the attack proposed upon Cascaes-bay was impracticable, because the bay is well defended by the fort of Cascaes and the other works constructed for its defence, and the ships of war could not approach sufficiently near to silence them. The landing in the Passa d'Arcos in the Tagus could not be effected without silencing fort St. Julian, which appeared to be impracticable to those who were to carry that operation into execution.

There are small bays within which might admit of landing troops, and others to the northward of the rock of Lisbon, but they are all defended by works which must have been silenced ; they are of small extent, and but few men could have landed at the same time. There is always a surf on them which affects the facility of landing at different times so materially, as to render it very doubtful whether the troops first landed could be supported in sufficient time by others, and whether the horses for the artillery and cavalry, and the necessary stores and provisions could be landed at all. These inconveniences attending a landing in any of the bays near the rock of Lisbon would have been aggravated by the neighbourhood of the enemy to the landing-place, and by the exhausted state of the country in which the troops would have been landed. It was obviously the best plan, therefore, to land in the northern parts of Portugal, and I fixed upon Mondego bay as the nearest place which afforded any facility for landing, excepting Peniché, the landing-place of which peninsula is defended by a fort occupied by the enemy, which it would be necessary to attack regularly, in order to place the ships in safety.

A landing to the northward was further recommended, as it would insure the co-operation of the Portuguese troops in the expedition to Lisbon. The whole of the corps placed under my command, including those under the command of general Spencer, having landed, I propose to march on Wednesday, and I shall take the road by Alcobaça and Obidos, with a view to keep up my communication by the sea-coast, and to examine the situation of Peniché, and I shall proceed towards Lisbon by the route of Mafra, and by the hills to the northward of that city.

As I understand from the secretary of state that a body of troops under the command of brigadier-general Ackland may be expected on the coast of Portugal before you arrive, I have written to desire he will proceed from hence along the coast of Portugal to the southward ; and I propose to communicate with him by the means of captain Bligh of the Alfred, who will attend the movements of the army with a few transports, having on board provisions and military stores. I intend to order brigadier-general Ackland to attack Peniché, if I should find it necessary to obtain possession of that place, and if not, I propose to order him to join the fleet stationed off the Tagus, with a view to disembark in one of the bays near the rock of Lisbon, as soon as I shall approach sufficiently near to enable him to perform that operation.   If I imagined that general Ackland's corps was equipped in such a manner as to be enabled to move from the coast, I should have directed him to land at Mondego, and to march upon Santarem, from which station he would have been at hand either to assist my operations, or to cut off the retreat of the enemy, if he should endeavour to make it either by the north of the Tagus and Almeida, or by the south of the Tagus and Elvas; but as I am convinced that general Ackland's corps is intended to form a part of some other corps which is provided with a commissariat, that he will have none with him, and consequently that his corps must depend upon the country; and as no reliance can be placed upon the re- sources of this country, I have considered it best to direct the gene- ral's attention to the sea-coast; if, however, the command of the army remainded in my hands, I should certainly land the corps which has lately been under the command of sir John Moore at Mondego, and should move it upon Santarem.   I have the honour to enclose a return of the troops, &c. &c.

(Signed)   ARTHUR WELLESLEY.

SIR ARTHUR WELLESLEY TO SIR HARRY BURRARD.
Camp at Lugar, 8 miles north of Lerya, August 10, 1808.
SIR,

Since I wrote to you on the 8th inst., I have received letters from Mr. Stuart and colonel Doyle at Coruña, of which I enclose copies. From them you will learn the state of the war in that part of Spain, and you will observe that Mr. Stuart and colonel Doyle are of opinion that marshal Bessieres will take advantage of the ineffici- ency of the Gallician army under general Blake to detach a corps to Portugal to the assistance of general Junot; we have not heard yet of that detachment, and I am convinced it will not be made till King Joseph Buonaparte will either be reinforced to such a degree as to be in safety in Madrid, or till he shall have effected his retreat into France, with which view it is reported that he left Madrid on the 29th of last month.

I conceive, therefore, that I have time for the operations which I propose to carry on before a reinforcement can arrive from Leon, even supposing that no obstacles would be opposed to its march in Spain or Portugal ; but it is not probable that it can arrive before the different reinforcements will arrive from England ; and as marshal Bessieres had not more than 20,000 men in the action at Rio Seco on the 14th July, I conceive that the British troops, which will be in Portugal, will be equal to contend with any part of that corps which he may detach.

The possibility that, in the present state of affairs, the French corps at present in Portugal may be reinforced, affords an additional reason for taking the position at Santarem, which I apprised you, in my letter of the 8th, I should occupy, if the command of the army remained in my hands after the reinforcements should arrive. If you should occupy it, you will not only be in the best situation to support my operations, and to cut off the retreat of the enemy, but if any reinforcements of the French troops should enter Portugal, you will be in the best situation to collect your whole force to oppose him, &c. &c.

(Signed)   ARTHUR WELLESLEY.

No. X.

ARTICLES OF THE DEFINITIVE CONVENTION FOR THE EVACUATION OF PORTUGAL BY THE FRENCH ARMY.

The generals commanding in chief, &c. &c., being determined to negotiate, &c. &c.

Article 1. All the places and forts in the kingdom of Portugal occupied by the French troops shall be given up to the British army in the state in which they are at the period of the signature of the present convention.

Art. 2. The French troops shall evacuate Portugal with their arms and baggage, they shall not be considered as prisoners of war, and on their arrival in France they shall be at liberty to serve.

Art. 3. The English government shall furnish the means of con- veyance for the French army, which shall be disembarked in any of the ports of France between Rochefort and L'Orient inclusively.

Art. 4. The French army shall carry with it all its artillery of French calibre, with the horses belonging thereunto, and the tum- brils supplied with sixty rounds per gun : all other artillery arms, and ammunition, as also the military and naval arsenals, shall be given up to the British army and navy, in the state in which they may be at the period of the ratification of the convention.

Art. 5. The French army shall carry with it all its equipments, and all that is comprehended under the name of property of the army; that is to say, its military chest, and carriages attached to the field commissariat and field hospital; or shall be allowed to dispose of such part of the same on its accounts, as the commander-in-chief may judge it unnecessary to embark. In like manner, all individuals of the army shall be at liberty to dispose of their private property of every description, with full security hereafter for the purchasers.

Art. 6. The cavalry are to embark their horses, as also the generals and other officers of all ranks. It is, however, fully understood that the means of conveyance for horses, at the disposal of the British commanders, are very limited; some additional conveyance may be procured in the port of Lisbon. The number of horses, to be embarked by the troops shall not exceed 600, and the number embarked by the staff shall not exceeed 200. At all events, every facility will be given to the French army to dispose of the horses belonging to it which cannot be embarked.

Art. 7. In order to facilitate the embarkation, it shall take place in three divisions, the last of which will be principally composed of the garrisons of the places, of the cavalry, the artillery, the sick, and the equipment of the army. The first division shall embark within seven days of the date of the ratification, or sooner if possible.

Art. 8. The garrison of Elvas and its forts, and of Peniché and Palmela, will be embarked at Lisbon. That of Almeida at Oporto, or the nearest harbour. They will be accompanied on their march by British commissaries, charged with providing for their subsistence and accommodation.

Art. 9 All the sick and wounded who cannot be embarked with the troops are entrusted to the British army. They are to be taken care of whilst they remain in this country at the expense of the British government, under the condition of the same being reimbursed by France when the final evacuation is effected. The English government will provide for their return to France, which will take place by detachments of about one hundred and fifty or two hundred men at a time. A sufficient number of Frence medical officers shall be left behind to attend them.

Art. 10. As soon as the vessels employed to carry the army to France shall have disembarked in the harbours specified, or in any other of the ports of France to which stress of weather may force them, every facility shall be given them to return to England without delay, and security against capture until their arrival in a friendly port.

Art. 11. The French army shall be concentrated in Lisbon, and within a distance of about two leagues from it. The English army will approach within three leagues of the capital, and will be so placed as to leave about one league between the two armies.

Art. 12. The forts of St. Julien, the Bugio, and Cascaes, shall be occupied by the British troops on the ratification of the convention. Lisbon and its citadel, together with the forts and batteries as far as the lazaretto or Trafaria on one side, and fort St. Joseph on the other, inclusively, shall be given up on the embarkation of the 2d division; as shall also the harbour and all armed vessels in it of every description, with their rigging, sails, stores, and ammunition. The fortresses of Elvas, Almeida, Peniché, and Palmela, shall be given up as soon as the British troops can arrive to occupy them. In the meantime, the general-in-chief of the British army will give notice of the present convention to the garrisons of those places, as also to the troops before them, in order to put a stop to all further hostilities.

Art. 13. Commissioners shall be named on both sides to regulate and accelerate the execution of the arrangements agreed upon.

Art. 14. Should there arise doubts as to the meaning of any article, it will be explained favourably to the French army.

Art. 15. From the date of the ratification of the present convention, all arrears of contributions, requisitions, or claims whatever, of the French government against subjects of Portugal, or any other individuals residing in this country, founded on the occupation of Portugal by the French troops, in the month of December, 1807, which may not have been paid up, are cancelled; and all sequestration laid upon their property, moveable or immoveable, are removed, and the free disposal of the same is restored to the proper owners.

Art. 16. All subjects of France, or of powers in friendship or alliance, domiciliated in Portugal, or accidentally in this country, shall be protected; their property of every kind, moveable and immoveable, shall be respected; and they shall be at liberty either to accompany the French army or to remain in Portugal. In either case their property is guaranteed to them, with the liberty of retaining or of disposing of it, and passing the produce of the sale thereof into France, or any other country where they may fix their residence, the space of one year being allowed them for that purpose. It is fully understood that shipping is excepted from this arrangement, only however in as far as regards leaving the port, and that none of the stipulations above mentioned can be made the pretext of any commercial speculations.

Art. 17. No native of Portugal shall be rendered accountable for his political conduct during the period of the occupation of this country by the French army; and all those who have continued in the exercise of their employments, or who have accepted situations under the French government, are placed under the protection of the British commanders ; they shall sustain no injury in their persons or property ; it not having been at their option to be obedient or not to the French government, they are also at liberty to avail themselves of the stipulations of the 16th article.

Art. 18. The Spanish troops detained on board ship, in the port of Lisbon, shall be given up to the commander-in-chief of the British army, who engages to obtain of the Spaniards to restore such French subjects, either military or civil, as may have been detained in Spain without having been taken in battle, or in consequence of military operations, but on occasion of the occurrences of the 29th of last May, and the days immediately following.

Art. 19. There shall be an immediate exchange established for all ranks of prisoners made in Portugal since the commencement of the present hostilities.

Art. 20. Hostages of the rank of field officers shall be mutually furnished, on the part of the British army and navy, and on that of the French army, for the reciprocal guarantee of the present convention. The officer of the British army shall be restored on the completion of the articles whichco ncern the army ; and the officer of the navy on the disembarkation of the French troops in their own country. The like is to take place on the part of the French army.

Art. 21. It shall be allowed to the general-in-chief of the French army to send an officer to France with intelligence of the present convention. A vessel will be furnished by the British admiral to convey him to Bordeaux or Rochefort.

Art. 22. The British admiral will be invited to accommodate his excellency the commander-in-chief and the other principal officers of the French army on board ships of war.

Done and concluded at Lisbon, this 30th day of August, 1808.

(Signed)   George Murray, quarter-master-general.

Kellerman, le général de division.

ADDITIONAL ARTICLES.

Art. 1. The inividuals in the civil employment of the army, made prisoners either by the British troops or by the Portuguese, in any part of Portugal, will be restored, as is customary, without exchange.

Art. 2. The French army shall be subsisted from its own magazines up to the day of embarkation. The garrisons up to the day of the evacuation of the fortresses. The remainder of the magazines shall be delivered over in the usual forms to the British government, which charges itself with the subsistence of the men and horses of the army from the above-mentioned periods till their arrival in France, under the condition of being reimbursed by the French government for the excess of the expense beyond the estimation to be made by both parties, of the value of the magazines delivered up to the British army. The provisions on board the ships of war in the possession of the French army will be taken on account by the British government, in like manner with the magazines of the fortresses.

Art. 3. The general commanding the British troops will take the necessary measures for re-establishing the free circulation of the means of subsistence between the country and the capital.

Done and concluded at Lisbon this 30th day of August, 1808.

(Signed)   GEORGE MURRAY, quarter-master-general.

KELLERMAM, le général de division.

Ratified, &c. &c.

_____

No. XI.

1st. LETTER FROM BARON VON DECKEN TO THE GENERAL COMMANDING THE ARMY IN PORTUGAL.

Oporto, August 18th, 1808.

SIR,

The bishop of Oporto having expressed to me his wish to see me in private, in order to make me an important communication, which he desired to be kept secret, I went to his palace last night at a late hour. The bishop told me that he had taken the government of Portugal in his hands to satisfy the wish of the people, but with the intention to re-establish the government of his lawful sovereign; and he hoped that his majesty the King of Great Britain had no other point in view in sending troops to this country. After having given him all possible assurance on that head, the bishop continued that as the prince regent, in leaving Portugal, had established a regency for the government of this country during his absence, he considered it his dury to resign the government into the hands of that regency as soon as possible. My answer was, that I had no instruction from my government on that head, but that I begged him to consider whether the cause of his sovereign would not be hurt in resigning the government into the hands of a regency which, from its having acted under the influence of the French, had lost the confidence of the nation, and whether it would not be more advisable for him to keep the government until the pleasure of the prince regent was known. The bishop allowed that the regency appointed by the prince regent did not possess the confidence of the people, that several members of it had acted in such a manner as to show themselves as friends and partisans of the French, and that, at all events, all the members of the late regency could not be re-established in their former power; but he was afraid that the provinces of Estremadura, Alemtejo, and Algarvé, would not acknowledge his authority if the British government did not interfere. After a very long conversation, it was agreed that I should inform our ministers with what the bishop had communicated to me, and in order to lose no time in waiting for an answer, the bishop desired me to communicate the same to you, expressing a wish that you would be pleased to write to him an official letter, in order to express your desire that he might continue the government until the pleasure of his sovereign was known, for the sake of the operations of the British and Portuguese troops under your command.

The secretary of the Bishop, who acted as interpreter, told me afterwards in private, that the utmost confusion would arise from the bishop resigning the government at this moment, or associating with people who were neither liked nor esteemed by the nation.

I beg leave to add, that although the bishop expressed the contrary, yet it appeared to me that he was not averse to his keeping the government in his hands, if it could be done by the interference of our government. I have the honour to be, &c. &c.

(Signed)   FREDERICK VON DECKEN, brig.-gen.

2d. DITTO TO DITTO.

Oporto, August 22, 1808.

Sir,

Your excellency will have received the secret letter which I had the honour to send you by brigadier-general Stuart, on the 18th, respecting the communication of his excellency the bishop of Oporto relative to his resignation of the government into the hands of the regency established by the prince regent. In addition to what I have had the honour to state upon that subject, I beg leave to add, that his excellency the bishop has this day desired me to make your excellency aware, in case it might be wished that he should keep the government in his hands until the pleasure of the prince regent may be known, that he could not leave Oporto; and the seat of government must in that case necessarily remain in this town. His excellency the bishop thinks it his duty to inform you of this circumstance as soon as possible, as he foresees that the city of Lisbon will be preferred for the seat of government, as soon as the British army have got possession of it. If the seat of the temporary government should remain at Oporto, the best method to adopt with respect to the other provinces of Portugal appears to be, to cause them to send deputies to that place for the purpose of transacting business relative to their own provinces; in the same manner as the provinces of Entre Douro y Minho and Tras os Montes now send their representatives. One of the principal reasons why his excellency the bishop can only accede to continue at the head of the government under the condition of remaining at Oporto is, because he is persuaded that the inhabitants of this town will not permit him to leave it, unless by order of the prince regent. It might also be advisable to keep the seat of government at Oporto, as it may be supposed that Lisbon will be in a state of great confusion for the first two months after the French have left it. I have the honour to be, sir, &c. &c.

   (Signed)   FREDERICK VON DECKEN, brig.-gen.

        3d.   *Oporto, August* 28.

SIR,

 Your excellency will have received my secret letters of the 18th and 22d instant relative to the temporary government of this kingdom. His excellency the bishop of Oporto has received lately deputies from the province of Alemtejo and the kingdom of Algarve. Part of Estremadura, viz. the town of Leria, has also submitted to his authority; and it may be therefore said that the whole kingdom of Portugal has acknowledged the authority of the temporary government, of which the bishop of Oporto is at the head, with the exception of Lisbon and the town of Setubal (St. Ubes). Although the reasons why these towns have not yet acknowledged the authority of the temporary government may be explained by their being in possession of the French, yet the bishop is convinced that the inhabitants of Lisbon will refuse to submit to the temporary government of Oporto, in which they will be strongly supported by the members of the former regency established by the prince regent, who of course will be very anxious to resume their former power. The bishop in assuming the temporary government complied only with the wishes of the people : he was sure that it was the only means of saving the country; but having had no interest of his own in view, he is willing to resign the authority which he has accepted with reluctance, as soon as he is convinced that it can be done without hurting the cause of his sovereign, and throwing the country into confusion. There is every reason to apprehend that the inhabitants of the three northern provinces of Portugal will never permit the bishop to resign the government, and submit to the former regency. They feel extremely proud of having first taken to arms, and consider themselves as the deliverers and saviours of their country ; and as the inhabitants of Lisbon will be as much disinclined to submit to the temporary government of Oporto, a division of the provinces, which will excite internal commotion, will naturally follow, if not supported by your excellency. It has appeared to me that the best way to reconcile these opposite parties would be in endeavouring to unite the present government at Oporto with such of the members of the former regency who have not forfeited by their conduct the confidence of the people ; and having opened my idea to the bishop, his answer was, that he would not object to it if proposed by you. I therefore take the liberty of suggesting, that the difficulty above mentioned would be in a great measure removed if your excellency would be pleased to make it known after Lisbon has surrendered, that until the pleasure of the prince regent was known, you would consider the temporary government established at Oporto as the lawful government, with the addition of the four members of the late regency, who have been pointed out to me by the bishop as such who have behaved faithfully to their sovereign and country—viz. *don Francisco Noronha, Francisco da Cunha, the Monteiro Mor, and the principal Castro.* These members to be placed at the head of the different departments, and to consider the bishop as the president, whose directions they are to follow—a plan which will meet with the less difficulty, as the president of the former regency, named by the prince regent, has quitted Portugal, and is now in France. The circumstance that Lisbon is now in a state of the greatest confusion will furnish a fair pretext for fixing the seat of the temporary government in the first instance at Oporto, to which place the gentlemen above-named would be ordered to repair without loss of time, and to report themselves to the bishop. Independent of the reasons which I had the honour of stating to your excellency in my letter of the 22d instant, why it is impossible for the bishop to leave Oporto, I must beg leave to add, that, from what I understand, the greater part of the inhabitants of Lisbon are in the French interest, and that it will require a garrison of British troops to keep that city in order. The bishop of Oporto, although convinced of the necessity of considering Lisbon at present as a military station, and of placing a British commandant and a British garrison there, yet from a desire that the feelings of the inhabitants might be wounded as little as possible, wishes that you would be pleased to put also some Portuguese troops in garrison at Lisbon, together with a Portuguese commandant, who, though entirely under the orders of the British governor, might direct the police in that town, or at least be charged with putting into execution such orders as he may receive from the British governor under that head. If your excellency should be pleased to approve of this proposal, the bishop thinks brigadier Antonio Pinto Bacelar to be the properest officer of those who are now with the Portuguese army to be stationed at Lisbon, and who might also be directed to organise the military force of the province of Estremadura. The bishop is fully convinced that the temporary government of the country cannot exist without the support of British troops: he hopes that our government will leave a corps of 6000 men in Portugal after the French have been subdued, until the Portuguese troops may be sufficiently organised and disciplined to be able to protect their own government. I have the honour to be, sir, your most obedient and humble servant,

FREDERICK VON DECKEN, brig.-gen.

No. XII.

(Translation.)

LETTER FROM GENERAL LEITE TO SIR HEW DALRYMPLE.

MOST ILLUSTRIOUS AND MOST EXCELLENT SIR,

Strength is the result of union, and those who have reason to be grateful should be most urgent in their endeavours to promote it. I therefore feel it to be my duty to have recourse to your excellency to know how I should act without disturbing the union so advantageous to my country. The supreme junta of the Portuguese government established at Oporto, which I have hitherto obeyed as the representatives of my sovereign, have sent me orders by an officer, dated the 1st instant, to take possession of the fortress of Elvas, as soon as it shall be evacuated. After having seen those same Spaniards who got possession of our strong places as friends, take so much upon themselves as even to prevent the march of the garrison which 1 had ordered to replace the losses sustained in the battle of Evora, which deprived me of the little obedience that was shown by the city of Beja, always favoured by the Spanish authorities; after having seen the Portuguese artillery which was saved after the said battle taken possession of by those same Spaniards, who had lost their own, without being willing even to lend me two three-pounders to enable me to join his excellency the Monteiro Mor; after having seen the arms which were saved from the destructive grasp of the common enemy made use of by those same Spaniards, *who promised much and did nothing ;* after having seen a Spanish brigadier dispute my authority at Campo Mayor, where I was president of the junta, and from whence his predecessor had taken away 60,000 crowns without rendering any account; in a word, after having seen the march of these Spaniards marked by the devastation of our fields, and the country deserted to avoid the plunder of their light troops, I cannot for a moment mistake the cause of the orders given by the supreme junta of Oporto.   A corps of English troops having yesterday passed Estrémos, on their road to Elvas, knowing that in a combined army no officer should undertake any operation which may be intended for others, thereby counteracting each other, I consulted lieutenant-general Herre (Hope), who has referred me to your excellency, to whom in consequence I send lieutenant-colonel the marquiss of Terney, my quarter-master-general, that he may deliver you this letter, and explain verbally everything you may wish to know which relates to my sovereign and the good of my country, already so much indebted to the English nation.

God preserve your excellency many years.

(Signed)   FRANCISCO DE PAULO LEITE, lieut.-general.
(Dated) *Estrémos*, 16*th September*, 1808.
To the most illustrious and most excellent
          sir Hew Dalrymple.

EXTRACT OF A LETTER FROM SIR HEW DALRYMPLE TO LIEUTENANT-GENERAL SIR JOHN HOPE.

Head-quarters, Benefico, 25th Sept. 1808.

SIR,

Impediments having arisen to the fulfilment of that article of the convention which relates to the cession of Elvas by the French to the British army, in consequence of the unexpected and unaccountable conduct of the commander-in-chief of the army of Estremadura, in bombarding that place, and endeavouring to impose upon the French garrison terms of capitulation different from those which were agreed upon by the British and French generals in chief; and as the British corps sent to take possession of the above fortress, and to hold it in the name of the prince regent until reinforced by a body of Portuguese troops, is not of sufficient strength to preclude the possibility of insult, should the general above-mentioned persevere in the contemptuous and hostile disposition he has hitherto shown ; I have therefore thought it advisable to order the remainder of your division, and general Paget's advanced guard, to cross the Tagus, and to occupy cantonments as near as possible to the place above-mentioned. In the mean time colonel Graham is gone to Badajos to expostulate with general Galuzzo on the singular and very inexplicable line of conduct he has seen cause to adopt. . . .

No. XIII.

JUSTIFICATORY EXTRACTS FROM THE CORRESPONDENCE OF SIR JOHN MOORE AND OTHER PERSONS.

SECTION I.—RELATING TO WANT OF MONEY.

Sir John Moore to lord William Bentinck, October 22, 1808.

' Sir David Baird has unfortunately been sent out without money. He has applied to me, and I have none to give him.' . . . ' I undertake my march in the hope that some will arrive ; if it does not, it will add to the number of a great many distresses.'

Sir John Moore to general Hope, October 22, 1808.

' Baird has sent his aide-de-camp Gordon to me : he is without money, and his troops only paid to September. He can get none at Coruña.

Sir John Moore to sir David Blair, October 22, 1808.

' We are in such want of money at this place, that it is with difficulty I have been able to spare 8,000*l.*, which went to you in the Champion this day.

Sir John Moore to lord Castlereagh, October 27.

' It is upon the general assurance of the Spanish government that I am leading the army into Spain without any established magazines. In this situation nothing is more essentially requisite than money, and unfortunately we have been able to procure very little here.'

Sir John Moore to Mr. Frere, November 10, 1808.

' I understand from Sir David Baird that you were kind enough to lend him 40,000*l.* from the money you brought with you from England. We are in the greatest distress for money. I doubt if there is wherewithal after the 24th of this month to pay the troops their subsistence.'

Sir John Moore to lord Castlereagh, November 24, 1808.

' I am without a shilling of money to pay, and I am in daily apprehension that from the want of it our supplies will be stopped. It is impossible to describe the embarrassments we are thrown into from the want of that essential article.'

Admiral de Courcy to Mr. Stuart, Coruña, October 21, 1808.

' Mr. Frere will have told you that the Semiramis has brought a million of dollars, in order to be at his disposal, besides 50,000*l*. in dollars, which are to be presented to the Marquis of Romana's army. In the mean time, the British troops remain in their transports at Coruña, uncertain whether they shall be invited to the war, and *without a shilling to pay their expenses.*'

SECTION II.—RELATING TO ROADS.

Sir John Moore to general Anstruther, at Almeida, dated Lisbon, October 12, 1808.

' A division under Beresford is marching upon Coimbra, and a part of it will proceed on to Oporto or not, as information is received from you, that the road from thence to Almeida is or is not practicable. Some officers of the Spanish engineers, employed in the quarter-master-general's department, with commissaries, are sent from Madrid to obtain information on the subjects you will want with respect to roads, subsistence, &c. &c. from Almeida to Burgos.'

Sir John Moore to lord William Bentinck, October 22, 1808.

' Colonel Lopez has no personal knowledge of this part of Spain; but what he has told me accords with other information I had before received, that the great Madrid road was the only one by which artillery could travel; the French brought theirs from Ciudad Rodrigo to Alcantara, but by this *it was destroyed.*' . . . .
' The difficulty of obtaining correct information of roads, and the difficulties attending the subsistence of troops through Portugal, are greater than you can believe.'

Sir John Hope to sir John Moore, Madrid, November 20.

' I sent Wills of the engineers by Placentia to Salamanca, and before this time I suppose he may have made his report to you of the roads from the Tagus at Almaraz and Puente de Cardinal to Salamanca.' . . . . . . ' Delancy is upon this road, and I have directed him to communicate with you at Salamanca, as soon as possible.'

Sir John Moore to lord Castlereagh, October 27, 1808.

' I am under the necessity of sending lieutenant-general Hope, with the artillery, &c. by the great road leading from Badajos to Madrid, as *every information* agreed that no other was fit for the artillery.'

Substance of a report from captain Carmichael Smyth of the engineers, 26th *December,* 1808.

' The country round about Astorga is perfectly open, and affords no advantage whatsoever to a small corps to enable it to oppose a large force with any prospect of success. In retreating, however, towards Villa Franca, at the distance of about two leagues from Astorga, the hills approaching each other form some strong ground; and the high ground in particular in the rear of the village of Rodrigatos appears at first sight to offer a most advantageous position. One very serious objection presents itself nevertheless to our making a stand near Rodrigatos, or indeed at any position before we come to the village of Las Torres (about one league from Bembibre), as the talus, or slope of the ground, from Manzanel (close to Rodrigatos) until Las Torres, would be in favour of an enemy, should we be forced at Rodrigatos, and we should be consequently, obliged to retreat down hill for nearly two leagues, the enemy having every advantage that such a circumstance would naturally give them.

' From Las Torres to Bembibre the ground becomes more open, but with the disadvantage, however, of the slope being still against us. From Bembibre to Villa Franca there is great variety of ground but no position that cannot easily be turned, excepting the ground in the rear of Calcavellos, and about one league in front of Villa Franca. This is by far the strongest position between Astorga and Villa Franca. It is also necessary to add, that the position at Rodrigatos can easily be turned by the Foncevadon road (which, before the establishment of the Camina Real, was the high road towards Coruña). This is not the case with the position in front of Villa Franca, as the Foncevadon road joins the Camina Real to Calcavellos in front of the proposed position.'

Major Fletcher, royal engineers, to sir John Moore, Betanzos, Jan. 5, 1809.

' I have the honour to report to your excellency that, in obedience to your orders, I have examined the neck of land between the harbour of Ferrol and the bridge of Puente de Humo. This ground does not appear to possess any position that has not several de-

fects.' . . 'I did not find any ground so decidedly advantageous
and containing a small space, as to render it tenable for the vanguard of an army to cover the embarkation of the main body.'
. . . 'I should have sent this report much sooner, but found
it impossible to procure post-horses until my arrival at Lugo, and
since that time I have had very bad ones.'

Ditto to Ditto,   Coruna, Jan. 6, 1809.

'I am therefore led to suggest, that as Coruña is fortified, reveted,
and tolerably flanked (though the ground about it is certainly not
favourable), as it could not be carried by a coup-de-main if pro-
perly defended, as it contains a great quantity of cover for men,
and as, even against artillery, it might make resistance for some
days, it may be worth consideration whether, under present circumstances, it may not be desirable to occupy it in preference to the
peninsula of Betanzos, should the army not turn off for Vigo.'

SECTION III.—RELATING TO EQUIPMENT AND SUPPLIES.

Sir John Moore to lord Castlereagh, Oct. 9, 1808.

'At this instant the army is without equipment of any kind,
either for the carriage of the light baggage of regiments, artillery
stores, commissariat stores, or other appendages of an army, and not a
magazine is formed on any of the routes by which we are to march.

Sir John Moore to lord Castlereagh, Oct. 18, 1808.

'In none of the departments is their any want of zeal, but in some
important ones there is much want of experience.' . . 'I have
no hope of getting forward at present with more than the light
baggage of the troops, the ammunition immediately necessary for
the service of the artillery, and a very scanty supply of medicines.'

Sir John Moore's Journal.

'My anxiety is to get out of the rugged roads of Portugal
before the rains.'

Sir John Moore to lord William Bentinck, Oct. 22, 1808.

'The season of the year admitting of no delay, there was a necessity for beginning the march, and trusting for information and supplies as we get on ; unfortunately our commissariat is inexperienced, and a **** of a contractor, Mr. Sattaro, has deceived us.'

Sir David Baird to sir John Moore, Oct. 29, 1808.

' The want of provisions for the men and forage for the horses
have been one of the most serious obstacles we have had to contend
with.   Nor do I at present feel at all easy upon that subject.' . .
' The horses are suffering very severely, both for want of proper
accommodations and food.'. . ' From lord Castlereagh's letter, I was
led to expect that every preparation for our equipment had
been made previous to our leaving England; I need hardly say
how different the case was, and how much I have been disappointed.'

Mr. Stuart to sir John Moore, November 17, 1808.

' The continued slowness of the junta is the only explanation I
can offer for the want of proper arrangements on the routes for
the reception of the English troops.'

SECTION IV.—RELATING TO THE WANT OF INFORMATION.

Sir John Moore's Journal, November 28, 1808.

' I am not in communication with any of the (Spanish) generals,
and neither know their plans nor those of the government.   No
channel of information has been opened to me, and I have no knowledge of the force or situation of the enemy, but what, as a
stranger, I pick up.'

Ditto Salamanca.

' It is singular that the French have penetrated so far (Valladolid), and yet no sensation has been made upon the people.   They
seem to remain quiet, and the information was not known through
any other channel but that of a letter from the captain-general of
the province to me.'

Sir David Baird to sir John Moore, Astorga, Nov. 19, 1808.

' The local authorities have not only failed in affording us the
least benefit in that respect (supplies), but have neglected to give us
any kind of information as to the proceedings of the armies or the
motions of the enemy.

Ditto, Astorga, 23d November.

' It is clearly apparent how very much exaggerated the accounts
generally circulated of the strength of the Spanish armies have
been.'   . . ' It is very remarkable that I have not procured the least

intelligence, or received any sort of communication from any of the official authorities at Madrid, or either of the Spanish generals.'

Sir David Baird to sir John Moore, Villafranca, Dec. 12, 1808.

' I also enclose a letter from the marquis of Romana; you will be fully able to appreciate the degree of reliance that may be placed on the *verbal* communication made to him by the extraordinary courier from Madrid. It was from the same kind of authority that he derived the information he conveyed to me of a *supposed* brilliant affair at Somosierra, which turned out to be an inconsiderable skirmish altogether undeserving of notice.'

Colonel Graham to sir John Moore, Madrid Oct. 4, 1808.

' The deputies sent over knew nothing but just concerning their own provinces, and *pour se faire valoir*, they exaggerated every thing ; for example, those of the Asturias talked louder than any body, and Asturias as yet has never produced a man to the army ; thus government, with all their wish to get information (which cannot be doubted), failed in the proper means.'

Lord Wm. Bentinck to sir John Moore, Madrid, Nov. 20, 1808.

' I must at the same time take the liberty of stating my belief, that reliance cannot be placed upon the correctness of information, even if such information should not be kept back, which does not come through the channel of a British officer. It is the choice of officers rather than the system, that seems to have failed.'

Mr. Stuart to sir John Moore, Madrid, Nov. 19, 1808.

' In your direct communications with Spanish generals, you must however, be contended with their version of the state of affairs, which I do not think can always be relied on, because they only put matters in the view in which they wish you to see them.'

Ditto, Nov. 29.

' The calculation of force which the junta hope may be united in the army under your command will be as follows, if no impediment prevents the different corps reaching the points selected for their junction.

		Remarks by Colonel Napier.
British	35,000	They were only 23,500.
La Romana	20,000	. . . only 5000 armed.
San Juan	15,000	Totally dispersed.
Levies from the south, say	10,000	None ever arrived.
	80,000	Real total, 28,500.

Lieut. Boothby, royal engineers, to sir John Moore, La Puebla, Jan. 1, 1809.

' I shall consider of any means that may more completely ensure the earliest information of the enemy's movements towards this quarter; but the Spaniards are the most difficult people in the world to employ in this way, they are so slow, so talkative, and so credulous.'

SECTION V.—RELATING TO THE CONDUCT OF THE LOCAL JUNTAS.

Sir David Baird to sir John Moore, Coruña, Oct. 24, 1808.

' The answer of the supreme government to our application, as read by Mr. Frere last night in the presence of the junta of this province, is certainly very different from what I expected. Instead of expressing an anxiety to promote our views, and dissatisfaction at the impediments thrown in the way of our measures by the Gallician government, it merely permits us to land here in the event of its being found impracticable to send us by sea to St. Andero, and directs that, if our disembarkation takes place, it should be made in detachments of 2000 or 3000 men each! to be successively pushed on into Castille, without waiting for the necessary equipment of mules and horses.'

Sir David Baird to sir John Moore, Coruña, Nov. 7.

' We have received no sort of assistance from the government.'

Ditto, Astorga, Nov. 19.

' Had the Spanish government afforded us any active assistance, the state of our equipments would have been much more advanced.'

Colonel Graham to sir John Moore, Madrid, Oct. 4, 1808.

' All this, instead of at once appointing the fittest men in the country to be ministers, looks much like private interest and patronage being the objects more than the public good.

Colonel Graham to sir John Moore, Tudela, Nov. 9, 1808.

It is hoped that the Aragonese army will come over to fill it ' (the line) ' up, but being an independent command, no order has yet been sent. An express went after Palafox, who will return here this morning, and *then it is hoped* that he will send an order to general O'Neil at Sanguessa to march instantly; and *further it is hoped* that general O'Neil will obey this order without waiting for one from his

immediate chief, Palafox, the captain-general of Arragon, who is at
Zaragoza ; at all events, there is a loss of above twenty-four hours
by the happy system of independent commands, which may make
the difference of our having 18,000 men more or less in the battle
that may be fought whenever the French are ready.' . . . .
' Making me compliments of there being no secrets with their allies,
they' (the members of the council of war) ' obliged me to sit down,
which I did for a quarter of an hour, enough to be quite satisfied of
the miserable system established by this junta.' . . . . ' In
short, I pitied poor Castaños and poor Spain, and came away
disgusted to the greatest degree.'

Col. Graham to lord W. Bentinck, Centruenigo, Nov. 13, 1808.

' If any thing can make the junta sensible of the absurdity of their
conduct this will.   It would indeed have been more felt if a great
part of the division had been lost, as might well have happened.
But the difficulty of passing so many men with artillery, and in
small boats, and the time that would have been required so great,
that I can hardly persuade myself these people can be so foolish as
ever seriously to have entertained the idea.   But with whatever
intentions, whether merely as a pretence for assuming the command for the purpose of irritating Castaños ; whether from the silly
vanity of exercising power, and doing something which, if by great
good luck it had succeeded, might have proved what might be
done with a more active commander ; or whether from a real conviction of the excellence of the scheme,—it must be equally evident
to every military man, indeed to every man of common sense, that
it is impossible things can succeed in this way ; and then the
junta itself interferes, and to worse purpose.

Castaños's Vindication.

' The nation is deceived in a thousand ways ; as an example, it
believed that our armies were greatly superior to those of the enemy,
reckoning 80,000 men that of the centre, when your excellencies'
(the junta) ' knew that it only amounted to 26,000 men.' . . ' Madrid
possessed money and riches ; the nobles and loyal inhabitants of
that capital wished to give both the one and the other ; but whilst
the armies were suffering the horrors of famine, naked, and miserable, the possessions and jewels of the good Spaniards remained
quiet in Madrid, and they might be soon seized by the tyrant, as
they were in the end.'

Stuart's Despatch, August 7, 1808.

' No province shares the succours granted by Great Britain, although they may not be actually useful to themselves. No gunboats have been sent from Ferrol to protect St. Ander or the coast of Biscay; and the Asturians have in vain asked for artillery from the dépôts of Gallicia. The stores landed at Gihon, and not used by the Asturians, have remained in that port and in Oviedo, although they would have afforded a seasonable relief to the army of general Blake. The money brought by the Pluto for Leon, which has not raised a man, remains in the port where it was landed.'

Major Cox to sir Hew Dalrymple, Seville, August 3, 1808.

' I freely confess that I cannot help feeling some degree of apprehension that this great and glorious cause may be ruined by the baneful effects of jealousy and division.'

Ditto, August 27.

' The fact is, their' (the junta of Seville) ' attention has been for some time past so much occupied by vain and frivolous disputes, and by views of private interest and advantage, and they seem to have neglected entirely every concern of real importance, and almost to have lost sight of the general interests of the country.'. . ' A million of dollars have, I understand, been sent out.'. . ' It certainly would not be prudent to intrust so large a sum to the management of the temporary government of a particular province, without having a sufficient security for its proper application. My own opinion is, that the less money which is given to them the better, until the general government is formed. This junta have shown too evident signs of a wish to aggrandize themselves, and a disinclination to afford those aids to other provinces, which they had it in their power to grant, not to afford just grounds of suspicion, that their boasted loyalty and patriotism have at times been mixed with unworthy considerations of self-interest and personal advantage.'

Ditto, Sept. 5.

' By Mr. Duff's present instructions, he would have had no option'(distributing the money),' even though the *iniquitous project of partition*, which your excellency knows was once contemplated, were still in existence.

Ditto, Sept. 7.

' A dispute between the two juntas' (Seville and Grenada),

'which had nearly been productive of the most serious consequences, and would probably have ended in open hostility, had it
not been prevented by the moderate, but decided, conduct of general
Castaños.'

Major Cox to sir Hew Dalrymple, Seville, Sept. 10.

' The supreme junta of Seville have latterly manifested very different views, and, I am sorry to say, they seem almost to have lost
sight of the common cause, and to be wholly addicted to their particular interest.   Instead of directing their efforts to the restoration of
their legitimate sovereign and the established form of national government, they are seeking the means of fixing the permanency of their
own, and endeavouring to separate its interests from those of the
other parts of Spain.   To what other purpose can be attributed the
order given to general Castaños, not to march on any account beyond
Madrid?   To what the instructions given to their deputy, don Andrea
Miniano, to uphold the authority and preserve the integrity of the
junta of Seville; to distinguish the army to which he is attached by
the name of the army of Andalusia; to preserve constantly the ap-
pellation, and not to receive any orders but what came directly from
this government?   And above all, what other motive could induce
the strong and decided measure of enforcing obedience to those orders, by withholding from general Castaños the means of maintaining his troops, in case of his refusing to comply with them?' ...
' What has been the late occupation of the junta of Seville?   Setting
aside the plans which were formed for augmenting the Spanish army
in these provinces, and neglecting the consideration of those which
have been proposed in their stead, their attention has been taken up
in the appointment of secretaries to the different departments, in
disposing of places of emolument, in making promotions in the army,
appointing canons in the church, and instituting orders of knight-
hood.   Such steps as these make their designs too evident.'

Captain Carrol to sir David Baird, Llanes, Dec. 17, 1808.

' This province' (Asturias), ' the first to declare war with France,
has, during seven months, taken no steps that I can discover to make
arrangements against the event of the enemy's entering the province.'
... ' What has been done with the vast sums of money that came
from England? you will naturally ask.   Plundered and misapplied:
every person who had or has anything to do with money concerns
endeavouring to keep in hand all he can, and be ready, let affairs
turn out as they may, to help himself.'

General Broderick to Mr. Stuart, Reynosa, 11th Sept. 1808.

' The fact is, the junta of Gallicia thinks that this army having marched to the assistance and protection of these countries, the latter ought to pay the expense, and therefore refuse the supplies, which Blake is unwilling to press'

Lord William Bentinck to sir Hew Dalrymple, Seville,
Sept. 19, 1808.

' Nothwithstanding the professions of the junta, their conduct has evidently fallen short of them, and I think it would be very desirable that more money should not fall into their hands.'

Major Cox to sir H. Dalrymple, Seville, 10th and 27th July.

' The proclamation of Florida Blanca was received here some time ago, but was carefully suppressed by the government.'

' Other publications, containing maxims similar to those inculcated by the proclamation of Florida Blanca, have appeared, but are suppressed here with equal care.'

SECTION VI.—CENTRAL JUNTA.

Mr. Stuart to Mr. Canning, Sept. 26, 1808.

' I have heard of several circumstances since my arrival at Aranjuez, which throw a light upon the conduct of general Cuesta, and, if well founded, go far to prove the existence of projects incompatible with the formation of any regular government in the country. I cannot say they are openly avowed by either party, although the measures of precaution, which the leading members of the junta have deemed expedient, go far to prove that the whispers which circulate are not altogether without foundation. It is said that the difficulty of forming a central junta induced Cuesta to propose to Castaños the establishment of a military power, alleging that, in the present situation of the corps under his command, he would take on himself to prevent the union of the central junta, and that his influence with the officers in other parts of Spain would enable him to crush all opposition, by the instant disorganization of the provisional government in the provinces of the kingdom. And I know, indeed, that the movement of Cuesta from Arevolo to Segovia gave so much alarm at Madrid, and so fully convinced the pnblic that he was going to carry this design into execution, that Castaños was formerly requested to give orders for the approach of a division to Madrid, to be ready to oppose any act of violence calculated to bias the determination of the persons about to form the government.'

Mr. Stuart to Mr. Canning, Oct. 9, 1808.

' I have received the paper (of which I enclose a copy) from the supreme junta. Although somewhat startled at the exorbitancy of the demand, I was no less so at the language in which the demand is conveyed, and the conversation I have subsequently had upon the subject. However willing I am to make every possible allowance for the embarrassments of this rising government, and the inexperience or intemperance of many among its members, I cannot but feel that the generosity of Great Britain not only called for some acknowledgment of what has been already done in favour of Spain, but that it likewise might have deserved a petition couched in terms less resembling a military requisition.' When it was observed to Mr. de Villar (the author of the note) that 'the demand for specie much exceeded the means of any country in the world, he said credit or specie was indifferent, provided they could obtain a part of what was requisite for present services. Mr. de Jovellaños was not so moderate, and *literally* proposed that I should draw bills at once on the treasury for the whole, or at least engage the faith of his majesty's government by such a promise as should enable them to raise money by anticipation, upon my signature, until the arrival of a British subsidy.' . . . . 'It was seriously demanded also, that the English government should seize the sums which the Prince of Peace and other friends of the French interest *are supposed* to have in the English funds; nor could my explanation, citing several well-known instances to prove the impossibility of such a measure, and the determination to keep inviolable whatever was deposited under the guardianship of the public faith, prevent Mr. de Jovellaños and others from testifying some ill-humour and incredulity at my answer.'

Lord William Bentinck to sir John Moore, Madrid, Oct. 4, 1808.

' I am sorry to say that the new government do not seem to proceed with the despatch and energy which the critical situation of the country demands.'

Ditto to sir H. Burrard, Madrid, Oct. 8.

' In my last letter I adverted to the inactivity and apparent supineness which prevailed in the central council in regard to the military, as well as to the other business of the government.'

Ditto to sir John Moore, Nov. 8.

' But it is upon the spot where the exact state of the armies, and the extraordinary inefficiency of the government, whose past conduct promises so little for the future, are known, that the danger must be more justly appreciated.' . . . ' The most simple order, however urgent the case, cannot be obtained from the government without a difficulty, solicitation, and delay that is quite incredible.'

Sir John Hope to sir John Moore, Madrid, Nov. 20, 1808.

' It is perfectly evident that they' (the junta) ' are altogether without a plan as to their future military operations, either in the case of success or misfortune. Every branch is affected by the disjointed and inefficient construction of their government.'

Mr. Stuart to sir John Moore, Madrid, Oct. 18, 1808.

' Lord William Bentinck, as well as myself, have made repeated representations, and I have given in paper after paper to obtain something like promptitute and vigour; but though loaded with fair promises in the commencement, we scarcely quit the members of the junta before their attention is absorbed in petty pursuits and the wrangling which impedes even the simplest arrangements necessary for the interior government of a country.' . . . ' In short, we are doing what we can, not what we wish; and I assure you we have infamous tools to work with.'

Ditto, Seville, Jan. 2, 1809.

' Morla's treason is abused, but passed over; and the arrival of money from Mexico, which is really the arrival of spoil for the French, seems to have extinguished every sentiment the bad views and the desperate state of things ought to have created.'

Ditto, Jan. 10, 1809.

' Castaños, Heredia, Castelar, and Galluzzo, are all here. These unfortunate officers are either prisoners or culprits, waiting the decision of government on their conduct in the late transactions. If the state of affairs should allow the government to continue in existence, they will probably wait many months, for no determination is to be expected from people who have in no one instance punished guilt or rewarded merit since they ruled the country. The junta indeed, to say the truth, is at present absolutely null, and although they represent the sovereign authority, I have never witnessed the exercise of their power for the public good.'

Mr. Frere to sir John Moore, Las Santos, Dec. 16, 1808.

' The subject of the ships in Cadiz had not escaped me, but I

thought it so *very dangerous* to suggest to the junta any idea
except that of living and dying on Spanish ground, that I avoided
the mention of any subject that could seem to imply that I entertained any other prospects.'

SECTION VII.—RELATING TO THE PASSIVE STATE OF THE PEOPLE.

Sir John Moore's Journal, Dec. 9, 1808.

' In this part the people are passive. We find the greatest
difficulty to get people to bring in information.

Sir John Moore to Mr. Frere, Sahagun, Dec. 23, 1808.

' If the Spaniards are enthusiastic, or much interested in this
cause, their conduct is the most extraordinary that was ever exhibited.'

Sir John Moore to lord Castlereagh, Astorga, Dec. 31, 1808.

' I arrived here yesterday, where contrary to his promise, and
to my expectation, I found the marquis la Romana, with a great
part of his troops. Nobody can describe his troops to be worse
than he does, and he complains as much as we do of the indifference of the inhabitants, his disappointment at their want of
enthusiasm ; and said to me, in direct terms, that had he known
how things were, he neither would have accepted the command,
nor have returned to Spain. With all this, however, he talks of
attacks and movements which are quite absurd, and then returns
to the helpless state of his army and of the country.'

Mr. Stuart to sir John Moore, Nov. 17, 1808.

' The tranquillity of Madrid is truly wonderful.'

Sir David Baird to sir John Moore, Dec. 6.

' Destitute as we are of magazines, and without receiving even
a show of assistance either from the government or inhabitants of
the country, who, on the contrary, in many instances, even
thwarted our plans and measures, we could not have advanced
without exposing ourselves to almost certain destruction.'

Sir David Baird to lord Castlereagh, Astorga, Nov. 22, 1808.

' Major Stuart, of the 95th regiment, who was despatched in
front of this place to obtain information, reports that the inhabitants appear perfectly depressed by their losses, and seem to
abandon all hope of making a successful resistance.'

Captain Carrol to sir John Moore, Dec. 17, 1808.

' On my arrival at Oviedo all was confusion and dismay ; the confidence between the people, the army, and the junta destroyed.' . . . .
' Is it to be expected that the peasantry can be as hearty in the cause of patriotism as if they were treated with justice ?'

Lieut. Boothby to sir J. Moore, La Puebla, Jan. 1, 1809.

' The Spanish soldiers now here (about 700) are merely on their way to the marquis de la Romana ; and as to any neighbouring passes, there are no people whom I can call upon to occupy them, or should expect to defend them, however naturally strong they may be, for I see no people who are thinking of the enemy's advance with any sentiments beyond passive dislike, and hopes of protection from God and the English army.'

Extract from general Fane's Journal, 1808-9.

' Five hundred and twenty-nine miles of our marches have been in Spain, and notwithstanding all we have read about Spanish patriotism, we have never been joined by *one man,* nor have we seen *one corps in arms.* The people have offered us *no* assistance ; while not even a cart or a guide have been to be procured, but by *force,* and by that measure we have generally been obliged to obtain our quarters. How our ministers could have been so deceived as to the state of the country is inconceivable.'

The prince of Neufchatel to the duke of Dalmatia,
Dec. 10, 1808.

' The city of Madrid is quite tranquil, the shops are all open, the public amusements are resumed.'

General Thouvenot to the prince of Neufchatel, St. Sebastian,
29th Nov. 1808.

' The successes obtained by the armies of the emperor, and those which are also foreseen, begin to make a sensible impression upon the authorities of the country, who become from day to day more affable towards the French, and more disposed to consider the king as their legitimate sovereign.'

The commandant Meslin to the prince of Neufchatel, Vittoria,
29th Nov. 1808.

' The public feeling is still bad, still incredulous of our successes.'
. . ' As to the tranquillity of the country, it appears certain.'

Mr. Frere to sir John Moore, Merida, Dec. 14, 1808.

' A thousand barriers would be interposed against that deluge of panic which sometimes overwhelms a whole nation, and of which at one time I was afraid I saw the beginning in this country.' . . . .
' *The extinction of the popular enthusiasm in this country,* and the means which exist for reviving it, would lead to a very long discussion.'

SECTION VIII.—MISCELLANEOUS.

Lord Collingwood to sir H. Dalrymple, Ocean, Cadiz, June 23, 1808.

' At Minorca and Majorca they describe themselves to be strong, and having nothing to apprehend. However, they made the proposal for entering into a convention with us for their defence, and in the course of it demanded money, arms, and the protection of the fleet. When, in return for them, it was required that their fleet should be given up to us, to be held for their king Ferdinand, or that a part of them should join our squadron against the enemy, they rejected all those proposals: so that whatever we did for them was to be solely for the honour of having their friendship.'

Captain Whittingham to sir Hew Dalrymple, June 12, 1808.

' 12th June. I returned to Xerez at three o'clock, A.M. The general sent for me, and requested I would go without delay to Gibraltar, and inform lieut.-general sir Hew Dalrymple that he at present occupied Carmona with three thousand men (regulars), having his head-quarters at Utrera, where his regular force would amount to twelve thousand men; that it was not his intention to attempt to defend Seville; that the heavy train of artillery, consisting of eighty pieces, was already embarked for Cadiz, under the pretext that they were wanting for the defence of its works; and that everything was prepared for burning the harness, timbers, &c. &c.., of the field-pieces; that he intended to fall gradually back upon Cadiz, if forced to retreat; and that he did not at present desire that any English troops should be landed till their numbers should amount to eight or ten thousand men, lest the ardour of the people should oblige him to commence an offensive system of warfare before the concentration of a considerable Spanish and English force should afford reasonable hopes of success.'

Capt. Whittingham to sir H. Dalrymple, Utrera, June 29, 1808.

' The president approves of the idea, condemned the policy which had led Spain to attempt to establish manufactories by force, and showed clearly that the result had been the loss of a considerable branch of the revenue, the increase of smuggling, and consequently an enormous expense, in the payment of nearly *one hundred thousand* custom or rather excise officers, distributed about the country, and the ruin of numberless families seduced by the prospect of immediate profit to engage in illicit traffic.'

Lord William Bentinck to sir H. Dalrymple, Madrid, Oct. 2, 1808.

' A passage of lord Castlereagh's letter, of which I received from you a copy, instructed you, if possible, to ascertain the intentions of the Spanish government after the expulsion of the French. Though not positively directed by you to ask this information, yet the occasion appeared to make the question so natural, and seemingly of course, and even necessary, that I availed myself of it, and gave to general Castaños, to be laid before count Florida Blanca, a memorandum of which I enclose a copy, marked **A.**'

Extract from the copy marked A.

' It seems probable, in such case, that no diversion could be more effectual or more formidable to Buonaparte than the march of a large combined British and Spanish army over the Pyrenees, into that part of France where there are no fortified places to resist their passage into the very heart of the country, and into that part where great disaffection is still believed to exist.'

No. XIV.

JUSTIFICATORY EXTRACTS FROM SIR JOHN MOORE'S CORRESPONDENCE.

Sir J. Moore to Mr. Frere, Salamanca, Nov. 27, 1808.

' The movements of the French give us little time for discussion. As soon as the British army has formed a junction, I must, upon the supposition that Castaños is either beaten or retreated, march upon Madrid, and throw myself into the heart of Spain, and thus run all risks and share the fortunes of the Spanish nation, or I must fall back upon Portugal.' . . . ' The movement into Spain is one of greater hazard, as my retreat to Cadiz or Gibraltar must be

very uncertain. I shall be entirely in the power of the Spaniards ;
but perhaps this is worthy of risk, if the government and people of
Spain are thought to have still sufficient energy, and the means to
recover from their defeats ; and by collecting in the south be able,
with the aid of the British army, to resist, and finally repel, the
formidable attack which is prepared against them.'

Sir John Moore's Journal, Salamanca, Nov. 30, 1808.

' In the night of the 28th I received an express form Mr. Stuart,
at Madrid, containing a letter from lieut.-colonel Doyle, announcing
the defeat of Castaños's army near Tudela. They seem to have
made but little resistance, and are, like Blake's, flying ; this renders
my junction with Baird so extremely hazardous that I dare not
attempt it ; but even were it made, what chance has this army,
now that all those of Spain are beaten, to stand against the force
which must be brought against it ? The French have eighty
thousand in Spain, and thirty thousand were to arrive in twenty
days from the 15th of this month. As long as Castaños's army
remained there was a hope, but I now see none. I am therefore
determined to withdraw the army.'

Ditto, Dec. 9.

' After Castaños's defeat, the French marched for Madrid, the
inhabitants flew to arms, barricadoed their street, and swore to die
rather than submit. This has arrested the progress of the French,
and Madrid still holds out : this is the first instance of enthusiasm
shown ; there is a chance that the example may be followed, and
the people be roused ; in which case there is still a chance that
this country may be saved. Upon this chance I have stopped
Baird's retreat, and am taking measures to form our junction
whilst the French are wholly occupied with Madrid. We are
bound not to abandon the cause as long as there is hope ; but the
courage of the populace of Madrid may fail, or at any rate they
may not be able to resist ; in short, in a moment things may be
as bad as ever, unless the whole country is animated and flock to
the aid of the capital, and in this part the people are passive.'

Sir John Moore to lord Castlereagh, Salamanca, Dec. 10, 1808.

' I certainly think the cause desperate, because I see no determined spirit anywhere, unless it be at Zaragoza. There is,
however, a chance, and whilst there is that I think myself bound
to run all risks to support it. I am now differently situated from

what I was when Castaños was defeated : I have been joined by general Hope, the artillery, and all the cavalry (lord Paget, with three regiments, is at Toro) ; and my junction with sir David Baird is secure, though I have not heard from him since I ordered him to return to Astorga.'

Sir John Moore to lord Castlereagh.   *Salamanca, Dec.* 12.

' I shall threaten the French communications and create a diversion, if the Spaniards can avail themselves of it ; but the French have in the north of Spain from eighty to ninety thousand men, and more are expected. Your lordship may, therefore, judge what will be our situation if the Spaniards do not display a determination very different from any they have shown hitherto.'

Sir John Moore's Journal.   *Sahagun, Dec.* 24, 1808.

' I gave up the march on Carrion, which had never been undertaken but with the view of attracting the enemy's attention from the armies assembling in the south, and in the hope of being able to strike a blow at a weak corps, whilst it was still thought the British army was retreating into Portugal; for this I was aware I risked infinitely too much, but something I thought was to be risked for the honour of the service, and to make it apparent that we stuck to the Spaniards long after they themselves had given up their cause as lost.'

Sir J. Moore to lord Castlereagh.   *Coruna, Jan.* 13, 1808.

' Your lordship knows that, had I followed my own opinion as a military man, I should have retired with the army from Salamanca. The Spanish armies were then beaten ; there was no Spanish force to which we could unite ; and from the character of the government, and the disposition of the inhabitants, I was satisfied that no efforts would be made to aid us, or favour the cause in which they were engaged. I was sensible, however, that the apathy and indifference of the Spaniards would never have been believed ; that had the British been withdrawn, the loss of the cause would have been imputed to their retreat ; and it was necessary to risk this army to convince the people of England, as well as the rest of Europe, that the Spaniards had neither the power nor the inclination to make any efforts for themselves. It was for this reason that I marched to Sahagun. As a diversion it has succeeded. I brought the whole disposable force of the French against this army, and it has been allowed to follow it, without a single movement being made by any of what the Spaniards call armies to favour its retreat.'

No. XV.

THIS despatch from the count of Belvedere to the count of Florida Blanca, relative to the battle of Gamonal, is an example of the habitual exaggerations of the Spanish generals.

[Translation.]

Since my arrival at Burgos I have been attacked by the enemy: in two affairs I repulsed him ; but to-day, after having sustained his fire for thirteen hours, he charged me with double my force, besides cavalry, as I believe he had three thousand of the latter, and six thousand infantry at least, and I have suffered so much that I have retired on Lerma, and mean to assemble my army at Aranda de Duero. I have sustained a great loss in men, equipage, and artillery ; some guns have been saved, but very few. Don Juan Henestrosa, who commanded in the action, distinguished himself, and made a most glorious retreat; but as soon as the cavalry attacked, all was confusion and disorder. I shall send your excellency the particulars by an officer when they can be procured. The volunteers of Zafra, of Sezena, of Valencia, and the first battalion of infantry of Truxillo, and the provincials of Badajoz, had not arrived at Burgos, and consequently I shall be able to sustain myself at Aranda, but they are without cartridges and ammunition. I lament that the ammunition in Burgos could not be brought off. The enemy followed me in small numbers: I am now retiring (10 P.M.), fearing they may follow me in the morning. I yesterday heard from general Blake, that he feared the enemy would attack him to-day, but his dispositions frustrated the enemy's designs, beginning the action at eleven at night.

(Signed)   CONDE DE BELVEDERE.

No. XVI.

EXTRACT FROM A LETTER FROM THE DUKE OF DAL-MATIA TO THE AUTHOR.

' Dans la même lettre que vous m'avez fait l'honneur de m'écrire, vous me priez aussi, Monsieur, de vous donner quelques lumières sur la poursuite de Mr. le général sir John Moore, quand il fit sa retraite sur la Corogne en 1809. Je ne pense pas que vous desiriez des détails sur cette opération, car ils doivent vous être parfaitement connus, mas je saisirai avec empressement l'occasion que vous me procurez pour rendre à la mémoire de sir John Moore le témoignage

que ses dispositions furent toujours les plus convenables aux circonstances, et qu'en profittant habillement des avantages que les localités pouvaient lui offrir pour seconder sa valeur, il m'opposa partout
la resistance la plus énergique et la mieux calculée ; c'est ainsi
qu'il trouva une mort glorieuse devant la Corogne, au milieu d'un
combat qui doit honorer son souvenir.

' *Paris, ce* 15 *Novembre,* 1824.'

No. XVII.

LETTER FROM MR. CANNING TO MR. FRERE.

London, Dec. 10, 1808.

Sir,

The messenger, Mills, arrived here yesterday with your despatches, No. 19 to No. 26 inclusive ; and at the same time advices
were received from lieutenant-general sir David Baird, dated on
the 29th ultimo at Astorga, which state that general to have received
intelligence from sir John Moore of the complete defeat of general
Castaños's army, and of the determination taken by sir John Moore,
in consequence, to fall back upon Portugal, while sir David Baird
is directed by sir John Moore to re-embark his troops, and to proceed to the Tagus. Thus at the same moment at which I receive
from you the caution entertained in your No. 20, that a retreat into
Portugal would be considered by the central junta as indicating an
intention to abandon the cause of Spain, his majesty's government
receive the information that this measure has actually been adopted,
but under circumstances which, it is to be supposed, could not have
been in the contemplation of the central junta. To obviate, however, the possibility of such an impression as you apprehend being
produced upon the Spanish government by the retreat of the British
armies, I lose no time in conveying to you his majesty's commands,
that you should forthwith give the most positive assurance, that the
object of this retreat is no other than that of effecting in Portugal
the junction which the events of the war have unfortunately rendered impracticable in Spain, with the purpose of preparing the
whole army to move forward again into Spain whenever and in
whatever direction their services may be best employed in support
of the common cause. In proof of this intention, you will inform
the Spanish government, that an additional reinforcement of cavalry
is at this moment sailing for Lisbon, and that the British army in
Portugal will be still further augmented, if necessary, so as to make
up a substantive and effective force, adequate to any operation for
which an opportunity may be offered in the centre or south of Spain,
according to the course which the war may take. But while you

make this communication to the Spanish government, it is extremely necessary that you should accompany it with a distinct and pressing demand for the communication to you and to the British general of whatever be the plan of operations of the Spanish armies. Sir John Moore complains that he had not received the slightest intimation of any such plan at the date of his last despatch of the 20th ultimo ; and I am afraid the appointment which you mention in your No. 20, of general Morla to discuss with the British commanders the mode of co-operation between the British and Spanish armies, will not have taken place till after the defeat of the Spanish armies will have entirely disposed of that question for the present. The language of sir David Baird, with respect to defect of information, is precisely the same as that of sir John Moore. Sir David Baird has indeed had the advantage of some intercourse with the marquis de la Romana ; but the marquis de la Romana himself does not appear to have been in possession of any part of the views of his government, nor to have received any distinct account of the numbers, state, or destination even, of either of the armies which he was himself appointed to command. The British government has most cautiously and scrupulously abstained from interfering in any of the counsels of the junta, or presuming to suggest to them by what plan they should defend their country. But when the question is as to the co-operation of a British force, they have a right and it is their duty to require that some plan should have been formed, and being formed, should be communicated to the British commander, in order that he may judge of, and (if he shall approve) may be prepared to execute the share intended to be assigned to him. You will recollect, that the army which has been appropriated by his majesty to the defence of Spain and Portugal is not merely a considerable part of the disposable force of this country ; it is, in fact, the British army. The country has no other force disposable. It may, by a great effort, reinforce the army for an adequate purpose ; but another army it has not to send. The proposals, therefore, which are made somewhat too lightly, for appending parts of this force, sometimes to one of the Spanish armies, sometimes to another, and the facility with which its services are called for, wherever the exigency of the moment happens to press, are by no means suited to the nature of the force itself, or consonant to the views with which his majesty has consented to employ it in Spain. You are already apprised by my former despatch (enclosing a copy of general Moore's instructions), that the British army must be kept together under its own commander, must act as one body for some distinct object, and on some settled plan.

It will decline no difficulty, it will shrink from no danger, when, through that difficulty and danger, the commander is enabled to see his way to some definite purpose. But, in order to this, it will be necessary that such purpose should have been previously arranged, and that the British army should not again be left, as that of sir John Moore and sir David Baird have recently been, in the heart of Spain, without one word of information, except such as they could pick up from common rumour, of the events passing around them. Previously, therefore, to general sir John Moore's again entering Spain, it will be expected that some clear exposition should be made to him of the system upon which the Spaniards intend to conduct the war; the points which they mean to contest with the advancing enemy, and those which, if pressed by a series of reverse, they ultimately propose to defend.

' The part assigned to the British army in the combined operation must be settled with sir John Moore, and he will be found not unambitious of that in which he may be opposed most directly to the enemy. The courage and constancy displayed by the junta, under the first reverses, are in the highest degree worthy of admiration.* And if they shall persevere in the same spirit, and can rouse the country to adequate exertions, there is no reason to despair of the ultimate safety of Spain. But it is most earnestly to be hoped that the same confidence which they appear to have placed in the ability of their armies, under Blake and Castaños, to resist the attacks of the enemy, will not be again adopted as their guide, again to deceive them in the ulterior operations of the war. It is to be hoped that they will weigh well their really existing means of defence against the means of attack on the part of the enemy, and that if they find them unequal to maintain a line of defence as extended as they have hitherto attempted to maintain, they will at once fall back to that point, wherever it may be, at which they can be sure that their stand will be permanent and their resistance effectual. It is obvious that unless they can resist effectually in the passes of the Guadarama, or in the Sierra Morena, the ultimate point of retreat, after a series of defeats more or less numerous and exhausting, according as they shall the sooner or the latter make up their minds to retreat, is Cadiz. Supported by Cadiz on one side, and by the fortress of Gibraltar on the other, the remaining armies of Spain might unquestionably make such a stand, as no force which France could bring against them could overpower; and

---

* The extract which follows this letter furnishes a curious comment on this passage.

the assistance of the British army would be in this situation incal-
culably augmented by the communication with Gibraltar and the
sea. I am aware of the jealousy with which the mention of a
British force of any sort coupled with the name of Cadiz will be
received. But the time seems to be arrived at which we must communicate with each other (the Spanish government and England)
without jealousy or reserve. His majesty has abjured, in the face
of the world, any motive of interested policy,—you are authorised
to repeat in the most solemn manner, if necessary, that abjuration.
But if in the midst of such sacrifices and such exertions as Great
Britain is making for Spain; if after having forgone all objects of
partial benefit, many of which the state of Spain (if we had been so
ungenerous as to take that advantage of it) would have brought
within our reach, the fair opinion of the British government cannot
be received without suspicion ; there is little hope of real cordiality
continuing to subsist under reverses and misfortunes, such as Spain
must but too surely expect, and such as are at all times the tests of
sincerity and confidence. It is the opinion of the British government, that the last stand (if all else fails) must be made at Cadiz.
It is the opinion of the British government, that this stand will
be made in vain *only* if the necessity of resorting to it is too late
acknowledged, and the means of making it effectually not provi-
dently prepared. It is the opinion of the British government that
on no account should the naval means of Spain be suffered to
fall into the hands of France, or those of France to be recovered
by her. It is their opinion that this may be prevented ; but to
prevent it, the object must be fairly looked at beforehand ; and
it is hoped that a spirit of distrust unworthy both of those who
entertain it, and of those with respect to whom it is entertained,
will not be suffered to interfere between an object of so great
importance and the means of ensuring its accomplishment. It is
absolutely necessary to lose no time in bringing this subject fairly
before the Spanish government ; and if, in doing so, you should
see either in M. Cevellos or in count Florida Blanca marks of
that distrust and suspicion which must fatally affect any measure
of co-operation between the British and Spanish forces, it will be
right that you should at once anticipate the subject, and you are at
liberty to communicate this despatch *in extenso*, as the surest mode
of proving the openness with which the British government is desirous of acting, and the disdain which it would feel of any imputation upon its disinterestedness and sincerity. But while this
object is thus to be stated to the central government, it is not to this

object alone that the services of the British army are to be appropriated. The commander-in-chief will have both the authority and the inclination to listen to any proposal for any other practicable undertaking. And it is only in the event of no such object or undertaking being presented to him in Spain, that he is directed to confine himself to the defence of Portugal.

I am, &c. &c. &c.

(Signed)   GEORGE CANNING.

EXTRACTS FROM A LETTER FROM MR. CANNING TO MR. FRERE, OF THE SAME DATE AS THE ABOVE.

December 10, 1808.

' The timely preparation of the fleets of France and Spain, now in the harbour of Cadiz, is also a point to be pressed by you with earnestness, but at the same time with all the delicacy which belongs to it. In the event of *an emigration to America*, it is obvious that this preparation should be made beforehand. And in the case of this project not being adopted, and of a resolution being taken to defend Cadiz to the utmost, it would still be desirable that the fleets should be prepared for removal to Minorca, in order to be out of the reach of any use which the disaffected in Cadiz (of whom General Morla is represented to have expressed considerable apprehensions) might be disposed to make of them for compromise with the enemy.'

EXTRACT FROM A LETTER FROM MR. CANNING TO MR. FRERE.

December 11, 1808.

' Sir,

' Complaints have been justly made of the manner in which the British troops, particularly those under sir David Baird, have been received in Spain.

' The long detention of sir David Baird's corps on board the transports at Coruña may but too probably have contributed to render the difficulties of a junction between the two parts of the British army insurmountable, by giving the enemy time to advance between them. In addition to this it is stated, that there was a total want of preparation for supply of any sort, and the unwillingness with which those supplies appear to have been administered, have undoubtedly occasioned as much disappointment as inconvenience to the British commanders. Unless some change is effected in these particulars when the army again moves into Spain, the advance of the British troops through that country will be attended with more difficulty than a march through a hostile country.'

No. XVIII.

ABSTRACT OF THE MILITARY FORCE OF GREAT BRITAIN IN 1808.

Extracted from the Adjutant-general's returns.

Cavalry............................... 30,000
Foot Guards.......................... 6,000
Infantry of the line.................... 170,000
Artillery 14,000

Total........ 220,000

Of these between fifty and 60,000 were employed in the Colonies in India; the remainder were disposable, because from 80 to 100,000 militia, differing from the regular troops in nothing but the name, were sufficient for the home duties. If to this force we add 30,000 marines, the military power of England must be considered prodigious.

RETURN OF BRITISH TROOPS EMBARKED FOR PORTUGAL AND SPAIN IN 1808.

Artil.	Cavalry.	Infantry.	Total.	
357	349	8688	9394	Commanded by sir A. Wellesley; embarked at Cork the 15th, 16th, and 17th June, 1808; sailed 12th July; landed at Mondego, August 1st.
379	..	4323	4702	Commanded by generals Acland and Anstruther; embarked at Harwich, July 18th and 19th; landed at Maceira, August 20th, 1808.
66	..	4647	4713	Commanded by general Spencer; embarked at Cadiz; landed at Mondego, August 3d.
712	563	10,049	11,324	Commanded first by sir John Moore, secondly by sir Harry Burrard; embarked at Portsmouth, April, 1808; sailed to the Baltic; returned, and sailed to Portugal, July 31st; landed at Maceira, August 29th.
..	672	..	672	Landed at Lisbon, Dec. 31st, 1808.
186	..	943	1129	Embarked at Gibraltar, sailed Aug. 14; landed at the Tagus in September.
94	..	929	1023	Commanded by general Beresford; embarked at Madeira, sailed Aug. 17th; landed at the Tagus in September.
..	672	..	672	Commanded by general C. Stewart; embarked at Gravesend, landed at Lisbon, September 1st.
798	..	10,271	11,069	Commanded by sir D. Baird; embarked at Falmouth, sailed Oct. 9th; arrived at Coruña, 13th Oct., landed 29th ditto.
..	..	1622	1622	Two regiments sent round to Lisbon from sir D. Baird's force.
..	2021	..	2021	Commanded by lord Paget; embarked at Portsmouth; landed at Coruña, October 30th.
2592	4277	41,472	46,719	
			1622	Add two regiments sent to Lisbon from Coruña.
			48,341	Grand total, of which 800 were artificers, waggon train, and commissariat

No. XIX.

RETURNS OF KILLED, WOUNDED, AND MISSING, OF THE ARMY UNDER THE COMMAND OF SIR A. WELLESLEY.

1808. August.	OFFICERS.			MEN.			TOTAL.
	Killed.	Wounded.	Missing.	Killed.	Wounded.	Missing.	
15th—Brillos..	1	1	0	1	5	21	29
17th—Roriça..	4	19	4	66	316	70	479
21st—Vimiero .	4	35	2	131	499	49	720
Grand total for the campaign	9	55	6	198	820	140	1228

No. XX.

BRITISH ORDER OF BATTLE. RORICA, 17th AUGUST, 1808.

Extracted from the Adjutant-general's states.

Regiments.

Right wing.
- 1st brigade, major-general Hill .. { 5th, 9th, 38th } 2780
- 3rd ditto, major-general Nightingale. { 29th, 82nd } 1722
- 5th ditto, C. Crawfurd.......... { 45th, 50th, 91st } 2744

7246

Left wing.
- 4th brigade, brigadier-general Bowes..................... { 6th, 32d } 1829
- 2nd ditto major-general Ferguson. { 36th, 40th, 71st } 2681
- 6th ditto (light) brigadier-general Fane .... { 95th, 2nd bn., 60th, 5th bn. } 1336

5846

Artillery, 18 guns, 6 and 9 lbs. .... 660 — 660
Cavalry .... 240 — 240

Total British 13,992

Portuguese, colonel Trant .. { Infantry of the line.. 1000, Light troops........ 400, Cavalry............ 250 } 1,650

Grand total, British and Portuguese, including sick men, &c. &c. 15,642

No. XXI.

BRITISH ORDER OF BATTLE. VIMIERO, 21st AUGUST, 1808.

Extracted from the Adjutant-general's states.

Regiments.

Right wing.	1st brigade, general Hill	5th 9th 38th	2780	2780
Centre.	6th ditto, brigadier-general Fane.	50th 60th 95th, 2nd bn.	2293	4953
	7th. ditto, brigadier-general Anstruther	9th 43rd, 2nd bn. 52nd, 2nd bn. 97th	2660	
Left wing.	2nd brigade, major-gen. Ferguson	36th 40th 71st	2681	7612
	3rd ditto, major-general Nightingale	29th 82nd	1722	
	4th ditto, brigadier-general Bowes	6th 32nd	1829	
	8th ditto, major-general Ackland	2nd 20th	1380	
Reserve	5th brigade, brig.-gen. C.Crawfurd	45th 50th 91st	2744	2744

Artillery, 18 guns, 6 and 9 lbs.   660   660
Cavalry, 20th light dragoons   240   240

                Total British   18,989

Portuguese, colonel Trant .... { Infantry, 1400 }   1,650
                         { Cavalry,   250 }

Grand total, including sick, wounded, and missing   20,639

No. XXII.

RETURN OF SIR HUGH DALRYMPLE'S ARMY, OCT. 1, 1808.

Head-quarters, Bemfica.

	Fit for duty.	Hospital.	Detached.	Total.
Cavalry....................	1402	128	28	1558
Artillery	2091	146	6	2243
Infantry	25,678	3196	454	29,328
Total.....................	29,171	3470	488	

Grand total, including artificers, waggon train, &c. &c.   33,129

No. XXIII.

EMBARKATION RETURN OF THE FRENCH ARMY UNDER GENERAL JUNOT.

| | PRESENT UNDER ARMS. | | | DETACHED. | | | ABSENT WITHOUT PAY. | | | | TOTAL. | | | CRIMINALS. |
| | | | | | | | Hospital | Prisons. | | | | | | |
	Officers.	Men.	Horses.	Officers.	Men.	Horses.	Officers.	Men.	Officers.	Men.	Officers.	Men.	Horses.	Men.
Infantry ..	273	15,860	....	52	2078	0	46	3281	17	895	..	22,635	..	13
Cavalry ..	48	1722	1176	..	1	1	..	195	1	....	..	1974	..	..
Artillery..	21	1015	472	..	6	..	..	....	3	....	..	1121	..	..
Engineers.	14	....	....	....	..	..	..	....	..	....	..	17	..	..

```
           Guns......................10   8 lbs. ⎫
           Ditto.....................16   4 lbs. ⎬30
           Howitzers ................ 4   6 inch.⎭
```
Grand total, 25,747 men, 1655 horses, and 30 pieces of artillery.

Note.—On the staff of each division there are—

1 General of division.	1 Inspector of reviews.
2 Generals of brigade.	1 Commissary of engineers.
7 Aides-de-camp.	2 Officers of engineers.

Artillery.............. ⎰ 1 General. / 4 Colonels. / 2 Chefs de bataillon.

Engineers .... ⎰ 1 Colonel. / 2 Captains. ⎱ The remainder in the divisions.

No. XXIV.

THE FOLLOWING EXTRACT FROM A MINUTE MADE BY HIS ROYAL HIGHNESS THE DUKE OF YORK IN 1808

Proves that sixty thousand men could have been provided for the campaign of 1808-9 in *Spain,* without detriment to other services:

' There are present in Portugal.. ⎰ Cavalry............ 1640 ⎱ 31,446
⎰ Infantry 34 battalions 29,806 ⎱

' Under orders to embark ...... ⎰ Cavalry............ 3410 ⎱ 14,829
⎰ Infantry ....11,419 ⎱

Total.....................46,275

' Of this force the 20th dragoons and eight battalions should remain in Portugal. The disposable force would then be—

	Cavalry.	Infantry.
From Portugal	1,313	23,575
Under orders	3,200	11,419
Force to be drawn from Sicily		8,000
Total	4,513	42,994
' To this may be added four regiments of cavalry } and the two brigades of guards .... }	2,560	2,434
Grand total....................	7,073	45,428

' When to this you add four battalions of infantry, which may be spared, and the artillery, it will form a corps of about sixty thousand rank and file.'

Note.—The details of names and strength of the regiments are omitted to save space.

No. XXV.

SIR J. MOORE'S ORDER OF BATTLE.

Third Division.	*Second Divison.*	*First Division.*
Lt.-gen. M'Kenzie Fraser.	Lieut.-gen. sir John Hope.	Lt.-gen. sir David Baird.
79th, 38th, 3d, 43d, 23d, 9th, 6th.	76th, 59th, 51st, 92d, 71st, 36th, 32d, 14th, 5th, 2d.	81st, 26th, 1st, 50th, 42d. 4th, 1st, and 3d bat. guards.
Wilmot's brig. of artillery, 6 pieces.	Drummond's brig. of art., 6 pieces.	Bean's brigade of artillery, 6 pieces.
Second Flank Brigade.	*Reserve.*	*First Flank Brigade.*
Brigadier-gen. C. Alten.	Major-general E. Paget.	Colonel R. Crawfurd.
1st battalion 2d battalion K.G.L. K.G.L.	21st, 28th, 1st bat. 95th, 52d, 20th. Carthew's brig. of artillery, 6 pieces.	2d bat. 95th, 2d bat. 52d, 1st bat. 43d.

Cavalry.

Lieut.-general lord Paget.

3d light dragoons K.G.L., 15th light dragoons, 10th, 18th, 7th hussars.

Dowman's and Evelin's troops of horse artillery, 12 pieces.

Artillery Parc and Reserve.

Colonel Harding.

5 brigades	30 pieces
6 ditto, attached to the divisions	36 ,,
	66 ,,

RETURN OF SIR JOHN MOORE'S ARMY, DECEMBER 19, 1808.

Extracted from the adjutant-general's morning state of that day.

	Fit for Duty.	Hospital.	Detached.	Total.	
Cavalry	2,278	182	794	3,254	
Artillery	1,358	97	..	1,455	
Infantry	22,222	3,756	893	26,871	
	25,858	4,035	1,687	31,580	3d regt. left in Portugal.
Deduct	2,275	Men composing four battalions, viz.			76th ⎫ Between Villa 51st ⎬ Franca and Lugo. 59th ⎭
	23,583	Total number under arms.			

Note.—Of 66 guns, 42 were attached to the divisions, the remainder in reserve, with the exception of one brigade of 3lbs.

***

No. XXVI.

THE following General Return, extracted from especial regimental reports, received at the Horse Guards, contains the whole number of non-commissioned officers and men, cavalry and infantry, lost during sir John Moore's campaign:—

Total.

Lost at or previous to the arrival of the ⎰ Cavalry .... 95 ⎱ 1397
army at the position of Lugo .... ⎱ Infantry .... 1302 ⎰

Of this number 200 were left in the wine-vaults of Bembibre, and nearly 500 were stragglers from the troops that marched to Vigo.

Lost between the departure of the army ⎱ Cavalry .... 9 ⎰ 2636
from Lugo and the embarkation at ⎰ Infantry .... 2627 ⎱
Coruña ....

Grand total 4033

Of the whole number, above 800 contrived to escape to Portugal, and being united with the sick left by the regiments in that country, they formed a corps of 1876 men, which being re-embodied under the name of the battalions of detachments, did good service at Oporto and Talavera.

The pieces of artillery abandoned during the retreat were six 3-pounders.

These guns were landed at Coruña without the general's knowledge : they never went beyond Villa Franca, and, not being horsed, they were thrown down the rocks when the troops quitted that town.

The guns used in the battle of Coruña were spiked and buried in the sand, but the French discovered them.

N.B. Some trifling errors may possibly have crept into the regimental states in consequence of the difficulty of ascertaining exactly where each man was lost, but the inaccuracies could not affect the total amount above fifty men more or less.

No. XXVII.

THE following states of the Spanish armies are not strictly accurate, because the original reports from whence they have been drawn were generally very loose, often inconsistent, and sometimes contradictory : nevertheless, it is believed that the approximation is sufficiently close for any useful purpose.

STATE I.

Army of Andalusia.

	Armed peasantry.	Regulars.
1808.		
19th July, Baylen	Unknown	29,000
1st Sept. { Madrid / La Mancha / Sierra Morena }	——	30,600

STATE II.

Numbers of the Spanish armies in October, 1808, according to the reports transmitted to sir John Moore by the military agents.

	Regulars.	Armed peasantry incorporated with the regular troops.	
Troops upon the Ebro, and in Biscay..	75,300	70,000	145,000
In Catalonia	20,000	..	20,000
In march from Aragon to Catalonia ..·	10,000	..	10,000
Ditto new levies from Grenada	..	10,000	10,000
In the Asturias	18,000	..	18,000
Total.............	123,000	80,000	——
Grand Total.............................			203,000

STATE III.

Real numbers of the Spanish armies in line of battle, in the months of October, November, and December. 1808.

1st Line.

	Cavalry.	Infantry.	Guns.	
Army of Palafox	550	17,500	20	} Defeated and dispersed at Tudela.
Army of Castaños	2200	24,500	48	
Army of Blake..........	100	30,000	26	} Ditto at the battles of Zornoza and Espinosa.
Army of Romana	1404	8,000	25	
Asturians	..	8,000	..	
Army of count Belvedere .	1150	11,150	30	Ditto at Gamonal.
Total	5404	99,150	149	
Deduct Romana's cavalry & guns, which never came into the line of battle .. }	1404	..	25	
Total, brought into 1st line battle .... }	4000	99,150	124	 103,150

2d Line.

	Infantry.	Cavalry.	
General St. Juan's division	12,000	..	{ Were beaten at the Somo-sierra 30th November; murdered their general at Talavera, December 7th, and dispersed.
Fugitives from Gamonal, commanded by general Heredia .... }	4000	..	{ Fled from Segovia and Sepulveda, Dec.2d, and dispersed at Talavera, 7th.
Fugitives from Blake's army, re-organised by Romana . }	6000	1400	{ Beaten at Mancilla,29th Dec.; retired into Gallicia. Infantry dispersed there.
Asturian levies under Ballasteros................ }	5000	..	Were not engaged.
Fugitives assembled by Galluzzo behind the Tagus.. }	6000	..	{ Defeated and dispersed, 24th December, by the 4th corps, at Almaraz.
Total, brought into 2d line..	33,000	1400	

To cover Moore's advance there were on the Ebro, in Biscay, and in the Asturias, according to the Spanish and the military agents' reports .... } 173,000

The real number brought into the field was 103,150

Exaggeration 69,850

Note.—The real amount includes the sick in the field hospitals.

No. XXVIII.

SECTION I.—STATE OF THE FRENCH ARMY, CALLED 'THE FIRST PART OF THE ARMY OF SPAIN,' DATED OCT. 1, 1808.

Head-quarters, Vittoria.

King Joseph, commander-in-chief.

General Jourdan, major-general.　General Belliard, chief of the staff.

Recapitulation, extracted from the Imperial states, signed by the prince of Neufchatel.

Officers included, present under arms.

	Men.	Horses.
Division imperial guard, commanded by gen. Dorsenne .	2,423	786
Do. reserve cavalry, imperial gendarmes, and other troops .... } gen. Saligny .	5,417	944
Corps of marshal Bessieres	15,595	2,923
Corps of marshal Ney	13,756	2,417
Corps of marshal Moncey 16,636 } Garrison of Pampeluna . 6,004 }	22,640	3,132
Garrisons of Vittoria, Bilbao, St. Sebastian, Tolosa, Montdragon, Salinas, Bergara, Villa Real, Yrun, and other places of less note .... } gen. Lagrange	8,479	1,458
Troops disposable at Bayonne and vicinity or in march upon that place .... } gen. Drouet, commanding 11th military division .... }	20,005	5,196
Troops employed as moveable columns in the defence of the frontier from Bayonne to Belgarde...................... }	6,042	261
In Catalonia, gen. Duhesme.................	10,142	1,638
Fort of Fernando Figueras, gen. Reille........	4,027	557
Division of gen. Chabot	1,434	..
Total...............	109,960	19,312

Note.—At this period the Spaniards and the military agents always asserted that the French had only from 35 to 45,000 men of all weapons.

STATE OF THE FRENCH ARMY, CALLED ' THE SECOND
PART OF THE ARMY OF SPAIN,' OCTOBER 1, 1808.

This army, composed of the troops coming from the grand
army and from Italy, was, by an imperial decree dated 7th September, divided into six corps and a reserve.

Present under arms.

	Men.	Horses.
1st corps, marshal Victor, duke of Belluno	29,547	5,552
5th do. ,, Mortier, duke of Treviso ..	24,405	3,495
6th do., destined for Ney, duke of Elchingen ..	22,694	3,945
Infantry of the viceroy of Spain's guards......	1,213	....
Cavalry ditto	456	551
1st division of dragoons	3,695	3,994
2d ditto	2,940	3,069
3d ditto	2,020	2,238
4th ditto	3,101	3,316
5th ditto	2,903	3,068
Division of general Sebastiani	5,808	185
5th regiment of dragoons....................	556	531
German division...........................	6,067	381
Polish ditto	6,818	....
Dutch brigade	2,280	751
Westphalian light horse	522	559
General Souham's division	7,259	....
General Pino's ditto	6,803	....
24th regiment of dragoons	664	731
Regiment of royal Italian chasseurs	560	512
Regiment of Napoleon's dragoons	500	474
Artillery and engineers in march for Perpignan..	1,706	1,430
Total of second part	132,517	34,782
Total of first part	109,960	19,312
Grand total	242,477	54,094

SECTION II.—GENERAL STATE OF THE FRENCH ARMY, OCTOBER 10th, 1808.

	PRESENT UNDER ARMS.		DETACHED.		HOSPITAL.	PRISONERS.	EFFECTIVE.		
	Men.	Horses.	Men.	Horses.	Men.	Men.	Men.	Cav. Hors.	Art. Hors.
1st corps, duke of Belluno	28,797	5,615	2,201	219	2,939	..	33,937	3,329	2,501
2d do. — Istria	20,093	3,219	7,394	1,199	5,536	30	33,054	3,616	802
3d do. — Cornegliano	18,867	3,186	11,082	2,472	7,522	219	37,090	4,537	821
4th do. — Dantzic	22,859	2,410	955	40	2,170	..	25,984	1,791	659
5th do. — Treviso	24,552	3,833	188	6	1,971	2	26,713	1,805	2,034
6th do. — Elchingen	29,568	4,304	3,381	257	5,051	33	38,033	2,465	2,096
7th do. — general St. Cyr	35,657	5,254	1,302	198	4,948	200	42,107	4,045	1,404
8th do. — duke of Abrantes	19,059	2,247	2,137	1	3,528	1,006	25,730	1,776	472
Reserve	34,924	23,604	3,533	733	3,553	392	42,382	21,225	3,112
1st hussars and 27th chasseurs	1,424	1,463	256	208	74	..	1,754	1,675	..
Artillery and engineers in march, coming from Germany	3,446	958	107	..	..	..	3,446	..	958
Moveable columns for defence of the frontiers of France	8,588	477	107	..	146	19	8,860	268	209
Total	247,834	56,670	32,643	5,333	37,438	1,901	319,690	46,822	15,068

	UNDER ARMS.						DETACHED.		HOSPITL.	PRSNRS.	EFFECTIVE.		
	Artillery.		Cavalry.		Infantry.								
	Men.	Horses.	Men.	Horses.	Men.		Men.	Horses.	Men.	Men.	Men.	Cav. Hors.	Art. Hors.
Of this number { French	17,868	15,107	34,172	35,761	152,770		29,647	5,052	31,401	1,771	267,629	41,565	14,253
Auxiliaries	1,503	968	4,782	4,831	36,739		2,889	277	6,018	130	52,061	5,263	815
Total	19,371	16,075	38,954	40,592	189,509		32,536	5,329	37,419	1,901	319,690	46,828	15,068

Grand total........ 319,690 men and 61,896 horses.

SECTION III.—STATE OF THE FRENCH ARMY OF SPAIN, THE EMPEROR NAPOLEON COMMANDING IN PERSON, 25th OCTOBER, 1808.

1148 Officers of the Staff. 298 Battalions. 184 Squadrons.

Present under arms.		Detached.		Hospitl.	Prisrs.	Total.		
Men.	Horses.	Men.	Hors.	Men.	Men.	Men.	Cav. H.	Art. H.
249,046	55,759	33,438	4,943	34,558	1,892	318,934	45,242	15,498

Grand total .. 318,934 men and 60,740 horses.

STATE OF THE FRENCH ARMY IN SPAIN, THE EMPEROR NAPOLEON COMMANDING, 15th NOVEMBER, 1808.

Officers of the Staff, 1064. Battalions, 290. Squadrons, 181.

Present under arms.		Detached.		Hospitl.	Prisrs.	Total.		
Men.	Horses.	Men.	Hors.	Men.	Men.	Men.	Cav. H.	Art. H.
255,876	52,430	32,245	8,295	45,107	1,995	335,223	43,920	16,808

Grand total .. 335,223 men and 60,728 horses.

SECTION IV.—STATE OF THE FRENCH ARMY IN PORTUGAL, 1st JANUARY, 1808.

[Extracted from the imperial returns.]

General Junot, commander-in-chief. General Thiebault, chief of the staff.

1st division, general De Laborde
2d " " Loison
3d " " Travot
Cavalry . " Kellermann
} 26 battalions, 7 squadrons.

10 guns of 8lbs.
22 " 4lbs.
4 6-inch howitzers
} 36 pieces.

	Under arms.		Effective.	
	Men.	Horses.	Men.	Horses.
	16,190	1,114	24,735	1,377
At Salamanca, or in march to join the army in Portugal	4,795	1,296	4,795	1,296
Total	20,985	2,310	29,530	2,673

STATE OF THE FRENCH ARMY IN PORTUGAL, 23d MAY, 1808.

	Under arms.		Detached.		Hospital.	Effective.		
	Men.	Horses.	Men.	Hors.	Men.	Men.	Horses.	Art.
French..........	24,446	2,789	..	..	2,449	29,684	3,586	629
Spanish division of gen. Quesnel ..	9,281	101	1,087	..	651	11,019	..	..
Do., gen. Caraffa .	6,309	844	174	13	141	6,624	13	..
Portuguese troops	4,621	483	570	234	116	5,307	234	..
Total......	44,657	4,217	1,831	247	3,357	52,634	3,833	629

Grand Total .. 52,634 men, 4,454 horses, and 36 guns.

SECTION V.—STATE OF 'THE SECOND ARMY OF OBSERVATION OF THE GIRONDE,' 1st FEB., 1808, SPAIN.

General Dupont, commanding.
20 battalions and 1 division of cavalry.
Head quarters, Valladolid.

Present under arms.		Detached.		Hospital.	Effective.	
Men.	Horses.	Men.	Horses.	Men.	Men.	Horses.
20,729	2,884	1,303	334	2,277	24,309	3,218

Total .. 21,309 men and 3,218 horses.

SECTION VI.—STATE OF 'THE ARMY OF OBSERVATION DE COTE D'OCEAN,' 1st FEB., 1808, SPAIN.

Marshal Moncey, commanding.
Head-quarters, Vittoria.

Present under arms.		Detached.		Hospital.	Effective.	
Men.	Horses.	Men.	Horses.	Men.	Men.	Horses.
21,878	2,547	2,144	..	4,464	28,486	2,547

Train of the guard........................ 225   509
Grand total .. 28,711 men and 3,391 horses.

No. XXIX.

THE following letters from lord Collingwood did not come into my possession before the present volume was in the press. It will be seen that they corroborate many of the opinions and some of the facts that I have stated, and they will doubtless be read with the attention due to the observations of such an honourable and able man.

TO SIR HEW DALRYMPLE

Ocean, Gibraltar, 30th August, 1808.

MY DEAR SIR,

I have been in great expectation of hearing of your progress with the army, and hope the first account will be of your success whenever you move. I have heard nothing lately of Junot at Cadiz; but there have been accounts, not very well authenticated, that Joseph Buonaparte, in his retiring to France, was stopped by the mass rising in Biscay, to the amount of fourteen thousand well-armed men, which obliged him to return to Burgos, where the body of the French army was stationed.

At Zaragoza, the French, in making their fourteenth attack upon the town, were defeated, repulsed with great loss, and had retired from it. There is a deputy here from that city with a commission from the marquis de Palafox to request supplies. The first aid upon their list is for ten or fifteen thousand troops. The deputy states they have few regulars in the province, and the war has hitherto been carried on by all being armed.   In this gentleman's conversation I observe, what I had before remarked in others, that he had no view of Spain beyond the kingdom of Aragon; and in reply to the observations I made on the necessity of a central government, he had little to say, as if that had not yet been a subject of much consideration.   I have great hope that general Castaños, Cuesta, and those captains-general who will now meet at Madrid, will do something effectual in simplifying the government.   In a conversation I had with Morla on the necessity of this, he seemed to think the juntas would make many difficulties, and retain their present power as long as they could.

I hope, my dear sir, you will give some directions about this puzzling island (*Perexil*), which it appears to me will not be of any future use ; but the people who are on it will suffer much in the winter, without habitations, except tents ; I conceive the purpose for which it was occupied is past, and will probably never return ; whenever they quit it, they should bring the stores away as quietly as possible ; for, if I am not mistaken, the emperor has an intention to keep them, and will remonstrate against them going.   I hope you have received good accounts from lady Dalrymple, &c.

*   *   *   *   *   *   *

I am to sail to-day for Toulon, where everything indicates an intention in the French to sail.   Mr. Duff brought a million of dollars to Seville, and has instructions to communicate with the junta ; but he appears to me to be too old to do it as major Cox has done ; he is still there, and I conclude will wait for your instructions.   Mr. Markland would accept with great thankfulness the proposal you made to him to go to Valencia.

I beg my kind regards, &c.

COLLINGWOOD.

P. S.   Prince Leopold is still here, and I understand intends to stay until he hears from England.   I have given passports for Dupont and a number of French officers to go to France on parole, ninety-three in number.   General Morla was impatient to get them out of the country.   The Spaniards were much irritated against them: they were not safe from their revenge, except in St. Sebastian's castle.

TO SIR HEW DALRYMPLE.

Ocean, off Toulon, October 18, 1808.

MY DEAR SIR,

I have received the favour of your letters of the 27th August and 5th September, and beg to offer you my sincere congratulations on the success of the British army in Portugal, which I hope will have satisfied the French that they are not those invincible creatures which Buonapare had endeavoured to persuade them they were.

It is a happy event to have rescued Portugal from the government of France; and their carrying off a little plunder is a matter of very secondary consideration; perhaps it may have the good effect of keeping up the animosity of the Portuguese who suffer, and incite them to more resistance in future.

The great business now is to endeavour to establish that sort of government, and organise that sort of military force, which may give security to the country; and the great difficulty in Portugal will be to find men who are of ability to place at the head of the several departments, who have patriotism to devote themselves to its service, and vigour to maintain its independence. In a country exhausted like Portugal, it will require much ingenious expedient to supply the want of wealth and of everything military. If it is not found in the breasts of those to whom the people look up, Portugal will remain in a hapless and uncertain state still.

I have not heard from sir Charles Cotton how he settled his terms with the Russian admiral; but as he has got possession of the ships to be sent to England, they cannot but be good. The hoisting the English flag on the fort which surrendered to our troops, I conclude, would be explained to the Portuguese as not to be understood as taking possession by England for other purpose than to be restored to its prince, as was done at Madeira; but in this instance it ought to have been thought necessary to deprive Siniavin of the argument he would have used of the neutrality of the Portuguese flag, with whom his nation was not at *war*.

I left Cadiz the moment everything in that quarter was pacific; and Mr. Duff arrived there with a million of dollars for their use; this money was sent to the junta of Seville, where I am afraid there are many members unworthy of the trust.

I have only heard once from Cox since I left that quarter. After getting the money, father Gil seemed to have dropt his communications with major C., and their discussions were not of a nature to excite much public interest; they consisted more in private bickerings than of grave consult for the public weal. Tilly seems to have been entirely disappointed in his project, both in respect to the annexation of southern Portugal to Andalusia and the pension of 12,000 dollars for his service in the supreme council: of those you will be informed by major Cox. I am afraid I related the proceedings to his majesty's ministers of events which were passing almost under my eye, and gave my opinion on them with too great freedom; I mean with a freedom that is not usual; but they were facts of which, without being possessed, his majesty's ministers could not have a knowledge of the real state of affairs in Spain; and the sentiments those facts inspired were necessary to explain my motives and the rule of conduct which I pursued. And still I consider the great and only danger to which Spain is now exposed is, the supposition that the whole nation is possessed of the same patriotism which, in Andalusia, Aragon, and Valencia, led to such glorious results. It is far otherwise. There are not many Castañoses, nor Cuestas, nor Palafoxes; and take from Spain the influence of the clergy, and its best source of power would be lost: wherever this influence is least, the war is languid.

I wrote to you some time since to represent the state of Catalonia. Nothing can be more indifferent to the cause than they appear to be; yet the common peasantry have not less spirit nor less desire to repel their enemy. They have no leaders. Palacio, the captain-general, stays at Villa Franca, west of Barcelona, talking of what he intends to do; and the people speak of him as either wanting zeal in their cause or ability to direct them; while the French from Barcelona and Figueras do just what they please. When the French attacked Gerona, he did nothing to succour it. The greatest discomfiture they suffered was from lord Cochrane, who, while they were employed at the siege, blew up the road, making deep trenches in a part where the fire of his ships could be brought upon; and when they came there he drove them from their guns, killed many, and took some cannon.

The French fleet is here quite ready for sea, and I am doing all that is in my power to meet them when they do come out. It is an arduous service: the last ten days we have had gales of wind incessantly; the difficulty of keeping a sufficient squadron is very great. I think the storms from those Alpine mountains are harder than in England, and of more duration.

I beg my best regards to captain Dalrymple, and my sincerest wishes for every success to attend you.

I am, my dear sir Hew,

Your obedient and most humble servant,

COLLINGWOOD.

P.S. In the letter which I wrote to you on the state of Catalonia I represented the necessity of sending a body of British troops to Catalonia. There is no other prospect of the French being kept in any bounds. The avenues to France are as open now as at any time they have been. I have kept a ship always at Rosas Bay; her marines have garrisoned the castle, and her company assisted in repairing the works. The French appear to have designs on that place. The presence of the English alone prevents them. If 18,000 men were here of our army, I think they would make Mr. Palacio come forward, and put the whole country into activity, which till then I don't think they ever will be.

COLLINGWOOD.

They want an English resident at Gerona, that they may have somebody to apply to for succour . . . .

[The rest torn off in the original.]

TO SIR HEW DALRYMPLE.

Ocean, off Minorca, April 8, 1809.

MY DEAR SIR,

I received the favour of your letter a few days ago, which gave me great pleasure, after all the trouble and vexations you have had, to hear you were all well.

I was exceedingly sorry when I saw the angry mood in which the convention in Portugal was taken up, even before the circumstances which led to it were at all known. Before our army landed in Portugal, the French force was reported to be very small. I remember its being said that a body of 5000 troops were all that was necessary to dispossess Junot. I conclude the same sort of report went to England; and this, with the victory that was obtained, led people to expect the extermination of the few French which were supposed to be there; and when once the idea is entertained, people shut their eyes to difficulties.

I remember what you told me, the last time I saw you off Cadiz, of the communication which might be made to you by an officer who possessed the entire confidence of ministers. I thought then, that whatever ministers had to communicate to a commander-in-chief, could not be done better than by themselves; for intermediate communications are always in danger of being misunderstood, and never fail to cause doubts and disturb the judgement. I hope now it is all over, and your uneasiness on that subject at an end.

My labours I think will never cease. I am worn down by fatigue of my mind, with anxiety and sorrow; my health is very much impaired; and while our affairs require an increased energy, I find myself less able to conduct them from natural causes. I give all my thoughts and time, but have interruptions, from my weak state of body, which the service will scarcely admit of. I never felt the severity of winter more than this last. They were not gales of wind, but hurricanes; and the consequence is, that the fleet has suffered very much, and many of the ships very infirm. I would not have kept the sea so long, because I know the system of blockading must be ruinous to our fleet at last, and in no instance that I can recollect has prevented the enemy from sailing. In the spring we are found all rags, while they, nursed through the tempest, are all trim. I would not have done it; but what would have become of me if, in my preserving the ships, the French had sailed, and effected anything in any quarter? The clamour would have been loud, and they would have sought only for the cause in my treachery or folly, for none can understand that there is any bad weather in the Mediterranean. The system of blockade is ruinous; but it has continued so long, and so much to the advantage of the mercantile part of the nation, that I fear no minister will be found bold enough to discontinue it. We undertake nothing against the enemy, but seem to think it enough to prevent him taking our brigs; his fleet is growing to a monstrous force, while ours every day gives more proof of its increasing decrepitude.

Of the Spaniards I would not say much; I was never sanguine in the prospect of success, and have no reason to change my opinion; the lower class of people, those who are under the influence of priests, would do anything were they under proper direction; but directors are difficult to be found. There is a canker in the state: none of the superior orders are serious in their resistance to the French, and have only taken a part against them thus far from the apprehension of the resentment of the people. I believe the junta is not free from the taint of the infection, or would they have continued Vives Don Miguel, in high and important command after such evident proofs as he gave of want of loyalty? I do not know what is thought of Infantado in England; but in my mind, the man, the duke (for his rank has a great deal to do with it,) who would seat himself in Buonaparte's council at Bayonne, sign his decrees, which were distributed in Spain, and then say he was forced to do it, is not the man who will do much in maintaining the glory or the independence of any country; no such man should be trusted now. The French troops are mostly withdrawn from Spain, except such as are necessary to hold certain strong posts, and enable them to return without impediment. Figueras, Barcelona, and Rosas, are held here in Catalonia, and of course the country quite open to them. Will the Spaniards dispossess them ? The junta does not seem to know any thing of the provinces at a distance from them. At Tarragona the troops are ill-clothed, and without pay ; on one occasion they could not march against the enemy, having no shoes, and yet at Cadiz they have fifty-one millions of dollars. Cadiz seems to be a general dépôt of everything they can get from England. If they are not active the next two months, Spain is lost.

I hope lady Dalrymple, &c. &c.

I ever am, my dear sir,

Your very faithful and obedient servant,

COLLINGWOOD.

END OF VOLUME I.